# THE CAPABILITY APPROACH TO LABOUR LAW

# The Capability Approach
# to Labour Law

Edited by
BRIAN LANGILLE

OXFORD

UNIVERSITY PRESS

Great Clarendon Street, Oxford, OX2 6DP,
United Kingdom

Oxford University Press is a department of the University of Oxford.
It furthers the University's objective of excellence in research, scholarship,
and education by publishing worldwide. Oxford is a registered trade mark of
Oxford University Press in the UK and in certain other countries

Published in the United States of America by Oxford University Press
198 Madison Avenue, New York, NY 10016, United States of America

British Library Cataloguing in Publication Data
Data available

Library of Congress Control Number: 2018961851

ISBN 978–0–19–883608–7

Printed and bound by
CPI Group (UK) Ltd, Croydon, CR0 4YY

# Acknowledgements

In October 2017, a meeting was convened at the University of Toronto Faculty of Law at which the chapters in this volume were first presented by their authors in a workshop setting. Funding for that meeting was provided as part of a multi-year insight grant from the Social Science and Humanities Research Council of Canada (SSHRC) for a project entitled 'Capability Theory Meets Labour Law'. I thank the SSRHC for providing the funds which made that meeting, and thus this volume, possible.

I also must acknowledge the very substantial support of many at the Faculty of Law at the University of Toronto and in particular the encouragement of Dean Ed Iacobucci, as well as the administrative support of my assistant Aleatha Cox, and of Annette Henry and her staff in the Faculty's Finance Office.

The production of this volume benefited enormously from the extraordinary editing and organizational skills of my research assistant, Sarah Kanko, a JD student in the Faculty of Law. Thank you, Sarah.

Finally, very real thanks to OUP and especially to Jamie Berezin, who supported this project from the beginning and to Eve Ryle-Hodges, who guided us to our destination.

# Contents

# Notes on the Contributors

**Pnina Alon-Shenker** is an Associate Professor in the Department of Law & Business at Ryerson University, Canada. She is the founding Academic Director of Ryerson Law & Business Clinic.

**Bruce P. Archibald** is Professor Emeritus of Law at Dalhousie University.

**Alan Bogg** is Professor of Labour Law at the University of Bristol Law School.

**Hugh Collins** is the Vinerian Professor of English Law at All Souls College, University of Oxford.

**Guy Davidov** is the Elias Lieberman Professor of Labour Law at the Hebrew University of Jerusalem.

**Simon Deakin** is Professor of Law at the University of Cambridge.

**Riccardo Del Punta** is Professor of Labour Law at the University of Florence.

**Clair Gammage** is Senior Lecturer in Law at the University of Bristol Law School.

**Virginia Mantouvalou** is Professor of Human Rights and Labour Law at University College London (UCL), Faculty of Laws.

**Pascal McDougall** is an SJD candidate at Harvard Law School.

**Martha C. Nussbaum** is Ernst Freund Distinguished Service Professor of Law and Ethics at the University of Chicago, appointed in the Law School and the Philosophy Department. With Amartya Sen, she is one of the Founding Presidents of the Human Development and Capability Association.

**Supriya Routh** is an assistant professor at the Faculty of Law, University of Victoria.

**Robert Salais** is an economist and former Director of the CNRS Research Centre—Institutions and Historical Dynamics of the Economy and the Society (IHDES)—at the *Ecole Normale Supérieure de Paris-Saclay*. He served as coordinator of European Programs of Research on the capability approach and its application to European employment and social policies.

**Lyn K.L. Tjon Soei Len** is a visiting assistant professor at Ohio State University.

**Laura Weinrib** is Professor of Law at the University of Chicago Law School and an associate member of the University of Chicago Department of History.

# Introduction

## The Capability Approach to Labour Law—Why are We Here?

*Brian Langille*

## I. Why is the Capability Approach Attractive to Labour Lawyers?

Forty years ago, Amartya Sen delivered his Tanner Lecture, 'Equality of What?', in which he introduced to the world a novel approach to the idea of equality by way of the notion of 'basic capability' as 'a morally relevant dimension'.[1] We can now see with hindsight that Sen's argument—that we should focus upon equality of basic capabilities ('a person being able to do certain basic things')—launched what has become an academic armada now proceeding under the flag of 'the Capability Approach'.[2] This is a volume of contributions about the Capability Approach (CA) and labour law. As such, it can be seen as another academic harbour in which the idea, set in motion forty years ago by Sen, has now arrived.

The CA is widely understood to have provided a major innovation, and interruption, in global debates in development theory and practice by offering an alternative account of what counts when measuring development and, indeed, in what counts as development. We see this expressed in the very idea of development captured in

---

[1] Amartya Sen, 'Equality of What?' (Tanner Lecture 1979) in Sterling M McMurrin (ed), *The Tanner Lectures on Human Values* (University of Utah Press, 1980) 197, 220.

[2] Or 'Capabilities Approach'. The chapters in this volume use both terms. Sometimes the term 'Human Development Approach' is used but this is controversial—see Ingrid Robeyns, *Wellbeing, Freedom and Social Justice: The Capability Approach Re-Examined* (Open Book Publishers, 2017) 197 https://www.openbookpublishers.com/product/682. Robeyns is currently the president of the Human Development and Capability Association (HDCA). The HDCA produces a peer-reviewed journal, the *Journal of Human Development and Capabilities* (see https://hd-ca.org/publication-and-resources/journal-of-human-development-and-capabilities). For further reading on the CA, see the bibliographies in Ingrid Robeyns, *Wellbeing, Freedom and Social Justice: The Capability Approach Re-Examined* (cited above); Ingrid Robeyns, 'Capabilitarianism' (2016) 17(3) *Journal of Human Development and Capabilities* 397, 397–414; Martha C Nussbaum, *Creating Capabilities: the Human Development Approach* (Harvard University Press, 2012). For reading on various applications of the CA, see the papers and bibliographies in Harry Brighouse and Ingrid Robeyns (eds), *Measuring Justice: Primary Goods and Capabilities* (Cambridge University Press, 2010); Flavio Comim, Mozaffar Qizilbash, and Sabina Alkire (eds), *The Capability Approach: Concepts, Measures and Applications* (Cambridge University Press, 2008).

the Human Development Index.[3] The CA has also offered a major intervention in fundamental debates in political theory as it set an alternative course to utilitarian or Rawlsian approaches. That indeed was the precise point of embarkation from which the Tanner lecture set the CA on its Odyssey.

The CA has travelled far and wide since. Ingrid Robeyns has drawn attention[4] to the many places to which the CA has found its way (either by adventure or hijacking), the myriad issues upon which the CA has been brought to bear, as well as many developments and distinctions in the different paths taken by many claiming allegiance to the approach. In her book *Wellbeing, Freedom and Social Justice*, she seeks to provide a 'helicopter view'[5] of the CA's now-expansive chart and its many uses, while also critically clarifying the whole of the approach.[6] She writes:

the range of fields in which the capability approach has been applied and developed has expanded dramatically, and now includes global public health, development ethics, environmental protection and ecological sustainability, education, technological design, welfare state policies, and many, many more.[7]

Labour law does not appear on this list nor, as far as I can see, in the surview offered by the book at all. And it is the point of this volume of chapters to address this absence.

It is true that there have been some beginnings, some points of connection between the CA and labour or work, if not labour law, dawning on the intellectual horizon. The 2015 Human Development Report provides such a data point, revealing a connection between the CA and labour. Its title is 'Work for Human Development'.[8] The 2015 UN Sustainable Development Goals could be invoked as a second place of connection.[9] In International Labour Organization (ILO) circles, for example, it is much celebrated that one of the goals mentions 'decent work'.[10]

---

[3] The Human Development Index (HDI) is 'a summary measure of average achievement in key dimensions of human development: a long and healthy life, being knowledgeable and have a decent standard of living'. See 'Human Development Reports' United Nations Development Programme http://hdr.undp.org/en/content/human-development-index-hdi for more details.
[4] In Ingrid Robeyns, 'Capabilitarianism' (n 2) and in Ingrid Robeyns, *Wellbeing, Freedom and Social Justice* (n 2).
[5] Robeyns, *Wellbeing, Freedom and Social Justice* (n 2) 4.
[6] Through what she now calls the 'modular approach' in *Wellbeing, Freedom and Social Justice* (n 2) 36.
[7] Sen, 'Equality of What?' (n 1) 9.
[8] The United Nations Development Programme, Human Development Report 2015: Work for Human Development (UNDP, 2015) http://hdr.undp.org/sites/default/files/2015_human_development_report.pdf.
[9] Division for Sustainable Development Goals, 'Sustainable Development Knowledge Platform' *United Nations Department of Economic and Social Affairs*. https://sustainabledevelopment.un.org.
[10] The 'Decent Work' as an ILO mantra was introduced by DG Juan Somavia. See the Press Release, International Labour Organization, 'ILO Director-General highlights need for "Decent Work", insists on employment as the best means of social inclusion and urges comprehensive employment policies to underpin globalization' (Turin, Italy: 10 November 2000) https://www.ilo.org/global/about-the-ilo/newsroom/news/WCMS_007916/lang--en/index.htm. And it was finally given some constitutional credibility in the 2008 declaration. See the ILO's 'Goal #8: Decent work and economic growth' https://www.ilo.org/global/topics/sdg-2030/goal-8/lang--en/index.htm and 'Decent Work and the 2030 Agenda for sustainable development', for multimedia accounts of the importance of Goal 8 for the 2030 Agenda https://www.ilo.org/global/topics/sdg-2030/lang--en/index.htm.

Goal 8 reads: 'Promote sustained, inclusive, and sustainable economic growth, full and productive employment, and decent work for all'. Some of Goal 8's specific sub-goals ('targets') mention specific labour law issues such as child and forced labour, and equal pay. And target 8.8 reads: 'Protect labour rights and promote safe and secure working environments for all workers, including migrant workers, in particular women migrants, and those in precarious employment'. Both of these international documents can be seen as establishing a connection between a general Human Development/CA and work and employment. But the connection established is often to work/employment/jobs, and to various desirable policies in that sphere, and not to our understanding of the role of law—labour law—in this enterprise.[11]

The general absence of a labour law dimension of the CA is somewhat puzzling, and for several reasons. To begin with, as Robeyns observes,

Many people who encounter the capability approach for the first time, find the ideas embedded in the approach intuitively attractive. The basic claim of the capability approach – that, when asking normative questions, we should ask what people are able to do, and what lives they are able to lead—resonates with widespread ideas on how to make policies, views about what social justice requires, or bottom-up views about the idea of development.[12]

No doubt this is true. It is intuitively attractive to think, as Jerry Cohen once put it, 'that capability is the right thing to look at when judging how well a person's life is going'.[13] But might it be the case that there are also dimensions of the CA which makes it particularly and specifically attractive for labour lawyers? I believe this to be the case. And for a number of reasons.

First, the CA and labour law share a commitment to an actual rather than a formal notion of freedom. The CA is an approach which focuses upon real freedom, real capability, to lead a life we have reason to value. Although it is interested in, it is not satisfied with, the absence of formal legal constraints upon freedoms (e.g., that you are not banned from voting) but is aimed at the real capability to do and to be (e.g. that you can participate in public debate, that you can get to a voting station, not be beat up on the way there, and so on). So too, has labour law's account of itself long been based on an understanding of, and a commitment to real, substantive freedom for workers. In labour law's context, this idea of substantive freedom was expressed in opposition to the formal freedom to contract in the labour market with buyers of labour power. Labour law's original legal architecture was provided by private law's regime of the law of contract with its twin commitments to freedom to contract (I am free to bargain with whom I choose—so I can refuse to bargain with you for racist reasons, or because you are a union member) and freedom of contract

---

[11] In so doing, or in failing to do so, these international documents reflect and help sustain a similar failure at the ILO. There is insufficient interest, in some quarters, in understanding how law, which is the ILO's central constitutional margin of advantage, can be deployed to secure its goals. See Francis Maupain, *The Future of the International Labour Organization in the Global Economy* (Hart Publishing, 2013).

[12] Robeyns, *Wellbeing, Freedom and Social Justice* (n 2) 7.

[13] GA Cohen, 'Amartya Sen's Unequal World' (1993) 28(40) *Economic and Political Weekly* 2156 at 2156.

(if I agree to bargain with you, I am free to insist on whatever terms I choose and can drive). Modern labour law is built on this foundation. It is designed to resist and alter these legal truths at private law.

There is a second fundamental shared dimension. The CA suggests, or demands in some hands, that we attend to the distinction between the 'opportunity aspect' of freedom and the 'process aspect of freedom'.[14] The basic structure of labour law's resistance to contract power reflects this duality as well. Labour law, to use its local way of speaking, consists of substantive labour standards (maximum hours, minimum wages, and so on) and also procedural labour rights/freedoms (to associate, to bargain collectively). That is, it too is concerned not only with the capabilities you have, but with how you come to have them. While both dimensions of labour law can be understood in terms of realizing real substantive freedom, they attend to these two aspects of freedom.

But a third deep dimension of consistency of approach between the CA and labour law lies in the insistence that we attend to intrinsic as well as the instrumental values. This is a delicate but vital point—and I am not sure I have found the best, or even an adequate, way of expressing it. But here is one way of approaching this point.

In a very early essay written for the ILO, and appearing in its *International Labour Review*,[15] Sen identifies three aspects of employment: the income aspect, the production aspect, and the recognition aspect. The critical distinction is between the third aspect—the recognition aspect—and the other two. The recognition aspect reminds us that, 'for those who have to work for a living, lack of 'employment' is not only a denial of income, it can also be a source of shame'.[16] This is a 'psychological' aspect that recognizes that employment 'gives a person the recognition of being engage in something worthwhile'.[17] On this view, employment or work has a personal as well as a productive aspect. It has intrinsic value as well as instrumental value as a means to other important ends. This is a theme which has long been attractive to labour lawyers—and, for example, to the Supreme Court of Canada. It is a theme which is fundamental to, and underwrites, our current labour law. One of it classic expressions is in David Beatty's wonderfully important essay, 'Labour is Not a Commodity',[18] where Beatty explores the personal meaning of employment:

As a vehicle which admits a person to the status of a contributing, productive, member of society, employment is seen as providing recognition of the individual's being engaged in something worthwhile. It gives the individual a sense of significance. By realizing our *capabilities* and contributing in ways society determines to be useful, employment comes to represent the means by which most members of our community can lay claim to an equal right of respect

[14] Amartya Sen, *The Idea of Justice* (Harvard University Press, 2009) 295–6; Amartya Sen, *Development as Freedom* (OUP, 1999) 291–2.
[15] Amartya Sen, 'Employment Institutions and Technology: Some Policy Issues' (1975) 112 *International Labour Review* 45.
[16] Sen, 'Employment Institutions and Technology' (n 15) 46.
[17] Sen, 'Employment Institutions and Technology' (n 15) 45.
[18] David M Beatty, 'Labour is not a Commodity' in Barry J. Reiter and John Swan (eds), *Studies in Contract Law* (Butterworths, 1979) 313. He then argues that the personal aspect of employment was sacrificed to its 'productive' aspect.

and of concern from others. It is this institution through which most of us secure much of our self-respect and self-esteem.[19]

After citing directly these very words of Beatty, former Chief Justice of Canada Brian Dickson went on to add:

Work is one of the most fundamental aspects in a person's life, providing the individual with a means of financial support and, as importantly, a contributory role in society. A person's employment is an essential component of his or her sense of identity, self-worth and emotional well-being. Accordingly, the conditions in which a person works are highly significant in shaping the whole compendium of psychological, emotional and physical elements of a person's dignity and self-respect.[20]

This idea of intrinsic and instrumental values is not only consistent with our view of the employment relationship, but also with our view of collective labour laws. As Justice Wilson once summed it up: unlike employment standards laws, which protect individuals from employer abuses through 'legislative protectionism' and may be about advancement, collective labour laws are much about 'self-advancement of working people'.[21]

This is a theme to which Sen returned explicitly when he addressed the idea of human capital and its relationship to human freedom. Some of the passages resonate deeply with the views of labour lawyers as expressed by Beatty's and the Chief Justice Dickson's soundings of both the instrumental and intrinsic:

If education makes a person more efficient in commodity production, then this is clearly an enhancement of human capital. This can add to the value of production in the economy and also to the income of the person who has been educated. But even with the same level of income, a person may benefit from education, in reading, communicating, arguing, in being able to choose in a more informed way, in being taken more seriously by others, and so on. The benefits of education, thus, exceeds its role as human capital in commodity production. The broader human-capability perspective would record—and value—these additional roles. The two perspectives are, thus, closely related but distinct.[22]

The charm of the CA and Sen's ideas for labour lawyers are thus, I think, both apparent and compelling. On the other hand, they are challenging. One way of putting this: the opening line of the first UNDP Human Development Report reads as follows: 'Human Development is a process of enlarging people's choices'.[23] This has a number of rather large and positive implications for labour law. But, this remark also carries a lot of freight, much of it negative, for labour lawyers. Any

---

[19] Beatty, 'Labour is not a Commodity' (n 18) 324 (emphasis added).
[20] *Reference Re Public Service Employee Relations Act (Alta)* [1987] 1 SCR 313, para 91. Dickson's strong words have been cited repeatedly by others, including Justice Iacobucci in *Machtinger v HOJ Industries Ltd.* [1992] 1 SCR 986. And then again in *Wallace v United Grain Growers Ltd* [1997] 3 SCR 701. Justice Iacobucci is then cited by Justice Abella, for example, in *Evans v Teamsters Local Union No 31* [2008] 1 SCR 661.
[21] *Lavigne v Ontario Public Service Employees Union* (1991) 81 DLR (4th) 545 at 607.
[22] Amartya Sen, 'Editorial: Human Capital and Human Capability' (1997) 25(12) *World Development* 1959 at 1959.
[23] UNDP, Human Development Report (1990) http://hdr.undp.org/en/reports/global/hdr1990.

account which takes choice, agency, or freedom seriously is likely to be resisted—or misunderstood—by labour lawyers. Hugh Collins puts this perspective well in his chapter in this volume:

the capability approach, with its strong emphasis on the goal of individual freedom for the achievement of well-being, appears to be pointing in the wrong direction. Instead of enhancing market freedoms, much of labour law consists of mandatory rights and institutions that are designed to inhibit freedom of contract out of the fear that unconstrained markets for labour often lead to social exclusion, exploitation, and the undermining of individual dignity.[24]

But there is more. Not only does the CA send out its intuitively charming message to labour lawyers, and not only is it a particularly charming (and challenging) message for them, but, in addition, labour lawyers have been listening keenly for such a signal from normative space. That is because many labour lawyers share the view that their discipline is in crisis and has suffered in recent times a near (at least) death experience. The world which their subject matter has long addressed—regulating contractual relations between employees and employers—is disappearing (or being disappeared).[25] And the redistributive, participatory values which underwrote labour law's substantive and procedural project have been seriously challenged. The world as we now know it is not kind to labour law, and it has not been for some time. Labour lawyers have been worried about these serious challenges and have been seeking ways of understanding the new world of work—globalized, platformed, outsourced, insourced, networked—and labour law's role in it. There has been a very significant, and necessary, revival in interest in very basic questions about labour law. Questions which did not need to be asked when things were going reasonably well, say, to use the French way of putting it, during the *trente glorieuses*. But the widely discussed and understood rise of conservative economic and libertarian political thought and politics, the breakdown of the post-war consensus of embedded liberalism, the rise of the Washington consensus, the entrenchment of what Dani Rodrik has called hyper-globalization,[26] the financial crisis of 2008, the pursuit of 'austerity' policies, the worry that the *trente glorieuses* were the exception not the norm,[27] and much more, has long put labour law well on the back foot as it seeks to articulate its role in this new and global dispensation. Labour lawyers now ask the questions

---

[24] Hugh Collins, 'What Can Sen's Capability Approach Offer to Labour Law?', Chapter 1 in this volume at p 21–22.
[25] See, for example, David Weil, *The Fissured Workplace: Why Work Became So Bad for So Many and What Can Be Done to Improve it* (Harvard University Press, 2014).
[26] Dan Rodrik, *The Globalization Paradox: Democracy and the Future of the World Economy* (WW Norton, 2011). See also Thomas Palley, 'Globalization Checkmated? Political and Geopolitical Contradictions Coming Home to Roost' *Political Economy Research Institute Working Paper Series No 466* (2018) and Thomas Palley, 'Three Globalizations, Not Two: Rethinking the History and Economics of Trade and Globalization' *Forum for Macroeconomics and Macroeconomic Policies, Hans-Böckler-Stiftung* No 18 (2018).
[27] Thomas Piketty, *Capital in the 21st Century* (Harvard University Press, 2014).

which have not been asked for a long time. They seek answers. Jeroboams of ink have been spilled in this endeavour in recent years.[28]

Thus labour law's encounter with the CA presents as a perfect academic storm: what is in general an intuitively appealing and developing approach, encounters an area of law (labour law) for which it is particularly salient, and at the very time when labour lawyers are worried and in need of inspiration. This storm has been, for the most part, until now, a scattered and approaching one. Some labour lawyers predict it will offer much needed rain, for all or at least for some of labour law's arid fields. For others it appears as a darkness on the edge of town—a potentially dangerous storm which could wipe out all of the fruits of labour law's carefully tended and historical vineyards. But thus far this storm has manifested itself in relatively isolated outbursts and exchanges—there has not been a concentrated effort by labour law scholars brought together for an exclusive focus upon, and intensive discussion and exchange about, the intriguing connection between the CA and labour law. And the skies overhead CA scholars from other disciplines have not often been obscured by worries about labour law.[29] This volume seeks to alter this existing academic climate and, in a preliminary way at least, to seed these intellectual skies.

## II. The Essays in This Volume

These contributions were written for, and presented to, a Workshop on Labour Law and the CA held at the Faculty of Law of the University of Toronto in October 2017. Funding for the Workshop was provided by The Social Sciences and Humanities Research Council of Canada. In constructing the invitation list for the Workshop, I hoped to attract those labour lawyers with philosophical inclinations who had expressed some interest, either positive or negative, in the CA. I was delighted when they responded positively to the idea of a Workshop. I was also concerned to invite theoreticians of the CA who are not labour lawyers. In this latter regard, I was delighted when Martha Nussbaum, one of two (along with Amartya Sen) principle

---

[28] See, for example, Guy Davidov and Brian Langille (eds), *The Idea of Labour Law* (Oxford University Press, 2011); Guy Davidov and Brian Langille (eds), *Boundaries and Frontiers of Labour Law* (Hart Publishing, 2006); Hugh Collins, Gillian Lester, and Virginia Mantouvalou (eds), *Philosophical Foundations of Labour Law* (Oxford University Press, 2018); Alan Bogg, Cathryn Costello, Anne CL Davies, and Jeremias Prassl (eds), *The Autonomy of Labour Law* (Hart Publishing, 2015); Guy Davidov, *A Purposive Approach to Labour Law* (Oxford University Press, 2016); Simon Deakin and Frank Wilkinson, *The Law of the Labour Market* (Oxford University Press, 2005); Mark Freedland and others (eds), *The Contract of Employment* (Oxford University Press, 2016); John Howe, Anna Chapman, and Ingrid Landau (eds), *The Evolving Project of Labour Law: Foundations, Development and Future Research Directions* (The Federation Press, 2017); Ruth Dukes, *The Labour Constitution: The Enduring Idea of Labour Law* (Oxford University Press, 2014).

[29] See, for example, Kirsten Sehnbruch, 'From the quantity to the quality of employment: an application of the capability approach to the Chilean labour market' in Flavio Comin, Mozaffar Qizilbash, and Sabina Alkire (eds), *The Capability Approach: Concepts, Measures, and Applications* (Cambridge University Press, 2008) 561.

architects and proponents of the CA, accepted my invitation. I thank the contributors for travelling to Toronto to present their drafts and for their work on the contributions which are presented in this volume.

At the conclusion of the workshop it became clear that the papers had organized themselves into three categories which are now reflected in the three-part structure of this volume. First, a number of contributions address the large issue of possibilities, positive or negative, for the CA and labour law. Much of the discussion here is whether the CA can provide a normative foundation for labour law. A second group of chapters were best seen as addressing the philosophical potential of the CA in relation to other perspectives (economic, historical, human rights, and so on) already brought to bear upon the discipline of labour law. The third set of chapters address the issue of 'the CA and labour law' through the lens of particular labour law issues (freedom of association, discrimination, sweatshop goods, etc.). There is no claim made here that in this latter part of the volume is comprehensive in this regard. Far from it. This final part of the volume is best viewed as a very limited, but interesting and widespread, sampling of specific interactions between the CA and discrete and concrete labour law topics. It is better viewed as a set of examples which constitute an invitation to others to bring the CA to bear upon the myriad of other, untouched, labour law issues.

## A. Part I

The chapters in Part I offer a spectrum of views and proceed in the following order: from those (Collins, Davidov, Nussbaum) expressing careful but very serious, if not ever complete, doubts about the potential of CA to illuminate or provide a normative basis for (much of) labour law; to a view expressing a general openness to the CA/labour law link (Del Punta); to two expressing a stronger view—that the CA is required to understand or justify what labour law is trying to accomplish (Routh, Langille).

In 'What Can Sen's Capability Approach Offer to Labour Law?' Hugh Collins sets out to assess the role the Capabilities Approach (CA) might play, as a theory of justice, in grounding labour law. He begins by addressing labour law's need for a theory of justice. It is difficult to reconcile the basic principles of private law, especially contract law and market freedom, with the paternalistic and mandatory rules of labour law that intrude upon employees and employers' freedoms. A justification of labour law must, as a result, be able to explain why these private institutions of justice are inadequate. Collins bases his discussion of the CA's ability to undertake this task on a critique of Brian Langille's arguments. According to Collins, Langille presents the CA as a broader and deeper way of justifying labour law, as either promoting or inhibiting freedom by recognizing labour law as the way in which human capital is created and deployed. Collins rejects Langille's argument with three main points. First, the CA is unable to explain what freedoms should be permitted or prohibited by labour law; the goal of the CA is to achieve substantive freedom for individuals, but it is not clear that the mandatory institutions of labour law can be justified to this end without something like the concept of inequality of bargaining.

Secondly, even if the CA is regarded as a theory of justice (which Collins doubts), it cannot provide guidance on the basic institutions that are required in a just society. It can only adjudicate issues of justice on an ad hoc basis, whereas liberal theories (like Rawls') provide arguments for institutional arrangements. Thirdly, the CA denies distributive justice as a principle in itself, and only values it as a means to the end of enhancing capabilities. Labour law has been based on disputes about distributive justice throughout its history, and it would be a mistake to deny that it is no longer a relevant principle. As a result of these problems, Collins concludes that the CA cannot be a theory of justice that provides a justification for labour law. He does note that the CA can be useful in establishing goals for the direction of certain areas of labour law, such as 'affirmative action'. And although he does recognize the fact that the traditional justifications of labour law may not be sufficient, be believes that the CA is not up to the task of grounding labour law.

In 'Capabilities and Labour Law', Guy Davidov continues his careful and philosophically nuanced explication of a 'purposive approach to labour law'.[30] The point of Davidov's chapter is to show the limits of the capabilities approach as a potential normative basis of labour law. He begins by arguing that the CA cannot offer a singular, exclusive justification of labour laws, nor can it provide a normative basis for labour law as a whole. In order for the CA to justify particular laws (or groups of laws) it must fit with those laws and provide a justification based on legal reasons (especially purposive interpretation). Davidov divides the CA into three strands. The first strand, *substantive freedom*, can only provide additional, defensive justifications to existing labour laws. The second strand, *specific capabilities*, seems to provide a justification for some labour laws. But it does not actually provide justifications on its own, and requires a list of capabilities specific to labour law. There are two readings of this kind of list. Either it is merely a descriptive account of capabilities that seem to be valued across legal systems, or it is a normative account that leads to a third strand. This third strand is the *effective enjoyment of rights*. In this strand, the CA is not a justification of labour law but a set of normative requirements that provides a means of evaluating existing institutions and labour laws which require separate justifications. None of the three strands fully fit with labour law, and so the extent to which the CA can justify labour law, alone, is thus limited.

Martha C Nussbaum continues this theme of caution in assessing the relationship of the CA and labour law. In 'Labor Law and the Capabilities Approach', Nussbaum clarifies a number of points about her version of the capabilities approach. She first notes that there is no such thing as *the* Capabilities Approach, and compares the different versions of CA's to utilitarianism. Like the theories of Mill, Bentham, and Sidgwick, different versions of the CA have general similarities and shared critiques while also being in profound disagreement. Nussbaum's version focuses on capabilities, that is, the substantial freedoms, in order to respect people's choices. Her aim is to use her idea of capabilities as a building block in a theory of basic social justice, using the ideas of a threshold and of 'a life worthy of inalienable human dignity'.

---

[30] Davidov, *A Purposive Approach to Labour Law* (n 28).

She argues that there must be a list of specific capabilities that protect the core political entitlements.

Of central importance in Nussbaum's chapter is her espousal of Rawls' political liberalism. She emphasizes the idea of a thin, narrow set of political principles that give equal respect to all individuals. The aim is an overlapping consensus. Nussbaum also argues for the importance of national sovereignty for ensuring that political decisions are left to self-determination for reasons of respect. Her focus is on ensuring central capabilities, and thereby a threshold of freedoms, for all citizens. She rejects Sen's aim of maximizing freedom as a mistaken goal. Nussbaum also argues that the individual must be at the centre of the CA. Groups, including labour unions, are helpful in securing capabilities, but individuals are the ultimate ends. Nussbaum summarizes these points by saying that her particular CA is a 'minimal' approach. In conclusion, Nussbaum illustrates different forms of women's labour in India, including the informal economy and domestic labour. Traditional labour law tools, like collective bargaining and unions, have been problematic in this context, and so it makes little sense to talk about labour law alone while ignoring other aspects of women's circumstances. Labour lawyers must be aware of such circumstances in applying the CA to labour issues.

In 'Is the Capability Theory an Adequate Normative Theory for Labour Law?', Riccardo Del Punta offers a reflection upon the (necessary, in his view) relationship of political theory and law, leading to a measured endorsement of a role for the CA. He argues this point by comparing two possible political theories—what he calls the traditional social-democratic basis of classical labour law and the capability approach—to see which can best account for existing labour law institutions while also being able to map out the directions in which labour law seems to be heading. On the first criterion, of accounting for existing institutions, Del Punta argues that both options are essentially equal in their explanatory power. The fact that labour law developed in conjunction (chronologically speaking) with social democratic theory does weigh in favour of that approach. On the second criterion, of anticipating the future course of labour law, Del Punta concludes that the CA is probably the better of the two options. His sense is that the CA is better suited to deal with changing labour markets and workplaces and that it is less paternalistic than traditional theories while still valuing social responsibility.

Supriya Routh's 'The Need to Become Fashionable' offers a much bolder defence of the CA's potential role in labour law. Routh begins his chapter with two questions: (1) whether the CA can justify the traditional account of labour law; and (2) whether the CA can help reconceptualize the regulation of work. Routh evaluates critiques made by Davidov about the way in which scholars, particularly Langille, Deakin, and Wilkinson, have applied the CA to labour law. Many of the criticisms, Routh argues, are the result of a misunderstanding of the CA. Routh argues that the CA should be seen as an 'approach' rather than a 'theory' in itself. That is to say, the CA has normative force, but needs supplementing in order to develop a full theory of distributive justice. It is easy, from this perspective, to justify existing labour law standards. Ultimately, Routh is dissatisfied with the theories based on the traditional conception of labour law and its reliance on the market. He argues that the CA allows for justification of legal entitlements, but that it is a piecemeal justification of legislative and substantive standards within the narrow perspective of traditional labour law. Routh moves on to consider how the CA might help to reconceptualize labour law. While the CA could be useful in understanding traditional labour and its regulation, it is most useful in helping with an understanding of work that goes beyond market-based industrial forms of employment to work performed outside the market space. Furthermore, in justifying substantive labour rights, the CA allows for the assessment of legal entitlements from the point of view of expanding workers' capabilities. The seeming indeterminacy of the abstract normative approach that the CA provides is actually a benefit, in that it allows for the approach to address a range of heterogeneous forms of work. The CA has potential in its role for labour law through this expanded understanding of labour to non-traditional forms. It is also important that the CA can provide an approach to policy creation that involves the participation of those directly affected.

In 'What is Labour Law? Implications of the Capability Approach' Brian Langille argues that the real potential of the CA for labour law lies in giving us a way of understanding labour law—of answering the question 'What is labour law?' That is, the salience of the CA lies not in providing an external justification for what we know as labour law—its content and its scope (to whom it applies)—but rather in conceptualizing the field in the first place. This view depends upon a view of how subject matters such as labour law are constructed, and a central idea is that of a necessary 'constituting narrative' which twines with what Langille calls law's 'grammar'. The real potential of the CA is to force lawyers to revisit both labour law's grammar and narrative—that is, to reveal a new answer to the question 'what is labour law' and not merely help answer the question 'what justifies our labour law as we have known it?' In proposing this view, Langille disagrees with Collins' insistence that labour law must be about justifying limits on contract law and agrees with Routh's emphasis that the CA is an approach, a view, which can structure a broader labour law.

## B. Part II

The conversations and disagreements about the possible role of the CA, in understanding or justifying our labour law, revealed in the chapters in Part I of this volume do not occur in a theoretical vacuum, or on an interdisciplinary open or 'green field'. Thus, one of the most interesting and important issues is how established, well-known approaches to labour law—economic, historical, human rights, and so on—cohere or conflict with the CA. This part can only offer a sampling of—and again, act as an invitation to other scholars to engage with—the many theoretical overlaps which the introduction of the CA makes possible, and inevitable.

Simon Deakin's chapter 'The Capability Approach and the Economics of Labour Law' addresses three questions central to the relationship of the CA and economic analysis of labour law. The first is about the nature of the labour market, and whether the capability approach can help us understand labour markets better than a neoclassical approach. The second is about whether the CA can be used to make sense of labour market regulation from a methodological point of view. And the third is whether, in light of the first two questions, the CA can provide a normative guide to labour law reform. In answering the first question, Deakin compares Sen's understanding of the CA (in particular, the ideas of functioning, capabilities, and conversion factors) to the neoclassical focus on preferences and prices that control the market. He notes that there are similarities—the idea of rationality and the possibility of market equilibrium—but argues that the CA goes further in helping us understand the nature of the labour market as an institution because it sees rationality and market function as contextual and constructed aspects of the labour market that are embedded within a wider range of institutions with market-constituting features. The CA can thus better help us understand the conflicts that arise between economic and socio-political considerations. Picking up on the idea of labour law as market constituting, Deakin argues, in answering the second question, that the CA is better able to understand the commodification of labour. Labour regulations should not be seen exclusively in economic terms; we need to look at labour law's market-building role and the way it expresses values that fall under the broader heading of social justice. Not only can the CA recognize this market-constituting reality, but it can also understand and measure the social and economic effects of labour regulation. This idea of measurement leads Deakin to answer his third question as follows: The CA approach can help generate empirical information about the effects of labour regulation, but alone the CA cannot provide a full normative grounding for labour reform. In sum, Deakin argues that the CA can help us escape the narrow constraints of the neoclassical economic analysis of labour law, and that it should be seen as offering a methodological approach, rather than a free-standing theory of law or the economy. It needs supplementation with other theories, methods, and techniques in order to generate a normative programme for labour law reform.

In 'Labor History and the Clash of Capabilities' Laura Weinrib gives a wonderful account of the history of labour law in the twentieth century and the various positions used to support labour claims. She uses this historical account to show how the CA, even if consistent with labour law today, does not exactly align with the various historical labour positions, particularly the subordination of the individual to group interests. Weinrib's historical account begins with the labour debates of 1914 and their focus on the broad aspirations and anti-government position of the labour movement. This beginning of a maximalist aim and anti-government means is the antithesis to the CA's minimalist goal for achieving capabilities and its reliance on the government to guarantee capabilities. She then explores the transition into the New Deal era and the labour movement's transition to reliance on government regulation. The United States Congress protected labour rights such as picketing in legislation, while in the courts, people were claiming (and the Court initially recognized) First Amendment protection of these labour rights (arguing that picketing was a form of expression and thus protected as free speech). Weinrib describes how labour activists have been wary of relying on constitutional protection in the way Nussbaum requires of the CA. Anti-union employees and employers have since put forward arguments—the converse of labour activists' claims—that requiring participation in a union or other such forced activity is a violation of their First

Amendment rights. These kinds of arguments have dominated labour discourse in courts since. Unions' power and economic tools have been eroded. Weinrib argues that, in an odd twist, unions might soon be able to claim protection under the First Amendment as voluntary associations. Weinrib's central point is about the difficulty of balancing the competing interests (and fulfilling the competing capabilities) of employees—pro- and anti-union—and employers. She is concerned that the CA will not be able to address the balancing issues that seem to be at the heart of the current labour law debates, and reminds us that it might be worthwhile to look back to arguments which labour law has expunged, but that could be relevant once again.

In 'Capabilities, Utility, or Primary Goods? On Finding a Conceptual Framework for (International) Labour Law', Pascal McDougall explores the encounter of the CA with the tradition of critical legal analysis. He argues that the CA has no intrinsic ideological or normative bent and is largely interchangeable with the other available approaches. As a consequence, whether or not we use the concepts elaborated by Sen and Nussbaum makes little difference to how we are able to tackle substantive questions of politics and ethics. McDougall does not deny that each capability theorist has taken positions that are unique and innovative, and he expresses agreement with several of the capability theorists. But he distinguishes the positions taken by the proponents of the CA from the approach itself, and suggests that these positions could have been expressed using other conceptual apparatuses, like utilitarianism and Rawlsianism. McDougall argues that this fact should change the way we write about the capabilities approach and labour law, in that critics and advocates of the CA should focus on engaging directly with their respective proposals on how to regulate work instead of debating which conceptual vocabulary to use.

McDougall begins by looking at ideas explored in various versions of the CA and by highlighting the similarities between the positions taken by Sen, Nussbaum, Langille, Salais, Villeneuve, Deakin, and Wilkinson, and traditional welfare economics, political philosophy, and labour law theory. McDougall then looks to the philosophical debates behind the CA for alternative concepts. He describes Nussbaum and Sen's critique of Rawls and utilitarianism, and argues that both rival theories can incorporate the critiques while remaining 'themselves', so that the contrast between the various theories may have been overstated.

McDougall then dedicates the second half of his chapter to fleshing out what he calls a 'first-order' analytical and normative approach to labour law, informed by critical legal theory. He insists that his approach is compatible with and could have been framed using the capabilities conceptual apparatus. His approach is based on American legal realism and the view of property and contract as 'bundles of rights', that is, amalgams of legal entitlements that can be arranged in many ways with widely varying distributive consequences, and concludes that many putative obstacles to redistribution are illusory. He combines that analytical approach with a normative approach he calls 'altruism'. McDougall then closes by arguing that the disciplinary boundaries of labour law are not intrinsically exclusionary and are fit for an 'altruist' project like his, provided that labour law is expanded to cover many heretofore excluded constituencies and that it is considered a subset of 'social law', that is, the law relating to social security and social insurance.

In 'Work, Human Rights, and Human Capabilities' Virginia Mantouvalou explores the connections between the CA and the human rights approach to labour law. She frames her chapter with questions that arise from the working conditions of an Amazon warehouse revealed by an undercover reporter, analysing these conditions through the two different normative frameworks (human rights and human capabilities). Mantouvalou notes many similarities—both are grounded in ideas of human dignity and both recognize the existence of positive and negative duties, particularly on governments. She notes that (Nussbaum's version of) the CA provides a more specific understanding of what justice requires, and that it fills in the content of underdetermined human rights. Mantouvalou then turns to the ways in which the human rights framework and the CA specifically address labour rights. She notes the distinction made between economic/social rights and civil/political rights, and how various labour rights fall into both categories. Civil and political rights are justiciable, while social and economic ones generally are not. There is no right, she notes, to meaningful work. In comparison, the CA has a broader scope in terms of the obligations it requires. Labour rights are grounded on the capabilities of practical reason, affiliation, and control over one's environment. These capabilities cover the kinds of rights that the human rights framework supports, but also go further to requiring some kind of meaningful work.

In 'Capabilities Approaches and Labour Law through a Relational and Restorative Regulatory Lens', Bruce Archibald argues that insights of the CA, combined with restorative approaches rooted in relational theory, can address current problems in labour law in order to provide a foundation for both rational labour law policy and sound labour market regulation. Like the capabilities approach, restorative approaches are embedded in values of equality, dignity, mutual respect, and concern for others. Restorative justice and relational theory are also significant for a capabilities approach because of their institutional applications. After establishing the potential connections between capabilities approaches and relational rights/restorative approaches to regulation and justice, Archibald examines two aspects of these matters in relation to labour and employment law: (i) capability-enhancing restorative approaches to workplace dispute resolution and (ii) restorative regulation of the legal construction of personal work relations. The first aspect involves an exploration of the role that mediation/arbitration and other more restorative processes can play in workplace disputes. The second aspect is the way in which the capabilities approach and restorative justice/relational principles might address changing structures of workplaces and labour markets.

## C. Part III

One of the great advantages of the engagement of law and philosophy is the relentless reversion to concrete examples, bearing out John Wisdom's remark: 'At the bar of reason, the final appeal is always to cases'.[31] In this part, a sampling of quite direct

---

[31] John Wisdom, *Paradox and Discovery* (Basil Blackwell, 1965) 102.

applications of the CA to discrete labour law issues is put on display. As has already been emphasized, no attempt has been—or could be, within the confines of a single volume—made to 'cover the field'. Rather, the topics selected for analysis are simply examples and, it is hoped, ones which offer inspiration to others to explore other concrete issues In this spirit, the examples are also intentionally wide spread across the field of contemporary labour law—both procedural and substantive, as well as domestic and transnational.

In 'The Constitution of Capabilities: the Case of Freedom of Association', Alan Bogg examines the connection between the CA and freedom of association. He begins by exploring Sen's version of the CA and, in particular, the applications of it to labour law by Langille and Oliphant. They have criticized some of the recent Supreme Court of Canada decisions that protect derivative rights (i.e. cases in which the Court impose duties on legislatures to impose duties on private parties) associated with labour claims. Bogg cites four main reasons why Langille and Oliphant support only a very limited use of derivative rights: (1) the argument from freedom; (2) the argument from democracy; (3) the argument against contextualism; and (4) the argument from equality. After addressing these arguments against derivative rights, Bogg turns to Nussbaum's account of the CA. He argues that her Aristotelian social democratic account can respond to each of the four arguments. He concludes the chapter by arguing, provocatively, that even though Nussbaum rejects the idea of directly promoting functionings, there are circumstances in which the best option is for the government to do exactly that (for example, in the context of exclusion of agricultural workers from collective bargaining laws) and describes the conditions under which it would be acceptable for the government to do so.

Pnina Alon-Shenker's 'Capabilities and Age Discrimination' explores, and takes a positive view of, the role that the CA might play in addressing age discrimination in the workplace. Alon-Shenker begins by reviewing the realities of age discrimination in today's world and the various debates, competing rationales, and controversies attached to it—including whether or not age discrimination is actually 'wrong'. In the face of these problems, Alon-Shenker argues that the CA provides an appealing way of approaching the issue of age discrimination. The CA can explain why age discrimination is wrong. Individuals' combined capabilities are, in part, determined by social structures and institutions. Older workers often face discrimination because of perceived deficits, and one of the roles of labour regulation ought to be as conversion factors that help older workers successfully participate in the labour market. Furthermore, Alon-Shenker argues, human worth is not measured solely through economic productivity, and so it is unacceptable to promote policies that reduce older workers' capabilities for the sake of younger workers' jobs. The idea of providing equal opportunity across lifespans, such that older workers are sacrificed for the sake of younger ones, is unjust. The CA not only focuses on each individual's achieving basic capabilities, but it also responds to intersectionality issues by recognizing that some older workers are in more disadvantaged positions than others. Alon-Shenker's final point is that the CA calls upon governments to promote policies and take positive action in the face of age discrimination and the problems it entails, in order to provide everyone, including older workers, with the support they need to achieve lives worthy of human dignity.

In '(Re)Imagining the Trade: Labour Linkage: The Capabilities Approach' Clair Gammage seeks to invert the dominant rationalist economic analysis of trade that sees development, consisting of economic growth, as the end of trade. Doing so, she argues, will allow for the '(re)conceptualisation' of the normative foundation of the international trade system to have human freedom as the real end of trade. Gammage begins by evaluating the development of international labour and trade regulations. Various social and labour regulations were proposed for international agreement, but were either rejected or were ineffectual and non-binding. While recasting labour standards as international human rights can impose legally binding commitments on trade partners, labour standards have increasingly been reframed in the context of sustainability, not rights. Sustainability has often been understood in economic terms, but Gammage presents an alternative version of the concept that is more aligned with the CA. In this CA version, the ends of economic activity ought to be the meeting of the needs of all within the means of the planet so that each individual can live in an ecologically safe and socially just space. After describing this alignment between sustainability and the CA, Gammage shifts her focus from the CA to international trade, workers' rights, and labour standards. The success of labour standards as fundamental and worthy of protection hinges, she argues, on the extent to which agency and participation can be facilitated through free trade agreements (FTAs). To explore this point, Gammage looks to examples of labour standards in FTAs in EU trade agreements and in a dispute between the USA and Guatemala about the latter's failure to meet labour obligations. Gammage concludes by noting ways in which the CA might be even more useful in the international trade-labour link going forward by highlighting the importance of human freedom—and not economic values—as the ends of trade, the need for increased involvement of non-governmental organizations, the importance of intersectionality, the need for more empirical data on the various social factors that affect capability deprivations, and the need for greater clarity in international sustainable development goals.

In his 'Freedom in work and the Capability Approach: Towards a politics of freedoms for labour?' Robert Salais explores the potential role of the capabilities approach in promoting freedom in work. He focuses specifically on moral harassment in the workplace (the need to be *free from* such attacks) and on the contradiction between asking workers to engage with their capabilities while still treating them as pure factors of production (the *freedom to* engage one's humanity in work). Salais begins by rejecting the 'European misunderstanding' of capabilities. Capabilities, especially those related to work, are not merely a measure for the binary fact of (un)employment. Instead, they provide a framework of principles of justice based on the real freedom of individuals to live lives they have reason to value. There is a sense in which the CA can act as a measure, but the point of the approach is to find a fair and complete way of evaluating lives in pursuit of the just ends of individual freedom. Salais moves on to consider two examples of unfreedom at work: first, moral harassment, which involves demeaning and demoralizing actions by management aimed to force individual workers to quit; and, second, the ways in which the concepts of individual freedom, agency, and capability are being used by firms to subject workers to strict standards of measurement established by management. In this latter case, the concept of worker freedom is, as a result, being used to create and perpetuate conditions of subordination and oppression in which workers are actually less free. Salais argues that the CA can help labour law move away from these problems associated with freedom. Of particular importance is the CA's understanding of freedom as both an instrument and an end. Salais argues that the 'situated state' (in contrast to a top-down or an absent state) is best positioned to achieve this CA application in labour law, by seeking collective knowledge and providing space in which everyone would be involved in specifying the rights to be implemented.

Lyn K.L. Tjon Soei Len's 'Capabilities, Contract, and Causality: The Case of Sweatshop Goods' deploys the capabilities approach to address minimum contract justice in the context of consumer contracts for sweatshop goods. By applying the CA, as a particular way of articulating minimum justice, Tjon Soei Len argues that sweatshop working conditions clearly do not meet a minimum threshold of capabilities. The question for her becomes whether contract law ought to enforce consumer contracts for sweatshop goods. The most common objection to the idea that contract law should not enforce these kinds of contracts is the 'causality objection'. Tjon Soei Len responds to this objection with two points: first, that it is based on a conception of 'the consumer' as weak and in need of protection, a conception which ignores the fact that consumers can (and should) make informed choices about consumption; and, secondly, that contract law does not depend on the concept of causality to determine liability. It is the concept of 'reasonable foreseeability' in contract law that provides an objective standard for those consequences.

Tjon Soei Len turns to her account of the capabilities-based approach to minimum contract justice. Rather than being about the internal, bilateral relationship between contracting parties, the CA sees contract law as the framework through which substantive freedoms are promoted and protected. The role of contract law is to ensure that market behaviours meet a minimum acceptable level of justice. Within this sphere, contract immorality offer a legal basis upon which courts can refuse the availability of state power to those private pursuits deemed contrary to society's fundamental values (i.e. those that diminish the fundamental capabilities of others). Len concedes that there will be conflicts between capabilities and that some freedom might be diminished at the cost of others. However, she argues, not all freedoms and capabilities are of equal importance, and few people would argue that the fundamental capabilities and freedoms of sweatshop workers are less important than the market freedoms of consumers to buy the latest fashion trends at cheap prices.

## III. Capability and Legality

Most of the chapters in this volume are written in an interdisciplinary spirit so central to legal education in our times. That is, they involve scholars who, having abandoned an old-fashioned sort of legal formalism of another age, are seeking inspiration from relevant disciplines as they seek to understand and sometimes improve our world though our laws, legal processes, and institutions. Some of the chapters in this volume, particularly in Part II, go a step further and explore the relationship between several of these disciplines, the CA and economic analysis of law of example, brought to bear upon the law. There is a risk in this sort of enterprise—a risk that some legal scholars see as very real—that what passes as interdisciplinary is really the replacement of one discipline with another, where law is displaced or becomes as an empty vessel filled with the insights from elsewhere and with nothing of its own to say.[32] This risk is a two-sided one and can be shared by lawyers and those non-lawyers offering their insights to the law. In this volume, this risk has been borne in mind and the results are evident. In these chapters both the idea of capability and legality have been taken seriously, and the chapters reveal a very real struggle to assess carefully the way the CA and labour law can inform each other. In this regard, Martha C Nussbaum has been a leader among CA theorists in concretely addressing the CA in a legal framework.[33] This is something Amartya Sen has expressly avoided.[34] He seeks an approach which is not centered upon, or stuck with, the 'limits' of law. This is a perfectly defensible position—not everyone has to be a lawyer and worry about what lawyers have to worry about. But some people are lawyers and have to take seriously what Sen calls the 'limits' of law—which, for lawyers, is another word for law's virtues. That is, there are many ways of thinking about the world and making it a better place; using law is one of them, and law comes with its limits/virtues. The chapters in the volume try to reflect the sort of interdisciplinary perspective which takes both law and the CA seriously. When we attempt to do so, we get a richer, more complex, and much needed debate. In this volume we see both lawyers and theoreticians of the CA carefully thinking about both the CA and labour law. We also see that there is much to be gained from doing so.

[32] Ernest Weinrib, 'Can Law Survive Legal Education?' (2007) 60 *Vanderbilt Law Review, Symposium on Legal Education* 401, 401–38.

[33] Martha C Nussbaum, 'Constitutions and Capabilities: "Perception" Against Lofty Formalism' (2007) 121 *Harvard Law Review* 4, 4–97 (Supreme Court Foreword).

[34] Amartya Sen, 'Human Rights and the Limits of the Law' (2006) 27 *Cardozo Law Review* 2913.

# PART I

# THE CAPABILITY APPROACH
# AND LABOUR LAW

*Fundamental Questions*

# 1

# What Can Sen's Capability Approach Offer to Labour Law?

*Hugh Collins**

What can the capability approach, as advocated by Amartya Sen, offer to labour lawyers?[1] The category of labour law includes both rights to form trade unions for the purpose of collective bargaining and individual employment protections such as rights to a minimum wage or against discrimination on grounds of gender or race. Can the capability approach provide a credible justification for the need for special legal rules to regulate work relations? Or can the capability approach at least provide fresh values for labour law to embrace at a time when the existing labour law traditions appears to be under attack?[2]

In several fascinating contributions,[3] Brian Langille has eloquently argued that Sen's capability approach can provide a grounding or justification for the whole field of labour law. Indeed, from one perspective, the capability approach looks potentially helpful, for its emphasis on the good of freedom to achieve well-being through what people are able to do in practice, and the requirement that justice must prioritize freedom, chimes with the aspirations of many of those who advocate strong labour laws for the sake of protecting workers against exploitation and improving their quality of life and self-respect. Yet, from another perspective, the capability approach, with its strong emphasis on the goal of individual freedom for the achievement of well-being, appears to be pointing in the wrong direction. Instead of enhancing market freedoms, much of labour law consists of mandatory rights and institutions that are designed to inhibit freedom of contract out of the

* I am grateful to Brian Langille for herding us towards this challenging project and to Virginia Mantouvalou for comments on an earlier draft of this chapter.

[1] Amartya K Sen, *Development as Freedom* (Oxford University Press, 1999); Amartya K Sen, *The Idea of Justice* (Penguin Group, 2009).

[2] Riccardo Del Punta, 'Labour Law and the Capability Approach' (2016) 32 *International Journal of Comparative Labour Law and Industrial Relations* 383.

[3] Brian Langille, 'Labour Law's Theory of Justice' in Guy Davidov and Brian Langille (eds), *The Idea of Labour Law* (Oxford University Press, 2011) 104; Brian Langille, 'Human Freedom: A Way Out of Labour Law's Fly Bottle' in Hugh Collins, Gillian Lester, and Virginia Mantouvalou (eds), *Philosophical Foundations of Labour Law* (Oxford University Press, 2018); Brian Langille, 'What is Labour Law? Implications of the Capability Approach', Chapter 6 in this volume.

fear that unconstrained markets for labour often lead to social exclusion, exploitation, and the undermining of individual dignity. Some labour laws may protect freedom, as in the case of laws against forced labour and trafficking, but for the most part the paternalism of mandatory labour laws overrides choices about terms of employment.

The chief reason why this issue matters is that there is a widespread view that labour law needs a better theory to justify its existence and that such a theory must be a theory of justice. Having considered why labour law needs a theory of justice and why current theories are criticized, we will consider whether the capability approach offers productive insights into the aims, structures, and principles of labour law. Although the capability approach benefits from the contributions of many philosophers, especially those of Martha C Nussbaum,[4] the focus here is on Sen's contribution for the reason that it has been relied upon by Langille and other legal scholars as the basis for claims about the potential of capability theory to provide a new, more profound justification for labour law. My argument will be that, although Sen's capability approach cannot on its own justify labour law or provide insights into many traditional parts of the subject, it does promise fresh insights with respect to topics such as affirmative action, voice at work, greater personal autonomy, the work/life balance, and rules about fair treatment within organizations.

## I. Labour Law's Need for a Theory of Justice

Labour law is not unique in looking to political theory for inspiration. In public law, especially constitutional law, views on complex issues in constitutional law are inevitably bound up with political theories. These theories may address such topics as the separation of powers, the proper relation between democratic sovereignty, the rule of law, and the protection of fundamental rights, all of which provide the core of constitutional law. In areas of private law, however, such as contract, tort, and property, the significance of political theory is rarely considered or acknowledged. In these private law fields, lawyers can often gain inspiration from some broad moral principles, such as promises ought to be kept or taking another's property without consent is wrong, without perceiving any need to consider the relevance of political theory. Nevertheless, these moral principles presuppose a basic legal institutional structure that respects private property, freedom of contract, the legal capacity of all persons, and other essential ingredients of a market society. Yet that basic legal structure of private law is inadequate for justifications and accounts of labour law.

The core of the subject of labour law concerns the regulation of work and employment relations. Since the demise of feudal societies and the rise of market societies,

---

[4] Martha C Nussbaum, *Frontiers of Justice: Disability, Nationality and Species Membership* (Harvard University Press, 2006); Martha C Nussbaum, *Creating Capabilities: The Human Development Approach* (Harvard University Press, 2011).

the legal framework for the exchange of work for payment has been found in the law of contract. But the basic institutional structure provided by contract law and free markets proves deeply unsatisfactory in connection with the employment of labour by owners of capital.

Indeed, labour law has as its main purpose the removal of general contract law (and private law more generally) from the regulation of many aspects of work relations. Contract law may still provide the scaffolding for personal work relations, but the bricks and mortar of the building derive from other sources. These sources include mandatory rules in legislation as well as the collective self-regulation mechanism of collective bargaining. To justify this substantial exclusion of general contract law from the laws governing work relations, labour law needs a theory of why the market and the basic institutions of justice that support it prove inadequate in the case of employment relations.

A popular justification for the exclusion of ordinary contract law is the claim that the employment relation is distorted by inequality of bargaining power. The meaning of inequality of bargaining power is this context is unclear. Whilst it is certainly correct that employers typically impose the terms of the contract unilaterally, that fact demonstrates that there is no competitive market for contract terms, but it does not reveal the absence of market competition with respect to the price of labour. The concept of inequality of bargaining power used in many justifications of labour law is not an economic description of the failure of a competitive labour market, but is rather an observation that the material and psychological risks to individual workers involved in obtaining and holding on to a job are far more significant to their well-being than the risks of gaining or losing a particular employee will be to the average employer. The stakes for an individual of having remunerated work or becoming unemployed are high, whereas the loss of a worker rarely harms the interests of employers because they can readily find a substitute. Given the significant impact on well-being of employment and job security, the ordinary freedom to enter and break contracts is regarded as conferring an unsatisfactory power on employers, because it may be used for the purpose of exploiting workers and depriving them of well-being. This is the problem of inequality of bargaining power, properly understood: there is no market failure, but rather the normal market creates opportunities for exploitation. Therefore, the basic institutions of private law need to be supplement by special rules for the institution of employment and workplace relations. These basic institutions need to be guided by a theory of justice that explains the shape and purpose of those labour laws.

Ideas of what justice requires may differ considerably, of course, but the case for having a labour law at all in place of the general law of contract depends ultimately on the appeal to some kind of theory of justice. Such a theory might emphasize the importance of general welfare or utility, or it might try to ground the theory in an appeal to individual rights such as human rights or labour rights. What any theory of labour law must do, in my view, is to explain and justify the substantial exclusion of the general law of contract.

## II.  A Critique of Existing Theories of Justice

In his essay entitled 'Labour Law's Theory of Justice',[5] Brian Langille appears to agree with what has been said so far about labour law's need for a theory of justice. But he announces that all prior theories of justice have failed.[6] His main attack is directed against theories that justify labour law by reference to the concept of inequality of bargaining power. Langille refers, probably accurately, to the existence of a 'traditional theory of justice' that relies heavily on the idea of inequality of bargaining power.[7] The role of labour law on this view is to be a 'countervailing force' either by promoting collective bargaining that will create greater equality of bargaining power or by removing the influence of superior bargaining power altogether by the imposition of mandatory rules such as protection against discrimination or unfair dismissal. Langille describes this theme of inequality of bargaining power to 'be basic to the received wisdom about our labour law'.[8] He also acknowledges that the slogan that 'labour is not a commodity' is also central to the labour law tradition.

As Langille rightly observes, neither of the claims about inequality of bargaining power and 'labour is not a commodity' would withstand much investigation within the framework of economic analysis.[9] Instead, as we have already noted, such claims should be regarded as reasons for excluding the ordinary private law of contract and property rights from employment relations. The claim about inequality of bargaining power means that the way that the private law market functions tends to lead employees into accepting poor terms and conditions that involve hard work for barely enough pay to live on. The claim that labour is not a commodity is fairly obscure, but, in my view, its primary meaning is a demand that employers ought not to treat workers like things or slaves, but should treat them rather with dignity and respect, even in the context of the relation of subordination that lies at the heart of the contract of employment. Why does Langille think that justifications for labour law based upon claims about inequality of bargaining power and 'labour is not a commodity' are failures?

His first point is to say that the idea of 'labour is not a commodity' has been treated as if it is the same as the idea of inequality of bargaining power. His exact words are:

We have reduced the power of the idea that 'labour is not a commodity' by tying it to, and seeing it intimately connected with, our other rallying cry of 'inequality of bargaining power.[10]

---

[5] Langille, 'Labour Law's Theory of Justice' (n 3).

[6] He is not alone in reaching that conclusion: e.g. Del Punta, 'Labour Law and the Capability Approach' (n 2) 387.

[7] Langille, 'Labour Law's Theory of Justice' (n 3) 104.

[8] Langille, 'Labour Law's Theory of Justice' (n 3) 105.

[9] Langille, 'Labour Law's Theory of Justice' (n 3) 106.

[10] Langille, 'Labour Law's Theory of Justice' (n 3) 110.

He adds a few lines later:

Labour law's understanding of the claim that 'labour is not a commodity' is too narrow. It places this claim in harness with the claim that labour law seeks to protect human beings who suffer from lack of bargaining power in the negotiation of terms of conditions of employment . . . This is our standard empirical, conceptual, and normative set-up.[11]

If this claim were true, it would certainly present a problem. The idea of inequality of bargaining power is vague, but it clearly has an inherent bias towards looking at issues of material welfare such as fair wages achieved through negotiations between parties of equal bargaining power rather than the protection of the dignity and human rights of workers. Although Langille concedes that sometimes discussions about the rationale for support of collective bargaining in terms of inequality of bargaining power may touch upon the idea that workers are 'agents' or 'participants', and not just things or objects to be protected, he nevertheless insists that justifications of labour law have been boiled down to concerns about inequality of bargaining power. Langille adds, as the final *coup de grace*, that if labour lawyers are asked 'the obvious question—why are we interested in that? we have no response'.[12] In other words, his claim is that 'inequality of bargaining power' is not really a theory of justice at all, but a normative idea masquerading as an economic concept that is merely 'an adjunct to market ordering's normativity',[13] which therefore cannot help us develop a proper rationale for labour law.[14]

Langille offers no supporting evidence for his claim that the normative justifications for labour law have been narrowed down to invocations of the obscure and unhelpful idea of inequality of bargaining power. It is true that judges often refer to the concept of inequality of bargaining power when discussing the context of employment disputes,[15] but those remarks are not intended to provide a comprehensive theory of the moral foundations for the law. Langille concedes that the two rather vague ideas of 'dignity' and 'decent work' are frequently referred to by scholars as justifications for labour law, but he seems to dismiss these ideas as lacking 'moral ammunition' and, surely unfairly, as being no more than restatements of the problem of inequality of bargaining power.

What is especially perplexing about Langille's claim that justifications of labour law have been reduced to concerns about inequality of bargaining power is that it is coming from an editor of the book entitled *The Idea of Labour Law*. A brief glance through that excellent book reveals arguments by legal scholars for a host of different ideas about the moral and political foundations of labour law. Indeed, one would be hard put to find any contributor to the volume who mentions inequality of bargaining power, let alone someone who reduces the justification for labour law down to that univocal claim. On the contrary, the general theme of the book is to advance

---

[11] Langille, 'Labour Law's Theory of Justice' (n 3) 110.
[12] Langille, 'Labour Law's Theory of Justice' (n 3) 110.
[13] Langille, 'Labour Law's Theory of Justice' (n 3) 111.
[14] Cf Brian Langille, 'Labour Law's Back Pages' in Guy Davidov and Brian Langille (eds), *Boundaries and Frontiers of Labour Law* (Hart Publishing, 2006) 13.
[15] E.g. *Autoclenz Ltd v Belcher* [2011] UKSC 41, [2011] ICR 1157 [35]; Wilson J in *Lavigne v Ontario Public Service Employees Union* [1991] 2 SCR 211 (Supreme Court of Canada).

and explain justifications for labour law that do not turn on inequality of bargaining power. Even Manfred Weiss, who is held up by Langille as a leading exponent of the shibboleth of inequality of bargaining power, in his essay in that book combines four justifications for labour law: labour is not a commodity; the personal dependency of employees; a concern for human dignity; and the protection of economic security through social security systems.[16] Similarly, in his essay, Harry Arthurs recognizes that stories about inequality of bargaining power have lost their shine, and so he argues instead in favour of three principles for the foundations of labour law: labour law should be embedded in, and help to advance, a regime of fundamental and universal human rights; labour law should empower workers by facilitating their accumulation of human capital and the realization of their human capacities; and to enable workers to seek justice in the workplace and labour market through all kinds of mobilization, both inside and outside the workplace.[17]

All this evidence tends to point to the conclusion that Langille is attacking a straw man or at least one that is a corpse. That is not to deny that labour law needs to renew its moral and political foundations. The pioneering book *The Idea of Labour Law* was needed in order to assess the traditional justifications and to revise them where they were inadequate. In that volume, Langille was the only scholar who wanted to discard the whole tradition and throw out the baby with the bathwater.[18] His purpose in so doing may have been to construct a similar critique and resolution to that presented by Sen in his discussion of development economics.

Sen was originally motivated to write *Development as Freedom* in order to challenge the orthodoxy within development economics that the sole measure of success was whether the dollar income of inhabitants of a developing country had increased. Sen argued that man does not live by bread alone, and that the purpose of contributing to development was not ultimately about levels of material wealth but rather about the degree of freedom enjoyed by inhabitants of developing countries. I see a parallel in Langille's argument. Langille attempts to describe the traditional justifications for labour law in a way that presents them in a narrow materialist way, so that he can then mount Sen's charger and insist that there is more to life than issues about wages and hours. For instance, later on in his essay, Langille argues that redistribution such as that achieved by collective bargaining or a minimum wage cannot be an end in itself, but is merely valuable insofar as it achieves, in line with Sen's definition of well-being as freedom, the good of human beings leading the lives we have reason to value. This devaluing of the importance of material wealth and relative deprivation in material terms as a social goal parallels Sen's attack on the economistic mentality of the World Bank. As I have argued, however, Langille's description of orthodox accounts of the justification of labour law as being solely concerned with

---

[16] Manfred Weiss, 'Re-inventing labour law?' in Guy Davidov and Brian Langille (eds), *The Idea of Labour Law* (OUP, 2011) 43.

[17] Harry Arthurs *Labour Law after Labour* in Guy Davidov and Brian Langille (eds), *The Idea of Labour Law* (OUP, 2011).

[18] I am not the first to accuse him of this: Guy Davidov, 'The (Changing) Idea of Labour Law' (2007) 146 *International Labour Review* 311.

material questions seem to me to be wide of the mark, so his attempt to imitate Sen's critique is not going to be convincing.

Where Langille makes an important point is with respect to the poverty of the normative orientation of many theories of labour law. In my view, the idea of inequality of bargaining power (in a non-economic sense) is essential to explain why the ordinary private law of contract cannot be accepted as the foundational institution for employment relations. Having made the case that ordinary labour markets lead to serious risks of exploitation, the question then becomes what values should shape the rules that replace the ordinary law of contract. The idea of inequality of bargaining power provides an inadequate answer to that question, for it seems to suggest that labour law should only provide a 'countervailing force' against the power of capital.[19] While such a countervailing force is important for the achievement of both material goals and the dignity of self-determination, it is true, as Langille urges, that labour law should set its sights on further ambitions such as social inclusion and dignity at work. Langille argues that we need a new normative theory for labour law and that such a theory can be derived from Sen's work. He writes:

… there is a broader, deeper morality which can be understood as underwriting in a more powerful and morally salient manner what we have known as labour law …[20]

## III.  The Capability Approach and the Justification of Labour Law

How does Langille present the potential contribution of the capability approach? He describes Sen as holding that our view of the 'good' or what we want everyone to achieve is 'the real capacity to lead a life we have reason to value'. Langille explains that, in Sen's view, it is important to have those 'real capacities', or human capital (in an extended sense), not only for the opportunities those capacities may give us, but also because the mere possession of them gives us a freedom, a freedom to choose among many different life options. For instance, being literate not only gives us the ability to do certain things such as read and write that may be essential for most well-remunerated jobs and careers, but we also have greater freedom by virtue of being literate, simply by having the choice about whether to read and write or not. We then reach the core of Langille's claim:

Labour law can be seen as that part of our law which structures the mobilization and deployment of human capital. Human capital is at the core of human freedom. Labour law is at its root no longer best conceived as law aimed at protecting employees against superior employer bargaining power in the negotiation of contracts of employment. That is now an empirically limited and normatively thin account of the discipline. Rather, we can say that labour law is

---

[19]  Paul Davies and Mark Freedland, *Kahn-Freund's Labour and the Law* (3rd edn, Stevens & Sons, 1983) 18; Karl Klare, 'Countervailing Workers' Power as a Regulatory Strategy' in Hugh Collins, Paul L Davies, and Roger Rideout (eds), *Legal Regulation of the Employment Relation* (Kluwer Law International, 2000).

[20]  Langille, 'Labour Law's Theory of Justice' (n 3) 111.

now best conceived of as that part of our law which structures (and thus either constrains or liberates) human capital creation and deployment.[21]

He goes on to repeat his claims that this view of the normative underpinnings of labour law provided by the capability approach is deeper, broader, more compelling, and more positive.

I have a number of reasons for believing that this claim is unsatisfactory as a new basis for a normative claim about the proper purposes and scope of labour law. Many critical points might be made, but here three principal concerns will be highlighted.

## A.  Freedom

The first issue concerns the role of the value of freedom in shaping labour law. Recall that it was argued above that the ordinary law of contract present in private law has to be rejected as the foundational legal structure for employment relations because of the risk that freedom of contract may lead to exploitation. A fundamental requirement of a justification for labour law is that it rejects the normative standard of freedom of contract between individuals (although perhaps supporting freedom of contract between collective groups or 'collective laissez-faire').[22] The theory of inequality of bargaining power may be morally thin and inadequate on its own, but at least it points towards a justification for mandatory protections for workers against exploitative managerial practices. The concern about the capability approach, especially that advocated by Sen, is that the emphasis on freedom as both a means and a goal of justice renders it hard to justify detailed mandatory laws. The whole emphasis on freedom in this capability approach suggests that everyone should have the opportunity to enter markets on the terms that they choose without paternalist controls.[23] Freedom of contract is an extremely important one of our capabilities, for without the ability to exchange goods and services, the benefits, and opportunities provided by a division of labour would be denied to us. My first concern is, therefore, that the emphasis on freedom and capabilities fails to achieve what any theory of labour law must achieve: to explain why the ordinary law of contract should not apply to the employment relation, or put the point another way, why labour should not be regarded solely as a market relation; or, in another manner of speaking, why labour should not be treated like a commodity.

Langille seems to be alert to this problem. He notes that labour lawyers tend to be worried about advocates of freedom and he recognizes that traditional theories about labour law were antagonistic to freedom in the context of freedom of contract.[24] Langille insists entirely fairly that Sen is not advocating formal freedom but a more substantive freedom. That is true, but what does the notion of substantive freedom mean in the context of labour law? What might substantive freedom mean in the context of workers looking for jobs in the labour market? A crucial question

---

[21] Langille, 'Labour Law's Theory of Justice' (n 3) 11, 2.
[22] Otto Kahn-Freund, 'Labour Law' in Otto Kahn-Freund, *Selected Writings* (Stevens & Sons, 1978) 1, 8.
[23] Ian Carter, 'Is the Capability Approach Paternalist?' (2014) 30 *Economics and Philosophy* 75.
[24] Langille, 'Labour Law's Theory of Justice' (n 3) 117.

is whether this substantive freedom permits the removal of almost all of the freedom of contract except the ability to walk away from a job, and the replacement of individual agreements with either collective agreements or mandatory rules. To put the issue another way, does the reduction and replacement of formal freedom in contracts of employment achieve, at the same time, as Langille must surely claim, an embodiment of the advancement of substantive freedom despite the evident restrictions on freedom of contract? For instance, can we say that workers have more substantive freedom if they cannot agree to be paid less than the minimum wage? That was Uber's spokesman's argument for not applying the minimum wage to their drivers using their IT platform: the drivers should have the freedom to use their capabilities (in this case a car, a smart phone, and a driving licence) to make a living. Famously, the Supreme Court of the United States held in *Lochner v New York*[25] that mandatory laws regarding working hours restricted freedom of contract of both employers and employees. Even if that case can be discounted as resting on a narrow conception of formal freedom, the same cannot be said of the judgment of the European Court of Justice in *Alemo Herron v Parkwood Leisure*,[26] where, in the name of the substantive and positive right to freedom to run a business in Article 16 of the Charter of the Fundamental Rights of the European Union,[27] the Court permitted an employer to abandon a collective agreement that was imposed on it by virtue of a European Directive.[28]

Anticipating this kind of objection coming from labour lawyers, Langille's riposte is, first, to say that his theory is much deeper than the received wisdoms of labour law. He makes the point that there is no such thing as a labour market that functions without rules that are guided by normative visions. It is correct that there is no such thing as an unregulated market. We have assumed that point throughout this discussion. The question is what rules should regulate the labour market: the ordinary law of contract or some special rules that address problems like exploitation and unfairness? If the answer given is that the choice should be in favour of the rules that maximize capabilities, why should we think that mandatory laws such as a minimum wage law that restrict freedom of contract are the ones to be chosen rather than a grant to the parties of freedom of contract? To that question, Langille offers no direct answer except to make a second riposte that the critics of capability theory are in error. This error seems to be the inability to see that freedom in some things can lead to greater freedom overall. For instance, freedom of association is a freedom for workers to help themselves through trade unions to improve their situation, which in turn may provide them with greater capabilities. That is a good example of how one freedom can enhance other freedoms. I doubt that any of the

---

[25] 198 US 45 (1905).

[26] Case C-426/11 *Alemo-Herron v Parkwood Leisure* ECLI:EU:C:2013:521, [2013] ICR 1116; Jeremias Prassl, 'Freedom of Contract as a General Principle of EU Law? Transfers of Undertakings and the Protection of Employer Rights in EU Labour Law' (2013) 42 *Industrial Law Journal* 434; Marija Bartl and Candida Leone, 'Minimum Harmonisation and Article 16 of the CFREU: Difficult Times Ahead for Social Legislation?' in Hugh Collins (ed), *European Contract Law and the Charter of Fundamental Rights* (Intersentia, 2017) 113.

[27] 2012/C 326/2, OJ 55, 26 10 2012, 391.          [28] Acquired Rights Directive 2001/23.

critics deny that point. Free markets undoubtedly liberate us to do things that we could not do without them.

Nevertheless, the question remains whether labour law in the form of mandatory rules is compatible with and more supportive of the ideas of substantive freedom that motivate the claims regarding the importance of capabilities. The answer provided by Langille seems to be:

> We need a theory which explains why market activity and economic growth are desirable in the first place. This justification has to be undertaken in terms of advancing the cause of real freedom.[29]

Instead of supporting the argument that the mandatory rules of labour law are needed to achieve substantive freedom, his last remark appears in fact to support the application of the ordinary law of contract that provides the legal foundation for market activity and economic growth. He is saying that free markets are valuable in the long run because they enhance substantive freedom. If that position is correct, it is unclear what scope is left for special regulation of employment contracts by labour laws.

## B. Justice and institutions

My second concern about the claim that we should adopt Sen's capability approach towards providing a justification for labour law relates to the adequacy of the capability approach to provide a suitable theory of justice. My question is whether the capability approach is a theory of justice or at least a theory that has sufficient elements of a theory of justice that it can be used to satisfy the requirement of providing a justification for labour law. Of course, that line of enquiry risks becoming mired in some unilluminating debate about what counts as a theory of justice. I will try to avoid that semantic trap, if at all possible.

John Rawls argues that a theory of justice comprises a normative guide to the basic structure of social institutions.[30] These institutions include the constitution, markets, property, and other institutions that make production and distribution possible. Rawls has been criticized for excluding other basic institutions such as the family and for being unclear what counts as an institution in the basic structure.[31] Those concerns do not need to detain us here, because what is evident is that Rawls' notion of justice will certainly regard the broad features of the market for personal performance of work as within the framework to be established by the principles of justice. As is well known, Rawls advances an argument that these institutions should be arranged according two principles of justice, the first principle that guarantees basic rights, and the second principle that ensures a degree of distributive equality

---

[29] Langille, 'Labour Law's Theory of Justice' (n 3) 119.

[30] John Rawls, *A Theory of Justice* (OUP, 1972); and John Rawls, *Political Liberalism* (Columbia University Press, 1993).

[31] Gerry A Cohen, 'Where the Action Is: On the Site of Distributive Justice' (1997) 26 *Philosophy & Public Affairs* 3; Liam B Murphy, 'Institutions and the Demands of Justice' (1999) 27 *Philosophy & Public Affairs* 251; Samuel Scheffler, 'Distributive Justice, the Basic Structure and the Place of Private Law' (2015) 35 *Oxford Journal of Legal Studies* 213.

in relation to material goods and opportunities. Although it is certainly possible to debate both the extent to which Rawls' work addresses the question of the need for labour law and the precise conclusions that should be drawn about the structures required by the theory of justice for labour law,[32] what cannot be doubted is that Rawls' theory of justice investigates the kind of issue that needs to be addressed in order to provide a justification for labour law. The question is whether Sen's capability approach can claim the same applicability. Sen claims to have a theory of justice, but is this kind of theory of justice going to provide labour lawyers with the kind of theory of justice that they crave?

Sen is writing from within a tradition in political theory that is closer to utilitarianism and welfarism than the liberal theory of John Rawls. He argues that the basic structure of social institutions is not a 'manifestation of social justice', but merely a means towards the goal of enabling people to live good lives.[33] So, in the jargon of political theory, Sen objects to Rawls' premise that it is possible to insist upon the priority of 'the right' over 'the good'; and therefore Sen objects to the idea that the structure of the basic institutions is itself an independent site of justice. For Sen, therefore, every question of justice can be resolved in principle on an ad hoc basis of asking in accordance with the capability approach which choice will favour the desired good, without the need to specify any particular kind of prior institutional arrangement. Sen acknowledges that institutions, laws, or principles like protection for equal basic rights, individual liberties, equal opportunities, equitable distributions, and fair procedures are all likely to be supported strongly by the capability approach. For Sen, civil and political liberties are important not just because they may indirectly contribute to economic growth (or some other kind of utilitarian goal), but are important because they normally provide constitutive institutional conditions for positive freedom.[34] In Sen's approach, it is this instrumental linkage between negative liberties and positive freedom that calls for the protection of civil and political liberties. In contrast, in rights-based liberal political theories, such as those of Rawls and Nozick,[35] individual rights provide the immutable foundation stones or starting-points for a theory of justice. As Sen says, 'In this approach, expansion of freedom is viewed as both (1) the *primary end* and (2) the *principal means* of development'.[36]

Sen seems to be reluctant to acknowledge that in his consequentialist approach logically this support for these principles and laws will always be subject to arguments that real freedom can be better achieved by dispensing with them in particular instances. In Sen's capability approach, rights should not be regarded as trumps over other claims and policy considerations, but as rules of thumb. Instead of acknowledging the provisional character of these basic liberal principles in his own theory, Sen goes on the offensive and argues that liberal theories like those of Nozick, Rawls, and Dworkin,[37] who insist upon the priority of the right over the good, never in

---

[32] Hugh Collins, 'Theories of Rights as Justifications for Labour Law' in Guy Davidov and Brian Langille (eds), *The Idea of Labour Law* (OUP, 2011) 101.

[33] Sen, *Development as Freedom* (n 1).     [34] Sen, *Development as Freedom* (n 1) 16–17.

[35] Robert Nozick, *Anarchy, State and Utopia* (Basic Books, 1974).

[36] Sen, *Development as Freedom* (n 1) 36.

[37] Ronald M Dworkin, *Taking Rights Seriously* (Duckworth, 1978).

fact stick to this position, but acknowledge all kinds of exceptions such as emergencies, wars, and natural disasters. Of course, it is true that those liberal writers have to presuppose a certain kind of society that has sufficient wealth and stability to establish institutional structures of the kind they support. Yet it is not clear why that presupposition or contingency should prevent them from articulating a theory of justice that gives priority of the right over the good. In any case, that should not matter to the enquiry in hand about the justification for labour law. Although Sen can fairly claim that his theory applies as much to stone-age cavemen as an industrial society, here, in the pursuit of a justification for labour law, we are only interested in the institutional arrangements to govern an industrial and post-industrial society. Theories of justice that presuppose such societies exist are exactly the kinds of theories of justice that labour lawyers need.

In sum, the problem with the capability approach from the point of view of the task in hand is that it does not offer a view of what permanent institutional structures are the kind of just arrangements that are needed to secure the basic elements of justice in a society. It therefore cannot offer a view on whether basic labour laws such as freedom of association, the right to work, or the protection from unjust dismissal are requirements of justice. Instead, the capability approach will tell us that each case will have to be reviewed on its merits: some workers in some situations may need such legal protections and others will not, according to what will maximize the good of real freedom. More generally, Sen's capability approach does not seem interested in describing what kinds of basic institutions are needed to establish a just society because he wants us to focus always on the overarching goal of freedom. This is a possible and in some ways attractive political theory, but it does not appear to offer any guidance on justifications for labour law. Although Sen gives general support to fairness and the protection of human rights, he is not interested in providing a guarantee of just institutions. As Samuel Freeman has commented about Sen's work on justice:

Conceiving of justice and respect for individual rights as if they were just one more good state of affairs to be maximally promoted, however, ignores the fundamental moral fact that justice is about social relations between persons and is not about persons' impartial relations to states of affairs. Rawls's social contract incorporates this fundamental moral fact. It is in danger of being compromised by Sen's disengaged spectator's impartial choice of the state of affairs that are best for people in one situation or another.[38]

In short, even if Sen's theory of 'the good' can be described as a theory of justice, it is not the kind of theory of justice that will provide any kind of serious defence of the need for the institutions of labour law. At most, it might offer some insights about the content of labour laws and some of the trade-offs that will be required. But on the fundamental need for labour law, Sen's capability approach has nothing to say, or, to repeat the previous concern, may even object to labour law altogether as an institution that interferes regularly and too much with real freedom.

---

[38] Samuel Freeman, 'A New Theory of Justice' (2010) LVII no 15, *The New York Review of Books* (14–27 October 2010) 58, 60.

## C.  Labour law and distributive justice

It is often part of the standard account of the aims of labour law to attribute to it an ambition to affect the distribution of wealth and power in society. The general idea is that the division of profits between capital and labour can be contested by labour law in order to improve the allocation to workers, or at least to prevent the risk of exploitation under ordinary market rules. This distributive aim can be fulfilled in a fairly straightforward way by ensuring that workers receive a fair or living wage for their work. A more ambitious approach is to support collective bargaining so that employers have to concede wage increases under the threat of industrial action. There are other potential redistributive mechanisms as well, such as a requirement for employers to pay for mandatory occupational pensions to help the elderly, or to give their employees a financial stake in the enterprise, or to avoid discrimination in payment systems against women and minority groups.

Langille argues, in contrast, that the goal of distributive justice is simply not really a goal in itself. He insists that the redistribution must have a deeper goal than a more egalitarian society (or however else it may be understood by political theorists). He argues that the point of redistributive measures is to achieve the goal formulated by Sen, which is real, substantive, human freedom—the real capacity to lead a life we have reason to value. Langille seems to be saying that inequalities in distribution do not matter in themselves; the point is rather whether those inequalities tend to inhibit the capabilities of disadvantaged individuals.

That argument seems to rule out the possibility of taking the view that an essential element of justice must be concerned with the distribution of material wealth and perhaps power as well. Rawls clearly disagreed with that argument. His second principle of justice was focused on helping the least well off in a manner that did not detract from the overall wealth of society. On the other hand, another rights theorist, Nozick,[39] took the position that inequalities produced by the ordinary market were not unfair, and that attempts to redistribute wealth through taxation and similar mechanism were tantamount to theft or slavery. Whilst I do not suppose Langille would go so far as to reject all redistributive taxation and welfare mechanisms, by denying that redistribution is an appropriate goal in itself for theories of justice, he certainly creates the possibility that any justification for labour law that is grounded in the capability approach, (a possibility that I have denied in my two previous points is even available), would not embrace laws that are designed for the aim of redistributing wealth from capital to labour. Among those laws we might include the laws of collective bargaining and strikes, a minimum wage law, an equal pay law, and a law about occupational pensions.

In short, my third concern about the capability approach towards a justification for labour law, as developed by Langille from the work of Sen, is that it would not provide a justification for what I regard as some of the essential ingredients of a labour law system such as laws on collective bargaining, minimum wage, and equal pay.

---

[39] Nozick, *Anarchy, State and Utopia* (n 35).

## D.  Summary

I have outlined here three reasons for doubting Langille's claim that Sen's capability approach can offer a superior theory of justice to those offered by current theories of justifications for labour law. The first difficulty is that the capability approach cannot tell us how much and what kinds of freedom should be permitted or prohibited by labour law. That tends to point to the conclusion that the inequality of bargaining power approach, which Langille caricatures and dismisses, may in fact have something significant to offer by justifying some mandatory institutions to regulate the market against exploitation of workers, although certainly this traditional theory needs to be supplemented. A second objection is that if the capability approach is properly regarded as a theory of justice (which I doubt), it is not the right kind of theory of justice to provide us with guidance on the basic institutions that a just society must have to have any chance of achieving justice. It is simply not up to the task of providing a justification for the core institutional arrangements required by a system of labour law. That is not to say that other theories such as Rawls' theory of justice provide us with a determinate account of the need for and the shape of labour law. Unfortunately, that is not the case.[40] Even so, these liberal theories about just institutions are at least making relevant and appropriate arguments, although admittedly their conclusions remain indeterminate. In short, justifications for labour law need to recognize the importance of the priority of the right over the good and Sen's capability approach deliberately rejects that kind of structure for his theory of justice. Thirdly, since the capability approach denies that principles of distributive justice, whether they adopt some version of egalitarianism or award priority to certain disadvantaged groups such as the elderly, are valuable parts of a theory of justice in themselves, as opposed to their possible contribution to the enhancement of capabilities, the capability approach risks a hollowing out of the tasks of labour law by ignoring its justification in terms of distributive justice. Historically, labour law was born through demands for distributive justice during the battles between capital and labour in early industrial society. Even though it may be heavily disguised by sham contracts and sophisticated technology, it would be a mistake to deny that the battle is still running.

## IV.  The Potential Contribution of the Capability Approach

Until this point, the argument has been that Sen's capability approach cannot provide the kind of theory of justice that would justify labour law regulation of work relations of the kind that most legal systems have today. It has been acknowledged, however, that the capability approach could contribute to the identification and exploration of a rich set of goals for labour law that go far beyond concerns about material well-being and exploitation. What sorts of interests of workers might the capability approach justify and articulate? As well as providing new reasons for

---

[40]  Hugh Collins, 'Theories of Rights as Justifications for Labour Law' (n 32) 101.

supporting some traditional labour laws, can Sen's capability approach help to set a new agenda for labour law by emphasizing new issues that should be addressed for the sake of enhancing positive freedom?

One obvious possibility for pushing labour law in particular directions is that the capability approach might support a worker's right to flexibility in hours or location of work or to be able to exercise greater autonomy at work.[41] The emphasis on freedom should also lead the capability approach to stress the importance of achieving a balance between working time and the opportunity to develop other capabilities relating to play and culture. It seems possible that the capability approach might support the shift from employment to self-employment, because the self-employed may have greater positive freedom to pursue their goals, although usually they do so whilst bearing greater risks of economic insecurity. Another possibility is that the capability approach might seek to expand the scope of employment protection laws to workers who are normally excluded from their protections because they lack formal contracts and a regular job.[42] With its emphasis on the workplace being a site for the development of capabilities, the capability approach may support an extended view of the responsibility of an employer to provide a workplace where workers are treated fairly and their autonomy is supported.[43] The capability approach might also require employers to provide work that can make a meaningful contribution to their employees' lives.[44] Yet all these directions that capabilities might take us are inherently speculative, as the criterion of enhancing capabilities or positive freedom remains indeterminate.[45] To try to tie down this argument that the capabilities approach can offer a fresh narrative for labour law, here we will focus attention on a plausible claim that is frequently made that the capability approach can justify strong legal support for the kinds of interests of workers that are proclaimed in charters of social and economic rights.

Although Sen does not discuss social and economic rights explicitly, he explains how the positive notion of freedom that distinguishes capability theory is necessarily interested in the social and material obstructions to an individual's actual ability to pursue valuable goals in life. Pointing to ways in which such obstructions can be overcome lies at the heart of Sen's proposals for development:

Development requires the removal of major sources of unfreedom: poverty as well as tyranny, poor economic opportunities as well as systematic social deprivation, neglect of public facilities as well as intolerance or over-activity of repressive states.[46]

---

[41] Del Punta, 'Labour Law and the Capability Approach' (n 2) 397. Cf Hugh Collins, 'The Right to Flexibility' in Joanne Conaghan and Kerry Rittich (eds), *Labour Law, Work, and Family: Critical and Comparative Perspectives* (Oxford University Press, 2005) 99.

[42] Supriya Routh, *Enhancing Capabilities through Labour Law* (Routledge, 2016) 166.

[43] Langille, 'Human Freedom: A Way Out of Labour Law's Fly Bottle' (n 3).

[44] Virginia Mantouvalou, 'Work, Human Rights, and Human Capabilities', Chapter 10 in this volume.

[45] A Bogg, 'Labour Law and the Trade Unions: Autonomy and Betrayal' in A Bogg and others (eds), *The Autonomy of Labour Law* (Hart Publishing, 2015) 73, 86–95.

[46] Sen, *Development as Freedom* (n 1) 3.

Sandra Fredman uses this capability approach to help to explain the importance of positive social and economic rights.[47] In order to achieve freedom to any worthwhile degree, individuals must be protected through human rights law against oppressive governments, but also they must have access to the necessary resources to achieve valuable goals. The essential resources for this purpose are often articulated in international conventions on social and economic rights. The rights listed in such conventions might include, for instance, food, shelter, education, and work. The social right to education illustrates such a capability: whatever one's level of intelligence and aptitude for study, one needs access to education in order to have the capability to explore a range of valuable alternatives, not just in work, but in other aspects of life such as culture. Social rights are important on this view because they provide legal support for capabilities in the sense that they permit individuals to use whatever abilities or endowments they have to achieve the goals or 'functionings' that they have reason to value. The social and economic rights place a correlative duty on the government to choose policies that are likely to protect and fulfil these rights. Building on Sen's conceptual scheme, Sandra Fredman can argue plausibly that the imposition of binding positive duties on government to promote and protect social and economic rights will provide a valuable contribution to the kind of positive freedom advocated in the capability approach.

While Fredman focuses her attention on housing, welfare, and education, Deakin and Wilkinson claim that Sen's theory provides support for the recognition and enforcement of those social and economic rights that serve as a precondition for the functioning of a labour market.

The social rights which we have in mind are therefore those which would empower individuals with the means needed to realize their potential in a sustainable way, thereby enhancing the wealth of well-being of society as a whole.[48] More precisely, constitutionalized social rights can be thought of as the juridical instantiation of the concept of capability.[49]

Many of these social and economic rights that are listed in international conventions apply to work relations. In the European Social Charter 1961 of the Council of Europe, for instance, the first six rights are in summary: the right to work, the right to just conditions of work, the right to safe conditions at work, the right to fair remuneration, the right to freedom of association in trade unions, and the right to collective bargaining and to strike. We can view those rights as forming part of the bedrock of labour law.

As a justification for social and economic rights, capability theory has considerable potential. As a goal-based theory, Sen's capability theory is always willing to consider making trade-offs between rights and goals, or between institutional structures and policy considerations. Unlike traditional human rights, social and economic rights are not generally regarded as fully imperative rights. It is generally

---

[47] Sandra Fredman, *Human Rights Transformed: Positive Rights and Positive Duties* (OUP, 2008) 10–12.

[48] Simon Deakin and Frank Wilkinson, *The Law of the Labour Market* (OUP, 2005) 277.

[49] Deakin and Wilkinson, *The Law of the Labour Market* (n 48) 345.

said that social and economic rights can be realized progressively and do not have to be met absolutely. For that reason, it is possible to have legitimate trade-offs between social policy and the allocation of budgets, on the one hand, and social and economic rights on the other. In other words, governments must fulfil a right like the right to education as far as possible in the light of the available resources and the competing demands of other social and economic rights. Capability theory may provide a way of balancing these competing considerations by evaluating measures against the standard of the goal of positive freedom. By using the concept of capability or positive freedom, it can explain why it is appropriate that rights should only be progressively realized and how trade-offs should be conducted.

On the other hand, as a goal-based theory, as we have already noted, the capability approach is unlikely to support strong mandatory legal protections for social and economic rights. Egalitarian or social inclusion theories of justice may view some social and economic rights such as rights to food and shelter as fixing minimum entitlements for everyone that should be legally enforceable against a government. In contrast—although no doubt extremely sensitive to problems of hunger and homelessness as they clearly impact on the ability to pursue one's goals in life—the capability approach is unlikely to support mandatory rules that cannot be challenged by reference to the competing demands of positive freedom. For that reason, advocates of social and economic rights may discover that capability theory may not provide reasons to give strong legal teeth to social and economic rights. Even so, by emphasizing the importance of dismantling obstacles to the realization of positive freedom, the capability approach certainly supports measures that protect and enhance the interests identified by social and economic rights, although not necessarily to the extent of constitutionalizing those rights.[50]

There is a further reason to question how far capability theory is likely to support those interests mentioned in social and economic rights that are applicable to employment relations and the labour market such as a fair wage and the rights to collective bargaining. In Sen's version of the capability approach,[51] he avoids any specification of basic goods that everyone should enjoy. Instead, he focuses on the obstacles that exist in any particular case for someone to realize their capabilities in practice. In contrast, most liberal theories rest on a conception of basic goods. For instance, in reasoning towards his principles of justice (and the priority accorded to freedom and civil liberties), John Rawls commences by identifying what he terms 'primary goods'.[52] The idea of a primary good is that it is something that everyone agrees would be an important element in their life-plans, whoever they are and whatever those plans might turn out to be. Everyone would want to include, according to Rawls, basic rights and liberties, freedom of movement, free choice of occupation protected by fair equality of opportunity, and sufficient income and wealth

---

[50] Cf Martha C Nussbaum, 'Human Rights Theory: Capabilities and Human Rights' (1997) 66 *Fordham Law Review* 273, 295.

[51] This is a crucial difference with the work of Martha C Nussbaum. See Nussbaum, *Frontiers of Justice: Disability, Nationality and Species Membership* (n 4).

[52] Rawls, *A Theory of Justice* (n 30) 90–5.

to provide the social basis for self-respect. As acknowledged by Nussbaum, this list of primary goods seems to be almost identical to the positive freedoms or capabilities that the capability approach is likely to insist should be the key criteria for assessing development plans and social justice.[53]

Although acknowledging the close similarity, Sen nevertheless criticizes this list of primary goods, not because they do not capture what he has in mind, more or less, in his notion of substantive freedom, but rather because they fail to ask the question of whether every individual will really enjoy those freedoms under Rawls' approach, owing to differences in their abilities to turn these opportunities into real substantive capabilities.[54] For instance, a person who has a severe disability such as blindness may not be able to do much with the primary goods without some additional support, either a health service cure for blindness or some additional resources for care and assistance. Rawls' response to this criticism is, essentially, that this is a matter of detail, to be sorted out later through the democratic legislative process.[55] He expresses confidence that any inability to access the primary goods under his second principle of justice of fair equality of opportunity will be remedied by, for instance, some kind of tax break or additional assistance. Rawls clearly regards Sen's objection as insignificant and therefore not a central issue in devising the framework of justice in a political theory.

But it seems to me that this difference is potentially critical. The difference is about starting points. In Rawls' work (and most liberal political theory), the discussion commences with an assumption that most individuals are roughly equal. Differences in talent, strength, mobility, etc are, in these liberal theories, morally irrelevant to the design of the basic structure of just institutions. It is only when the basic structure of just institutions has been set that the theorist turns to the issue of potential inequalities created by differences in personal characteristics. In Sen's work, his starting point concerns these differences: people's actual capabilities are what matters above all. Furthermore, he includes in these differences not only physical characteristics but also the cultural situation of individuals, such as the inequality of women or castes under the social conventions of a particular society. His aim is to maximize the enjoyment of the primary goods or capabilities for all members of a society (their 'functionings', as he terms it), and this objective necessitates taking into account the actual position the individuals find themselves in.

Consider the example of discrimination laws. Standard liberal theories provide a robust defence of anti-discrimination laws in employment. Given that the right to work is, in one legal form or another, central to the pursuit of primary goods, liberal theories will certainly wish to insist upon fair equality of opportunity in the labour market. This principle will justify laws against discrimination based upon considerations other than merit (although defining merit is sometimes tricky). But more positive kinds of discrimination, such as affirmative action for minorities, prove much more difficult to reconcile with the principle of fair equality of opportunity. On Sen's approach, however, the disadvantages of personal starting points

[53] Nussbaum, 'Human Rights Theory' (n 50) 290.
[54] Sen, *Development as Freedom* (n 1) 74.      [55] Rawls, *Political Liberalism* (n 30) 185.

are central to the theory, and the social exclusion resulting from unemployment is one of the major obstacles to capability. His theory has the potential, therefore, to justify positive action within the framework of anti-discrimination laws.[56] With its development of a duty of accommodation for disabilities, the current law seems to match more closely Sen's starting point than the formal equality in the work of Rawls and other liberal political theories. Deakin and Wilkinson apply a similar analysis of how the capability approach supports laws against pregnancy discrimination.[57] These laws are, in effect, positive action in the form of a duty of accommodation in favour of women who are pregnant. Whereas standard liberal theories with their emphasis on equal rights and equal treatment experience difficulty in accounting for any kind of positive action in favour of disadvantaged groups, such affirmative action is central to the ambition of Sen's capability approach because it is targeted at obstacles to the effective use of capabilities. This illustration shows that in respect of some aspects of labour law, in this case laws against discrimination, Sen's capability approach may have the edge over liberal theories in justifying and accounting for the current law. But that advantage will not exist in every case.

Consider, in contrast, the attempt by Deakin and Wilkinson to apply the capability approach to justify a minimum wage law.[58] The problem with this argument is that it will have to be demonstrated that in most or perhaps all cases where the minimum wage is applied that it serves the goal of enhancing positive freedom or capabilities. A liberal theory of primary goods or one that stresses equality can support a minimum wage on grounds of the need for workers to receive a living wage or a fair wage as a requirement of justice in itself. In contrast, the capability approach must demonstrate that the mandatory legislation enhances positive freedom.[59] In some instances a minimum wage may enhance freedom, as Deakin and Wilkinson point out. If, for instance, employers respond to the minimum wage by improving the workers' training with a view to enhancing productivity, as a form of education, the training may well improve the capabilities of workers since it may open up other opportunities for work. But it is as well to remember that Sen, himself, advised against confusing 'human capital' with capability and freedom. He was concerned that 'human capital' was defined typically as resources that would improve the productivity of a worker, and therefore normally improve the wealth of the worker. Yet wealth-maximization, although often helpful to the enlargement of capacities, is not a goal in itself in the capability approach, but only an indirect means towards the goal of positive freedom. If, on the other hand, the employer responds to the minimum wage by replacing labour with technology or simply by reducing the numbers employed, it is hard to discern how the minimum wage in such instances where workers become unemployed has improved their capabilities. Whilst it is possible that in some instances the application of a minimum wage law may lead to

[56]  Sen, *Development as Freedom* (n 1) 21.
[57]  Deakin and Frank Wilkinson, *The Law of the Labour Market* (n 48) 293.
[58]  Deakin and Frank Wilkinson, *The Law of the Labour Market* (n 48) 293.
[59]  Cf Guy Davidov, 'The Capability Approach and Labour Law: Identifying the Areas of Fit', Chapter 2 in this volume.

an enhancement of capabilities, that outcome may be rare. It follows that Sen's capability approach will have difficulty in finding reasons to support a minimum wage or indeed any mandatory regulation that may lead to unemployment effects. The trade-off in liberal political theories between liberty and an equal society permits restrictions on positive liberties such as the right to work for the sake of egalitarian principles. But the capability approach rejects fairness or equal resources as a relevant consideration except insofar as the unfair distribution prevents a person from realizing their capabilities.

A similar difficulty confronts attempts to use a capability approach to support collective labour laws in the form of union organization, collective bargaining, industrial action, and other aspects of collective labour law. If we view collective bargaining as primarily an attempt by organizations of workers to use their greater bargaining power when united to obtain better terms and conditions of employment including better pay, this material and redistributive ambition is hard to justify as an institution that enhances positive freedom. If, in contrast, we emphasize the dimension of 'voice' or 'industrial democracy' that may arise from institutions of collective bargaining or other forms of information and consultation, it is plausible to argue that these collective institutions may enhance individual positive freedom.[60] It is questionable whether, in practice, a right of workers to information and consultation with their employer enhances the freedom of people to lead the lives they have reason to value and to enhance the real choices they have. The causal link is thin, but perhaps participation in decision-making is part of positive freedom in the workplace and counterbalances the purely instrumental and materialist aspects of work. As with the minimum wage example, a liberal political theory has less difficulty than the capability approach in accounting for a legal right to engage in collective bargaining, because it is concerned with a fair distribution of wealth as well as individuals having a say in their lives for the sake of dignity and self-realization. In contrast, the capability approach emphasizes positive freedom at the expense of distributive justice and therefore will not regard collective labour rights as crucial to its agenda.

## V. Conclusion

My question has been: what can Sen's capability approach offer to labour law? Despite claims to the contrary by Brian Langille, my answer is that this version of the capability approach cannot address the key existential demand of labour law for a theory of justice that requires the exclusion of the ordinary law of contract from the regulation of the labour market. The capability approach of Sen provides the wrong kind of theory of justice (if indeed it is a theory of justice at all) to ground a sound institutional basis for labour law as a system for regulating the labour market. Even if Brian Langille is correct that all the current theories of justice that support labour law are out of date and superficial, what we can say with confidence is that his

---

[60] Alan Bogg, 'The Constitution of Capabilities: The Case of Freedom of Association', Chapter 12 in this volume.

proposed alternative of a capability approach cannot provide a complete answer or even a significant part of an answer. Nevertheless, an assessment of our labour laws from the point of view of how, if at all, they enhance positive freedom or capabilities is surely a worthwhile line of enquiry. Although Sen's capability approach will not have much to say about large swathes of labour law, it does promise insights with respect to topics such as affirmative action, voice at work, greater personal autonomy, and rules about fair treatment within organizations.

# 2

# The Capability Approach and Labour Law

## Identifying the Areas of Fit

*Guy Davidov* *

## I. Introduction

The capability approach (CA) has been highly influential in labour law discourse in recent years. Originally conceived by Amartya Sen,[1] and further developed mainly by Martha C Nussbaum,[2] it has led an increasing number of labour law scholars to argue that the CA can be used as a normative justification for labour laws.[3] Sen developed the CA as a critique of Rawls' focus on the distribution of resources in his theory of justice. If resources are just means to an end ('the successful execution of a rational plan of life', for Rawls[4]), we have to wonder whether the same level of resources will give different people the same opportunities and abilities to reach their goals. Surely people with disabilities, or otherwise detrimental conditions, will be able to do much less if given the same resources.[5] Ronald Dworkin attempted

---

\* Elias Lieberman Professor of Labour Law, Hebrew University of Jerusalem. Some small parts in this chapter have been reproduced from Guy Davidov, 'Distributive Justice and Labour Law' in Hugh Collins, Gillian Lester, and Virginia Mantouvalou, *Philosophical Foundations of Labour Law* (OUP, 2018).

[1] See especially Amartya Sen, *Development as Freedom* (OUP, 1999).

[2] See especially Martha C Nussbaum, *Women and Human Development: The Capabilities Approach* (Cambridge University Press, 2000).

[3] Simon Deakin and Frank Wilkinson, *The Law of the Labour Market: Industrialization, Employment and Legal Evolution* (OUP, 2005) 290; Brian Langille, 'Labour Law's Theory of Justice' in Guy Davidov and Brian Langille, *The Idea of Labour Law* (OUP, 2011) 101; Judy Fudge, 'The New Discourse of Labor Rights: From Social to Fundamental Rights?' (2007) 29 *Comparative Labor Law and Policy Journal* 29; Judy Fudge, 'Labour as a "Fictive Commodity": Radically Reconceptualizing Labour Law' in Guy Davidov and Brian Langille, *The Idea of Labour Law* (OUP, 2011) 132; Mark Freedland and Nicola Kountouris, *The Legal Construction of Personal Work Relations* (OUP, 2011) 377; Supriya Routh, *Enhancing Capabilities through Labour Law: Informal Workers in India* (Routledge, 2014); Kevin Kolben, 'Labour Regulation, Capabilities, and Democracy' in Colin Fenwick and Shelley Marshall (eds), *Labour Law and Development* (Edward Elgar Publishing, 2016) 60; Riccardo Del Punta, 'Labour Law and the Capability Approach' (2016) 32 *International Journal of Comparative Labour Law and Industrial Relations* 383. And see the contributions by these authors and others in the current volume.

[4] John Rawls, *A Theory of Justice* (Harvard University Press, rev edn 1999, originally published 1971) 380.

[5] Sen, *Development as Freedom* (n 1) 74.

to rectify this problem with his scheme for redistribution to compensate for brute bad luck,[6] and luck egalitarians later suggested a shift of focus to 'opportunity for welfare', or 'access to advantage'.[7] Sen offered a different solution. He argued that we should focus on 'capabilities' instead of resources. What's important for people is *effective, real freedom* to pursue their plans of life. Sen described our needs and wants as 'functionings', and drew attention to the importance of capabilities to achieve these functionings. Nussbaum later explained that capabilities are the appropriate political goal—not functionings—because 'citizens must be left free to determine their own course after that'.[8]

Although Sen originally developed this idea in response to the question 'equality of what',[9] his focus was more on freedom than equality (capabilities being a way to understand effective human freedom). In principle, one could argue in favour of redistribution towards full equality of capabilities, but Sen himself is sceptical about this idea.[10] He supports equality of capabilities only in the 'sufficientarian' sense: ensuring that everyone has a set of basic capabilities. Nussbaum similarly advocates only a *threshold* level of capabilities.[11] With this approach in mind, it becomes clear why the CA is better understood as advancing freedom rather than equality.

In the current chapter I will not discuss critiques of the CA. Rather, I will assume that it is valuable in general and concentrate on whether it can also prove valuable for labour law theory. I will also refrain from any discussion of the CA as a descriptive tool,[12] concentrating instead on its potential usefulness at the normative level. Where Sen, himself, refused to consider his theory as a basis for legal duties, and Nussbaum limited herself to legal duties at the constitutional level,[13] the question addressed here is whether the CA can justify labour *legislation*.

If one wants to use the CA as a normative guide regarding which laws (and/or social policies) to adopt, one must address the question, 'what do we (as a society) want people *to be capable of*?' There are three possible answers to this question. One option is 'whatever they want'. People should have capabilities to do and be what they themselves value. Sen adds the caveat of whatever people have 'reason to value', but he has not developed this idea at length and it does not appear to be a major

---

[6] Ronald Dworkin, 'What is Equality? Part 2: Equality of Resources' (1981) 10 *Philosophy & Public Affairs* 283.

[7] Richard Arneson, 'Equality and Equality of Opportunity for Welfare' (1989) 56 *Philosophical Studies* 77; GA Cohen, 'On the Currency of Egalitarian Justice' (1989) 99 *Ethics* 906.

[8] Nussbaum, *Women and Human Development* (n 2) 87.

[9] Amartya Sen, 'Equality of What?' in Sterling M McMurrin (ed), *Tanner Lectures on Human Values* (Cambridge University Press, 1980). See also Amartya Sen, *Inequality Re-examined* (Harvard University Press, 1992).

[10] Amartya Sen, *The Idea of Justice* (Harvard University Press, 2009) 295.

[11] Martha C Nussbaum, *Creating Capabilities: The Human Development Approach* (Harvard University Press, 2011) 38.

[12] For an illuminating discussion at this level, see Simon Deakin, 'The Capability Approach and the Economics of Labour Law', Chapter 7 in this volume.

[13] For further development at this level, in the specific context of labour rights, see Alan Bogg, 'The Constitution of Capabilities: The Case of Freedom of Association' and Virginia Mantouvalou, 'Work, Human Rights, and Human Capabilities', Chapters 12 and 10 in this volume (discussing freedom of association and the right to work, respectively).

restriction. Sen believes that the choice of capabilities (assuming a choice is needed) should be left to the democratic process, and he can be understood as advancing the view that we should generally enhance people's (non-specific) capabilities—their freedom to make their own personal choices.[14] I will call this option the *substantive freedom strand*.

A second option is to identify a list of capabilities that are especially important. This option requires an additional normative theory to support the choice of capabilities. Nussbaum developed an influential list of ten basic capabilities that she argued are necessary for reasons of human dignity.[15] Elizabeth Anderson has similarly proposed a list of capabilities in three general areas, which she argued are needed to advance 'democratic equality'.[16] These are different versions of what can be called the *specific capabilities strand*.

Finally, a third option is to rely on a variety of other (non-specific) theories and goals—like the rich body of human rights law and the many justifications for various rights—to decide what we want. More specifically, we could rely on the already-existing body of labour laws with their own purposes and justifications. With this option, the CA is not independent, but rather an 'add-on', or (in Sen's terms in a slightly different context) a 'supplementary device'.[17] It puts the emphasis on ensuring that the rights are *effective*—that people are actually in a position (or have a real opportunity) to enjoy them. In the context of the current chapter, the aim could thus be described as giving people a real opportunity to choose to work under decent conditions that labour laws are designed to secure. It is different from the substantive freedom strand because, here, freedom is not the main normative idea, but a supplement to some other idea (that certain rights are justified). It is also different from the specific capabilities strand because it does not require a fixed list of capabilities, nor does it require a specific normative basis for them. Accordingly, this third option can be used to justify some means and choices that will enhance the ability to enjoy the rights, but it does not offer justifications for the rights themselves. I will call this the *effective enjoyment of rights strand*.

In the growing literature on capabilities and labour law, it is possible to find all three strands (the first two explicitly, the third with some imagination). The goal of this chapter is to assess to what extent the CA can be used to explain and justify labour laws, more or less as we currently know them. To address this issue, section II

---

[14] See, e.g., Sen, *The Idea of Justice* (n 10) 231–8. And see Nussbaum, *Creating Capabilities* (n 11) 70: 'Sen sometimes speaks as if all capabilities were valuable zones of freedom and as if the overall social task might be to maximize freedom'.

[15] Nussbaum, *Women and Human Development* (n 2) 70–80. The capabilities are: life (being able to live to the end of a human life of normal length); bodily health; bodily integrity (being able to move freely from place to place, to be secure against violent assault, etc); senses, imagination, and thought (being able to use the senses, to imagine, think, and reason); emotions; practical reason (being able to form a conception of the good, etc); affiliation; other species (being able to live with concern for and in relations to them); play (being able to laugh, play, and enjoy recreational activities); control over one's environment (political and material).

[16] Elizabeth Anderson, 'What is the Point of Equality?' (1999) 109 *Ethics* 287; Elizabeth Anderson, 'Justifying the Capabilities Approach to Justice' in Harry Brighouse and Ingrid Robeyns (eds), *Measuring Justice: Primary Goods and Capabilities* (Cambridge University Press, 2010) 81.

[17] Sen, *Development as Freedom* (n 1) 82.

sets the stage by asking what we can expect from a normative theory of labour law, and by introducing several distinctions that can prove helpful to understand the potential—and also the limits—of a CA for labour law. The following sections then move to consider the different strands in this light: section III examines substantive freedom, which has attracted most attention so far, and section IV is dedicated to specific capabilities and effective enjoyment of rights, which are somewhat related insofar as both require additional justifications.

## II. What to Expect from a Normative Theory of Labour Law

### A. The purpose of identifying a purpose

There are five possible reasons (that I can think of) for identifying and articulating justifications of labour laws. First, understanding the purpose of a law is necessary when performing purposive interpretation of it (including the filling of lacunas). Secondly, when a law is challenged as unconstitutional, the examination of its constitutionality requires an assessment of the means chosen in light of the importance of the goal, a process which again requires lawyers and judges to identify the goal itself. Thirdly, when labour laws need to be reformed and adapted to new realities and challenges, it is necessary to start by asking what we are trying to achieve with these laws.[18] Fourthly, we need to articulate justifications for legal regulations intervening in the 'free market'—such as labour laws—in order to defend them against neo-liberal critiques and calls for deregulation. Fifthly, for those who believe that we need to re-conceive the entire field and its boundaries, that is, those who wish to propose radical changes to the existing model of regulating work and its role within the welfare state, it is, again, necessary to start with identifying goals and justifications. Unlike the third reason above, here the idea is not simply to improve labour laws while trying to achieve the same goals, but to transform the system radically.

Labour law scholars sometimes also suggest a need to create a new 'narrative',[19] or a new 'paradigm',[20] for the field. This need is not an independent reason for identifying the goals of labour law. A new narrative can indeed be useful to 'sell' labour law to people (employers? legislatures?) and gain their support; but this will be a *by-product* of adopting a theory that can be used for one of the five reasons mentioned above.

The first three reasons can be grouped together under the heading of 'legal' reasons because they are necessary as part of the processes of legislating, adjudicating, enforcing, and amending labour laws. In this context, in many legal systems (although not all) it is clear that purpose has to be identified at the level of *normative* justification, rather than merely at the level of the legislature's intent at a given historical

---

[18] For more on the first three reasons, see Guy Davidov, *A Purposive Approach to Labour Law* (OUP, 2016) ch 2.
[19] Langille, 'Labour Law's Theory of Justice' (n 3) 102.
[20] Richard Mitchell, 'Where are we Going in Labour Law? Some Thoughts on a Field of Scholarship and Policy in Process of Change' (2011) 24 *Australian Journal of Labour Law* 45.

moment. Importantly, if our goal is to identify purposes (justifications) for *legal* reasons, it is necessary to show a 'fit' with current labour laws. Accordingly, a crucial question to be examined in the following sections is this: to what extent is there 'fit' between existing labour laws and the CA? If (and only if) such 'fit' exists, the CA can be useful for practical and important tasks such as purposive interpretation of labour laws, examining their constitutionality, and proposing reforms to improve existing labour laws and/or adapt them to new realities and new challenges.

The other two reasons are not relevant for the legal process but they are important at the political level.[21] The fourth reason can be described as *defensive*; in many contexts, it provides a necessary support for labour laws under attack. The ability to offer a reply to a critique could have an important role in sustaining a law, but it is doubtful whether it can be used for practical legal purposes like purposive interpretation. Arguably, there is a distinction between defensive and positive justifications. I will return to this issue in the next section.

Finally, the *radical* approach is not concerned with existing labour laws at all. Several advocates of a CA for labour law have been focusing on trying to show a 'fit' with existing laws, while in fact their main goal is to use this approach to advance radical changes or entirely new laws.[22] If this is the real need, then a 'fit' is arguably not necessary. The radical potential should be examined independently by asking 'to what extent can the CA be used to support entirely *new* work-related laws, outside of the existing contours of labour law?' This last question is out of the scope of the current chapter, which will focus on identifying the areas of 'fit' with existing labour laws.

To clarify, I am not arguing against radical changes. Such changes will have to be examined based on the details of specific proposals.[23] I argue that we should distinguish between the need to justify existing laws and the desire of some scholars to propose something entirely new. Assume that existing labour laws are X1, X2, X3, and so on. They are a family of laws that have separate goals behind them, but also some shared idea. Articulating the normative justifications of these laws can be useful—indeed, I argue that it is necessary—for purposive interpretation, constitutional adjudication, and reforms that improve such laws and adapt them to new realities. I distinguish between these kinds of reforms—reforms that do not change the basic structure and that can still be seen as part of the X family—and radical changes. If one wants to suggest something entirely different—a new Y family of laws—then it is neither necessary nor required to claim that the Y family shares the same normative foundations as the X family. A proposal to expand the same laws to a broader group of employees or quasi-employees is still within the X family; a

---

[21] I realize, of course, that the distinction between legal and political is not clear-cut. I still find it helpful to employ it in the current context, to emphasize the differences between the different reasons for articulating goals.

[22] See Langille, 'Labour Law's Theory of Justice' (n 3); Fudge, 'Labour as a "Fictive Commodity"' (n 3); Routh, *Enhancing Capabilities through Labour Law* (n 3).

[23] Routh, in his chapter in this volume, 'The Need to Become Fashionable', is therefore mischaracterizing my arguments in his introduction. In previous writings as well, I have not argued that the CA cannot be used to justify radical changes.

proposal to place responsibility on the state for work-related rights (as opposed to placing responsibility on an employer) is something entirely different. The focus of the current chapter is only on the family of laws currently known as labour law (in the international rather than the US sense).

## B. Monist versus pluralist theories

Consider next the distinction between a theory that purports to be complete—offering a monist, exclusive way to think about justice—and a pluralist view that allows different theories and justifications to co-exist. Sen rejects a 'unifocal' approach to justice, acknowledging instead a plurality of concerns.[24] This approach seems very sensible to me, unless a theory rises to an unhelpful level of abstraction. There is little point in answering the question 'what is the right thing to do' with something that comes close to 'do the right thing'; and, once we get more specific, it should be expected that there is more than one thing that we value.

None of the proponents of a CA for labour law has argued that it should be accepted as an *exclusive* normative basis for the field, at least not explicitly.[25] I will not assess the CA in light of this impossible standard, but rather ask whether it can be useful as one justification alongside others. It is often more plausible and more direct to understand labour laws as advancing workplace democracy, dignity, equality, distributive justice, or other such goals. At another level of abstraction, it may be more plausible to understand labour laws as designed to confront the vulnerabilities of subordination and dependency that characterize employment relationships.[26] The question for the following sections is therefore this: to what extent can the CA offer *another* justification for labour laws?

## C. General versus specific justifications

It is also useful to distinguish between general and specific justifications, with regard to the law(s) they aim to explain and justify. Specific justifications focus on one concrete piece of law, or sometimes several specific laws. General justifications aim to justify the entire body of labour laws, although not necessarily with a monist, exclusive justification (see above). A general justification can be presented as part of a pluralist approach. The idea is to treat labour law as a unified project and say that, *as a whole*, it is needed because of a certain justification (or several justifications). On

---

[24] Sen, *Inequality Re-examined* (n 9) 317; Sen, *Development as Freedom* (n 1) 77. See also Sen, *The Idea of Justice* (n 10) 96–102, where he critiques 'transcendental' theories, arguing in particular that they cannot help 'in comparative assessments of justice and therefore in the choice between alternative policies', at 100.

[25] Langille came close to that in previous writings (see Langille, 'Labour Law's Theory of Justice' (n 3)), where he put much focus on rejecting traditional justifications before proceeding to argue for the CA as an alternative justification. But in his chapter in the current volume (Chapter 6), he clarifies that he considers the CA as coming *alongside* other justifications.

[26] On all of these goals and their connection to labour laws see Davidov, *A Purposive Approach to Labour Law* (n 18) chs 3–5.

the face of it, when looking for justifications for practical-legal reasons, it may not be clear why a general justification is needed. When we perform purposive interpretation of a provision in legislation, for example, we only need to know the purposes of this specific legislation. Nonetheless, there are terms that appear in every labour law—such as 'employer' and 'employee'—and it makes sense to interpret them in a coherent way. Not necessarily the same for every piece of legislation, but at least while taking into account the meaning given to this term in the context of other related laws (i.e. within the same body of laws). For these purposes, identifying general goals/justifications—to the extent there are any—is helpful. Of course, it can also be helpful for defensive and radical (i.e. non-legal) purposes.

Note that a combination of a monist (non-pluralist) approach with a general justification for the field is especially problematic. An attempt to find a *single* normative justification for the *entire* body of labour laws entails two significant risks. On the one hand, some of the laws can be left without justification, with the risk of being abolished, even though they can be supported with other justifications. Alternatively, if the monist justification is broad enough to cover all the current laws, it is likely to justify any other regulation in favour of workers without offering any 'stopping point' or any help with where to draw the line.

Leaving aside the monist view, can we consider enhancing human freedom or capabilities a *general* (even if not exclusive) goal of labour law? This could be possible when articulating a defensive justification, designed at a general level to deflect critiques that labour laws (as a whole) are an assault on freedom. But when searching for *positive* justifications needed for *legal* purposes, the CA cannot serve as a general goal.[27] Labour law is an amalgamation of solutions to various different problems concerned with employment relations.[28] Connecting *all* of these laws are the vulnerabilities that justify distinguishing between employment relations and other contractual relations. Therefore, the only way to explain and justify existing labour law *as a whole* is by deciphering the unique characteristics of employment relations. Elsewhere, I have argued that democratic deficits (subordination, broadly conceived) and dependency (economic as well as for the fulfilment of social/psychological needs) characterize the employment relationship.[29] These vulnerabilities explain why intervention (i.e. labour law) is needed and why private laws setting the 'free market' should not apply. Additional justifications at this level include inequality of bargaining power and market failures, and other articulations are surely

---

[27]  I have made this argument in a separate recent paper, not only for the CA but for any other high-level (abstract, philosophical) justifications as well. See Guy Davidov, 'Using Moral and Political Philosophy to Justify Labour Law: Potential and Limits' (unpublished draft, presented at LLRN3, June 2017).

[28]  Matthew W Finkin, 'The Death and Transfiguration of Labor Law' (2011) 33 *Comparative Labor Law & Policy Journal* 171; Matthew W Finkin, 'Introduction: The Past and Future of Labor Law in Comparative Perspective' in Bob A Hepple and Otto Kahn-Freund (eds), *XV International Encyclopedia of Comparative Law* (Mohr Siebeck, 2014); Davidov, *A Purposive Approach to Labour Law* (n 18) 34.

[29]  Guy Davidov, 'The Three Axes of Employment Relationships: A Characterization of Workers in Need of Protection' (2002) 52 *University of Toronto Law Journal* 357; Davidov, *A Purposive Approach to Labour Law* (n 18) ch 3.

possible. The point here is simply that only at this level—which is not only normative but also descriptive, identifying problematic characteristics of employment—a general justification is possible. I do not argue here that such a general theory is sufficient to explain and justify labour law; it must be coupled with abstract justifications that are needed to further explain, in the context of specific laws, why these vulnerabilities are problematic.

Can the CA be conceptualized as being at the level of identifying vulnerabilities? In another recent article,[30] I asked whether the republican idea of non-domination can be considered a general justification for labour law. I argued that just like subordination, domination can be seen as descriptive and normative at the same time; that is, identifying a problem in real life (domination) and explaining why it must be addressed by law. I concluded, however, that the idea of domination as defined (for other purposes) mostly by Philip Pettit does not have sufficient 'fit' with the characteristics of the employment relationship. As a result, it can be useful as a justification for some specific labour laws, but not for the entire body of laws. One could raise a similar question with regard to the CA, by moving from the level of abstract ideas (enhancing capabilities) to the level of identifying vulnerabilities, and suggesting that employment relations can be characterized by 'capability deprivations'.[31] However, such a claim seems on the face of it extremely hard to sustain. In a study of capability deprivations, Supriya Routh[32] focused on rights/needs that are not available to the examined group of workers (waste pickers in India) rather than using this concept to identify the inherent characteristics of the group.

I will therefore proceed with the understanding that the CA cannot be used as a general justification for labour law (for legal purposes), and ask which specific laws (if any) it can justify. For this kind of analysis, it will be useful to divide labour law into several groups of regulations: collective labour laws, the 'procedural' group of laws that set the 'rules of the game' for the parties to negotiate on equal footing (including the right to organize, bargain collectively, and strike); workplace equality laws (including anti-discrimination, pay equity, sexual harassment laws, parental leave, right to request flexible work); obligations of fairness (limitations on unjust dismissals, duties to act in good faith, and proportionality); human rights/citizenship at work (privacy, free speech); wage protection (duties to ensure that wages are paid in time and regulating how they are paid, including obligations to record wages, hours, etc); workers' health and well-being (maximum hours, public holidays, vacation rights, health and safety laws, limitations on child labour); and distributional laws (shifting resources by setting a minimum wage, overtime payments, pensions, notice period, severance payment, intellectual property rights, etc). There is obviously some overlap between the groups, and several laws can reasonably be included in more than one group, but this is not critical for current purposes. Each law was

[30] Guy Davidov, 'Subordination vs Domination: Exploring the Differences' (2017) 33 *International Journal of Comparative Labour Law and Industrial Relations* 365.
[31] This term was used by Sen to define poverty. See Sen, *Development as Freedom* (n 1) ch 4.
[32] Routh, *Enhancing Capabilities through Labour Law* (n 3).

assigned to a group based on what appears to be its dominant feature.[33] In the following sections, the connection between the CA and each of those groups will be examined.

## III. Using Substantive Freedom to Justify Labour Law

Understanding labour law as advancing freedom is counter-intuitive. We usually understand labour law as an intervention in the 'free market'—which almost by definition *limits* the freedom of the parties, to enter into contracts that society finds unacceptable (for example, for payment below the minimum wage). Nonetheless, Kahn-Freund has argued that protective legislation actually *enlarges* the worker's freedom, by restraining the power of management. When the law puts limits on the duty of the worker to obey employer rules, it enlarges the worker's freedom 'from the employer's power to command, or, if you like, his freedom to give priority to his own and his family's interests over those of his employer'.[34]

This line of thought has been developed more recently by Brian Langille on the basis of Sen's theory.[35] Langille does not focus on capabilities or functionings, but relies instead on a rich concept of 'human freedom'. This 'human freedom' is not freedom in the traditional liberal sense, which can quickly lead to freedom of the employer to impose detrimental work conditions and the 'freedom' of the worker to accept such conditions without interference from the state. Instead, Langille focuses on *substantive* human freedom, meaning 'the real capacity to lead a life we have reason to value'.[36] He argues that one of the components of this freedom is human capital, which is not only instrumental, 'but also an end in itself (directly contributing to a more fulfilling and freer life)'.[37] He then argues that we should understand (or reframe) labour law as the law which 'structures . . . human capital creation and deployment'[38] and its goals are 'both the instrumental and intermediate end of productivity and the intrinsic and ultimate end of the maximizing of human freedom'.[39] Langille sees the focus on specific capabilities as useful only for 'reinforcing' the traditional view of labour law; by contrast, he considers his preferred view which focuses on substantive freedom to be more radical, leading to an entirely new

---

[33] An additional group of laws is designed to prevent evasion from other laws. That group includes, for example, the regulation of employment through temporary work agencies. In the current context, it seems sufficient to focus on 'primary' laws as opposed to 'supportive' ones.

[34] Paul Davies and Mark Freedland, *Kahn-Freund's Labour and the Law* (Stevens & Sons, 1983) 24. Kahn-Freund adds: 'To restrain a person's freedom of contract may be necessary to protect his freedom, that is, to protect him against oppression which he may otherwise be constrained to impose upon himself through an act of his legally free and socially unfree will' (at 25).

[35] Langille, 'Labour Law's Theory of Justice' (n 3), and see n 30 there for a list of his previous contributions on this subject. See also, more recently, Brian Langille, ' "Take These Chains from My Heart and Set Me Free": How Labor Law Theory Drives Segmentation of Workers' Rights' (2015) 36 *Comparative Labor Law & Policy Journal* 257.

[36] Langille, 'Labour Law's Theory of Justice' (n 3) 112.

[37] Langille, 'Labour Law's Theory of Justice' (n 3).

[38] Langille, 'Labour Law's Theory of Justice' (n 3).

[39] Langille, 'Labour Law's Theory of Justice' (n 3) 114.

vision of the field. At the same time, he insists that it explains and justifies *existing* labour laws and not only new proposals for expansion: 'much of what our subject is about is not only protecting humans, it is liberating them, i.e. removing obstacles to the realisation of their human capital'.[40]

## A. Substantive freedom as a defensive justification

The idea that labour laws advance substantive human freedom is certainly convincing and helpful as a *defensive* justification; when labour laws are critiqued as an assault on freedom, it is useful to redirect attention to the freedom-enhancing aspects of these laws. Moreover, when we focus on substantive/positive freedom, rather than specific capabilities, it becomes clear that there is a strong connection between the CA and the republican idea of non-domination.[41] Both theories point their attention to the ability to pursue one's goals freely. Republicanism focuses on removing barriers to this pursuit, while the CA is about building the capacity to do so. But there is a lot of overlap, because removing barriers is necessary for building capacity, which is hard to do when facing barriers. And non-domination, like the CA, is not focused only on negative freedoms, but also—indeed, mostly—on positive rights. Given that the main idea of republicanism, at least as articulated by Pettit, is to advance the understanding of freedom as non-domination (as opposed to non-interference), which can be used to *support* interference in the 'free market', the CA and republicanism share the same defensive potential of protecting labour laws.

Simon Deakin and Frank Wilkinson have used the CA to justify social rights more generally.[42] They understand the concept of capabilities as capturing the ability of individuals to access 'the processes of socialization, education and training which enable them to exploit their resource endowments'.[43] Deakin and Wilkinson explain that the right to housing, for example, is necessary as part of the need to provide 'security in the face of risks'—which in turn is a necessary precondition for people to realize their potential, work flexibly, and so on.[44] The rules of 'social law' thus

---

[40] Brian Langille, 'Labour Law's Back Pages' in Guy Davidov and Brian Langille, *Boundaries and Frontiers of Labour Law* (Hart Publishing, 2006) 13, 34.

[41] The connection between non-domination and capabilities is explicitly made in Philip Pettit, *Republicanism: A Theory of Freedom and Government* (OUP, 1997) 158, and Philip Pettit, 'Capability and Freedom: A Defence of Sen' (2001) 17 *Economics and Philosophy* 1, 17–19; and in Sen, *The Idea of Justice* (n 10) 305–309. For further discussion of this connection see Del Punta, 'Labour Law and the Capability Approach' (n 3) 394–5, and Riccardo Del Punta, 'Is the Capability Theory an Adequate Normative Theory for Labour Law?', Chapter 4 in this volume.

[42] Deakin and Wilkinson, *The Law of the Labour Market* (n 3) 347: 'Social rights should be understood as institutionalized forms of capabilities which provide individuals with the means to realize the potential of their resource endowments and thereby achieve a higher level of economic functioning'. This is based on joint work also with Jude Browne, starting in Simon Deakin and Jude Browne, 'Social Rights and the Market Order: Adapting the Capability Approach' in Tamara Harvey and Jeff Kenner (eds), *Economic and Social Rights under the EU Charter of Fundamental Rights: A Legal Perspective* (Hart Publishing, 2003) 27.

[43] Deakin and Wilkinson, *The Law of the Labour Market* (n 3) 291.

[44] Deakin and Wilkinson, *The Law of the Labour Market* (n 3) 347–8, who rely on the Supiot Report; (Alain Supiot, *Beyond Employment: Changes in Work and the Future of Labour Law in Europe* (OUP, 2001)) for this point.

have a 'market-creating' function.[45] Unlike Langille, Deakin and Wilkinson rely on the concept of capabilities rather than substantive freedom; but, like Langille, they refrain from listing specific capabilities, preferring the more general/abstract level of 'aiming to enable individuals to develop their capacity to make substantive choices from a range of economic functionings'.[46] Their understanding of the CA shares significant similarities with the *substantive freedom strand*. The general goal of Deakin and Wilkinson appears to be to defend labour law against neo-classical economists and libertarians: to explain why social laws, including labour laws, are needed to allow people to actualize their potential in the market.[47] They thus provide further support for the CA defensive role.

## B. Substantive freedom as a justification for legal purposes

Can we also use the idea of substantive freedom (or the related idea of advancing non-specific capabilities) for *legal* purposes, as described in the previous section? The ultimate question is this: does it make sense to understand existing labour laws as designed to create opportunities/open choices for workers? There is a strong fit between this idea and workplace equality laws, which are needed to prevent artificial barriers to labour market opportunities.[48] Health and well-being laws can also be seen as a precondition to entering the labour market. It is also plausible to conceive of collective labour laws as enhancing freedom because they open up possibilities for 'self-help' that are not available for a worker acting individually,[49] but this enhancement becomes rather indirect. Such opportunities open up because the law shifts power from employers to employees (compared to the default private law rules). In this respect, it is quite similar to distributional labour laws that shift resources (such as the minimum wage).[50] Indirectly, every resource we get potentially opens up more choices and opportunities, thus enhancing our freedom,[51] but the whole idea of the CA is to move away from the focus on resources—presumably they are not a good enough proxy—and concentrate directly on capabilities/real opportunities. It is extremely difficult to justify distributional labour laws with the idea of enhancing freedom, given that this freedom (to do more with the additional resources or

[45] Deakin and Wilkinson, *The Law of the Labour Market* (n 3) 348. See also Simon Deakin, 'The Contribution of Labour Law to Economic and Human Development' in Guy Davidov and Brian Langille, *The Idea of Labour Law* (OUP, 2011) 162.
[46] Deakin and Wilkinson, *The Law of the Labour Market* (n 3) 353.
[47] Deakin and Wilkinson, *The Law of the Labour Market* (n 3) 348.
[48] Deakin and Wilkinson, *The Law of the Labour Market* (n 3) 291–2 bring the example of a prohibition against dismissals of pregnant women. They explain that it is necessary in order to make it possible, in practice, for women to enter the labour market (i.e. ensures that their freedom to enter the labour market is not merely formal, but substantive). They also discuss domestic responsibilities of women as detrimental to their capabilities (at 286), which can provide support for work-family balance laws.
[49] Brian Langille, 'Core Labour Rights: The True Story (Reply to Alston)' (2005) 16 *European Journal of International Law* 409 (focusing on freedom of association).
[50] On this point, see also Laura Weinrib's chapter in this volume.
[51] For such an argument see, e.g., Brian Langille, 'What is Labour Law? Implications of the Capabilities Approach' and Riccardo Del Punta, 'Is the Capability Theory an Adequate Normative Theory for Labour Law?', Chapters 6 and 4 in this volume, respectively.

powers) comes at the expense of the employer's resources and power (and therefore freedom).[52]

Admittedly, when we define the idea of labour law so generally, one can connect almost any regulation indirectly to such a goal. But it does not help us decide when to intervene in the 'free market' and does not offer any 'stopping point' to regulatory intervention. It has been argued by Alan Bogg, as well as by Tonia Novitz and Colin Fenwick, that the CA is not sufficiently specific to offer normative guidance for labour law,[53] and this seems especially true for the view that focuses on substantive freedom.

Deakin and Wilkinson have tried to offer a CA defence for the minimum wage by focusing on non-distributional aspects of this law. They argue that a minimum wage forces employers to invest in new technologies, training, skill development, and health and safety—all strategies enhancing capabilities, which employers have no incentive to pursue when they have the power to lower wages below their market rate.[54] This argument is certainly logical, but it seems odd to see this as the main (or even a major) goal of minimum wage laws.[55]

The incompatibility between distributional labour laws and the CA appears fundamental, given the nature of these laws. This significant and important part of labour law is clearly and unapologetically *paternalistic*, while the CA is decidedly *anti*-paternalistic; the focus on capabilities (as opposed to functionings) is designed to give people freedom to choose their own ways.[56] Langille is well aware of that fact,[57] so when he argues that labour laws should be 'liberating, not constraining',[58] it suggests that he sees no need for substantive standards such as a minimum wage unless he ignores the fact that they are 'constraining' for the employer. The same is true for human rights/citizenship at work and wage protection laws. An attempt to connect them to human freedom or non-specific capabilities seems artificial and forced. It is much more fitting to understand them as placing *constraints* on employers.

---

[52] Alan Bogg supports an interpretation of freedom of association constitutional provisions that includes the rights to bargain collectively and strike, and finds support in the CA for this view (see Alan Bogg, 'The Constitution of Capabilities: The Case of Freedom of Association', Chapter 12 in this volume). While I wholeheartedly share his views about the proper interpretation, his arguments seem to be based on other justifications, perhaps showing that this interpretation is *not incompatible* with the CA, but not really based on it.

[53] Alan Bogg, 'Labour Law and the Trade Unions: Autonomy and Betrayal' in Alan Bogg and others (eds), *The Autonomy of Labour law* (Hart Publishing, 2015) 73, 86–95; Tonia Novitz and Colin Fenwick, 'The Application of Human Rights Discourse to Labour Relations: Translation of Theory into Practice' in Colin Fenwick and Tonia Novitz (eds), *Human Rights at Work: Perspectives on Law and Regulation* (Hart Publishing, 2010) 1, 30–3.

[54] Deakin and Wilkinson, *The Law of the Labour Market* (n 3) 293.

[55] For a similar view see Hugh Collins, 'What Can Sen's Capability Approach Offer to Labour Law?', Chapter 1 in this volume.

[56] Ingrid Robeyns, 'The Capability Approach' in *The Stanford Encyclopedia of Philosophy* (Winter 2016 edition) section 3.1, https://plato.stanford.edu/entries/capability-approach/.

[57] As Langille himself acknowledges in Langille, 'Core Labour Rights: The True Story (Reply to Alston)' (n 49) 429.

[58] Langille, 'Take These Chains from My Heart and Set Me Free' (n 35) 277.

There is also some inherent incompatibility between obligations of fairness and the CA. One of the reasons behind these obligations (notably, limitations on unjust dismissals) is to facilitate trust and allow the parties to make job-specific long-term investments.[59] In this respect, they strengthen the commitments and co-dependence of the parties, which is *detrimental* to freedom. Sometimes, perhaps often, this is what people want; after all, notwithstanding the great importance of freedom, it is also true that, in some contexts, 'freedom is just another word for nothing left to lose'.[60] To enjoy the benefits of a long-term relationship, we sometimes have to relinquish some of our freedom. Labour law supports that; the CA, at least in its substantive freedom strand, does not.

We have seen that there is some 'fit' between the substantive freedom justification and existing labour laws, but only to a limited extent. With this in mind, it is problematic to rely on substantive freedom for practical-legal tasks like setting the scope of labour law, unless this refers to a specific piece of legislation from those noted above. Langille has argued that substantive freedom can help us by getting 'old ideas out of the way', moving directly from purpose to scope without being bothered by tests to decide who is an employer/employee.[61] He brings two examples from Canadian case law. One is of a person who did sewing work at her home for a contractor, who was engaged by another contractor, eventually leading at the top of a production chain to a big brand (J Crew). The legal question was whether J Crew should be responsible for non-payments by the contractor who directly hired the worker. The second case involved a law firm with a partnership agreement requiring all partners to retire at the age of 65. Canadian legislation prohibits mandatory retirement of employees—it is considered age discrimination—and the legal question was whether a partner is an employee for this purpose. Langille calls for a 'worker-centered conception of labour law... that does not seek a relationship'[62] as the basis for labour regulation. In his view, labour law should not be about the employment relationship or any other relationship, but simply about workers—we should focus on maximizing their substantive freedom. This unsurprisingly leads him directly to concluding that J Crew was an employer and that the lawyer-partner was an employee. But this conclusion is too easy. As far as existing laws are concerned—in Canada and elsewhere—labour law *is* about a relationship. The legal question is not whether the sewing worker is entitled to her wages from the state, but whether she has a right vis-à-vis J Crew—that is, whether J Crew has a legal duty towards her. Similarly, the lawyer who had to retire at 65 does not ask for a remedy from society at large: the question is whether his partners at the law firm have a duty towards him, in

---

[59] On trust, see Simon Deakin and Frank Wilkinson, 'Labour Law and Economic Theory: A Reappraisal' in Hugh Collins, Paul Davies, and Roger W Rideout (eds), *Legal Regulation of the Employment Relation* (Kluwer, 2000) 29, 45–6.

[60] As eloquently articulated by Kris Kristofferson in his song *Me and Bobby McGee* (1969). In the song, the narrator leaves his girlfriend when she wants to settle down—a decision he later regrets. He gained freedom but lost the relationship.

[61] Langille, 'Take These Chains from My Heart and Set Me Free' (n 35) 278.

[62] Langille, 'Take These Chains from My Heart and Set Me Free' (n 35) 266.

their bilateral relationship, with the understanding that, by law, business associates who do not employ one another do not have such duties.

It is of course possible to suggest a radical departure from this model. As noted, this option is beyond the scope of the current chapter. But if the goal is to justify, explain, and describe the idea behind *existing* labour laws, it is not possible to ignore the fact that they are based on an employment relationship. Labour laws very explicitly and unquestionably place responsibilities on an employer towards its employees.[63] Note that there are also ways in which society invests in human capital through the state using tax money. Langille's analysis, being at such a high level of abstraction, glosses over this crucial difference and its distributional implications. There are areas in which we want the market to operate 'freely', without regulatory intervention (other than the background rules of private law); areas where we want employers to stand up to certain standards towards those who work for them, which includes redistributing resources from employers to employees; and areas where we want the state to invest in improving the lives of its citizens, or residents, or workers (depending on the context). The difficult questions of labour law are often concerned with how to put the lines between these three areas. The idea of human freedom does not offer much help with this task.

## IV. Combining Capabilities with Additional Justifications to Justify Labour Law

### A. Specific capabilities and labour law

The substantive freedom strand of the CA has its advantages, but also some obvious drawbacks when one is looking for guidance for social policy. To achieve more specificity, Nussbaum developed a list of capabilities that was later adopted by other scholars as well. It is important to note at the outset that the list is meant to capture 'areas of freedom so central that their removal makes a life not worthy of human dignity'.[64] With this approach, capabilities can justify fundamental constitutional rights, but everything else 'will be left to the ordinary workings of the political process'.[65] This does not seem to leave open the possibility of justifying the many specific labour laws that every modern economy has, unless one wants to argue that all of these laws are constitutionally *necessary* and should be left out of the political process. That would be quite extreme. The question, however, is whether we can use the same ideas—the same list of capabilities—to support, propose, and justify labour legislation even if it is *not* constitutionally mandated.

---

[63] There are some specific contexts in which the scope of labour law is broadened to cover workers who are not 'employees'. But, even in such cases, except for very rare exceptions, labour laws are still based on the existence of a bilateral relationship.

[64] Nussbaum, *Creating Capabilities* (n 11) 31.

[65] Nussbaum, *Creating Capabilities* (n 11) 32.

Nussbaum herself refers to labour laws only indirectly, when discussing two of her ten capabilities. The first is the ability to control one's environment; she specifies that this capability includes 'the right to seek employment on an equal basis with others' as well as 'being able to work as a human, exercising practical reason and entering into meaningful relationships of mutual recognition with other workers'.[66] The second capability is 'play'. In this context, she notes that: 'working at a job and then coming home to do all the domestic labor, including child care and elder care, is a crushing burden, impeding access to many of the other capabilities on the list: employment opportunities, political participation, physical and emotional health, friendship of many kinds'.[67] Arguably, then, the labour laws that can be justified based on Nussbaum's list of capabilities include workplace equality laws and health and well-being laws.

It is also possible to use other capabilities listed by Nussbaum to support labour laws. Kevin Kolben has argued that life, bodily health, bodily integrity, play, affiliation, and the ability to control one's environment are all relevant for labour law. He uses them to justify health and safety laws, working time laws, protections against sexual harassment, workplace equality, and freedom of association.[68] These justifications are, often, quite indirect. But in any case, the focus remains on the same groups of laws that were also supported by the substantive freedom strand.

Further development of the CA was offered by Jonathan Wolff and Avner de-Shalit, who argued that alongside the level of functionings, we must be concerned with the ability to sustain functionings. *Insecurity* of functionings creates risk and vulnerability, which are in themselves problematic. Wolf and de-Shalit give casual employees as an example, characterizing the insecurity of being possibly out of work at any given time as a disadvantage requiring societal response.[69] In an attempt to identify the least advantaged members of society, they show how disadvantages 'cluster' together, multiplying in severity.[70] Possibly this idea can be used to justify specific protections for casual workers.

Elizabeth Anderson listed three aspects of functionings, which she derived from the goal of 'democratic equality': as a human being, as a participant in a system of cooperative production (the market), and as a citizen of a democratic state. The second of those is most relevant for current purposes. Anderson argued that it requires 'effective access to the means of production, access to the education needed to develop one's talents, freedom of occupational choice, the right to make contracts and enter into cooperative agreements with others, the right to receive fair value for one's labor, and recognition by others of one's productive contributions'.[71] This

---

[66] Nussbaum, *Creating Capabilities* (n 11) 34. For an analysis see Del Punta, 'Labour Law and the Capability Approach' (n 3).

[67] Nussbaum, *Creating Capabilities* (n 11) 36.

[68] Kolben, 'Labour Regulation, Capabilities, and Democracy' (n 3) 67–70.

[69] Jonathan Wolff and Avner de-Shalit, *Disadvantage* (OUP, 2007) 9, 70. They further argue that 'the government should guarantee genuine opportunities for secure functionings' (at 14).

[70] Wolff and de-Shalit, *Disadvantage* (n 69) ch 7.

[71] Anderson, 'What is the Point of Equality' (n 16) 318. Although Anderson used the term 'functionings', in substance she phrased them as capabilities, with a focus on opportunities.

functioning appears to provide some basis for a small number of labour laws. Most notably, the idea of 'fair value' is an attempt to support a minimum wage law, but Anderson does not explain how it fits into the logic of capabilities. Note also that in more recent writings, when Anderson turned her attention to the specific context of justifying labour laws, she relied first on the republican idea of non-domination,[72] and later on the non-democratic characteristics of the employment relationship.[73] In these later writings, there is no mention of capabilities.

Anderson's work on the CA—later also adopted by Judy Fudge and by Supriya Routh in the context of labour law[74]—relies on a combination of the CA with the goal of democratic equality. Wolff and de-Shalit, in turn, rely on a combination of the CA with the goal of security, as a supplement to Nussbaum's work which combines the CA with dignity. The question arises: is the CA really necessary here? Is it stronger/better to justify health and safety laws, for example, by deriving them from capability for life (or bodily health, or control of one's environment), which in turn is derived from dignity, instead of relying *directly* on dignity? Similarly, is it better to justify maximum hour laws by reference to capability for play which is derived from dignity, rather than simply referring to the latter as justification? Or to justify anti-discrimination laws by relying on 'effective access to the means of production', which in turn is derived from democratic equality, as opposed to directly relying on equality?

These questions have recently received some illumination from Riccardo Del Punta, who took the specific capabilities approach one step further by developing a list of capabilities tailored for labour law. Deriving the list from advanced systems of labour law, based on the idea that they reflect the result of public reasoning and democratic deliberation, Del Punta includes the following capabilities: capability for work (having a job that is fairly paid, etc); capability for human respect and dignity (working conditions compatible with that); capability for professional skills (occupational training, etc); capability for work-life balance (sufficient amount of free time, etc); and capability for voice (including by joining trade unions, etc).[75] He is well aware that this could be seen as 'a mere translation of labour rights into the language of capabilities',[76] but ultimately finds this language useful because of its focus on freedom and autonomy. The main point is the understanding and justification of labour law not as protecting helpless workers, but as opening more choices for them and thus enhancing their freedom.

One way to understand this approach is as going back to the substantive freedom strand: people should be free (and capable) to pursue whatever they want, and in the context of work, it turns out (based on a reading of existing labour laws) that this set

[72] Elizabeth Anderson, 'Equality and Freedom in the Workplace: Recovering Republican Insights' (2015) 31 *Social Philosophy and Policy* 48.

[73] Elizabeth Anderson, *Private Government: How Employers Rule Our Lives (and Why We Don't Talk about It)* (Princeton University Press, 2017).

[74] Fudge, 'Labour as a "Fictive Commodity"' (n 3); Routh, *Enhancing Capabilities through Labour Law* (n 3).

[75] Del Punta, 'Labour Law and the Capability Approach' (n 3).

[76] Del Punta, 'Labour Law and the Capability Approach' (n 3) 392.

of capabilities is what they want. On this reading, the specific labour capabilities do not provide a *justification* for specific labour laws that can be derived from them, but rather offer a descriptive supplement to substantive freedom. An alternative reading is that Del Punta proposes to combine the CA with the many different justifications for labour laws. I turn to this last idea in the next section.

## B. The capability approach as effective enjoyment of rights

As noted in the introduction, the basic idea of the CA is that people should be capable to *be* and *do* things—that people should have choices and real opportunities—and this raises the question of *what* they should be capable of. The two common replies, discussed above, are 'whatever they want', or alternatively, to develop a list of specific capabilities. The latter option requires an additional theory to decide which capabilities are the most important or necessary.[77] It is here that philosophers turned to human dignity or to 'democratic equality' for answers. But why should we limit ourselves to one specific justification from which all rights (or capabilities) should be derived? I doubt that this is the best approach, certainly not when we no longer aim to justify fundamental, constitutional rights, but rather aim to justify a multitude of labour laws that intervene in private relations. Assume, therefore, that the choice of capabilities is based not on one specific high-level goal/value, but on a multitude of justifications that already exist in the rich literature on labour law. It is possible to understand Del Punta's list of labour capabilities this way.[78]

With such a combination between the CA and labour law's many justifications, what is the normative force or significance of the CA? The answer suggests a modest option for the project of a CA for labour law. In this strand, the CA is not a justification for labour laws, which have to rely on other justifications. The CA is rather a supplement—an 'add-on'—that requires that we ensure effective enjoyment of the laws. This in turn can justify the choice of certain *means* to improve the enjoyment of the rights, that is, the achievement of the goals. Take for example the idea of *voice*. It has long been considered one of the justifications for collective labour laws, sometimes as part of a more general justification of workplace democracy. When we combine this justification with the CA, it continues to stand independently and support collective bargaining laws. But on top of that, there is recognition that voice also requires *capability for voice*, which could justify certain means that can make these laws effective. The right to bargain collectively is not enough by itself to ensure voice; we have to make sure that people have the capability—a real opportunity—actually to engage in collective bargaining.

---

[77] To be more precise, I should note that the first option was articulated by Sen as whatever people 'have reason to value', which on the face of it also requires an additional theory to decide which activities or conditions fit the qualification of *reason*. In practice, as noted above, the literature in this strand has not developed this idea at length, putting instead the focus on freedom of choice.

[78] Del Punta himself notes that the CA demands 'actual fulfilment' of labour rights (Del Punta, 'Labour Law and the Capability Approach' (n 3) 399), although he clearly sees this as coming *on top* of a normative justification for the rights themselves. I suggest here the possibility of understanding this as coming *instead*.

An application of this approach can be found, I believe, in a study by Simon Deakin and Aristea Koukiadaki.[79] After noting that 'the CA provides a normative framework for judging the effectiveness of institutional mechanisms in terms of how far they extend the substantive freedom of action of individuals',[80] they move to examine a specific labour law in this light: the law dealing with information and consultation. They argue that information and consultation rights can be

> conceptualized as 'social conversion factors' for the development of a 'capability for voice' in corporate decisions making. Their success can be judged on how far they induce a process of institutional learning, based on deliberation, through which employees are provided with effective opportunities to shape the workplace environment.[81]

The study then uses this sophisticated approach to assess the impact of the regulations on employee voice *in practice*. In other words, arguably, it ultimately leads to an examination of the effectiveness of the law in light of the purpose (in this case, voice). In the particular study this question was examined empirically, leading to proposals on how the potential of information and consultation rights can be materialized effectively.

This approach is consistent with the purposive approach, which can be used not only for purposive interpretation, but also to ensure that the legal means can achieve the goals, and solve the problems that I described elsewhere as a 'mismatch' between goals and means.[82]

# V. Conclusion

The CA is a welcome addition to labour law theory. It enriches the discourse on justifications for labour law and offers new insights on the need for such laws and on the best way to structure them. Others have already made the case for a CA for labour law. The goal of the current contribution was to assess this endeavour from a friendly yet critical perspective in order to help the understanding of the CA's proper role within labour law theory.

As a starting point, I showed that the CA cannot offer a monist, exclusive justification for labour laws, and also that it would be difficult to use it as a normative basis for the labour law project as a whole, rather than only for specific laws. A further distinction that should be acknowledged is between attempts to explain and justify *existing* labour laws (which can also include some concrete corrections or

---

[79] Simon Deakin and Aristea Koukiadaki, 'Capability Theory, Employee Voice and Corporate Restructuring: Evidence from UK Case Studies' (2012) 33 *Comparative Labor Law and Policy Journal* 427.

[80] Deakin and Koukiadaki, 'Capability Theory, Employee Voice and Corporate Restructuring' (n 79) 433–4.

[81] Deakin and Koukiadaki, 'Capability Theory, Employee Voice and Corporate Restructuring' (n 79) 434.

[82] Guy Davidov, 'Re-Matching Labour Laws with Their Purpose' in Guy Davidov and Brian Langille (eds), *The Idea of Labour Law* (OUP, 2011) 179; Davidov, *A Purposive Approach to Labour Law* (n 18) ch 1.

amendments) and proposals for radical changes to the system of work regulation. The chapter did not address the latter issue, except to argue that is has to be assessed independently; if the CA is invoked to justify a radical change, there is no need to show a 'fit' with existing labour laws.

In contrast, justifying existing labour laws requires such a 'fit', and the chapter looked for the areas in which it can be found. At this juncture I employed another distinction, between articulating justifications for *legal* reasons (notably, purposive interpretation) and doing so for *defensive* reasons (i.e. supporting the project against libertarian and neo-classical economic critiques, which is important in itself but does not positively provide a normative basis). In this light, I examined three strands within the CA to labour law, distinguished by their approaches towards the question of what people ought to be capable of.

The first strand, concerned with substantive freedom, is not focused on any specific capabilities, but on enhancing people's capabilities (and thus freedom) generally. This is very helpful as a defensive justification. As for legal purposes, it can be connected with workplace equality law, health and well-being laws, and possibly collective bargaining laws. Substantive freedom can hardly be seen as the *only* or *main* justification, in either of these cases, but it is certainly useful as an *additional* justification in this significant part of the labour law apparatus. The second strand focuses on a specific list of capabilities, derived from a high-level justification like dignity. The list of capabilities developed for constitutional law purposes proved to be partially helpful for labour law as well—it can be used as a justification for some of the same laws mentioned above. Again, it is not the only or main justification, and the list certainly cannot support all labour laws. Most notably, labour laws that are designed mostly to redistribute resources from employers to employees are difficult to justify by these freedom-centred approaches.

This difficulty has led scholars, understandably, to develop a list of capabilities unique to labour law, rather than relying on a list designed for other purposes. But if we compile a list based on existing labour laws, the question arises whether it adds a normative justification or simply describes existing labour laws with the addition of the word 'capability' before them. I offered two possible readings, both of which maintain that developing this new list is a worthwhile exercise, but perhaps more modest than some have argued. On one interpretation, the list of labour capabilities is not normative but descriptive; it involves listing capabilities that, as a matter of practice, people across legal systems consider valuable. This list can be used to support the basic normative idea of substantive freedom (i.e. support for the first strand). The second interpretation leads to what I identified as a third strand: the CA not as offering justification for labour laws but, more modestly, as demanding effective enjoyment of these laws—a real opportunity (and thus, capability) for workers to benefit from labour laws as a matter of practice. In such a case, the laws require their own separate justifications—that can be found, of course, in the rich labour law literature—and the CA adds a justification for *means* that will make them effective.

Overall, the chapter shows several ways in which a CA for labour law can be useful, while at the same time arguing that such a justification should not be over-extended.

Hopefully, this analysis can assist future research on this topic by identifying the areas of 'fit' between the CA and labour law, which offer the most promise for further development, and also by suggesting for those seeking to use the CA as a vehicle for radical reforms to skip the unnecessary efforts to show a 'fit' with existing laws and move directly to proposing concrete reforms that the CA can justify.

# 3

# Labor Law and the Capabilities Approach

*Martha C. Nussbaum*

## I.  Not an "It" but a "They"

Many people, including labor lawyers, use the idea of capabilities for many different purposes. Our international Human Development and Capability Association, officially founded in 2004, is highly diverse, containing 800–1,000 members from over seventy nations; but actually a lot more people are active workers on the approach, since being a "member" means paying dues, and many work on the approach without wanting or being able to pay dues. The approach long preexisted the founding of the Association, and its reach is far broader. We have an annual meeting every year, and different parts of the world are deliberately involved: meetings have been held in Argentina, South Africa, Japan, India, Jordan, and Nicaragua, as well as Italy, the Netherlands, and the United States. We also publish a journal, the *Journal of Human Development and Capabilities*, which has a very wide range of topics. The aim of the Association is to build bridges across countries and regions, and also between theory and practice. Thus, many who work with the approach do so as practitioners, so the diversity of projects cannot even be judged by looking at publications.

Members of the Association pursue many types of projects, in areas as diverse as education, health, feminism, measurement, constitutional law, disability rights, environmentalism, and animal rights. This list of topics already points to an important way in which members disagree: for our journal and our Association use the word "Human" in their titles, and yet many members, including I myself, think that the normatively best way to use the approach involves protecting the capabilities of all animals. Some think, instead, of ecosystems as ends, in that way jettisoning the usual commitment of the approach to treating each individual as an end and none as a means to the ends of others.[1] But a more moderate view treats ecosystems as

---

[1] A good starting point for people interested in those debates is the symposium "Human Capabilities and Animal Lives: Conflict, Wonder, Law: A Symposium," *Journal of Human Development and Capabilities* 18 (2017): 317–69, including three symposium papers, of which my contribution is "Scientific Whaling? The Scientific Research Exception and the Future of the International Whaling Commission" (with Rachel Nussbaum Wichert), 356–69. See also Martha C. Nussbaum, "Working with and for Animals: Getting the Theoretical Framework Right," *Denver Law Review* 94 (2017): 609–25. A longer version published in the *Journal of Human Development and Capabilities* 2018; Martha C. Nussbaum and Rachel Nussbaum Wichert, "The Legal Status of Whales and Dolphins: From

The Capability Approach to Labour Law. Edited by Brian Langille. Chapter 3 © Martha C. Nussbaum 2019. Published 2019 by Oxford University Press.

instrumental means to the capabilities of human beings (in some cases) or all sentient beings (in others, e.g. my own).[2]

Amartya Sen and I were the two Founding Presidents of the Association, and our own views differ in significant respects, some of which I will describe later. Other thinkers have expressed their own vision of the Approach, for example our current President, Ingrid Robeyns, in her recent book.[3] Soon these differences will be exhaustively summarized by a wide range of our affiliates, in the forthcoming *Handbook of the Capability Approach*.[4] Many, following Amartya Sen, use the idea of capabilities as a space of comparison, arguing against the ranking of nations and regions by gross domestic product (GDP) and in favor of a capability-based ranking. Many are focused on much smaller units: for example comparing the capabilities of inpatients in nursing homes in a nation or region. All of this is fine and illuminating, and there is no confusion so long as people say what they are doing.

More generally, it's clear that there really is no such thing as *the* Capabilities Approach, except in a very loose generic sense conveying a lot of overlap and common dissatisfactions. I would compare "the CA" to Utilitarianism: it means something to call Jeremy Bentham, John Stuart Mill, Henry Sidgwick, and Peter Singer all Utilitarians. They share some common ideas and some common discontents with other moral theories. They all call themselves Utilitarians, attaching themselves to the tradition, and defending the tradition in some respects. But ever since Mill's wonderful essay "Bentham,"[5] it has also been obvious that on some extremely important matters, Bentham and Mill disagree: on the significance of qualitative differences, on whether activities (or only feelings) are ends, on whether pleasure is single and what exactly it is, on how to surmount egoism in society, and much more. As for Sidgwick, although he appears in many respects to agree with Bentham more than with Mill, things are otherwise once we probe the depth of Sidgwick's commitment to "common sense" and ordinary Victorian morality, especially now that we are able to contrast Sidgwick's writings with Bentham's recently published works on sexuality. Indeed I am inclined to say that Bentham and Sidgwick are poles apart as regards their fundamental philosophical motivations. Bentham is a radical and

Bentham to the Capabilities Approach," forthcoming in Lori Keleher and Stacy J. Kosko (eds.), *Agency, Democracy, and Participation in Global Development* (Cambridge University Press, 2019); and "Legal Protection for Whales: Capabilities, Entitlements, and Culture," in Luis Cordeiro Rodrigues (ed.), *Animals, Race and Multiculturalism: Contemporary Moral and Political Debates* (Palgrave Macmillan, 2017) 95–120.

[2] See Breena Holland, *Allocating the Earth: A Distributional Framework for Protecting Capabilities in Environmental Law and Policy* (Oxford University Press, 2014); Breena Holland, "Environment as Meta-Capability: Why a Dignified Life Requires a Stable Climate System," in Allen Thompson and Jeremy Bendik-Keymer (eds), *Ethical Adaptation to Climate Change: Human Virtues of the Future* (MIT Press, 2012) 145–64; Breena Holland, "Justice and the Environment in Nussbaum's 'Capabilities Approach': Why Sustainable Ecological Capacity is a Meta Capability," *Political Research Quarterly* 6 (2008): 319–22.

[3] Ingrid Robeyns, *Well-Being, Freedom, and Social Justice: the Capability Approach Re-Examined* (Open Book Publishers, 2014); see also Ingrid Robeyns, and Brighouse, Harry (eds.), *Measuring Justice: Primary Goods and Capabilities* (Cambridge University Press, 2010).

[4] Mozaffar Qizilbash (ed.), (Cambridge University Press, 2019).

[5] John Stuart Mill, "Bentham," *London and Westminster Review* (August 1838).

naturalist, seeking in the body an objective criterion of norms and laws, to replace the (to him) diseased beliefs of his culture about virtue. He thinks most of "common sense" is not sense at all, but smug special pleading that oppresses many people and groups. He uses Utility as a knife to slice away hypocrisy and special pleading, and ends up recommending radical positions on homosexuality, women's position, and the rights of animals. (Mill is also radical, though more polite.)

Sidgwick, by contrast, holds as a matter of philosophical method that the main deliverances of common sense must be preserved, and he uses this commitment to justify some of the most repressive ideas of Victorian morality, such as a strict re-tributive view of punishment and even the need for society to ostracize the unchaste woman. (This is not personal special pleading, in fact just the opposite: Bentham was a celibate with romantic inclinations toward women; Sidgwick was a gay man who denied himself sexual expression because he feared disgrace, as Bart Schultz has now shown.[6] Ironically, the shy and recessive Mill seems to have been the only one who had a happy—and unconventional—romantic life.) In general, then: Bentham and Mill would each think that the other was wrong about quite a few significant philosophical points, but they would be in general sympathy about the radical aims and social goals of Utilitarian philosophy. By contrast, Bentham would not care beans about Sidgwick's superior philosophical refinement, and he would judge plausibly that Sidgwick had thrown away the entire purpose and animating spirit of Utilitarianism. My relationship to Sen's views is similar to the Bentham/Mill relation, not the Bentham/Sidgwick relation. I think Sen is wrong about some philosophical matters, but I also think that the underlying intellectual and political motivations for his work are not just admirable but basically the same as mine. In general we are pursuing complementary projects.

My general point is this: we can point to general similarities that link Sen and me, and link, as well, many other people who use the CA (among whom we find natural law Catholics, radical environmentalists, Marxist, liberals, and yet others). We can point to general dissatisfactions. But none of this should be taken to suggest that there are not profound disagreements, both at the level of concrete views and at the level of method. I am pursuing a type of ideal theory; Sen says he repudiates ideal theory, though at times he also uses a type of ideal theory, particularly in discussing the Human Rights Movement, or so I argue.[7] Sen is more sympathetic to perfec-tionist political principles than I am (see below); I endorse Rawlsian political liber-alism. Sen uses capabilities for comparative purposes only. I use them as an element in a theory of basic justice. (That one is less a disagreement than a difference of aim.) Sen is drawn to the idea of maximizing freedom; I believe (see below) that even when we take account of Sen's important distinction between maximizing and optimizing, this project is not one we should endorse, and it may well be incoherent (see below). Sen is averse to inflicting pain on animals, but up until now he has framed his cap-abilities approach in terms of human capabilities only, as is the dominant approach

---

[6] Bart Schultz, *Henry Sidgwick: Eye of the Universe* (Cambridge University Press, 2004).
[7] See Martha C. Nussbaum, "Aspiration and the Capabilities List," *Journal of Human Development and Capabilities* 17 (2016): 1–8.

in our Association; I have long focused on a project of protecting animal capabilities, alongside that of protecting human capabilities. So we are like Bentham and Mill: sharing a very general space and some criticisms of other views, but differing in significant ways.

I think it is unfortunate that young people in our Association, imbued with a spirit of missionary zeal, sometimes ignore these differences and think of us as a great church of humane economics. I always say this, urging debate and contestation, and I make many criticisms of Sen, though in the Aspirations paper I decided to emphasize the points of agreement; for both rhetorical and institutional purposes I underplayed disagreement, rather as Mill does in "Utilitarianism." Labor lawyers would also do well to attend to the agreement and disagreement within this "general space" of capabilities.

I shall now describe the shared terrain of (virtually) all practitioners and theorists of the CA, and then turn to a description of my own philosophical project, in the process noting differences between me and Sen.[8]

## II. The Shared Terrain

The CA was born out of a dissatisfaction, within development economics, with the prevalent practice of ranking countries by GDP per capita alone, and then treating that ranking as a good proxy for the normative notion of "development" and the related notion of "quality of life."[9] It is in that sense an oppositional or critical theory directed at a very particular set of ideas: I call it "a necessary counter-theory." I view our role as rather like that of a lawyer retained by poor people and activists on their behalf, to argue their case in the halls of the World Bank and other international and national fora. If one should ask why theorists needed to intervene on behalf of the poor, and whether this work of ours is not objectionably paternalistic, I think the answer is similar to the answer to the question why people whose lives are on the line in a legal proceeding need lawyers. Discussions in economic and policy fora tend to be technical and top-down, and development economists typically don't listen to poor people a lot. So we hoped to create a sophisticated theory that corresponds to the lived experience of poverty and exclusion. For similar reasons, our theory could not simply be a philosophical theory, although philosophy lies at its heart. Economists don't read philosophy, and they tend to be contemptuous of it because

---

[8] The most succinct statement of my view is in Martha C. Nussbaum, *Creating Capabilities: the Human Development Approach* (Harvard University Press, 2012); more detailed philosophical accounts are in Martha C. Nussbaum, *Women and Human Development: The Capabilities Approach* (Cambridge University Press, 2000) and Martha C. Nussbaum, *Frontiers of Justice: Disability Nationality, Species Membership* (Harvard University Press, 2006). In what follows I shall refer to these as *CC, WHD,* and *FJ* respectively. See also Martha C. Nussbaum, "Capabilities, Entitlements, Rights: Supplementation and Critique," *Journal of Human Development and Capabilities* 12 (2011): 23–38. *CC* has a detailed bibliography of all relevant work by me, by Sen, and by a range of other authors. A work that uses my account and that has enriched my own is Jonathan Wolff and Avner De-Shalit, *Disadvantage* (Oxford University Press, 2007).

[9] The "shared terrain" is described more fully in *CC* (n. 8) ch. 3.

of its (usually) non-mathematical character. Thus, the leadership of Amartya Sen, who has daunting technical credentials, was essential to getting the new theory a hearing, even though Sen is also a philosopher and his contributions to the theory are primarily philosophical.

Insurgent proponents of the CA point out, first, that even should one want a single number to measure a nation's quality of life, average GDP would not be the best single number, because the proceeds of foreign investment are often repatriated by the investing country and do not trickle down to improve lives in the region. But we then go on to criticize the GDP idea with two further arguments. First, average GDP neglects distribution and thus, can give high marks to nations that contain alarming inequalities. Second, average GDP runs together different aspects of a human being's quality of life, such as health, education, and employment opportunities. These vary independently, and are not just a function of GDP.

We then go on to criticize a different opponent, also significant in development and policy circles, namely the metric of average utility, where utility is conceived as desire-satisfaction. This approach at least has the merit of talking to people about things that matter to them. But it has four defects. First, utility aggregates across persons, and thus, it, too, effaces distribution. Second, it aggregates across components of lives, and thus, it, too, effaces their separateness. Third, there is the problem of "adaptive preferences," much discussed by Sen and others:[10] People tailor their satisfactions, all too often, to what they believe they can achieve, or what they are taught is proper for them. In some areas this adaptation is unobjectionable: it's a good thing that we learn that flying like birds is not for us. But so often women and other excluded groups learn not to desire to seek employment outside the home, to attain a high level of education, to participate in politics, etc. The metric of desire-satisfaction thus, can bias things toward an unjust status quo. Finally, the satisfaction is a state, not activity. As Robert Nozick famously pointed out, it could be attained by a person plugged into an "experience machine" who only had the illusion of acting, but really did nothing. Most people would not choose to be plugged in![11] One's own agency is very important (as J. S. Mill already saw, criticizing Bentham). For these four reasons, the metric of average utility fails to be a good measure of quality of life.

One further alternative theory remains to be considered. This theory measures life quality by looking at the quantity of some all-purpose resources, such as income and wealth, adjusted for distribution (according to some theory of adequate distribution).[12] This view is obviously a lot better, but it still falls short, for reasons repeatedly given by Sen. People vary both in their needs for resources and in their ability to convert resources into functionings. Some of these needs are straightforwardly physical: a child needs more protein than an adult; a pregnant or lactating woman needs more calories than a non-pregnant woman. But some are connected to traditional

---

[10]  For a summary, see my book *WHD* (n. 8) ch. 2.

[11]  Robert Nozick, *Anarchy, State, and Utopia* (Basic Books, 1974), 42–5.

[12]  Sen often presents this view as Rawls's account of "primary goods," but it isn't accurately so considered, so I simply present it independently as a view Sen criticizes.

sources of disadvantage: a person who uses a wheelchair will need more resources connected to mobility in order to attain the same level of ability to move around as a so-called "normal" person. (I would add that some of the pertinent resources are not personal financial resources at all, but social and political: wheelchair ramps in building, access on busses, etc.) To produce female literacy in a country that has traditionally denied women schooling requires more expenditure than producing male literacy. If what matters is what people are actually able to do and to be, the income theory falls short. Affirmative action to aid the traditionally disadvantaged is frequently needed.

To all these prevalent theories, the CA poses a simple question: What are people actually able to do and to be? That, we argue, is the pertinent question, and that is the pertinent space of comparison. The answer to the question is an account of that person's *capabilities*: the substantial freedoms a person has to choose this or that functioning. The trick for theorists is to find a way of measuring this all-important capability space, and much of our attention has been devoted to that question.

The reason to focus on capability rather than actual functioning is to respect people's choices. A person with adequate nutritional choices can always choose to fast for religious or personal reasons; but there is a huge difference between fasting and starving, and it is that difference that we aim to capture.

Human capital theorists in economics typically use the word "capability" to mean "skill" or "personal ability." That is not our usage. To make this clear, I have identified three types of capabilities; although this language is mine, the ideas behind it are common to the group. First, there are what I call *basic capabilities*, the innate material of persons that enables them to develop higher-level capabilities. (Even this is partly social on account of maternal nutrition and maternal stress, but let me bracket this for now.) Second are what I call *internal capabilities*, the developed abilities of persons thanks to maturing and social care: for example the ability to read and write. But a person may have all sorts of internal capabilities while being deprived of a chance to use them in action. Many people are able to think and form beliefs but live in societies that deny them the freedom of speech. Most people the world over can form religious ideas, but many of these people lack the freedom of religion. *Combined capabilities* are internal capabilities plus a social-political environment that makes choice a live possibility—or, to use Sen's words, "substantial freedoms."[13] All CA theorists agree that the pertinent space of comparison is combined capabilities (and not actual functionings and also not simply internal capabilities).

That is the shared position of capability theorists: that the space of capabilities, so defined, is superior as a space of comparison to the space of average GDP, or desire satisfaction, or income and wealth, and that this critical theory helps development theory and policy make progress in making human lives better.

---

[13] Amartya Sen, *Development as Freedom* (Alfred A. Knopf, 2000), 18.

## III. Nussbaum's Normative Theory: An Approach
## to Basic Political Principles, Not to Everything

Many people who use and further develop the CA focus on the space of comparison, arguing in favor of measuring quality of life in a nation or region with reference to capabilities, not average GDP or average utility. This has been Sen's primary endeavor: as in the Human Development Index, which he helped to originate, to recommend to countries a new space of comparison. For these purposes it is not necessary to make any distinction between the political and the social or personal. One may apply the approach anywhere. If one wishes, one may compare the capabilities of students in elective postgraduate classes that nobody would regard as a basic political entitlement. And where there is controversy about political entitlements, one may apply the comparative metric anyway. Nor is there any need to say which capabilities are central, although in any particular comparative exercise one must focus on something and say why it matters. Thus, the framers of the HDI chose to focus on health and education, suggesting their importance in thinking about quality of life, but not stating that these are more important than many other capabilities or that they are basic political entitlements. Throughout his writings Sen certainly gives us a robust sense of the capabilities that matter to him, but he remains reluctant to go further and say which ones might be basic constitutional (or otherwise political) entitlements.

What I am doing, by contrast, is something specific and quite restricted. It is to use the idea of capabilities as one building block in a theory of basic social justice (which has implications for global justice that I then describe). The list of capabilities is intended as an element in a theory of basic political entitlements, when combined with an idea of a threshold and the idea of a life worthy of people's inalienable human dignity. What I am trying to do is to frame some highly abstract principles that nations could then embody in the fundamental rights section of their constitution, or some other basic law if there is no written constitution. The idea is that if a nation does not give its citizens a threshold level of each of these capabilities, it has fallen short of even minimal justice. What this means in my terms is that it has not given them the chance to live lives worthy of their human dignity, which is seen as equal and inalienable. They may attain lives worthy of their dignity anyway, through private efforts, but the government has not executed a task that lies at the very heart of what government is for, as I articulate that idea.[14]

In one way, my project is more ambitious than that of the capability comparatists: it goes beyond normatively pregnant comparison to normative theory. In another way, however, it is more restricted, since it focuses on core political entitlements inherent in the very idea of a life worthy of human dignity, rather than the many other things people have reason to value and to measure. The two projects are

---

[14] See my "Constitutions and Capabilities: 'Perception' Against Lofty Formalism," Supreme Court Foreword, *Harvard Law Review* 121 (2007): 4–97.

complementary, though one might happily pursue the comparative project while remaining agnostic on the value of the normative project, or critical of my version of it.

Obviously, then, I am not talking about the entirety of law, only that part of law
that describes or directly bears upon people's core entitlements. Some statutes do
bear on core entitlements; that is why judicial review of legislation is a necessary aspect of political structure in my account.[15] But a lot of statutory law does not bear
on core entitlements, and that means that my view has nothing to say about it, nor
anything to say about civil society institutions. That does not mean that the idea of
capabilities could not be used fruitfully in these other domains by capability comparatists.[16] But that is not my project. Thus, labor lawyers would need to work out
what aspects of labor law inhere in the very idea of a life worthy of human dignity
if they want to use my approach, though they could also be content with the project of the comparatists—or, obviously, adopt a different account of fundamental
entitlements.

The nature of my project explains why, in my theory, there has to be a list. It is not
possible to have a constitution that just says "All citizens are entitled to freedoms, but
we won't say which ones." Furthermore, since I reject the whole idea of maximizing
freedom (see below), I think it very important to be definite: *these* freedoms are
fundamental entitlements based on justice, but others (for example the freedom to
keep all one's earnings without taxation) are not. The same point was elegantly made
to John Rawls by Herbert Hart in his excellent review of *A Theory of Justice*: Rawls,
said Hart, should not speak of "the priority of liberty," but rather the priority of an
enumerated list of liberties (speech, conscience, association).[17] Rawls immediately
accepted that critique.[18]

The rather small and finite list is also entailed by my espousal of Rawlsian political
liberalism, to be discussed below. We ask all citizens to agree on a relatively small list
of core political entitlements, but we leave other matters to be filled in by each in accordance with their comprehensive doctrines. Thus, the list is not a way of imposing
on people, it is actually a way of limiting imposition: we protect certain things for
all, but we leave the rest to you. Sen's view is in some respects more perfectionist,
I believe, and will shortly argue.[19]

[15] Although I might be satisfied with the weaker power of the British judiciary to issue a declaration
that legislation conflicts with core principles, I am surely not satisfied with the weaker stance of the New
Zealand Supreme Court, which so far refuses to issue such declarations.
[16] See Alan Bogg, "The Constitution of Capabilities: The Case of Freedom of Association,"
Chapter 12 in this volume.
[17] H. L. A. Hart, "Rawls on Liberty and Its Priority," *University of Chicago Law Review* 40 (1973): 534–55.
[18] Rawls's response to Hart is discussed in *Political Liberalism* (Columbia University Press, 1996)
289–340, and in *Justice as Fairness: a Restatement* (Harvard University Press, 2001), 42–50.
[19] Here is the list:
The Central Capabilities
  1. Life.
    Being able to live to the end of a human life of normal length; not dying prematurely, or before
    one's life is so reduced as to be not worth living.
  2. Bodily Health. Being able to have good health, including reproductive health; to be ad-
    equately nourished; to have adequate shelter.

## IV. The Moral Importance of National Sovereignty

In *Frontiers of Justice* and other writings on the global community, I follow Hugo Grotius in attaching fundamental importance to national sovereignty.[20] Nations are the largest units we know that are decently accountable to people's voices, and I argue that this means that we must think of the borders of the nation as having moral salience. They are key vehicles of human choices and autonomy in the literal sense of giving law to oneself. Intervention with the affairs of another nation, if that

3. Bodily Integrity. Being able to move freely from place to place; to be secure against violent assault, including sexual assault and domestic violence; having opportunities for sexual satisfaction and for choice in matters of reproduction.
4. Senses, Imagination, and Thought. Being able to use the senses, to imagine, think, and reason—and to do these things in a "truly human" way, a way informed and cultivated by an adequate education, including, but by no means limited to, literacy and basic mathematical and scientific training. Being able to use imagination and thought in connection with experiencing and producing works and events of one's own choice, religious, literary, musical, and so forth. Being able to use one's mind in ways protected by guarantees of freedom of expression with respect to both political and artistic speech, and freedom of religious exercise. Being able to have pleasurable experiences and to avoid non-beneficial pain.
5. Emotions. Being able to have attachments to things and people outside ourselves; to love those who love and care for us, to grieve at their absence; in general, to love, to grieve, to experience longing, gratitude, and justified anger. Not having one's emotional development blighted by fear and anxiety. (Supporting this capability means supporting forms of human association that can be shown to be crucial in their development.)
6. Practical Reason. Being able to form a conception of the good and to engage in critical reflection about the planning of one's life. (This entails protection for the liberty of conscience and religious observance.)
7. Affiliation.
   A. Being able to live with and toward others, to recognize and show concern for other human beings, to engage in various forms of social interaction; to be able to imagine the situation of another. (Protecting this capability means protecting institutions that constitute and nourish such forms of affiliation, and also protecting the freedom of assembly and political speech.)
   B. Having the social bases of self-respect and non-humiliation; being able to be treated as a dignified being whose worth is equal to that of others. This entails provisions of non-discrimination on the basis of race, sex, sexual orientation, ethnicity, caste, religion, national origin.
8. Other Species. Being able to live with concern for and in relation to animals, plants, and the world of nature.
9. Play. Being able to laugh, to play, to enjoy recreational activities.
10. Control over one's Environment.
    A. Political. Being able to participate effectively in political choices that govern one's life; having the right of political participation, protections of free speech and association.
    B. Material. Being able to hold property (both land and movable goods), and having property rights on an equal basis with others; having the right to seek employment on an equal basis with others; having the freedom from unwarranted search and seizure. In work, being able to work as a human being, exercising practical reason and entering into meaningful relationships of mutual recognition with other workers.

[20] I offer a detailed reading of Grotius on this issue, and further reflections of my own, in Martha C. Nussbaum, *The Cosmopolitan Tradition: A Noble but Flawed Ideal* (Harvard University Press, forthcoming 2019).

nation meets a minimal standard of legitimacy (far lower than justice), is justified only in very extreme circumstances, those covered in traditional legal accounts of genocide and crimes against humanity. The capabilities theory is a template for persuasion held out to the international community, but its implementation is left to the people of each nation. So the approach absolutely does not license, indeed forbids, intervention with other sovereign nations either by military force or by stringent economic measures.[21] Even when there is a genocide, as was the case in Gujarat in 2002,[22] international military intervention would have been prudentially a huge error, though surely there should have been much more protest than there was.

Because people have a right to make their own laws, it is appropriate for nations to make their constitution or basic law somewhat differently, in accordance with different histories and circumstances. So the account of capabilities is deliberately left vague, much vaguer than constitutions typically are, although a good constitution is also usually rather vague, gaining incremental precision through adjudication.

Needless to say, this Grotian defense of the moral importance of a nation's "basic structure" (to use Rawls's phrase) has nothing to do with aggressive saber-rattling nationalism of the type all too common today. Indeed, in its historical origins (in Grotius and Kant) it is closely linked to the pursuit of world peace and national cooperation. As for supranational federations such as the EU, the view I have taken is that they need to be sufficiently accountable to the voices of their citizens, a goal that the EU has not always fulfilled. To the extent that it is fulfilled, such a federation will become a federated nation such as the U.S. or India (both composites out of originally independent entities), and will therefore be protected as such, under my view. (I note that India, with twenty-two official languages and 350 or so that are actually in use, shows that a nation needn't be homogeneous in language and culture.)

It will likely remain a matter for debate which national choices are permissible variations and which violate the core commitments of my capabilities theory. I myself have changed my mind on specific cases. (I used to say that Germany's legal restrictions on the free speech of anti-Semites were a permissible expression of Germany's history, so different from that of the U.S., but I have come around to a more absolutist view, according to which speech may not justly be limited in this way—for reasons irrelevant to our current purposes, and inspired by some unfortunate events in India.[23])

Furthermore, some variations result from morally problematic material inequalities between nations that should be corrected over time. (Thus, if one nation can guarantee its people only an elementary education and another can guarantee college education to all, there is something wrong with this picture.) But in any case the

---

[21] See *FJ* (n. 8) and *CC* (n. 8). (I say that persuasive use of foreign aid may occasionally be ok, but usually one would want to be assured that the aims of the aid are supported by the people of the aided country.)

[22] See Martha C. Nussbaum, *The Clash Within: Democracy, Religious Violence, and India's Future* (Harvard University Press, 2007).

[23] See, if you're interested, http://indianexpress.com/article/opinion/columns/jnu-row-freedom-of-speech-ekla-cholo-re/ and http://indianexpress.com/article/opinion/columns/law-for-bad-behaviour/.

spirit of the theory is to be humble and to leave many important things for national self-determination, *for reasons of respect.*

So far as I am aware, other capability theorists do not discuss this question. They do proceed as if the nation is the fundamental unit for comparative purposes, but this choice may be an artifact of the world as it is, or the importance of the nation within the UN system. I am sure some would be more interested in the idea of a world state than I currently am.

## V. The Centrality of Political Liberalism

No central part of my philosophical theory is more neglected than its espousal of John Rawls's *political liberalism*, the view articulated in his book of that name.[24] I have insisted on this in all three of my books, and I wrote a 2011 article to expand further—and yet I find that friendly summaries typically leave this crucial bit out.[25] (I first espoused the political-liberal view in 1995,[26] and yet the different more Aristotelian view that I held in several articles of the 1980s is still sometimes imputed to me.) For that reason I reprinted and expanded the 2011 paper in an edited collection on the CA in 2014,[27] but it still has not had the desired effect, and much of what I write is consequently misunderstood.

In my view, agreeing with Rawls's second book, all modern societies (and to his emphasis on Western societies I add, in the Comim/Nussbaum volume, an extension to non-Western democracies) contain a reasonable plurality of comprehensive doctrines of the good or flourishing life, some religious and some secular. Protestants, Catholics, Muslims, Jews, Hindus, Buddhists, Marxists, Utilitarians— all these people have different comprehensive doctrines. It would be disrespectful to people, I argue, for the constitution of any nation to include the whole comprehensive doctrine of any one group. (In effect my view is a slightly expanded version of the US Constitution's Establishment Clause.) Political liberalism is grounded in an idea of equal respect for persons. Its upshot is that political principles ought to be both thin and narrow: narrow in that they do not pronounce on many important aspects of human life, such as the nature of death or the survival of the soul; thin in that they avoid using contentious metaphysical or even epistemic notions, such as the notion of the soul, or the notion of self-evident truth. They should use a thin ethical language that different religious and metaphysical traditions can accept but also thicken, each in their own way. (I often note that the Universal Declaration of Human Rights has a similar abstemiousness, as one of its primary architects, Jacques

[24] John Rawls, *Political Liberalism* (Columbia University Press, 1986).
[25] "Perfectionist Liberalism and Political Liberalism," *Philosophy and Public Affairs* 39(1) (2011): 3–45.
[26] See "The Good as Discipline, the Good as Freedom," in David A. Crocker and Toby Linden (eds.), *Ethics of Consumption: The Good Life, Justice, and Global Stewardship* (Rowman and Littlefield, 1998), 312–41 (written in 1995).
[27] Flavio Comim and Martha C. Nussbaum (eds.), *Capabilities, Gender, Equality: Towards Fundamental Entitlements* (Cambridge University Press, 2014).

Maritain, often emphasized:[28] it uses a thin ethical notion of human dignity rather than the thicker notions the various participants would use in their own comprehensive doctrines, such as the notion of the soul.) The aim will be a Rawlsian "overlapping consensus": all the comprehensive doctrines that are reasonable, in the sense of accepting the idea of equal respect for persons (I discuss the proper interpretation of "reasonable" in the PAPA article[29]) can accept these principles and agree to live by them as political principles, though they will want to say a lot more.

Political liberalism and capabilities go well together. Capabilities are options, but nobody is forced to use them. A religion that doesn't want people to function in certain ways can often accept the capability to do so as an option protected for all citizens. Thus, the Old Order Amish don't want their members to participate in politics, but they happily live in a nation that gives people political rights. Some types of Christian doctrine forbid interreligious marriage for their members, but few, today at least, oppose the availability of such marriages. Even divorce, though forbidden in some religions, is usually understood to be a perfectly acceptable aspect of political principles open to all. Members of the religions that forbid divorce will just not use that option. (I think that the uproar over same-sex marriage will eventually resolve itself in the same way.)

Furthermore, many comprehensive doctrines that citizens hold do not support a comprehensive doctrine of personal freedom or autonomy, as do the political views of Mill and Raz. Instead, they ask citizens to chart their course to some extent by religious authority. Raz and Mill both say that such authoritarian religious comprehensive doctrines, while they will not be suppressed, will be strongly denigrated in the public realm: political leaders should tell people that these doctrines are mistaken. In PAPA I call this "expressive subordination," comparable to a situation in which religious freedom is protected but one religion is endorsed as THE public religion.[30] I argue that expressive subordination is at odds with basic norms of equal respect. So my own capabilities approach is carefully designed to show equal respect to citizens who espouse authoritarian religions. They do not have to agree on anything but the fact that certain opportunities or capabilities ought to be available, *for political purposes*, to all citizens. I think they can agree on this, provided that they are "reasonable" in the sense of extending equal respect to their fellow citizens. (In PAPA I argue that this is the correct reading of "reasonable" in Rawls, despite certain other things he says.)

What the espousal of political liberalism means for our purposes is that every putative central capability needs to be carefully examined to see whether it is consistent with mutual respect in a nation of diverse equals. Abstemiousness is not cowardice, it is a core moral principle.

In the Comim/Nussbaum volume, I point out that every modern democracy is in the same situation that Rawls described for Europe and North America. Namely, every single one contains a plurality of different religious and secular conceptions,

---

[28] See, for example, Jacques Maritain, *Man and the State* (University of Chicago Press, 1951), Ch. IV.
[29] "Perfectionist Liberalism and Political Liberalism" (n. 25).
[30] "Perfectionist Liberalism and Political Liberalism" (n. 25) 35.

basically the same ones that the U. S. contains. Only the proportions differ, and these do not matter for normative purposes. Moreover, these same considerations obtain when we try to frame principles in the international community. So when we make international accords and principles we should think about respect in a similar way. But in the transnational case, there's even further reason for caution in the respect we attach to national sovereignty. International accords must not simply respect people, they must respect the right of people to make laws as citizens of nations.

What is Sen's view on this all-important matter? Many capability theorists seem to espouse the sort of comprehensive preference for freedom as autonomy that I find in Mill and Raz. Sen's view is less clear. He seems unfamiliar with Rawls's second book, which does not even appear in the Index in his *The Idea of Justice*, a book largely concerned with Rawls.[31] Clearly Sen is a pluralist about freedom: he supports the freedoms of individuals to pursue what they "have reason to value," a phrase often used, and rejects the idea that politics should focus on a single value. As we shall see, his distinction between maximizing and optimizing comes from that commitment to pluralism. On the other hand, like Raz and Mill, he expresses a strong preference for religions or other comprehensive doctrines grounded in reason rather than mysticism, faith, or authority.[32] My conclusion is that he agrees here with Raz and Mill: while not limiting the freedom of other types of religion, he would allow the state to announce a preference for the rationalistic sort. Obviously, this difference makes a difference when we begin to talk about freedom.

It is crucially important that I make no claim that the goal of politics is to maximize the development of each person's human capital. I don't think this is even the view of human capital theorists, and James Heckman has eloquently commented on the relationship between his version of human capital theory and my theory.[33] But certainly it isn't my view. That sort of comprehensive doctrine would in any case run afoul of political liberalism. Most of the major religions would reject it.

Is there any other sense in which I would support the goal of maximizing freedom? Capabilities are freedoms, but mine is a threshold view, and I have not commented on how to handle inequalities over the threshold. In some cases, the threshold level is equality: Thus, freedom of speech, voting rights, religious freedom, and others, must all be distributed equally. I do not say maximally, though I am sympathetic with Rawls's idea of "the most extensive liberty compatible with a like liberty for all"—in the case of some enumerated liberties.[34] But I don't hold this about voting, for example: I think it is fine for many offices to be filled by appointment, or appointment plus confirmation. And in the socio-economic area I am very skeptical of such ideas: we should figure out what adequate education and adequate health care are, rather than trying to maximize the amount of education and health care.

---

[31] Amartya Sen, *The Idea of Justice* (Harvard University Press, 2009).

[32] See Amartya Sen, *Identity and Violence: The Illusion of Destiny* (W. W. Norton, 2006). I am also drawing on recent personal correspondence about this point.

[33] See the Appendix on Heckman in *CC*. Heckman has also given an eloquent Plenary Lecture to the HDCA in 2016, as yet unpublished.

[34] John Rawls, "Justice As Fairness," in Samuel Freeman (ed.), *John Rawls: Collected Papers* (Harvard University Press, 1999) ch. 3 at 48.

My view is demanding enough: up to a high threshold of adequacy, which in certain cases requires equality, the ten freedoms should be secured. This view is, I believe, compatible with political liberalism, in that it could become the object of an overlapping consensus among the reasonable comprehensive doctrines. I don't think Sen's view can. But we must describe it.

Sen does often speak of maximizing freedom, but caution is needed. Since he is a pluralist about conceptions of the good, he makes an important distinction between maximizing and optimizing, arguing that the result can only be a partial ordering.[35] Even so, there is a recognizable sense in which he does think that an appropriate goal for politics would be to promote the freedoms of persons to pursue "what they have reason to value." Since he has no list, this is potentially quite a demanding goal.

I think it is a mistaken goal. First, coherence: some freedoms limit others. The freedom of industry to pollute the air interferes with the freedom of you and me to breathe clean air. Second, good and bad: the freedoms sought by racists should be limited. They should not be allowed to put up placards in the workplace saying "No blacks here." The freedoms of polluters should also be limited. Men should not have the freedom to harass women in the workplace. And so forth. Perhaps Sen could try to argue that these freedoms are not things that people "have reason to value," but then the notion of reason would be so normatively freighted and tendentious that I can't imagine how he would do that. People clearly have arguments for bad goals! My view does not get enmeshed in this problem because it focuses abstemiously on a small group of central capabilities, leaving it to the democratic process to sort out these other matters (but using the list to constrain some of the bad freedoms). Finally, some freedoms are simply trivial. Some people are crazy about riding a motorcycle without a helmet, and they may put forward some pieces of reasoning to support this. But surely that doesn't mean that it's an important job of government to listen to them with approval or to subsidize their activities. Again, by sticking to central matters, I avoid committing myself to the cause of the helmetless bikers.

On specific cases, Sen and I basically agree. He is no libertarian, favoring heavily regulated markets and ample taxation. I am therefore puzzled by his talk of maximizing freedom. Perhaps it is a legacy of his anti-colonialism, perhaps a repudiation of his youthful Marxism, perhaps a vestige of utilitarian economics. Whatever the case may be, even apart from the issue of political liberalism, he should not speak of maximizing freedom. People are not so good a lot of the time, and law needs to make them do things that create a decent egalitarian society with an ample social safety net, a point on which both he and I actually agree.

In short, insofar as the idea of maximizing freedom makes any sense at all, it is a very bad idea, which only a die-hard libertarian could even entertain. Most libertarians, however, don't want people to be totally free: they want contract law, tort law, taxation to support the legal system and the courts. So what is really going on is that they want legal rules and legal constraint in some areas and not others. Sen

---

[35]  See Amartya Sen, "Maximization and the Act of Choice," *Econometrica* 65 (1997): 745–80.

is not in harmony with those choices, and I think on substantive policy matters he and I basically agree.

## VI. The Individual a Goal not a Limit

What role does "individualism" play in my approach? I have long insisted that the word "individualism" has been used to mean confusingly many things, and that more clarity is needed before we can ask whether "individualism" is good or not.[36] Some of the things to which people at times refer with the term "individualism," for example psychological egoism and ethical egoism, can be rejected decisively as inadequate theories. Other ideas (for example, the norm that one should strive for self-sufficiency, as the Stoics taught) are more interesting, but ultimately, I believe, to be rejected.[37] But there is a type of normative individualism that is not to be rejected. It lies at the heart of the liberal tradition, in its Kantian form and at least John Stuart Mill's version of its Utilitarian form. This is the idea that each person is an end, a being with dignity, to be treated with respect, and that none should be used as a mere means to the ends of others. That is the form that I endorse in my version of the Capabilities Approach, and Sen does too. (I also endorse this view concerning non-human animals, but let us not discuss that question further here.)

In other words: the goal is to extend capabilities to *each*, rather than to some corporate entity, whether a family or a class or a religious group or a labor union. Each person is an end, and none a mere tool of the ends of others. All groups, including groups in which people work (the household, the labor union) may house and conceal gross inequalities among members. Groups may certainly be crucial to securing capabilities to people, but it is each person who ultimately matters, and each should be treated as an end. Groups are instruments. This commitment has been particularly important in the world of women's development projects where much of my work has been done, since women have so often been valued as support structures for men, not as people of worth in their own right.

Most practitioners of the CA are normative individualists in just this sense. Sen clearly is, and the primary exception of which I am aware would be those environmentalist scholars who think that the capabilities of ecosystems should take priority.

---

[36] See my "The Feminist Critique of Liberalism," in my *Sex and Social Justice* (Oxford University Press, 1999).

[37] I note parenthetically that many global feminists are far more enamored of individual self-sufficiency as a norm than I am. When I walked into the offices of SEWA, I was astonished to see SELF-SUFFICIENCY on the wall among other norms such as literacy and access to credit. Hadn't I spent years trying to convince anti-liberals that liberalism endorsed only Kantian individualism and not Stoic self-sufficiency? I soon found out that their idea had Gandhian roots. Just as Gandhi insisted that India would achieve dignity only to the extent that she became self-sufficient vis a vis her colonial master, Britain, so too, thinks SEWA, women will achieve dignity only to the extent that they achieve self-sufficiency (economic, political, and even emotional) vis a vis their colonial masters, viz., men. These women see Western feminists like me as all too lovey-dovey in their preference for marriage and the nuclear family. I do have romantic views, but in chapter 4 of *WHD* I try to show that many groups may reasonably be supported in a society's effort to raise children—including women's groups like SEWA, formed as sources of emotional and economic self-sufficiency for each.

None of this means that groups are unimportant. The fact that their importance is instrumental rather than intrinsic does not mean that they are not extremely important. (Food is important instrumentally, but who would say that it is not really important?) Nor does it mean that capabilities cannot involve relational aspects, as several of those on my list clearly do. Thus, one of the most important capabilities, as I often state, which organizes and suffuses all the others, is a person's opportunity to form a variety of relationships, and I include work relationships of equality and dignity among those.

## VII. Why a "Minimal" Approach?

By now we can see several distinct reasons why I insist that my theory is a "minimal" theory of social justice, a claim that has sometimes been misunderstood. Some of these are normative reasons, some reasons of (deliberate) incompleteness. I have never gathered these together, and I may have given rise to confusion by not doing so.

a. *Inequalities over the threshold.* My threshold view says nothing at all about how we ought to regard inequalities above the threshold, or whether and when those raise problems of justice. So the theory is to that extent incomplete. However, I think it is likely that we could not achieve an overlapping consensus on anything beyond a threshold view, so perhaps there is little more to be said.

b. *Humble and revisable.* I list ten capabilities, but I repeatedly insist (see CC) that this list is to be regarded as "humble and revisable," a kind of "talking points" paper for further debate. I myself changed the list in the early days, in response to criticisms I received. At this point I have stopped doing this because it is too confusing for people to operate with eight or ten different lists, and I am pretty satisfied with this one, but I have emphasized that other crucial ingredients (the importance of care, for example) need to be recognized as we further interpret the list.

c. *Political liberalism.* This commitment suggests abstemiousness and thinness as matters of respect. Here the theory is minimal for normative reasons. As I have remarked, this may mean that the theory, as a threshold theory, is not actually incomplete.

d. *National sovereignty.* Another normative reason for keeping the theory pretty abstemious is the space this leave for nations to flesh things out in their own way. That is why the list is so abstract.

e. *The threshold is not so minimal, and in some cases it is equality.* The word "minimal" might be read as suggesting that not much is guaranteed. I make it clear, however, that this is not the case with my view. Concerning a large group of capabilities, including all of those corresponding to traditional guarantees of free speech, voting rights, freedom of religion, and freedom of association, I make it clear that the only satisfactory position is full equality of persons.

I tentatively say the same for education rights.[38] Concerning other matters such as housing, I suggest that there is latitude: a constitutional housing right would fetishize material goods too much if it were understood to guarantee everyone houses of the same price or size. But nonetheless, an ample threshold is what I have in mind. Here I reason normatively, thinking of what the idea of a life worthy of human dignity implies in each area.

f. *Constitutions must contain more than capabilities: structure, national security.* No theory of a just nation could be simply a list of fundamental entitlements. In effect my list corresponds to Part III of the Indian Constitution, its list of Fundamental Rights. But there are other things a constitution must include: political structure, procedures, qualifications for office, and provisions for national security. So my theory is incomplete, and, if you will, "minimal," in this further sense. I do think and say that the separation of powers, an independent judiciary, and judicial review of legislation are entailed by the idea of protecting human capabilities, but that's about as far as I have gone. I tend to think that other matters of political structure are highly contextual. Thus, the best method of selecting Supreme Court judges depends on facts about the nation: average educational level, especially. In recent writings about the Indian Supreme Court I have defended Ambedkar's move in creating a very large Court (it currently has 29 members) so that people and NGOs can approach the Court directly by petition.[39] This seems very important for a nation like India, where access to legal services is so unevenly distributed, although it creates large problems, in that cases are heard by three-judge panels that may come out differently from one another, with no higher Court to resolve the differences. Still, it is best for India. It would not be so good for the U.S., I believe.

## VIII. Capabilities and Women's Work

In concluding, let me turn more briefly to the topic of labor[40] As any reader of any of my books will know, my views were developed and continue to be developed in the context of international development policy, and with the situation of women in developing countries at its heart. India has been my particular focus. *Women and Human Development* includes a sustained confrontation with women's history and current struggles in that country, and my later writings on Indian politics (e.g. my

[38] See *FJ* and *CC* (n. 8).

[39] Martha C. Nussbaum, "Ambedkar's Constitution: Promoting Inclusion, Opposing Majority Tyranny," in Tom Ginsburg and Aziz Huq (eds.), *Assessing Constitutional Performance* (Cambridge University Press, 2016), 295–336.

[40] I have written specifically about the topic of labor in: "Women and Equality: The Capabilities Approach," *International Labour Review* 138 (1999), reprinted in Martha Fetherolf Loutfi (ed.), *Women, Gender, and Work: What is Equality and How Do We Get there*, ed. (International Labour Office, 2001), 45–68; and in my preface to the 2017 second volume of *Women, Gender and Work*.

2007 book *The Clash Within*) include a substantial focus on India's women and the gender politics of the Hindu right.[41] My own fieldwork has focused on women's development organizations in many different regions of the country. I co-authored, at UNDP Delhi, a report on Gender and Governance.[42] And I have been involved closely with The Lawyer's Collective, a Delhi-based NGO that has two arms, one working on women's equality and one on HIV/AIDS and sexual orientation equality (another primary topic of my work in general).

Moreover, insofar as I am a constitutional law academic (albeit with no law degree!) my publications on law have focused insistently, in a long series of papers, on India's constitution, and particularly on aspects of relevance to women's equality and, more recently, sexual orientation.[43] Most recently, I have been running a large bi-national project, funded by our University of Chicago Delhi Center, studying stigma and prejudice comparatively with a team of scholars from the US and India. The fruits of this work appeared in 2018 in the volume *The Empire of Disgust: Prejudice, Discrimination, and Policy in India and the U. S.*, co-edited by Zoya Hasan, Aziz Huq, Martha C. Nussbaum, and Vidhu Verma, from OUP-Delhi; I wrote the theoretical part of the Introduction, and my two contributions focus on (1) age discrimination, and (2) the legal aspects of sexual orientation discrimination under Indian constitutional law. I consider India my second country, and I regularly write political commentary in the Indian press, most recently an essay on Trump and Modi co-authored with Zoya Hasan, and a June 2018 interview on lynchings of Muslims.[44] I say all this to indicate the world from which I approach and have long approached human (and animal) capabilities.

This is truly a different world from the world inhabited by most contributors to the present volume. More than ninety percent of India's women work in the informal economy, meaning that they are either home-based workers, or hawkers and vendors, or employed in cottage industries too small to be subject to formal labor law. (Thus, it's a mistake to say that in the informal economy there is no employer; and even home-based workers need middlemen who often exploit them. Thus, a

---

[41] Martha C. Nussbaum, *The Clash Within* (Belknap Press of Harvard University Press, 2009).

[42] "Gender and Governance: An Introduction," in *Essays on Gender and Governance*, with Amrita Basu, Yasmin Tambiah, and Niraja Gopal Jayal (United Nations Development Programme Resource Centre, 2003), 1–19.

[43] One can find an overview of this work in "India, Sex Equality, and Constitutional Law," in Beverly Baines and Ruth Rubio Marin (eds.), *Constituting Women: The Gender of Constitutional Jurisprudence* (Cambridge University Press, 2004), 174–204. But there are about ten other papers, some more recent.

[44] Seema Chishti, "Professor Martha Nussbaum interview: 'Govts must make it clear that hate crimes are unacceptable … This is not taking place,'" *The Indian Express* (New Delhi, 2 July 2018) https://indianexpress.com/article/technology/sponsored/five-competitors-one-clear-winner-the-best-smartphone-you-can-buy-under-rs-25000-5294574/; Zoya Hasan and Martha C. Nussbaum, "India & US, spot the difference." *The Indian Express* (New Delhi, 24 July 2017) https://indianexpress.com/article/opinion/columns/donald-trump-narendra-modi-demonetisation-education-radical-islam-employment-beef-lynching-cow-slaughter-love-jihad-india-us-spot-the-difference-4763976/ reprinted on ABC in Australia as Zoya Hasan and Martha C. Nussbaum, "The Narcissist and the Ideologue: Trump, Modi and the Threat They Pose to Democracy," *Australian Broadcasting Corporation* (27 July 2017) http://www.abc.net.au/religion/articles/2017/07/27/4708861.htm.

flower-garland twiner working at home in Tamil Nadu works for an entrepreneur who sells the product to flower shops.)

Getting the ILO to take home-based work seriously as work has been a long struggle, engaged in not so much by me directly but by close colleagues, such as Martha Chen and Ela Bhatt, the co-founders of WIEGO (Women in the Informal Economy Globalizing and Organizing).[45] (Bhatt is also the founder of SEWA, the Self-Employed Women's Association, which I discuss in both WHD and CC.) In addition to the primacy given informal work in my examples and the resulting theory, I have also long been concerned with unpaid domestic labor and care labor, as work that is not recognized at all in national income accounts and whose lack of recognition causes a variety of legal and political problems, mostly for women. The work of economists Nancy Folbre and Bina Agarwal on this issue has been at the heart of my own concern and my teaching.[46]

Again: this is a different world from the world of collective bargaining and labor unions. First of all, to someone interested in the equality of women in poor countries, it would make no sense at all to consider labor in isolation from other aspects of women's situation, such as education, access to credit, political participation, and strategies to combat domestic violence. SEWA in Ahmedabad, as I describe in *WHD* and *CC*, does some informal-sector labor organizing, but it does many other things. It has literacy classes, it engages with the police to prod them to deal better with domestic violence, it gives loans and runs a woman's bank. All these activities are interrelated, and most good organizations in India use a similar combined approach. Labor opportunities and protections are not very useful if women are illiterate; if they are beaten and afraid to go outside; if they have no access to credit to start an informal business enterprise. And of course women's political voice is crucial to advancing all these goals. So my account of Vasanti, used in two of my books, shows clearly the interrelationship of all the capabilities and the importance of addressing them all together.

Second, in the world where I work, the focus on unions and collective bargaining has often been not the solution, but part of the problem. It is the old story: men defining "work" as what they do, and refusing to grant that dignified title to what women do. (A fine biography of Ela Bhatt by Kalima Rose chronicles her struggles with the ILO and the initial mockery that greeted her dignified and eventually successful advocacy for women's work, comparing her to Draupadi in the *Mahabharata*, whom the men attempt to strip naked, but whose sari reweaves itself so that she is always clothed with perfect dignity.[47]) This condescending attitude is part of the

[45] See "WIEGO at 20: Accomplishments and Gaps" www.wiego.org. See also Bhatt's book *We Are Poor But So Many: The Story of Self-Employed Women in India* (Oxford University Press, 2006).

[46] See, for example, Nancy Folbre, Barbara Bergmann, Bina Agarwal, and Maria Floro (eds.), *Women's Work in the World Economy* (Palgrave Macmillan, 1992); Bina Agarwal, *A Field of One's Own* (Cambridge University Press, 1994); Bina Agarwal, *Gender and Green Governance* (Oxford University Press, 2010); Bina Agarwal, *Gender Challenges, Vols 1, 2, and 3* (Oxford University Press, 2016); Nancy Folbre, "Valuing Non-market Work," 2015 UNDP Human Development Report Office: http://hdr.undp.org/sites/default/files/folbre_hdr_2015_final_0.pdf.

[47] Kalima Rose, *Where Women are Leaders: The SEWA Movement in India* (Zed Books, 1993).

history of the ILO's marginalization of informal work, and its continuing resistance to counting unpaid domestic labor as work. It was a remarkable achievement of the commission on welfare and quality of life convened by former President Sarkozy of France and chaired by Amartya Sen, Jean-Paul Fitoussi, and Joseph Stiglitz, that, despite its location in a highly unionized industrial nation, the report highlighted the issue of informal work and domestic work, heeding the proposals of commission members Folbre and Agarwal.[48] I think it is time for the world of labor law to follow this lead.

One way of beginning would be to study the history of interactions between advocates for informal-sector workers and the ILO, and the standards for home-based work that eventually emerged from that struggle. Another way would be to study efforts to unionize such workers in more affluent nations, for example the effort in the U.S. to unionize home-based health care workers.

Only after such a study, I believe, would it make sense to face the question of labor law's autonomy or non-autonomy. In the case of informal work, many considerations dictate a non-autonomous approach. But the whole picture will emerge from further study.

It would certainly be odd if the area of most urgent focus for the creators of the CA, an area of urgent human importance, were utterly neglected by thinkers who are using the CA to pursue issues of labor law. Let us hope that future work will take up this challenge!

---

[48] Joseph E. Stiglitz, Amartya Sen, and Jean-Paul Fitoussi, "Report by the Commission on the Measurement of Economic Performance and Social Progress," Commission on the Measurement of Economic Performance and Social Progress (Paris, 2009) http://ec.europa.eu/eurostat/documents/ 118025/118123/Fitoussi+Commission+report

# 4

# Is the Capability Theory an Adequate Normative Theory for Labour Law?

*Riccardo Del Punta*

## I. On Labour Law and Political Philosophy

Hugh Collins recently wondered[1] whether it makes sense to use political theory in order to find a normative foundation for labour law, and ended up by expressing several doubts or caveats in this regard. And although acknowledging that certain operations can be attempted, he queried (in particular with reference to the capability theory) whether they could be successful.

Collins' remarks are, as always, very perspicacious, and his idea of the three possible strategies (methodological imitation, reapplication of key philosophical concepts, exegesis of philosophers' positions) that can be followed in making use of political philosophy to establish (or re-establish) the foundations of labour law is enlightening.

In my view, while the methodological copy is hardly feasible and the exegesis of political theorists' positions may be too focused on the philosopher's text, the *reapplication of philosophical concepts* could, in principle, be a productive strategy.

Actually, one could speak directly of an *application*, since it should be normal for concepts drawn up in the abstraction of normative theories to be contextualized in the various fields of social action. This is commonly done through examples provided by the philosophers themselves; hence, lawyers or other social scientists should be allowed to do the same from a different viewpoint.

Moreover, the philosopher should be willing to accept that, once the concepts concerned are handled by legal scholars, they may be *adapted* to some extent, without this resulting in a betrayal of the original idea. Conversely, the legal scholar should not expect to find a perfect correspondence in the philosophical theory with the conceptual framework inherent in her specific field of interest.

---

[1] In the paper, presented at the third LLRN conference held in Toronto on June 2017, based on Hugh Collins, Gillian Lester, and Virginia Mantouvalou, 'Introduction: Does Labour Law Need Philosophical Foundations?' in Hugh Collins, Gillian Lester, and Virginia Mantouvalou (eds), *The Philosophical Foundations of Labour Law* (OUP 2018).

The Capability Approach to Labour Law. Edited by Brian Langille. Chapter 4 © Riccardo Del Punta 2019. Published 2019 by Oxford University Press.

The legal scholar should also be aware that the fact of connecting to a more general value, which can be referred to a wider range of situations, is able to give the context-specific values a greater consistency even when it may not add much to them in strictly conceptual terms.

It follows that no inevitable alternative exists between either general or context-specific explanations once they are both given their rightful place.

That said, it still has to be demonstrated why a close comparison with political philosophy, in addition to being an exciting intellectual exercise (at least for jurists with a philosophical bent), should also be productive for labour lawyers. I see three main reasons for this, the first related to law in general, and the other two inherent in labour law.

The *first* reason is that if one opens up, as a labour lawyer should basically be inclined to do, to a non-positivist theory of the law, then ethical and social values cannot be kept out of legal discourse since they are relevant not only to the making of the law but also to its interpretation and application.

From this perspective, law is, indeed, subject to a process of *permanent justification* of its functioning, which tends to go beyond a strictly legal discourse.[2] This should leave a natural space for a dialogue with philosophy.

The *second* reason why labour lawyers, in particular, should pay special attention to political philosophy is that the connection with values is a key component of the discipline's DNA, owing to the fact that it differs from private law, as a paradigmatic example of Max Weber's material law, with a view to pursuing specific social goals.

However, this immanency of values, which since its beginning has infiltrated the labour law discourse, has not brought it closer to the philosophical debate. The opposite has instead occurred, but this is a paradox that can be understood.

A simple explanation could be that labour law's spectacular success during the second half of the 20th century was so evident and in harmony with the *zeitgeist* of the time that labour lawyers did not feel the need to verify their value assumptions in the light of political philosophy.

But a deeper reason may be that labour law has always been openly *partisan*, in that it has only cared for a particular category of people, albeit socially important and vulnerable, such as the subordinate workers.

As a consequence, although the discipline has a natural inclination towards social justice, it has rarely felt the need to be supported by a universalistic theory of justice rather than, at best, mere *arguments of justice* focused on the employee's condition. This has meant that labour law, in parallel with its growing realizations, has elaborated its own values as though they needed no further ground.

However, despite their importance (and enduring relevance also in the light of the reappraisal proposed hereafter), each of these values could entail more basic

---

[2]  That is also true for those civil law systems with a strong *constitutional foundation*, in which social values are internalized by the legal system through the Constitution's principles (many of which, as regards 20th century constitutions, are dedicated to labour). This is not sufficient, in fact, for determining an operational closure of the legal system from outside, since constitutional statements are also subject to interpretation, which puts values back into the argumentative game.

questions: why should subordinate workers alone deserve protection aimed at correcting the imbalance of bargaining power inherent in their relationship, and what comes afterwards?[3] Is it not true that a labour market exists and, therefore, that labour is at least partially commodified? What kind of equality is pursued by labour law?

Given these and other questions for which there are obviously no simple solutions, the time might have come to resume contact with the philosophical debate in search of some new spark.

This leads to a *third*, albeit more contingent, reason for a philosophical revival, which has to do with the need to give stronger foundations to labour law in order to enable it to better resist, at least at a theoretical level, the neo-liberal attack.

The search for a new foundation, however, cannot be merely a matter of resistance, but also that of constructively finding a new value paradigm that is more fitting than the older ones for rationalizing the current stage of labour law. This is exactly why some scholars have recently become interested in the capability approach,[4] in much the same way as others have shown interest in other ideas taken from philosophical literature.

## II. Which Foundation?

In my view, therefore, the question is not if, but how, to make correct use of political philosophy in the field of labour law.

An essential difference between the methodology of political theories and that of a legal discipline emerges.[5] Political theories usually start with a 'tabula rasa', that is, with very few assumptions about people and the world, on the basis of which they try to justify their general theories.

But looking for the normative foundation of something that already exists, such as labour law, is a different kind of undertaking, as it requires us to take account of both the theoretical references and a rich and highly differentiated (as well as imperfect) legal material.

In short, from both viewpoints, the attempt to find in a political theory new foundational arguments for a legal discipline that is not an exercise of applied ethics,[6] but has developed hand in hand with history, and often as a result of harsh social conflicts, could seem *artificial*.

---

[3] For a closer criticism of the mainstream labour law narrative, see Brian Langille, 'Labour Law's Theory of Justice' in Guy Davidov and Brian Langille (eds), *The Idea of Labour Law* (OUP 2011), especially at 110.

[4] This chapter represents an expansion of the reflections developed in Riccardo Del Punta, 'Labour Law and the Capability Approach' (2016) 32 *International Journal of Comparative Labour Law and Industrial Relations* 383.

[5] This and the following paragraphs are based on Collins, Lester, and Mantouvalou, 'Introduction' (n 1).

[6] Bob Hepple, 'Factors Influencing the Making and Transformation of Labour Law in Europe' in Guy Davidov and Brian Langille (eds), *The Idea of Labour Law* (OUP 2011) 30.

Nonetheless, I would insist that the comparison between the two perspectives can be enriching, provided their differences are well conceptualized. A first choice must be made in this respect.

On the one hand, most normative philosophers could be inclined to look at workers' fundamental entitlements, which involve general considerations of justice (although not necessarily a complete theory of justice).

A good example of this is represented by Martha C Nussbaum's version of the capability approach, where the emphasis is on the ten basic capabilities that make a life worth living and which should be supported by all democracies in the name of the Kantian value of human dignity[7] (even though Nussbaum refuses Kant's and Rawls'[8] contractarianism).

In particular, she mentions 'control over one's environment', which is specified, with concern for the 'material' condition of life, as 'having a right to seek employment on an equal basis with others' and 'being able to work as a human, exercising practical reason and entering into meaningful relationships of mutual recognition with other workers'.[9]

Nussbaum admits that this list is open to greater specification, but her approach remains of a sufficientarian kind,[10] even though, according to a plausible reading of her position, concentrating the theory on a decent 'social minimum' does not entail being indifferent to addressing inequalities above this threshold.[11]

This approach has clear connections with a *human rights* perspective, which is equally in search of a universal threshold that should apply to all human beings for the mere fact of existing and possessing human dignity.[12]

Labour lawyers, on the other hand, (attracted as they might be by a sufficientarian approach) could be even more interested in searching for a philosophical explanation of labour law as a whole and not only with regard to its minimum standards.[13] Amartya Sen's assumption that the list of capabilities must be the product of public reasoning and democratic deliberation[14] may be helpful in this regard.

---

[7] Martha C Nussbaum, *Frontiers of Justice: Disability, Nationality and Species Membership* (HUP 2006) 76–8.

[8] Nussbaum, *Frontiers of Justice* (n 7) 9 ff in general terms and 220–1 specifically on Kant.

[9] Nussbaum, *Frontiers of Justice* (n 7) 77–8.

[10] Nussbaum, *Frontiers of Justice* (n 7) 75: 'The capabilities approach is not intended to provide a complete account of social justice. It says nothing, for example, about how justice would treat inequalities above the threshold'.

[11] See John M Alexander, *Capabilities and Social Justice: the Political Philosophy of Amartya Sen and Martha Nussbaum* (Ashgate Publishing 2008) 75.

[12] Nussbaum, *Frontiers of Justice* (n 7) 284 ff. For the proposal to take recognized human rights as a basis for deriving a 'minimum core' list of capabilities, see Polly Vizard, Sakiku Fukuda-Parr, and Diane Elson, 'Introduction: The Capability Approach and Human Rights' (2011) 12(1) *Journal of Human Development and Capabilities* 1.

[13] In the same vein, the proposal to find a foundational basis of labour law in the human rights view does not seem capable of exhausting the topic. The normative field should at least be broadened by looking at *fundamental* rather than human rights, such as those laid down by the European Charter of Fundamental Rights.

[14] Amartya Sen, *The Idea of Justice* (Penguin Group 2009) 321 ff.

Indeed, as labour law is deeply entrenched in the democratic process of socially advanced countries, Sen's approach may suggest that labour-related capabilities—selected and promoted through public action—could be derived from the driving values of consolidated labour legislation, thereby establishing an open and viable channel of communication between the philosophical and legal perspectives.[15]

This implies that the labour lawyer can reasonably assume that the best selection of the relevant capabilities[16] has already been made by labour law itself, to the extent that it can be conceptualized from a capability perspective.

This assumption could be criticized for reversing the relationship that should exist, from a normative perspective, between the is (labour law as it is) and the ought (labour law how it should be according to certain abstract values).

However, such criticism would be misplaced. What is developed here cannot be but an *interpretive legal analysis* that tries to open up to a philosophical perspective while remaining of an *inductive* kind. The materials that are taken into primary consideration are therefore the legal institutions at a certain stage of their evolution. In other words, these institutions are both something that must be taken as a matter of fact to be decoded, and something on which a normative discourse, albeit at a lower level of abstraction than in philosophy, can be built. In turn, this allows for the discovering of a possible rationalization of their development.

A normative approach is intrinsically *foundational*. However, up to this point it should also be evident that when I refer to the search for a revised foundation of labour law, I am applying the concept of foundation in a non-metaphysical sense, that is, by attributing a weak epistemological status to it.

Indeed, the analysis is aimed at reinforcing the normative status of the discipline in terms of a discursive conception of the law, which focuses on the reliability of the lines of reasoning developed within a certain knowledge context while leaving out the possibility of a foundation of the law in the strict sense.[17]

## III. When Can a Political Theory Be Relevant to Labour Law?

Within the perspective described above, two main requirements for labour law can be identified to make a certain political theory relevant to labour law, despite not necessarily being the most adequate.

---

[15] However, the difference between Sen's and Nussbaum's positions, which undoubtedly exists (Nussbaum, *Frontiers of Justice* (n 7) 166), could be less than it seems, since Nussbaum herself acknowledges 'that the item on the list ought to be specified in a somewhat abstract and general way, precisely in order to leave room for the activities of specifying and deliberating by citizens and their legislatures and courts' (Nussbaum, *Frontiers of Justice* (n 7) 78–9).

[16] This is a debated topic in capability literature: on the possible complementarity between the 'democratic' and the 'philosophical' approaches in the selection of relevant capabilities; see Morten Fiebeger Byskov, 'Democracy, Philosophy and the Selection of Capabilities' (2017) 18(1) *Journal of Human Development and Capabilities* 1.

[17] I addressed this topic more in depth in Riccardo Del Punta, 'Epistemologia breve del diritto del lavoro' (2013) *Lavoro e diritto* 37.

The *first* requirement is that the theory is able to give a satisfactory explanation/ justification in light of a conceptual analysis (rather than a vague narrative), of *qualified institutions of labour law*—that is, of a group of institutions that belong to different representative areas of the discipline—so that systemic importance can be assigned to the theory under examination.

Consequently, Guy Davidov and others are right in assuming that no grand theory is able to give a justification for *all* labour law.[18]

However, it does not follow that theories providing only *partial justifications* for labour law are irrelevant, therefore, it is better to redirect the investigation to the labour law discourse. For instance, Davidov acknowledges that the capability theory can be considered a possible justification for equality laws, regulations of working time, health and safety laws, and freedom of association.[19] This is already enough to make it an important theory for labour law, even though it has to be complemented by other theories.

In the end, the labour law sky would be populated by a *constellation of values*, each of which is capable of giving an account of some of labour law's realizations.

The *second* requirement I would propose is that a theory should be able to cast light on the main *directions of development* of a discipline, especially if this is subject, as labour law is, to continued transformation that depends on changing economic and social conditions. In this evolving context, it is essential for a theory to be able to capture, almost with a geological eye, the movements affecting the most recent stratifications (also in their replacement of older ones), as these express the most characterizing trends. In this case, a theory can be helpful in rationalizing what it is happening beneath the surface and for providing an orientation for further developments.

In addition, the relevance of a theory may differ depending on the system of labour law to which it is applied. Its political impact may also vary accordingly: if one looks at the capability theory from a Continental European perspective, it has a certain liberal (although definitely not neo-liberal) flavour that may not be greatly appreciated by mainstream labour lawyers. Conversely, from the perspective of other systems characterized by a looser regulation, the language of capabilities could aim at reinforcing the workers' protection.

I will now examine whether the capability theory can be considered an adequate normative theory for labour law according to the assumed standards. Political theories, however, do not function in isolation, so intersections with other theories will be possible.

## IV. Exploitation, Domination, Subordination

At first glance, the fact of bringing the capabilities, that is, the spirit of *liberty*, into the world of labour could seem a typical 'mission: impossible'. In order to

---

[18] Guy Davidov, 'Using Moral and Political Philosophy to Justify Labour Law: Potential and Limits', paper presented at the third LLRN conference (2017).
[19] Davidov, 'Using Moral and Political Philosophy to Justify Labour Law' (n 18).

figure it out, we just need to look at the well-known characteristics of this dimension of social life. Over the centuries labour has been considered—exactly the
opposite of liberty—as belonging to the realm of *necessity*, from the perspective
of the human relationship with nature, and to that of *authority*, with regard to
the master's power over slaves and their more modern descendants (servants,
employees, etc).

Karl Marx, himself, who is quoted by Nussbaum as an important source of the
idea of human development,[20] wanted on one hand to free labourers through the
revolutionary overthrow of the capitalist system, while on the other aspired to free
men and women from labour in the future communist society. There is an ambivalence, there, between freedom *in* and *from* labour that has been stigmatized by
Hannah Arendt.[21]

In any case, Marx clearly did not see any possibility of emancipation in the condition of wage labour within a capitalist system that he considered inescapably
grounded in the workers' exploitation. Therefore, although free in a classical liberal
or economic sense, the person who, by signing the employment contract, agreed
to be bound by contractual duties towards the employer, was only really as free, according to Marx, as any 'modern slave' could be.[22]

The Marxian critique of the employment contract as a bourgeois mystification
has had a great influence on labour law, providing a powerful basis for its differen-
tiation from contract-based private law. However, in Marx's perspective, labour law
(although in its very early stages at that time) was part of the capitalist plot. That is,
it was not the solution but, rather, a further worsening of the contradiction inherent
in the relations of production.

But even admitting that this was an ideological assumption, in the early era of
industrialization, the harsh reality of a relationship in which one party was affected
by a structural weakness with respect to the other—as Marx and Engels themselves
had vividly described[23]—was undeniable.

With regard to this 'original state' of the employment relationship, to speak of
inequality of the bargaining power (as the labour law narrative was to do in the following century), was indeed a euphemism. According to Philippe Pettit's classical
account, which defines domination as exposure to someone else's arbitrary power,[24]

---

[20] Nussbaum, *Frontiers of Justice* (n 7), for instance 74. Marx is also quoted by Sen (*The Idea of Justice* (n 14) xvi) among those philosophers (Condorcet, Wollstonecraft, Bentham, John Stuart Mill are also mentioned) with a cultural affinity with his approach.

[21] Hannah Arendt, *Karl Marx and the Tradition of Western Political Thought* (Jerome Kohn, Trustee, Hannah Arendt Bluecher Literary Trust 2002).

[22] However, this did not entail the denial by Marx that wage labour had represented a huge improvement with respect to slave labour: Sen, *The Idea of Justice* (n 14) 22.

[23] Guy Davidov, 'Subordination vs. Domination: Exploring the Differences' (2017) 33 *International Journal of Comparative Labour Law and Industrial Relations* 365, 369 ff.

[24] Philippe Pettit, *Republicanism: A Theory of Freedom and Government* (OUP 1997) 52. On the latest evolutions of Pettit's positions, see Davidov, 'Subordination vs Domination' (n 23) 374 ff.

the employee's condition could hardly be defined as other than total domination by the employer.[25]

However, even though this state culminated in the condition of subordination and dependency deriving from the employment contract,[26] it had already taken place on the labour market[27] owing to the incomparably higher value, for the worker, of what was at stake in the negotiation.[28] Therefore, an empirical continuity existed, and still exists, between the worker's external and internal dependency.[29]

That said, even though in the early industrial period, the substance of the workers' condition was not so different from that described by Marx or Engels, it is well known that the social-democratic and reformist strands of the socialist movement began to look at it from a more pragmatic perspective, which activated a process of change despite being fiercely opposed.

It is the same as saying that while structural *exploitation* could not be modified by definition, except with a revolution, the employer's *domination* was an empirical fact that could be potentially reduced, although not eliminated, by human will and political action. In the gap between these two concepts a path opened up that entailed a totally different political perspective and a change of direction of the historical course.

It was just at this point that labour law began to develop its long-term corrective action, which brought on stage a third and more institutionalized concept, that of

---

[25] In Pettit's words ('A Brief History of Liberty—And Its Lessons', (2016) 17(1) *Journal of Human Development and Capabilities* 5, 14), 'the mines and factories of the of the world's rapidly industrialising countries were little better than slave camps. Men, women and even children were driven for want of a better alternative into accepting conditions that clearly denied them an undominated status in relation to their betters. They might have signed up freely for the employment offered, but the contract they entered into allowed employers unrestrained discretion in how they treated their workers. Employees had no alternative but to live under such discretion: if they did not, they could be fired at will and, as often happened, find that they were black-balled among other potential bosses'.

[26] I accept these concepts in Davidov's sense ('Subordination vs. Domination' (n 23) 368–74), although, according to Article 2094 of the Italian Civil Code, the term subordination indeed refers to the legal definition of the employment contract, which includes both hetero-direction of work and dependency.

[27] I prefer not to speak of 'structural dependency' (Davidov, 'Subordination vs. Domination' (n 23) 369) in referring to the worker's weakness on the market, simply so as not to create confusion with the dependency inside the employment relationship. No doubt, however, this formula captures 'the vulnerability of being dependent on wages from unknown others for income': Davidov (n 23).

[28] Within the neo-republican school, this aspect seems better captured by the more articulated notion of domination proposed by Lovett, the elements of which are a market power imbalance, a condition of dependency, and the possibility of arbitrary interference with someone else; see Frank Lovett, *A General Theory of Domination and Justice* (OUP 2010) 120. For insights into this theory, see David Cabrelli and Rebecca Zahn, 'Theories of Domination and Labour Law: An Alternative Conception for Intervention?' (2017) 33 *International Journal of Comparative Labour Law and Industrial Relations* 339; Davidov, 'Subordination vs. Domination' (n 23), 374–84. This reference to Lovett does not entail, however, acceptance of the policy implications that he draws from his political theory: see below on this point.

[29] Although, internal dependency may occur as an effect of the employment contract, also without a structural dependency on the market, as in the case of a worker with great bargaining power: Davidov (n 23) 381–3.

*subordination.* Subordination was understood as two-faceted: on the one hand, as the epitome of the fact that labour law's action was internal to the capitalistic model of production and had not gone so far as to affect the structural features of the employee's condition; on the other, as a field open to legal as well as social regulation, within which that action could progressively reduce the level of submission inherent in the employment relationship and eventually make space for the employee's freedom within the relationship at the cost of partially sacrificing the employer's economic freedom.

## V. Labour Law Aimed at Reducing the Employer's Domination Over the Employee

Labour law has tried to change the described state of things by means of regulation with a dual goal corresponding to the dual dimensions of labour.

Labour is indeed both a means of acquiring the resources necessary for life (in Sen's words, the 'income aspect' of labour), and an end in itself, as it implies the worker's personal involvement and also represents, albeit not to the same extent for everyone, a factor of personal esteem and fulfilment (the 'recognition aspect' of labour), with a decisive role in generating (or hindering) well-being.[30]

In order to have an impact on this complex reality, labour law's action has to include a wide spectrum of measures based on different techniques. The need for this spectrum is also attributable to the fact that, due to the incompleteness of the employment contract, it was not enough to intervene in the genesis of the contract, but it was required that the reach of the regulation was extended to include the performing, over the time, of the employment relationship.

In this spirit, the insertion of mandatory rights in the employment contract was supplemented by the provision of limitations of both a substantive[31] and procedural[32] nature to the employer's powers, as well as bans aimed at protecting the employees' fundamental rights.[33] The workers' empowerment was completed through the full development of collective actions, which progressively penetrated the workplace, and also owing to the recognition of representation rights at that level.[34]

---

[30] Amartya Sen, *Employment, Technology and Development* (Clarendon Press 1975) 5–6.

[31] The champion of this kind of regulation is the 'just cause' rule in the event of a dismissal, which is given special emphasis in the European approaches as the prerequisite for an effective guarantee of all the workers' rights. Other classical examples include the bans on the employee's demotion and the most intrusive forms of control, the limits to the working time, and the duty to respect the employees' health and safety.

[32] Procedural fairness ensures that the counterparty's position is taken into due account, which improves the quality of the relationship. Moreover, procedural limitations are often complementary to substantive ones: e.g., the fact that the employer has previously been obliged to clarify the reasons for the disciplinary dismissal makes it easier for the employee to allege its unfairness before the judge.

[33] Such as the bans on discrimination and both moral and sexual harassment.

[34] Instead, according to Cabrelli and Zahn, 'Theories of Domination and Labour Law' (n 28) 360, these rights ultimately fail to weaken the employer's enjoyment of arbitrary power.

This has essentially been the story of a progressive power struggle aimed at reducing the degree of the employer's domination over the employee and inducing it to evolve into a more democratic subordination.

Admittedly, the inequality-of-bargaining-power narrative has grasped this crucial point. This has naturally put labour law—if I may hazard this connection for the sake of my overall analysis—in line with the freedom as non-domination perspective. Rather, in a sense, the discipline practised this value before it was rediscovered by the neo-republican theorists.

In particular, as far as the Pettit's concept of freedom from domination is concerned,[35] it is logical to derive from it the need for a public action aimed at pursuing, not only (in the negative) the mere absence of interference, but also a positive 'security against interference, in particular against interference on an arbitrary basis',[36] and this broadly evokes labour law's mission.

Pettit himself has referred, as an example, to a legislation that bans at-will dismissal,[37] although this measure and others are only able, unless subverting the logic of the employment contract, to reduce and not to cancel subordination.[38]

It is disputed, however, that this reference to the neo-republican perspective allows some relevant gain. It might be seen, rather, as purely tautological, or at best as no more than an 'ex post' rationalization of certain labour laws.[39]

Even more serious objections have been raised. Alan Bogg has stressed that the pursuing of freedom from domination in Lovett's broader perspective, which includes market power imbalance,[40] could lead to paradoxical policy implications—that is, to consider a precarious work as less dependent, or independent contracting as preferable, to the employment contract.[41]

What Lovett seems to ignore in this passage is that the employment contract both constitutes and, as far as it is integrated by labour law, restrains domination.[42] Therefore, the point is to enlarge the scope of labour's freedom within the contract while not mistakenly thinking that the therapy against dependency can be looked for on the free market.

Nonetheless, the freedom as non-domination view remains important as it reminds us that one of the main values pursued by labour law is not related to a supposed uniqueness of our field but is the expression of a more universal ideal that has

---

[35]  Pettit, *Republicanism* (n 24).          [36]  Pettit, *Republicanism* (n 24) 51.

[37]  Philippe Pettit, *Just Freedom. A Moral Compass for a Complex World* (Norton & Company 2014) 90.

[38]  This does not seem adequately considered by Davidov, 'Subordination vs. Domination' (n 23) 377.

[39]  See Davidov (n 23) 388–9, to whom I object, seeing the glass half full, that should this political theory only offer a justification for the dismissal regulation or other specific laws, it would nonetheless be important to labour law.

[40]  Lovett, *A General Theory of Domination and Justice* (n 28) 120.

[41]  Alan Bogg, 'Republican Non-Domination and Labour Law: New Normativity or Trojan Horse?' (2017) 33 *International Journal of Comparative Labour Law and Industrial Relations* 391, 393 ff. Bogg passes a different judgement on Pettit's conception, in which he sees 'a powerful new normativity for re-conceiving the rights, institutions, and governance structures of worker-protective labour law', even though with concerns about the distrust that Pettit seems to have for the employees' collective empowerment: Bogg, 'Republican Non-Domination and Labour Law' (n 41) 401 ff.

[42]  Bogg, 'Republican Non-Domination and Labour Law' (n 41) 398.

to do with everyone's freedom with respect to everyone else and with the democratic character of social relationships. I tend not to see this normativity as a really 'alternative' one, but instead as 'a more refined incarnation or amalgam of the traditional inequality of bargaining power and social objective constructs'.[43]

Also much in harmony with labour law's spirit is the neo-republican emphasis on the fact that people must be protected against the *possibility* of someone else's interference. In this regard, if the example of the benevolent slave-master might seem (at least in part) outdated, the same cannot be said for Pettit's reference to Nora's story, as told by Henrik Ibsen in his famous *A Doll's House*.[44] The 'good employer' could indeed act the part of Torvald, Nora's 'good husband;' just like Nora, an employee who can only rely on the employer's goodwill or social responsibility, is not free according to the neo-republican standard.[45]

In short, the perspective which has been highlighted up until now, in close connection with the labour law 'acquis', has the virtue of focusing on the topic of power, that is, of looking—to use Pettit's famous expression[46]—into power's eyeballs.

This leads us to wonder whether this genetic tendency of labour law could also be read through the language of capabilities, in view of which the non-domination perspective is essentially, in the context of this analysis, a point of passage.

## VI. Capabilities and Power

Indeed, the dimension of power does not have a recognized place within the capability theory, partly owing to the fact that it appears more focused on the unrelated individual rather than on the social relationships in which individuals operate.

This has been said, in particular, of the approach of Nussbaum, whose Aristotelian background 'is a sort of universalism informed by the concept of a "flourishing human life" ',[47] which tends to leave out asymmetric relationships or to consider them inevitable.

But Sen too seems to share the methodological individualism borrowed from economic thought, which, at first sight involves an insurmountable difference from the labour law perspective that is entirely *relational*.

However, a broad area of convergence emerges between the anti-domination and capability views,[48] which may, in turn, lay a first bridge between the capability theory and labour law, to the extent that a significant part of the latter can be considered as a realization, albeit imperfect, of the value of freedom from domination.

---

[43] Which is one of the possibilities contemplated by David Cabrelli and Rebecca Zahn, 'Guest Editors' Introduction' (2017) 33 *International Journal of Comparative Labour Law and Industrial Relations* 334.

[44] Pettit, *Just Freedom* (n 37) xiii–xvii.

[45] This does not, however, mean ruling out that regulation may promote good voluntary practices (such as those of CSR) by employers, within the framework of 'reflexive law' as developed by Ralf Rogowski, *Reflexive Labour Law in the World Society* (Edward Elgar Publishing 2013).

[46] Pettit, *Just Freedom* (n 37).          [47] Alexander, *Capabilities and Social Justice* (n 11) 70.

[48] Mozaffar Qizilbash, 'Some Reflections on Capability and Republican Freedom' (2016) 17 *Journal of Human Development and Capabilities* 22.

It may be conceptually helpful to start, in this regard, from Pettit's argument, on occasion of a famous dialogue with Sen, when he stressed the deep affinities between his theory of freedom and the capability theory.[49] In particular, he argued that Sen's commitment to our freedom to enforce our preferences independently from their *content* logically entailed (although this aspect had not been explicitly considered by Sen) that such freedom was also asserted independently from the *context*, and as a consequence, that it was independent of the favour or benevolence of others.[50]

Sen accepted Pettit's point and admitted 'that if the capability approach is supplemented to define freedom in a context-independent form, then the amended theory will, in this respect, be very like Pettit's republican approach'.[51] In the end, however, he concluded that the two approaches capture different aspects of freedom, for which they must both be maintained: the capability theory 'concentrates on whether someone is actually free and able to achieve those functionings that she has reason to want', while the republican theory 'on whether the capability enjoyed is conditional on the favours and goodwill of others'.[52] One of the examples given by Sen was that of a disabled person who, helped by volunteers, is thus fully able to go out of her house whenever she wanted and to move around freely; this is an acceptable condition for the capability theorists, but an unfree one for the neo-republicans.[53]

Later on, in *The Idea of Justice*, Sen more or less kept to the same position, denying that the two theories totally overlap but acknowledging that the capability view could be enriched by *supplementing* its notion of freedom, both negative (which Sen takes for granted and which was also considered a priority by Rawls[54]) and positive or substantial (which lies at the core of Sen's conception), with the concept of freedom as non-domination.[55]

As for Nussbaum's position, her complex relationship with Pettit's conception has been brilliantly analysed:[56] she is generous in acknowledging the merits of the non-domination approach, while remaining convinced that, in particular on certain topics such as disability (which had inspired a powerful critique of Rawls[57]), the capability approach retains a comparative advantage.

In short, it would be senseless to consider the two views, which are both inspired by the primary value of each individual's independence and autonomy, as adversarial. Rather, they partially overlap and are capable of complementing each other depending on the topic under examination.

A difference between the two approaches may remain, in our perspective, on how to treat the case of the 'socially responsible employer', but not on giving a negative

---

[49]  Philippe Pettit, 'Capability and Freedom: a Defence of Sen' (2001) 17 *Economics & Philosophy* 1, 8.
[50]  Conversely, Nora's 'decision to leave her husband here is driven by the need to be positively free and to expand her capabilities, not merely a desire to be free from domination ... she seems to implicitly invoke Marx's 'rich human being ... in need of a totality of human life-activities' (Qizilbash, 'Some Reflections on Capability' (n 48) 26).
[51]  Amartya Sen, 'Reply' (2001) 17 *Economics & Philosophy* 51, 53.
[52]  Sen, 'Reply' (n 51) 55.      [53]  Sen, 'Reply' (n 51) 54.
[54]  Sen, *The Idea of Justice* (n 14) 300.      [55]  Sen, *The Idea of Justice* (n 14) 304–309.
[56]  Qizilbash, 'Some Reflections on Capability' (n 48) 29 ff.
[57]  Nussbaum, *Frontiers of Justice* (n 7) 96 ff and 176 ff.

evaluation of the 'bad employer'. A capability theorist, however, could end up by accepting that it is too risky to leave the employer totally free to exercise her powers on employees, counting only on her goodwill.

It follows that the rules aimed at banning the various forms of an employer's abuse of power, which have been dealt with in the previous section and identified as the classical core of labour law, can also be seen as aimed at *safeguarding workers' capabilities*, which expand in proportion to the withdrawal (albeit partial) of said powers.

Does this imply, therefore, that a labour lawyer will be indifferent about using either one language or the other? As far as the area of labour law that has been traced is concerned, the anti-domination idea, broadly seen in continuity with the inequality-of-power labour law narrative here, seems indeed to be more powerful in addressing the bare reality of the employment relationship and in calling for the adoption of concrete measures aimed at reducing the employee's submission.

Nonetheless, the purpose of this kind of regulation fundamentally remains a *negative* one, as it consists of countering an imbalance of power that affects one party with respect to another. But this is still not *sufficient* for giving people the chance to realize their life aspirations.[58] It is in this broader perspective that another line of European labour law must be taken into account.

## VII. Labour Law Aimed at Developing the Workers' Capabilities

In addition to the norms aimed at limiting the employer's powers, even in its classical version, labour law has provided other mandatory rules the purpose of which is to give workers the capability to fulfil their basic needs and that concern both the identified dimensions of work.

By considering labour as an instrument for earning a living, collective bargaining as well as minimum wage provisions are easy examples to mention. These institutions can be seen as capability-enhancing (as well as equality-enhancing), since the fact of being fairly paid, in proportion to the quantity and quality of work, is obviously a necessary condition of people's independence, and therefore of their capacity to be or to do what they value.

Admittedly, it is well known that the capability approach goes beyond income, but this does not mean denying the fact that resources are essential.[59] As a result, treating labour also as a means does not imply any return to resource-based theories, such as those of John Rawls and Ronald Dworkin, nor does it mean overlooking the fact that, from a capability perspective, what matters most is the rate of conversion of capabilities into functionings.

---

[58] Pettit himself acknowledges that people should enjoy protection and resources in order to ensure their capacity to function properly in their local communities, as emphasized by the capability approach: see 'A Brief History of Liberty' (n 25) 16.

[59] Ingrid Robeyns, 'The Capability Approach: a Theoretical Survey' (2005) 6(1) *Journal of Human Development and Capabilities* 93, 99–100.

As regards the personal or existential dimension of work, the right to annual leave, sick leaves, and maternity/paternity leaves can be mentioned; their effect is not that of limiting an employer's power, but of giving employees the right not to work (in some cases with pay) in order to satisfy basic needs.[60]

In the wake of these regulations, the latest generation of labour law has proposed new regulatory perspectives which can be seen, more and more clearly, as *capability-enhancing*.

The transformation processes of business models and work organizations, often conceptualized in terms of transition to post-Fordism (or advanced Fordism) must first be taken into consideration, as they tend to entail a potentially deep change in the *employee's role within the organization of work*.

The IT revolution, the last frontier of which is the 4.0 industry, must be included among the main causes of such changes. In the most advanced experiments of 'intelligent factories', the employee is practically no longer subject to the employer's hierarchical power, but rather, is similar to an independent contractor who essentially works by objectives (and often in teams) and is required to play a proactive and possibly creative role.

Something even more radical may occur with *smart working*, which entails a virtualization of the workplace, provided one's work can effectively be managed remotely.

In relation to the described changes, a whole new emphasis is put on the worker's *agency*, which is more and more considered a crucial competitive resource by companies, as well as an opportunity for the worker's personal growth and self-fulfilment.

Agency requires knowledge, skills (both hard and soft), professional training, spirit of initiative, and responsibility; in a nutshell, it requires the building of *human capital*, which it is the employer's responsibility (and interest) to invest in.[61] This does not magically transform the firm into a democratic garden, but it can change the terms of the balance of interests between the two parties, creating a potentially win-win situation in which the enhancement of the worker's position is also in the employer's ultimate interests.[62]

Labour market institutions should encourage these transformations, as they are already doing to some extent. Collective action must first be recalled in this perspective, with particular regard to its growing tendency to penetrate firms also thanks to *representation and participatory rights* that were initially provided by law in critical

---

[60] Moreover, some of the traditional labour law legislation, such as the anti-discrimination law, can naturally create the conditions for further development of the capabilities of subjects, such as female workers, who are protected by the latter.

[61] On the key relevance of the idea of human capital from a capability perspective, see Langille, 'Labour Law's Theory of Justice' (n 3) 112–13.

[62] This also entails a change in the philosophy of HR management, which breaks away from the reductionist understanding of employees as mere resources, considered from the sole viewpoint of economic efficiency, by adopting an integrated approach which embraces both economic and human development. For an (admittedly problematic) attempt to apply the capability approach to the field of human resource practices, see Dilip Subramanian, Joan Miquel Verd, Josiane Vero, and Bénédicte Zimmermann, 'Bringing Sen's Capability Approach to Work and Human Resource Practices' (2013) 34(4) *International Journal of Manpower* 292.

situations such as the transfer of undertakings or collective dismissal, and later in a broader spectrum of cases entailing a joint governance of at least some aspects of the work organization. A trend towards decentralization of collective bargaining followed and is still underway. A virtuous circle between the enhancement of the worker's roles and skills and their greater participation in the firm is often activated.

Legislation, too, can play a role in establishing new social rights, such as the worker's right to have *professional training*, both by the employer, particularly in the event of organizational changes,[63] and by the state, in terms of an entitlement to *lifelong learning*.[64]

The labour law under scrutiny is also characterized by a whole new emphasis, which is genuinely capability-friendly, on creating an equality of opportunity in the access to work and in professional careers on behalf of various categories of *disadvantaged workers*. The most obvious example is represented by all the affirmative measures aimed at promoting *female work* and closing the gender gap.

Another significant case, which is particularly in line with Nussbaum's ideas,[65] is that of legislation aimed at enhancing *disabled people*'s capability for work. Such laws, including those that oblige companies of a certain size to hire a quota of disabled persons, are hardly new. But the 'quid pluris' which has been added by an EU directive is that employers must adopt 'reasonable accommodations' to enable these disadvantaged workers to integrate into the work environment without, however, being required to change the pre-existing work organization.[66]

The renewed European emphasis on *privacy protection* (also) at work, which culminated in the entry into force of the General Data Protection Regulation,[67] must also be emphasized in this respect; the essential premise of this model, as opposed to the US one,[68] is that the worker is also considered a full citizen in the workplace, therefore with a capability to do private things and prevent the employer from knowing them, although her right must be balanced with the employer's prerogatives.

A natural corollary of this vision is then represented by a growing promotion of the capability for *work-life balance*, thanks to a number of various arrangements: the spread (often via second-level collective bargaining) of company welfare schemes, which allow employees to benefit from a range of discounts and personal services (e.g., medical care);[69] the measures aimed at making the working

---

[63]  Such a right has been provided by Article 2103 of the Italian Civil Code, as amended in 2015.

[64]  In the age of robotics and the development of artificial intelligence , a consensus has formed around the belief that the traditional model of education—with a burst at the start and top-ups through company training—is no longer sufficient to cope with today's necessities, which include the need for new, and constantly updated, skills. New policy measures should promote new modes of lifelong learning in order to make adult learning accessible to all, especially to disadvantaged people.

[65]  See the chapter on 'Capabilities and Disabilities' in Nussbaum, *Frontiers of Justice* (n 7) 155–223.

[66]  See Article 5 of Directive 2000/78/EC.        [67]  See the Regulation (EU) 2016/679.

[68]  Matthew W Finkin, 'Some Further Thoughts on the Usefulness of Comparativeness in the Law of Employee Privacy' (2010) 14 *Employee Rights and Employment Policy Journal* 11.

[69]  These arrangements have a direct effect on increasing the workers' capabilities because, among other things, they give them the possibility of choosing between different combinations of goods, therefore meeting their concrete life needs.

time more flexible or switching to a part-time contract in the event of employees' personal necessities or choices; the experimental attempts to contain the invasion of work in one's private life (such as the right to disconnect provided by French and Italian legislation, though still vague to a certain degree); and the provision of new forms of leave, characterized by greater attention to employees' special needs[70] and parental duties.[71]

Finally, the capability perspective is relevant in the broader dimension of the *labour market*. This in particular seems to be the ideal yardstick for the 'security' element of European 'flexicurity' policies, as it focuses on strengthening the worker's position on the labour market, therefore possibly reducing the 'structural dependency' of job-seekers. The key concept here, which has long been at the core both of ILO statements[72] and EU social policies,[73] is that of *employability* (or capability for work).[74]

Support for the unemployed during labour market transitions is often conditional on the person's active engagement. These conditions also raise capability questions, but this chapter is not the place to deal with them.

## VIII. Capabilities, Rights, and Positive Freedoms

The political theories that have been discussed from a labour lawyer's viewpoint certainly share a common humanistic inspiration, as they believe in the incommensurable value of each individual's freedom. Moreover, they have a 'positive', in the sense of 'substantial', view of freedom (in addition to the 'negative' one) in common and assume that public action must be directed towards defending and promoting such a view.

To this end, these theories also recognize the important role of *legal rights*, which is obviously significant from a lawyer's perspective.

Indeed, in the literature on the capability approach, the recognition of the importance of legal codification of individual rights is most closely associated with Nussbaum, who has placed emphasis on the instrumental role of positive law, and in particular, constitutional law (which highlights the importance of her thinking on a

---

[70] For instance, the provision of special sick leaves in the event of cancer or other serious illnesses.

[71] Such as the extension of the time in which maternity and paternity leave can be enjoyed and the provision of an almost total interchangeability between mother and father in the interests of promoting gender equality.

[72] See, in particular, the Human Development Recommendation [2004] R195, and the Global Jobs Pact [2009].

[73] See, most recently, point No 4 of the EU Commission Recommendation on the European Pillar of Social Rights [2017].

[74] Anneleen Forrier and Luc Seals, 'The concept of employability: a complex mosaic' (2003) 3(2) *International Journal of Human Resources Development and Management* 103. For a critical approach, see Bernard Gazier, 'Les dynamiques des versions operationnelles de l'employabilité, entre individuel et collectif' in Guillaume Tiffon, Frédéric Moatty, Dominique Glaymann, and Jean-Pierre Durand (eds), *Le piège de l'employabilité. Critique d'une notion au regard de ses usages sociaux* (Presses Universitaires de Rennes 2017).

discipline with a strong constitutional foundation such as labour law), in protecting and promoting capabilities.[75]

Conversely, Sen is normally thought to focus more on moral rights than on legal rights. Actually, the ways in which the ethical notion of rights (and, in particular, human rights) can provide a foundation for legal initiatives, is an important issue for Sen too. It induced him to argue, in a famous address to the ILO, that goal-based formulations of social ethics are usefully integrated by rights-based reasoning, as the fulfilment of rights (of the Marshallian kind[76]) should be included among the goals to be pursued.[77]

It must not be forgotten, however, that according to a rights-as-goals approach, rights are important, but not sufficient[78] in a dual sense: firstly, what matters (at least from Sen's consequentialist perspective[79]) is that rights which are considered valuable by an individual are actually fulfilled; secondly, rights are only one of the many possible ways of promoting workers' capabilities, since other institutional mechanisms, eventually combined with rights, may be used for this purpose with equivalent or even better results.[80]

That said, if both views that have been identified uphold the need for a public regulation of the market and recognition of the role of rights, what is the news regarding the capability theory?

I have already observed that the anti-domination perspectives are more suited to capturing the mission of classical labour law—that is, the counteracting of the employer's bargaining supremacy, which is still a *'freedom from'*, even though much more advanced, and with affirmative policy implications—than the classical negative freedom.

But the second part of the story is that the capability theory appears indispensable, instead, for giving an account of other norms of labour law as well as, and above all, the discipline's latest trends of development,[81] at least in the Continental European context.[82]

This reading entails the placing of new emphasis on the *positive* side of labour law, which is aimed not only at reducing domination and safeguarding dignity, but also at valuing and promoting the worker's knowledge and skill, to the point of

---

[75] Nussbaum, *Frontiers of Justice* (n 7) 273 ff and 284 ff.

[76] Alexander, *Capabilities and Social Justice* (n 11) 88–91.

[77] Amartya Sen, 'Work and Rights' (2000) 139(2) *International Labour Review* 119, 123–5.

[78] For criticism of Ronald Dworkin's 'institutional fundamentalism', see Sen, *The Idea of Justice* (n 14) 267. For Dworkin's reply, see *Justice for Hedgehogs* (HUP 2011) 480–1.

[79] Sen, *The Idea of Justice* (n 14) 23–4, 210–21.

[80] For example: the efficiency of assistance services for job-seekers is much more important than any solemn declaration about the right to work; the legal guarantee of a job for a disabled person is a starting point, but the fact that the disabled can be usefully integrated into the workplace is no less decisive; in the sphere of health and safety protection, legal rights are much less important than organizational models designed to protect workers from labour-related risks.

[81] See section VII above.

[82] This perspective is echoed by the EU Commission Recommendation of 26 April 2017 (C2017 2600 final), on the European Pillar of Social Rights, which expresses 'principles and rights essential for fair and well-functioning labour markets and welfare systems in 21st century Europe'.

cultivating the major ambition of bringing substantial freedom (a *freedom to*) into the dimension of work.

Therefore, once it has been accepted that in order to be relevant, a theory must be able to cast light on the direction of development of a discipline, the capability theory appears to have a comparative advantage, in that it potentially covers the most dynamic area of labour law which presides over the discovery of the worker's subjectivity.

On this basis, I will conclude my analysis with an overall assessment of the implications that following the capability perspective could have for labour law.

## IX.  Market Liberalism, Paternalism, and Capabilities

Labour law has never had any problem with being socially paternalist; rather, it has always been proud of this status. Its paternalism has always been grounded, at least in the European version, not so much on a supposed inability of workers to make rational choices and pursue their true interests,[83] as more simply on the asymmetry of power that leaves workers in need of protection.

In this regard there has been a subtle shift from a statement of fact to a judgement of value, since the dual subjection of the employee to the employer (before and after the contract) has been considered a structural and inescapable feature of the employment relationship.

The next step is not hard to imagine: if an objective is declared unattainable 'a priori', it easily becomes something not even worth pursuing. This is exactly the point where the labour law's paternalism has taken on its mature form, with the consideration that the market is an irreparably hostile environment for subordinate workers, so that the only way to serve their interests is to protect them from the market.

This view has been typically represented by *social-democratic* political conceptions. But the recognized crisis of this model has instead coincided with the great advance of *market liberalism*, which labour law had always been contrary to.

Where does the capability theory locate itself with respect both to the neo-liberal attack and the social-democratic tradition? To my mind, in an innovative position.

*On the one hand*, it goes without saying that the capability theory, while not being hostile to the market as such, clearly distinguishes itself from market liberalism, even though this endorses the aim of increasing individual choice as a central value as well.

The conception of freedom at the basis of the two approaches is totally different. Namely, from a capability perspective (as well as the neo-republican one), every possible means or policy must be used to grant everybody the substantial freedom to do or be what she values, which presupposes the fact of being free from an unrestrained

---

[83] Such as in the non-intrusive version of paternalism proposed by Horacio Spector, 'Philosophical Foundations of Labour Law' (2006) 33 *Florida State University Law Review* 1119, 1139–44 and 1147–8.

domination. This leads to accepting that, in order to guarantee these freedoms as far as possible, others' freedoms must be restricted, such as the employer's freedom to make use of employees, and more broadly, to appreciating the state's active intervention in order to improve the living conditions of employees and all citizens.

But does this mean, *on the other hand*, that the capability view, in particular, is still *paternalist* to such an extent that nothing substantially new would come to be, in the end, under the sun of labour law? The answer is inevitably complex and must be articulated.

In principle, the capability view tries to keep together the concept of social responsibility and the *freedom of choice* of each individual. The more this freedom of choice is guaranteed, the more the perspective focuses on the capabilities rather than on the functionings, as happens in both Sen's[84] and Nussbaum's[85] perspectives.

Nussbaum also acknowledges, however, that when the goal is the protection of self-respect and human dignity, the emphasis should switch to functioning, as in some ways it is difficult to envisage having to make a choice.[86]

This also seems to be the point with many labour rights that tend to override the dimension of capabilities as they jump directly onto the corresponding functioning. Take for instance the workers' health and safety regulation: it can be seen as aimed at protecting the worker's capability 'not to die prematurely' or 'to have good health' (No 1 and No 2 on Nussbaum's list[87]), but without adding much to the simple fact that the protection of the workers' life, health, and safety—namely a certainly essential functioning—is already provided.

In other words, no real choice comes into play in this dynamic, as what is important is the safeguarding of the worker from an external risk that is inherent in the fact of being dominated by the employer (in addition to the natural risks of the work activity), therefore not having control over her environment. On the contrary, in reference again to health, other life events are really a matter of individual choice, which raises the problem of the point up to which the regulation should intervene, say, to oblige the individual to eat a certain food, have a certain life-style, and so on.

The same could be said of the capability not to be discriminated on the grounds of race, sex, sexual orientation, etc. (No 7b on Nussbaum's list), which has to do with being treated 'as a dignified being whose worth is equal to that of others'.

When fundamental goods are at stake, it is also difficult to envisage, 'a fortiori', the possibility of a choice among different combinations of alternative functionings (to which Sen attaches great importance as an indication of a higher level of capabilities). Examples are easy to find: a choice between salary and health, or between time off work and protection from harassment. In addition to being unacceptable, because those mentioned must be non-negotiable goods, these choices would not make any sense.

In short, as far as the norms aimed at reducing the employer's domination and guaranteeing the bases of the employee's dignity and self-respect are concerned, a

---

[84]  Sen, *The Idea of Justice* (n 14), for instance 235–8.
[85]  Nussbaum, *Frontiers of Justice* (n 7) 171 ff.
[86]  Nussbaum, *Frontiers of Justice* (n 7) 172.          [87]  Nussbaum, *Frontiers of Justice* (n 7) 76.

certain degree of paternalism appears to be inevitable, since it is inherent in the logic of protective intervention. This would confirm that the capability view might not be very much in sync with this legislation.

Instead, as regards the other line of regulation that has been identified, the degree of paternalism significantly decreases compared to a classical social-democratic approach. These provisions, although still aimed at protecting workers (which could lead a classical liberal to consider them as paternalist as well[88]), attempt to do so in a profoundly different way, that is, by developing each worker's capability to exercise, eventually in a participatory context, her own autonomy and responsibility. Some of these rights also encapsulate a possibility of choice for the employee, as they are designed to meet personal reasons or needs.

Therefore, in a nutshell, these rights and practices are not statically focused on containing the stronger party of the relationship; rather, they are dynamically aimed at an expansion of each individual worker's capacities, skills, and opportunities, as well as contractual autonomy.

This also highlights why this kind of labour law lends itself to being conceptualized in terms of the law-of-the-labour-market perspective, which has been extensively theorized by Simon Deakin and Frank Wilkinson,[89] and which intersects, once again, with the capability view, even though observed from an economic rather than a normative viewpoint (nonetheless, these two approaches can be complementary).

What this view fundamentally suggests is that *market freedom* can also be built by norms aimed at limiting pure *contract freedom*. This does not mean to say, however, that all the labour law norms are necessarily market-friendly,[90] and therefore the conceiving of a complete break with the labour law tradition,[91] but merely to point out an *evolutionary path* which will probably allow the hard core of classical labour law to survive, while refocusing the discipline on new perspectives.

These observations should explain why, from a Continental European labour lawyer's point of view, the switch to the capability theory would be *an anti-paternalistic move*, as it would mean placing emphasis on the value of individual autonomy and responsibility, which is almost unknown in the mainstream European approach, inspired as it is by a social-democratic background.

Conversely, although it is not for me to say, if all this is viewed from an Anglo-American perspective, the impression could be different, or perhaps even the opposite.

---

[88] This aspect has been examined by Ian Carter, 'Is the Capability Approach Paternalist?' (2014) 30 *Economics & Philosophy* 75.

[89] See Simon Deakin and Frank Wilkinson, *The Law of the Labour Market* (OUP 2005).

[90] For the suggestion to look at protective norms as market-friendly, that is, as an enhancement of the market and not as an escape from it, see also Simon Deakin, 'Contract Law, Capabilities and the Legal Foundations of the Market' in Simon Deakin and Alain Supiot (eds), *Capacitas* (Hart Publishing 2009) 4.

[91] I see a grain of truth in Ruth Dukes' criticism (*The Labour Constitution: The Enduring Idea of Labour Law* (OUP 2014), especially 194 ff) of the exclusively win-win features of the law-of-the-labour-market perspective, even though this does not entail sharing all the implications of her approach, such as the emphasis on a certain political characterization of labour law in the wake of Sinzheimer's heritage.

Instead, from both perspectives, but especially from the European one, the criticism could be raised that freedom, substantial as it may be, fundamentally remains *an individualistic value*, which in effect is the reason why the capability approach still belongs, albeit with the examined additions, to the liberal tradition.[92]

This is indeed a disputed point in capability literature,[93] even though it may be accepted that Sen's individualism is a purely ethical, rather than an ontological, individualism.[94] In other words, there is nothing, not even in Sen, that amounts to a negation of the collective dimension of social action[95] and, as a consequence, of the possibility of developing 'collective' capabilities.[96]

Admittedly however, in this regard, the adopting of the capability view would mark a significant break with a certain labour law tradition that has always endeavoured to go beyond ethical individualism, conceived as being too liberal and opposed to the leading values of equality and solidarity, up to the point of embracing, in the most extreme versions, a kind of 'ontological collectivism'.

In conclusion, in my opinion, the major virtue of the proposed approach lies in the fact that the capability theory establishes (with a broader reach than the neo-republican theory of freedom) an innovative balance between social and individual responsibility while, at the same time, providing a possible compromise between the European and the Anglo-American traditions.

On the one hand, in no way does it give up the idea of *social responsibility*, which is instead refocused and reinforced in comparison with other liberal theories, such as those of Rawls and Dworkin. In this respect, the theory should be reassuring to a Continental European labour lawyer.

On the other hand, as the capability theory insists on *individual autonomy and responsibility*,[97] this entails major opportunities for the growth of each worker but, at the same time, a passage to adulthood which breaks away from the all-protective philosophy of classical labour law while inevitably bringing with it a number of anxieties.

A *social liberalism* perspective is thus advanced, which seems well equipped to revive the discipline's humanistic commitment, while at the same time helping the baby to grow up and in this way extend the reach of labour law.

---

[92] Robeyns, 'The Capability Approach' (n 59) 95.

[93] Sabina Alkire, 'Using the Capability Approach: prospective and evaluative analyses' in Flavio Comim, Mozer Quizilbash, and Sabina Alkire (eds), *The Capability Approach: Concepts, Measures and Applications* (CUP 2008) 34–8.

[94] Robeyns, 'The Capability Approach' (n 59) 107–108: 'Ethical individualism makes a claim about who or what should count in our evaluative exercises and decisions. It postulates that individuals, and only individuals, are the units of moral concern ... In contrast, ontological individualism states that only individuals and their properties exist, and that all social entities and properties can be identified by reducing them to individuals and their properties'.

[95] However, in this regard, Sen (*The Idea of Justice* (n 14) 247) takes his distance from Marx's approach, which considered the working class as the only relevant group.

[96] Robeyns, 'The Capability Approach' (n 59) 109–10.

[97] Alexander, *Capabilities and Social Justice* (n 11) 124.

# 5

# The Need to Become Fashionable

*Supriya Routh**

## I. Introduction

In a recent—and I must add, influential—reflection on the purported goal of labour law, Guy Davidov notes that some legal scholars are inappropriately becoming
fashionable in invoking the capability approach to conceptualize the normative goal
of labour law.[1] Davidov understands that the objective of engaging philosophical
perspectives (such as the capability approach) for the study of labour law ought to
be to justify the discipline of labour law as it exists. Accordingly, he retorts, the capability approach does not have much to offer in debates about labour law concerns
such as minimum wages or collective bargaining. If this claim were true, then labour
law scholars engaged in justifying the discipline should surely discard the capability
approach. However, the question that will still remain is whether the capability
approach could prove useful in (re)conceptualizing regulation of work (or, if one
wishes, 'labour law'), not merely justifying the traditional discipline. In this chapter,
I evaluate the capability approach against both of these challenges.

I examine Davidov's and other scholars' perspectives on the role of the capability
approach in debates on labour law, particularly in the normative (re)conceptualiza-
tion project of labour law. I argue that, while the capability approach is capacious
enough to account for minimum wages and other pluralistic concerns of labour
law, its significance goes much beyond merely justifying the existing account of labour law. The capability approach helps conceptualize a coherent idea on regulation
of work in its societal complexity (i.e., catering to the empirical reality of the increasingly complex world of work) without assuming a now out-dated institutional
framework of industrial employment or other behavioural patterns of workers and
their collectives. I contend that the fashion—defined as 'expression of the sensibility,
preoccupations and pressures of society',[2]—of employing the capability approach
in conceptualizing the goal of legal regulation of work is, perhaps, *a need* in view of

* I thank participants of the Capability Approach Meets Labour Law Workshop at the Faculty of
Law University of Toronto, 20-21 October 2017, for their comments on an earlier version of the arguments presented in this chapter. Special thanks to Brian Langille and Sarah Kanko.

[1] Guy Davidov, *A Purposive Approach to Labour Law* (Oxford University Press, 2016) 65–7.
[2] Jane Ashford, *Dress in the Age of Elizabeth I* (BT Batsford, 1988) 7.

The Capability Approach to Labour Law. Edited by Brian Langille. Chapter 5 © Supriya Routh 2019.
Published 2019 by Oxford University Press.

the dramatically altered social realities from the one that existed at the dawn of the industrial revolution and that labour law originally catered to.

In section II, I evaluate labour lawyers' engagement with the capability approach insofar as they justify existing/traditional labour law regime. In section III, I analyse those perspectives that employ the capability approach in order to articulate a new(er) idea of labour law. Locating myself in the latter category, in section IV, I discuss how some of the purported challenges posed to the capability approach to legal regulation of work result from misunderstandings of the capability approach. I also note how some of the justified criticisms might be overcome in (re)conceptualizing legal regulation of work for heterogeneous working situations. The chapter ends with a brief conclusion.

## II. Justifying Labour Law

Some labour law scholars think that the role of philosophy ought to be to justify existing (i.e., traditional) labour law jurisprudence, that is, to help articulate a coherent narrative of labour law that offers 'a solution to . . . labour "problem" '.[3] In surveying the likely values of—or possible interests advanced by—labour law, Davidov charts them along a spectrum of more concrete to abstract universal values.[4] The values that Davidov identifies are (moving from less abstract to more abstract ones): workplace democracy; redistribution of resources, power, and risks, mainly between employers and employees; dignity or human rights; social inclusion or citizenship through work; stability of work or security through work; maximizing market efficiency; promoting human freedom and capabilities; and emancipation or social equality.[5] From among these purported values of labour law, Davidov is particularly critical of the 'fashionable' capability approach as an underlying value of labour law.[6] He contends that since the capability approach is articulated at a high level of abstractness as an ideal that will 'please everyone', it cannot lead to any concrete programmes for labour law;[7] 'because they can support everything, in practice they support nothing'.[8] In criticizing Brian Langille's invocation of the capability approach in articulating a normative goal of labour law, Davidov notes that Langille fails to account for the conflict of interest and imbalance of power between employers and employees in articulating labour law's normative goal.

Davidov also criticizes Langille for his over inclusive scope of labour law.[9] He notes that, although substantive freedom might be relevant in issues such as unpaid

---

[3] For example, Davidov, *A Purposive Approach to Labour Law* (n 1) 55; also see Riccardo Del Punta, 'Is the Capability Theory an Adequate Normative Theory for Labour Law?', Chapter 4 in this volume; also Hugh Collins, 'What Can Sen's Capability Approach Offer to Labour Law?', Chapter 1 in this volume.
[4] Davidov, *A Purposive Approach to Labour Law* (n 1) 55.
[5] Davidov, *A Purposive Approach to Labour Law* (n 1) 56–68.
[6] Davidov, *A Purposive Approach to Labour Law* (n 1) 65–7.
[7] Davidov, *A Purposive Approach to Labour Law* (n 1) 66.
[8] Davidov, *A Purposive Approach to Labour Law* (n 1).
[9] Davidov, *A Purposive Approach to Labour Law* (n 1) 66.

work, education, or child care, Langille incorrectly categorizes these as issues pertaining to labour law. What Davidov thinks more useful, however, is the more concrete articulation of labour law employing the capability approach as undertaken by Simon Deakin and Frank Wilkinson.[10] He notes that, in justifying social rights, including those that are traditionally not associated with an employment relationship framework, Deakin and Wilkinson point out that social rights enable individuals to 'exploit their resource endowments'.[11] By exploiting their resource endowments, so the argument goes, individuals can become effective market participants. In this sense, social rights perform a market-creating function. Davidov considers this a better approach because it can justify concrete labour laws and is not fixated on an 'all-encompassing idea of labour law' seeking to maximize capabilities.[12]

Davidov argues that abstract values such as the capability approach, which claim to be good for everyone—employees, employers, and society at large—may not be useful at all in constituting the narrative of labour law. What he overlooks is that several of the other values he mentions, such as workplace democracy, dignity, and human rights, citizenship and social inclusion, and market efficiency are all values that are largely expressed as overall social virtue, and thus, good for all—workers, employers, and society at large. The capability approach does not have any unique claim to this comprehensiveness or moral aspiration. Davidov's other worry is that the capability approach (or similar abstract theories with universal aspirations) does not justify—or, more precisely, labour lawyers using the capability approach have not justified—existing labour laws on the basis of the capability approach.[13] For example, he notes that if goals of labour law are fixated at such an abstract level, laws securing minimum wages, collective bargaining, or unjust dismissal could not be adequately explained with such theoretical aspirations.[14]

This contention that the capability approach is unable to explain the logic behind specific labour laws reflects Davidov's misunderstanding of the implications of the capability approach. The capability approach is expressed as an approach rather than as a theory in itself. What this implies is that while the capability approach could be employed in normative terms, there are other tools that are necessary in developing a fuller account of a capability approach-sensitive theory of distributive justice. Once this additional step is taken, it is not difficult to justify existing labour standards on the basis of the capability approach, as I will show later in this section.

In any case, Davidov is so attached to existing labour standards that he thinks the goals of labour law should be expressed in such a manner that justifies only those standards. Strangely, however, while Davidov agrees with Matthew Finkin that labour law is too all-encompassing to be justified by a single 'catchphrase' (such as the capability approach), he opines that he is particularly weary of too all-encompassing goals (of the capability approach) that seem good for society at large, including

[10] Davidov, *A Purposive Approach to Labour Law* (n 1) 67.
[11] Davidov, *A Purposive Approach to Labour Law* (n 1).
[12] Davidov, *A Purposive Approach to Labour Law* (n 1).
[13] Davidov, *A Purposive Approach to Labour Law* (n 1) 66, 69–71.
[14] Davidov, *A Purposive Approach to Labour Law* (n 1) 73–112, 252.

employees and employers.[15] There is a logical inconsistency here. If labour laws are too all-encompassing, it should then be appropriate to explicate it by means of all-encompassing theories at an abstract level. The all-encompassing nature of labour law cannot surely be deployed as a critique against the all-encompassing (as Davidov sees it) capability approach.

As I mention, amongst the several attempts to justifying labour (including so-cial) laws, the one that impresses Davidov the most is presented by Deakin and Wilkinson.[16] Deakin and Wilkinson seek to offer an *evaluative agenda to judge* ex-isting 'labour market regulation ... within the *framework of a market-based economic system*'.[17] Their objective is to challenge the free market efficiency model based on neo-liberal deregulatory logic. They are interested in ascertaining the nature of a regulatory framework that will make the labour market function in the interests of society, including that of promoting market efficiency.[18] Their thesis is that social and labour rights are not hostile to the market efficiency agenda. These legal rights empowering individuals should be seen as constituting the core of the market order that helps full realization of social resources. Social and labour rights, then, should be seen as entitlements to those means necessary for individuals to attain 'economic self-sufficiency'.[19] Criticizing Friedrich Hayek for his minimalist approach to market regulation—that is, the permissibility of market interference only by means of private laws of property and contract—and drawing on Robert Sugden, Deakin and Wilkinson suggest that redistributive concerns pursued by labour law should also be part of a free market order.[20]

Deakin and Wilkinson note that free markets may work to everyone's benefit when everyone is positioned to participate unhindered in market exchanges by pro-viding something that others want.[21] But the free market will not work for those people's advantage who have no goods of exchangeable value. They observe that extreme inequality in resource endowments makes it impossible for some people to participate in the market, which results not only in their impoverishment and marginalization but also signifies an overall loss for the society. In this context, the role of redistribution is not of correcting market failures, but of securing the very conditions (i.e., necessary resource endowments) of the market.

Resource endowments of individuals consist of labour power, accumulated assets, and entitlements to public and private transfers.[22] In arguing for the role of legal en-titlements in furthering resource endowments, Deakin and Wilkinson employ the

---

[15] Davidov, *A Purposive Approach to Labour Law* (n 1) 65–7; also see Matthew W Finkin, 'The Death and Transfiguration of Labour Law' (2011) 33 *Comparative Labor Law & Policy Journal* 171, 183.
[16] See Simon Deakin and Frank Wilkinson, *The Law of the Labour Market: Industrialization, Employment, and Legal Evolution* (Oxford University Press, 2005).
[17] Deakin and Wilkinson, *The Law of the Labour Market* (n 16) 275 (emphasis mine).
[18] Deakin and Wilkinson, *The Law of the Labour Market* (n 16) 277.
[19] Deakin and Wilkinson, *The Law of the Labour Market* (n 16).
[20] Deakin and Wilkinson, *The Law of the Labour Market* (n 16) 283, 295–6; also see Simon Deakin, 'Social Rights in a Globalized Economy' in Philip Alston (ed), *Labour Rights as Human Rights* (Oxford University Press, 2005) 25–60, 55–6.
[21] Deakin and Wilkinson, *The Law of the Labour Market* (n 16) 283–4.
[22] Deakin and Wilkinson, *The Law of the Labour Market* (n 16) 285.

capability approach or, more particularly, the concept of conversion factors articulated by Sen.[23] Conversion factors, in the sense Sen uses it, are abstract factors that are responsible for converting resources, including those delivered by socio-political institutions, into capabilities.[24] An individual's capability, then, depend on their physical and mental endowments, including their agency, and the resources they have access to. Leveraging this idea of conversion factors, Deakin and Wilkinson note that social norms, legal rules, and other socio-political institutions, inter alia constitute the institutionalized conversion factors enabling people to expand their capabilities.[25] If legal institutional resources are to expand people's actual capabilities to attain a wide range of functioning sets, they cannot be limited only to legal rights pertaining to property or contract; people also need to access health care, education, training, and other similar resources for a more wholesome expansion of their capabilities.[26] On this reasoning, Deakin and Wilkinson conclude that 'mechanisms of redistribution' (i.e., social norms, legal rules, legal-political institutions) are 'precondition to ... the operation of the labour market'.[27]

Deakin and Wilkinson's support for labour law is conditional primarily upon its compatibility with the market order.[28] According to them, the 'enduring values of labour law' (but not all aspects of 'existing labour law systems')[29] should be seen as preconditions to the market. They contend that the redistributive and protective labour laws have a '*market-creating* function': '[s]ocial rights [including labour rights] should be understood as *institutionalized forms of capabilities which provide individuals with the means to realize the potential of their resource endowments and thereby achieve a higher level of economic functioning*'.[30] They support this perspective by employing the capability approach: '[t]he idea of capabilities as substantive economic freedoms provides the foundation for this new conceptualization of social rights'.[31] They make it clear that by economic freedom, they actually mean market freedom: '[t]he version of the capability approach which we are outlining here offers a response which is based on the market-creating function of the rules of social law'.[32]

Unfortunately, however, no version of the capability approach articulates a market-creating justification for an individual's capability expansion. In fact, one of the central premises of the capability approach is that human capabilities do not—and

[23] Deakin and Wilkinson, *The Law of the Labour Market* (n 16) 290.
[24] Amartya Sen, *Commodities and Capabilities* (North Holland, 1985) 13; Amartya Sen, *Development as Freedom* (Alfred A. Knopf, 1999) 74; Ingrid Robeyns, 'The Capability Approach: a theoretical survey' (2005) 6(1) *Journal of Human Development* 93 99; Supriya Routh, *Enhancing Capabilities through Labour Law: Informal Workers in India* (Routledge, 2014) 98–100.
[25] Deakin and Wilkinson, *The Law of the Labour Market* (n 16) 290–3.
[26] Deakin and Wilkinson, *The Law of the Labour Market* (n 16) 291.
[27] Deakin and Wilkinson, *The Law of the Labour Market* (n 16).
[28] Deakin and Wilkinson, *The Law of the Labour Market* (n 16) 294.
[29] Deakin and Wilkinson, *The Law of the Labour Market* (n 16) 275, 294.
[30] Deakin and Wilkinson, *The Law of the Labour Market* (n 16) 284, 347 (emphasis added).
[31] Deakin and Wilkinson, *The Law of the Labour Market* (n 16) 347.
[32] Deakin and Wilkinson, *The Law of the Labour Market* (n 16) 348; also see Deakin, 'Social Rights' (n 20) 56–60.

should not—cater only to the market.[33] The market, rather, plays an instrumental role in expanding an individual's capability.[34] It is on the basis of this premise that Sen distinguishes the capability approach from the human capital approach.[35] Sen notes that human development in terms of capability is not aimed at becoming market-enabling; it is aimed at facilitating a better quality of life.[36] Of course, this expanded freedom (i.e., capability) may be used by individuals to participate in the market if that is what they value in their lives. Accordingly, any market-creating role of human capability is secondary—a by-product—to intrinsic human freedom.[37] From this point of view, Deakin and Wilkinson somewhat mischaracterizes the capability approach and its foundational principles.

However, in his most recent contribution (see Chapter 7 in this volume), Deakin offers a more nuanced articulation of the labour law-capability approach relationship, although he has not abandoned his rational economic-exchange perspective in the market-constitutive role of labour law (i.e., market-creating capabilities furthered by labour law).[38] Deakin notes that the market-constituting role of an individual's capabilities is just one of several possible capabilities (i.e., functioning-sets) that an individual could possess: '[t]here may well be others'.[39] He recognizes that the capability approach does not allow any preeminent status for the market.[40] If individuals (or communities) so aspire, it is possible that market-creating capabilities (or functioning-sets) may be less valued by such individuals (or communities) than other non-market capabilities.[41] After all, capabilities are those freedoms of individuals (and communities) that 'they value—and have reason to value'.[42]

In fact, Hugh Collins, too, ignores this insight of the capability approach.[43] Collins contends that, in order for the capability approach to claim the high place of philosophically justifying the discipline of labour law, it must specify why the market, that is, the law of contract (promoting freedom of contract), is inadequate for governing work relations. Happily, the capability approach does offer an answer to Collins. According to the capability perspective, capability expansion is a social commitment whereas the market is a domain of private exchange.[44] Since private exchanges are not efficient in delivering public goods, which are essential for overall capability expansion of individuals, public regulation and social support are often complimentary to the market.[45] While capabilities promoted by non-market

---

[33] Sen, *Development* (n 24) 116, 124.     [34] Sen, *Development* (n 24) 6-7, 116–17.
[35] Sen, *Development* (n 24) 293–7.     [36] Sen, *Development* (n 24) 144–5, 293–7.
[37] Sen, *Development* (n 24) 144.
[38] Simon Deakin, 'The Capability Approach and the Economics of Labour Law', Chapter 7 in this volume.
[39] Simon Deakin, 'The Capability Approach and the Economics of Labour Law', Chapter 7 in this volume.
[40] Simon Deakin, 'The Capability Approach and the Economics of Labour Law', Chapter 7 in this volume.
[41] See Sen, *Development* (n 24) 18.     [42] Sen, *Development* (n 24).
[43] See Hugh Collins, 'What Can Sen's Capability Approach Offer to Labour Law?', Chapter 1 in this volume.
[44] Sen, *Development* (n 24) xii, 128; Amartya Sen, *The Idea of Justice* (The Belknap Press of Harvard University Press, 2009) 91, 98, 126–8.
[45] Sen, *Development* (n 24) 6–7, 25–6, 112–29.

institutions are equally important as capabilities expanded by the market, market imperfections often limit the market's capacity to expand people's capabilities.[46] Accordingly, notes Sen, there needs to be justified—but not arbitrary—regulation of the market or freedom of contract.[47] To be sure, Sen himself thinks that the market is one of the valuable spaces of interaction and exchange, but he is far from imposing this judgment on specific individuals and communities.[48]

On the contrary, by prioritizing the market, what Deakin and Wilkinson do is they take away the decision-making and judgmental power from the hands of actual individuals and communities, and take on the role of proselytizers. It is the role of specific individuals, communities, and societies to determine which values they want to further as their desired capabilities and functionings by means of discursive and deliberative processes. Arguing that one central role (if not the preeminent one) of the capability approach-focused labour law is to promote market-creating functionings is to deny that capacity to the community. This perspective thus denies the very agency to individuals that is one of the foundational components of the capability approach. Moreover, market participation requires a specific set of skills. Proposing that a goal of the capability approach is to constitute the markets is to articulate that it is those skill sets that should be prioritized by the law and policy (for our discussion, labour law). In the context of labour law, this proposal would mean that labour rights developed originally for an industrial marketplace should prevail over other possible substantive entitlements that might be more relevant in heterogeneous working situations. This way of seeing the role of labour law is paternalistic and somewhat imperialistic (because of the assumption that regulatory cognizance of labour is confined only to the industrial market).

What this economic-exchange perspective also does is to conflate intrinsic and instrumental trajectories of individual capability. Individual capability is important, primarily in its intrinsic sense, that is, a more expansive capability set goes on to make life better per se.[49] This role of capability is different from (only at a conceptual evaluative level) the instrumental trajectory of capability, that is, the role that capability plays in furthering other agendas that individuals may value, such as market participation. Expansive capability in specific spheres of action as human beings, as democratic citizens, and as participants in a cooperative production process is inherently important for a life lived well.[50] Instrumental significance of individual capability is secondary to the quality of life (i.e., intrinsic importance) questions. By de-emphasizing the capability approach in its intrinsic (and more fundamental) sense, Deakin and Wilkinson lay their justification of labour law too narrow.

The justification of labour law that Deakin and Wilkinson offer is better supported by the human capital approach rather than the capability approach. While I will discuss the human capital theory in a later part of the chapter, for now it is

---

[46] Sen, *Development* (n 24) 116–17.     [47] Sen, *Development* (n 24) 25–6.
[48] Sen, *Development* (n 24) 112–13; Sen, *The Idea* (n 44) 7–8, 79–81, 117–23, 410–12.
[49] Sen, *Development* (n 24) xii, 36–7, 90–2.
[50] See Elizabeth S Anderson, 'What is the Point of Equality' (1999) 109(2) *Ethics* 287 317–18.

useful to note that the theory is concerned with the creation of capital in human beings (i.e., resources in people) by means of healthcare, education, training, and other socio-economic conditions.[51] The primary use of this capital (just as physical and financial capital[52]) is its deployment in economic productivity.[53] Human capital is, thus, valuable in terms of its 'economic and physical return', or 'future real income' through market participation.[54] On the other hand, human capability, although expanded by similar factors (e.g., education, healthcare, social security, and so on) is aimed primarily at living a life inherently more flourishing; human capability does not have to be justified on the basis of its economic (or social) productivity.[55] Thus, in order theoretically to substantiate their argument, Deakin and Wilkinson do not need the aid of the capability approach—the human capital theory would more appropriately articulate what they envisage.

Be that as it may, if our agenda is merely to justify the existing regulatory framework taking cognizance of only market-based employment relationships, the capability approach could still be useful, but not necessarily in a market-constitutive sense. As Elizabeth Anderson suggests, one of the spaces of capability that integrates market functions is the idea of 'cooperative production process', by which she means cooperative interaction amongst participants (including employers and workers) of the overall production process.[56] Against this backdrop, market-based and employment relationship-centred labour law could be seen as a factor in promoting democratic equality in this conceptual space. From this perspective, the role of statutory minimum wages, unfair dismissal laws, anti-discrimination laws, or collective bargaining laws is not market-constitutive, but to expand the overall capability of workers so that, in addition to living a rich life, they are able to participate equally in determining the contours of the production process. In addition to this overarching normative justification of labour law, more specific justification of statutory regimes is also possible along similar lines.

For example, the capability approach objects to income or wealth measured in terms of gross domestic product (GDP) as an evaluative proxy to determine the developmental state of a society.[57] When a society's income or wealth is measured, Sen and Nussbaum argue, it does not tell us how each member of the society is doing in terms of their capability expansion. In order to assess each individual's capability, we

---

[51] Gary Becker, 'Investment in Human Capital: A Theoretical Analysis' (1962) 70(5) *Journal of Political Economy* 9, 9–49; Yoram Weiss, 'Gary Becker on Human Capital' (2015) 81 *Journal of Demographic Economics* 27, 27–31; Margherita Bussi, 'Going beyond Work-First and Human Capital Approaches to Employability: the Added-Value of the Capability Approach' (2014) 12(2) *Social Work & Society* 1, 1–15.

[52] Alan Burton Jones and J-C Spender, 'Introduction' in Alan Burton Jones and J-C Spender (eds), *Oxford Handbooks Online* (Oxford University Press, 2015) 1–47, 2.

[53] Weiss, 'Gary Becker on Human Capital' (n 51); Sen, *Development* (n 24) 292–7.

[54] Bussi, 'Going beyond Work-First and Human Capital Approaches to Employability' (n 51) at 9; Becker, 'Investment in Human Capital' (n 51) 9.

[55] Sen, *Development* (n 24).

[56] Anderson, 'What is the Point of Equality' (n 50) 317–18.

[57] See, for example, Martha C Nussbaum, *Creating Capabilities: The Human Development Approach* (The Belknap Press of Harvard University Press, 2011) at ix–xii.

must assess their personal conversion factors and their command over resources.[58] Although what I am calling factors are not only economic factors, it is often the case that such economic factors directly contribute to an individual's ability to expand their capability. In this context, if GDP does not express actual wealth available to individuals, there are evaluative and policy reasons to focus on each individual's access to a minimum level of income. But, since markets as spaces of private interest are ill-equipped to adopt public agendas such as furthering democratic equality in the space of the cooperative production process, it is the government (more broadly, the state) that has to secure a minimum level of income to members (i.e., workers) engaged in the cooperative production process.[59] Similarly, legal rights to association and collective bargaining are factors that cater to democratic equality by expanding workers' capabilities.

A capability approach-based justification of unfair dismissal and anti-discrimination laws are slightly different. Although Sen thinks that a rough equality of individual capability could be a worthy normative goal, he refrains from proposing complete equality of capability among individuals in a society.[60] He argues that often the quest for equality of capability may lead to adverse conclusions about fairness.[61] He offers equal healthcare as an example: given all things constant, just because women may tend to live longer than men cannot be a ground to give more medical attention to men than women in order to equalize their capability to live a long life.[62] The concern of strict equality of capability has to give way to human right to non-discrimination and right against unfair dismissal. Although existing employment relationship-based labour law including specific statutes could be explained through a capability approach-sensitive interpretation, a far greater challenge is to conceptualize a regulatory framework that takes notice of valuable work that is not captured by the juridical employment relationship model or performed within the market-space. In the following section, I engage those attempts.

## III. Imagining a New Labour Law

The evolution from a feudal master-servant-based model of production to a capitalist industrial employment model in Europe and then elsewhere has given rise to a specific form of industrial relations model.[63] This form of industrial relations model

---

[58] Sen, *Development* (n 24) 74; Amartya Sen, *Commodities and Capabilities* (North Holland, 1985) 13; Ingrid Robeyns, 'The Capability Approach: A Theoretical Survey' (2005) 6(1) *Journal of Human Development* 93, 99.

[59] Sen, *Development* (n 24) at 120–1, 128–9, 295, 297.

[60] Sen, *The Idea* (n 44) at 265, 295–8.

[61] Sen, *The Idea* (n 44); also see Amartya Sen, 'The Place of Capability in a Theory of Justice' in Harry Brighouse and Ingrid Robeyns (eds), *Measuring Justice: Primary Goods and Capabilities* (Cambridge University Press, 2010) 239, 248–50.

[62] Sen, *The Idea* (n 44).

[63] See generally Deakin and Wilkinson, *The Law of the Labour Market* (n 16); also see the different chapters in Douglas Hay and Paul Craven (eds), *Masters, Servants, and Magistrates in Britain and the Empire, 1562-1955* (The University of North Carolina Press, 2004).

is characterized by a neatly defined employment relationship; duties of employers; obligations of employees; specific job profiles; definite workplaces; bureaucratic and legislative involvement in furtherance of public interest; *sui generis* judicial structures; and integration of ideals underlying human rights. That this form of industrial employment is shrinking has now been widely noted by labour relations scholars.[64] Since our present idea of labour law developed with reference to this specific form of organizing industrial production, newer forms of organizing economically productive work are posing challenges to existing labour laws, both conceptually as well as from an enforcement point of view. While legal scholars' responses to these challenges have been varied, they are in broad agreement that the foundations of labour law need revisiting.[65] Some of them have employed the capability approach to imagining a new way to regulating work.[66]

One such capability approach-sensitive revisitation has been made by Mark Freedland and Nicola Kountouris.[67] Freedland and Kountouris are concerned that activities such as self-employment, commercial agency, freelancing, public service, voluntary work, labour intermediary, casual work, care work, and so on are not adequately addressed by the existing dispensation of labour law.[68] They offer a private personal relational concept of labour law as an alternative to the standard employment contract-based idea of labour law.[69] By standard employment contract, they understand a stable long-term bipartite employment relationship with adequate level of social security and grievance disposal mechanisms. They consider public service employment, tripartite contracts, subcontracts, short-term contracts, and single-job contracts as personal work relations beyond the employment relationship-based form of industrial organization, and hence, outside the current scope of labour law.[70] They propose that labour law needs to take notice of these

[64] For example, see Alain Supiot and others, *Beyond Employment Changes in Work and the Future of Labour Law in Europe* (Oxford University Press, 2001); also Katherine V W Stone, *From Widgets to Digits: Employment Regulation for the Changing Workplace* (Cambridge University Press, 2004); also Ela R Bhatt, *We Are Poor but So Many: The Story of Self-Employed Women in India* (Oxford University Press, 2006); also Mark Freedland and Nicola Kountouris, *The Legal Construction of Personal Work Relations* (Oxford University Press, 2012); also Jennifer Gordon, *Suburban Sweatshops: The Fight for Immigrant Rights* (The Belknap Press of Harvard University Press 2005); also Bob Hepple, 'The Future of Labour Law' (1995) 24(4) *Industrial Law Journal* 303; also Judy Fudge, 'Fragmenting Work and Fragmenting Organizations: The Contract of Employment and the Scope of Labour Regulation' (2006) 44(4) *Osgoode Hall Law Journal* 609; also see the different chapters in Guy Davidov and Brian Langille (eds), *The Idea of Labour Law* (Oxford University Press, 2011) and Guy Davidov and Brian Langille (eds), *Boundaries And Frontiers Of Labour Law* (Hart Publishing, 2006).
[65] See n 59.
[66] See, for example, Judy Fudge, 'Labour as a "Fictive Commodity": Radically Reconceptualizing Labour Law' in Guy Davidov and Brian Langille (eds), *The Idea of Labour Law* (Oxford University Press, 2011) 120; Brian A Langille, 'Core Labour Rights: The True Story (Reply to Alston)' (2005) 16(3) *European Journal of International Law* 409; Judy Fudge, 'The New Discourse of Labor Rights' (2007) 29 *Comparative Labor Law and Policy Journal* 29; Brian Langille, 'Labour Law's Theory of Justice' in Langille and Davidov, *The Idea of Labour Law*, ibid, 101; Mark Freedland and Nicola Kountouris, *The Legal Construction of Personal Work Relations* (Oxford University Press, 2011).
[67] Freedland and Kountouris, *The Legal Construction of Personal Work Relations* (n 66).
[68] Freedland and Kountouris, *The Legal Construction of Personal Work Relations* (n 66) 35.
[69] Freedland and Kountouris, *The Legal Construction of Personal Work Relations* (n 66) 358–69.
[70] Freedland and Kountouris, *The Legal Construction of Personal Work Relations* (n 66) 29–36.

personal work relations and construe a personal work profile of each worker over her life course for legal entitlement purposes.

Although Freedland and Kountouris' personal relational frame of reference to labour law does integrate certain work-related relationships into its fold (i.e., outside the traditional contractual employment form), they do exclude some important socially (and economically) valuable activities such as house work, care work, domestic employment, street vending, waste recycling, smallholder and subsistence agriculture, and so on from their conceptualization.[71] Some of these exclusions are surprising, given their stated claim that they offer a relational concept of work.[72] These exclusions are also surprising in view of their assertion that they see the legal personal relational conceptualization of work in both its economic as well as its social significance.[73] Thus, although they seem to recognize that legal cognizance of socially valuable work is important, in their final analysis they exclude those relational activities that are not economically productive from legal cognizance.[74]

For the personal work relationships that they do include in their framework, the normative aim of labour law is to promote dignity, enhance capability, and further stability.[75] Freedland and Kountouris capture these values as constituting the overall notion of personality at work.[76] This articulation of dignity, capability, and stability as distinct values creating an idea of personality is somewhat problematic and confusingly underspecified.[77] Stability at work is a social factor, creating conditions necessary for an individual worker to convert their personal characteristics into their capability. It is not a distinct value contributing to workers' personalities at work, although one does not know what exactly are the substantive qualities of personality at work in Freedland and Kountouris' conceptualization. Similarly, the idea of capability as the value underlying unconstrained autonomous exercise of choice in the life course could possibly be part of the overarching conceptualization of dignity, depending on the version of dignity one articulates. As Christopher McCrudden shows, there are several competing ideas of dignity with different contours.[78] Some of these ideas are closer to the capability approach, while others cover only a minimalist ground characterized by so-called negative rights.

---

[71] Freedland and Kountouris, *The Legal Construction of Personal Work Relations* (n 66) 351–2, 347–9, 354–6. Judy Fudge notes this inconsistency in their approach to defining work beyond employment relationship. See Judy Fudge, 'Feminist Reflections on the Scope of Labour Law: Domestic Work, Social Reproduction, and Jurisdiction' (2014) 22 *Feminist Legal Studies* 1, 12–16.

[72] Freedland and Kountouris, *The Legal Construction of Personal Work Relations* (n 66) 346–9.

[73] Freedland and Kountouris, *The Legal Construction of Personal Work Relations* (n 66).

[74] Freedland and Kountouris, *The Legal Construction of Personal Work Relations* (n 66) 364–81.

[75] Freedland and Kountouris, *The Legal Construction of Personal Work Relations* (n 66) 371–82.

[76] Freedland and Kountouris, *The Legal Construction of Personal Work Relations* (n 66) 372.

[77] See Christopher McCrudden, 'Labour Law as Human Rights Law: A Critique of the Use of Dignity by Freedland and Kountouris' in Alan Bogg, Cathryn Costello, ACL Davies, and Jeremias Prassl (eds), *The Autonomy of Labour Law* (Hart Publishing, 2015) 275, for a critique of their account of personality at work, in particular human dignity.

[78] McCrudden, 'Labour Law as Human Rights Law' (n 77); also see Christopher McCrudden, 'Human Dignity and Judicial Interpretation of Human Rights' (2008) 19 *European Journal of International Law* 655.

Freedland and Kountouris' explication of human dignity in terms of autonomy and equality[79] seems to share substantial common ground with the capability approach. As I note, the capability approach proposes a somewhat rough equality in basic capabilities. The substance of capability is articulated as the unconstrained freedom to be and to do, that is, an idea of autonomous life-trajectory. In this manner of conceptualizing dignity both values (i.e., dignity and capability) end up doing the same thing in their regulatory agenda. Freedland and Kountouris note that: 'at a prescriptive level, one of the objectives of labour law should be that of enhancing human capabilities for the purposes of fostering human autonomy and equality at work, and a rewarding existence'.[80] At another point, they assert that the value of stability will require shaping 'the regulation of contractual termination rules in a way that promotes job security for workers and allows them to enjoy dignity and capability entitlements to the full ...'.[81]

Here, one is unable to assess as to what they mean by capability entitlements. It is one thing to say that the normative goal of labour law ought to be enhancement of workers' capabilities. It is an altogether different proposition to assume entitlements to capability. By capability entitlements, do they mean legal entitlements to specific capabilities? Or is there an entitlement to broad overarching capability? Is it possible for legal standards alone to secure capability (i.e., freedom to do or to be), especially when the very idea of capability is expressed as a combination of access to resources and individual's agency? It is overambitious (if not outright wrong) to conceive that law alone can offer entitlements to substantive freedom or capability. Legal entitlements can secure resources and create conducive circumstances (what I collectively called factors) for individuals to exercise their agency in expanding their capability (or specific capabilities). In absence of individual agency, it is difficult to see how legal entitlements per se might enhance overall capability of workers.

Thus, Freedland and Kountouris' account of capability remains too unclear and burdensome to be of much use in conceiving a regulatory framework capable of taking cognizance of work that is performed outside the industrial employment form. Their account is also problematic in the sense that they do not offer any justification as to why they exclude several socially and economically valuable kinds of work, including unpaid work from their personal relational conceptualization of labour law.

While Freedland and Kountouris' articulation has several limitations in its reimagination of labour law, Brian Langille's account of capabilities as a normative goal of labour law is more useful in taking cognizance of a range of heterogeneous activities performed by workers. In offering what he calls 'labour law's theory of justice', Langille delivers perhaps the most persuasive reasoning for a new normative goal of labour law.[82] He notes that the 'received wisdom' about labour law's

[79] Freedland and Kountouris, *The Legal Construction of Personal Work Relations* (n 66) 372–6.
[80] Freedland and Kountouris, *The Legal Construction of Personal Work Relations* (n 66) 378.
[81] Freedland and Kountouris, *The Legal Construction of Personal Work Relations* (n 66) 381.
[82] Langille, 'Labour Law's Theory' (n 66); also see Brian Langille, 'What is Labour Law? Implications of the Capability Approach', Chapter 6 in this volume.

normative goal, of striking equality in bargaining between employer and employees, is inadequate in view of empirical realities. The logic of inequality of bargaining power (and labour not being a commodity) is unable to carry the weight of a regulatory idea involving work in its heterogeneous manifestations. In addition to the industrial organization *form*, the other categories of work that he has is mind are 'non-contractual approaches to work relations (informal activities, for example) and other non-traditional labour law subjects (unpaid work, education, child care, and so on)'.[83]

Noting that the crisis of labour law has three dimensions—empirical (i.e., transformations in the world of work); conceptual (i.e., the employment relationship basis); and normative (i.e., salience of moral ideals)—Langille proposes a new normative basis of labour law based on the capability approach.[84] Langille is searching for an idea of regulation that might be capable of taking cognizance of work, irrespective of the form in which it is organized.[85] This is an important but largely ignored task for academic labour lawyers. The industrial employment-based labour law never covered those undocumented and unmonitored (but in no imagination, illegal) domestic workers, unpaid agriculturists, street vendors eking out a living, forest collectors, waste recyclers, home-based workers (often connected to global value chains), paid goat rearers, tailors, transport workers, and so on, that are not organized in the same (or similar) industrial employment form. Additionally, labour law finds it increasingly difficult to engage with fragmented workplaces and a heterogeneity of working relationships.

In this context, Langille proposes that the capability approach ought to constitute labour law's theory of justice.[86] By treating workers as subjects—as participants in the labour law discourse rather than objects and as actors regulated by labour law—the capability approach focuses on 'our true ends' rather than the means of achieving those ends.[87] Emphasizing the connection that he sees between human freedom and human capital, Langille notes that labour law could mediate this connection in furthering overall capability of workers.[88] Citing Sen, he argues that human capital should not be seen here as merely an instrumental tool in economic development, but also an end in itself.[89] Langille proposes that '[l]abour law ... be seen as that part of our law which structures the mobilization and deployment of human capital'.[90] The 'agenda for labour law', then, is human development insofar as it relates to *work*.[91]

I am generally in agreement with Langille's broader regulatory agenda of work, although certain internal disagreements (i.e., an insider's constructive criticism)

---

83  Langille, 'Labour Law's Theory' (n 82) 114.
84  Langille, 'Labour Law's Theory' (n 82) 111–14.
85  Langille, 'Labour Law's Theory' (n 82) 112.
86  Langille, 'Labour Law's Theory' (n 82) 103.
87  Langille, 'Labour Law's Theory' (n 82) 111–12.
88  Langille, 'Labour Law's Theory' (n 82) 112.
89  Langille, 'Labour Law's Theory' (n 82).
90  Langille, 'Labour Law's Theory' (n 82) 112–14.
91  Langille, 'Labour Law's Theory' (n 82) 113.

remain. First, instead of employing the capability approach in furthering a theory of justice of labour law, it is perhaps more useful to view labour law as a constituent of the overall narrative of distributional justice furthered by the capability approach. A theory of justice needs a metric, which is offered by the capability approach; but it also needs a distributional criterion in order to distribute the metric, which the capability approach is silent on. Additionally, it is also a responsibility of a theory of justice to specify a manner of taxation for distributional purposes. While these social justice concerns may have relevance in the context of work, should it be the role of a regulatory framework of work to be concerned with all of these issues? I doubt it (although this judgment will also depend on how the scope of work regulation is defined). Moreover, theories of justice aim to offer optimum formulae that are good for all societies under all circumstances.[92] Such an agenda might be problematic for an idea of labour law given the fragmentation of workplace and the heterogeneity of work relations across the globe. It is therefore more useful to adopt a contextual-distributional perspective on labour law rather than a complete theory of justice.

The second disagreement that I have with Langille is on his emphasis of human capital. His contention that labour law is to mobilize and deploy human capital, in my view, is a problematic proposition. As I mention, the human capital approach adopts an instrumental view of capital in human beings, which is to be employed primarily for economic productivity. But, as Sen notes, economic productivity cannot itself be valuable unless it is able to promote people's aspirations (i.e., what they value).[93] In this sense, the human capital approach tells us only about means (i.e., that economic productivity is important) rather than ends (i.e., whether people's valuable capabilities are expanded).[94] Thus, the emphasis on human capital rather than directly on human capability goes against Langille's stated intention of pursuing ends ('workers as subjects') rather than means through legal regulation of work.

However, I must mention that Langille does discuss the relationship between human capital and human capability, and recognizes the fact that human capability is a much broader ends-focused concept. In spite of this recognition, he sees the role of a regulatory framework of work as mobilizing and deploying human capital. Human capital as a conceptual idea emerged mainly to explain income growth that could not be explained by the growth of physical capital and labour.[95] It is understood as a:

[c]ollection of productive skills embodied in a person that can be used to generate earnings in the labour market and to augment household's consumption options. It is a dynamic concept, as individuals can choose to invest in their own human capital and this investment decision can be analyzed by economic tools that are usually applied to financial investments based on forward looking considerations.[96]

---

[92] See generally Sen, 'The Place of Capability' (n 61).    [93] Sen, *Development* (n 24) 295.
[94] Sen, *Development* (n 24).    [95] Weiss, 'Gary Becker on Human Capital' (n 51) 27.
[96] Weiss, 'Gary Becker on Human Capital' (n 51) 27.

Thus, even at the cost of repetition, human capital is an instrumental idea conveying the usefulness of human capabilities for future income growth; and hence, it is analysed as an investment—not an end-goal per se. Health, education, training, and access to market-information are all seen as investments to human capital, which in turn is to be invested for wealth creation.[97] Even when scholars of human capital assess non-monetary values of human capital, they do so in terms of 'profitability' and 'achievement' of personal relationships.[98] Thus, (human) capital is something that needs to 'produce value over time'.[99] Accordingly, juridical aspirations such as mobilization and the deployment of human capital seem to further an income-focused—or, at least, market-constitutive—idea of human development. If regulation is to mobilize and deploy human capital in this sense then it remains bound primarily to an economic logic that Deakin and his colleagues further.

Perhaps this instrumental and primarily economic perspective is not what Langille has in mind when articulating the normative goal of regulation of work. If human beings are not viewed as economic instrumentalities (i.e., capital), then an alternative manner of explicating the juridically mediated facilitation of individual autonomy is by means of human agency, something that Sen calls the agency aspect of freedom.[100] If the significance of the capability approach lies in its intrinsic idea of freedom, as I argue it does, then regulatory intervention should seek to generate conditions wherein individuals (i.e., workers) have real freedom to exercise their agency in furtherance of lives they value and have reason to value rather than mobilization of their human capital. However, the challenge for regulatory entitlements in the modern world of work is that, depending on the context, substantive entitlements would have to be differently conceptualized in order to create conditions of real freedom. Can context-specific heterogeneous substantive legal entitlements become part of a coherent idea of regulation of work? I discuss this issue in the following section.

## IV. Regulation of Work for Heterogeneous Workers: A Social Justice-focused Approach

Langille notes that labour law needs liberating by 'expand[ing] its justificatory horizons' and he proposes the capability approach as one of the better means of doing it.[101] The capability approach offers a basis for evaluating distributional concerns in a society from an objective point of view—objective because, instead of focusing merely on individual happiness or desire fulfilment (which are subjective emotions), the capability approach emphasizes the real freedom of individuals to

---

[97] See generally Weiss, 'Gary Becker on Human Capital' (n 51).
[98] Weiss, 'Gary Becker on Human Capital' (n 51) 30.
[99] Jones and Spender, 'Introduction' (n 52) 4.
[100] Amartya Sen, 'Well-Being, Agency and Freedom: The Dewey Lectures 1984' (1985) 82(4) *Journal of Philosophy* 169, 203–204.
[101] Langille, 'Labour Law's Theory' (n 66) 102.

live the life they value. Rather than focusing on the means of human development (such as participation in the market or government welfare), the capability approach centralizes the ends of human development, which is the expansion of individual capability. Since development is seen as substantive freedom to do things that are valued and determined by communities themselves (i.e., not externally imposed), communities' freedom becomes a social commitment in this perspective. In the capability approach, individuals are not seen as mere beneficiaries of social policies; they are seen as dynamic participants in the development process of themselves and of the society.

As I note, freedom in this perspective has two trajectories: well-being freedom and agency freedom. While well-being freedom evaluates how 'well' an individual is doing in terms of her health, nutrition, educational level, community participation, and so on, agency freedom mainstreams an individual's own initiative in doing the things that she values doing. These two trajectories of freedom are irreducible to each other. Thus, the capability approach is not merely a recipe for socio-economic-political entitlements; it is also an agenda for human flourishing. This capacious idea of freedom in terms of capability makes the capability approach particularly attractive for labour law or, more broadly, the regulation of work debates.

At a level of generality, the claim in employing the capability approach for regulatory concerns involving work is that the normative goal of such regulatory agenda ought to be the expansion of a worker's freedom to decide a thought-out plan for her life and enable her to pursue that life (i.e., to promote the agency aspect of freedom). This perspective could be channeled in two directions: bounded and unbounded. The bounded perspective could see such expansion of freedom to choose and pursue a life course within a given space, such as the one offered by Anderson of democratic equality in the space of a cooperative production process. The unbounded perspective could mandate equal participation as one of the factors in expanding individual capability and leave the space (i.e., aspirations of individuals) indeterminate. The regulatory agenda in this indeterminate space could aim at a rough (i.e., approximate) equality of capability, but this equality should not be pursued at the cost of fairness, which is often secured through fundamental human rights to equal treatment.

It is true, then, that the capability approach is an abstract overarching normative perspective often appearing indeterminate in its exposition. But the problem lies in taking this abstractness to be a weakness in employing the capability approach for the purpose of thinking about theoretical conceptualization of labour law. Instead of seeing this abstract generality as a weakness, it should be seen as one of the strengths of the capability perspective. If regulatory concerns about work need to be cognizant of heterogeneous activities performed both within the traditional industrial employment form as well as those performed outside that form, a higher-level normative goal is essential. Otherwise, we may end up reinforcing those regulatory initiatives that do not seem to work for the majority of workers globally. Although legal entitlements in relation to the industrial employment form could be explained by the capability approach, its analytical strength becomes more prominent in the context of work that is performed outside that form.

My primary interest lies in articulating a normative goal of legal regulation of work for workers who fall outside the industrial employment form.[102] I do not employ the capability approach in justifying the existing labour law regime; this, however, is not to say that the existing regime cannot be explained through the capability approach. Neither do I take a position that the labour law of industrial employment form cannot be salvaged. Of course, there are situations that diverge slightly from the industrial employment form (e.g., tripartite employment, multiple employer, agency-mediated work, electronic platform-mediated work) and some modifications of the existing labour law regime might be able to address these divergences. This is a useful project to pursue. However, if we need to conceive of a more general logic to legal regulation when work is performed, we might need to think outside the proverbial labour law box.

As I have argued elsewhere, existing labour rights that emerged through the experience of industrial revolution-induced organization of economic production are often unable to account for the specific and varied experiences of non-industrial workers.[103] Under these circumstances, the capability approach helps mainstream those factors (both resources as well as socio-economic-political-environmental circumstances) that might be more pertinent to the situated experiences of specific categories of heterogeneous workers. From this point of view, the capability approach could be seen as underpinning those entitlements (i.e., legally institutionalized factors) that have not attained the status of labour rights, yet are central in promoting workers' capabilities. This simultaneity of existing labour rights and capability-expanding entitlements is one of the strengths of the capability approach in conceptualizing a normative goal for labour law.

The polycentric theoretical underpinnings of existing labour law have been enumerated as redistribution, dignity and human rights, and democracy (among other perspectives). As I specify earlier, it is also argued, although without much elaboration, that the capability approach ought to be inadequate in explaining these polycentric goals of labour law. This view, unfortunately, is incorrect. The capability approach is able to explain—and does explain—the above-mentioned concerns. There is a wealth of literature that documents the relationship between the capability approach and the above-mentioned theoretical perspectives. A brief stock-taking could be undertaken in the following manner. First, the capability approach is directly concerned with redistribution. It specifies that the metric of redistribution should be capabilities rather than utilitarian happiness, Dworkinian resources, or Rawlsian primary goods. Thus, instead of redistributing rights and resources, the capability approach mandates that legal regulation considers capability as the subject matter of redistribution. Secondly, the capability approach constitutes and enriches ideas of human dignity and supplements fundamental human rights. For example, if autonomy and equality are constituents of a dignity conceptualization

---

[102] See generally Routh, *Enhancing* (n 24).
[103] Supriya Routh, 'Do Human Rights Work for Informal Workers?', forthcoming in Diamond Ashiagbor (ed), *Re-imagining Labour Law for Development: Informal Work in the Global North and Global South* (Hart Publishing, 2019).

(among other conceptualizations of dignity), the capability approach is inherently linked to such perspective. And as I already mention, human rights and the capability approach often occupy similar spaces complementing each other. Finally, even a cursory look at Sen, Nussbaum, and other capability scholars' scholarship is enough to suggest the integral nature of democracy—as people's actual participation and deliberation—in the capability perspective.

Several of these misunderstandings about the capability approach emanate from the misperception that the capability approach offers a complete theory of justice.[104] It does not, at least in the variation that Sen offers (and most labour lawyers use Sen's perspective on capability approach). There is a reason why Sen calls his contribution *The Idea of Justice* rather than the theory of justice.[105] Although Nussbaum offers a capability approach-centred theory of justice for the constitutional organization of societies, her endeavour is far from being a closed theory.[106] She allows for democratic space and situated experiences of societies and communities to inform and modify her perspective within the broad parameters of her theory.[107] The capability approach offers an approach to evaluate human development. The approach needs to be supplemented by other perspectives and theories including theories of power, public choice, and collective action in order to construct a satisfactorily developed theory of justice,[108] although it is doubtful whether a theory of justice will be helpful in offering a satisfactory answer to the heterogeneous working situations in widely varied contexts.

In any case, we would do well to recognize that substantive rights, resources, and entitlements in accordance with the capability approach are inherently linked with participation and dialogue involving workers. The capability approach answers the question, 'what constitutes knowledge for policy-making?' by centralizing experiences of individuals (i.e., workers). The integral nature of participation and dialogue in the capability approach means that scholarly engagement with the capability approach should devise a mechanism for the participation of workers in developing regulatory entitlements, rather than asserting workers' aspirations in life on their behalf.

## V. Conclusion

I begin by asking two questions in the introduction to this chapter: first, whether the capability approach could be employed (coherently) to justify the traditional account of labour law and, secondly, whether the capability approach could prove

---

[104] See, for example, Hugh Collins, 'What Can Sen's Capability Approach Offer to Labour Law?', Chapter 1 in this volume.

[105] Sen, *Idea of Justice* (n 44).

[106] See generally Nussbaum, *Creating Capabilities* (n 57); also see Martha C Nussbaum, *Women and Human Development: The Capabilities Approach* (Cambridge University Press, 2000); also Martha C Nussbaum, *Frontiers of Justice: Disability, Nationality, Species Membership* (The Belknap Press of Harvard University Press, 2006).

[107] See the references cited in n 106.

[108] Ingrid Robeyns, 'Sen's Capability Approach and Gender Inequality: Selecting Relevant Capabilities' (2003) 9(2–3) *Feminist Economics* 61, 67; Fudge, 'Labour as a "Fictive Commodity": Radically Reconceptualizing Labour Law' (n 66) 65.

useful in (re)conceptualizing regulation of work for heterogeneous working arrangements. Although I argue that the capability approach could do both of the above, the full potential of the capability perspective will be used when it is employed to conceptualize a broader account of the regulation of work that not only takes cognizance of market-based employment, but also recognizes work performed outside the market space.

When the capability approach is employed to justify substantive labour rights, it does the following things: first, it assesses legal entitlements from the point of view of their ability to expand every worker's capability; and, secondly, it allows enough scope to justify legal entitlements that are consistent with the capability approach (e.g., those based on fairness) even if they may not strike a rough equality of capability. While the capability approach can justify piecemeal legislation and substantive standards, this is a narrow application of the perspective. A much more capacious engagement of the capability perspective leads to a critique of traditional labour law exclusions such as socially reproductive work, informal work, and other atypical work, and a critique of traditional labour rights that are insensitive to increasingly diverse contexts. Though dissimilar and diverse substantive legal entitlements are necessary for the expansion of workers' capability in heterogeneous contexts, and yet it is possible to develop a coherent account of a discipline (i.e., regulation of work) is the fundamental usefulness of the capability approach.

In this contribution, I assess labour lawyers' critique of using the capability approach as an inspiration for (re)conceptualizing the normative aim of legal regulation of work. Taking their objection seriously, I considered why some of the concerns that they express are not damaging, but rather helpful, in the (re)conceptualization project of work regulation. It is true that the capability approach offers an abstract overarching concept and hence might appear detached from, and to underspecify, the specific concerns of labour law. However, the problem lies in assuming that the capability approach per se can overcome the shortcomings of legal regulatory framework on work. The capability approach needs further specifications and development, depending on the context to which it is applied. And it is the job of labour lawyers to specify the capability approach in the (re)conceptualization project of legal regulation of work. It is no wonder that this is an attractive scholarly proposition—catching the imagination of a society of scholars—thereby becoming 'fashionable'.

# 6

# What is Labour Law? Implications of the Capability Approach

*Brian Langille*

> The point of providing an account of the form of thought in an area of legal doctrine is not to invent that area, or give someone else credit for inventing it. Instead, it is to make it intelligible, to show how the characteristic modes of reasoning, the questions asked, and the inferences permitted or refused fit into an intelligible pattern. That pattern is composed of conceptual and normative structures rather than causes and effects.
>
> Arthur Ripstein, *Private Wrongs* (p xi)*

> Every subject studied in the university or elsewhere is a structure to be entered into ...What inspires a good teacher is a clarified view of his own subject.
>
> Northrop Frye, *On Education* (pp 80 and 50)

## I. Introduction: 'Light dawns gradually over the whole'

This is a chapter about labour law.[1] But it is not about any particular part of our labour law, nor any particular legal or doctrinal dispute, nor any specific legislative scheme or initiative, nor indeed any constitutional controversy about our labour laws. It is also not about any specific labour law regime in place in any particular legal jurisdiction.[2] Further, this project is not just about domestic labour law regimes.

---

\* PRIVATE WRONGS by Arthur Ripstein, Cambridge, Mass.: Harvard University Press, Copyright © 2016 by the President and Fellows of Harvard College.

[1] Ludwig Wittgenstein, *On Certainty* (Blackwell, 1969) para 141: 'When we first begin to believe anything, what we believe is not a single proposition, it is a whole system of propositions. (Light dawns gradually over the whole)'.

[2] I am a Canadian labour law academic who also received, a long time ago, some of my labour law education in England. I know more about these (sorts of) labour law regimes than other domestic examples—almost all of which I know very little or nothing about by way of legal details. But I have taught and lectured about these ideas in several parts of the world and I find that there is not much lost in translation. That is, I find that my concerns and approach are understood. Not agreed with all the time, but understood. Another way of putting this—where there is disagreement, it is real disagreement and not a talking past one another. See Brian Langille, 'Eight Ways to Think about International Labour Standards' (1997) 31 *Journal of World Trade* 27 at 27 (where I described lack of communication and engagement between groups of citizens and scholars as an example of what Canadians call 'two solitudes').

It has ramifications for international and transnational labour law. But again, it is not about any particular aspect of that 'labour law beyond borders'.[3]

What then is this chapter all about? It is about how we think about labour law. Further, this chapter explores how certain ideas developed by Amartya Sen and Martha Nussbaum can assist us in our thinking.

This chapter takes seriously issues such as how we know what law is labour law, and what law is not labour law. What makes labour law, labour law? What is labour law? The answers to these questions, it turns out on the view taken here, depend upon our answer to questions such as 'What is labour law for?' And 'why do we have it?' Many distinguished scholars,[4] some of them labour lawyers,[5] have insisted upon a 'purposive approach'. They are certainly correct. But I sometimes doubt whether this insight is driven all the way to the conclusions it demands or constantly kept in mind. Nietzsche said: 'The most common form of stupidity is forgetting what we are trying to accomplish'.[6]

At the core of the enterprise of taking these sorts of questions as central, and answering them, is another set of ideas. These are ideas about how some legal subject matters such as labour law (or family, or environmental, or trade law) 'work'; or are made possible as legal subjects; or what gives them a 'structure which can be entered into', to use Frye's formulation; or, in virtue of what can we discern 'an intelligible pattern', to use Ripstein's words. Central to this line of thinking are the ideas that legal subjects have whatever coherence they have as legal subjects in very different ways. Some subject matters cohere in virtue of a legal idea—tort, contract, trusts, for examples. Yet, some other subject matters, such as labour law, operate very differently. They are centred not on a legal idea but on a part of real life. Whatever coherence they have is structured and made possible by what I have called a 'constituting narrative', which performs three tasks. First, it tells us what part of the real world is the focus of our, in this case labour law's, concern. This enables us, when we look out of the window at the hurly-burly, the motley of activities, the complexity of the real lives of human beings, to say 'this is the aspect of real life, the slice of reality, which is of important legal concern'. Say, 'employment'. Secondly, it provides the concepts—the legal concepts—necessary to frame that reality and express it in legal terms. Say, 'employer/employee/contract of employment' and so on. Thirdly, it provides a normative, that is, moral, justification for taking this part of our lives as a vital focus of concern—that is, what is morally at stake, why we need labour law, what it is for, and why it is important. Say, redressing power imbalances in the negotiation and administration of employment contracts.

---

[3] To use the words of my colleague Patrick Macklem—see 'Labour Law beyond Borders' (2002) 5 *Journal of International Economic Law* 605.

[4] See e.g. Aharon Barak, *Purposive Interpretation in Law* (Princeton University Press, 2005).

[5] See e.g. Guy Davidov, *A Purposive Approach to Labour Law* (Oxford University Press, 2016).

[6] Friedrich Nietzsche, 'The Wanderer and His Shadows' in Human, All Too Human: A Book for Free Spirits, trans. R. J. Hollingdale (Cambridge University Press, 1996) 360. See also Lon L Fuller with William R Perdue, Jr, 'The Reliance Interest in Contract Damages: 1' (1936) 46 *Yale Law Journal* 52, 52.

It is a significant accomplishment of modern labour law, as we now know it, that it does possess such a constituting narrative—the one just outlined. I refer to this currently dominant constituting narrative as 'the received wisdom'.[7]

This articulation of the three elements of labour law's constituting narrative lays bare the ways in which legal subject matters such as labour law can go 'off the rails'. They can, and do so in just these three ways. And going off the rails in just these three ways dominates our current discussions of the fate of labour law in our world. Labour law is viewed as 1. empirically irrelevant, 2. conceptually obstructive, and 3. normatively challenged—both by those who do and those who do not agree with its normative stance. First, it is observed that labour law is increasingly empirically irrelevant to the world we now see outside our windows. The world our labour law has long made sense of—long term employment on what is now called 'the standard model'—is now being 'disappeared' by changes in the organization of work in which we see fewer employees, fewer contracts of employment, more 'fissured workplaces', more independent contractors, 'gig' employment—that is, globalized, networked, 'uberized', platformed, crowd-sourced, outsourced, and all the rest.[8] Second, the legal concepts which structure this now declining proportion of the working population are manipulated and operate perniciously as conceptual barriers to the application of our labour laws to the new world of productive activity. That is, our familiar and basic legal concepts, such as 'employee' are not only inadequate but harmful, easily manipulated, and constitute a barrier or hurdle for workers who seek the protection they need.[9] Third, labour law can go off the rails by failing to find an adequate moral justification for itself and attaching itself to a narrow morality inadequate to its true calling. We can become locked into a certain morality and fail to see more robust accounts which are available. An out-of-date picture can hold us captive. All three sorts of pitfalls are now on display in our law. They are of course closely connected, as they must be to constitute a coherent and compelling story capable of structuring and making possible legal subject matters such as labour law. There are exceptions and contradictions—new points of light, hints of the possibility of a new

[7] In my thinking the content of what I now call the received wisdom was visible early on. See Brian Langille, 'Labour Law Is a Subset of Employment Law' (1981) 31(2) *University of Toronto Law Journal* 200. It was later that I saw its role as a constituting narrative. See Brian Langille, 'Labour Law's Back Pages' in Guy Davidov and Brian Langille (eds), *The Boundaries and Frontiers of Labour Law* (Hart Publishing, 2006) 13.

[8] See e.g. Harry W Arthurs, 'Labour Law without the State?' (1996) 46 *University of Toronto Law Journal* 1; Harry W Arthurs, *The New Economy and the Demise of Industrial Citizenship* (Don Wood Lecture: Industrial Relations Centre, Queen's University, 1996); Katherine VW Stone, *From Widgets to Digits: Employment Regulation for the Changing Workplace* (Cambridge University Press, 2004); Judy Fudge, 'Fragmenting Work and Fragmenting Organizations: The Contract of Employment and the Scope of Labour Regulation' (2006) 44 *Osgoode Hall Law Journal* 609; David Weil, *The Fissured Workplace: Why Work Became So Bad for So Many and What Can Be Done to Improve it* (Harvard University Press, 2014); Valerio De Stefano, 'The Rise of the "Just-in-Time Workforce": On-Demand Work, Crowd Work and Labour Protection in the "Gig-Economy"' (2016) 37(3) *Comparative Labor Law & Policy Journal* 471.

[9] See Brian Langille and Pnina Alon-Shenker, 'Law Firm Partners and the Scope of Labour Law' (2015) 4(2) *Canadian Journal of Human Rights* 211; Brian Langille, '"Take These Chains from my Heart and Set Me Free": How Labor Law Theory Drives Segmentation of Workers' Rights' (2015) 36 *Comparative Labor Law & Policy Journal* 257.

dawn, in some real legal decisions and in other parts of our law. We are at a point at which we can still ignore such aberrations—or, see them as constituting a demand that we come up with a new narrative in order to make sense of them.[10]

Many in the academic labour law community have spilled a great deal of ink exploring the stresses upon the first two elements of our received narrative—upon the empirical and conceptual dimensions. Some scholars have stressed the new empirical realities of work,[11] while others have attended to the challenges posed by the new forms and ways of working to our basic conceptual apparatus—employee,[12] employer,[13] contract of employment,[14] and so on. But, following the demands of a purposive approach, I have come to the view that it is the third dimension of any constituting narrative for labour law—the normative or moral dimension—which is the key to our current difficulties.[15] Only by starting with questions such as 'What are we trying to do?' and 'What is labour law for?' can we hope to be rational in our thinking about the empirical dimension (who and what part of their world falls within the scope of our concerns) and about the legal conceptual framework we need to deploy to bring that aspect of the world into legal view as part of a system of law. All of the interesting questions of labour law—the 'who', the 'what', the 'how', and all the rest—must all be addressed in light of the answer to the question 'why?' That is what dedication to the purposive and rational approach means and requires. Of course, all of the three dimensions of any constituting narrative must fit together—just to be a compelling, and useful in understanding and dealing with the world in a legal way. But the question 'what are we trying to accomplish?' is basic.

## II. Understanding Labour Law: Grammar and Narrative

A number of the other chapters in this volume make the claim that the capabilities approach (CA) of Sen and/or Nussbaum cannot provide a normative justification for all of our labour law, but at most can be helpful here and there in providing the moral underpinning of bits of our labour law.[16] But one can only say that if one has

---

[10] See Brian Langille, 'Human Freedom: A Way Out of Labour Law's Fly Bottle' in Hugh Collins, Gillian Lester, and Virginia Mantouvalou (eds), *Philosophical Foundations of Labour Law* (Oxford University Press, 2019) forthcoming.

[11] See e.g. Weil (n 8).

[12] See e.g. Guy Davidov, 'Who is a Worker?' (2005) 34 *Industrial Law Journal* 57.

[13] See e.g. Jeremias Prassl, *The Concept of the Employer* (Oxford University Press, 2015).

[14] See e.g. Mark Freedland, 'From Contract of Employment to the Personal Work Nexus' (2006) 35(1) *Industrial Law Journal* 1; Mark Freedland, 'The Legal Characterization of Personal Work Relations and the Idea of Labour Law' in Guy Davidov and Brian Langille (eds), *The Idea of Labour Law* (Oxford University Press, 2011); Mark Freedland and Nicola Kountouris, *The Legal Construction of Personal Work Relations* (Oxford University Press, 2011).

[15] Some insisted it has not changed and should not change (see e.g. Guy Davidov, 'The (Changing?) Idea of Labour Law' (2007) 146 *International Labour Review* 311), while some agree (see e.g. Harry Arthurs, 'Labour Law as the Law of Economic Subordination and Resistance: A Counterfactual?' (2012) Comparative Research in Law & Political Economy, Research Paper No 10/2012 http://digitalcommons.osgoode.yorku.ca/clpe/9).

[16] Guy Davidov, 'The Capability Approach and Labour Law: Identifying the Areas of Fit' (Chapter 2 in this volume), Hugh Collins, 'What Can Sen's Capability Approach Offer to Labour Law?' (Chapter 1

a different idea of 'justifying' labour law in mind. A different picture. A different explanation of the role of the normative. On my view, the normative enters as part of our account of what labour law is. As part of our constituting narrative. It does not simply enter 'after the event'. We cannot proceed by saying 'well, here is our labour law—what in heaven's name could possibly justify that from a moral point of view?' On such a view we just know what labor law is and then scour the normative theory marketplace for a justification of it. On this view, normative theory is external to our account of labour law. That is not the view taken here. I believe that subject matters such as labour law require a constituting narrative with an internal normative dimension in order for us to know what is and is not labour law in the first place. On my view labour law does have—and must have—a normative account of the whole of labour law. Labour law's normative stance does not come in bits and pieces. Light does dawn over the whole. There is a 'structure to be entered into', as Frye put it.

So, the role which the CA, or any normative dimension of any account of labour law plays, is part of an account of what labour law is and not simply a normative claim about something we independently identify as labour law. That is, it is not simply a claim about justifying or criticizing labour law or various parts of it from an external point of view. It is a claim about our internal understanding of labour law. In Ripstein's words: 'The point of providing an account of the form of thought in an area of legal doctrine is . . . to make it intelligible'.

Here is another important point. We are actually after a view of labour *law*. We seek an understanding of an area of law—its structure. But we hold that, for subjects such as labour law, we need an important normative reason for isolating this part of our reality as worthy of our attention. But the normative underpinning of labour law—its theory of justice if you will—must be an account expressed in law. Our commitment to the rule of law means that we need not only a legal narrative but also a legal grammar. Legal grammar does not tell us what we want or need or should aspire to. Rather, it tells us how to express our moralities, in law. Grammar instructs us as to how we must articulate any narrative in such a way for it to be law, to live up to the idea of legality, and not merely a philosophy or an economics chapter. Thus, I have come to see the following 'structure' as basic: grammar (legality) and narrative (capability).

The legal grammar of labour law has not always been that of contract—but it has been for a long time. I have written before about contract law as the beginning and continuing legal framework for our account of labour law.[17] Our current constituting narrative begins there and continues to be organized around that legal idea and our reactions to it (both substantive (employment standards legislation) and procedural (collective bargaining laws)). It is where labour law has found legal traction and expression. Hugh Collins also understands this point about the legal grammar of our labour law. He sets out what I take to be labour law's received wisdom, accurately, as follows:

in this volume), and Simon Deakin, 'The Capability Approach and the Economics of Labour Law' (Chapter 7 in this volume), for examples.

[17]   Langille, 'Back Pages' (n 7). See also Langille, *The Idea of Labour Law* (n 14).

The core of the subject of labour law concerns the regulation of work and employment relations. Since the demise of feudal societies and the rise of market societies, the legal framework for the exchange of work for payment has been found in the law of contract. But the basic institutional structure provided by contract law and free markets proves deeply unsatisfactory in connection with the employment of labour by owners of capital.

Indeed, labour law has as its main purpose the removal of general contract law (and private law more generally) from the regulation of many aspects of work relations. Contract law may still provide the scaffolding for personal work relations, but the bricks and mortar of the building derive from other sources. These sources include mandatory rules in legislation as well as the collective self-regulation mechanism of collective bargaining. To justify this substantial exclusion of general contract law from the laws governing work relations, labour law needs a theory of why the market and the basic institutions of justice that support it proves inadequate in the case of employment relations.[18]

But Collins then objects to the ideas I express regarding inequality of bargaining power as underwriting our current labour law. I find this puzzling. This is particularly so because he agrees with me that this is not an economic idea but rather a way of criticizing that way of thinking about things. He writes:

A popular justification for the exclusion of ordinary contract law is the claim that the employment relation is distorted by inequality of bargaining power... The concept of inequality of bargaining power used in many justifications of labour law is not an economic description of the failure of a competitive labour market, but is rather an observation that the material and psychological risks to individual workers involved in obtaining and holding on to a job are far more significant to their well-being than the risks of gaining or losing a particular employee will be to the average employer... This is the problem of inequality of bargaining power, properly understood: there is no market failure, but rather the normal market creates opportunities for exploitation. Therefore, the basic institutions of private law need to be supplement by special rules for the institution of employment and workplace relations. These basic institutions need to be guided by a theory of justice that explains the shape and purpose of those labour laws.

Ideas of what justice requires may differ considerably, of course, but the case for having a labour law at all in place of the general law of contract depends ultimately on the appeal to some kind of theory of justice. Such a theory might emphasise the importance of general welfare or utility, or it might try to ground the theory in an appeal to individual rights such as human rights or labour rights. What any theory of labour law must do, in my view, is to explain and justify the substantial exclusion of the general law of contract.[19]

This is, on my way of thinking, just perfect as a classic statement of labour law's contractual legal grammar and the discontents it produces for those interested in a narrative of real justice for workers. That is, it provides the grammatical stage upon which labour law's theory of justice enters the scene, comes on stage, to take on, civilize, constrain, humanize contract. Absolutely classic. Then the question for Collins is whether the CA can fill the need, 'do what any theory of labour law must do', that is, 'explain the substantial exclusion of the general law of contract'.

---

[18] Hugh Collins, 'What Can Sen's Capability Approach Offer to Labour Law?' Chapter 1 in this volume at p 23.
[19] Collins, 'What Can Sen's Capability Approach Offer to Labour Law?' (n 18) p 23.

And the answer Collins gives is essentially 'no' (with a few reservations about filling a role here and there). This is an answer quite close to that offered by Davidov, and perhaps Deakin.[20]

Collins is certainly correct to express labour law's dilemmas and needs in these terms, in this way. He is committed, as he should be, to the idea that there is and must be a legal structure for expressing our desires about workplace justice in legal terms and not simply moral terms. A legal structure is critical. As well as the normative story which it invites and with which it is entwined.

But here is a way in which I think he misunderstands and underestimates the potential of the CA. Its potential role is not to simply answer the dilemma for justice posed by our familiar account of the history and current structure of our labour law. Rather its potential is greater: to force us to reconsider that basic structure. It may offer us a way out of the grasp of the familiar legal account, a way out of the contractual (and needed reactions to contract) fly bottle. If grammar and narrative are intertwined, as they are, and as Collins lays bare, then a new narrative must and does have large implications for law's grammar—the grammar of contract.

If this is the potential of the CA then we have something of real interest at hand. Something reasonably radical, in fact. This is not a return from the normative shopping mall with a bag full of new normative ideas ('non-domination'!) which come to the normative rescue of what we know as labour law.[21] Rather, it is a way of reconceiving labour law.

If this is possible we will be able to say: yes, our legal way of thinking about labour law was contract, and then the various procedural and substantive alterations, glosses, removals, replacements of the general rules of contract both procedural and substantive, etc. But now contract as a legal scaffold has dropped away, along with our standard objections to it, as our basic legal understanding—our constituting narrative—of our labour law. All of that will become like a ladder we can throw away having climbed up it.[22] We will be able to see a new set of reasons for what we have been doing in labour law. A new structure, pattern, frame which opens up much that we were blocking ourselves from doing. A new whole over which light dawns. With a new and broader scope adequate to the work realities we see as we look out our windows today.[23]

The task of our normative ideas will not simply be to 'explain and justify the substantial exclusion of the general law of contract'.[24] The task will be larger and more interesting than that. We will no longer start or end with contract. Contract is one of many ways that work can be performed. And while there are many forms

[20] Although Deakin is much closer to understanding the nature of the project at hand—what he calls 'framing' or understanding in the best way possible, what labour law is.

[21] Say, Philip Pettit's ideas regarding non-domination. See, for example, the discussion of these ideas in David Cabrelli, Rebecca Zahn, 'Theories of Domination and Labour Law: An Alternative Conception for Intervention?' (2017) 33 *International Journal of Comparative Labour Law and Industrial Relations* 339, 339–64.

[22] See proposition number 6.54 of Wittgenstein's *Tractatus Logico-Philosophicus*.

[23] Including but not limited to contractual regulation.

[24] Collins, 'What Can Sen's Capability Approach Offer to Labour Law?' (n 18).

of work contracts, those are also now legal details. Furthermore, the incentives to use one or another form of contract will be substantially altered on another understanding of our labour law. So, for example, our current legal solutions to massive 'mischaracterization' of employees as independent contractors, or simply 'not employees', will begin to look like bloodletting as a surgical cure—a useless or even harmful response to a problem badly theorized.[25]

But, it will be rightly objected, how can we jettison the legal scaffold of contract? Law is inherently relational.[26] It's about the rights and duties of each of us to each other. And the rule of law demands that these be knowable, certain, etc. A part of labour law's problem with its current account of itself is that it has insisted that the relationship which counts is a contractual one—and a contractual one of a certain sort.

But what if our problem were deeper—with our insistence upon a contractual relationship and of a certain sort as a necessary ingredient in all labour law cases? In many cases there will be a contract—and that is one sort of relationship. And in the modern world we may be able to think rationally about all sorts of new work arrangements by expanding our relevant contractual category when smart to do so. But there are many aspects of the modern world where this is not an available move. So, to take a very real example, we simply must take note of Supriya Routh's reminders about the informal economy.[27] Or, again, consider the problems coming to grips with the labour law problems generated by commodity or supply or production chains. Or franchising arrangements. We can all construct the facts of a typical case involving a franchisor–franchisee–employee. Sometimes we need to, and do, impose responsibility on the franchisor for violations of employees' labour rights committed by the franchisee[28] even though—and this is largely the labour law point of franchising—there is no contract between the franchisor and the employee of the franchisee.[29] The legal solution required, and at hand, is a simple one. We have to recognize the limitations of the law of contract in a more fundamental way. Not by tinkering with it and curing its defects, but forgetting about it as our required legal grammar. The Supreme Court of Canada got this right at least once in a remarkable case of sexual harassment at work.[30] In finding an employer responsible for the acts of a supervisor in harassing a fellow employee the Court rejected all private law explanations as unnecessary and unhelpful. Liability (and the legal relation between

---

[25] Many leading scholars have spent a lot of time developing useful ways of expanding the categories of contract to meet new working arrangements. The classic is Harry W Arthurs, 'The Dependent Contractor: A Study of the Legal Problems of Countervailing Power' (1965) 16 *University of Toronto Law Journal* 89. The idea is that after these alterations to our idea of what may count as the right sort of contract we can then bring the relevant statutory or common law rules to bear and do their work.

[26] Ernest Weinrib, *The Idea of Private Law* (Harvard University Press, 1995).

[27] Supriya Routh, 'The Need to Become Fashionable', Chapter 5 in this volume; also see Supriya Routh, *Enhancing Capabilities through Labour Law: Informal Workers in India* (Routledge, 2014).

[28] See cases discussed in Langille, 'Human Freedom' (n 10).

[29] Langille, 'Human Freedom' (n 10).

[30] *Robichaud v Canada (Treasury Board)* [1987] 2 SCR 84. See the discussion in Langille, 'Human Freedom' (n 10).

plaintiff and defendant) was 'purely statutory'.[31] A labour law untethered to contract was required. And found to exist.

So, if we take on board the idea of the CA providing a way of understanding labour law—that is, of providing an answer to the question 'what is labour law?' (and not simply, 'we know what labour law is, what could possibly justify that?')—we arrive at point in our thinking where we need both a new narrative and a new grammar. And my proposal is that we can now shed the traditional accounts of both; we can move beyond contract and beyond our traditional normative problems with contract (the position so well articulated by Hugh Collins). At the core of the empirical world is the idea of work, or productive activity, and the idea of contractual relationship, and of a certain sort, is dropped as a threshold issue. We are pragmatic and rational in seeking where to place incentives and liability to deliver, effectively, capabilities for decent work. This way of thinking now occupies the territory once dominated by increasingly frustrating discussions of who is an employee or employer. The idea of inequality of bargaining power cannot be the necessary or foundational building block of our thinking, and our problem is not responding to simply that problem. We need something larger in normative scope to cover a larger empirical terrain, one no longer tethered to, or 'captureable' by, the traditional or expended concepts of employer, employee, etc. What sort of normative idea could be adequate to such an idea of labour law?

First, the normative focus would, obviously, have to be broader that the one labour law has been familiar with. It will probably be the sort of normative idea which can be seen as underwriting other important aspects of our life and other legal subject matters but will be part of our account of this particular area, that is, labour law. The idea will have to be capacious enough to comprehend the many elements of labor law we know—freedom of association, minimal terms, health and safety, non-discrimination, anti-harassment laws, and so on. That is, it will have to be able to address at least most of the issues addressed by our current conception of labour law's normative point. But it will also offer a better account, and cover more ground.

This is the potential of the CA.

## III. Pushback: the CA is too Narrow, or too Broad for Labour Lawyers

This way of thinking leads to two types of pushback. First, it is said that the CA is too narrow and cannot cover, let alone offer a better account of or expand, labour law's traditional terrain and concerns. Many critiques of the CA even argue that the CA is normatively opposed to labour law's fundamental project of restraining contract power. This is a point made by some critics of the CA. It is an external criticism.

Secondly, there are two claims made which argue that either the CA is too broad to be of use to labour law, or labour law too broad for the CA. These are both claims made by those who take the CA seriously. These are both internal critiques, and both

---

[31] Langille, 'Human Freedom' (n 10) para 17.

are made by Martha C. Nussbaum. The first is about the over-breadth of Sen's idea of human freedom (an argument also made by Alan Bogg, Guy Davidov, and Hugh Collins, among others). On this view, Sen's commitment to human freedom is too broad to be coherent, and thus of no use to labour lawyers. On the other hand, on the Nussbaum view, the limitations of the CA's ambition need to be kept in mind. This second point is tied to her view that the CA is 'not a theory of everything', and is best seen as being concerned with fundamental or constitutional freedoms and capabilities.[32] This view admits that the CA may be of some normative relevance to labour law.[33] But because there is much more to labour law than constitutional labour law, a broader normative account is required. And on Nussbaum's account of the CA, it is not designed to perform that task.

## A. Too narrow—critics of the CA

Over the past few years many scholars have critiqued an account of labour law which relies upon Sen's idea of Human Freedom, or the Capabilities, or the Human Development Approach. This critique may be subdivided into several main themes. But for the purpose of this chapter, we will focus on one theme in particular, advanced by those who claim that Sen's work –including my account—is individualistic, lacks any interest in associations and unions, and is resistant and even hostile to collective rights. Specifically, my account has been critiqued for neglecting to consider collective action and power relations theories and for making a flawed distinction between procedural and substantive rights.

For example, Judy Fudge criticizes Sen's ideas for emphasizing individual choice and responsibility, failing to appreciate the significance of collectivities and the relationship between individuals and collectivities, and not devoting sufficient attention to social relations of exploitation and obligations.[34] Fudge maintains that human freedom requires organized collectivities to formulate and pursue shared values and preferences in the face of powerful opposition.[35] According to Fudge, Sen fails to take into account how distribution of economic power might undermine this process and the conditions of democratic deliberation needed to determine the set of human functionings a society values.[36] Similarly, Adrian Smith argues that Sen fails to consider the effects of capitalist power over labour relations as an affront to freedom. Consequently, Sen's account fails to consider the centrality of market dependence ('the compulsion used to ensure that … people secure subsistence or

---

[32] Martha C Nussbaum, 'Labor Law and the Capabilities Approach', Chapter 3 in this volume.

[33] Alan Bogg, 'The Constitution of Capabilities: The Case of Freedom of Association', Chapter 12 in this volume.

[34] Judy Fudge, 'Labour as a "Fictive Commodity": Radically Reconceptualizing Labour Law' in Guy Davidov and Brian Langille (eds), *The Idea of Labour Law* (Oxford University Press, 2011) 120 at 128–9, 133. See also Simon Deakin, 'Social Rights in a Globalized Economy' in Philip Alston (ed), *Labour Rights as Human Rights* (Oxford University Press, 2005) 25, 59–60.

[35] Fudge, 'Labour as a "Fictive Commodity" ' (n 34) 133–4.

[36] Fudge, 'Labour as a "Fictive Commodity" ' (n 34) 134; Judy Fudge, 'The New Discourse of Labour Rights: From Social to Fundamental Rights?' (2007) 29 Comparative Labor Law & Policy Journal 29, 63.

survival through market exchange'), and thus runs the risk of reproducing a set of excluded and marginalized others.[37] Marlese von Broembsen argues, too, that Sen's account is unsuitable as a constituting narrative for labour law; it is conceptualized in individual rather than collective terms, which she argues are essential to engaging with the political economy in pursuit of values and preferences that may encounter powerful opposition—especially when faced with corporate power.[38]

More specifically, Fudge describes my account as a primarily procedural characterization of fundamental labour rights resting on a 'thin' conception of capabilities.[39] Fudge takes issue with the distinction between procedural and fundamental labour rights, questioning whether so-called procedural rights of self-determination and participation can be achieved given the current distribution of rights and entitlements.[40] She also critiques the individualistic emphasis of my conception of fundamental labour rights, particularly my approach to freedom of association.[41] Even more critically, Supriya Routh accuses me of a misleading interpretation, and oversimplification, of Sen's account. He notes that a prioritization of core procedural rights over substantive standards 'misses the centrality of Sen's approach' because Sen's approach extends beyond negative civil, political, or procedural rights and gives equal weight to social and substantive rights.[42] Routh maintains that Sen's objective was to allow each society to determine the nature and extent of their freedoms through participation and deliberation processes, not to predetermine the priority of procedural or substantive rights.[43]

What are we to make of all of that? At the centre of all this seems to be a common allegation. Marlese von Broembsen and Shane Godfrey put it as follows: 'Herein lies the problem: Labour law's normative agenda has to be able to contest market power, which the capabilities approach fails to do'.[44] They later make it even clearer that

---

[37] Adrian A Smith, 'Racism and the Regulation of Migrant Labour' in Adelle Blackett and Anne Trebilcock (eds), *Research Handbook on Transnational Labour Law* (Edward Elgar Publishing, 2015) 138, 142–4.

[38] Marlese von Broembsen, 'A New 'Constituting Narrative' for Labour Law: A Critique of Development and Making a Case for Fraser's Conception of Social Justice' (June 2013) http://www.upf.edu/gredtiss/_pdf/2013-LLRNConf_VonBroembsen.pdf.

[39] Fudge, 'The New Discourse of Labour Rights' (n 36) 58.

[40] Fudge, 'The New Discourse of Labour Rights' (n 36) 60–1. See also Philip Alston, 'Facing Up to the Complexities of the ILO's Core Labour Standards Agenda' (2005) 16(3) *European Journal of International Law* 467, 477; Adelle Blackett, 'Situated Reflections on International Labour Law, Capabilities, and Decent Work: The Case of *Centre Maraîcher Eugène Guinois*' (2007) *Revue Québécoise De Droit International* 223, 227; Tonia Novitz and Colin Fenwick, 'The Application of Human Rights Discourse to Labour Relations: Translation of Theory into Practice' in Colin Fenwick and Tonia Novitz (eds), *Human Rights at Work: Perspectives on Law and Regulation* (Hart Publishing, 2010) 1, 32.

[41] Fudge, 'The New Discourse of Labour Rights' (n 36) 62–3. See also Blackett, 'Situated Reflections on International Labour Law, Capabilities, and Decent Work' (n 40) 229; and Guy Davidov, *A Purposive Approach to Labour Law* (Oxford University Press, 2016) 66. Alan Bogg develops this last point into a full critique. We will return to this later.

[42] Routh, *Enhancing Capabilities through Labour Law* (n 27) 157.

[43] Routh, *Enhancing Capabilities through Labour Law* (n 27) 157–8.

[44] Marlese von Broembsen and Shane Godfrey, 'Labour Law and Development Viewed from Below: What do Case Studies of the Clothing Sectors in South Africa and Lesotho tell us?' in Shelley Marshall and Colin Fenwick (eds), *Labour Regulation and Development: Socio-Legal Perspectives* (Edward Elgar Publishing, 2016) 127, 133.

labour law's 'axiomatic normative agenda . . . is to act as a countervailing force to the power of capital'.[45] This is a classic statement of what I am calling labour law's received wisdom—that is, its current (and in my view limited) constituting narrative. And the charge is that the CA will not carry its normative freight.

In taking this line, it seems that there are two themes. The first is that labour law's current account of itself is immutable as well as axiomatic. No new account can take its place. The second is that the CA is not up to the job of underwriting that self-understanding and is in fact either uninterested in, or a denier of, labour law's fundamental beliefs about its role in our lives.

We need to be careful about how we respond to these ideas, for they are widely shared and, as we have just seen, are at the basis of much of the resistance to the CA among thoughtful labour lawyers. But I hold that the correct way of approaching these claims is as follows. First, the ideas of Sen and Nussbaum do not challenge labour law's basic, 'axiomatic' truths. The CA is quite comfortable with confronting the world as we really do find it, unequal bargaining power and all. One might say, on the contrary, that the CA is so taken with the insight of classic labour law that it seeks to extend its reach and expand our true understanding of what labour law has put its limited finger upon. This is so because the CA is interested in the real capabilities of persons to lead lives we have reason to value, that is, real human freedom. On this view, bargaining, in a private law way, over contractual terms and conditions for the deployment of labour power is 'merely' one site, one location, one example, of a larger and more important problem. (Or, the private law of contract is merely one bad 'conversion factor', which needs to be corrected.)

But there is more. By sticking to its standard account of itself, labour law blinkers and limits us—for example, as Routh points out, by making it impossible to see the informal sector (no contract, no bargaining, no employer or employee) as part of labour law's world at all. Labour law's normative vision and empirical scope are not rejected by the CA, but expanded, reformulated, and given a solid foundation. It explains to us how and why inequality of bargaining power is a concern in light of our basic values and our true ends. So our problem is not that the CA offers us a 'radically *underspecified*' account of labour law, as Bogg may want us to think.[46] Rather, what we are really doing here is liberating labour law from a constricting and radically *over-specified* narrative. We are showing this fly the way out of this particular fly-bottle.[47] It allows us to begin the project of a more specified labour law on a sound foundation. It gets us over the hurdle we have placed in our way in the form of the received wisdom. It lets us get on with the important tasks at hand, unhindered and blinkered—for example, to a better understanding of the scope of our human rights laws.[48]

[45] von Broembsen and Godfrey, 'Labour Law and Development Viewed from Below' (n 44) 159.
[46] Alan Bogg, 'Labour Law and the Trade Unions: Autonomy and Betrayal' in Alan Bogg and others (eds), *The Autonomy of Labour law* (Hart Publishing, 2015) 73, 88–9.
[47] Ludwig Wittgenstein, *Philosophical Investigations* (4th edn, Wiley-Blackwell, 2009) 309.
[48] This is an issue addressed in Langille and Alon-Shenker, 'Law Firm Partners and the Scope of Labour Law' (n 9).

Or to improving much of our constitutional law of freedom of association.[49] It makes cases like *Robichaud*[50] understandable. And so on.

So, it seems to me that the needed responses to the two claims underlying much of the fuss about the CA are as follows. First, the CA does not reject labour law's current insights. Rather, it sees them, valid as they may be, as limited and limiting. Secondly, the CA brings the resources to the table required to escape that limited and limiting self-understanding, while not undermining or endangering labour law's valid accomplishments.

And of course we all agree that any constituting normative account of labour law cannot overlook issues of distribution of economic and political power. That would miss a rather large point which has been basic to labour law's self-understanding for a long while. And our point is not to deny this truth but to see it as part of a larger picture which has the advantage of explaining why this basic truth about distribution of power is of concern to us. Similarly, we do not deny that freedom of association and collective bargaining are fundamental facets of any labour relations system and of any labour law theory. To the contrary, we believe the CA can help us explain, in a more profound way, why this is so.

It is evident to me that the CA has been improperly understood and mischaracterized as individualistic. However, there is no necessary alignment between the CA and anti-collectivism. As Ingrid Robeyns explains, the CA may be concerned with normative individualism (which 'postulates that individuals, and only individuals are the units of ultimate moral concern') and therefore 'when evaluating different states of social affairs, we are only interested in the (direct and indirect) effects of those states on individuals'.[51] But, as Robeyns rightly notes, 'a commitment to normative individualism is not incompatible with an ontology that recognizes the connections between people, their social relations, and their social embedment'.[52] Indeed, it is hard 'to see how the CA can be understood to be methodologically or ontologically individualistic, especially since Sen himself analysed some processes that are profoundly collective ... [and] acknowledged persons as social embedded'.[53] Robeyns then cites[54] Sen's joint work with Dreze to prove this point:

The [capability] approach used in this study is much concerned with the opportunities that people have to improve the quality of their lives. It is essentially a 'people-centered' approach, which puts human agency (rather than organizations such as markets or governments) at the centre of the stage. The crucial role of social opportunities is to expand the realm of human agency and freedom, both as an end in itself and as a means of further expansion of freedom. The word 'social' in the expression 'social opportunity' ... is a useful reminder not to view individuals and their opportunities in isolated terms. The options that a person has depend greatly *on relations with others and on what the state and other institutions do*. We shall be

[49] See Alan Bogg, 'The Constitution of Capabilities: The Case of Freedom of Association', Chapter 12 in this volume.
[50] *Robichaud* (n 30).
[51] Ingrid Robeyns, *Wellbeing, Freedom and Social Justice: The Capability Approach Re-Examined* (OpenBook Publishers, 2017) 184.
[52] Robeyns, *Wellbeing, Freedom and Social Justice* (n 51) 184.
[53] Robeyns, *Wellbeing, Freedom and Social Justice* (n 51) 185.
[54] Robeyns, *Wellbeing, Freedom and Social Justice* (n 51) 185.

particularly concerned with those opportunities that are strongly influenced by social circumstances and public policy.[55]

Robeyns also argues that the CA does consider social and power relations and the
constraints and opportunities of societal structures and institutions on individuals.
First, it recognizes the social and environmental factors which influence the con-
versions of commodities into functionings. Secondly, it recognizes choice, which is
required to transform capabilities into achieved functionings, and that this choice
may be influenced by societal structures and constraints.[56]

Importantly for labour lawyers, the CA emphasizes both process (procedural
rights) and opportunity (substantive rights). That is, the fact that procedural rights,
such as those expressed in the ILO's 1998 Declaration, are supported as a good idea
does not mean that there are no other good substantive ideas.[57] This is in fact, as has
been pointed out, fundamental to the structure of labour law—it has procedural and
substantive (outcome) concerns. This is what any constituting narrative must make
sense of. And these procedural rights (e.g. freedom of association and the procedural protections labour law accords to the processes of unionization and collective
bargaining) are intrinsically valuable as 'an exercise in self-government' and instrumentally valuable in securing favourable substantively decent working conditions
(which in turn will likely advance freedoms in other areas).[58]

## B. Too narrow—defenders of the CA

One of the well discussed differences between Sen and Nussbaum is that Nussbaum
believes that in order for the CA to move beyond a restatement of what counts when
it comes to assessing how things are going—that is to say the 'what to measure'
issue vital to debates in development economics—to a normative theory of what
we ought to do, one needs to articulate a list of central capabilities. Nussbaum in-
vokes the idea of 'dignity' to generate her list of ten central capabilities (ten CCs).[59]
On her view, without such a list, Sen is left with the dubious project of promoting
freedom as an undifferentiated good and not being able to tell which freedoms are
the important ones. But we need to narrow our focus. The list of ten CCs enables
her, she says, to embark on the development of a direct link between the capabilities
approach and law, and in particular a way of understanding constitutional entitlements. This is a move Sen does not attempt. So we are faced with a vital question: is

---

[55] Jean Dreze and Amartya Sen, *India: Development and Participation* (Oxford University Press, 2002), 6.

[56] Robeyns, *Wellbeing, Freedom and Social Justice* (n 51) 186–94.

[57] See Philip Alston, '"Core Labour Standards" and the Transformation of the International Labour Rights Regime' (2004) 15(3) *European Journal of International Law* 457. See contra Philip Alston, Brian Langille, 'Core Labour Rights: The True Story (Reply to Alston)' (2005) 16(3) *European Journal of International Law* 439.

[58] See Paul C Weiler, *Reconcilable Differences: New Directions in Canadian Labour Law* (Carswell, 1980) 33.

[59] Martha C Nussbaum, *Creating Capabilities: The Human Development Approach* (Harvard University Press, 2011) 17 ff and 70 ff.

Nussbaum correct to say that one needs to narrow down to a list of (ten, or any number) capabilities we are to view as central, and that without that list we are left adrift with an open-ended commitment to freedoms no matter how trivial? This is an important question for labour law because if Nussbaum is right then the CA cannot be a theory of labour law, but only bits of it—the fundamental, ie constitutional bits. These are no doubt fundamental bits—certainly in Canada where the constitutionalization of labour law reaches to collective bargaining and the right to strike.[60] But there is much more to labour law on which her view of the CA would remain normatively silent.

It is very unclear to me that Sen is too hopelessly broad to be of interest to labour lawyers. One might say, to the contrary, that labour law's existence and content are better viewed as credible evidence that his approach is manageable and capable of giving guidance on the issue of when, and how, we know that real substantive freedom is at stake. And it should be noted that Nussbaum's invocation of the idea of dignity to sort out which CCs are vital and make it to the list (leading to constitutional conclusions as well) has a particular structure. The idea of dignity becomes a litmus test for the identification of CCs. On Nussbaum's account, this provides a normative program for governments, and indeed a way of understanding entrenched constitutional rights. The test is whether a particular capability is vital to 'a life that is worthy of human dignity', which we all possess. The focus is thus upon 'the protection of areas of freedom so central that their removal makes a life not worthy of human dignity'.[61]

And is Sen's formulation so different and radically open-ended in the way Nussbaum suggests? Sen does not speak of human freedom in the abstract. Rather, his own formulation of his central concern is not simply human freedom but 'ability—the substantive freedom—of people to lead the lives they have reason to value'.[62] This important qualification of freedom can be seen as clearly aimed at performing at least a part of the work which Nussbaum says needs to be undertaken and for her is captured by the idea of a life of human dignity. But this important qualification of freedom also has an advantage which is central to the ideas of human agency and of development: what matters is not only what set of capabilities one ends up with, but how one comes to have them. This is what Sen describes as the 'process' aspect of freedom and not simply the 'opportunity aspect'.[63] This idea is central to Sen's pluralistic, democratic, and deliberative understanding of real human freedom. It is also central, for our purposes, to the real importance of basic labour rights to association and collective action. This is something labour lawyers have known for a very long time. As Paul Weiler—one of the greatest defenders of collective bargaining in North America—argued, while unions have

    [60] See Alan Bogg, 'The Constitution of Capabilities: The Case of Freedom of Association', Chapter 12 in this volume.
    [61] Nussbaum, *Creating Capabilities* (n 59) 31.
    [62] Amartya Sen, *Development as Freedom* (OUP, 1999) 17; and Amartya Sen, *The Idea of Justice* (The Belknap Press of Harvard University Press, 2009) 228.
    [63] Sen, *Development as Freedom* (n 62) 17.

economic impact as well as a 'civilizing' or a 'rule of law' impact, the true defence of collective bargaining actually comes from an intrinsic value and not those other accomplishments, valuable as they are:

[c]ollective bargaining is not simply an instrument for pursuing external ends, whether these be mundane monetary gains or the erection of a private rule of law to protect dignity of the worker in the face of managerial authority ... Rather, collective bargaining is intrinsically valuable as an experiment in self-government.[64]

At the centre of the 'human development' approach, shared by Sen and Nussbaum,[65] is the idea of focussing upon what is important—our true ends, and not just the means, or epiphenomenon. In Sen's formulation, this means focusing upon the substantive freedom to lead a life that we have reason to value. In Nussbaum's terms, it means the capability to lead a life worthy of human dignity. As noted above, Nussbaum famously lists ten central capabilities. Labour law concerns explicitly appear on Nussbaum's list at number ten under the heading 'control over one's environment', and divided into two parts, 'political' and 'material'. Nussbaum defines 'material' control over one's environment as:

Being able to hold property (both land and movable goods), and having property rights on an equal basis with others; having the right to seek employment on an equal basis with others; having the freedom from unwarranted search and seizure. In work, being able to work as a human being, exercising practical reason and entering into meaningful relationships of mutual recognition with other workers.[66]

This is an interesting formulation which tracks a number of labour law themes. Most notably, it tracks entering into employment and the conditions of employment. In labour law's standard formulation, these are articulated as subordination and submission.[67] But what is significant are the links one can easily discern between these labour capabilities and the other central capabilities—life, bodily health, bodily integrity, affiliation (including non-discrimination), and so on. This is because access to decent work is not only an important capability in itself, and a large/everyday dimension of our lives in which many capabilities are in play, but also because work is instrumental to the securing of other central capabilities (whether in formal employment or in the informal sector without an employer of any sort). It seems that decent work has some characteristics of what Wolff and De-Shalit call a 'fertile functioning'.[68] A functioning is, on the CA, what your capabilities enable you to be or do—such as working for a living. They are what happen in your life. In Wolff and De-Shalit's view, disadvantages 'cluster'. This is a result of 'corrosive disadvantages' which are disadvantages 'which cause other disadvantages'.[69]

---

[64] Weiler, *Reconcilable Differences* (n 58) 33.
[65] I use this term, as does Nussbaum (and Routh), to cover both the 'human freedom' approach of Sen and the 'capabilities approach' of Nussbaum.
[66] Nussbaum, *Creating Capabilities* (n 59) 34.
[67] Hugh Collins, 'Theories of Rights as Justifications for Labour Law' in Guy Davidov and Brian Langille (eds), *The Idea of Labour Law* (OUP, 2011) 137.
[68] Jonathan Wolff and Avner De-Shalit, *Disadvantage* (OUP, 2007) 131.
[69] Wolff and De-Shalit *Disadvantage* (n 68) 131.

A 'fertile functioning' is the mirror image—functionings which 'benefit other functionings'. And as Nussbaum points out, they are functionings which benefit other capabilities.[70]

On my view we can say: work can turn out to be either a corrosive, or a fertile, functioning. The job of labour law is to prevent the former and promote the latter.

In spite of important differences, then, there is perhaps a common structure to the basic approaches of Sen and Nussbaum. There is a resolute focus on starting with ends rather than means. The end is real human agency: our real substantive human freedom to choose a life worthy of dignity, a life we have reason to value. The shared focus is on capabilities, not what we do with them (functionings). Functionings do matter. After all, as Jerry Cohen put it, 'a person's functionings matter because they *are* his life ...'.[71] But the key to the CA is its focus on real freedom, real capability to choose a life worth living, a life worthy of human dignity. It is not simply on how things turn out for you, but how you get there. There is, as Sen points out a large difference between starving and fasting.[72] That should resonate with all labour lawyers—as it did with Paul Weiler.[73]

Nonetheless, we need to look the 'freedom is not a coherent goal' objection to Sen right in the eye. And if we do so, it blinks. The incoherency thesis is, upon reflection, very odd. The idea, as expressed by Collins, is that

the capability approach, with its strong emphasis on the goal of individual freedom for the achievement of well-being, appears to be pointing in the wrong direction. Instead of enhancing market freedoms, much of labour law consists of mandatory rights and institutions that are designed to inhibit freedom of contract out of the fear that unconstrained markets for labour often lead to social exclusion, exploitation, and the undermining of individual dignity.[74]

Davidov also criticizes the role of freedom as the justifying goal of labour law. He writes that

It is also plausible to conceive of collective labour laws as enhancing freedom because they open up possibilities for 'self-help' that are not available for a worker acting individually ... Every resource we get potentially opens up more choices and opportunities, thus enhancing our freedom, but ... [i]t is extremely difficult to justify distributional labour laws with the idea of enhancing freedom, given that this freedom (to do more with the additional resources or powers) comes at the expense of the employer's resources and power (and therefore freedom).[75]

---

[70] Nussbaum, *Creating Capabilities* (n 59) 44–5. See also Amartya Sen, 'Inequality, Unemployment and Contemporary Europe' (1997) 136 *International Labour Review* 156 for an exploration of the corrosive disadvantages of unemployment.

[71] GA Cohen, 'Amartya Sen's Unequal World' (1993) 28(40) *Economic and Political Weekly* 2156, 2156.

[72] Sen, *Development as Freedom* (n 62) 76.        [73] Weiler, *Reconcilable Differences* (n 58).

[74] See Hugh Collins, 'What Can Sen's Capability Approach Offer to Labour Law?', Chapter 1 in this volume.

[75] See Guy Davidov, 'The Capability Approach and Labour Law: Identifying the Areas of Fit', Chapter 2 in this volume.

Similarly, Nussbaum writes that Sen's goal for politics 'to promote the freedoms of persons to pursue "what they have reason to value"' is mistaken.[76] She argues that it is incoherent, since 'some freedoms limit others', and that the notion of 'reasons', in order to be able to distinguish between good and bad freedoms that individuals have 'reason to value', would be 'so normatively freighted and tendentious that [Nussbaum] can't imagine how [Sen] would do that'.[77]

If we were to take this idea seriously we would have to give up on the project of escaping the state of nature (i.e. competition between actors unconstrained by law in the exercise of their freedom to do what they choose regardless of the impact of their exercise of their freedoms upon others). But, as Bora Laskin succinctly put it,

law exists for the sake of enlarging the liberty of man, and as a consequence there must be restrictions on the liberty of man; based on this premise law is to regarded as primarily a system of duties, involving the proper recognition of the interests of others as a necessary limitation on self-interest.[78]

What Sen's formulation offers is, at a general level, a way of understanding why and how we might go about 'the proper recognition of the interests of others'. This is not a detailed shopping list of what labour law requires. Sen offers a compass, not a map. In Simon Deakin's words, the CA 'reframes'[79] the way we think by providing an alternative answer to our question, 'what are we trying to accomplish?' Its is an answer which must be offered at a general level. But it is not a useful criticism to say it does not tell us what exactly to do across labour law's (now broader) internal self-understanding of its reason for existence. The old normative story of redressing inequality of bargaining power was, and had to be, general as well. Working out the particulars of labour law's agenda (recognizing when and how legitimate interests 'trump' or constrain the freedom of others) will be, as it has always been, sometimes a matter of contract, sometimes collective bargaining, sometimes judicial/administrative interpretation, sometimes public agitation and legislative processes, sometimes constitutional law (to which Nussbaum would limit the CA), and so on. And on the view taken here we will do so un-hobbled by a view which was wonderfully progressive in its day, but increasingly unhelpful in the world as we now find it.

## IV. Conclusion

The potential and the achievements of the CA have been explored and deployed to assist in our thinking about many issues, some quite large. What does development

---

[76] See Martha C Nussbaum, 'Labor Law and the Capabilities Approach', Chapter 3 in this volume.

[77] Martha C Nussbaum, 'Labor Law and the Capabilities Approach', Chapter 3 in this volume.

[78] Bora Laskin, 'The Protection of Interests and the Problem of Contracting Out' (1937) 15 *Canadian Bar Review* 270. In Hohfeldian terms, a move from a world of liberty and no rights to a system of rights/duties restricting freedom in the name of expanding it—and in the name of the rule of law and eliminating 'might makes right'.

[79] See Simon Deakin, 'The Capability Approach and the Economics of Labour Law', Chapter 7 in this volume.

consist in? What should we focus upon in evaluating how people's lives are going? In addition, the CA's lens has been trained upon, as Robeyns reminds us, many public policy problems ('global public health, development ethics, environmental protection and ecological sustainability, education, technological design, welfare state policies, and many, many more'[80]). Martha Nussbaum has invoked the CA as a method or approach to constitutional interpretation. But the way the CA should enter discussions about labour law, in my view, seems to be quite unique. This is because the significance of the CA for labour law lies in its ability to illuminate—put in a new and better light—and provide a frame, a pattern, and a structure for, a legal subject matter. That is, the CA is not invoked here as a position in a political/philosophical dispute about development, nor as providing the right empirical focus for measurement of success or failure in our efforts to make the world a better place, nor indeed to provide a detailed roadmap to the understanding and solving of any concrete social problem, including labour law problems. Rather, it is important because it is an approach which can be deployed to understand, and provide a new way of seeing, a new structure, a new and liberating narrative, for a discipline, a subject—labour law.

---

[80] Robeyns, *Wellbeing, Freedom and Social Justice* (n 51).

# PART II

# THE CAPABILITY APPROACH
# TO LABOUR LAW FROM OTHER
# DISCIPLINARY PERSPECTIVES

# 7

# The Capability Approach and the Economics of Labour Law

*Simon Deakin*

## I. Introduction

This chapter addresses three questions which arise at the intersection of the capability approach and labour law. The first is: how far can we use the capability approach to understand how labour markets work? This level of analysis is essentially about modelling or conceptualizing the labour market in a way that may help us better analyse and examine it. Thus, it lies within the scope of positive or descriptive social science, and has an ontological dimension in the sense of addressing questions concerning the nature of social reality in a labour market context.

The second question is: how far can we use the capability approach to understand the nature of labour law as a mode of labour market regulation? This issue can be addressed at a number of levels. One is to look at labour law discourse and argumentation. This mode of analysis is interpretive or hermeneutic, as it is concerned with the degree to which we can discern the presence of a capability-based logic within juridical language. Another is to conduct empirical studies of the social and economic effects of labour law rules and related forms of labour regulation.

The third question is: can we use the capability approach as a normative guide to labour law reform? This is the point at which many legal discussions of the use of the capability approach begin their analysis: legal research, in contrast to most (although not all) social science analysis, generally has a policy or normative dimension, but is less frequently concerned with the empirical questions addressed by the social sciences, or with issues of ontology. It will be argued here that questions posed at this third level can be most effectively addressed after the first two questions have been explored and at least provisionally resolved.

## II. The Capability Approach and the Institutional
## Nature of the Labour Market

This section takes as its starting point the presentation of the capability approach by Amartya Sen in *Capabilities and Commodities*[1] and *Development as Freedom*.[2] Sen's analysis is located within the general framework of welfare economics. His approach is not an orthodox one but it shares certain features with a more standard neoclassical or new-institutional approach, and it is relevant to consider to what extent he occupies common ground with these more 'mainstream' paradigms and to what extent he departs from them.

Sen develops a conceptual framework consisting of (at least) three elements: functionings, capabilities, and conversion factors. A 'functioning' reflects subjective values; it is reflection of 'the things a person may value doing or being'. It could be either more or less complex depending on context: 'valued functionings may vary from elementary ones, such as being adequately nourished and being free from avoidable disease, to very complex activities or personal states, such as being able to take part in the life of the community and having self-respect'.[3]

A capability is something a person possesses when they are able to achieve, to some degree or other, one or more of their desired functionings. Thus, 'a capability is a kind of freedom: the substantive freedom to achieve certain alternative functioning combinations'.[4] Whereas a functioning, it would seem, is the result of the subjective value individuals place upon particular activities or states, a capability has an objective existence, relating to the degree to which, in a given society, individuals are able to achieve, or not, given functionings.

A conversion factor is a feature or mechanism which enables capabilities to be translated into functionings.[5] A conversion factor could be an aspect of the natural world, such as a biological process, for example the workings of the human body, or a physical feature of a city, such as a transportation system. Conversion factors can also operate in the social world and so can include routines, norms, and institutions.[6] An anti-discrimination law which reverses a social norm or practice such as the gender-based division of labour is a conversion factor in this sense.[7] Its presence, or absence, in a given society is one of the factors affecting the degree to which individuals, depending on their gender, can access paid employment or a career. The law is a conversion factor in the sense that it may enable some people to achieve their desired functionings who would otherwise be unable to do so (it may also negatively

---

[1] Amartya Sen, *Commodities and Capabilities* (North Holland, 1985).
[2] Amartya Sen, *Development as Freedom* (OUP, 1999).
[3] Sen, *Development as Freedom* (n 2) 75.    [4] Sen, *Development as Freedom* (n 2) 75.
[5] Sen, *Commodities and Capabilities* (n 1) 17.
[6] Jude Browne, Simon Deakin, and Frank Wilkinson, 'Capabilities, Social Rights and European Integration' in Robert Salais and Robert Villeneuve (eds), *Towards a European Politics of Capabilities* (CUP, 2004).
[7] Simon Deakin and Frank Wilkinson, 'Capabilities, Ordineo Spontaneo del Mercato e Diritti Sociali' (2000) 2 *Il Diritto del Mercato del Lavoro* 317.

affect the capabilities of those who were previously in a more advantaged position). The presence or absence of this conversion factor will therefore materially affect the capabilities (substantive freedoms) of individuals.

Are these concepts which together make up the capability approach— functionings, capabilities, and conversion factors—useful in understanding how labour markets operate? The ontological framework of the capability approach differs from that of neoclassical economics. Among the basic elements of neoclassical models are preferences and prices. Preferences are subjective wants which are exogenously given: *de gustibus non est disputandum.*[8] Individuals, acting rationally, rank their preferences for particular outcomes from exchange, taking account of prices. Prices result from the interaction of supply and demand and so are a collective expression of individuals' decisions on when and how to trade. In this sense they are endogenous to individuals' subjective wants. However, if the market is competitive, no single individual can affect prices. In this sense, prices have an objective existence and so operate as an exogenous constraint on action.

The market clears when supply and demand are in equilibrium. This occurs when there is sufficient competition on both the supply side and demand side of the exchange. Competition enables preferences to be optimally expressed through exchange. If there is no exogenous interference with prices, the market clears at the equilibrium price or wage. The resulting allocation is optimal in the sense of aggregating the individual wants of market participants to the greatest possible extent. Welfare is measured in terms of the collective value of individual wants.

How does the capability approach differ from this picture? While a functioning is an expression of the value an individual places on particular states or activities, and so is subjective, it is not the same as a preference. A preference is a 'taste' or 'want' which can be ranked and ordered by reference to other wants in the process of market-based exchange. A functioning does not just describe a want which is expressed through exchange. In the case of a functioning, the desired activity or state of being is more complex than the expression of a taste. A functioning is a state of being or activity which could result from one or more market-based exchanges, and also from non-market (non-priced) forms of resource allocation. Functionings are complex: they may be derived from many exchanges, which could be interrelated, or autonomous from each other, or they could be the composite result of a range of market and non-market allocations.

Is a functioning similar to a preference in that it is a subjective given, the origin of which cannot be determined, and which is taken for granted in the analysis of how the market functions? It would seem not. A functioning, Sen tells us, could be more or less complex, depending on context. In one context it could be the freedom to avoid hunger. In another it could be the freedom to have a professional career. Rather than functionings being tastes whose origin cannot be, and need not be, understood in order to appreciate the operation of the market, it would seem that

[8] George Stigler and Gary Becker, 'De Gustibus non est Disputandum' (1977) 67 *American Economic Review* 76.

the idea of a functioning involves a degree of reflexivity between an individual's preferences and the environment they are in; functionings are subjective but, in contrast to preferences, contextual. Functionings, unlike preferences but like prices, have an objective existence and can be empirically mapped.

What, then, about the idea of capability as a substantive freedom to achieve a desired functioning? It could be said that the neoclassical model of the market does need this idea, but simply assumes it; in other words, it is assumed that each individual market agent has a certain basic capability to rank outcomes from exchange according to how far they satisfy their wants, and decide to trade on that basis. In other words, the characteristic of individual behaviour which the neoclassical model describes as 'rationality' is a kind of capability.

This does not mean that we can fold the capability approach into the neoclassical model. Far from it: the capability to engage in market exchange is just one of the means by which individuals, in the capability approach, can achieve their desired functionings. There may well be others. Thus, it is the capability approach which enfolds the case of the market, rather than the other way round. The capability approach recognizes the potential for the market to operate in such a way as to enhance substantive freedoms, but it does not grant the market any kind of exclusive or prior status in this respect, when compared to other modes of resource allocation.

Do capabilities have an objective existence which makes them susceptible to empirical analysis? This is not straightforward. One way to measure capabilities is to measure outcomes. Thus, the human development index (HDI) attempts to measure the degree to which, in a given society, well-being has been achieved, using a basket of indicators.[9] It is not altogether clear that the HDI is measuring capabilities in the sense of freedoms. It seems instead that much of the time it is measuring functionings. A society with a high HDI score, insofar as that score is indicative of a high level of well-being, is one in which functionings of a certain kind are regularly achieved. We can infer the existence of capabilities from the presence of functionings by a kind of backwards induction, but outcomes may be, in a given society, an imperfect measure of freedoms. We may need other measures to obtain a clearer understanding of capabilities.

But whether the focus is on capabilities or functionings, and whatever measurement method is used, the capability approach differs from the neoclassical one in its conception of social welfare. The neoclassical approach measures social welfare by reference to the aggregation of wants. A measure such as gross domestic product (GDP),[10] which captures the extent of trade in an economy, expresses this idea in a quantitative form. In this perspective, economic growth and societal welfare are essentially the same thing.

The capability approach takes a different path: aggregate growth is not irrelevant, but nor is it the sole benchmark of whether a given society has succeeded in

---

[9]  United Nations Development Programme (UNDP), *Human Development Index* (2018) http://hdr.undp.org/en/content/human-development-index-hdi (last accessed 13 August 2018).
[10]  See Diane Coyle, *GDP: A Brief but Affectionate History* (Princeton UP, 2014).

advancing human development or well-being more generally. Whether the HDI is as good as GDP in capturing the underlying variable which it is aiming to measure is a question of statistical methodology. For present purposes, what matters most is that they are trying to measure different things.

How then does the idea of a conversion factor fit into the neoclassical approach? The neoclassical approach could be said to assume the existence of conversion factors in the same sense that it assumes the existence of capabilities. The conversion factor in question is the resource allocation function of the market itself. Through the price mechanism, the market allocates scarce means to alternate uses. In the world of pure competition, this happens automatically: individuals who try to trade at prices which do not reflect a market equilibrium are penalized. Employers offering wages below the market-clearing wage will not be able to hire workers, and workers with a too-high reservation wage will not be able to find employment. The various parties will (rationally) change their behaviour when they observe the reaction to their original choices. It is because this process is automatic that neoclassical economics pays little attention to it. The idea that the market will move spontaneously to equilibrium is a foundational axiom of the neoclassical approach: if markets are able to function unimpeded, they will necessarily arrive at optimal allocations, without the need for centralized coordination.

Through the idea of a conversion factor, the capability approach opens up a debate about how far the neoclassical model of the market conforms to observable reality. What was an assumption becomes a testable claim. The capability approach, therefore, takes on board the possibility that the market works costlessly to achieve efficient outcomes, but it does not regard this as the only case or even the most likely one in practice.

The price mechanism is therefore one particular type of conversion factor. In markets of a certain kind, those characterized by a very high degree of transactional security, the symmetrical availability of price information, the absence of collusion between actors, and the absence of endogenously occurring market imperfections such as sunk costs, externalities, and inter-dependencies—in other words, a very unusual context—the price mechanism enables individuals to maximize their wants to the greatest extent possible.

The qualifier 'to the greatest extent possible' is important: through market-based exchange, the preferences of each individual are maximized to the greatest extent possible given the preferences of other individuals. It is only welfare in the aggregate, not the well-being of a given individual, which is maximized in the perfectly competitive market. Thus, Pareto optimal distributions may be compatible with highly unequal and illiberal outcomes.[11] The market may help some individuals to realize their functionings to a greater extent than would be possible if there were no such mechanism of allocation. It may, at the same time, inhibit the capabilities of others, in particular those with resources which other market actors do not value highly.[12]

---

[11] Amartya Sen, 'The Impossibility of a Paretian Liberal' (1970) 78 *Journal of Political Economy* 152.
[12] Robert Sugden, *The Economics of Rights, Cooperation and Welfare* (Basil Blackwell, 1986).

The market, even when working 'perfectly', will not necessarily bring about equality of capabilities, understood as substantive freedoms, nor will it inevitably maximize the sum total of functionings, understood as outcomes.

But the perfect market is such a rare case in practice that consideration of its properties is, in any event, more than a little artificial. Markets are characterized in practice by externalities, information asymmetries, and transaction costs. These are the subject matter of new institutional economics, which, to this extent, marks a departure from the neoclassical approach.

The conversion factors which the market needs to function go far beyond the 'invisible hand' of spontaneous resource allocation. Non-market institutions, among them the legal system, but also conventions with their roots in shared conceptions of what amounts to a regular and hence enforceable through exchange, are a precondition of market-based ordering. Through the concept of the conversion factor, the capability approach directs our attention to the wide variety of institutions, formal and informal, which support market-based exchange. In this sense, it goes beyond the agenda of new institutional economics which, despite its focus on laws, norms, and practices, tends to see the market as the principal mode of allocation in society, against which others are to be compared and ranked, and to which they are subsidiary.[13] There is no sense, in the capability approach, of the market necessarily occupying this prior or superior position. Hence there is no need for the capability approach to proceed on the basis that the function of institutions is to try to reproduce or mimic perfect market outcomes. In this sense it differs, for example, from neoclassically orientated economic analysis of law.

In short, there are some overlaps between the ontology of the capability approach and those of neoclassical and new institutional economics. The capability approach proceeds on the basis of a duality between agency and structure, that is, between the individual market agent and the context in which market exchanges take place, which is also recognizable in the neoclassical and new-institutional paradigms (and indeed in those of other social sciences). The capability approach does not involve a full refutation of the idea of rationality, nor does it reject the empirical possibility of market equilibrium.

However, in contrast to the neoclassical and new institutional models, the capability approach sees rationality as contextual and constructed. In other words, the capability to enter into a market exchange is not a natural or spontaneous feature of the economy; it is constructed by reference to institutions and norms. The market itself is not a given or natural phenomenon, but a complex institution, or set of institutions, in its own right. The market depends on the presence of non-market institutions for its successful functioning, including the legal system. In the capability approach, the market may operate to allocate scarce means to alternate uses, but while this outcome may maximize aggregate welfare if that is understood to mean

---

[13] 'In the beginning there were markets': Oliver Williamson, *Markets and Hierarchies: Analysis and Anti-Trust Implications: A Study in the Economics of Internal Organization* (Free Press, 1975) 20. See also Geoffrey Hodgson and David Gindis, 'An Interview with Oliver Williamson' (2007) 3 *Journal of Institutional Economics* 373, 378–9.

the sum total of the subjective wants of market actors, it may not, at the same time, maximize the sum total of either functionings (outcomes related to individual well-being) or capabilities (the freedom to achieve such outcomes).

Understood in this way, the capability approach offers a set of ontological building blocks which can form the basis for a more realistic model of the labour market. This is one in which the scale and scope of market-based exchange are enhanced by the presence of institutional conversion factors of various kinds. This is a particularly helpful focus for labour lawyers interested in thinking about the various ways in which the institutions of the legal system constitute, shape, and structure markets.[14]

This is not to say that labour law only has a market-building function. Labour law aims to achieve many other goals, such as economic security, human dignity, freedom of collective action, and democratic participation. No one disputes this. The argument for labour lawyers taking the capability approach seriously is not that labour laws should be seen in exclusively economic terms. The argument, rather, concerns the relationship between labour law's market-building role and the way it articulates and seeks to operationalize values which are not intrinsically economic in nature, but go under the broad heading of social justice.

The capability approach is particularly relevant to the debate about the economic effects of labour law because it suggests that there are situations in which labour law constitutes and shapes the labour market precisely by articulating the interests and claims of workers as social rights.[15] In the capability approach, market transactions are not self-enforcing. They depend upon institutional conversion factors which facilitate market access and preserve the value which workers have in their labour power, or capacity to work. To this extent, the identification of mechanisms which enhance capabilities, in the sense of substantive freedoms to participate in labour market relations, are also those which recognize the claims of workers to access economic and social justice.

Inevitably, considerations of social justice will not always coincide with those of economic efficiency. Working out when these aspects of labour law are complements and when they involve trade-offs is a task for analysis at multiple levels: methodological, conceptual, and empirical. Conducting this project from the ontological starting point of the capability approach marks an advance compared to doing so

---

[14] For labour law analyses in this vein see Richard Mitchell (ed), *Redefining Labour Law: Perspectives on the Future of Teaching and Research* (Centre for Employment and Labour Relations Law, Melbourne, 1995); Simon Deakin and Frank Wilkinson, *The Law of the Labour Market: Industrialization, Employment, and Legal Evolution* (OUP, 2005); Chris Arup, Peter Gahan, John Howe, Richard Johnstone, Richard Mitchell, and Anthony O'Donnell (eds), *Labour Law and Labour Market Regulation* (Federation Press, 2006); Judy Fudge, 'Labour as a Fictive Commodity: Radically Reconceptualizing Labour Law' in Guy Davidov and Brian Langille (eds), *The Idea of Labour Law* (OUP, 2011); Judy Fudge, 'The Future of the Standard Employment Relationship: Labour Law, New Institutional Economics and Old Power Resource Theory' (2017) 59 *Journal of Industrial Relations* 374. For discussion of the 'law of the labour market' approach to labour law, see Ruth Dukes, *The Labour Constitution: The Enduring Idea of Labour Law* (OUP, 2014) chs 1, 5, and 8.

[15] Browne and others, 'Capabilities, Social Rights and European Integration' (n 6).

from the viewpoint of the standard neoclassical or new institutional economic analysis of law.[16]

## III. The Capability Approach and the Market-constituting Role of Labour Law

If the capability approach can help us better understand the nature of the labour market as an institution, can it also aid understanding of labour law as a mode of regulation? The issue can be addressed in two ways: through an examination of juridical discourse (exploring through hermeneutic methods the linguistic structure of legal concepts, principles, and rules) and via the empirical study of labour law systems (using statistical and other methods to estimate the effects of labour regulation).

It is not suggested that legal concepts provide a map of social reality. Thus, if we find analogues to the capability concept in legal discourse, this is not, in and of itself, an indication that capabilities exist in the social realm.[17] Legal concepts are discursive forms which lawyers use to mobilize and apply legal rules to particular fact situations. The existence of the concept of capability within legal discourse is thus a sign of its usefulness in the operationalization of rules; it is functional rather than descriptive. However, for legal rules to be operationalized, the concepts underpinning them cannot be too far out of synch with social structure. Thus, the appearance of the capability concept within juridical discourse can, at one remove, tell us something about the nature of social reality beyond the legal text.[18]

According to neoclassical law and economics, labour law rules operate in ways which are often taken to have the effect of restricting exchange and distorting prices. By inserting mandatory norms into contracts for the protection of workers against employers, labour law rules interfere with bargaining and prevent the parties from making an optimal exchange.[19] By allowing workers to organize collectively in ways which would otherwise be a breach of antitrust or competition law, labour law allows the labour market to be distorted, preventing optimal resource allocations.[20]

One answer to this line of argument is that it assumes that markets work perfectly, which is implausible. In the presence of monopsony and information asymmetry, labour law rules may function to eliminate or reduce transaction costs, and thereby

---

[16] Robert Salais, 'Libertés du travail et capacités: une perspective pour une construction Europénne?' (1999) 5 *Droit Social* 467; Alain Supiot (ed), *Au delà de l'emploi: Transformations du travail et devenir du droit du travail en Europe* (Flammarion, 1999).

[17] Simon Deakin, 'Juridical Ontology: The Evolution of Legal Form' (2015) 40 *Historical Social Research* 170.

[18] Simon Deakin and Alain Supiot (eds), *Capacitas: Contract Law and the Institutional Foundations of a Market Economy* (Hart Publishing, 2009).

[19] Richard Epstein, 'In Defense of the Contract at Will' (1984) 51 *University of Chicago Law Review* 947.

[20] Richard Epstein, 'A Common Law for Labor Relations: A Critique of New Deal Labor Legislation' (1983) 92 *Yale Law Journal* 1357; Richard Posner, 'Some Economics of Labor Law' (1984) 51 *University of Chicago Law Review* 988.

restore more efficient market outcomes. Private cost is not the same as social cost, and many labour regulations reduce social cost and so have positive aggregate welfare effects even if they add to the private costs of individual firms. The 'fallacy of composition' means that what is rational for firms collectively is not rational for each individual firm; there are incentives on the part of individual firms for regulatory avoidance. It does not follow that society will be better off, or economic growth enhanced, if the 'regulatory burden' on firms is removed.[21] The more likely consequence is a worsening of the collective action problem which is inherent in any large-number bargaining context of this kind.[22]

But while this line of argument can take us a certain way to countering the critique that 'laws created to protect workers often harm them,'[23] it does not exhaust the possible ways in which labour law can be analysed from an economic perspective. Viewing labour law's role more broadly, it is not confined to correcting market imperfections, but extends to creating the conditions under which the market operates: in this sense it has a more fundamental market-constituting role.

One of the ways in which labour law does this is to provide institutional recognition to the commodification of labour, or, more precisely, of labour power or capacity. In a capitalist economy, the commodity 'labour power' signifies the worker's capacity to work. It is labour power, and not finished labour, which is exchanged in the contract of employment. Through that arrangement, the worker is placed at the disposal of the employer for a limited time and space. The distinction between the sale of finished labour and the sale of labour power is not only foundational to the capitalist modes of production.[24] It is also foundational to the juridical discourse of labour law, as it is the basis for the distinction between the independent work contract (generally outside the scope of labour law regulation, or at its margins) and the contact of service or employment (generally inside the scope of labour law protection and in many respects its core case).[25]

In the framework of the capability approach, commodities are not self-forming, but are socially and institutionally constructed.[26] The commodity 'labour power' is formed in numerous ways, some of which find expression at the level of social norms and routines, while others find expression in the operation of the legal system and hence in juridical discourse. Labour law constructs labour capacity by identifying it as the subject matter of the exchange which is inherent in the contract of employment;[27] it protects it through rules which recognize the physical, economic, and psychological

[21] For a review of these pro-efficiency arguments for labour regulation, see Simon Deakin and Frank Wilkinson, 'Labour Law and Economic Theory: A Reappraisal' in Gerrit De Geest, Jacques Siegers, and Roger van den Bergh (eds), *Law and Economics and the Labour Market* (Edward Elgar Publishing, 1999).

[22] Alan Hyde, 'What is Labour Law?' in Guy Davidov and Brian Langille (eds), *Boundaries and Frontiers of Labour Law* (Hart Publishing, 2006).

[23] World Bank, *Doing Business 2008: Measuring Business Regulations* (World Bank, 2007) 19.

[24] Karl Marx, *Capital Volume 1* (translated by Samuel Moore and Edward Aveling, Lawrence and Wishart, 2003) ch 7.

[25] Deakin and Wilkinson, *The Law of the Labour Market* (n 14); Fudge, 'Labour as a Fictive Commodity' (n 14).

[26] Sen, *Capabilities and Commodities* (n 1).

[27] Alain Supiot, *Critique du droit du travail* (PUF, 2015, first published 1994).

interests at stake in the employment exchange;[28] and it promotes its social reproduction, a role it shares with social security law and the law of the welfare state more generally.[29]

In legal discourse, the idea of 'capacity' expresses the conditions under which the law grants market access to individuals and entities. Without legal capacity, a person cannot hold property or make contracts with legal support and underpinning. Thus, the way in which the concept of capacity is framed within legal analysis reveals one of the means by which the legal system defines the market and sets its boundaries. As the meaning of capacity has shifted over time, its evolution can be studied to reveal the way that the boundaries of the market have also changed through time.[30]

With the expansion of markets in the nineteenth century, the idea developed that legal capacity should be available to all market participants: as Savigny put it, 'every single human being—and only the single human being—enjoys capacity'.[31] This was a revolutionary sentiment as prior to that point capacity was confined to a narrow segment of society. Married women did not acquire full capacity in most Western European countries until the later decades of the nineteenth century. Even as the right to contract was being extended to all adult citizens, the second part of Savigny's precept was being undermined as business firms and other trading entities began to acquire legal personality in their own right. As Savigny recognized, this development had the effect of undermining equality of capacity, strengthening some (mostly the holders of the capital interest in the enterprise) at the expense of others.

Today, the capacity to contract is still denied to certain persons: to the young, and also those deemed, by virtue of their physical or mental condition, to be unable to form a consistent view of their own interests. The former are safeguarded against contracts which are not to their benefit on the basis that they would otherwise be liable to self-exploitation. The latter lack rationality in the economist's sense of the capacity to make choices from alternatives in a preference-consistent way. The inability to make a contract is a form of protection as well as exclusion, which cuts both ways: not just those unable to contract with the help of legal enforcement, but also those who would contract with them, are protected against fragile and unreliable transactions. Thus, the integrity of the market is also protected by the concept of capacity.[32]

It is not just the concept of capacity which sets a boundary to the market. The concept of public policy does the same when it denies enforcement to certain illegal contracts.[33] One of these is the contract for slavery. The law does not enforce an unfree labour contract. Thus, the law states a preference for the employment contract

---

[28] Guy Davidov, *A Purposive Approach to Labour Law* (OUP, 2016).
[29] Deakin and Wilkinson, *The Law of the Labour Market* (n 14).
[30] Deakin and Supiot, *Capacitas* (n 18).
[31] For discussion of Savigny's conception of capacity, see Alain Wijffels, 'Rationalisation and Derationalisation of Legal Capacity in Historical Perspective: Some General Caveats' in Deakin and Supiot, *Capacitas* (n 18).
[32] Sandrine Godelain, 'Le concept de capacité dans le droit des contrats français' in Deakin and Supiot, *Capacitas* (n 18).
[33] Simon Deakin, 'Capacitas: Contract Law, Capabilities, and the Legal Foundations of the Market' in Deakin and Supiot, *Capacitas* (n 18).

over indenture and other unfree labour forms. This is not a natural or spontaneously generated rule; prior to the eighteenth century in England, and the nineteenth century in the USA, contracts involving slavery were enforceable. Slavery was only ended by concerted political action. A political choice and a publicly instituted legal norm, not a spontaneous order as claimed by Hayek,[34] underlie the institution of 'free labour' in modern Western societies.

So there is nothing 'unnatural' about regulating the terms upon which labour power is contracted. When labour law inserts into the employment contract norms for the protection of the worker against the employer, it is not upsetting a spontaneous bargain. It is setting the conditions under which labour power is initially commodified and reproduced as a commodity. The process is more akin to establishing property rights than to undermining them.

With the advent of modern social legislation on matters such health and safety and working time in the final decades of the nineteenth century and the early decades of the twentieth, the notion of capacity was again the focus of juridical debates. Opponents of mandatory labour regulation characterized it as an illiberal reversal of the extension of capacity which had been achieved in the 'age of reason'. Those who defended it argued that laws protecting workers from the injurious effects of long hours were protecting their physical 'capabilities'. This divergence can be seen, for example, in the iconic *Lochner* decision[35] of the US Supreme Court.[36] In this challenge to working time legislation, the opponents of social reform were successful, but in the long run they lost the constitutional argument and the Supreme Court eventually validated most of the social legislation of the 'age of reform' which culminated in the New Deal of the 1930s, in the process rejecting the 'naturalistic' reasoning underlying *Lochner*.[37]

Thus, the legal system operates with an implicit ontology of the labour market. This is one in which the labour market is institutionally constituted, shaped by politics, and characterized by the exercise of power. It is also a context in which fairness norms set parameters within which exchange takes place. This is very far removed from the economic model of the market as a self-correcting spontaneous order. If we remove regulation from the picture and focused just on private law, which some suggest would be a feasible mode of governance for the labour market and one to be preferred by comparison to the current mix of judge-made law and statutes,[38] the doctrines of capacity and public policy are even then a reminder that the market is not self-constituting.

The juridical notion of capacity therefore has more than a superficial linguistic connection to the economic concept of capability. Through a consideration of capacity in its juridical context, we can come closer to an understanding of the role played by the legal system in constituting the conditions for market activity.

---

[34] Friedrich A. Hayek, *Law, Legislation and Liberty* (Routledge, 1980).
[35] *Lochner v. New York*, 198 U.S. 45 (1905).
[36] Deakin, 'Legal Foundations of the Market' (n 33).
[37] Cass Sunstein, 'Lochner's Legacy' (1987) 87 *Columbia Law Review* 873.
[38] Epstein, 'A Common Law for Labor Relations' (n 20).

To avoid any confusion on this point, it may be worth re-emphasizing that seeing labour law in these terms is not to argue that other, non-instrumentalist justifications might not be given for social rights. It is to point out that there might be less than meets the eye to the supposed 'big trade-off'[39] between equity and efficiency.

There are other ways in which it is helpful to use the capability approach to approach the issue of the economic and social effects of labour regulation. The first point to consider here is one of framing. The capability approach implies that when we are considering the effects of labour regulation, we should use a range of benchmarks when evaluating its impact, in addition to GDP and other growth-related indicators. These other benchmarks can include inequality data and the HDI,[40] as well as more conventional indicators such as GDP,[41] employment and unemployment levels, and productivity.

A second point to consider is a methodological one: the capability approach, in its emphasis on conversion factors which may include institutions, points to the importance of getting better measures of institutional variables. To that extent it reinforces the growing interest in 'leximetric' indicators of labour law and related areas of legal regulation of the economy.[42]

The relatively recent development of law-related indicators for large numbers of countries and covering extended time periods makes it possible to test, in a newly systematic way, the claim that labour laws have harmful effects on growth and on employment. This field of research is in the course of developing, but the consensus which is emerging from panel data analysis (in which the data from large numbers of countries are pooled) is that worker-protective labour laws tend to be correlated with reduced inequality, measured by labour's share of national income, so that while the labour share has mostly been falling around the world since the start of the 1990s, labour law slows the rate of decline.[43] For present purposes, it is relevant to note that higher worker protection is mostly correlated with higher HDI scores.[44] In terms of the effects of labour laws on more conventional economic indicators, the impact of increases in employment protection on employment and productivity is mostly positive, although the effects are small.[45]

What these findings imply is that if we adopt the ontological and methodological perspective implied by the capability approach, with its focus on institutional conversion factors, and take into account a wide range of outcome variables which make

---

[39] Arthur Okun, *Equality and Efficiency: The Big Tradeoff* (Brookings Institution, 1975).

[40] UNDP, 'Human Development Index' (n 9).          [41] Coyle, 'GDP' (n 10).

[42] Zoe Adams, Parisa Bastani, Louise Bishop, and Simon Deakin, 'The CBR-LRI Dataset: Methods, Properties and Potential of Leximetric Coding of Labour Laws' (2017) 33 *International Journal of Comparative Labour Law and Industrial Relations* 59.

[43] Zoe Adams, Louise Bishop, Simon Deakin, Colin Fenwick, Sara Martinsson Garzelli, and Giudi Rusconi, 'The Economic Significance of Laws Relating to Employment Protection and Different Forms of Employment: Analysis of a Panel of 117 Countries, 1990-2013' forthcoming, *International Labour Review*.

[44] This may not be true of strike laws. See Simon Deakin, Colin Fenwick, and Prabirjit Sarkar, 'Labour Law and Inclusive Development: The Economic Effects of Industrial Relations Laws in Middle Income Countries' in Michèle Schmiegelow and Henrik Schmiegelow (eds), *Institutional Competition between Common Law and Civil Law* (Springer, 2014).

[45] Deakin, Fenwick, and Sarkar, 'Labour Law and Inclusive Development' (n 44).

reference to equality and developmental indicators, we will see a more nuanced picture of the social and economic effects of labour laws than the one derived from the neoclassical economic approach. Thus, the capability approach has the potential to reframe the debate about the relationship between labour law and economic development in a way that is empirically revealing.

## IV. The Capability Approach and the Developmental Role of Labour Law

We have much more information today on the relationship between law and economic development than we did only a decade or so ago. The amount of data available on the workings of legal systems and related institutions has increased along with the emergence of new methodologies for tracking and quantifying institutional change. We also have the benefit of new techniques for analysing very large and complex data sources. This new availability of data poses challenges as well as opportunities. The variability of results arrived at through 'leximetric' methods of different kinds suggests that more work needs to be done to ensure that data are being coded consistently and transparently.[46]

But even with these caveats, we can say that thanks to the emergence of statistical methods for coding labour law data in a consistent way over long periods of time and for large numbers of countries, we are in a better position now than in the past to make empirical assessments of the long-run relationship between labour law and development. At a descriptive level, we know that labour laws across the world have gradually been becoming more protective over time.[47] Developed countries, on average, have a higher level of protection than developing ones. Systems which experience deregulation in one period (most of Latin America in the 1970s, or the UK in the 1980s, for example) tend to see this trend reversed in a following period. The recent trend towards deregulation in parts of the global north, which has been driven by austerity policies since the onset of the global financial crisis in 2008, has led to a relatively small push-back in the level of protection when compared to the advances achieved since the 1970s. The largest gains in worker protection in the last decade have been in middle-income countries, including China, South Africa, and most of Latin America. The United States, while the focus of some of the most influential and highly cited work in the social sciences on the economics of labour regulation, is, in terms of its regulatory system, an outlier even compared to other common law systems such as the UK or Canada. What is happening in the United States to labour regulation is not necessarily going to be a good guide to experience elsewhere.

Seen in the wider context of what is known about developmental outcomes, we can make some assessment of the long-run contribution of worker-protective labour law to economic development and growth. In general (there are exceptions,

[46] Adams and others, 'Methods, Properties and Potential' (n 41).
[47] Adams and others, 'Methods, Properties and Potential' (n 41).

most notably the USA), the higher the level of development in a given country, the more likely it is to have strong labour law protections, as well as more extensive social security provision, effective state capacity, and a functioning rule of law. Middle income countries aiming to transition to a higher and more stable level of development are not mostly trying to do so by pushing back on worker protection (again, there are exceptions, with India, for example, attempting a different route from China or South Africa). In the global north, the picture is similar: deregulation is not, on the whole, correlated with higher growth or with better outcomes on other relevant indicators such as health and education.[48]

When we descend from the level of aggregated analysis using pooled, cross-national data, to look instead at the policies adopted in individual countries and their outcomes, we see a varied picture which statistical aggregates tend to mask. There are some high profile cases of countries and regions in which deregulatory strategies have been chosen as the pathway to growth. This type of strategy generally involves carving out special economic zone (SEZ) status for fast-growing regions. In SEZs, firms benefit from a relaxation of worker protections along with fiscal subsidies and exemptions from planning laws. This is the model followed in the Indian state of Gujarat since the 1990s. With the elevation of Gujarat's former premier Narendra Modi to the position of prime minister of India in 2014, Gujarat's growth model has become the focus of national level economic policy, and a broadly deregulatory agenda for labour law has been proposed. However, it has yet to lead to significant changes in the national legal framework for labour and employment relations, and there is downside to the Gujarat model, with high economic growth on the one hand but a weak performance on other social and economic indicators including literacy and mortality rates.[49]

In contrast to the Gujarat model is the approach taken in the Pearl River Delta region of southern China. Although there are SEZs in Guangdong province, the best known being in the city of Shenzhen, they do not confer exemption from national labour laws, but focus on fiscal and planning regulations. Unlike India, which has a federal system of labour law regulation (enabling Gujarat to opt out of more stringent national standards for dismissal protection), China's labour laws apply across the country. The local state in China, at city and provincial level, has the capacity to enforce labour standards and has adopted a strategic approach to doing so in the coastal regions where industry is most developed, focusing on larger multinationals and locally owned firms.[50] From 2007, China's national labour laws were significantly strengthened in the areas of basic labour standards (wages and working time), employment protection, regulation of temporary agency work, and the right to a written contract of employment. Parallel reforms expanded the labour arbitration system to provide for low-cost access to dispute resolution. There is evidence

[48] See generally Steven K Vogel, *Marketcraft: How Governments Make Markets Work* (OUP, 2018).
[49] Simon Deakin and Antara Haldar, 'How Should India Reform its Labour Laws?' (2015) 50 *Economic and Political Weekly* 48.
[50] Simon Deakin, Shelley Marshall, and Sanjay Pinto, 'Labour Laws, Informality, and Development: Comparing India and China' forthcoming in Diamond Ashiagbor (ed), *Reimagining Labour Law for Development: Informal Work in the Global North and Global South* (Hart Publishing, 2019).

of a growing formalization of employment relations in Guangdong, with surveys reporting that a majority of workers now received written employment contracts despite employment being highly precarious in many sectors, and widespread use of labour arbitration to resolve disputes.[51]

Thus, developing countries have choices when framing their developmental strategies. The point about the contrast between Gujarat and Guangdong is not that one is necessarily superior to the other. In Guangdong there is a high degree of precarious work together with labour intensification in many of the factories, including those run by multi-nationals. In Gujarat, as elsewhere in India, there are formal legal guarantees for freedom of association, which are lacking in China, although enforcement of collective labour rights in India is incomplete at best.[52] The point of the comparison, however, is that the Gujarat model is not the only one available. The Guangdong experience suggests that worker-protective labour law can form part of a strategy for development based on social and economic upgrading.

Empirical evidence of this kind is relevant for normative labour law analysis, since it suggests that serious reappraisal is needed of the claim that, in developing country contexts, the application of global labour standards needs to be tailored to take into account potentially negative effects of labour law rules on economic growth. While labour standards do need to take into account local conditions and the particular trajectories of countries and regions, the idea that labour law in general harms development would seem to be mistaken. On the contrary, labour law can operate as a developmental institution, addressing labour market risks and promoting social cohesion as part of the wider process of economic transition currently being experienced, in particular, by middle-income countries.[53]

## V.  Conclusion

This chapter has considered issues arising at the intersection of the capability approach and the economic analysis of labour law. It has sought to show that the concept of capability can be used to reframe understandings of the labour market and of the way labour law operates in relation to it. It can also help us get better measurements of institutional phenomena and of human well-being. By these means it can help us find a way of out of the narrow constraints of the neoclassical economic analysis of labour law.

---

[51] Enying Zheng and Simon Deakin, 'Pricing Labour Capacity: the Unexpected Effects of Formalising Labour Contracts in China' CBR Working Paper No 479 (2016) https://www.cbr.cam.ac.uk/publications/working-papers/2016/ (last accessed 13 August 2018).

[52] Richard Mitchell, Petra Mahy, and Peter Gahan, 'The Evolution of Labour Law in India: An Overview and Commentary on Regulatory Objectives and Development' (2014) 1 *Asian Journal of Law and Society* 413.

[53] Shelley Marshall and Colin Fenwick, 'Labour Law and Development: Characteristics and Challenges' in Shelley Marshall and Colin Fenwick (eds), *Labour Regulation and Development: Socio-Legal Perspectives* (Edward Elgar Publishing, 2016).

The chapter has also argued that capability-based analysis should therefore be understood as offering a methodological *approach* rather than a free-standing *theory* of law or the economy. If we are to engage in the process of making proposals for labour law reform, we need to supplement the capability approach with other theories, methods, and techniques, which will help us to predict the likely effects of particular reforms, and to evaluate them on that basis.

It is doubtful that the capability approach can be used to generate a normative programme for labour law reform in isolation from other theories and methods. Rather, the capability approach offers a series of ontological and methodological moves, which can be used to reframe the debate over the economic effects of worker-protective labour laws. The resulting project, which is partly theoretical but must, in the final analysis, also be empirical in orientation, points the way to a conception of labour law as a 'developmental' institution, that is, one promoting sustainable economic and social development.

# 8

# Labor History and the Clash of Capabilities

*Laura Weinrib*

This chapter argues that the congruity between the capabilities approach and the American labor movement's ambitions and tactics has shifted over time. In the early twentieth century, labor activists embraced coercion, rejected minimalism, and disavowed state intervention. Over the course of the twentieth century, however, the American administrative state actively structured the bargaining relationship between unions and employers, and unions surrendered much of their coercive power. In the new legal landscape, it may be plausible to ground labor law in the Capabilities Approach (CA), which combines an emphasis on full equality of freedom of speech and association with support for a strong social safety net. This compatibility, however, is premised on the labor movement's relinquishment of its most effective historical weapons. That is, the same modifications that have accommodated labor law to the capabilities approach have also eroded labor's strength and accelerated its decline.

## I. Introduction

"Political liberalism is dead," declared Roger Baldwin, a staunch labor advocate and a co-founder of the American Civil Liberties Union (ACLU), in 1925: "The only power that works is class power."[1] Baldwin's was a curious assessment, coming from

---

[1] "Where are the Pre-War Radicals," *Survey*, February 1, 1926, p. 560 (entry by Roger Baldwin). Baldwin, of course, did not use the term "political liberalism" in the technical sense specified by John Rawls in his book of that title (and subsequently adopted by Martha C. Nussbaum in her discussion of the CA), where he identifies the conditions for securing an overlapping consensus within a "(liberal) constitutional democratic regime" encompassing "free and equal citizens profoundly divided by reasonable religious, philosophical, and moral doctrines." John Rawls, *Political Liberalism* (Columbia University Press, 1993), xxv, xxxix. Nonetheless, Baldwin's Marxian class analysis, which explicitly rejects democratic institutions in favor of naked class organization, is incompatible with political liberalism in its Rawlsian usage, as well. See Baldwin, ibid., 560 ("The world has lost faith in parliaments; political democracy is recognized only as a form under which capitalism controls society, just as feudalism controlled it through kings."). For an argument that "if a Marxist analysis of social conflict is right in certain respects, a commitment to accept advances toward the difference principle in societies that do not embody it would not emerge from the original position," see Richard Miller, "Rawls and Marxism," *Philosophy & Public Affairs* 3 (1974): 167–91, 167.

The Capability Approach to Labour Law. Edited by Brian Langille. Chapter 8 © Laura Weinrib 2019. Published 2019 by Oxford University Press.

the helm of an organization that helped to craft America's distinctive form of constitutional liberalism, with its commitments to state-centered social welfare on the one hand and judicial enforcement of free speech and minority rights on the other. Indeed, on the eve of resigning his directorship of the ACLU a quarter-century later, Baldwin expressed satisfaction that "political liberalism ... [was] stronger than ever."[2]

If Baldwin's 1925 pronouncement was premature, it also captured something fundamental about the orientation of the American labor movement and its allies toward the principles of liberalism in the decades before the World War II.[3] In the early twentieth century, labor advocates forthrightly rejected not only the label of liberalism, but also some of its basic tenets, including several that are central to the CA as articulated by Martha C. Nussbaum.[4] As they were initially conceived, the tools of concerted activity were designed to entrench rather than remediate the antagonist relationship between labor and capital, in service of robust redistributive goals. Moreover, the most influential theories of labor power before the New Deal disavowed state action on behalf of workers. Above all, many early labor advocates endorsed an exercise of coercion incompatible with the valorization of individual choice.

These historical commitments have important implications with respect to the candidacy of the CA for what Brian Langille has described as labor's "constituting narrative."[5] In elaborating them, this chapter seeks to redress the relative inattention

---

[2] ACLU press release (Dec. 14, 1949) in American Civil Liberties Union Records, The Roger Baldwin Years, 1917–1950, Seeley G. Mudd Manuscript Library, Public Policy Papers, Princeton University, Princeton, NJ (ACLU Papers), vol. 146.

[3] The United States experience is, of course, hardly generalizable. On the contrary, I hope to emphasize the contingency of the modern regime. Moreover, I accept Simon Deakin's assessment that the United States regulatory system is "an outlier even compared to other common law systems," and that "what is happening in the United States to labour regulation is not necessarily going to be a good guide to experience elsewhere." Simon Deakin, "The Capability Approach and the Economics of Labour Law," Chapter 7 in this volume at 155. Acknowledging these caveats, I nonetheless believe that the U.S. example is instructive, insofar as it lays bare an unresolved tension at the heart of labor law as it historically was conceived.

[4] For Nussbaum's views, see Martha C. Nussbaum, *Creating Capabilities: The Human Development Approach* (Harvard University Press, 2012); Martha C. Nussbaum, *Women and Human Development: The Capabilities Approach* (Cambridge University Press, 2000); and Martha C. Nussbaum, *Frontiers of Justice: Disability, Nationality, Species Membership* (Harvard University Press, 2006). Some of the disagreement about the relevance of the CA to labor law is driven by competing accounts of the CA, a problem that many of the papers in this volume, including Nussbaum's, grapple with explicitly. Alan Bogg, for example, rejects the commitment to maximizing freedom espoused by Amartya Sen and embraced by Langille, but finds promise in the constitutionalization of central capabilities preferred by Nussbaum, as long as functionings are given sufficient weight. Alan Bogg, "The Constitution of Capabilities: The Case of Freedom of Association," Chapter 12 in this volume. Similarly, Guy Davidov distinguishes between Sen's "substantive freedom strand" and Nussbaum's "specific capabilities strand" and concludes that both are useful as supplementary justifications for some labor laws, although even the latter is unlikely to compel particular solutions as a matter of constitutional law. Guy Davidov, "The Capability Approach and Labour Law: Identifying the Areas of Fit," Chapter 2 in this volume at 44. This chapter focuses on Nussbaum's account, which is specified with precision and allows for careful engagement.

[5] Brian Langille, "Labour Law's Back Pages," in Guy Davidov & Brian Langille (eds.), *Boundaries and Frontiers of Labor* (Hart Publishing, 2016), 13–36, 13.

in the existing literature on labor law and the CA to the strained relationship between unions and individual rights, an issue that dominates both public and scholarly debate about labor law in the United States but appears to be more muted elsewhere.[6] On the conventional American understanding, efforts to enhance the decisional autonomy of individual workers are often at odds with measures to improve their collective welfare.[7] To be sure, labor lawyers have argued poignantly that "the well-being of the individual and the well-being of the group are not experienced as antagonistic."[8] It is nonetheless a core premise of American labor law that "the concepts of individual action for personal gain and 'concerted activity' are intuitively incompatible," as Justice O'Connor famously expressed the point.[9] That is, it is an assumption of labor law theory and doctrine that members of a union subordinate their own particular interests to the interests of the group—or, framed more antagonistically, that the objectives of the union overbear the interests of its individual members. To the extent this is true, it poses a significant challenge to any attempt to ground labor law in the CA, which insists that "[e]ach person is an end, and none a mere tool of the ends of others."[10]

The flip side of this intervention is to recognize—against a backdrop of the "centrality of choice in the whole notion of capability as freedom"[11]—that the language of choice, no less than freedom, has long been deployed by anti-union advocates in an effort to undermine labor's collective power. In the early twentieth century, employers reluctantly conceded the right of workers to organize into unions and to engage in so-called "simple strikes," even as they fiercely opposed labor's most potent weapons, including the closed shop, secondary boycotts, and mass picketing. Their open-shop campaigns purported to respect the autonomy of antiunion employees. It is tempting to dismiss this framing as disingenuous and detached from material reality, a species of the *Lochner*-era thinking that Nussbaum has described as "lofty formalism."[12] Yet in a real sense, union tactics depended for their success on constraining workers' choices. In its celebratory strain, unionism is about preserving employee choice and enhancing employee voice: it is a voluntary and

---

[6] American labor law has almost as much to say about conflicts among workers—including majority rule and exclusivity, the illegitimacy of wildcat strikes and minority unions, and the duty of fair representation—as it does about disputes between unions and employers. See, for example, Kenneth Dau-Schmidt et al. (eds.), *Labor Law in the Contemporary Workplace* (2nd ed. West Academic Publishing, 2014).

[7] See Reuel E. Schiller, "From Group Rights to Individual Liberties: Post-War Labor Law, Liberalism, and the Waning of Union Strength," *Berkeley Journal of Employment and Labor Law* 20 (1999): 1–73. This chapter focuses primarily on labor law, as opposed to employment law. Insofar as employment law vindicates individual rights, it is generally regarded as orthogonal to or even inconsistent with the motivating vision of labor law, namely, to enhance collective power.

[8] Staughton Lynd, "Communal Rights," *Texas Law Review* 62 (1984): 1417–41, 1426.

[9] *NLRB v. City Disposal Systems, Inc.*, 465 U.S. 822, 842 (1984) (O'Connor, J., dissenting).

[10] Martha C. Nussbaum, "Labor Law and the Capabilities Approach," Chapter 3 in this volume at 76. It is significant that unions are often analogized to the family, an institution that the CA regards with ambivalence because of its tendency to treat some members as means rather than ends. See, for example, Staughton Lynd, "Communal Rights" (n. 8) 1427 (casting unions in terms of "families-at-work").

[11] Nussbaum, *Creating Capabilities* (n. 4) 39.

[12] Martha C. Nussbaum, "Foreword: Constitutions and Capabilities: "Perception" Against Lofty Formalism," *Harvard Law Review* 121 (2007): 4–97.

collaborative effort to resist domination by employers. The reality of labor activism has often deviated sharply from this anodyne picture. In practice, unions have regularly called upon their members to foreclose choices that the CA would characterize as capability-enhancing.[13]

In this chapter, I suggest that while the CA may well justify many of labor law's current commitments, it is ill suited to the labor movement's most ambitious past aspirations, many of which contemporary labor law has either contained or discarded. Over the course of the twentieth century, as the administrative state actively structured the bargaining relationship between unions and employers, unions steadily surrendered their coercive power. Today an employee in a unionized workplace may choose to cross a picket line and, in many states, decline to contribute to union expenses. In this new legal landscape, it may be more plausible to ground what remains of labor law in the CA, which combines an emphasis on "full equality" of freedom of speech and association with support for a strong social safety net. But the same modifications that have accommodated labor law to the CA have also eroded labor's strength and accelerated its decline. In other words, the labor movement's recent doctrinal successes in defending its activity in terms compatible with the CA may stem directly from its relinquishment of its historical tactics, and its corresponding loss of power.

To elaborate this trajectory, I turn in the following sections to some historical conceptions of labor power. I begin with the premise that the early labor movement was not satisfied with minimalism; it demanded redistribution on a larger scale than the capabilities approach would support. To achieve this redistribution, early labor activists vacillated between methods premised on private coercion, on the one hand, and direct legislative intervention into labor relations, on the other. During the New Deal, it was the latter approach that prevailed, notwithstanding objections articulated by certain segments of the labor movement. That development, in turn, undermined the legitimacy of the powerful economic weapons that had once seemed necessary to counteract employer dominance. Today, the United States Supreme Court is dismantling the last vestiges of union security under the banner of employee choice.

My argument here is a descriptive one. There may be reason to conclude that the historical vision of union power is either inimical to social justice or unsuited to a modern global economy. Moreover, I am not arguing that the CA *must* fit labor law in its past or current form to provide valuable insights and guidance; it is surely a permissible goal of normative theory to transcend traditional paradigms and imagine normatively preferable alternatives. Still, it is important to assess whether a theory of social justice that expressly endorses political liberalism is consistent with the aspirations from which our contemporary labor law has evolved, and which many labor activists no doubt still harbor. Riccardo Del Punta has suggested that for many generations, "labour law *history* seemed so successful that labour lawyers didn't

---

[13] At bottom, I suspect that disagreement about the usefulness of the CA as an organizing framework for labor law turns as much on disagreement about the legitimacy of such tactics—that is, the authors' deep views about the goals and methods of labor law—as it does on disagreement about the CA itself.

much feel the need to complicate their lives with *philosophy*," and that the "quality of the normative reflection" within labor law discourse has consequently suffered.[14] It does not follow, however, that labor's legal history has become expendable. On the contrary, the apparent *failure* of labor law history has, in my view, made it even more indispensable to normative reflection.

## II. Labor's Maximal Goals

The capabilities approach is, by design, a '"minimal' theory of social justice."[15] In particular, Martha C. Nussbaum's threshold view "says nothing at all about how we ought to regard inequalities above the threshold, or whether and when those raise problems of justice."[16] Labor advocates, by contrast, have ordinarily demanded far more than threshold capabilities. Indeed, they have often regarded the pursuit of minimums as counterproductive.

Perhaps the most influential explication of labor's maximalist commitment is the well-known 1914 debate between labor lawyer Morris Hillquit, a founder of the Socialist Party of America, and Samuel Gompers, president of the American Federation of Labor, in testimony before the United States Commission on Industrial Relations. "Will the organized labor movement," Hillquit asked Gompers, "stop in its demands for an ever greater share in the product at any time before it has received or does receive the full product, and before in its eyes complete social justice shall have been done?" Although Gompers refused "to be labeled by any particular 'ism,'" he reluctantly conceded the AFL's expansive aspirations:

MR. GOMPERS: The working people are pressing forward, pressing forward, making their claims and presenting those claims with whatever power they have, to exercise it in a normal, rational manner, to secure a larger, and constantly larger share of the products. They are working to the highest and best ideals of social justice.

MR. HILLQUIT: . . . In your experience with the labor movement and in its ever forward march toward greater and greater improvement, and a greater and greater share of social justice, can you point out any line where the labor movement will stop and rest contented so long as it may receive short of the full product of its work?

MR. GOMPERS: I say that the workers, as human beings, will never stop in any effort, nor stop at any point in the effort to secure greater improvements in their condition, a better life in all its phases.

. . .

---

[14] Riccardo Del Punta, "Is the Capability Theory an Adequate Normative Theory for Labour Law?" draft of Chapter 4 in this volume (on file with author).

[15] Nussbaum, "Labor Law and the Capabilities Approach" (n. 10) 77.

[16] Nussbaum, "Labor Law and the Capabilities Approach" (n. 10) 77. Notably, many of the chapters in this volume point to the indeterminacy of the CA and its inability to justify particular regulatory solutions or to adjudicate among them. Nussbaum accepts this assessment but regards it as a strength rather than a weakness of the CA; her theory of social justice is "minimal" as a matter of respect. As she explains, "a lot of statutory law does not bear on core entitlements, and that means that [her] view has nothing to say about it." Ibid., 69. Of course, that does not mean that "the idea of capabilities could not be used fruitfully in these other domains." Ibid.

The working people will never stop … [i]n their effort to obtain a better life for themselves and for their wives and for their children and for humanity.

MR. HILLQUIT: Then, the object of the labor union is to obtain complete social justice for themselves and for their wives and for their children?

MR. GOMPERS: It is the effort to obtain a better life every day.… In other words, we go further than you. You have an end; we have not.[17]

Stripped of some obsolete scaffolding, the exchange between Gompers and Hillquit captures a core tension between labor law and the CA. Despite profound disagreement over methods, labor advocates have overwhelmingly aspired to more than an adequate social minimum, even a generous one. The CA does not purport to guarantee Hillquit's benchmark, "complete social justice"; in fact, it is deliberately and explicitly *incomplete*.

There are clearly many issues on which strong forms of early-twentieth century labor activism are patently irreconcilable with the CA, not least of which is Nussbaum's inclusion of property rights—which radicals regarded as fundamentally illegitimate, at least in relation to private ownership of the means of production—in her list of basic capabilities. Still, the CA's agnosticism regarding inequality over the threshold is a particularly difficult challenge because the labor movement's focus on equalization bore a lasting imprint on labor law.

That the CA does not rule out a more vigorously redistributive agenda is an insufficient response. It is true that in Nussbaum's conception, basic justice requires a minimum threshold that is quite high, and in some domains—including voting rights, speech rights, education rights, and religious liberty—it commands full equality. Moreover, the CA preserves the possibility that additional equalization may be justice-enhancing. In contrast to some versions of sufficientarianism, it treats entitlement to threshold levels of particular capabilities as necessary to human flourishing without assuming that redistribution above the threshold is either unimportant or inefficient.[18] It is explicitly a partial theory of justice.

Yet Hillquit and Gompers's comments to the Commission on Industrial Relations suggest that something more than completeness is at stake. Indeed, many labor theorists and activists have repudiated minimalism as itself incompatible with social justice, on the assumption that a basic safety net would obscure exploitation and perpetuate false consciousness. This impulse motivated not only the socialist repudiation of the Progressive Party planks as "mere palliatives and nostrums," but

---

[17] U.S. Congress, Senate, *Final Report and Testimony Submitted to Congress by the Commission on Industrial Relations,* 64th Cong., 1st sess., S. Doc. 415, 2 (Government Printing Office, 1916) (CIR Testimony), 1526–9.

[18] Sufficientarian accounts accept inequality provided that basic needs are met. See, for example, Harry Frankfurt, *On Inequality* (Princeton University Press, 2015). On the historical ascendance of sufficientarian approaches to human rights, including discussion of Amartya Sen's evolving views, see Samuel Moyn, *Not Enough: Human Rights in an Unequal World* (Harvard University Press, 2018). For an argument that Nussbaum's view is sufficientarian, see Richard Arneson, "Distributive Justice and Basic Capability Equality: 'Good Enough' Is Not Good Enough," in *Capabilities Equality: Basic Issues and Problems*, ed. Alexander Kaufman (Routledge, 2006), 17–43. Alexander Kaufman disputes that interpretation in Alexander Kaufman, "A Sufficientarian Approach? A Note," in Alexander Kaufman (ed.), *Capabilities Equality: Basic Issues and Problems* (Routledge, 2006), 71–8.

also Gompers's rejection of a maximum-hours law for adult male workers.[19] For the AFL, whose reliance on economic weapons in reserve would eventually become the template for U.S. labor law, ameliorative concessions were mere distractions from the "strenuous struggle of all America's organized workers" against their employers.[20] Organized labor proceeded gradually, but it never wavered in its "aims and aspirations for still better and better and still better things."[21]

To be sure, just as Marxists wrote off the lumpenproletariat, U.S. labor advocates understood that desperate workers would never hold a picket line. Gompers learned that lesson firsthand when he failed to mobilize tenement house cigar workers in nineteenth-century New York and thereafter shunned involvement with unskilled workers.[22] In subsequent generations, unions would argue (unsuccessfully) against the suspension of federal food stamps to striking workers, recognizing that access to a social safety net would enhance their bargaining position by prolonging their ability to strike.[23] But before the New Deal, the solution to economic desperation was instead a strong union, whose dues would support sick relief, unemployment compensation, and an ample strike fund. Providing this minimum was part and parcel of labor's maximalist goals.

## III. Labor Law and State Power

The labor movement's ambivalent attitude toward state-sponsored social programs in the period before the New Deal also implicates a second feature of the capabilities approach: the function of government in securing human capabilities. The CA, as Nussbaum explains, "ascribes an important role to government in human life."[24] This emphasis stems from the insight that state inaction often enables oppression and violence. It is government, rather than private entities (whether charitable institutions or unions), that "is charged with securing for citizens a comprehensive set of necessary conditions for a life worthy of human dignity."[25] To leave the vindication of basic capabilities to the happenstance of benign circumstances or successful private resistance is an abdication of government responsibility.

The early labor movement shared with the CA a conviction that individuals acting alone were ill equipped to counter domination, and that a just society requires affirmative mechanisms for preserving human dignity. As a descriptive matter, many also insisted that the most vulnerable and impoverished class of workers had "lost the conventional relationship to women and child life, lost its voting franchise, lost its habit of common comfort or dignity, and gradually become consciously a social class

---

[19] CIR Testimony (n. 17), vol. 2, 1575.  [20] CIR Testimony (n. 17), vol. 2, 1576.
[21] CIR Testimony (n. 17), vol. 2, 1576–7.
[22] William E. Forbath, *Law and the Shaping of the American Labor Movement* (Harvard University Press, 1991), 39–45.
[23] *Lyng v. UAW*, 485 U.S. 360 (1988).
[24] Nussbaum, "Constitutions and Capabilities" (n. 12) 11.
[25] Nussbaum, "Constitutions and Capabilities" (n. 12) 11.

with fewer legal or social rights than are conventionally ascribed to Americans."[26] Many labor leaders nonetheless rejected the notion, core to the CA, that indignities were best remediated by the state. They worried that government largesse was subject to political whim and that depending on the state to improve wages and working conditions would endanger the strong social-movement core necessary to sustain their demands, which were premised on power. As late as the New Deal, labor sympathizers like Roger Baldwin professed their commitment to "human rights" (which they contrasted with "property rights"), even as they hesitated to rely on government to protect the "organized workers … and racial minorities" whose rights were "most commonly violated."[27]

The complicated attitude of the interwar labor movement toward state intervention in labor relations is a staple of American labor history.[28] The AFL (after early flirtation with legislative reform) had long espoused a principle of voluntarism, which presumed that labor activity should take place outside the realm of state power, perhaps extending even to government's background role in enforcing common law property rights and contractual agreements.[29] Samuel Gompers worked with the state when it suited his ends, but he remained skeptical of a strong role for government regulation, and he endorsed the "constant struggle of the workers through the ages, to get the tentacles of governmental agencies from off the throats of the workers."[30] More radical groups, including the Industrial Workers of the World (IWW), contrasted *direct action* with *political action* and eschewed the latter entirely.[31]

There was of course considerable support for legislation to protect strikes and boycotts from judicial injunctions. Because the early labor movement understood the courts as arms of the state, however, they regarded such measures as state-constraining. Occasionally, labor advocates asked the "Government [to] take some steps to protect the workers in their right to organize,"[32] but the solutions they espoused bore little resemblance to progressive proposals for workers' compensation and minimum wage laws. To take an illustrative example, one witness before the Commission on Industrial Relations urged legislation withholding government

[26] National Civil Liberties Bureau, *The Truth about the IWW* (National Civil Liberties Bureau, 1918), 11.

[27] Roger Baldwin, "The Main Issues of Civil Liberties under the New Deal" (Dec. 8, 1934), ACLU Papers, vol. 721.

[28] See, for example, Melvyn Dubofsky, *The State and Labor in Modern America* (University of North Carolina Press, 1994); Ruth O'Brien, *Workers' Paradox: The Republican Origin of New Deal Labor Policy, 1886-1935* (University of North Carolina Press, 1998); Karen Orren, *Belated Feudalism: Labor, the Law, and Liberal Development in the United States* (Cambridge University Press, 1991); Christopher Tomlins, *The State and the Unions: Labor Relations, Law, and the Organized Labor Movement in America, 1880–1960* (Cambridge University Press, 1985).

[29] On the AFL and the state, see Nelson Lichtenstein, *State of the Union: A Century of American Labor* (Princeton University Press, 2002), 12; Nick Salvatore, "Introduction" in Samuel Gompers (ed.), *Seventy Years of Life and Labor: An Autobiography* (ILR Press, 1984).

[30] Samuel Gompers, "Voluntary Social Insurance vs. Compulsory: Shall the Toilers Surrender Their Freedom for a Few Crumbs," *American Federationist* 23 (1916): 347.

[31] See generally Melvyn Dubofsky, *We Shall Be All: A History of the Industrial Workers of the World* (Quadrangle Books, 1969).

[32] E. B. Ault (Seattle Union Record), August 12, 1914, CIR Testimony, vol. 5, 4192–93.

enforcement of the property rights of any employer that denied its employees the right to organize.[33]

By the 1930s, however, a new cohort of labor advocates rejected voluntarism as an "archaic philosophy."[34] On this ascendant understanding, unions in a modern industrial economy required active government assistance; according to David Saposs, the NLRB's chief economist from 1935 to 1940, organized labor had accomplished most during "periods of widespread government intervention in industrial relations."[35] Not everyone was convinced. Despite lofty promises to organized labor, labor legislation often proved disappointing or damaging, and the 1933 National Industrial Recovery Act was roundly condemned as a failure.[36] Meanwhile, some craft unions had thrived on the voluntarist model and resisted potential incursions on their interests.[37] On the left, the concerns varied from pragmatic to ideological. Radical unions worried that exclusive bargaining rights would assist established unions in edging out insurgents (mainstream labor experts countered that minority group recognition would prop up company unions).[38] The more fundamental opposition came from those "radicals who oppose[d] state capitalism as a form of economic fascism, denying to the working class a chance to develop its power." In their view, "the state [was] always an instrument of violence and compulsion in the hands of the dominant economic class"; the "real fight [was] on the job, not in Washington."[39] In the end, however, Senator Robert F. Wagner's National Labor Relations Act passed with overwhelming labor support. Over time, the American labor movement came to regard state-mandated employer recognition of a majority union as a prerequisite for meaningful labor rights.[40]

The New Deal deployment of federal power on labor's behalf marked a dramatic break with past policy, and employers and their allies were quick to argue that it contravened constitutional limitations.[41] Until the 1930s, courts regularly enjoined labor activity—and invalidated the effort of state legislatures to protect it—for

---

[33] E. B. Ault (Seattle Union Record), August 12, 1914, CIR Testimony, vol. 5, 4192–3.

[34] David J. Saposs, "The American Labor Movement since the War," *Quarterly Journal of Economics* 49 (1935): 236–54, 239.

[35] Saposs, "The American Labor Movement since the War" (n. 34) 239.

[36] See James A. Gross, *The Making of the National Labor Relations Board: A Study in Economics, Politics, and the Law* (SUNY Press, 1974), 7–40.

[37] James Gray Pope, "The Thirteenth Amendment versus the Commerce Clause: Labor and the Shaping of American Constitutional Law, 1921–1958," *Columbia Law Review* 102 (2002): 1–123, 1, 7–17, 61–5; Tomlins, *The State and the Unions* (n. 28).

[38] Cletus Daniel, *The ACLU and the Wagner Act: An Inquiry into the Depression-Era Crisis of American Liberalism* (New York State School of Industrial and Labor Relations, Cornell University, 1980), 34; David Montgomery, *The Fall of the House of Labor: The Workplace, the State, and American Labor Activism, 1865–1925* (Cambridge University Press, 1987), 357 (attributing early embrace of exclusive bargaining to Woodrow Wilson's belief that "employers should be encouraged to negotiate with legitimate unions and to shun the IWW and other groups deemed 'outlaw' by the AFL").

[39] Roger Baldwin, "Coming Struggle for Freedom" (Nov. 12, 1934), ACLU Papers, vol. 717; Roger Baldwin and Morris Ernst, "The New Deal and Civil Liberties" (radio debate over the Blue Network of NBC), Jan. 27, 1934, ACLU Papers, vol. 717. See generally Gross, *Making* (n. 36) 41–72.

[40] Today, American labor unions are actively debating the principles of majority rule and exclusivity.

[41] Gross, *Making* (n. 36) 149–253; Peter H. Irons, *The New Deal Lawyers* (Princeton University Press, 1982), 201–71.

infringing employers' property rights, as well as the "liberty of contract" purportedly contained within the Due Process Clause of the Fourteenth Amendment.[42] They also struck down federal efforts to ameliorate economic hardships for exceeding the federal government's authority to regulate interstate commerce. It was widely expected that the Supreme Court would invalidate the Wagner Act on precisely those grounds. Instead, Chief Justice Hughes, in upholding the statute, described the right to organize as a "fundamental right."[43]

At first blush, then, it appears that on the eve of American entry into World War II, labor law in the United States had found a firm basis in the principles of the CA. In 1935, the Social Security Act created a minimal social safety net. With the 1938 Fair Labor Standards Act (FLSA), Congress extended a minimum wage and other basic protections to individual employees. The United States Department of Justice began to deploy state power actively to investigate the conditions of private work arrangements and even to prosecute employers for unduly repressive relationships.[44] And the Supreme Court abandoned its longstanding exercise of "substantive due process," tolerating state incursions on liberty of contract to support the right to organize.

Taken as a whole, however, the New Deal labor law regime fits rather awkwardly with the social democratic exercises of state power envisioned by the CA. The Wagner Act was the anchor of the emerging system, and it was designed to enhance union power, not to dictate substantive outcomes. It protected workers from employer retaliation against concerted activity, and it required an employer to bargain with a union designated by a majority of its employees. Most important, it created a three-member board to monitor and evaluate unfair labor practices and made its decisions enforceable by federal courts. Yet it also allowed for private ordering, at least where newly empowered unions, rather than isolated individuals, negotiated the terms of employment.[45]

In this arrangement, labor's strength was secured above all by economic weapons. The NLRA garnered broad union support only because of Senator Wagner's solemn assurances that it would not curtail the right to strike, which explicitly was preserved in the statute. This commitment was so central to labor advocates' interwar understanding that some were unwilling to surrender the fate of labor's weapons to electoral politics. I have written elsewhere about the efforts by the small band of self-described labor "partisans" who founded the ACLU to inscribe a strong form of free

---

[42] See, for example, Forbath, *American Labor Movement* (n. 22); Victoria C. Hattam, *Labor Visions and State Power: The Origins of Business Unionism in the United States* (1993); Christopher L. Tomlins, *Law, Labor, and Ideology in the Early American Republic* (Harvard University Press, 1993).

[43] *NLRB v. Jones and Laughlin Steel Corp.*, 301 U.S. 1, 33 (1937).

[44] Laura Weinrib, *The Taming of Free Speech* (Harvard University Press, 2016), 258–61, 64–5. During the 1940s, the Civil Rights Section of the United States Department of Justice pursued Thirteenth Amendment peonage and involuntary servitude charges on behalf of domestic servants on the theory that government bore a duty to ensure all citizens surpassed a minimal threshold of personal and economic security, with strong resonances to the CA. Risa Lauren Goluboff, *The Lost Promise of Civil Rights* (Harvard University Press, 2007).

[45] On the drafting and legislative history of the NLRA, see Irving Bernstein, *The New Deal Collective Bargaining Policy* (University of California Press, 1950); Gross, *Making,* (n. 36) 130–48.

speech into American constitutional law as a means of protecting mass picketing, secondary boycotts, and the right to strike.[46] In 1940, in apparent vindication of their strategy, the Supreme Court recognized a First Amendment right to picket in *Thornhill v. Alabama*. "Free discussion concerning the conditions in industry and the causes of labor disputes," the court's majority concluded in *Thornhill*, was "indispensable to the effective and intelligent use of the processes of popular government to shape the destiny of modern industrial society."[47]

But as state power played an increasingly central role in shaping labor relations an unintended consequence emerged. The weapons that the New Deal labor movement fought so fiercely to preserve rested on a strong form of economic pressure that shaded into coercion.[48] And as the postwar period unfolded, it became clear that state action—even in its tepid intermediate form—rendered union coercion legally and politically intolerable.[49]

Once unions were invested with government authority, judges and administrators insisted that they respect individual freedom.[50] Labor lawyers sought desperately to reframe picketing and boycotts as expressive activity instead of instruments of economic power, but their efforts largely misfired. Barely a decade after the labor movement's historic victories, the United States Supreme Court withdrew First Amendment protection of labor picketing and imposed on unions a duty of fair representation as a matter of statutory interpretation in the shadow of constitutional law. For its part, Congress abolished the closed shop, prohibited secondary boycotts, and created a category of union unfair labor practices to protect both employers and individual rights.

## IV. The Problem of Conflicting Capabilities

With this progression in mind, I turn to a final set of tensions between labor law and the capabilities approach. First, the CA assumes the "centrality of choice."[51] As Nussbaum puts it, "respect for people's power of choice is at the center of the entire approach."[52] Political liberalism and the CA "go well together" because "capabilities

---

[46] Weinrib, *Taming of Free Speech* (n. 44); Laura Weinrib, "The Right To Work and the Right To Strike," *University of Chicago Legal Forum* 2017 (2018): 513–36.

[47] *Thornhill v. Alabama*, 310 U.S. 88, 95 (1940).

[48] See, for example, Ahmed White, *The Last Great Strike: Little Steel, the CIO, and the Struggle for Labor Rights in New Deal America* (University of California Press, 2016).

[49] Reflecting on the early opposition to the Wagner Act within the ACLU and Communist Party, Staughton Lynd poignantly observed: "Now it took a lot of backtracking by the Supreme Court to get there, but maybe that was part of the prediction, at least in its more sophisticated form: no matter how the law was written, once you had the government that far into controlling the labor movement, given the nature of power in American society it was going to wind up controlling the labor movement for the sake of business." Len Calabrese, "An Interview with Staughton Lynd," *Radical History Review* (1977): 60–75, 69.

[50] Of course, many courts had regarded union power as illegitimate precisely because it operated as an alternative and independent legal regime and thus threatened the state's monopoly on coercion. Forbath, *American Labor Movement* (n. 22) 65.

[51] Nussbaum, "Constitutions and Capabilities" (n. 12) 14.

[52] Nussbaum, "Constitutions and Capabilities" (n. 12) 14.

are options," and "nobody is forced to use them."[53] Second, and relatedly, the CA insists that "each person is treated as an end, and none as a mere adjunct or means to the ends of others."[54]

Both principles are difficult to reconcile with the labor theory and tactics that produced our modern labor law regime, which rested fundamentally on the suspension of individual choice for the benefit of workers collectively. While it is possible to repackage those tactics (if not the theory) in terms compatible with the CA, and with political liberalism more broadly, the reconfiguration requires significant adjustments that directly undermine their effectiveness as tools. Put differently, to the extent contemporary labor law can be captured by the CA, it is only because unions have been drained of their coercive power—a development that is at least partly responsible for decreasing union density and the diminishing effectiveness of strikes.[55] If a goal of reorienting labor law around the CA is to justify and thus revitalize the labor movement in an era of declining union power, these constraints will pose a significant barrier.

Among the legal conflicts that foreground this problem, the most salient example in the United States is the Supreme Court's recent decision in *Janus v. AFSCME*, in which public sector non-union employees successfully asserted a First Amendment right not to subsidize union activities.[56] Alan Bogg has suggested that the CA might support a claim to constitutional associational status for unions—and moreover, that such a strategy may be the most promising path forward for organized labor, insofar as "constitutional courts have been the only forums in which workers' voices have been heard so as to impede the legislative curtailment of freedom of association rights."[57] From an American perspective, this confidence in judicial enforcement of constitutional rights as a lifeline for the labor movement is difficult to fathom; for the past half-century such claims have served to undermine rather than strengthen unions. The notion of grounding labor rights in freedom of speech and association seems both fanciful and misguided at a time when the judiciary has "weaponiz[ed]" the First Amendment to hamstring public sector unionism by invoking precisely those constitutional values.[58]

Critics have denounced the new antiregulatory campaign as a distortion of the First Amendment, an unprecedented departure from such core values as democratic deliberation and informed public debate. They have attributed the recent success of

---

[53] Martha C. Nussbaum, "Labor Law and the Capabilities Approach," Chapter 3 in this volume at 73.

[54] Martha C. Nussbaum, "Capabilities as Fundamental Entitlements: Sen and Social Justice," in Alexander Kaufman (ed.), *Capabilities Equality: Basic Issues and Problems* (Routledge, 2006), 44–70, 51.

[55] Efforts to explain the decline of union density abound and account for specific political and legal developments in the United States as well as international trends and globalization. See, for example, Cynthia Estlund, "The Ossification of American Labor Law," *Columbia Law Review* 103 (2002): 1527–612; David Weil, *The Fissured Workplace: Why Work Became So Bad for So Many and What Can Be Done to Improve It* (Harvard University Press, 2014); Kate Andrias, "The New Labor Law," *Yale Law Journal* 126 (2016): 1–100.

[56] *Janus v. American Federation of State, County, and Municipal Employees*, Council 31, No. 16-1466, 585 U.S. ___ (2018).

[57] Alan Bogg, "Labour Law and the Trade Unions: Autonomy and Betrayal," in Alan Bogg et al. (eds.), *The Autonomy of Labour Law* (Hart Publishing, 2015), 73–106, 102.

[58] *Janus v. AFSCME* (n. 56) (Kagan, J., dissenting).

claims of this type to what legal scholars have tellingly dubbed the "Lochnerization" of the First Amendment, that is, businesses' reliance on freedom of speech, association, and religion claims to invalidate unwelcome regulatory measures (a trend that raises its own set of puzzles for the CA).[59] Ironically, however, the best analogue to the current First Amendment strategy lies within labor law itself. To constitutionalize the right to strike, civil liberties advocates in the 1920s and 1930s argued that picketing and boycotts were protected expressive activity. In so doing, they inadvertently laid the groundwork for courts to invest *non*-participation in union activities with First Amendment significance. It was they who recast the concrete economic objectives of concerted labor activity in terms of individual self-fulfillment and informed democratic debate.[60]

Of course, many within the labor movement had always considered it perilous to shield labor's economic weapons from state interference as constitutionally protected speech. For one, the effort risked legitimating a judiciary that labor leaders lambasted for its antagonism to workers' rights.[61] The champions of judicial review before World War II, most prominently the bar and the business lobby, envisioned the courts as a bulwark against state meddling in putatively private economic exchanges. To pursue civil liberties through constitutionalism thus threatened to prop up and legitimate an institution that progressives resented almost as much as labor activists did, and which New Deal court-curbing initiatives were on the verge of curtailing. These historical attitudes do not track the CA, which presumes that "many of the most central human capabilities, given their enormous importance to basic social justice, should be placed beyond majority whim through constitutionally protected status."[62] Nussbaum has urged constitutional protection of social rights along with their civil and political counterparts, and she has therefore described the failed ambitions of "liberal jurisprudence" in the late 1960s and early 1970s as "very much in the spirit of the CA"[63]: it was "an approach to basic welfare" that aspired not to

---

[59] See, for example, Jack M. Balkin, "Some Realism About Pluralism: Legal Realist Approaches to the First Amendment," *Duke Law Journal* (1990): 375–430, 384; Morton Horwitz, "Foreword: The Constitution of Change: Legal Fundamentality Without Fundamentalism," *Harvard Law Review* 107 (1993): 30–117, 109–16 (discussing "The Lochnerization of the First Amendment"); Robert Post & Amanda Shanor, "Adam Smith's First Amendment," *Harvard Law Review Forum* 128 (2015): 165–82; Amanda Shanor, "The New Lochner," *Wisconsin Law Review* (2016): 133–206; Jeremy K. Kessler & David E. Pozen, "The Search for an Egalitarian First Amendment," *Columbia Law Review* 118 (2018): 1953–2010; Genevieve Lakier, "Imagining an Anti-Subordinating First Amendment," *Columbia Law Review* 118 (2018): 2117–59. Scholarship examining the significance of the deregulatory First Amendment in the labor context includes Charlotte Garden, "The Deregulatory First Amendment at Work," *Harvard Civil Rights-Civil Liberties Law Review* 51 (2016): 323–62; Cynthia Estlund, "Truth, Lies, and Power at Work," *Minnesota Law Review* 101 (2017): 349–62; Weinrib, "The Right to Work and the Right to Strike" (n. 46); Catherine Fisk, "A Progressive Labor Vision of the First Amendment: Past as Prologue," *Columbia Law Review* 118 (2018): 2057–93; and Kate Andrias, "Janus's Two Faces," *Supreme Court Review* (forthcoming).

[60] See generally Weinrib, *Taming of Free Speech* (n. 44).

[61] See Laura Weinrib, "From Left to Rights: Civil Liberties Lawyering between the World Wars," *Law, Culture, and the Humanities* (May 2016) doi:10.1177/1743872116641871.

[62] Nussbaum, "Constitutions and Capabilities" (n. 12) 56.

[63] Nussbaum, "Constitutions and Capabilities" (n. 12) 67. In the 1960s and 1970s, lawyers and scholars in the United States sought and failed to introduce poverty as a suspect classification for Fourteenth Amendment purposes. See, for example, Archibald Cox, "Foreword: Constitutional

"equalization," but rather "(as in the CA) [to] the provision of a decent social min-imum."[64] The New Dealers responsible for the major capabilities-enhancing social welfare programs of the 1930s would have been unsurprised that even this modest poverty law project would founder in the courts, which had consistently thwarted economic redistribution. They would have wondered instead at the CA's predilec-tion for a countermajoritarian judiciary.

Even aside from the question of judicial enforcement, however, it is no wonder that most labor lawyers dismissed the interwar endeavor to ensconce a sweeping vision of labor power in the First Amendment as quixotic or counterproductive.[65] After all, the constitutional case for the right to picket and boycott was a strained one. The ACLU advanced a "right of agitation," which encompassed activity far more disruptive than the ordinary soapbox oratory that was itself routinely suppressed in this period.[66] When unions stationed mass pickets to block strikebreakers, they im-peded access to employer property. Where direct recognitional strikes were unsuc-cessful, unions adopted more drastic measures. Secondary strikes placed pressure on "innocent" third parties to discontinue business with the primary target, regardless of the secondary's relationship with its own employees. In other words, a unionized employer that failed to terminate dealings with an "unfair" employer—perhaps be-cause of a contractual commitment to purchase its products—might find its own employees on strike. Meanwhile, the dreaded secondary boycott extended effective sanctions to unionized employers. Whereas workers were unable to sustain the lost wages of strikes for long periods, refusal to purchase or handle an unfair product might continue indefinitely and entangle parties far removed from the primary dis-pute. In resisting a powerful union, an employer risked lost profits, spoilage, con-tractual liability, and reputational damage. Many struck businesses, including small shopkeepers or artisans, were forced to close their doors. The courts that considered whether labor picketing and boycotts were constitutionally protected activity in the early twentieth century typically dismissed the argument out of hand. Most ac-cepted the assessment of the National Association of Manufactures that enjoining "the use of [a man's] hands or his feet or his head to do some unlawful thing" was functionally indistinguishable from the "use of the injunction in connection with the use of the tongue."[67]

Adjudication and the Promotion of Human Rights," *Harvard Law Review* 80 (1966): 91–122; Frank Michelman, "Foreword: On Protecting the Poor Through the Fourteenth Amendment," *Harvard Law Review* 83 (1969): 7–59; Peter B. Edelman, "The Next Century of Our Constitution: Rethinking Our Duty to the Poor," *Hastings Law Journal* 39 (1987): 1–61; William E. Forbath, "Caste, Class and Equal Citizenship," *Michigan Law Review* 98 (1999): 1–91.

[64] Nussbaum, "Constitutions and Capabilities" (n. 12) 67.
[65] Other advocates sought to embed labor rights within the Thirteenth and Fourteenth Amendments. See, for example, Pope, "Thirteenth Amendment" (n. 37); James Gray Pope, "Labor's Constitution of Freedom," *Yale Law Journal* 106 (1997): 941–1031. Many labor lawyers resisted the pursuit of anti-employer injunctions for similar reasons. See Arthur Garfield Hays, Clement Wood, and McCalister Coleman, *Don't Tread on Me: A Study of Aggressive Legal Tactics for Labor* (1928) (discussing reaction of labor lawyers); Forbath, *American Labor Movement* (n. 22) 118–27.
[66] Weinrib, *Taming of Free Speech* (n. 44) ch. 3.
[67] James A. Emery, May 18, 1915, CIR Testimony, vol. 11, 10823.

To the extent union methods undermined employer interests, they might none-theless be reconciled to the CA, which treats some freedoms as either trivial or per-nicious and therefore undeserving of protection.[68] The abstract adulation of liberty that American scholars associate with classical legal thought has no place in the CA, which is concerned with the "material and institutional conditions that turn mere words on paper into a working reality."[69] The CA is therefore consistent with the labor movement's longstanding emphasis on the material underpinnings of bargaining and with the conclusion (forcefully expressed in the Norris-LaGuardia Act) that "under prevailing economic conditions, developed with the aid of govern-mental authority for owners of property to organize in the corporate and other forms of ownership association, the individual unorganized worker is commonly helpless to exercise actual liberty of contract and to protect his freedom of labor."[70] From the perspective of the CA, the right to counter concentrated employer power with the power of organized workers—whether secured by legislation or constitutional law—would seem uncontroversial.

Nonetheless, there are formidable obstacles to assimilating labor agitation in its strong form to the CA. Labor laws will inevitably entail tradeoffs not only between employers and employees, but also among workers. To be sure, some such tradeoffs are less intractable than others. Even if there were sound empirical evidence that minimum wage laws raised aggregate unemployment and therefore foreclosed op-portunities for the least fortunate workers, the CA would not necessarily preclude them, provided they were coupled with an ample safety net. Even where affirmative action impedes the discrete opportunities of individual members of a dominant group, the CA has a response: it does not guarantee anyone a particular job, and the privileged have no special or vested rights in their traditional privileges.

But the compliance a union demands is more than the diminishment of oppor-tunity or material gain. At the heyday of union power, the underlying objective of picketing and boycotts was often to close the shop—an outcome, when successful, that compelled the discharge of non-union employees. The hardship wrought by the closed shop was particularly stark with respect to those employees who were not eligible to join for reasons of gender or race. Early advocates for racial justice (along with subsequent scholars) rightly emphasized the failure of the American labor movement to remediate racism within its ranks, despite its ostensive commit-ment to equality.[71] Yet while discrimination of this kind was arguably orthogonal

---

[68]   Nussbaum, *Frontiers of Justice* (n. 4) 90. Given Nussbaum's preference for "heavily regulated mar-kets," the notion that improving the capabilities of workers might entail material loss to employers does not seem to me an insurmountable obstacle. After all, Nussbaum is quite explicit that many commit-ments demanded by the CA "will not be justifiable as mutually advantageous in the narrow economic sense of advantage." As she explains, "Justice is also one of our ends, and we limit our pursuit of it too much when we think of it as the outcome of a contract for mutual advantage." Ibid., 90.

[69]   Nussbaum, "Constitutions and Capabilities" (n. 12) 23.

[70]   29 U.S.C. §§ 101–15 (2016).

[71]   See, for example, Paul Frymer, *Black and Blue: African Americans, the Labor Movement, and the Decline of the Democratic Party* (Princeton University Press, 2008); Herbert Hill, *Black Labor and the American Legal System* (The University of Wisconsin Press, 1985); Mark V. Tushnet, *The NAACP's Legal Strategy against Segregated Education, 1925–1950* (University of North Carolina Press, 1987); Sophia Z. Lee, *The Workplace Constitution from the New Deal to the New Right* (Cambridge University Press, 2014).

to unionism, and even contemporaries recognized that it was counterproductive, other discriminatory practices were core to labor's tactics. A union member who failed to honor a picket line could expect expulsion from the union and, in a densely organized industry, might forfeit future employment. An individual worker who defied a union faced a genuine possibility of social ostracism and impoverishment. Occasionally, discipline even extended to members' families. Testifying before the Commission on Industrial Relations, one labor witness acknowledged the harshness of such tactics but explained there were "a great many instances [in which] we are unable to bring any effective pressure to bear on an employer except through this form of discrimination."[72]

When the Supreme Court did afford First Amendment protection to labor picketing in *Thornhill*, labor scholars balked. Charles O. Gregory of the University of Chicago Law School accepted the usefulness of labor's tactics but considered "the claim that such coercive union practices are justifiable as constitutional freedom of speech" to be a "perversion of an American ideal."[73] Violent or not, picketing was "a type of coercion" rather than an "argument intended to achieve an intellectual conquest," he explained. By framing their economic weapons as instruments of persuasion, union leaders had "won the support of thousands of intellectual leaders who are actuated by the social movement aspects of unionism and who seem to have ignored the dangers of the sort of power which federated universal closed shops may bring."[74]

To be clear, there was plenty of coercion on the other side, as well. Employers often professed commitment to the open shop, which guarded the employer's prerogative to hire non-union labor but ostensibly left employees free to join the union. In reality, they typically relied on labor spies to identify and eliminate pro-union workers, and they disseminated blacklists of agitators. Many required workers to sign "yellow-dog" agreements not to unionize, which rendered would-be organizers liable for tortious interference with contract.[75] Finally, employers routinely hired security guards to evict union organizers from their property and to keep picketers at bay; where private guards proved inadequate to break a strike, government officials reliably proved willing to dispatch police officers or the National Guard.[76] Still, unions' far-reaching tactics helped to justify such assistance, and the courts that issued labor injunctions often emphasized employee choice. As one typical judge explained, "The labor unions and [their] officers meddle into a member's daily affairs deeper than does the law; restrict him in matters that the law leaves free."[77]

---

[72] E. B. Ault (Seattle Union Record), Aug. 12, 1914, CIR Testimony, vol. 5, 4199.
[73] Charles O. Gregory, "Peaceful Picketing and Freedom of Speech," *ABA Journal* 26 (1940): 709–15, 714.
[74] Gregory, "Peaceful Picketing and Freedom of Speech" (n. 73) 714.
[75] Daniel R. Ernst, *Lawyers Against Labor: From Individual Rights to Corporate Liberalism* (University of Illinois Press, 1995); Daniel Ernst, "The Yellow-Dog Contract and Liberal Reform, 1917–1932," *Labor History* 30 (1989): 251–74, 268–70.
[76] Dubofsky, *The State and Labor in Modern America* (n. 28).
[77] Transcript of Record at 627, *Gompers v. Buck's Stove & Range Co.* (D.D.C. Dec. 23, 1908) (No. 372).

Cognizant of this history, labor leaders were ambivalent about tethering labor rights to the Constitution. They worried that the Supreme Court would not adhere to a strong form of constitutional protection for labor speech (a concern that proved prescient); even advocates of the First Amendment strategy insisted that "power wins rights," and consequently that the "direct action of open conflict" was far more effective "than all the legal maneuvers in the courts to get rights that no government willingly grants."[78] More fundamentally, they were ambivalent about a staunchly speech-protective analysis of labor activity. For example, labor leaders and the NLRB considered it necessary and legitimate to curtail employers' anti-union communications. In their view, a union's anti-union expression was coercive rather than persuasive, and therefore subject to regulation consistent with the First Amendment. The ACLU, by contrast, worried that suppression of employer speech would lead to the curtailment of labor speech as well, and urged the courts to protect both.[79]

With respect to employer speech, the courts obliged. Just months after *Thornhill*, the Seventh Circuit concluded that the Ford Motor Company was free to distribute antiunion propaganda to its employees, notwithstanding its security force's brutal attack on union organizers at the notorious Battle of the Overpass. According to the court, the old power disparity between master and servant might once have invested the former with disproportionate power, but the NLRA had leveled the playing field: "The servant no longer [had] occasion to fear the master's frown of authority or threats of discrimination for union activities, express or implied."[80] The Supreme Court soon adopted a speech-protective rule, which Congress formalized in the 1947 Taft-Hartley Act. Today, an employer may go so far as to require employee attendance at "captive audience meetings" for the purpose of discouraging unionization, where it may compel employees to listen quietly, at the risk of discipline or discharge.[81]

But the Supreme Court's expansion of the First Amendment quickly proved to be partial. Only a year after the *Thornhill*, the Supreme Court explained, in a decision upholding a state's injunction against picketing by a union that had previously engaged in violence, that "[u]tterance in a context of violence can lose its significance as an appeal to reason and become part of an instrument of force."[82] In subsequent cases, the Court described even peaceful picketing as an exercise of "economic power" as opposed to speech.[83] In one such case, it upheld an injunction against peaceful recognitional picketing, which the state court had justified on the basis that economic pressure would "interfere with the free choice of the *employees*" by inducing the *employer* to encourage unionization.[84] Just two decades after it rejected

---

[78] Roger Baldwin, "Free Speech Fights of the IWW," in Roger Baldwin (ed.), *Industrial Workers of the World. Twenty-Five Years of Industrial Unionism* (The Industrial Workers of the World, 1930), 15.

[79] Weinrib, *Taming of Free Speech* (n. 44) ch. 7.

[80] *NLRB v. Ford Motor Company*, 114 F.2d 905, 914 (6th Cir. 1940).

[81] See, for example, Paul M. Secunda, "The Contemporary 'Fist Inside the Velvet Glove,' Employer Captive Audience Meetings Under the NLRA," *FIU Law Review* 5 (2010): 385–410.

[82] *Milk Wagon Drivers Union v. Meadowmoor Dairies, Inc.*, 312 U.S. 287, 293 (1941).

[83] *Giboney v. Empire Storage & Ice Co.*, 336 U.S. 490.

[84] *Stacey v. Pappas*, 350 U.S. 870 (1955) (emphasis added); *Pappas v. Stacey*, 116 A.2d 497 (Me. 1955).

employers' arguments that the NLRA was an unconstitutional infringement of their constitutional liberty of contract, the Supreme Court—in an opinion the dissent described as a "formal surrender"—clarified that regulation by states could rarely be invalidated for infringing on workers' constitutional freedom of speech. Notably, the pro-union picketing at issue, as it was characterized by the Wisconsin Supreme Court, was "for the purpose of coercing the employer to coerce his employees."[85]

As unions surrendered constitutional protection for their tactics, employers and antiunion employees enjoyed increasing solicitude for theirs. At the end of the New Deal, employer organizations described the "right to work"—that is, an asserted right neither to join or subsidize a union nor be bound by its decisions—as a "fifth freedom, quite as important as … worship, speech, the press and assembly."[86] They quickly learned to frame that fifth freedom in First Amendment terms.[87] There was an inescapable symmetry in the strategy: by investing union activity with expressive and associative significance, unions had opened the door to a First Amendment refusal to join, quite aside from the question whether financial contributions are equivalent to protected speech. Whereas employers and antiunion employees had once rooted the right to work in liberty of contract, cases like *Thornhill* made it possible to imagine it as a First Amendment freedom instead.

At their prompting, the Supreme Court recognized a First Amendment right of a public-sector employee not to "contribute to the support of an ideological cause he may oppose," though it preserved space for agency fees directed toward "collective bargaining activities."[88] In the private sector, the Court fashioned the same compromise approach. Although the decision was issued as a matter of (specious) statutory interpretation rather than constitutional law, everyone understood that the First Amendment was lurking in the background.[89] What made the private sector "right to work" cognizable as a constitutional question was the very state action that the New Deal labor movement had reluctantly invited.[90] What made it plausible as a claim to free expression was the growing constitutional commitment, endorsed by the CA, to "full equality" of freedom of speech.

In 2018, the industry-funded right-to-work campaign invalidated public-sector agency fees for infringing the First Amendment rights of "public employees who would not subsidize a union if given the option."[91] It is widely expected that the Court will soon extend the same rule to private sector unions.[92] Even then, the

---

[85] *International Brotherhood of Teamsters, Local 695 v. Vogt, Inc.*, 354 U.S. 284 (1957).

[86] "Rights and Duties of Business," Address by Albert W. Hawkes, President, Chamber of Commerce of the United States, Dec. 1, 1941, p. 5, Chamber of Commerce of the United States records (acc. 1960), Hagley Museum and Library, Wilmington, DE, box 12.

[87] See generally Lee, *The Workplace Constitution* (n. 71).

[88] *Abood v. Detroit Board of Education*, 431 U.S. 209 (1977).

[89] *Communications Workers of America v. Beck*, 487 U.S. 735 (1988).

[90] Lee, *The Workplace Constitution* (n. 71). On choice and private versus state power in relation to Nussbaum's work, see Tracy E. Higgins, "Feminism as Liberalism: A Tribute to the Work of Martha Nussbaum," *Columbia Journal of Gender and Law* 19 (2010): 65–87.

[91] *Janus v. AFSCME* (n. 56).

[92] Currently, employers are challenging union access to their property and communications systems on First Amendment grounds.

lawsuits will continue. By its very nature, after all, union representation requires trade-offs among member interests, and some employees inevitably would fare better bargaining on their own. The ability of today's unions to extract concessions from employers turns directly on their ability to privilege the welfare of the group over individual preferences, and to keep wayward workers in check. The eventual aim of the antiunion litigation strategy is the dismantlement of majority rule and exclusive representation, and it is no wonder that its architects have often adopted the rhetoric of choice. That was precisely the language employed by the petitioner in *Janus v. AFSCME*, who complained that "if he had the choice, he 'would not pay any fees or otherwise subsidize [the Union].' "[93]

None of this is to say that it is impossible to justify strike activity in terms of expressive and associational capabilities.[94] Some strikes have always been spontaneous outpourings of shared grievances and solidarity.[95] More to the point, as legislatures and the courts have stripped unions of their coercive power, the First Amendment frame has become increasingly apt. That is, over the course of the twentieth century, unions have relinquished the authority to negotiate closed shop agreements, engage in prolonged recognitional picketing, undertake secondary strikes and boycotts, fine non-members for crossing picket lines, and prevent employees from resigning their union membership during strikes. Simultaneously, they have been burdened with new obligations toward individual members, including the duty of fair representation and the restrictions imposed by the 1959 Landrum-Griffin Act, with its employee "bill of rights." Many such limitations were imposed in direct or implicit concessions to speech and association concerns.

In this new legal landscape, unions may be well positioned as voluntary associations to claim constitutional rights, including the First Amendment rights to expend resources on political campaigns,[96] to decline to represent non-members,[97] and even to picket and strike.[98] Indeed, it is my view that the new openness among lower courts to protecting secondary boycotts on First Amendment grounds is a direct reflection of unions' declining power. More than ever, unions now operate by

---

[93] *Janus v. AFSCME* (n. 56).

[94] That unions themselves cling to the language of choice is evident from a major (if failed) attempt during the Obama administration to counter employer coercion along the path to union representation, which sponsors labeled the Employee Free Choice Act.

[95] Josiah Bartlett Lambert, *"If the Workers Took a Notion": The Right to Strike and American Political Development* (Cornell University Press, 2005).

[96] Benjamin I. Sachs, "Unions, Corporations and Political Opt-Out Rights After Citizens United," *Columbia Law Review* 112 (2012): 800–69; Catherine Fisk & Erwin Chemerinsky, "Political Speech and Associational Rights After *Knox v. SEIU*, Loc. 1000," *Cornell Law Review* 98 (2013): 1023–91.

[97] Catherine L. Fisk & Margaux Poueymirou, "*Harris v. Quinn* and the Contradictions of Compelled Speech," *Loyola of Los Angeles Law Review* 48 (2015): 439–92; Catherine Fisk & Benjamin Sachs, "Restoring Equity in Right-to-Work Law," *U.C. Irvine Law Review* 4 (2014): 857–80. In *Janus v. AFSCME* (n. 56), the Court seemingly suggested that doing so would itself be unconstitutional.

[98] Charlotte Garden, "Citizens, United and Citizens United: The Future of Labor Speech Rights?" *William and Mary Law Review* 53 (2011): 1–53; Catherine Fisk & Jessica Rutter, "Labor Protest Under the New First Amendment," *Berkeley Journal of Employment and Labor Law* 36 (2015): 277–329, 295–300.

moral suasion rather than coercion—not by design, but because they have lost the ability to coerce.

## V. Conclusion

What are the implications of this historical trajectory for adopting the CA as labor's constituting narrative? On the hand, it is possible to argue that the Supreme Court has failed to undertake the nuanced accounting of historical circumstances and practical power that the CA requires. "The good judge, as the CA imagines that role, will read a case the way an attentive reader reads such a novel, asking what the people are actually able to do and to be, what the history of their efforts is, and whether the freedoms and rights at issue are real for them, or distant and unavailable abstractions."[99] On such a reading, the reality of subordination in the workplace would generate many more victories for workers. In the end, however, any attempt to ground labor's rights in the CA will also have to grapple with the rights claims of individual antiunion employees, as clashes between capabilities or as competing exercises of a single capability.

It is a bedrock principle of the CA that "[o]ne person loses any legitimate claim to exercise their capabilities in a certain way when such action undermines the central, or fundamental, capabilities of others."[100] But vindicating multiple capabilities, or even any given capability, will sometimes be a zero-sum game. Moreover, it is often difficult to ascertain where one individual's capabilities end and another's begins. Courts themselves have long understood this problem. In its 1940 decision in *Ford v. NLRB*, the Seventh Circuit acknowledged the difficulty of "reconcil[ing] the conflicting claims of liberty and authority, or when one liberty collides with another"— a challenge for the CA as much as the judiciary.[101] It is significant, in my view, that the judge in that case elected to subordinate the right of workers to organize (though "clearly recognized as a fundamental right," by the court's own concession) to "the freedom of speech guaranteed without exception to all."[102]

In the United States, there has been a sense among some labor law scholars and activists since at least the 1980s that the New Deal's skeptics had it right: that reliance on the state to secure picketing and boycotts inevitably have undercut their power, and that labor's economic weapons are something other than individual rights. Today, it has become fashionable to contemplate abandonment of the New Deal apparatus, which would eliminate the specter of constitutionally problematic state suppression and perhaps free unions to coerce. Brian Langille has implicitly rejected this approach in suggesting that labor law is clinging to a "once valuable (indeed revolutionary) narrative which is now past its 'best before' date."[103] Whether history

[99] Nussbaum, "Constitutions and Capabilities" (n. 12) 32.
[100] Rosalind Dixon & Martha C. Nussbaum, "Children's Rights and a Capabilities Approach: The Question of Special Priority," *Cornell Law Review* 97 (2012): 549–94, 565–6.
[101] *NLRB v. Ford Motor Company*, 114 F.2d 905, 914 (6th Cir. 1940).
[102] *NLRB v. Ford Motor Company* (n. 101) 914.
[103] Brian Langille, "What is Labour Law? Implications of the Capability Approach," draft of Chapter 6 of this volume (on file with author).

counsels a different course is largely a question of normative judgment.[104] Still, it is worth contemplating the reminder of historian Christopher Tomlins that the "fragile, centuries-long threads of ideas" that construct political consciousness are "only ever rendered 'out of date' ... in teleological and developmental accounts of human affairs and intellects."[105] Indeed, it is clear that in a disaggregated economy, unions' old weapons are even more valuable to their traditional redistributive goals.[106] Perhaps today's labor movement will yet find something useful in the historical aspirations that contemporary labor law has expunged.

---

[104] On the normative dimensions of this problem, including a defense of workers' right to use coercive strike tactics to resist oppression, see Alex Gourevitch, "The Right to Strike: A Radical View," *American Political Science Review* 112 (2018): 905–17.

[105] Christopher Tomlins, "From Slavery to the Cooperative Commonwealth: Labor and Republican Liberty in the Nineteenth Century," *Civil War Book Review* 17 (2015), art. 5. I embrace Hugh Collins's historical assessment that "labour law was born through demands for distributive justice during the battles between capital and labour in early industrial society." I also share his diagnosis of the present: that "[e]ven though it may be heavily disguised by sham contracts and sophisticated technology, it would be a mistake to deny that the battle is still running." Hugh Collins, "What Can Sen's Capability Approach Offer to Labour Law," Chapter 1 in this volume at 34.

[106] It is true that the modes of industrial employment that shaped our current model of labor law are declining, and in fact never represented more than a slice of productive labor. For the early labor movement, however, industrial production within vertically integrated firms was hardly the only contemplated model. The organizers who targeted migrant workers in the mining and lumber industries encountered many of the same obstacles as contemporary unions do. In fact, it was precisely the decentralized nature of early twentieth-century work—and the prevalence of piecework, casual work, and unpaid labor—that required workers to organize outside their own workplaces. And dense organization of this kind, in an era when the state prohibited rather than protected most forms of concerted activity, required aggressive tactics to enforce solidarity.

# 9

# Capabilities, Utility, or Primary Goods?
# On Finding a Conceptual Framework
# for (International) Labour Law

*Pascal McDougall\**

The 'capabilities approach' (CA), developed inter alia by Martha C Nussbaum and Amartya Sen, has attracted the interest of labour lawyers for a while now, as this volume demonstrates. In a growing body of literature, proponents of that approach argue that it has the potential to reconcile labour law with economic performance and/or individual freedom and rights, while left-wing critics denounce the CA as inherently 'individualist' or complicit with right-wing economic thought.[1] As a result, much engagement by labour lawyers with the CA is framed in terms of whether to 'adopt' that approach in order to think differently about labour law.

I present here a different take, one that I have never seen articulated. My position is that the CA has no intrinsic ideological bent and is largely interchangeable with the alternative approaches available. As a result, whether or not we use the concepts elaborated by Sen and Nussbaum makes little difference for first-order questions of political philosophy and law.

This is not at all to deny that each capability *theorist* has taken positions that are unique and defended those positions with innovative and creative arguments. And I agree with many positions taken by both Sen and Nussbaum. I agree even more with Robert Salais, Simon Deakin, and Frank Wilkinson (albeit less with Brian Langille). But I distinguish the positions taken by the proponents of the CA from the approach itself, and suggest that these positions could have been expressed using other conceptual apparatuses.

Registering this fact should change the way we write about the capabilities approach and labour law. Indeed, if I am right, both critics and advocates of the CA should spend much less time attributing good or bad characteristics to the approach and to competing conceptual frameworks themselves, and more time developing their own first-order proposals on how to regulate work.

\* SJD Candidate, Harvard Law School. I thank the Social Sciences and Humanities Research Council of Canada for financial support.

[1]  See the references collected by Brian Langille in his contribution to this volume.

This chapter proceeds as follows. In section I, I lay out some of the themes explored by capability theorists and emphasize that they have been extensively debated by labour lawyers already, with no recourse to the concepts of the CA. I touch on debates about both domestic and international labour law.

In section II, I revisit the philosophical debates out of which the CA emerged, and survey the possible alternatives to capabilities (and functionings) as a philosophical organizing concept. The most prominent alternatives are (1) utility/welfare, including the economist's 'choice' and/or 'wealth'-based variants, and (2) Rawlsian primary goods—essentially income, power, and legal rights. These are the two main contenders I assess, although I also deal in passing with Ronald Dworkin's 'resources' and GA Cohen's 'access to advantage'.[2] I argue that all these concepts supply different ways of getting at roughly the same issues, and that they can accommodate roughly the same array of positions as to what makes a life good and how to maximize and/or equalize that.

In section III, I briefly introduce my own proposed approach to the regulation of employment, focusing on questions that emerge from my exploration of the capability theorists' work. My approach, which I call 'left legal realism', essentially argues that labour laws on collective bargaining and employment standards are not deviations from competition, freedom of contract, and private property, but are mere reconfigurations of those abstract ideas from one possible instantiation to another. Relying on this 'bundle of rights' approach to property and contract, I then provide the briefest of sketches of my normative ideals, which revolve around 'altruism' and redistribution along class, gender, and racial lines.

I end section III by addressing Nussbaum's suggestion in this volume that labour law's disciplinary boundaries might be inadequate from the point of view of a redistributive normative project like hers (and mine). I argue that is not the case, but acknowledge that there is much analytical and normative work to do in order to have a better discipline of labour law.

## I.  Capabilities and Contemporary Labour Law Debates

### A.  Sen and Nussbaum

I propose to start with Amartya Sen. I assume basic familiarity with Sen's arguments, at least in their well-known iteration in *Development as Freedom*.[3] I will thus not rehearse Sen's advocacy of 'freedom' as the valuable end and his downplaying of economic growth as a mere means to that end. Instead of this conventional way of presenting Sen's work, I want to jump to what I see as the analytical core of Sen's theory.

A big part of that core seems to me to be in Chapter 5 of *Development as Freedom* where, drawing on his earlier work,[4] Sen relies on the Arrow-Debreu general

---

[2]  See Ronald Dworkin, 'What Is Equality? Part II: Equality of Resources' (1981) 10 *Philosophy and Public Affairs* 283; GA Cohen, 'On the Currency of Egalitarian Justice' (1989) 99 *Ethics* 906.

[3]  Amartya Sen, *Development as Freedom* (Anchor Books, 1999).

[4]  Amartya Sen, *Inequality Reexamined* (Harvard University Press, 1992) 143–4.

equilibrium model to assert that 'individual freedoms' ('capabilities', in the earlier work[5]), just as much as 'utility (or welfare)', are maximized by a 'competitive market equilibrium', such that 'no one's freedom can be increased any further while maintaining the freedom of everyone else'.[6] The viability of this move stems from the fact that freedom (like capabilities) is defined in part as the 'substantive'[7] capacity to attain a valuable life (this connects or even overlaps with utility, which people get by using their capabilities to satisfy preferences in the market).[8]

Sen himself makes clear that this idea of Pareto efficiency could be, and almost always has been, framed in utilitarian/welfarist terms, and that he is merely restating the classic theorems at the foundations of modern welfare economics. But it is nevertheless worthwhile to emphasize just how much this policy issue is fundamental and long-standing, including for labour lawyers.

The theorems of welfare economics model 'profit maximization' in perfectly competitive markets. This ensures that entrepreneurs respond as price-takers to consumer good prices (determined according to marginal utility) and thereafter price labour according to the value of the product of the marginal worker (determined, among other things, by worker productivity and technology).[9] Against this background, economists came to model unions as pushing wages above the level of individualized bargaining under 'competition' and 'freedom of contract', which is also the level at which wages are envisioned to be equal to the value of the product of the marginal worker.[10] This above-equilibrium wage level is said to create a surplus in the market, that is, unemployment.[11] It also results in a 'deadweight loss', a net loss of output caused by supra-competitive wages,[12] which is a loss of freedom and capabilities in Sen's analysis.

Sen immediately qualifies this perfectly conventional welfare analysis so that it does not lead to the absolute freedom of contract and *laissez-faire* traditionally associated with conservatives and the Washington Consensus. He insists that environmental protection, 'elementary' health care, and 'basic' education are public goods that are under-provided by the free market.[13] He also acknowledges welfare arguments against 'intervention' to provide those goods, including the risk of 'budget deficits and inflation (and generally of 'macroeconomic instability')' and the issue of 'incentives', that is, 'the effects that a system of public support may have in discouraging initiative and distorting individual efforts'.[14]

Sen then launches an intricate discussion of these two issues, coming out in favour of *some* unemployment insurance, public health care and education, and fiscal/monetary stimulus, but countervailed by *some* means testing, fiscal discipline, and contractionary central bank policies.[15] The details of this discussion are less

---

[5] Sen, *Inequality Reexamined* (n 4) 143–4.     [6] Sen, *Development as Freedom* (n 3) 117.
[7] Sen, *Development as Freedom* (n 3) 19.        [8] Sen, *Development as Freedom* (n 3).
[9] See Francis Bator, 'The Simple Analytics of Welfare Maximization' (1957) 47 *American Economic Review* 22.
[10] George Borjas, *Labor Economics* (5th edn, McGraw-Hill, 2009) 432.
[11] N Gregory Mankiw, *Principles of Microeconomics* (7th edn, Cengage Learning, 2015) 118.
[12] Borjas, *Labor Economics* (n 10) 432.        [13] Sen, *Development as Freedom* (n 3) 127–9.
[14] Sen, *Development as Freedom* (n 3) 130.
[15] Sen, *Development as Freedom* (n 3) 129–45.

important than its general tenor. It is a staple of our good old discussions on the virtues of economic 'regulation' (including through labour laws) to ensure a fair distribution of the good things.[16]

In addition to this welfarist discussion, Sen grants autonomous value, as a component of 'equity', to 'basic social opportunities'[17] as well as to 'rights', which are seen to be to in large measure efficiency-compatible, and valuable even to the extent they are not efficiency-compatible.[18] This analysis involves on the part of Sen a typical (and useful) economic emphasis on the need for a 'social welfare function'.[19] This concept was progressively taken beyond its initial narrow use in welfare economics—merely to choose among different Pareto-efficient resource allocations stemming from different distributions of income (the fairness of which could not be scientifically determined[20])—to a wider role of balancing rights with efficiency and performing the 'efficiency/equity trade-off' necessary to make political choices.[21]

The foregoing discussion might be taken to suggest that Sen is mostly a welfarist but subject to some ad-hoc balancing of rights and equity with efficiency. In fact, Sen has a lot to say about rights, in ways that resonate with longstanding debates in labour law. For instance, in *The Idea of Justice,* he closes off a path that many would have wanted to take by pronouncing against the equalization of capabilities as an unqualified goal. Equality of capabilities is limited both by 'efficiency' and by the 'process aspect of freedom',[22] defined as 'choice', 'decid[ing] for [one]self what to do', and as the opposite of 'duress'.[23] The 'process aspect of freedom' is Sen's way of referring to individual, negative rights,[24] in contrast to the 'opportunity aspect of freedom', which is the positive or substantive side of freedom.[25]

In a famous 1993 text, Sen added useful details to this picture, stating the following:

[I]t may be appropriate to see the claims of individuals on society in terms of the *freedom* to achieve well-being (and thus in terms of real opportunities) rather than in terms of *actual achievements.* If the social arrangements are such that a responsible adult is given no less freedom (in terms of set comparisons) than others, but he still 'muffs' the opportunities and ends up worse off than others, it is possible to argue that no particular injustice is involved.[26]

---

[16] See on incentives-based objections to labour laws and social rights Cass R Sunstein, *The Second Bill of Rights: FDR's Unfinished Revolution—and Why We Need It More Than Ever* (Basic Books, 2004) 194 7. On macroeconomic troubles stemming from labour laws (including inflation and 'crowding out' of private investment) see Daniel Mitchell, 'Inflation, Unemployment and the Wagner Act: A Critical Reappraisal' (1986) 38 *Stanford Law Review* 1065, 1074–5.

[17] See among many passages Sen, *Development as Freedom* (n 3) 144–5.

[18] See Amartya Sen, *The Idea of Justice* (Harvard University Press, 2008) 289.

[19] Amartya Sen, 'Personal Utilities and Public Judgements: Or What's Wrong With Welfare Economics' (1979) 89 *Economic Journal* 537, 546–7.

[20] On this traditional use see Bator, 'The Simple Analytics of Welfare Maximization' (n 9).

[21] Mankiw, *Principles of Microeconomics* (n 11) 5, 421–4.

[22] Sen, *The Idea of Justice* (n 18) 296.    [23] Sen, *The Idea of Justice* (n 18).

[24] Sen, *The Idea of Justice* (n 18) 282.

[25] Sen, *Development as Freedom* (n 3) 281–2, 285, 297.

[26] Amartya Sen, 'Capability and Well-Being' in Martha C Nussbaum and Amartya Sen (eds), *The Quality of Life* (Oxford University Press, 1993) 30, 39 n 23.

This passage concerns the limits to equalization imposed not by efficiency but by individual freedom and rights. The extent of those limits would depend on the extent to which we consider the 'opportunity aspect of freedom' in assessing whether a given responsible adult is given 'no less freedom ... than others'.

There is, of course, an answer to this question that any labour lawyer will identify as classically *laissez faire*. This is the idea that the only responsibilities we have to each other are not to harm each other, where harm is defined as impinging on others' rights and freedoms and, in turn, rights and freedoms are defined as respect for inter alia private property, freedom of contract, and bodily integrity. In other words, only the 'process aspect' of freedom matters. Any altruistic duties over and above those responsibilities, in this classical view, are not legally enforceable; they are merely moral and discretionary. Similarly, the state cannot obligate people to take care of themselves; this is the problem of paternalism, which is not related to respect for others' rights and therefore not a proper object of state regulation. Jeremy Bentham and Immanuel Kant agreed on this: duties to respect others' individual rights and freedoms ('probity' for Bentham and 'duty of right' for Kant) are fit for state enforcement, but not altruism and self-care ('beneficence' and 'prudence'[27] for Bentham and 'duty of virtue' to others and self[28] for Kant, respectively).

When one defines the relevant individual rights in the Bentham/Kant view as free contract and private property, and assimilates those rights to the common law rules of the eighteenth and nineteenth centuries, we arrive at territory familiar to labour lawyers. This familiar territory is the *laissez-faire* rights talk that contemporary Anglo-American political philosophers often associate with Robert Nozick.[29] Lawyers are likely to associate it with Lochnerism, or the idea that workers as a general rule cannot be subject to labour laws because they 'are in no sense wards of the State' and 'are ... able to assert their rights and care for themselves without the protecting arm of the State, interfering with their independence of judgment and of action'.[30]

So, assuming Sen identifies the concept of freedom of contract with the specific 'free market' legal rules of the eighteenth and nineteenth centuries (a point I will revisit in part III below), the extent to which he considers substantive, 'opportunity aspect' differences in his assessment of the threshold beyond which responsible adults cannot be helped for 'muffed' opportunities is the only thing that distinguishes his approach from *Lochner*-type *laissez-faire*. I note that he might be open to considering many substantive opportunity differences to excuse much 'muffing'. My goal is only to point out how familiar the debate is to labour lawyers.

I now turn to Martha C Nussbaum's version of the capabilities approach, which is famously based inter alia on socio-economic rights advocacy—another important object of debate by employment lawyers—rather than on Sen's welfare economics.

---

[27] Jeremy Bentham, *An Introduction to The Principles of Morals and Legislation* (Hafner Publishing Co, 1970; 1823) 321–2. I am indebted to Mikhail Xifaras and Duncan Kennedy for pointing out the parallels between Bentham and Kant on this point.

[28] Immanuel Kant, *The Metaphysics of Morals* (Cambridge University Press, 1996; 1797) 20–1.

[29] Robert Nozick, *Anarchy, State and Utopia* (Blackwell, 1974).

[30] *Lochner v. New York*, 198 U.S. 45, 58 (1905).

In fact, Nussbaum's version is explicitly hostile to the latter. I think this hostility is what lies behind Nussbaum's criticism of the fact that Sen emphasizes 'measurement' over 'substance'[31] and does not 'introduc[e] an objective normative account of human functioning' that would lead not (only) to market maximization but to 'fundamental political entitlements and constitutional law'.[32] Nussbaum is also notably—and very productively, as I argue below—opposed to Sen's invocation of the idea of 'freedom'.

For Nussbaum, then, the main governing concept is human dignity, which is used to derive basic socio-economic entitlements and then to determine who is entitled to what above the minimum; for example, recognizing no right to housing above the minimum, but recognizing a right to equal education and voting rights way above the minimum.[33] We must debate in each case whether 'a given liberty is implicated in the idea of human dignity' and entailed by an individual or group's 'full equality as citizens and workers'.[34] This idea of dignity is embedded in an Aristotelian philosophical conception that deduces rights from the requirements of human 'nature', understood as a mixed factual and normative inquiry.[35] Another (Rawlsian) condition is that each socio-economic right or capability potentially be part of an 'overlapping consensus' between 'reasonable comprehensive views' dealing narrowly with the 'political domain', as opposed to the 'domain of human conduct generally'.[36]

These criteria revolving around dignity, then, rather than Sen's efficiency and 'process aspect of freedom' analyses, are what supply the limits to state-mandated redistribution in Nussbaum's account. Of course, human dignity is a trope that has been used extensively to debate labour laws, with no reference to the notion of capabilities.[37]

## B. The labour lawyer capability theorists

I now turn to positions by labour lawyers framed using the capabilities approach. I start with a famous debate among labour lawyers as to the adequacy of the International Labour Organization (ILO)'s 1998 Declaration on Fundamental Principles and Rights at Work. In that declaration, the ILO gave priority status to four of its labour standards: (1) freedom of association and collective bargaining; (2) the prohibition of forced labour; (3) the prohibition of child labour; and (4) the elimination of discrimination at work.

---

[31] Martha C Nussbaum, *Creating Capabilities: The Human Development Approach* (Belknap Press of Harvard University Press, 2011) 19, 27.
[32] Nussbaum, *Creating Capabilities* (n 31) 70.
[33] Nussbaum, *Creating Capabilities* (n 31) 40.
[34] Nussbaum, *Creating Capabilities* (n 31) 31.
[35] Martha C Nussbaum, *Frontiers of Justice: Disability, Nationality, Species Membership* (The Belknap Press of Harvard University Press, 2006) 36, 159.
[36] Martha C Nussbaum, 'Perfectionist Liberalism and Political Liberalism' (2011) 39 *Philosophy and Public Affairs* 3, 5–6, 9, 22.
[37] E.g. 'Introduction: Labour Rights, Human Rights' (1998) 137 International Labour Review 127, 127; David Yamada, 'Human Dignity and American Employment Law' (2009) 43 *University of Richmond Law Review* 523.

Brian Langille elaborated his version of the capabilities approach in part in defending this move by the ILO.[38] He famously claimed that the ILO's four 'core labour rights' were justly prioritized because they provide 'procedural protection' instead of 'substantive entitlements'.[39] This priority of procedural rights is good be-cause, 'while there is much room for and need of other laws and institutions to make for a just workplace, the most valuable legal technique (instrumentally and as an end in itself) has always been, and is, to unleash the power of individuals themselves to pursue their own freedom'.[40]

That this argument would infuriate many labour lawyers and social rights ad-vocates, specifically those not wed to the 'industrial pluralist' procedure/substance distinction,[41] is not very surprising. Their worry was that the prioritization of the four core civil and political rights might marginalize the more socio-economic ILO conventions, including those on social security, working conditions, occupational health and safety, etc. Philip Alston, Judy Fudge, and Adelle Blackett are three of such scholars, critical of Langille, who have framed their opposition at least in part in the terms of the capabilities approach.[42] They each argued that the CA, prop-erly understood, entails substantive entitlements just as much as procedural em-powerment.[43] This controversy about the conceptual possibility and desirability of focusing on procedural empowerment and not on substantive protections is, of course, a classic labour law debate both at the global and domestic level.[44]

I turn to another example. Robert Salais and Robert Villeneuve, in their in-spiring call for a reform of European employment policies, take capability theory in some new and surprising directions. Among other things, they speak of *firm* capabilities, putting those 'at the core of an agenda centred on work issues that, via collective bargaining and law, aims at developing economic competition through collective learning and quality, not between national social models via price and cost-cutting'.[45]

I am not sure whether other proponents of the CA would accept the idea of *firm* capabilities or reject it as an economistic deviation from *human* dignity

---

[38] Brian Langille, 'Core Labour Rights: The True Story (Reply to Alston)' (2005) 16 *European Journal of International Law* 409, 430.

[39] Langille, 'Core Labour Rights' (n 38) 429.

[40] Langille, 'Core Labour Rights' (n 38) 433–4.

[41] See Katherine Stone, 'The Post-War Paradigm in American Labor Law' (1981) 90 *Yale Law Journal* 1509, 1514–5.

[42] Philip Alston, '"Core Labour Standards" and the Transformation of the International Labour Rights Regime' (2004) 15 *European Journal of International Law* 457, 477–8; Judy Fudge, 'The New Discourse of Labor Rights: From Social to Fundamental Rights?' (2007) 29 *Comparative Labor Law and Policy Journal* 29, 61–3; Adelle Blackett, 'Situated Reflections on International Labour Law, Capabilities, and Decent Work: The Case of *Centre Maraîcher Eugène Guinois*' (2007) *Revue québécoise de droit international* 223, 243.

[43] Ibid.

[44] E.g. Christopher McCrudden and Anne Davies, 'A Perspective on Trade and Labour Rights' (2000) 21 *Journal of International Economic Law* 43, 51–2; Stone, 'The Post-War Paradigm in American Labor Law' (n 41) 1514–5.

[45] Robert Salais and Robert Villeneuve, 'Introduction: Europe and the Politics of Capabilities' in Robert Salais and Robert Villeneuve (eds), *Towards a European Politics of Capabilities* (Cambridge University Press, 2005) 1, 15 (see also 7–8).

and freedom. But I do not dislike Salais and Villeneuve's idea. To return to the point I am belabouring, note that they rely on very established justifications of labour law that have to do with disincentivizing competition through wage cutting in favour of the 'high road' of product quality, good management, and innovation.[46]

I analyse one last example. Simon Deakin and Frank Wilkinson have offered what I can only describe as a monumental contribution to our understanding of employment regulation, relying on the capabilities approach. One element of their contribution that interests me is the insistence that any market order can only be instantiated in law, and that therefore social/labour rights are 'market-constituting' in the sense that they can redress pre-market inequalities in income and bargaining power.[47]

Deakin and Wilkinson also have a radically institutionalist outlook, according to which path dependence and cumulative causation can cause sub-optimal legal-economic 'market' structures to persist.[48] So, social/labour rights raising the compensation of labour can incentivize 'high-road' investment strategies by firms aiming to maintain a healthy and skilled labour force, enabling labour laws to act as 'conversion factors' leading to more substantive freedoms for workers.[49] Labour laws can also compensate for employer monopsony power, described with brio by Deakin and Wilkinson as stemming from social undervaluation of certain (e.g. female) jobs and the comparative lack of barriers to entry for firms and workers in certain sectors.[50]

It is not possible for me to do justice to Deakin and Wilkinson's work here. My only purpose is to illustrate that their contribution, like that of the other capability theorists, builds on long-standing themes and could well have been articulated with no reference to the capabilities approach.[51]

## II. The Debate about Capabilities in Political Philosophy

In this section, I hone in on debates among philosophers as to what measuring unit should be used to assess social states in order to further suggest that capabilities,

---

[46] E.g. Richard Freeman and James Medoff, *What Do Unions Do?* (Basic Books, 1984) 163–79; Alice Amsden, *The Rise of the Rest: Challenges to the West from Late-Industrializing Economies* (Oxford University Press, 2001) 31–50.

[47] Simon Deakin and Frank Wilkinson, *The Law of the Labour Market: Industrialization, Employment and Legal Evolution* (Oxford University Press, 2005) 275.

[48] Deakin and Wilkinson, *The Law of the Labour Market* (n 47) 9, 26, 290.

[49] Deakin and Wilkinson, *The Law of the Labour Market* (n 47) 293.

[50] Deakin and Wilkinson, *The Law of the Labour Market* (n 47) 293.

[51] On labour law as incentivizing 'high road' investment strategies see above n 46. On countering employer monopsony power see e.g. Bruce Kaufman, 'Labor Law and Employment Regulation: Neoclassical and Institutional Perspectives' in Kenneth G Dau-Schmidt, Seth D Harris, and Orly Lobel (eds), *Labor and Employment Law and Economics* (Edward Elgar Publishing, 2009) 3, 29–35; Michael H Gottesman, 'Whither Goest Labor Law: Law and Economics in the Workplace' (1991) 100 *Yale Law Journal* 2767, 2782 ff.

Rawlsian primary goods, and utility (as well as Dworkinian 'resources' and GA Cohen's 'access to advantage') are, to a large extent, interchangeable.

Before I start, I want to touch briefly on GA Cohen's illuminating description of the capabilities approach (and his 'access to advantage', as well as Dworkin's 'resources', I would add) as a 'middle' point between Rawlsian goods and utility.[52] That is, thinking in terms of capabilities allows us to consider the different needs of people so that we look beyond equal shares in goods. But we do not quite look to the utility created by the use of the goods because we want a judgment on a person's actual state that does not depend solely on her own perceptions. Cohen's example is helpful: in those 'middle' approaches, we look at a person's 'nutrition level, and not just, as Rawlsians do, at her food supply, or, as welfarists do, at the utility she gets out of eating food'.[53]

It strikes me that Cohen is describing a spectrum that goes from more objective (Rawlsian goods) to more and more subjective and individual indicators (ending with utility, i.e. subjectively felt pleasure or happiness). Conceiving of these indicators on a spectrum from objective to subjective will be useful as I make the point below that we can adjust each indicator so that it leads to the same result as the others.

Now on to the debates I want to analyse. One reason offered by Nussbaum and Sen for departing from Rawlsian primary goods, and from the goal of equalizing them to the extent required by the difference principle, was that this did not account for the special needs of groups like persons with disabilities, children, and pregnant women, who need more than an equal share of income and rights.[54] In Nussbaum's useful twist on this idea, with a capabilities approach we can 'look further into social context' and find more 'variety' to be compensated, for instance when it comes to 'children from minority groups'[55] (and this seems to open the door to socio-economic disadvantage more generally).

I note two things about this point. The first is that it seems perfectly compatible with Rawls' primary goods approach; nothing in that concept logically precludes varying the amount of primary goods to account for differences in needs and capacity to attain desired states. In fact, despite many qualifications, Rawls himself eventually 'agree[d] with Sen that basic capabilities are of first importance and that the use of primary goods is always to be assessed in the light of assumptions about those capabilities'.[56] I will not insist on this point, seeing as Nussbaum herself notes that 'it is not clear that the core of the Rawlsian approach to justice could not be reformulated in a way that would preserve most of Rawls' essential insights but would meet my criticisms'[57] on points that include the different needs of certain groups in

---

[52] GA Cohen, 'Equality of What? On Welfare, Goods and Capabilities' in *The Quality of Life* (n 26) 9, 18.

[53] Cohen, 'Equality of What?' (n 52) 19.

[54] Nussbaum, *Creating Capabilities* (n 31) 57; Sen, *The Idea of Justice* (n 18) 252–65.

[55] Martha C Nussbaum, 'Aristotelian Social Democracy' in BB Douglass and others (eds), *Liberalism and the Good* (Routledge, 1990) 203, 211.

[56] John Rawls, *Political Liberalism* (Columbia University Press, 1993) 183.

[57] Nussbaum, *Creating Capabilities* (n 31) 87.

society. The second point I want to make about this debate is that Nussbaum and Sen's move is best seen as a subjectivization of the metric, that is, a move away from objectively defined primary goods towards the subjective end of the spectrum—the end of individual differences in capacity to use the goods.[58]

In addition to dissenting from Rawls' objective approach to primary goods distribution, Nussbaum and Sen have advocated for a move away from subjectivist utility assessments towards more objective judgments on the desirability of social outcomes. 'Adaptive preferences' were a key concept here. This is the idea that certain subjective preferences and utility experiences are to be disregarded because they are misguided, including when they are the product of oppressive social conditions. The classic example of this phenomenon is some women's lack of desire for economic opportunities and gender equality due to social conditioning.[59]

A related problem with utilitarianism was said to lie in offensive and oppressive preferences (e.g. the sadist who is very unhappy unless others suffer and very happy when they do),[60] as well as expensive tastes that would require us to cater to individual capricious desires (e.g. we would have to give more to the person who is unhappy without caviar and champagne than to a poor person in order to maximize utility).[61] Another complaint was that utilitarianism does not account for the value of the process of generating utilities, which could be brought about through violations of rights or without active involvement of the persons concerned.[62] A final complaint was that utilitarianism is intrinsically blind to distributive justice, wed as it is to maximum aggregate utility (expressed, for instance, in GDP).[63]

To sum up, then, the capabilities approach was said to be preferable to utilitarianism in order to correct for adaptive, offensive, and expensive preferences (all to be disregarded); to account for the process by which utility is generated (and whether it also enhances capabilities); and to judge distributive outcomes (i.e. how utilities are distributed).

I think those criticisms of (certain forms of) utilitarianism are all sound, but they underestimate the extent to which utilitarianism can be reformed while remaining 'itself'. Taking the criticisms in reverse order, let me start by mentioning that many utilitarianisms have been very friendly to distributive concerns. We can follow some economists in holding that under certain conditions interpersonal comparisons of utility are admissible, opening the door to interventions that maximize total utility

---

[58] Note the strong analogy between this move and Ronald Dworkin's idea of giving more 'resources' to people who suffer from bad 'luck' or have lesser 'native skills'; see Dworkin, 'What Is Equality? Part II' (n 2) 327. It seems safe to assume that disability and the social disadvantages discussed by the capability theorists and Rawls would be compensated in the same way by a Dworkinian. The same could be said of GA Cohen's 'advantage' (and 'equal access' thereto); see 'On the Currency of Egalitarian Justice' (n 2) 921–2.

[59] Martha C Nussbaum, *Women and Human Development: The Capabilities Approach* (Cambridge University Press, 2000) 98; Sen, *Inequality Reexamined* (n 4) 55; Sen, *Development as Freedom* (n 3) 62–3.

[60] Sen, *The Idea of Justice* (n 18) 218–19.

[61] On this see Ronald Dworkin, 'What Is Equality? Part I: Equality of Welfare' (1981) 10 *Philosophy and Public Affairs* 185, 197–201.

[62] Nussbaum, *Women and Human Development* (n 59) 120–1; Sen, *The Idea of Justice* (n 18) 218–19.

[63] Nussbaum, *Creating Capabilities* (n 31) 50–6.

through redistribution.[64] Indeed, this fact has even led non-utilitarian observers with very different outlooks to deplore utilitarianism's excessive amenability to the redistribution of wealth![65]

We can, alternatively, follow the traditional welfare economists and hold that comparing utilities interpersonally is perfectly admissible, albeit unscientific.[66] In fact, this more modest acceptance by welfare economists that they cannot exclude distributive judgment (however unscientific they may think it) from an account of the good underlines the extent to which utilitarianism can in fact be reformed. That is to say that we can even displace *maximization* as the goal and go after some equalization of utilities without contradicting any tenet of the welfare economists' utilitarianism.

Moving on to the next objection to utilitarianism, it seems to me that we can easily account for the value of the process used to generate utilities *in utility terms.* In other words, we can prefer processes that have desirable utility consequences (of the maximizing or the distributive kind), including, for example, because they respect 'rights', either justified on rule-utilitarian grounds or as desired by the people involved.

As for the correction of adaptive, offensive, and expensive tastes, I just note that I do not see why we would constrain the utilitarian to favour *only* subjective preferences on pain of not being utilitarian anymore. One can coherently want to honour subjective preferences as much as possible—to be as far away from objective Rawlsian primary goods and as close to pure subjective utility on the spectrum I described above—while being open to compromising with objective desiderata in certain cases.[67] Theorists have accepted several of these objective modifications to utility as permissible within utilitarianism, holding that other modifications were irreconcilable with it. Thus for Nussbaum, offensive preferences—and possibly expensive ones—can be corrected while staying within the utilitarian framework, but adaptive preferences cannot, because they 'involv[e] people's entire upbringing in a society' and '[a]daptation is not just lack of information'.[68] For Cohen, offensive preferences can be corrected within utilitarianism, but it is the correction of expensive tastes that takes us out of utilitarianism.[69]

Any position on these questions (including my own) must rest on a game of definitions of the various approaches or theories that will often refer to a particular historically-existing version of each theory; we might look to Bentham instead of John Harsanyi, for example, to fix the contours of utilitarianism. But anyone who

---

[64] E.g. Arthur C Pigou, *The Economics of Welfare* (Transaction Publishers, 2009; 1920) 850–1; Abba Lerner, *The Economics of Control: Principles of Welfare Economics* (Macmillan, 1944) 26–35.

[65] Richard Posner, 'Utilitarianism, Economics, and Legal Theory' (1979) 8 *Journal of Legal Studies* 103, 115; John M Alexander, *Capabilities and Social Justice: The Political Philosophy of Amartya Sen and Martha Nussbaum* (Ashgate Publishing, 2008) 53.

[66] Lionel Robbins, *An Essay on the Nature and Significance of Economic Science* (2nd edn, Macmillan, 1935) 136–40; Bator, 'The Simple Analytics of Welfare Maximization' (n 9).

[67] For a similar analysis of utilitarianism, see Jonathan Riley, *Liberal Utilitarianism: Social Choice Theory and J.S. Mill's Philosophy* (Cambridge University Press, 1988) 6–8.

[68] Nussbaum, *Creating Capabilities* (n 31) 83.

[69] Cohen, 'Equality of What?' (n 52) 12.

chooses to work within a tradition can also change its definition and expand it beyond its past limits. Defining theories very broadly has the advantage of helping us avoid being entangled in the resulting complicated debates about the 'nature' of various theories in light of historical antecedents. My choice of defining utilitarianism very broadly as being amenable to objective corrections of subjective preferences will likely seem even more plausible to the reader in light of my suggestion below, in section III, that disregarding the will and subjective preferences of individuals ('paternalism') is pervasive even in the daily administration of a legal system purporting to honour people's freedom of choice.

Before leaving the topic of the interchangeability of the various approaches to measuring the good, I want to make a final point. If we trace the role of 'choice' in the various alternative theories, we get the following portrait, which further shows the similarities between all of them. According to the capability theorists, we should maximize and/or equalize capabilities (not functionings) defined as the substantive ability to choose things that presumably procure pleasure (thereby preserving choice by definition and resting on a conception of desert[70]). For a utilitarian economist we should maximize the pleasure derived from people's choices as expressed in a marketplace, perhaps sometimes also equalizing substantive opportunities to choose with lump-sum transfers.[71] For Rawlsians, we should equalize primary goods except where that is economically inefficient, and leave people free to choose how they will pursue the good life (or pleasure) with their primary goods.[72] Finally, as briefly noted above,[73] Dworkin and Cohen would equalize resources and access to advantage except to the extent that discrepancies thereof are freely chosen.

This summary, which leaves out several of the nuances I have touched on above, nevertheless brings out just how close these theories are. They all rest on the idea of countering inequalities that are not freely chosen and tolerating those that are. Of course, it will make much difference how we use the concept of capabilities, or of utility and primary goods, for that matter. We can, for example, maximize them on the market (Sen) or distribute them based on 'dignity' (Nussbaum), and do either in many different ways. My point has only been that nothing much hangs on the adoption of the concept of capabilities instead of the alternatives.

As a result, it seems to me that the stakes of adopting one or the other conceptual framework are rhetorical and strategic, and have to do with how one's anticipated audience is likely to perceive the various possible frameworks. I, for one, mostly stay clear of the capabilities language in my own work because I often find it to be associated by my audiences to a centre-left orientation. Since I am quite to the left of the political spectrum, I am inclined to frame my work in concepts more traditionally accepted by the right, like utility, to appeal to a broader group. But this is a very personal decision, and one about which we cannot easily generalize.

---

[70] See my discussion of Sen (nn 26–30) and accompanying text.
[71] See Bator, 'The Simple Analytics of Welfare Maximization' (n 9).
[72] Rawls, *Political Liberalism* (n 56), 186–7.    [73] See n 58.

## III.  A Brief Sketch of a First-order Approach to Labour Law

In this section I try to practise what I preach by addressing the first-order question of how we should regulate employment. I provide a brief sketch of my own approach, which I call left legal realism. My approach is perfectly compatible with, and could be articulated using, the capabilities concept, although I make no particular effort to do so here. This introductory account can only be incomplete and maybe even somewhat cryptic, but because no other contributor to this volume is part of the otherwise quite large family of left legal realist approaches, hopefully my chapter can put those approaches on the map for the reader.

### A.  A primer on Hohfeld and legal realism

Above, I described a view of 'rights' that I attributed to Kant, Bentham, and Nozick, according to which individuals have a zone of freedom in which they can do whatever they want with their bodies and property, provided they do not infringe on others' rights. This zone might entail private property, freedom of contract, the right to bodily integrity, and freedom of expression and religion, among others.

Laura Weinrib, in her contribution to this volume, helpfully reminds us of a historical period, in the late nineteenth and early twentieth centuries, during which this philosophical outlook was invoked to justify the judicial and legislative repression of the labour movement. For instance, the employer's legal liberty to hire non-union labour as well as its proprietary interest in its business and existing non-union (sometimes 'yellow-dog'[74]) employment contracts were held to be violated by union tactics like boycotts aiming to obtain union recognition, strikes, or even union recruitment *tout court*. Faced with these legal challenges, legal realist thinkers like Wesley Hohfeld developed an analysis of law and rights that I propose we adopt in thinking about employment.

The Kantian/Benthamite/Nozickian idea of equal freedom is often dealt with in the 'harm principle' formulation given to it by John Stuart Mill, who famously defined liberty as 'doing what we like ... without impediment from our fellow-creatures, so long as what we do does not harm them'.[75] Hohfeld is best understood as demonstrating that the idea of equal freedom qualified by the harm principle is question-begging and useless for fixing specific legal rules. Indeed, according to a Hohfeldian approach, the harm principle is only coherent if we ignore the gigantic pockets of legal harm (or *damnum absque injuria*) that are—and always have been—permitted by all legal systems.[76] Contemporary examples of such harms include non-negligent damages in tort (or otherwise excusable damages under another standard like strict liability), some competitive tactics but not others (e.g. stealing

---

[74]  These are contracts in which the employee commits to not joining a union.
[75]  John S Mill, *On Liberty* (Norton, 1975) 13.
[76]  Joseph W Singer, 'The Legal Rights Debate in Analytical Jurisprudence from Bentham to Hohfeld' (1982) *Wisconsin Law Review* 975, 1012.

market share by cutting prices, but not 'dumping' or 'exclusionary practices'), interrupting performance after some types of breach but not others, etc.

The critical idea, worked out by legal theorists like Oliver Wendell Holmes and John Salmond in the late nineteenth century and culminating in Hohfeld's work, is that legal harm to some freedom/right is the corollary of any other existing freedom/right. To exercise one's freedom of action is, very often if not always,[77] to impinge on the other's freedom from harm (or on her rights to security). It is in light of this relationship that we must understand Hohfeld's famous insistence that the imprecise catch-all term 'right' be disaggregated into the two possible 'claim-right'/duty and privilege/no-right pairs of correlatives.[78] To take the example of the judicial repression of the labour movement, which Hohfeld used as an application of his analytic,[79] we would say that a 'general' right or freedom (like the employer's property right or freedom of contract) is no good authority to justify imposing a duty on another party not to interfere with a particular act. This is because to assert a general right or freedom is not useful; given the ubiquity of legal harm or *damnum absque injuria*, we need to make more specific decisions as to whether a particular harm will be allowed.

It follows that the courts that justified enjoining union organizing and boycotts by invoking previous cases establishing the employer's legal right/freedom to fire non-union employees (this was Hohfeld's example) were reading the earlier cases much too broadly and committing an error of logic. The possibility of firing a union employee did not establish a general right against any interference with 'freedom of contract', because interference with freedom of contract is, and can only be, omnipresent. Those earlier cases must be taken to have established something narrower, that is, merely a rule as to when employees can be fired.[80] In short, the abstract concept of freedom of contract is compatible with both allowing and banning union organizing and boycotts/strikes (which in Hohfeld's example aimed to pressure an employer into not firing union employees).

Hohfeld's analysis led to the famous view of property (and freedom of contract) as a 'bundle of rights'[81] (or 'bundle of sticks'), constituted by a set of narrow rules establishing some vulnerabilities ('no-rights') and some protections ('rights'), as well as some authorizations to harm ('privileges') and some prohibitions on harming others ('duties'). According to the 'bundle of rights' approach, rights and freedom are question-begging concepts that cannot be invoked to justify a given allocation of legal permissions to harm because they can correspond to multiple different such

---

[77] There might be a residuum of some acts that absolutely do not affect others, but the claim here is that this area is extremely small, much more than the harm principle suggests.

[78] Wesley N Hohfeld, 'Some Fundamental Legal Conceptions as Applied to Judicial Reasoning' (1913) 23 *Yale Law Journal* 16. I am leaving aside the power/liability and disability/immunity part of the Hohfeldian *schema*.

[79] See Hohfeld's discussion of the English case of *Quinn v. Leathem* [1901] AC 495, 36–7.

[80] See similarly Walter W Cook, 'Privileges of Labor Unions in the Struggle for Life' (1918) 27 *Yale Law Journal* 779, 788.

[81] Jane B Baron, 'Rescuing the Bundle of Rights Metaphor in Property Law' (2013) 82 *University of Cincinnati Law Review* 57, 61–79.

allocations. Hence Hohfeld's insistence that legal rights and no-rights can only be coherently distributed by reference to 'policy',[82] a famous *leitmotif* of legal realist thought.[83]

Successive generations of scholars have explored the kinds of arguments that may be considered under the rubric of policy, holding that we can look at things like morality, expectations, social utility, and 'administrability' (the flexibility of general standards versus the certainty of rigid narrow rules).[84] The important thing to emphasize here is that 'rights', on the Hohfeldian view, cannot be part of the policy calculus, either as 'trumps' or merely 'balanced' against other non-rights considerations. Because rights are circular assertions of the very legal entitlements to be distributed, they have no role in justificatory legal reasoning. They are also not good descriptions of any legal system, because they are compatible with a multitude of legal regimes that contain the bundles but arrange the sticks within each bundle very differently.

I note, in passing, that my reading of Hohfeld is the opposite of that of Brian Langille, who uses Hohfeld to support what he calls the 'right/freedom' distinction.[85] My reading is much closer to Alan Bogg and Keith Ewing's 'molecule' metaphor,[86] which is premised on a rejection of the distinction between freedoms (which would be negative) and rights (which would be positive or 'derivative' as well as correlated with duties). In fact, the 'molecule' described by Bogg and Ewing (but not mentioned by Bogg in this volume) is the equivalent of the bundle of rights I have been mentioning, and applies to both rights and freedoms. That is, both rights and freedoms are complex amalgams of privileges, rights, duties, and no-rights that can be configured in many different ways. I wish I had space to elaborate, but I must leave full exploration of this difficult point for another time.

I also want to note that the Hohfeldian analysis is not akin to the idea, often attributed to HLA Hart and his critique of Rawls,[87] that we should speak of an adequate scheme of enumerated liberties rather than of pursuing the 'greatest liberty'. Rawls, in accepting this idea, insisted that the liberties in such a scheme can be 'adjusted' against one another but never against 'considerations of all kinds—political, economic, and social'.[88] A Hohfeldian would counter that there is a multitude of ways to 'adjust' the liberties against one another by shifting sticks from one bundle to another, encompassing both radically egalitarian and anti-egalitarian labour laws, for instance. 'Political, economic, and social' considerations will thus inevitably enter the analysis of just which adjustment of the liberties we will choose. These

---

[82]  Hohfeld, 'Some Fundamental Legal Conceptions as Applied to Judicial Reasoning' (n 78) 36.

[83]  Cook, 'Privileges of Labor Unions in the Struggle for Life' (n 80) 783; Arthur L Corbin, 'Offer and Acceptance, and Some of the Resulting Legal Relations' (1917) 26 *Yale Law Journal* 169, 206.

[84]  E.g. Melvin Eisenberg, *The Nature of the Common Law* (Harvard University Press, 1988) 37–42; Jack Balkin, 'The Crystalline Structure of Legal Thought' (1986) 39 *Rutgers Law Review* 1, 28.

[85]  See Brian Langille, 'Why the Right/Freedom Distinction Matters to Labour Lawyers: and All Canadians' (2011) 34 *Dalhousie Law Journal* 143, 149.

[86]  Alan Bogg and Keith Ewing, 'A (Muted) Voice at Work: Collective Bargaining in the Supreme Court of Canada' (2012) 33 *Comparative Labor Law & Policy Journal* 379, 397.

[87]  HLA Hart, 'Rawls on Liberty and Its Priority' (1973) 40 *University of Chicago Law Review* 538.

[88]  Rawls, *Political Liberalism* (n 56) 357.

conflicts may well divide people along the lines of their 'comprehensive views' of the good life or their ideologies.

The Hohfeldian analysis does resemble Nussbaum's critique of Sen's use of the concept of 'freedom' as something to be maximized. Nussbaum suggests that this idea is incoherent because 'some freedoms limit others' and 'the very idea of freedom involves the idea of constraint: for person P is not free to do action A unless other people are prevented from interfering'.[89] She concludes that promoting capabilities will involve curtailing some freedoms that stand in the way, as 'some freedoms involve basic social entitlements, and others do not'.[90] Nussbaum then proceeds to justify several 'rights' on the basis of her system described above.[91]

I agree with Nussbaum's critique of Sen, but I would go further. The Hohfeldian circularity critique applies as much to rights as to freedoms; in fact, it relativizes that distinction. So, the idea is that freedoms and rights are incoherent categories because they tell us nothing about how to trade-off the competing freedoms and rights (this would be my Hohfeldian reformulation of Nussbaum's critique).

The Hohfeldian analysis deals only with the concepts of rights and freedoms, and not with the possibility of an analysis that does not rely on such concepts. Since many kinds of policy analysis do not straightforwardly appeal to rights and freedoms, yet ultimately incorporate or assume those concepts (e.g. Posnerian law and economics), the Hohfeldian analysis covers a lot of ground. That said, it is at least theoretically possible to imagine 'balancing' the importance of, for example, honouring expectations of security versus expectations of freedom of action, or the importance of equitable flexibility versus certainty, or the importance of taking care of others versus self-reliance, without framing those interests and values as equal rights and freedoms.

We therefore need to address the possibility of such 'balancing'. In a long-standing tradition of legal realism and critical legal studies, scholars have argued that there are very often multiple equally defensible trade-offs between those different values and interests traceable to a fundamental conflict between individualism and altruism, both as ideals and as inspirations for particular legal rules.[92] The take-away of this line of analysis is that such balancing, even one that would not rely implicitly or explicitly on the circular concepts of rights and freedoms, does not help us choose among the many possible legal regimes of property and contract.

## B. Implications for political and moral philosophy

The implications of this bit of legal theory for political and moral philosophy are manifold. One is Robert Hale's point, which he explicitly ties to Hohfeld's approach,

---

[89] Nussbaum, *Creating Capabilities* (n 31) 71–2.
[90] Nussbaum, *Creating Capabilities* (n 31) 72.      [91] See nn 31–7 above.
[92] Duncan Kennedy, 'Form and Substance in Private Law Adjudication' (1976) 89 *Harvard Law Review* 1685, 1774–5; P Gabel, 'Intention and Structure in Contractual Conditions: Outline of a Method for Critical Legal Theory' (1977) 61 *Minnesota Law Review* 601, 612–13; Singer, 'The Legal Rights Debate in Analytical Jurisprudence from Bentham to Hohfeld' (n 76) 980; JM Feinman, 'Critical Approaches to Contract Law' (1983) 30 *UCLA Law Review* 829, 847.

that the market value of a worker's product is not a function only of productivity and skills but of the legal rules that distribute bargaining power.[93] In other words, Hale gives the legal system an independent role in causing the distribution of income. This point has the potential to justify the promotion of Sen's 'positive', 'substantive', or 'opportunity aspect' freedom,[94] but it goes beyond it by dissolving the distinction between that and the negative or 'process aspect' freedom.

The distinction between process and substance is dissolved because the procedural legal rules (e.g. those defining consideration, mistake, duress, and permissible bargaining tactics including the legality of collective bargaining and strikes) exist on a very wide spectrum depending on how the bundles are constituted. And moving along the spectrum (e.g. by having broader or narrower definitions of consideration, mistake, or duress) can dramatically change the substantive outcome of transactions.[95] There is no set of procedural rules that is neutral as to the outcome, so choosing one set of procedural rules over another amounts to choosing an outcome. Fixing the content of contracts, for instance through compulsory terms, is thus functionally indistinguishable from applying the merely procedural rules of the free market.

My discussion here follows a trend in the literature of focusing on a situation of bargaining between two parties: the employer and a union or a single employee. It is easiest to grasp the 'bundle of rights' point that way, because applying it to a situation of multiple employees bargaining with an employer requires us to address not only the rules that structure bargaining but also the rules about when an employee can 'undercut' the deal struck by another employee. This raises the question, on which Laura Weinrib helpfully focuses in her contribution, of the extent to which labour laws and union tactics might violate (negative) freedom of association and constitute cartels that restrict competition—two distinct but overlapping points.

Scholars have brought legal realism to bear on this question and argued that unions are no more derogatory of freedom or competition than the regular rules of the free market or than compulsory terms imposed by the legislature.[96] But it is fair to say that this theme has been underdeveloped in the literature as compared to the more straightforward scenario where two parties, a union and an employer, bargain and exert pressure tactics against one another. I intend to contribute to filling this gap in future work. Nevertheless, the more general point about the importance of procedural free market rules in determining substantive contractual outcomes already gives us a lot to build on.

This analysis has implications for the important question of the place to be given to choice and subjective desires in a legal system. On that front, I applaud Sen and Nussbaum's emphasis on the fact that preferences have to be corrected, including

[93] See Robert Hale, 'Bargaining, Duress, and Economic Liberty' (1943) 43 *Columbia Law Review* 603, 628.

[94] Sen, *Development as Freedom* (n 3) 281–2, 285, 297.

[95] Hale, 'Bargaining, Duress, and Economic Liberty' (n 93) 626–8; Duncan Kennedy, 'The Stakes of Law, or Hale and Foucault!' in *Sexy Dressing Etc.: Essays on the Power and Politics of Cultural Identity* (Harvard University Press, 1993) 83, 84–92.

[96] E.g. Hale, 'Bargaining, Duress, and Economic Liberty' (n 93).

when they are adaptive, offensive, or expensive.[97] Emphasizing the need to correct adaptive preferences is an important contribution that dovetails quite nicely with work in behavioural law and economics on the impossibility of a neutral 'choice architecture' and on the often-determinative role that default rules can play in steering people towards certain choices.[98] I also salute Nussbaum's insistence that we make socio-economic rights non-waivable.[99] This is common practice in labour law. Nussbaum and the behavioural legal economists nevertheless insist that they are committed to choice and opposed to paternalism, through slightly different argumentative moves that need not detain us here.

The better attitude seems to me to be to acknowledge that paternalism is pervasive and that we must engage in it, although such a project is not without its dangers. I rely here on Duncan Kennedy's work on the inevitability of paternalism, even in routine institutions of our legal system like the law of consideration (the famous 'cautionary function' of which is meant to allow courts to ignore unwise decisions to contract) and promissory estoppel (which operates to override unwise decisions not to seek adequate consideration), among many other examples.[100] Because paternalism is pervasive and because the distinction between correcting for imperfect information and paternalism is blurry,[101] one can confidently impose compulsory terms and substantive regulation of contracts without being deterred from doing so by the mere invocation of choice and anti-paternalism in the abstract.

So far I have used legal realism and Hohfeld mainly for negative purposes; I have shown how they dissolve putative obstacles to redistribution, including through labour laws. Fleshing out a positive normative agenda that we could combine with legal realism would take up too much space. But here is a glimpse of where I end up normatively without much in the way of explication. I start on the 'altruist' side of the individualist/altruist conflict I described above, that is, the side that tends towards compensating low income as well as excusing mistakes and failures to self-insure. The grounds for this starting place include Rawls' argument that we are not (entirely) responsible for our characters, such that the concepts of effort and choice must be relativized.[102] Further supporting grounds include the idea that productivity, skills, and income are the product of self-reinforcing familial class dynamics, and of social and institutional networks that are biased against have-nots,[103] not to mention discrimination and exclusion based on identity status.

The foregoing claims are quite conventional for left liberals and socialists. The crucial added component is that, as I have said several times already, the legal rules of

---

[97] See nn 59–61 above and accompanying text.

[98] E.g. Richard H Thaler and Cass R Sunstein, *Nudge: Improving Decisions About Health, Wealth and Happiness* (Yale University Press, 2008) 3–6.

[99] Nussbaum, *Women and Human Development* (n 59) 93–4.

[100] Duncan Kennedy, 'Distributive and Paternalist Motives in Contract and Tort Law, with Special Reference to Compulsory Terms and Unequal Bargaining Power' (1982) 41 *Maryland Law Review* 563, 635.

[101] Kennedy, 'Distributive and Paternalist Motives in Contract and Tort Law' (n 100).

[102] John Rawls, *A Theory of Justice* (Harvard University Press, 1971) 104.

[103] See Pierre Bourdieu, 'Cultural Reproduction and Social Reproduction' in Jerome Karabel and Albert H Halsey (eds), *Power and Ideology in Education* (Oxford University Press, 1977) 487.

property and contract are themselves given a crucial role in causing the distribution of income. That is, there is no single 'market' to which we can default as instantiating choice or freedom even after tax-and-transfer compensation for character and social-familial determinisms. It is thus impossible to straightforwardly separate, as many liberal political philosophers purport to do, the effects of 'luck' and innate 'talent' (which should not be rewarded) from 'choice' and 'ambition' (which can be rewarded).[104]

That said, in the end the guiding principle is indeed the extent to which an individual deserves her plight, and luck, historical-social-familial determinism, and control over our own characters are central issues. It is just that the prevailing distribution of income resulting from existing laws has no claim to being presumptively even remotely close to a neutral one produced by freedom. This point leads me to advocate a lot of redistribution and altruism, perhaps falling short of complete equality, but much closer to it than to the current distribution of income anywhere. These kinds of judgments about the other's psychology, family, and history can only be approximate, but my general direction is towards radical altruism and redistribution.

This account is perforce fragmentary and would require more fleshing out. Even if I were to provide that, however, it would still be the case that my normative agenda remains self-consciously partisan, ideological, and subjective rather than neutral, logical, and objective. That is, I accept that my own altruist approach is one possible moral and political outlook, and that one could have another (although not any other), more individualist outlook that would be equally rationally defensible. In so doing I follow a long string of 'pluralist' and 'decisionist' thinkers that include Max Weber, Isaiah Berlin, Hans Kelsen, the logical positivists, and neoclassical economists like Lionel Robbins and Kenneth Arrow. I therefore find it productive that Sen emphasizes so much in recent work that 'there can exist several distinct reasons of justice, each of which survives critical scrutiny, but yields divergent conclusions'.[105] I see this as forming part of the pluralist and decisionist approach that I espouse, alongside my altruist and leftist commitments.

## C. Thoughts on labour/employment law as a discipline

Rather than develop the above philosophical sketch any further, I want to close by dealing with an issue raised insistently by Martha C Nussbaum in this volume, but which labour lawyers have been debating for decades now: the question of the relationship of labour/employment law to informal, domestic, and non-subordinate work. Nussbaum suggests that the very discipline of labour/employment law (which I have been calling labour law for short) is intrinsically complicit with the marginalization of women and informal workers because of its focus on wage labour. My position is that, on the contrary, the categories of labour law can be made capacious

---

[104] E.g. Cohen, 'On the Currency of Egalitarian Justice' (n 2) 922; Dworkin, 'What Is Equality? Part II' (n 2) 315, 327.
[105] Sen, *The Idea of Justice* (n 18) at x.

enough to encompass much of the excluded groups, and that the well-established category of 'social law' as a broader ensemble of which labour law is a part can do the rest of the work of providing politically satisfying disciplinary boundaries.

Start with informal work, which can be any work not covered by formal labour laws. When no labour laws are applied, workers become independent contractors subjected to a more generic form of contract law, even if not the law of the state.[106] Informal work is in this regard obviously similar to the 'fissured workplace'[107] relationships in the contemporary Global North, that is, independent contracting, work for temporary worker agencies, franchising, and flexible work contracts more generally.

Rather than attribute informality to the nature of the societies of the Global South and fissured work relations in the Global North to the nature of the 'new economy' or 'globalization', I follow Simon Deakin in considering that, to a large extent, it is law that constitutes and creates the fissured workplace (and informality), rather than merely tracking or following the economy.[108] That is to say that law and the state could very well defissure the workplace and make workers out of independent contractors. Similarly, law and the state could eliminate (much) informality in the Global South.

Now, of course, there are economic consequences and costs to making workers out of informal or independent contractors; my claim is that the indispensable analysis of those economic consequences and costs should proceed just like the analysis of the impact of the enactment of, say, late nineteenth century labour laws in the Global North. This economic analysis might reveal that in some cases employee status is too rigid or costly; we already have many innovative forms of labour law to deal with those cases, including 'craft' (as opposed to 'industrial') models of production and unionism.[109] This economic analysis might also reveal that in the Global South, lack of growth and development makes some formal labour laws too costly (contrast this left-wing perspective with the neoliberal account of informality as caused by labour laws themselves).[110] In that case, the solution could lie in more growth and development, of the 'inclusive' and redistributive type.

In short, my position is that labour/employment law can be (and sometimes has been) expanded to carry much of the abstract altruist agenda sketched above, in the Global South and North. It therefore seems wrong to reify its current shrunken scope and label it as necessarily exclusionary.

---

[106] See Guillermo Perry and others, *Informality: Exit and Exclusion* (World Bank, 2007) 4.

[107] David Weil, *The Fissured Workplace: Why Work Became so Bad for so Many and What Can be Done to Improve it* (Harvard University Press, 2014).

[108] Simon Deakin, 'The Comparative Evolution of the Employment Relationship' in Guy Davidov and Brian Langille (eds), *Boundaries and Frontiers of Labour Law: Goals and Means in the Regulation of Work* (Hart Publishing, 2006) 89, 104.

[109] See Michael J Piore and Charles Sabel, *The Second Industrial Divide: Possibilities for Prosperity* (Basic Books, 1984) 115–24.

[110] See L Josh Bivens and Dominick S Gammage, 'Will Better Workers Lead to Better Jobs in the Developing World?' in Tony Avirgan, L Josh Bivens, and Dominick S Gammage (eds), *Good Jobs, Bad Jobs, No Jobs: Labor Markets and Informal Work in Egypt, El Salvador, India, Russia* (Economic Policy Institute, 2005) 1, 21–2.

It is true, however, that there are limits to expanding the dependent work relationship. The clearest example would be domestic and care work—at least a residuum thereof that couldn't or shouldn't be taken over by a welfare state and therefore made into public sector jobs. I think there we do need more than labour law, but that we can do with the existing (European) category of 'social law'—a broad term that has been taken to include social security, social insurance, and the legal regulation of care and reproductive work—in addition to labour/employment law. This seems to me to be the take-away of many analyses by feminist labour lawyers dealing with just these questions.[111]

Some forms of independent contracting (including, for example, by small-holding agricultural producers) might also be irredeemably ill-suited for labour law, however adapted and modified. It might be that there we need not labour law but 'petty bourgeois socialism'[112] to carry through my legal realist altruist programme. That said, it is unclear to me that such a project would ultimately be very different from labour law, especially in its craft unionism variant that treats workers more as collectively bargaining independent contractors than as subordinate wage earners.[113]

Labour law, understood as a component of social law, therefore seems to me politically viable as a discipline, including for the kind of altruist normative project that Nussbaum and I to a certain extent share. Of course, this is not to say that labour law or social law should be the only vehicles for such a project, but merely that they can be important *loci* of political thought and activity.

## IV.  Conclusion

There is a lot to be done in labour law theory that can inform political philosophy and economic analysis. In section III of this chapter I have tried to cover as many important questions of legal theory as I could in order to illustrate the issues on which I think labour lawyers should focus. My claim has been that much of the discussion around whether to 'adopt' the capabilities approach is not very useful. This is because those arguing for or against a conceptual vocabulary often underestimate the extent to which the various possible vocabularies, say of utility, primary goods, and capabilities, can be used to take the same positions on first-order questions. I should say that critics of the CA have been, in my view, more guilty of this error than advocates, who have tended a bit less to reify the CA as a fixed apparatus with clear normative consequences. However, reification has been frequent on all sides of the debate.

---

[111]  E.g. Joanne Conaghan, 'Work, Family, and the Discipline of Labour Law' in Joanne Conaghan and Kerry Rittich (eds), *Labour Law, Work and Family: Critical and Comparative Perspectives* (Oxford University Press, 2005) 19, 41.

[112]  Cui Zhiyuan, 'China's Future: Suggestions from Petty Bourgeois Socialist Theories and Some Chinese Practices' in Fred Dallmayr and Zhao Tingyang (eds), *Contemporary Chinese Political Thought: Debates and Perspectives* (University of Kentucky Press, 2012) 209.

[113]  See Piore and Sabel, *The Second Industrial Divide* (n 109) 115–24.

Rather than attacking or defending any given conceptual scheme, I have advocated for an engagement with Sen, Nussbaum, Langille, Salais, Deakin, and Wilkinson as individual theorists taking specific first-order positions. I have begun to describe my own normative and analytical approach to labour regulation, comparing and contrasting it with Sen, Nussbaum, and the others' positions. And I propose that we labour lawyers proceed on that basis, in the spirit of renewal and contestation that has characterized the past work of many of the contributors to this volume.[114] That, rather than debating which conceptual vocabulary to use, seems to me a promising way forward.

---

[114] See e.g. the contributions to Guy Davidov and Brian Langille (eds), *The Idea of Labour Law* (Oxford University Press, 2011); Joanne Conaghan, Richard Michael Fischl, and Karl Klare (eds), *Labour Law in an Era of Globalization: Transformative Practices and Possibilities* (Oxford University Press, 2002).

# 10

# Work, Human Rights, and Human Capabilities

*Virginia Mantouvalou**

## I. Introduction

A BBC undercover reporter got a job as an agency worker at Amazon's Swansea warehouse. His job as a picker involved collecting orders at an 800,000 square feet warehouse, where Amazon stores products. He was given a handset, which said exactly what he needed to collect and put in the trolley, and which gave him a set period of time—a few seconds—to find each product. The machine also counted down the time, and beeped if he made a mistake. Discussing his experience working with Amazon, he said: 'We are machines, we are robots, we plug our scanner in, we're holding it, but we might as well be plugging it into ourselves. We don't think for ourselves, maybe they don't trust us to think for ourselves as human beings, I don't know'.[1] Amazon responded that they got legal advice to ensure that working conditions in its warehouses comply with all relevant legislation.[2] Should the law prohibit or prevent jobs that are robotic in the nature of their performance?

It is not obvious that the kind of work that Amazon requires of its employees amounts to a human rights violation. Many jobs are robotic in nature, but appear to be above the threshold of what most people would consider to be an assault on human rights. On the other hand, robotic jobs are certainly incompatible with notions of meaningful and fulfilling employment. For this reason, this chapter considers the question of robot-like jobs against two normative frameworks: first, the framework of human rights, and second, the framework of human capabilities. These two frameworks might justify controls, albeit not necessarily the same, over the sorts of jobs that are available.

* Professor of Human Rights and Labour Law, UCL Faculty of Laws. A version of this chapter was presented at the University of Toronto workshop on 'Theory of Capabilities and Labour Law' in October 2017, and the Oxford Labour Law Discussion Group in January 2018. Many thanks are due to Brian Langille and to all participants for comments and suggestions. I am also very grateful to Alan Bogg, Hugh Collins, and George Letsas for comments on a draft.

[1] 'Amazon Workers Face "Increased Risk of Mental Illness"', 25 November 2013 http://www.bbc.com/news/business-25034598.

[2] 'Amazon Hits Back Over Panorama Claims About Working Conditions at Swansea Warehouse', 25 November 2013 http://www.walesonline.co.uk/news/wales-news/amazon-hits-back-over-panorama-6337773

The structure of the chapter is as follows: the second section presents the theory of human capabilities, and its relationship to human rights.[3] It finds that there are strong links between Nussbaum's list of capabilities, human rights theory, and the international law of human rights. Both human capabilities and human rights identify important areas of well-being that people should be free to pursue, and which are interdependent and mutually supportive. They share some common values, such as human dignity. They impose negative and positive obligations on the state, and challenge the divide between the public and the private sphere. They demand a basic minimum of social justice. For Nussbaum and others, both rights and capabilities must be constitutionally guaranteed. Yet there are also certain differences. The capabilities approach is a theory of human flourishing, while human rights protect important human interests and prohibit moral wrongs. For this reason, the capabilities approach may impose more demanding duties on the state and others, than the duties imposed by human rights.

In order to assess whether working conditions such as those described above are compatible with human rights and human capabilities, we need to consider what each framework provides in relation to employment as a human interest and as an element of human flourishing. The third section of the chapter therefore examines the human right to work and human rights at work, including safe working conditions and private life, which are recognized both in morality and in law.[4] Morally, some elements of these rights are grounded on interests such as self-esteem and self-realization,[5] while components that involve working conditions are grounded on the prohibition of exploitation.[6] In law, aspects of the right to work and rights at work have been identified and protected primarily in the context of non-judicial mechanisms of economic and social rights, but also in judicial decisions on civil and political rights. The right to work includes components, such a right to employability, which imposes duties to educate and train individuals in order to be able to

---

[3] Literature on this includes Amartya Sen, 'Human Rights and Capabilities' (2005) 6 *Journal of Human Development* 151; Martha C Nussbaum, *Creating Capabilities: The Human Development Approach* (OUP, 2011) ch 4; Martha C Nussbaum, 'Capabilities and Human Rights' (1997) 66 *Fordham Law Review* 273; Pablo Gilabert, 'The Capability Approach and the Debate Between Humanist and Political Perspectives on Human Rights: A Critical Survey' (2013) 14 *Human Rights Review* 299.

[4] See James Nickel, 'Is There a Human Right to Employment?' (1978–79) X *Philosophical Forum* 149; Virginia Mantouvalou (ed), *The Right to Work: Legal and Philosophical Perspectives* (Hart Publishing, 2011). There are some accounts of human rights that may not necessarily ground a right to work as framed in law. See James Griffin, *On Human Rights* (OUP, 2008) 207.

[5] See Nickel 'Is There a Human Right to Employment?' (n 4). See also Hugh Collins, 'Is There a Human Right to Work?' in V Mantouvalou (ed), *The Right to Work* (Hart Publishing, 2011).

[6] Literature on exploitation includes Andrew Reeve (ed), *Modern Theories of Exploitation* (Sage Publications, 1987); Robert Goodin, *Reasons for Welfare* (Princeton University Press, 1988); Alan Wertheimer, *Exploitation* (Princeton University Press, 1999); Ruth Sample, *Exploitation: What It Is and Why It's Wrong* (Rowman & Littlefield, 2003); Jonathan Wolff, 'Structures of Exploitation' in H Collins, G Lester, and V Mantouvalou (eds), *Philosophical Foundations of Labour Law* (OUP, 2018); Virginia Mantouvalou, 'Legal Construction of Structures of Exploitation' in H Collins, G Lester, and V Mantouvalou (eds), *Philosophical Foundations of Labour Law* (OUP, 2018); H Spector, 'A Risk Theory of Exploitation' in H Collins, G Lester, and V Mantouvalou (eds), *Philosophical Foundations of Labour Law* (OUP, 2018); Virginia Mantouvalou, 'The Right to Non-Exploitative Work' in V Mantouvalou (ed), *The Right to Work* (Hart Publishing, 2011).

pursue work. In relation to working conditions, human rights protect a right not to be exploited at work, by guaranteeing workplace rights, including a right to fair working conditions, and a right to paid time off work. In addition, human rights law recognizes, to a certain degree, the role of self-development and the development of relations with others at work. However, human rights do not necessarily prohibit working in monotonous conditions. The duties that human rights impose include the creation of work opportunities and the prohibition of exploitation at work, rather than the creation of meaningful work.

If human rights do not prohibit working like a robot, can it be said that this kind of work is incompatible with human flourishing understood in terms of human capabilities? The fourth section of the chapter turns to this question. Nussbaum has developed a list of central human capabilities, which has close links to human rights as moral claims, and to human rights law.[7] This list does not include a capability to work. However, a capability to work, as well as certain requirements on working conditions, can be derived from it. People need to be able to have access to employment in order to obtain the means to control the material environment, which is one of Nussbaum's central capabilities. Duties that involve working conditions can also be derived from Nussbaum's so-called architectonic capabilities of affiliation and practical reason. There are important overlaps in the duties at work imposed by Nussbaum's capabilities and human rights law. In addition to the overlapping duties, there are some differences. Unlike the requirement of human rights law, for Nussbaum, work has to be meaningful in order to be conducive to human flourishing, as this section explains.[8] Working like a robot, or like a cog in a machine, is not conducive to human development. It undermines both architectonic capabilities of practical reason and affiliation, the exercise of which affects all other capabilities. It is therefore incompatible with Nussbaum's capabilities approach. Even though boring and monotonous work is incompatible with this approach, it is less clear whether there should be a state duty to prohibit it, according to the theory of human capabilities. The value of meaningful work may not ground a duty to prohibit boring and monotonous work. This is because work, even if boring and monotonous, may still be conducive to human flourishing for it is good for the enjoyment of several human capabilities. This lack of clarity as to the duties imposed in this area is a weakness of the capabilities approach.[9]

The concluding section returns to the conditions of workers employed by Amazon. It suggests that the main problem with these working conditions is not that they offer no opportunities of decision-making and other such features that are associated with meaningful work. The heart of the moral wrong suffered by workers employed in Amazon warehouses is not that the working conditions are not meaningful. Not being meaningful is not a sufficient condition for their wrongfulness.

---

[7] See literature cited above in n 3.

[8] On meaningful work, see for instance, Adina Schwartz, 'Meaningful Work' (1982) 92 *Ethics* 634; Andrea Veltman, *Meaningful Work* (OUP, 2016); Ruth Yeoman, *Meaningful Work and Workplace Democracy* (Palgrave MacMillan, 2014).

[9] See also Hugh Collins, 'What Can Sen's Capability Approach Offer to Labour Law?', Chapter 1 in this volume.

The presence of other factors suggests that they are exploitative, and that they should be prohibited.

## II. Human Capabilities and Human Rights

What are human capabilities? For Amartya Sen, who first developed the theory, the idea of capabilities can serve to understand the value of freedom, which is a social good that ought to be maximized.[10] According to him, state authorities in a good society have an obligation to make people capable to pursue a series of valuable functionings. A functioning is an achievement, while a capability is the ability to achieve.[11] A capability can also be described as a substantive opportunity or freedom to engage in a functioning.[12] Choice is of central importance, as capabilities theory is not only about what someone ends up doing, but primarily about what someone is actually able to do. Unlike Sen, Nussbaum developed a concrete list of capabilities, and made commitments as to their content.[13] According to her, the central capabilities are: 1. Life; 2. Bodily health; 3. Bodily integrity; 4. Senses, imagination, and thought; 5. Emotions; 6. Practical Reason; 7. Affiliation (friendship and respect); 8. Other species; 9. Play; 10. Control over one's environment (political and material).[14]

Human rights are moral norms, which are also often protected in law.[15] Rights identify fundamental human interests of such importance that they impose duties on others.[16] As they are very weighty, they are given priority when they come into conflict with other goals, e.g. the promotion of economic efficiency. In law, human rights purport to reflect moral rights. They are usually divided in two categories: civil and political rights that we find in the UN International Covenant on Civil and Political Rights 1966 (ICCPR) and the Council of Europe's European Convention on Human Rights 1953 (ECHR), which include the protection of the right to life and freedom of expression; and economic and social rights that we find in the UN International Covenant on Economic, Social and Cultural Rights 1966 (ICESCR)

---

[10] Amartya Sen, *The Idea of Justice* (OUP, 2009) 231.

[11] Amartya Sen, 'The Standard of Living: Lives and Capabilities' in Geoffrey Hawthorn (ed), *The Standard of Living* (Cambridge University Press, 1987) 20, 36.

[12] Amartya Sen, *Development as Freedom* (OUP, 1999) 74–6. For the implications of Sen's account for labour law, see B Langille, 'Labour Law's Theory of Justice' in G Davidov and B Langille (eds), *The Idea of Labour Law* (Oxford University Press, 2011) 104; B Langille, 'Human Freedom: A Way Out of Labour Law's Fly Bottle' in H Collins, G Lester, and V Mantouvalou (eds), *Philosophical Foundations of Labour Law* (Oxford University Press, 2018); B Langille, 'What is Labour Law for? Implications of the Capability Approach', this volume. See also Hugh Collins, 'What Can Sen's Capability Approach Offer to Labour Law?', Chapter 1 in this volume. On capabilities and labour law, see further Riccardo Del Punta, 'Labour Law and the Capability Approach' (2016) 32 *International Journal of Comparative Labour Law and Industrial Relations* 383.

[13] Nussbaum, *Creating Capabilities* (n 3) 70.

[14] Nussbaum, 'Capabilities and Human Rights' (n 3) 287–8.

[15] Nickel 'Is There a Human Right to Employment?' (n 4) 153.

[16] On interests and rights, see, for instance, Joseph Raz, *The Morality of Freedom* (OUP, 1986) 166, 180–3, 208.

and the Council of Europe's European Social Charter 1961 (ESC), which safeguard rights such as the right to housing and the right to education. In many national legal orders, human rights are protected in constitutions or other legislation with a higher status than ordinary laws. Even though there is disagreement on which rights belong in a list of human rights that merit special protection, and how these rights should be interpreted, human rights are generally viewed as constitutional essentials in a decent society.[17]

What is the relationship between human rights and human capabilities? Both frameworks purport to set moral standards against which we can assess whether treating people in a certain way is fair or unfair. On Sen's view, the main connection between rights and capabilities is that both rights and capabilities make the idea of freedom concrete: they help us understand what specific freedoms we have.[18] This is a function that is also pursued by Nussbaum's account of capabilities.[19] Nussbaum's list brings to mind human rights that we find in civil, political, economic, and social rights documents, such as the right to life and bodily integrity, the right to healthcare, freedom of conscience and expression, the right to education, the right to private and family life, the right to leisure, and the right to work. Other social rights, such as the right to housing or adequate nutrition, can be viewed as necessary preconditions for the exercise of Nussbaum's capabilities.

Nussbaum explains that her version of the capabilities approach focuses on areas of freedom that are of such importance that their violation makes a life undignified.[20] Human rights are also typically grounded on human dignity.[21] In addition, Nussbaum endorses a liberal account of capabilities. She is clear that her theory does not require that people pursue functionings, but simply that they are capable of pursuing them.[22] Capability, namely freedom to pursue functionings, is the central idea, and not functionings themselves.[23] This interpretation of capabilities theory brings it close to an understanding of human rights as preconditions of a good life.[24]

The capabilities approach focuses on actual fulfilment of human capabilities, namely that each person can really do and be certain things in diverse circumstances that affect different individuals.[25] This concern also emerges from human rights

---

[17] The term 'constitutional essentials' was used by Rawls. See John Rawls, *Political Liberalism* (3rd edn, Columbia University Press, 2005) 227. Rawls did not include social rights in the constitutional essentials. For an argument that welfare rights are constitutional essentials, see L Sager, 'The Why of Constitutional Essentials' (2003–2004) 72 *Fordham Law Review* 1421.

[18] Sen, 'Human Rights and Capabilities' (n 3) 152.

[19] Nussbaum, *Creating Capabilities* (n 3) 25.

[20] Nussbaum, *Creating Capabilities* (n 3) 31.

[21] See, for instance, the preambles of the Universal Declaration of Human Rights, the ICCPR and the ICESCR. For the role of the concept of human dignity in human rights adjudication, see Christopher McCrudden, 'Human Dignity and Judicial Interpretation of Human Rights' (2008) 19 *European Journal of International Law* 655.

[22] Nussbaum, *Creating Capabilities* (n 3) 25.

[23] Nussbaum, 'Capabilities and Human Rights' (n 3) 289.

[24] See, for instance, S Matthew Liao, 'Human Rights as Fundamental Conditions for a Good Life' in Rowan Cruft, S Matthew Liao, and Massimo Renzo (eds), *Philosophical Foundations of Human Rights* (OUP, 2015).

[25] Gilabert, 'The Capability Approach and the Debate Between Humanist and Political Perspectives on Human Rights' (n 3) 306 ff.

practice. For instance, it was expressed by one of the delegates during the drafting of the ECHR: 'What indeed does freedom mean?' It was asked, '[w]hat does the inviolability of the home mean for the man who has got no home? What is the value of sacred family rights and family liberties for the father who is permanently haunted by the spectre of unemployment?'[26] The concern about the actual fulfilment of rights can also be traced in the case law of the European Court of Human Rights (ECtHR), and particularly the principle of effectiveness that we find therein. According to this principle, rights cannot be theoretical and illusory: they have to be practical and effective.[27] This means, for instance, that for the right to a fair trial to be practical and effective, financial support in the form of legal aid by the state may be necessary.[28] The focus on what individuals are in fact able to do and to be, and on whether they are in reality able to exercise their rights, questions the traditional separation between civil and political, and economic and social rights.[29] It supports the idea that all human rights (as with capabilities) are indivisible and interdependent.[30]

Both capabilities theory and human rights take a broad view of duties that are imposed by each of these two normative frameworks. There is a line of human rights scholarship and case law that supports the view that rights impose only negative obligations on state authorities to refrain from acting in ways that violate them. As Robin West put it in relation to US constitutional law (in order to criticize this view): 'Rights protect us against the paternalistic state that might otherwise regard the "good society" as its business'.[31] This concern primarily involves accounts of constitutional and other human rights that, first, focus on civil and political rights, and, secondly, impose obligations of non-interference only. At the international level, when rights were first protected in international human rights law, their primary purpose was to impose duties of non-interference on state authorities. However, over the years, courts and other monitoring bodies developed a long list of positive obligations imposed by human rights.[32] These are obligations on the state to act in order to protect individuals from the arbitrary exercise of private power. In this way, human rights law nowadays imposes obligations not only on

---

[26] European Convention on Human Rights, *Travaux préparatoires*, Vol I (Martinus Nijhoff, 1985) 42.

[27] *Demir and Baykara v Turkey* 2008 DR; 48 EHRR 54, para 66.

[28] *Airey v Ireland* A 32 (1979); [1980] 2 EHRR 305.

[29] Nussbaum, *Creating Capabilities* (n 3) 66–7. See also Sandra Fredman, *Human Rights Transformed* (OUP, 2008).

[30] James Nickel, 'Rethinking Indivisibility: Towards a Theory of Supporting Relations Between Human Rights' (2008) 30 *Human Rights Quarterly* 984.

[31] Robin West, 'Rights, Capabilities, and the Good Society' (2001) 69 *Fordham Law Review* 1901, 1906.

[32] See, for instance, Dean Spielmann, 'The European Convention on Human Rights: The European Court of Human Rights' in D Oliver and J Fedtke (eds), *Human Rights and the Private Sphere* (Routledge, 2007) 427; Alastair Mowbray, *The Development of Positive Obligations under the European Convention on Human Rights by the European Court of Human Rights* (Hart Publishing, 2004); Virginia Mantouvalou, 'Labour Rights in the European Convention on Human Rights: An Intellectual Justification for an Integrated Approach to Interpretation' (2013) 13 *Human Rights Law Review* 529; Laurens Lavrysen, 'Positive Obligations in the Jurisprudence of the Inter-American Court of Human Rights' (2014) *Inter-American and European Human Rights Journal* 94; Andrew Clapham, *Human Rights Obligations of Non-State Actors* (OUP, 2006).

state authorities, but also, usually indirectly, on private actors.[33] Similarly, the capabilities approach supports both negative and positive duties, because what matters is that people are capable to do and be what they have reason to value. In order to be able to exercise their functionings, the state may have positive obligations to provide education, healthcare, and other such goods.[34] On the basis of capabilities theory, West criticized certain liberal accounts of constitutional human rights, such as the one endorsed in the main analyses of the US Constitution, which do not impose any obligations on state authorities to protect human capabilities, and may even limit the state's authority to secure the basic material preconditions of a good life.[35]

Moreover, both capabilities and rights reject a sharp distinction between the public and private sphere. Even though human rights law initially involved the public sphere, and did not interfere with activities in the privacy of one's home, in recent years courts, including the ECtHR, have ruled that protection of human rights may require state intervention in the private sphere, in someone's home, for example when faced with instances of domestic violence.[36] Capabilities also impose obligations to intervene in the private sphere.[37]

Finally, Nussbaum has suggested that rights should be understood in terms of capabilities, and that the capabilities approach 'can embrace the language of rights and the main conclusions of the international human rights movement, as well as the content of many international human rights documents'.[38] She also envisaged capabilities as a basis for constitutional guarantees.[39] She suggested that commitment to her list of central capabilities is required for a Government to be even minimally just, and that this commitment imposes positive obligations on Government, and not just negative ones.[40] On her view, by constitutionalizing capabilities, we are securing them, and courts have an important role to play in this context.[41] Moreover, both Sen and Nussbaum claim that capabilities can help us understand better the foundations, nature, content, and implementation of human rights,[42] and in this way help address criticisms that international human rights are wish-lists that are aspirational and undertheorized.[43]

---

[33] Fredman, *Human Rights Transformed* (n 29), analyses positive obligations imposed by human rights by reference to the capabilities approach.

[34] See Fredman, *Human Rights Transformed* (n 29).

[35] West, 'Rights, Capabilities, and the Good Society' (n 31).

[36] See, for instance, *Opuz v Turkey* 2009 DR; Application No 33401/02, 9 June 2009.

[37] Nussbaum, *Creating Capabilities* (n 3) 66–7.

[38] Nussbaum, *Creating Capabilities* (n 3) 67.

[39] Nussbaum, *Women and Human Development* (CUP, 2000) 74.

[40] Nussbaum, *Creating Capabilities* (n 3) 64–5.

[41] Martha C Nussbaum, 'Foreword: Constitutions and Capabilities: "Perception" Against Lofty Formalism' (2007) 121 *Harvard Law Review* 4.

[42] See the literature cited above in n 3.

[43] Of course, there is theoretical literature that examines the content, and guides the interpretation of human rights and other areas of law, without invoking human capabilities. See, for instance, Ronald Dworkin, 'In Praise of Theory' (1997) 29 *Arizona State Law Journal* 353; George Letsas, *A Theory of Interpretation of the European Convention on Human Rights* (OUP, 2008).

## III. Work and Human Rights

What is the place of work in the normative frameworks of human rights and human capabilities? In human rights theory work is identified and protected as an important human interest, grounded in values of self-esteem and self-realization.[44] It also has a prominent place in human rights law that generally recognizes many labour rights as human rights.[45] The right to work and rights at work are guaranteed, explicitly or implicitly, in several declarations and conventions. What does it mean to say that we have a human right to work in this context? One of the most influential documents, the Universal Declaration of Human Rights (UDHR), states in Article 23(1) that '[e]veryone has the right to work, to free choice of employment, to just and favourable conditions of work and to protection against unemployment'. The right to work, here, is not only a right to choose a job freely, but also involves the quality of the work that a person is required to do. The fact that the right to work and fair working conditions were included in the UDHR indicates that the drafters viewed unemployment as an ill, and that working in unjust conditions is a wrong that the state has to address.

When the international community separated civil and political from economic and social rights, rights to work and fair working conditions were explicitly protected in social rights documents, including the ESC and the ICESCR, which were not justiciable through individual petition.[46] Some other limited labour rights, such as the right to form and join a trade union and the prohibition of slavery, servitude, forced and compulsory labour, were included in civil and political rights treaties. The right to work was protected in the ICESCR, Article 6, which states in its first paragraph: 'The States Parties to the present Covenant recognize the right to work, which includes the right of everyone to the opportunity to gain his living by work which he freely chooses or accepts, and will take appropriate steps to safeguard this right'. Article 7 of the Covenant protects the right to fair and just conditions of work, and Article 8 protects trade union rights. The Committee on Economic, Social and Cultural Rights (CESCR) provides authoritative interpretations of the Covenant through its General Comments,[47] and has issued General Comment 18 on the Right to Work. In this General Comment, the Committee explained that the right to work should be read holistically: Articles 6–8 are interdependent, and the

---

[44] See, for instance, Nickel, 'Is There a Human Right to Employment?' (n 4). See also the essays in Virginia Mantouvalou (ed), *The Right to Work* (Hart Publishing, 2011).

[45] See generally Virginia Mantouvalou, 'Are Labour Rights Human Rights?' (2012) 3 *European Labour Law Journal* 151. On different theoretical accounts of human rights as justifications for labour law, see Joe Atkinson, 'Human Rights as Foundations for Labour Law' in H Collins, G Lester, and V Mantouvalou (eds), *Philosophical Foundations of Labour Law* (OUP, 2018).

[46] There is now a Collective Complaints Protocol under the ESC, and an individual communications Protocol under the ICESCR. For analysis of the interpretation of the right to work in these two documents, see Colm O'Cinneide, 'The Right to Work in International Human Rights Law' in V Mantouvalou (ed), *The Right to Work* (Hart Publishing, 2011) 99.

[47] See, generally, M Langford and J King, 'Committee on Economic, Social and Cultural Rights' in M Langford (ed), *Social Rights Jurisprudence* (CUP, 2008) 477.

right to work should be viewed as a right to decent work.[48] The ESC protects several labour rights, including the right to work, with a focus on a high and stable level of employment, free choice of occupation, free employment services, and provision of vocational training (Article 1); the right to just working conditions (Article 2); the right to health and safety at work (Article 3); and freedom of association and the right to collective bargaining (Articles 5 and 6).

According to the interpretation of authoritative bodies, the right to work means that the state and its citizens have to refrain from pursuing policies that lead to massive unemployment, and also pursue policies that create opportunities for employment.[49] This latter aspect of the right to work is a right to employability. On this basis, state authorities have positive duties to promote education and training of individuals in a way that will make them capable of accessing jobs. Moreover, economic policies of the state have to lead to the creation of jobs, so that everyone has the opportunity to work. This is how international human rights law, such as Article 1 of the ESC that refers to the aim of full employment as well as vocational guidance and training, is understood. In relation to the more concrete state duties, such as the promotion of full employment, the European Committee of Social Rights, which is the monitoring body of the ESC, examines a range of indicators in order to assess whether states comply with their relevant obligations.[50]

It was said earlier that the CESCR that issues authoritative interpretations of the ICESCR has interpreted the right to work in a manner that integrates both having access to work, and being employed in decent conditions. It has said that '[w]ork as specified in Article 6 of the Covenant must be *decent work*'. Decent work 'respects the fundamental rights of the human person as well as the rights of workers in terms of conditions of work safety and remuneration', 'provides an income allowing workers to support themselves and their families', and is compatible with the 'physical and mental integrity of the worker in the exercise of his/her employment'.[51] An analysis of working conditions as an essential aspect of the right to work is in line with international labour law.[52]

The right to decent work, which focuses on fair working conditions, is not a right to be employed in meaningful work that leads to human flourishing. It is better understood as a right not to be exploited at work.[53] Exploitation can be defined as taking advantage of the vulnerability of a worker, which is due to the economic imbalance that characterizes the employment relation, or other individual or structural

---

[48] General Comment No 18 (paras 7–8).
[49] Gilabert, 'The Capability Approach and the Debate Between Humanist and Political Perspectives on Human Rights (n 3) 309.
[50] O'Cinneide, 'The Right to Work in International Human Rights Law' (n 46) 114–15.
[51] General Comment No 18 (para 7) (italics in the original).
[52] On the meaning of decent work in international human rights law, see for instance, O'Cinneide, 'The Right to Work in International Human Rights Law' (n 46) 105–107. On the meaning of decent work in international labour law, see the ILO Decent Work Agenda https://www.ilo.org/global/topics/decent-work/lang--en/index.htm.
[53] Virginia Mantouvalou, 'The Right to Non-exploitative Work' in V Mantouvalou (ed), *The Right to Work* (Hart Publishing, 2011). See also Mantouvalou, 'Legal Construction of Structures of Exploitation' (n 6).

factors, by violating their human and other labour rights.[54] It is a moral wrong, which is in breach of several provisions of social rights treaties, such as the right to a fair remuneration that is protected in Article 4 of the ESC.

Another important labour right, which is one of the most controversial ones in human rights scholarship, is the right to rest and leisure, which we find in Article 24 of the UDHR. The right was criticized by some for being a luxury rather than a necessity.[55] Its inclusion in a list of human rights was viewed as leading to an inflation of rights. However, it is important to appreciate that being unable to rest is exhausting and can be destructive, as we know from examples of workers in sweatshops.[56] Leisure, including paid holidays as provided in the UDHR, is essential for a worker, and most workers will not be able to exercise their right to rest and leisure unless they are paid during their leave. The necessity of a right to leisure explains why Luban suggested that those who criticize Article 24 of the UDHR probably 'include academic critics writing during their sabbaticals—[who] have not considered seriously what a working life would be for someone whose day-to-day survival depends on a regular paycheck and who must work at a grinding job fifty-two weeks a year from age fifteen until premature death at fifty'.[57] This analysis of the right to rest and leisure as a necessity, rather than a luxury, also supports the view that the wrong that Article 24 aims to address is that of labour exploitation.

In the case law of the ECtHR, which examines the protection of civil and political rights under the ECHR, we find, first of all, certain obligations not to deprive individuals of their work arbitrarily. In *Sidabras and Dziautas v Lithuania*,[58] the ECtHR considered the applicants' dismissal and ban from access to public and various parts of the private sector employment for a period of ten years, for the reason that they were former KGB members. Considering the question whether the right to private life was engaged, the Court said that the ban 'affected their ability to develop relationships with the outside world to a very significant degree and has created serious difficulties for them in terms of earning their living, with obvious repercussions on the enjoyment of their private lives'.[59] The extensive implications of the restriction engaged the right to private life, and led to a violation of Article 14 (prohibition of discrimination) together with Article 8 (the right to private life).

In addition, civil and political rights documents contain the prohibition of slavery, servitude, forced and compulsory labour,[60] and a right to form and join a trade union.[61] From the ECHR Article 4 case law, we can derive a prohibition of exploitation at work, but the definition of exploitation here is much narrower than that emerging from the interpretation of social rights treaties, and provides

---

[54] See the literature cited above in n 6.

[55] Maurice Cranston, *What Are Human Rights?* (The Bodley Head, 1973).

[56] For an overview of the issues, see Jeremy Snyder, 'Exploitation and Sweatshop Labor: Perspectives and Issues' (2010) 20 *Business Ethics Quarterly* 187.

[57] David Luban, 'Human Rights Pragmatism and Human Dignity' in Rowan Cruft, S Matthew Liao, and Massimo Renzo (eds), *Philosophical Foundations of Human Rights* (OUP, 2015) 263, 276.

[58] *Sidabras and Dziautas v Lithuania*, App Nos 55480/00 and 59330/00, Judgment of 27 July 2004.

[59] *Sidabras and Dziautas v Lithuania* (n 58) para 48.

[60] See, for instance, art 4 of the ECHR.          [61] See, for instance, art 11 of the ECHR.

safeguards against the worst forms of ill-treatment and humiliation at work.[62] *Siliadin v France*,[63] for instance, involved the living and working conditions of a minor migrant domestic worker who was seriously exploited and abused by her employers, who had also confiscated her passport. In its ruling, the ECtHR found that the applicant's treatment breached the prohibition of servitude, which involves 'particularly serious form of denial of freedom',[64] as well as the prohibition of forced and compulsory labour.

Jurisprudence on the protection of human rights at work recognizes that the workplace is a place of human interaction where people form deep and meaningful relationships. This is observed particularly in cases that involve the protection of the right to private life. The ECtHR said, for instance, that 'it is, after all, in the course of their working lives that the majority of people have a significant, if not the greatest, opportunity of developing relationships with the outside world'.[65] Intrusive employer practices, such as extensive monitoring in the workplace, would undermine the right to privacy, for they would not allow workers to develop valuable relations. As the Court emphasized in a recent judgment: 'an employer's instructions cannot reduce private social life in the workplace to zero. Respect for private life and for the privacy of correspondence continues to exist, even if these may be restricted in so far as necessary'.[66] This line of cases does not impose on employers a duty to promote the development of meaningful relations at work, but protects people's personal relations from employer intrusions when they are at work.

This section sketched central elements of the right to work and human rights at work that we find in human rights law. It suggested that work is an important human interest that imposes obligations on the authorities to promote full employment, prohibit discrimination, and address workplace exploitation. Courts have also recognized some elements of the ability for human flourishing at work by underlining the value of developing social relationships in the workplace, particularly in case law on the right to private life. The very close monitoring of employees by Amazon, as described in the introductory passage, may give rise to issues of protection of the right to privacy. But working in a boring and monotonous job, like a robot or a cog in a machine, alone, without other elements of wrongdoing, does not necessarily violate the right to work or other human rights at work. The right to work is not a right to meaningful work. This is in line with theoretical scholarship that suggests that the duties that a right to meaningful work would impose cannot become concrete enough or that they are too subjective.[67] That there is no human right

---

[62] Virginia Mantouvalou, 'The Right to Non-Exploitative Work' in V Mantouvalou (ed), *The Right to Work* (Hart Publishing, 2011). For criticisms of the focus on the most severe forms of labour exploitation and a theoretical discussion of the concept of exploitation, see Mantouvalou 'Legal Construction of Structures of Exploitation' (n 6).

[63] *Siliadin v France*, App No 73316/01, Judgment of 26 July 2005.

[64] *Van Droogenbroeck v Belgium*, Commission's report of 9 July 1980, Series B no 44, p 30, paras 78–80.

[65] *Niemietz v Germany* A 251-B; Application No 13710/88, Merits, 16 December 1992, para 29.

[66] *Barbulescu v Romania*, App No 61496/98, Judgment of 5 September 2017, para 80.

[67] See the discussion in Veltman, *Meaningful Work* (n 8) 187 ff.

to meaningful work does not signify that governments have no duty to distribute such work. But this duty may be grounded on the promotion of human well-being, rather than human rights.[68] Could boring and monotonous work be contrary to the capabilities approach?

## IV. Work and Human Capabilities

Nussbaum does not include a capability to work explicitly in her list and has been criticized for this reason for underestimating work as a basic human good.[69] However, she recognizes a capability to exercise control over one's material environment, by inter alia having a 'right to seek employment on an equal basis with others ...'.[70] Work is one of the functionings through which people can exercise control over the material environment through the income generated from work. On this analysis, work is valuable for the resources it generates for it is seen as a means by which we get access to material goods.

The existence of opportunities for work, alone, is not sufficient on a capabilities account, unless these opportunities are sensitive to people's individual circumstances, because the capabilities approach pays attention to what people are *actually* able to do and be. When it comes to people with disabilities, for instance, the opportunity to work has to be sensitive to, and accommodating of, their needs.[71] Protection of pregnant workers in hiring and from dismissal, and special arrangements during pregnancy, if needed, would also be a case in point.[72] Moving on, a duty to work as a condition for welfare support, which we find in several legal orders, is incompatible with human capabilities. As was explained above, capabilities theory places special weight on individual freedom and the value of choice. An obligation to work would violate this choice. People should be free not to work if they so choose, and they should not be forced to work in order to have access to essentials for survival, in the form of basic income support.

Some scholarship that embraces the theory of capabilities has questioned the role of work in relation to them:

labor is nothing we like to do if it was not for the money earned by labor, and it is odd to demand to secure someone a disliked activity. Rather than protecting us against the evil of unemployment by a right to labor, we should protect us against the social causes that make unemployment an evil by a right to a life without the coercion of employment if productivity allows for this.[73]

---

[68] James Bernard Murphy, *The Moral Economy of Labour* (Yale University Press, 1993) 228.
[69] Veltman, *Meaningful Work* (n 8) 49.      [70] Nussbaum, *Creating Capabilities* (n 3) 34.
[71] See further Einat Albin, 'Universalising the Right to Work of Persons with Disabilities: An Equality and Dignity Based Approach' in V Mantouvalou (ed), *The Right to Work* (Hart Publishing, 2011) 61.
[72] See discussion in Simon Deakin and Frank Wilkinson, *The Law of the Labour Market* (OUP, 2005) 291.
[73] Ulrich Steinvorth, 'The Right to Work and the Right to Develop One's Capabilities' (2009) 1 *Analyse & Kritik* 101, 102.

For this reason and on this view, there should be no right to work, but there should be a right to develop one's capabilities instead. This position may under-estimate the role of work for a flourishing life, and the role of the workplace as a space where people develop a range of capabilities. It is important to appreciate that for many people work is not only about resources. Having a right to work in most modern societies is important not just in order to obtain means for living, but also in order to have actual opportunities of living, through self-development and the development of valuable relations through work. That the relationship between work and well-being does not only consist in the income generated through work has been recognized both in normative political theory and in empirical scholarship. For instance, it has been argued that the central goods of work consist in excellence, social contribution, community, and social recognition.[74] People may be unable to access these goods in the modern world, unless they work.

Similarly, the position that we do not need a right to work but that we need in-stead a right to develop our capabilities does not appreciate sufficiently the fact that capabilities are interrelated, and that neglecting some capabilities risks undermining others. As Nussbaum has argued, women who can look for work outside home have options that help protect their physical integrity at home.[75] Work is empowering, both financially and emotionally, and this argument reflects that. Moreover, work outside the home means, for many, having a significant opportunity of thought and reason in order to plan and execute their work. The capability to look for work, in other words, creates opportunities to not only control the material environment, but also to escape physical or emotional abuse that is suffered mostly by women at home, as well as opportunities to develop one's capabilities of thought and reason. This brings to mind the idea of the indivisibility of human rights, too, that was dis-cussed earlier, which suggests that there are several kinds of supporting relations between them.[76]

The capabilities approach also contains requirements on the content of work. According to Nussbaum, in work, a person has to be 'able to work as a human being, exercising practical reason and entering into meaningful relationships of mutual recognition with other workers'.[77] The capabilities of practical reason and affili-ation come into play here. The capability of practical reason, namely 'being able to form a conception of the good and to engage in critical reflection about the plan-ning of one's life',[78] and the capability of affiliation, namely being able 'to engage in various forms of social interaction', and 'having the social bases for self-respect and non-humiliation; being able to be treated as a dignified being whose worth is equal

---

[74] Anca Gheaus and Lisa Herzog, 'The Goods of Work (Other than Money!)' (2016) 47 *Journal of Social Philosophy* 70. See also David L Blustein, 'The Role of Work in Psychological Health and Well-Being' (2008) 63 *American Psychologist* 228; Kara Arnold and others, 'Transformational Leadership and Psychological Well-Being: The Mediating Role of Meaningful Work' (2007) 12 *Journal of Occupational Health Psychology* 193.

[75] Nussbaum, *Creating Capabilities* (n 3) 81. On the relationship between different capabilities, see also Jonathan Wolff and Avner de-Shalit, *Disadvantage* (OUP, 2007).

[76] Nickel, 'Rethinking Indivisibility' (n 30).

[77] Nussbaum, *Creating Capabilities* (n 3) 34.

[78] Nussbaum, *Creating Capabilities* (n 3) 34.

to that of others',[79] both play an architectonic role in Nussbaum's account, which means that the exercise of these two capabilities affects all other capabilities.[80] The capability of affiliation at work supports protection of developing personal relations at work, as well as protection of workers' associations, which can also be supported by the capability to control the material environment. This can include collective bargaining and a right to strike.[81] The capability of practical reason can lend support to freedom of expression at work. In addition, Nussbaum's list of capabilities also includes a capability to play, which is about being able to engage in recreational activities. This capability brings to mind the inclusion of a right of workers to paid time off work.

On the basis of the capabilities of practical reason and affiliation, work 'must involve being able to behave as a thinking being, not just a cog in a machine; and it must be capable of being done with and toward others in a way that involves mutual recognition of humanity'.[82] For work to meet Nussbaum's requirements, it has to be meaningful, because working like a cog in a machine undermines the architectonic capabilities of affiliation and practical reason. What is 'meaningful work'? Adina Schwartz argued that in a fair society that cares about the autonomy and development of all its members, nobody should be employed in routine jobs with little opportunity for forming aims, deciding by what means they will achieve their aims, or choosing and changing their methods in light of their experience.[83] On this account, people are not only autonomous when they can exercise a capacity, but when they plan and act on the basis of a rational belief on what they want in life.[84] Meaningful work, in other words, is work which is varied, complex, and provides opportunities of decision-making to the worker.[85] Others have argued that what makes work meaningful is the unity between conception and execution.[86] Workplace participation has also been presented as an essential characteristic of meaningful work, in literature suggesting that what is required is a system of workplace democracy with, on the one hand, democratic authority, and on the other, agonistic participatory practices.[87] People whose work consists in completing routine, monotonous tasks, and who exercise no initiative at work, are less likely to live autonomous lives outside work, in their private lives.[88]

---

[79] Nussbaum, *Creating Capabilities* (n 3) 34.
[80] Nussbaum, *Creating Capabilities* (n 3) 39.
[81] See further, Brian Langille (n 12); Alan Bogg, 'The Constitution of Capabilities: The Case of Freedom of Association', Chapter 12 in this volume; Bruce C Archibald, 'The Significance of the Systemic Relative Autonomy of Labour Law' (2017) 40 *Dalhousie Law Journal* 1.
[82] Nussbaum, *Creating Capabilities* (n 3) 82.
[83] Schwartz, as above 'Meaningful Work' (n 8) 634–5.
[84] Schwartz, 'Meaningful Work' (n 8) 635.
[85] Schwartz, 'Meaningful Work' (n 8) 634 and 641; R Arneson, 'Meaningful Work and Market Socialism' (1987) 97 *Ethics* 517, 521.
[86] Murphy, *The Moral Economy of Labour* (n 68) 226. See also Collins, 'Is There a Human Right to Work?' (n 5) 36.
[87] Yeoman, *Meaningful Work and Workplace Democracy* (n 8) 96.
[88] Schwartz, 'Meaningful Work' (n 8) 638, discussing empirical literature. See also Veltman, *Meaningful Work* (n 8) ch 2.

For the capabilities approach, it is not sufficient for work to be non-exploitative, which is what human rights law requires. It has to be conducive to human flourishing, which is a duty that we do not find in human rights. Working like a robot is ruled out by the capabilities approach. This suggests that the division of labour that we find in several industries, where managers decide and dictate, and workers simply execute the decisions, is not compatible with it. However, the capabilities approach does not explicitly require the prohibition of boring and monotonous jobs. This is probably because a relatively monotonous job with little opportunity to take initiatives, such as a supermarket cashier, may be meaningful because of the opportunities that it provides to the worker to make a living, and form friendships and other valuable relations at work. Having a boring and monotonous job is better, in terms of human development (for reasons such as the promotion of people's material well-being and abilities for social interaction), than having no job at all. On this issue, then, the capabilities approach is not sufficiently clear as to the normative standards against which we can assess treatment at work, and the duties that are imposed.

## V. Conclusion

This chapter examined the value of work and the requirements of the content of work against two normative frameworks: first, human rights, and secondly, human capabilities. Its main question was whether working like a robot should be prohibited. The chapter identified certain overlaps in the requirements imposed by the two frameworks, such as a duty to create opportunities to work and the prohibition of being forced to work. When it comes to the content of work, both frameworks prohibit workers' exploitation, and both recognize the value of self-development in the workplace, up to a certain extent. The overlap is justified given that there are connections between human dignity and human flourishing, both values that are also linked to human rights.[89] However, it was also suggested that capabilities theory, as a theory of human flourishing, requires the promotion of meaningful work for everyone. This requirement is more demanding than the duties imposed by human rights, which are primarily about identifying and addressing moral wrongs. Whether boring and monotonous jobs should be prohibited as a moral wrong, though, is not specifically addressed within capabilities theory. The lack of specificity as to the duties imposed is a weakness of the capabilities approach.

Before concluding, I need to return to the Amazon warehouse conditions that I described in the introduction. Even though it is clear that these conditions are not conducive to human flourishing, this is not the end of the story. Experts have warned that the conditions in the business's warehouses can have serious effects on mental and physical health,[90] while further evidence also supports the view that working

---

[89] John Kleining and Nicholas G Evans, 'Human Flourishing, Human Dignity, and Human Rights' (2013) 32 *Law and Philosophy* 539. See also Nussbaum, *Creating Capabilities* (n 3) 64.
[90] 'Amazon Workers Face "Increased Risk of Mental Illness"' (n 1).

like a robot is not the only problem.[91] For instance, presenting his experience as an Amazon worker, James Bloodworth explained the effects of having extremely high productivity targets: 'The cumulative effect of the monstrous amounts of walking you are expected to undertake is felt most keenly on your feet, which in my case began to resemble two ragged clods of wax gone over with a cheese grater ... Over the course of a week the tiredness crept up on me to the point where it felt as if someone had fastened manacles around my ankles'.[92] And then referring to some of his co-workers, he said: 'Just a few days later they'll be curled over their trolleys, covertly trying to snatch a morsel of sleep out of sight of the roving supervisors'.[93]

In these examples, working as a robot is accompanied by an intensity that gives rise to questions of whether Amazon respects workers' human rights to fair and safe working conditions. It may therefore be in breach not only of duties imposed by the framework of human capabilities, but also of duties imposed by human rights that focus on minimally just treatment, and with the protections that we find in human rights law.

---

[91] See James Bloodworth, *Hired: Six Months Undercover in Law-Wage Britain* (Atlantic Books, 2018). See also 'Accidents at Amazon: Workers Left to Suffer After Warehouse Injuries' *Guardian*, 30 July 2018.
[92] Bloodworth, *Hired* (n 91) 44.      [93] Bloodworth, *Hired* (n 91).

# 11

# Capabilities Approaches and Labour Law through a Relational and Restorative Regulatory Lens

*Bruce P. Archibald*

## I. Introduction

Human capability development approaches, whether in variants rooted in the theories of Amartya Sen ('fundamental capabilities and functionings')[1] or Martha C Nussbaum ('central capabilities'),[2] can make an important contribution to the principled evolution of both restorative justice practices in workplaces and restorative labour market regulation writ large. Restorative approaches grounded in relational values of equality, dignity, mutual concern, and respect, and flex/stability dovetail with the key elements of human capability development theory.[3] These theoretical foundations allow one to explain the essential nature of existing practical, but sophisticated, multi-level approaches to dispute resolution in workplaces. This can occur via adjudication, mediation/arbitration, restorative workplace conferencing, and varying degrees of enterprise co-regulation.[4] These same theoretical foundations can ground broad restorative labour market regulation. This involves the legal construction of varieties of personal work relations,[5] supported by coordinated

---

[1] Amartya Sen, *Development as Freedom* (Oxford University Press, 1999).

[2] Martha C Nussbaum, *Creating Capabilities: The Human Development Approach* (Belknap Press, 2011).

[3] The literature on relational theory is vast and multi-faceted, but for present purposes I will rely on articulations of relational theory by Jennifer J. Llewellyn and Jennifer Nedelsky: see Jennifer J. Llewellyn, 'Restorative Justice: Thinking Relationally about Justice' in Jocelyn Downie and Jennifer J. Llewellyn (eds), *Being Relational: Reflections on Relational Theory and Health Law* (University of British Columbia Press, 2011) 89–108; Jennifer Nedelsky, *Law's Relations: A Relational Theory of Self, Autonomy, and Law* (Oxford University Press, 2011).

[4] See Bruce Archibald, 'Progress in Models of Justice: From Adjudication/Arbitration through Mediation to Restorative Conferencing (and Back)' in R Murphy and P Molinari, *Doing Justice: Dispute Resolution in the Courts and Beyond* (Canadian Institute for the Administration of Justice, 2007).

[5] See Mark Freedland and Nicola Kountouris, *The Legal Construction of Personal Work Relations* (Oxford University Press, 2011).

social and economic policies,[6] which can enhance competitive and efficient enterprises[7] while promoting individual and collective human flourishing.[8] Exploration of these notions and their inter-relationship in both theory and practice constitutes the essence of subsequent sections of this chapter. However, it is necessary to begin by setting the discussion in the context of the current academic uproar in labour and employment law and uncertainties about the fit between traditional labour law and contemporary social and economic realities.

## II.  Transcending Labour Law's Contradictions through a Relational Capability Analysis

There may be a consensus around the claim that laws regulating work emerged historically from political demands by vulnerable workers for protection from exploitative conditions which rendered their lives miserable, and perhaps brutish and short in the Hobbesian sense.[9] Lawyers are sometimes said to carry in their heads a simple narrative which characterizes standard forms of work regulation in either substantive or procedural terms: one can change terms and conditions of work substantively by legislated rules which establish set minimum wages, maximum hours of work vacation entitlements, and the like; or one can establish procedural rules which increase the bargaining power of workers through forms such as collective bargaining and its possible regulatory extensions.[10] In more recent historical terms, the regulation of conditions of work has been cast in the language of basic rights and human dignity, and embodied in national and international 'bills of rights', human rights conventions, treaties, and the like.[11]This approach can be buttressed by rhetoric to the effect that 'labour is not a commodity'.[12] Both protective and human rights justifications for labour law can be seen to be legitimate on their own terms, and will undoubtedly continue to maintain considerable currency and political clout. However, both the protective and human rights rationales for labour and employment regulation have been subjected to corrosive neo-liberal criticisms

---

[6] For a comprehensive vision of such an approach, see Alain Supiot, *Beyond Employment: Changes in Work and the Future of Labour Law in Europe* (Oxford University Press, 2001).

[7] See Simon Deakin, 'The Capability Approach and the Economics of Labour Law', Chapter 7 in this volume.

[8] Which I take to be the general goal of the capabilities approach: see Martha C Nussbaum, 'Labor Law and the Capabilities Approach', Chapter 3 in this volume.

[9] S Deakin and F Wilkinson, *The Law of the Labour Market: Industrialization, Employment and Legal Evolution* (Oxford University Press, 2005).

[10] Brian Langille, 'Labour Law's Back Pages' in Guy Davidov and Brian Langille (eds), *Boundaries and Frontiers of Labour Law* (Hart Publishing, 2006).

[11] Philip Alston (ed), *Labour Rights as Human Rights* (Oxford University Press, 2005). For a critical assessment of this phenomenon, see Hugh Collins, 'Theories of Rights as Justifications for Labour Law' in Guy Davidov and Brian Langille (eds), *The Idea of Labour Law* (Oxford University Press, 2011).

[12] See Judy Fudge, 'Labour as a 'Fictive Commodity'' in Davidov and Langille (eds), *The Idea of Labour Law* (n 11).

of radical free-market advocates.[13] Their view, essentially, is that from the point of view of economic efficiency, such regulations impose costs on enterprises and, to the extent that they are state-imposed, constitute unjustifiable 'taxes' on production. This creates a debate where incommensurable values are compared, and which is ultimately unfruitful and inconclusive. Traditional 'right versus left' arguments are often deployed in this context which generate more tension and conflict than they do understanding and progress. Moreover, the attractiveness of this simplistic and dichotomous framework for argument has led some politicians to successfully convince electorates that protective labour standards or processes can be sacrificed to notions of competitive economic efficiency, despite human rights defences of their merits. Globalization of production has increased the temptations of this reasoning. Jurisdictions can compete with one another in a harmful 'race to the bottom' in terms of lowering labour standards to attract investment.[14] Moreover, technological change has led to out-sourcing, off-shoring, just-in-time production, casualization of employment, franchising, the fissuring of workplaces and the litany of other bases for precarious employment.[15] The scholarly literature is now replete with conflicting perspectives on how one can conceive of new approaches to labour law that can successfully respond to what appears to be the increasing irrelevance of old models of labour law to today's regulatory needs.[16]

Capabilities approaches arguably have the potential to alter the terms of the discourse surrounding this conceptual and practical uncertainty in the domain of labour and employment law, providing more sensible ways of moving forward on some degree of common understanding. The literature on capabilities approaches to human development is inter-disciplinary and heterodox,[17] but as suggested above, this chapter will take as its starting point the work of Sen and Nussbaum. However, as asserted by Robeyns, 'the core characteristic of the capability approach is its focus on what people are effectively able to do and be; that is on their capabilities'. Being capable of doing *work* in various settings seems of irresistible relevance to labour

---

[13] J Buchanan, *Liberty, Market and State: Political Economy in the 1980s* (New York University Press, 1986); F Hayek, *Individualism and Economic Order* (University of Chicago Press, 1996); Milton Friedman and Rose Friedman, *Free to Choose: A Personal Statement* (Harcourt Brace Jovanovich, 1980).

[14] Simon Deakin, 'The Contribution of Labour Law to Economic and Human Development' in Davidov and Langille, *The Idea of Labour Law* (n 11); Ronald B Davies and Krishna Chaitanya Vadlamannati, 'A Race to the Bottom in Labor Standards? An Empirical Investigation' (2013) 103 *Journal of Development Economics* 1; and Bob Hepple, *Labour Laws and Global Trade* (Hart Publishing, 2005).

[15] Leah F Vosko (ed), *Precarious Employment: Understanding Labour Market Insecurity in Canada* (McGill-Queen's University Press, 2006).

[16] Much of this literature is neatly summarized in Davidov and Langille, *The Idea of Labour Law* (n 11) passim; see also J Conaghan, M Fischl, and K Klare, *Labour Law in an Era of Globalization: Transformative Practices and Possibilities* (Oxford University Press, 2001); C Barnard, S Deakin, and G Morris (eds), *The Future of Labour Law: Liber Americorum Bob Hepple QC* (Hart Publishing, 2004); J Craig and M Lynk (eds), *Globalization and the Future of Labour Law* (Cambridge University Press, 2006); B Bercusson and C Estlund (eds), *Regulating Labour in the Wake of Globalization: New Challenges, New Institutions* (Hart Publishing, 2008); A Supiot, *The Spirit of Philadelphia: Social Justice vs. the Total Market* (Verso, 2012).

[17] See I Robeyns, 'The Capabilities Approach: A Theoretical Survey' (2005) 6 *Journal of Human Development* 93 and I Robeyns, 'Capabilitarianism' (2016) 17 *Journal of Human Development and Capabilities* 397.

and employment law in their narrow senses,[18] and to broader regulatory areas such as occupational health and safety, workers compensation, employment insurance, pensions, and the like.[19]

Sen identifies five instrumental freedoms which sustain people's capabilities and 'contribute, directly or indirectly to the overall freedom that people have to live the way they would like to live'.[20] These are (1) *political freedoms*; (2) *economic facilities*; (3) *social opportunities*; (4) *transparency guarantees*; and (5) *protective security*.[21] As Sen points out, these instrumental freedoms are interconnected and complement one another in creating the capability for individuals to choose how to convert such capabilities into concrete instantiations that are their life activities, which Sen calls 'functionings'. Clearly, *work* is a functioning chosen by most of us at various points in our lives, and the degree to which our capabilities are enhanced by Sen's instrumental freedoms will heavily influence the quality and the potential remunerative character of the work, with obvious implications for our private lives (to say nothing of the impact on the societies in which we live). In other words, capabilities set essential parameters for the degree of autonomy with which we can function in labour markets, as well as in other spheres of human activity. However, it is critical to understand that from Sen's perspective, the development of human capabilities is much more that the development of 'human capital'. The latter, based on education, training, and the like, is oriented to efficiency in production and may be seen as a sub-set of capability enhancement, but the former encompasses a wider range of potential functionings, oriented not merely to economic goals but rather to the expansion of capabilities to allow individuals to choose to live lives they have reason to value.[22] Nonetheless, Sen asserts that societies that enhance human capabilities through the institutional freedoms which he catalogues tend to promote efficient economic development[23] in addition to other, arguably more important, forms of human flourishing. This insight is critical to the contribution that relational theory and restorative regulatory approaches can make to linking a capabilities approach to labour law.

Nussbaum provisionally defines the capabilities approach as ' ... an approach to comparative quality-of-life assessment and to theorizing about basic social justice' in relation to which the key question is 'what is each person able to do and be?'[24] Not unlike Sen, Nussbaum's capabilities approach 'takes each person as an end', and is 'focused on choice or freedom'.[25] Nussbaum asserts that the approach is 'pluralist about value' in its deference to individual choices, but nonetheless says the

  [18] Labour law here refers to the North American convention that the phrase covers unionized labour relations, whereas employment law refers to regulation of the non-union sector.
  [19] See Christopher Arup and others (eds), *Labour Law and Labour Market Regulation: Essays on the Construction, Constitution and Regulation of Labour Markets* (The Federation Press, 2006) for a comprehensive survey of the notion of labour market regulation and its relationship to labour and employment law in a common law system.
  [20] Sen, *Development as Freedom* (n 1) 38.        [21] Sen, *Development as Freedom* (n 1) 38–40.
  [22] Sen, *Development as Freedom* (n 1) 292–8.
  [23] Sen, *Development as Freedom* (n 1) 41, 49, and 143–4.
  [24] Nussbaum, *Creating Capabilities* (n 2) 18.        [25] Nussbaum, *Creating Capabilities* (n 2).

approach is concerned with 'entrenched social injustice and inequality'.[26] Moreover, Nussbaum claims the approach 'ascribes an urgent task to government and public policy – namely, to improve the quality of life for all people as defined by their capabilities'.[27] Her version of the capabilities approach employs a specific list of ten 'central capabilities': (1) *life*; (2) *bodily health*; (3) *bodily integrity*; (4) *senses, imagination, and thought*; (5) *emotions*; (6) *practical reason*; (7) *affiliation*; (8) *other species*; (9) *play*; and (10) *control over one's environment*.[28] There is a substantial overlap here between Nussbaum's central capabilities and the values and freedoms which are foundational for constitutional democracy.

It is worth quoting verbatim Nussbaum's description of the central capability of 'material control over one's environment', since it is both important to the subject of this chapter and has been the object of some criticism. The exact wording is as follows:

Being able to hold property (both land and moveable goods), and having property rights on an equal basis with others; having the right to seek employment on an equal basis with others; having the freedom from unwarranted search and seizure. In work, being able to work as a human being, exercising practical reason and entering into meaningful relationships of mutual recognition with other workers.[29]

There has been critical comment on the fact that a 'right to seek work', is different from a 'right to work',[30] or perhaps one could say with the International Labour Organization 'a right to decent work', although the reference to work 'exercising practical reason' might take us in the latter direction.[31] Furthermore, 'being able to enter into meaningful relationships of mutual recognition with other workers' gives no sense of what the practical content of such a capability might mean, but it seems far from recognizing a right to collective bargaining as a central capability.[32]

Given the emphasis in the work of both Sen and Nussbaum on individual choice and agency in the conversion of capabilities to functionings or lives lived, one might be tempted to conclude that both are simply embracing liberal individualism with its stress on individual autonomy, individual preferences, and the like. But this fails to take account of the way in which both characterize the enhancement of human capabilities as embedded in societal institutions rather than as the result of individual human efforts of people pulling themselves up by their own bootstraps. They are explicit about rejecting utilitarianism with its aggregation and weighing of individual preferences, as well as rejecting welfarist and resource theories of development in the bargain.[33] However, they have not explicitly adopted a relational theory of

---

[26] Nussbaum, *Creating Capabilities* (n 2) 19.     [27] Nussbaum, *Creating Capabilities* (n 2).
[28] Nussbaum, *Creating Capabilities* (n 2) 33–34. This list is presented in a condensed fashion, but provides in italics the key words as they appear in Nussbaum's list. These will be used in the text below.
[29] Nussbaum, *Creating Capabilities* (n 2) 34.
[30] See T Weidel, 'Moving Towards a Capability for Meaningful Labour' (2018) 19 *Journal of Human Development and Capabilities* 70.
[31] On the right to work from various perspectives, see Virginia Mantouvalou (ed), *The Right to Work* (Hart Publishing, 2015).
[32] For more on this, see below.
[33] Sen, *Development as Freedom* (n 1) ch 3; Nussbaum, *Creating Capabilities* (n 2) ch 3.

social justice in procedural terms. This may in part result from their human development focus which is oriented to equality and dignity in a substantive and distributive sense rather than a procedural one. Concern with substantive equality is familiar territory to labour law scholars and practitioners steeped in the protective rationale for the discipline who see minimum wages and collective bargaining as mechanisms for enlarging the labour share of the economic pie. But these preoccupations can be encased in an ironically individualist world view, sometimes associated with business unionism, oriented to improving the lot of individual workers as consumers rather than as citizens, and focused merely on increasing the size of employee pay cheques. Restorative justice, on the other hand, began with procedural practices in criminal law that have implications for participatory voice in other institutional regulatory contexts. The emergence of relational theory, as the primary grounding for such restorative approaches, can also have a transformative impact on workplaces and labour markets. What is more, the relational theory which underlies the most sophisticated restorative approaches to dispute resolution and institutional regulation is strongly compatible with both capabilities approaches to development and to the world of work. These latter issues will be addressed next.

## III. Relational Theory and Restorative Regulation in the World of Work

Relational theory, with its roots in feminist theories of social analysis,[34] proceeds from the undeniable premise that all of us are quite literally the product of relationships between our parents and are brought up in social circumstances which require nurturing relations with care-givers to achieve a gradual transition to mature citizenship. We live our lives in relationship with our families, friends, school contacts, and social groups to which we belong, not least of which are our relationships in the world of work. Unlike liberal individualist understandings of the legal world which conceive of people as rights-holders exercising rights-claims autonomously against others, the relational view of society accepts that we all operate out of relationships that structure and mediate our autonomy. Such relative autonomy is often exercised in cooperation with significant others, although from time to time will clearly be exercised in opposition to those with whom we nonetheless have relationships. Relational theorists argue that rights are not simply trumps which autonomous individuals play to assert the superiority of their claims over the rights of others, but that rights and duties, in fact, represent values which structure relationships.[35] In this context, relational theorists often assert that the primary values which enable societies to function in a just manner from a relational perspective are those that promote equality, dignity, mutual respect, and mutual concern in one's relations with others.[36] These values clearly overlap with the manner in which Sen articulates the

---

[34] Llewellyn, 'Restorative Justice' (n 3) and Nedelsky, *Law's Relations* (n 3).
[35] Nedelsky, *Law's Relations* (n 3).    [36] Llewellyn, 'Restorative Justice' (n 3).

dimensions of certain institutional freedoms and Nussbaum elaborates her central capabilities.

Restorative justice, often implicitly but sometimes explicitly, employs relational values in procedural and institutional contexts. Let us look first at the procedural context. When wrongs are perpetrated or harms are caused to others, restorative responses privilege voluntary, inclusive, and deliberative processes which aim to repair the harm or right the wrong in a context which restores or creates egalitarian, respectful relationships among those affected.[37] This is in contrast to adversarial adjudicative decision-making, which often vindicates rights in ways that may drive people apart and sustain animosities rather than addressing dysfunctional relationships which can be the causes of the harms or wrongs. In the criminal context, restorative approaches, implemented by trained facilitators, go beyond victim-offender mediation and involve family members or supporters of both victims and offenders, as well as community representatives who may bring to the deliberations resources and expertise that can make agreed upon solutions more effective.[38] Different jurisdictions have implemented restorative approaches to criminal wrongs in different ways, including police-led restorative conferencing,[39] circle sentencing,[40] or restorative processes led by community facilitators.[41] In the civil context, collaborative family law practices are being brought to bear in the resolution of domestic disputes,[42] and can be helpfully employed in corporate management.[43] Human rights commissions can employ restorative approaches in the resolution of complaints in matters which can range from domestic tenancy issues to consumer related discrimination and frequently to workplace discrimination.[44] In all of these instances, restorative approaches to dispute resolution embedded in values of equality, dignity, mutual respect, and concern for others are central to inclusive, deliberative processes which can harness the capabilities of all participants to achieve outcomes which garner community respect.

---

[37] Bruce Archibald and J Llewellyn, 'The Challenges of Institutionalizing Comprehensive Restorative Justice: Theory and Practice in Nova Scotia' (2006) 29 *Dalhousie Law Journal* 297.

[38] Bruce Archibald, 'Let My People Go: Human Capital Investment and Community Capacity Building via Meta/Regulation in a Deliberative Democracy: A Modest Contribution For Criminal Law and Restorative Justice' (2008) 16 *Cardozo Journal of International and Comparative Law* 1.

[39] New Zealand, see Nessa Lynch, 'Respecting Legal Rights in the New Zealand Youth Justice Family Group Conference' (2007–2008) 19 *Current Issues in Criminal Justice* /5. For Australia, see Kathleen Daly and Hennessey Hayes, 'Restorative Justice and Conferencing in Australia' and Jenny Bargen, 'Kids, Cops, Courts, Conferencing and Children's Rights: A Note on Perspectives' (1996) 2 *Australian Journal of Human Rights* 209.

[40] Barry Stuart, 'Circle Sentencing in Canada: A Partnership of the Community and the Criminal Justice System' (1996) 20 *International Journal of Comparative and Applied Criminal Justice* 291.

[41] See Archibald and Llewellyn (n 37).

[42] Susan Swain Daicoff, 'Families in Circle Process: Restorative Justice in Family Law' (2015) 53 *Family Court Review* 427.

[43] Jerry Goodstein and Karl Aquino, 'And Restorative Justice For All: Redemption, Forgiveness and Reintegration in Organizations' (2010) 31 *Journal of Organizational Behavior* 624; Jerry Goodstein and Kenneth Butterfield, 'Extending the Horizon of Business Ethics: Restorative Justice and the Aftermath of Unethical Behavior' (2010) 20:3 *Business Ethics Quarterly* 453.

[44] See e.g. the Nova Scotia Human Rights Commission's dispute resolution process, 'Restorative Approaches', online: Nova Scotia Human Rights Commission <http://humanrights.gov.ns.ca/resolution>.

The second dimension of relational rights theory and restorative approaches that is significant to a capabilities approach is their application to restorative or responsive regulation in a variety of institutional settings. Restorative approaches are being used in education in numerous jurisdictions to deal with matters ranging from school discipline on playgrounds to participatory approaches to classroom teaching and curriculum development and delivery.[45] Municipalities and local governments in some jurisdictions are applying relational principles and restorative approaches to management of the delivery of health services[46] and social services with the participation of clients.[47] In other jurisdictions, regulation of industries involved in delivery of key services are abandoning pure command and control methods of regulatory enforcement, for a more sophisticated mix of 'smart' or responsive regulation which has its origins, to some degree, in relational theory and participatory restorative justice approaches.[48] Recognizing the dignity of students, social service recipients, and regulatees of various sorts is surely a matter of showing concern and respect for them by supporting their capabilities in order to allow the people in question to make enlightened choices which help them live lives they have reason to value or to improve their quality of life.

Let us be explicit about the possible connections and compatibilities between relational rights principles, restorative justice, and the capabilities approaches of Sen and Nussbaum. In fact, it is the latter's central capabilities which are most easily linked to restorative justice. In engaging with a response to wrong-doing in an inclusive, deliberative manner, circle or restorative conference participants are using their *senses, imagination, and thought* to develop a notion of what is the right thing to do and they are engaged in the exercise of *practical reason.* The circle or conference creates or reinforces existing *affiliations* which work themselves out in dignified and non-discriminatory ways that instantiate concern for others. Experience has shown that restorative conference interactions elicit strong *emotions* on the part of participants which can indeed embody justified anger which can transform itself into gratitude and social solidarity when agreement on a way forward can be found. Moreover, circle or conference participants are engaged in a process of asserting *control over their environment* by making what amount to politico-legal choices in the discussions. These may result in reparations or compensation which recognize material *property rights* vindicated in *meaningful relationships of mutual recognition*

---

[45] Leeds (for example, at Carr Manor Community School, see 'Restorative Learning: Carr Manor Community School (2014)' <https://restorativejustice.org.uk/sites/default/files/resources/files/Schools%20article%20-%20Resolution%2052_0.pdf>).

[46] J Braithwaite, J Healy, and K Dwon, *The Governance of Health and Safety Quality* (Australia: Commonwealth of Australia, 2005).

[47] Birmingham (West Midlands Police and Crime Commissioner, *Making Sense of the Restorative Justice Landscape in Youth Justice in the West Midlands* (2015), < https://www.westmidlands-pcc.gov.uk/media/429373/11-SPCB-Restorative-Justice-for-Young-People-Annex-1.pdf>); Bristol (see 'Restorative Bristol' http://restorativebristol.co.uk/); Hull (Laura Mirsky, 'Hull, UK: Toward a Restorative City' (2009) *Restorative Practices E-Forum,* www.iirp.org.

[48] I Ayres and J Braithwaite, *Responsive Regulation: Transcending the Deregulation Debate* (Oxford University Press, 1992); Julia Black and Robert Baldwin, 'Really Responsive Risk-Based Regulation' (2010) 32(3) *Law & Policy* 181.

*with others.* Restorative circles or conferences thus activate and reinforce Nussbaum's central capabilities, treating people as ends in themselves in ways which respect their freedom of choice and action in determining significant outcomes in a cooperative process. This is the antithesis of formal, professionalized judicial proceedings where lawyers and judges do most of the talking and determine outcomes for others who are treated as the means (witnesses) to achieve results that conform to 'the law'. In standard adjudication, professional players do things *to* or *for* others rather than *with* them, in a spirit of equality, dignity, and mutual concern and respect.

Sen's instrumental freedoms dovetail with the values and processes found in restorative approaches in a more indirect and abstract way than Nussbaum's central capabilities, but the connections are still there. Sen's articulation of *political freedoms* focuses on the institutions of representative democracy (engaging in political discussion, participating in political parties, voting for legislators or executives, etc.), but surely participation in restorative processes connected to legal dispute resolution is a kind of direct participation in governance which turns capabilities into a kind of 'functioning' that is more immediate even than acting as a juror in civil or criminal proceedings. In addition, restorative conferences or circles, when properly authorized by law and recognized as an aspect of the administration of justice, are ideally characterized by openness, disclosure, and trust which for Sen come under the rubric of *transparency guarantees* associated with the rule of law.[49] Finally, there is the question of Sen's approach to *economic facilities*. In his view, the latter are not to be confused simply with markets. While recognizing the importance of markets for efficient distribution of resources and production and distribution of goods, Sen is acutely aware of potential market inadequacies or failures and the need for public regulation of markets to ensure that they do not become destructive of capabilities. In this context, the complementarity of Sen's approach to capabilities and restorative or responsive regulation of markets and other public and private institutions becomes evident.

While relational/restorative theory's emphasis on the values of equality, dignity, and mutual concern and respect may comport nicely with the capabilities approaches of Sen and Nussbaum, there is another value, or a balancing of conflicting values, which arguably constitutes an important element in the assessment of capability theory as a justification for or explanation of labour and employment law. This is the notion of what has become known in Europe as 'flex/security'[50] or what I am tempted to call 'flex/stability'.[51] In a globalized world of international competition in the provision of goods and services, it has become clear that 'flexibility' on the part of firms to engage in forms of production which can respond to rapidly changing market conditions has become a kind of mantra. Just in time production, the changing of product lines, competitive pricing, out-sourcing, off-shoring, and

[49] Bruce Archibald, 'Restorative Justice and the Rule of Law: Rethinking Due Process through a Relational Theory of Rights' SSRN, https://papers.ssrn.com/sol3/papers.cfm?abstract_id=2395224
[50] Manfred Weiss, 'Re-Inventing Labour Law' in Davidov and Langille, *The Idea of Labour Law* (n 11).
[51] Bruce Archibald, 'The Significance of the Systemic Relative Autonomy of Labour Law' (2017) 40 *Dalhousie Law Journal* 1.

the like, which are common mechanism to allow firms flexibility, have an impact on workers and labour markets. Part-time and casual employment, lay-offs, and abrupt termination of employment can be the result of corporate planning for flexibility, with negative impacts on workers. In the best of all possible worlds, these negative impacts can be alleviated by employment insurance, re-training, and the like, which are linked to Sen's *social opportunities* and *protective security* categories of instrumental freedoms. Instability in employment could also be thought to cripple Nussbaum's central capability of *practical reason,* if the latter indeed involves 'being able to form a conception of the good and engage in critical reason about the planning of one's life'. Thus, an important value underlying these capabilities from a worker's perspective is having sufficient security or stability in one's work environment to plan one's life in a general sense, and in particular to be able to plan in advance for changes in employment forced upon one by an employer responding to market conditions. On the other hand, the reality is that institutional support for workers wishing to change jobs or careers is often in short supply, despite private and public claims to the contrary. Nonetheless, flex/security or flex/stability is important for labour market regulation in a broad institutional sense. It is also an important value or policy goal to be reflected in relevant capabilities to support workers' variable functionings in an individual sense.

Having thus explored the potential connections between capabilities approaches and both relational rights and restorative approaches to various forms of socio-legal regulation, it follows that we can now examine two broad aspects of these matters in relation to labour and employment law. These are (i) restorative approaches to workplace dispute resolution which can enhance capabilities and arguably improve the quality of workers' experience in the workplace, as well as that of economic productivity; and (ii) restorative regulation of the legal construction of personal work relations in ways which can help achieve these same ends.

## IV.  Restorative Approaches to Workplace Dispute Resolution that Enhance Capabilities

As society industrialized, from the common law's origins in the 'master and servant' setting, inegalitarian stability was replaced by exploitatively 'egalitarian' legal flexibility. Labour standards and collective bargaining institutions of the nineteenth and twentieth centuries developed to redress certain 'modern' notions of formal legal equality, which masked the inequality of economic duress suffered by many employees and not legally recognized.[52] However, it should be noted that in some common law jurisdictions, the common law, now applicable largely to more affluent workers, has evolved to recognize needs for what might be termed a modest form of 'flexstability'. In response to the vulnerable situation of employees as compared

---

[52] A Fox, *History and Heritage: The Social Origins of the British Industrial Relations System* (George Allen and Unwin, 1985).

to employers, the common law came to recognize 'reciprocal' requirements for reasonable notice before termination by the latter or resignation by the former, in the absence of exigent circumstances on either side.[53] Nonetheless, the common law has never recognized the principle that termination should only be for 'just cause', even if latterly it has moved toward imposing a duty of fairness on employers in administering employment contracts as a counterweight to the employees' duty of loyalty.[54] The upshot of this common law evolution, broadly speaking, might be thought in some instantiations to be an implicit recognition of values of dignity, mutual concern, and respect, although not equality in employment relations. The common law's contribution to labour and employment regulation must still be said to be relatively distant from a substantive capabilities approach. In procedural terms, its primary reliance on enforcement through expensive adversarial litigation in common law courts puts the common law of employment at the other end of the spectrum from restorative justice. To the extent that some jurisdictions seem to countenance stipulations in employment contracts requiring dispute resolution before arbitrators chosen by the employer, the common law may simply be off the restorative scale completely.[55]

Collective bargaining regimes, at least in their North American variants, would seem to rely on restorative—or at least deliberative and participatory—dispute resolution processes. Labour boards, established by statute and regulating certification or decertification and unfair labour practice complaints, are usually tri-partite in that they are composed of members associated with both unions and employers, with a 'neutral' chair.[56] Arbitration boards deciding disputes under collective agreements are similarly structured through partisan 'wingers' chosen by the parties who then try to agree on a neutral chair. Where the latter does not occur, the chair is appointed through the ministry of labour, as is the case where a collective agreement calls for dispute resolution by a single arbitrator, but where the union and the employer are unable to agree on an appointee.[57] These participatory institutional arrangements were intended to be responsive to the culture of labour relations, and to be relatively informal, inexpensive, and quicker than courts. However, over the decades of their evolution, these adjudicative institutions have become bureaucratized, professionalized, burdened with human rights and constitutional issues, subjected to judicial review, and have seen their decisions turned into a virtual system of precedents, collected by publishing houses and cited by labour lawyers from both sides in a highly legalistic fashion.[58]

---

[53] Peter Barnacle and others, *Employment Law in Canada* (4th edn, LexisNexis Canada, 2005).
[54] C Mummé, 'A Comparative Reflection from Canada: A Good Faith Perspective' in M Freedland and others, *The Contract of Employment* (Oxford University Press, 2016).
[55] A Colvin, 'Organizational Primacy: Employment Conflict in a Post Standard Contract World' in K Stone and H Arthurs (eds), *Rethinking Workplace Regulation: Beyond the Standard Contract of Employment* (Russell Sage Foundation, 2013).
[56] George W Adams, *Canadian Labour Law* (2nd edn, Canada Law Book, 1993) (loose-leaf revision, 2016).
[57] Adams, *Canadian Labour Law* (n 56) ch 12.
[58] Archibald, 'Progress in Models of Justice' (n 4).

In reaction to this procedural sclerosis, labour boards, arbitration boards, and individual arbitrators, with the encouragement of the parties, have created more responsive and restorative approaches. Sometimes this can simply be mediation, but more often it is mediation/arbitration, or 'med/arb' in the vernacular, where the arbitrator, with the consent of the parties, will act as a mediator but put on his or her arbitrator's hat and decide the matter where the mediation fails.[59] Med/arb has been so successful in some jurisdictions that it has been regularized in statutory form and given protection from certain forms of judicial review.[60] Mediation caucuses can allow for free ranging and direct discussion of issues between med/arb practitioners and the parties relatively un-mediated by counsel. Counsel is usually there to ensure there is focus on the issues and relevant material is brought to the attention of the med/arbitrator, but grievers, union officials, managers, and supervisors (and sometimes experts for each side) are often able to cut to the chase in an informal assessment of the situation. This informality can also occur when everyone is called into the same room as well. Even where the mediation does not achieve a settlement, the med/arbitrator can give direction on what issues need more evidence or analytical clarification.[61] Hearings can be shortened and decisions given expeditiously. In other words, people in the workplace are thus exercising their own capabilities (in the Nusbaum sense, relating their own sense observations in context with others, exercising *practical reason*). They are also doing so in circumstances which, in the Sen view, feel as though they are achieving collective disclosure and transparency in their relations, although the med-arbitrator has a delicate role in this latter regard.[62] Therefore, in appropriate cases, med/arb can be more participatory and restorative than straight, formal, adjudicative arbitration.

There is a role, however, even in unionized workplaces, for more comprehensive restorative approaches. In the toxic workplace, for example, where the culture is tainted by racism, sexism, or other pervasive attitudes which sap morale or interfere with positive and efficient interaction, restorative approaches can be most effective. Sometimes such processes can be initiated by a grievance which alleges a violation of the collective agreement, but at other times they can be generated by a complaint to a human rights commission or a regulatory body,[63] or even a simple complaint to management.[64] These restorative processes may be most useful when problems

---

[59] D Elliott, 'Med/Arb: Fraught with Danger or Ripe with Opportunity?' (1995) 34 *Alberta Law Review* 163.

[60] Archibald, 'Progress in Models of Justice' (n 4).

[61] E.g. Trade Union Act, RSNS 1989, c 475 (as amended) s 46D.

[62] Parties may reveal matters to med/arbitrators which they do not wish the other side to know. If the time comes to shift from mediation to adjudication, the arbitrator will have to decide how to sort out this conundrum.

[63] See, for example, Nova Scotia Human Rights Commission, 'Annual Accountability Report for the Fiscal Year 2016-2017' https://novascotia.ca/government/accountability/2016-2017/2016-2017-Human-Rights-Commission-Accountability-Report.pdf.

[64] Collective bargaining legislation may preserve the right of individual employees to take complaints or grievances directly to management without going through the union: e.g. Trade Union Act, RSNS 1989, c 475 s 15.

cross lines between different work units or between groups of employees and various managers. In such cases, participatory and deliberative approaches rooted in values of equality, dignity, mutual respect, and concern in an environment where flexibility may be required for solutions but where everyone knows they still must work together when it's over, can transform workplaces. *Affiliation* as a capability is nurtured by restorative facilitators who are consciously supporting efforts by all concerned to assert *control over their environment* in ways characterized by '*entering into meaningful relationships of mutual recognition with other workers*', and indeed, management personnel. In other words, restorative workplace dispute resolution can be used to great effect as encouragement for the instantiation of capabilities or operative functionings. This is particularly true in unionized workplaces where just cause for dismissal is an arbitrable issue and unionized employees can be protected by the grievance process against risk of retaliation which restorative approaches might possibly generate.

The last point moves us to the question of how to promote restorative approaches to dispute resolution which engage people's capabilities in non-union workplaces. This is particularly important in a world of work where union density, at least in the private sector, is declining and where labour standards complaint remedies are widely recognized as ineffective (often only used by employees who have quit or been fired to get retroactive entitlements, rather than by the rare activist employee who will take an employer to task before a labour standards tribunal and risk retaliation). In this context, the occupational health and safety model is of significance. At least in workplaces of a minimum size, statutory schemes require the appointment of occupational health and safety officers or the creation of occupational health and safety committees composed of equal numbers of employee and management representatives, who must regularly consider occupational health and safety issues.[65] This, of course, is in a situation where there are statutory rights for employees to be informed of safety risks and statutory duties on employers to disclose such dangers. There is also the statutory right of employees to a self-help remedy, the right to refuse to do unsafe work, buttressed by inspectorates which can investigate such claims and provide protection against retaliation.[66] It has been suggested that this model could be used to improve labour standards by essentially expanding the jurisdiction of occupational health and safety officers and committees to deal with other workplace issues.[67] Despite the potentially immense political barrier here posed by the rise of illiberal authoritarianism, one can see in principle that safe, deliberative forums in large numbers of workplaces could encourage worker choice and the transformation of capabilities into functionings in accordance with restorative values and processes in ways consistent with both the Sen and Nussbaum analyses.

---

[65]  D Dyck, *Occupational Health and Safety: Theory, Strategy and Industry Practice* (3rd edn, LexisNexis Canada, 2015).

[66]  Dyck, *Occupational Health and Safety* (n 65).

[67]  C Estlund, *Regoverning the Workplace* (Yale University Press, 2010); also D Doorey, 'A Model of Responsive Workplace Law' (2012) 50 *Osgoode Hall Law Journal* 47.

## V. Restorative Regulation of Personal Work Relations

There is currently a good deal of scholarly discussion about debilitating precarity in labour markets which flows in large part from the search for flexibility in the production of goods and services as described above.[68] However, there are two dimensions of this situation which merit exploration in relation to how labour and employment law can benefit from capabilities approaches in developing restorative paths to improved quality of life for workers. The first is a concern with how firms are increasingly structured in negative ways in relation to the needs and aspirations of workers who provide the goods and services which such firms market. Some describe this as the vertical and horizontal disintegration or disaggregation of enterprises,[69] although recently the concept of 'the fissured workplace' has gained popularity.[70] The second concern is with market segmentation mainly through the use of casual or part-time employees or purportedly independent contractors to do work which is indistinguishable from that done by full-time, long-term employees in 'standard contracts of employment'.[71] This has been usefully been called the problem of 'the legal construction of personal work relations'.[72] A labour lawyer might encapsulate the first concern in the question 'who or what is an employer for purposes of labour regulation?' and refer to the second concern by asking 'who is an employee?' for those same purposes. The questions are clearly linked. Both will be examined briefly in relation to capabilities approaches and restorative solutions to issues raised for labour and employment law.

Until fairly recently, the most prominent global or multi-national corporations tended to be huge, vertically and horizontally integrated companies which controlled almost all aspects of the production, marketing, and sale of the goods and services for which they were known, either directly or through wholly-owned subsidiaries.[73] Many such firms were conglomerates engaged in wide ranges of different businesses. Such companies were said to be taking advantage of economies of scale and employed huge workforces to accomplish their manufacturing and commercial endeavours. These workforces were composed mostly of full-time employees with health plans, defined benefits pension plans, and were often unionized. In that context, such workforces constituted internal labour markets where employees usually

---

[68] L Vosko (ed), *Precarious Employment: Understanding Labour Market Insecurity in Canada* (McGill-Queen's University Press, 2006); Law Commission of Ontario, *Vulnerable Workers and Precarious Work* (December 2012).

[69] H Collins, 'Independent Contractors and the Challenge of Vertical Disintegration to Employment Protection Laws' (1990) 10(3) *Oxford Journal of Legal Studies* 353.

[70] D Weil, *The Fissured Workplace: Why Work Became So Bad for So Many and What Can Be Done to Improve It* (Harvard University Press, 2014).

[71] For a comparative treatment of this topic, see Stone and Arthurs, *Rethinking Workplace Regulation* (n 55).

[72] Freedland and Kountouris, *The Legal Construction of Personal Work Relations* (n 5).

[73] K Levitt, *Silent Surrender: The Multi-national Corporation in Canada* (McMillan, 1970) for a left critique of the phenomenon.

had preferred access to jobs within the corporate network and could climb up the 'corporate ladder' or make lateral transfers inside the corporate family.[74]

However, in the last few decades there has been a revolution in the way in which enterprises structure their operations. Institutional investors began to demand the streamlining of corporate structures to emphasize immediate profitability, and firms began to concentrate on 'core competencies', leading them to jettison unprofitable or peripheral operations.[75] Cutting costs was increasingly managed through reducing the number of employees by contracting out marginal functions, outsourcing product lines, or franchising many operations. For many such companies, defining, marketing, and controlling the standards of 'the brand' became the primary focus, while the actual production of goods or provision of services to customers was in the hands of other subordinate entities.[76] The brand holder typically has a contract—or, more likely a chain of subcontracted arrangements—with actual producers or service providers. This model is widespread throughout the globalized economy, but a striking example is the hospitality industry.[77] Many hotel 'brands' own virtually no hotels: their branded properties are mostly owned by franchisees, and almost all functions within each hotel are contracted out by those franchisees (accounting, marketing, front desk services, room services, restaurants, maintenance, and the like …) to separate smaller business entities.[78] Rather than a protected internal labour market with hotel employees engaged in doing the brand's business, long-term, in a career of indeterminate length, workers are now employed within competitive commercial markets for each internal hotel function. Those who work in the establishment may wear brand logos, but actually work in precarious and largely dead-end jobs for a plethora of different companies. Evasion of labour standards by sub-contractors in these circumstances is a way of commercial life, and unionization efforts are almost inevitably unsuccessful. Who is the ultimate authority in these arrangements? In fact, in many cases it appears that brand holders control to the extent of minute detail virtually all aspects of franchise operations *except* labour standards, for which they purport to eschew any responsibility.

The stereotypical 'fissured workplace' as described above is clearly not the paradigmatic employer for which labour and employment laws were developed in the 'Thirty Glorious Years' of the welfare state after the Second World War:[79] that is, expansive employers with large, stable workforces. But can those labour and employment regimes nonetheless be modified to enhance capabilities and improve the quality of life of workers? Are not brand holders who pursue rigorous fissuring strategies really in practical terms the effective employer? Some legislatures, administrative tribunals, and courts have been willing to declare that this is the case. Recently, some common law courts have applied 'common employer' doctrines where owners

---

[74] See P Weiler, *Governing the Workplace* (Harvard University Press, 1990).
[75] Jeremias Prassl, *The Concept of the Employer* (Oxford University Press, 2015).
[76] Weil, *The Fissured Workplace* (n 70).     [77] Weil, *The Fissured Workplace* (n 70).
[78] This a striking example with which millions of consumers unwittingly come in contact daily.
[79] Reference to *les Trente Glorieuses* is widely used in critical French social commentary. See Jean Fourastié, *Les Trente Glorieuses, ou la révolution invisible de 1946 à 1975* (Fayard, 1979). See also T Piketty, *Capital in the Twenty- First Century* (Belknap/Harvard University Press, 2014) 96, 96–9.

of enterprises have played corporate shell games in attempts to avoid their contractual employment obligations to employees.[80] Finding such equitable doctrines to exist at common law is not, however, a universal judicial approach. In an in/famous example, a class action applicant seeking the enforcement of minimum labour standards against a brand for those working at the bottom of an international garment supply chain was rejected.[81] On the other hand, many North American labour relations acts, employment standards codes, and occupational health and safety statutes have explicit statutory 'related' or 'joint' employer doctrines.[82] These were clearly intended to prevent employers from using multiple corporate vehicles to hide their true employment or labour relations arrangements so as to leave beleaguered employees with remedies only against the formally employing entity, while lead brand holders take the profits from—or leave significant assets in—other corporations beyond 'legal' reach of wronged employees. Formal common law rules about privity of contract and narrow statutory interpretation seem to predominate in those cases where workers are arguably left in the lurch, while purposive approaches to related or joint employer statutes or flexible equitable principles about common employers have presented workers with remedies.[83] The important question for this chapter is to ask whether capabilities approaches and relational restorative values are relevant to resolving some of these interpretive tensions in labour market regulation.

Sen's macro approach to capabilities would seem at first glance to provide the most promising leads in the interpretive exercise, but on closer examination some of Nussbaum's central capabilities also provide useful arguments. As noted above, Sen's instrumental freedom dealing with *economic facilities* is not to be equated with unregulated markets. Sen is clear that markets can be regulated in the public interest to ensure capabilities are not irreparably damaged, and has a chapter devoted to 'poverty as capability deprivation'. A labour market structured, in some considerable measure, to place many people in precarious part-time and casual employment, can surely be seen to deprive them of capabilities. Furthermore, those struggling to put together a family income based on several part-time or casual jobs have little time to devote to their career enhancement through further studies or training, and may not have time or courage to communicate with others in political activities aimed at the same purpose. This surely is the curtailment of Sen's capability to have access to relevant *social opportunities*. From the perspective of Nussbaum's analysis, precarious employment can negatively affect the central capability of *affiliation* where work/family balance is concerned and where simultaneous work for different employers creates consistently difficult scheduling. Similarly, the Nussbaum capability of *control over one's own environment* can be impaired by fissured work arrangements inhibiting one's ability to 'work as a human being, exercising practical reason and

---

[80] *Downtown Eatery Ltd v Ontario* (2001), 54 OR (3d) 161 (Ont. CA).

[81] *Lian v J Crew Group Inc and Others*, 54 OR (3d) 239, [2001] OJ No 1708.

[82] E.g. Occupational Health and Safety Act, Stats NS, 1996, c 7, ss 13–23 where joint, if proportionate, responsibility for safety violations is imposed on employers, contractors, constructors, suppliers, employees, self-employed persons, owners, service providers, architects, and engineers.

[83] See Guy Davidov, *A Purposive Approach to Labour Law* (OUP, 2016).

entering into meaningful relationships of mutual recognition with other workers'. In terms of appropriate relational values underlying restorative approaches to workplace interaction, precarious employment in legally fragmented work settings fails to promote equality with others who have 'decent work', is damaging to a worker's dignity, and does not bespeak a labour market characterized by mutual concern and respect for the worker's quality of life in the workplace. Surely, all the above reinforce an interpretive approach to the common, related, or joint employer issues which can enhance the possibilities for regulating that particular labour market problem in ways which enhance worker capabilities and their own freedom to make choices they have reason to value.

Now we can address the second major concern related to restorative labour market regulation through recognizing the importance of capabilities approaches which are responsive to the ills of labour market segmentation. In other words, this is the question of 'who is an employee for purposes of labour and employment law?' seen from the perspective of the legal construction of personal work relations.[84] Early on, the common law saw attempts by either category of worker (servant/employees or tradesperson/independent contractors) to band together to negotiate better terms of engagement to be illegal conspiracies in the restraint of trade—such was the common law's ideological integration with early mercantile affairs. In the twentieth century, trade unions of employees were granted legislative status to act in protection of their members by negotiating on wages, terms, and conditions of work, but commercial providers of goods and services continued to be the subject of anti-trust acts or pro-competition regulation. By this time, of course, the standard contract of employment had become a preferred platform by which to link the welfare state to many of its citizens: pension contributions, unemployment insurance premiums, workers' compensation assessments, and income taxes were deducted from employee wages, while independent contractor fees were not subject to such regulation.[85] The latter were expected to provide for retirement and economic down-turns out of savings garnered from their profits. All of this is a familiar story, but it needs to be told to understand how this legal construction of personal work relations created the foundations for distortions in labour markets as businesses responded to the burdens and opportunities which the system provided.

Many of the same economic pressures which led to the fissuring of workplaces also led to employers seeking efficiencies and competitive advantages to engage in what has been called workforce or labour market segmentation.[86] While there is obvious legitimacy to the distinction between employees and independent contractors, it has provided incentives for some employers to develop practices known as 'disguised employment'.[87] That is where people who work for a single employer are

---

[84] Freedland and Kountouris, *The Legal Construction of Personal Work Relations* (n 5).
[85] Brian Langille, 'Labour Policy in Canada: New Platform, New Paradigm' (2002) 28 *Canadian Public Policy* 133.
[86] Brian Langille, ' "Take these Chains from my Heart and Set me Free": How Labour Law Theory Drives Segmentation of Workers' Rights' (2015) 36(2) *Comparative Labor Law and Policy Journal* 257.
[87] Brian Langille and Guy Davidov, 'Beyond Employees and Independent Contractors: A View from Canada' (1999) 21 *Comparative Labor Law and Policy Journal* 7.

categorized as 'independent contractors', thus allowing the employer to reduce costs by avoiding the accounting and financial burdens of contributions to employee befits and the like. Such workers are subject to the same controls over their work as regular employees, but with none of the attendant benefits associated with standard employment. Certain public regulatory practices associated with the presumed predominance of standard, full-time employment provided incentives to employers to engage in other forms of labour market segmentation. Casual employment has always been a feature of advanced economies, where fluctuating work requirements lead employers and employees alike to engage in employment contracts for irregular hours on an as-needed basis. Regulators, however, responded to it by exempting casual employees from some minimum employment standards and benefits, and from access to collective bargaining, as available to regular full-time employees. This, in turn, became an incentive for employers to fragment or 'casualize' workforces and reduce the regulatory burdens and costs of hiring people on a full-time basis.[88] Another technique used by some employers in some industries is to pay workers on a 'piece-work' basis, while still insisting on their presence in the workplace, which can disguise both the full-time or regular part-time basis of their work and the legal requirements of employer to adhere to labour standards regimes. The current controversies in various jurisdictions around the world concerning the legal status of drivers working for Uber, the taxi business or ride-sharing platform (depending on your perspective), has elements of most of the above problems.[89] The point is that the legal constructions associated with work regimes have created incentives for hirers to make distinctions among workers doing indistinguishable personal work and reduce the quantity of work, quality of pay, and working conditions. These practices are highly problematic for the workers and, ultimately, for society at large. How does a capabilities approach in tandem with policies based on restorative principles allow for the construction of work relations which embody values of equality, dignity, mutual concern, and respect, and flex/stability, rather than the above inversions associated with labour market segmentation in its various guises?

From the point of view of equal treatment in the workplace, characterized by regard for the dignity of those involved in hiring arrangements as well as notions of mutual concern and respect, it may be too simplistic to say merely that those doing similar work should be treated in a similar manner. However, analytical clarity can be achieved by moving to a broader category, the 'personal work relation', as the concept which requires analysis for assessing the proper regulatory scope of labour and employment law in so far as the status of hirees is concerned.[90] There are two aspects to this notion: (i) a relation or *nexus*, and (ii) personal work. Freedland and Kountouris provide a careful definition of the concept:

---

[88] Geoffrey England, *Part-time, Casual and Other Atypical Workers: A Legal View* (Research and Current Issues Series No 48, IRC Press, 1987); Harry Arthurs, *Fairness at Work: Labour Standard for the 21st Century* (Federal Labour Standards Review, 2006) 109–110.

[89] J Prassl and M Risak, 'Uber, Taskrabbit, and Co.: platforms as Employers? Rethinking the Legal Analysis of Crowdwork' (2015–2016) 37 *Comparative Labor Law and Policy Journal* 619.

[90] Freedland and Kountouris, *The Legal Construction of Personal Work Relations* (n 5).

The personal work relation is a connection or set of connections between a person – the worker – and another person or persons or an organization or organizations, arising from an engagement or arrangement or set of arrangements for the carrying out of work or the rendering of service or services by the worker personally, that is to say wholly or primarily by the worker himself or herself.[91]

They suggest that this definition could be considered as the basis for 'presumptions rather than hard rules about the personal or relational scope for labour laws or labour rights'.[92] In fact, the law already does this to certain degrees in certain circumstances. Adjudicative decisions and statutory provisions have sometimes assimilated 'dependent' or 'non-self-dependent' contractors to the status of employee for the purposes of attaching labour standards and collective bargaining rights to individuals doing work under such arrangements.[93] Similarly, workers labelled by employers as 'casual' or 'temporary' have been characterized by adjudicators as regular part-time or even full-time employees, where their patterns of working hours and working conditions justify such classifications, and thereby entitle them to the rights and benefits of the latter.[94] A parallel example is the possibility for certain own-account personal workers to be treated the same way as employees for purposes of access to public pension plans.[95] Regulation of own-account workers in franchise arrangements is another instance in which the personal work relation idea can assist in clarifying policy questions.[96] Arguably, the personal work relation notion could also assist in resolution of policy debates around piece-work arrangements which consistently provide remuneration below the minimum wage for hours worked or for dealing with the problem of 'zero-hours contracts'.[97] Conceptualizing these problems as aspects of the 'legal construction of personal work relations' is a relational approach which analyses the substance rather than the form of the *nexus* between hirer and worker. The real question, however, is whether the personal work relation idea, and its restorative potential, is clarified or enhanced by seeing it in terms of capabilities approaches.

From the perspective of Nussbaum's central capabilities, the personal work relation analysis comports well with her articulation of an aspect of *affiliation* as 'being able to be treated as a dignified being whose worth is equal to that of others'. But

[91] Freedland and Kountouris, *The Legal Construction of Personal Work Relations* (n 5) 31.
[92] Freedland and Kountouris, *The Legal Construction of Personal Work Relations* (n 5).
[93] See Langille and Davidov, *Boundaries and Frontiers of Labour Law* (n 10) 88; These distinctions have been applied in Nova Scotia: see *International Alliance of Theatrical Stage Employees, Moving Picture Technicians, Artists and Allied Crafts, Local 849 v Egg Films Inc*, 2012 NSLB 120, aff'd 2014 NSCA 33, [2014] NSJ No 150, leave to appeal to SCC refused, [2014] SCCA No 242. The current author must disclose that he was the Vice-Chair of the Labour Board panel which made this decision.
[94] See *NSGEU v Metro Community Living Support Services Ltd*, 2017 NSCA 15 (Again, the author must disclose he chaired the original panel in this case).
[95] Expert Commission on Pensions, *A Fine Balance: Safe Pensions, Affordable Rules, Fair Rules* (Queen's Printer for Ontario, 2008); Pension Review Panel, *Promises to Keep* (Government of Nova Scotia, 2009).
[96] For an Australian approach to this issue, see Richard Johnstone and others, *Beyond Employment: The Legal Regulation of Work Relationships* (Federation Press, 2012) 47–76.
[97] This phrase is used in Europe, but is not well known in North America. For a British case describing regulatory strictures on the phenomenon, see *Autoclenz Ltd v Belcher* [2011] UKSC 41.

perhaps the more direct connection to Nussbaum's approach is to be found in using a personal work relation analysis in the development of labour and employment law policy as having enhanced *material control over one's environment* in the sense of 'having the right to seek employment on an equal basis with others'. As to Sen's *instrumental freedoms*, even-handed approaches to the legal construction of parallel personal work relations must be an aspect of fair *economic facilities* which he characterizes as 'the opportunities that individuals respectively enjoy to utilize economic resources for the purposes of consumption, production or exchange'. Furthermore, the implications of the personal work relation analysis are consistent with *transparency guarantees* which ' ... deal with the need for openness that people can expect ...' in terms of lucidity, disclosure, and trust in ensuring egalitarian treatment in the workplace. In other words, the personal work relation concept reinforces the relevance of the capabilities analysis oriented to improving the choices that people exercise to live lives they have reason to value and to improve their quality of life. Personal work relation analysis points to ways in which to engage in potentially restorative labour and employment law characterized by the embodiment of relational values of equality, dignity, mutual concern, and respect, which support flex/stability in labour market regulation.

## VI. Conclusion: Prospects for Getting from Here to There

Capabilities insights combined with restorative approaches rooted in relational theory provide a foundation for rational labour law policy and sound labour market regulation. Elaborating labour and employment law in accordance with values of equality, dignity of all people, and mutual concern and respect for their needs and choices becomes more than the mere assertion of ideals when understood through the practical complementary lenses of capabilities theory and restorative justice. However, the exercise of achieving such goals is, in considerable part, a political one, and the prospects for attaining consensus are less than certain in the current climate of political polarization. We are reliably told that levels of economic and social inequality in 'Western' nations now reflect those of the 1920s.[98] Financial institutions were bailed out after the Great Recession of 2008, but the recovery has not 'trickled down' to general populations. It never does. People seem angry and frustrated. The recovery from the Great Depression of the 1930s and the devastation of the Second World War was based on conscious government intervention on Keynesian principles. While history never repeats itself exactly, and while Piketty may be right that the Thirty Glorious Years of social and economic progress after the Second World War were an historical aberration,[99] the general lesson learned from that turn-around bears close analysis. We need another 'New Deal' and not a return

[98] Chrystia Freeland, *Plutocrats: The Rise of the New Global Super-rich and the Fall of Everyone Else* (Doubleday Canada, 2012); Piketty, *Capital in the Twenty- First Century* (n 79); Branko Milanovic, *Global Inequality: A New Approach for the Age of Globalization* (Harvard University Press, 2016).
[99] Piketty, *Capital in the Twenty- First Century* (n 79).

to fascism. Sen, the economist, asserts that capabilities approaches make economic sense—a view shared by others.[100] Moreover, there are economists who agree that sensible government policies, consistent with egalitarian redistribution of income, are within our grasp.[101] Righting the current imbalances in labour law and labour market regulation are arguably an important aspect of this process. Political forces opposed to such approaches are formidable.[102] However, the survival of constitutional democracies may depend on overcoming them.[103] Advancing capabilities approaches in the domain of labour and employment can be an important element in overcoming these challenges. In this endeavour, there is nothing so practical as good theory, although the divine is in the details—and nobody does this alone. We're all in it together, using our capabilities, functioning relationally, and, one hopes, restoratively.

[100] Simon Deakin, 'The Contribution of Labour Law to Economic and Human Development' in Davidov and Langille, *The Idea of Labour Law* (n 11); and Simon Deakin, 'Concepts of the Market in Labour Law' in A Numhauser-Henning and Mia Ronmar (eds), *Normative Patterns and Legal Developments in the Social Dimension of the EU* (Hart Publishing, 2013).

[101] P Krugman, *End this Depression Now* (WW Norton and Company, 2013); A Atkinson, *Inequality: What can be Done?* (Harvard University Press, 2015).

[102] See Jane Meyer, *Dark Money: The Hidden History of the Billionaires behind the Rise of the Radical Right* (Doubleday, 2016); and Mark Lilla, *The Shipwrecked Mind: On Political Reaction* (New York Review of Books, 2016).

[103] J Stieglitz, *The Price of Inequality: How Today's Divided Society Endangers Our Future* (WW Norton and Company, 2012).

# PART III

# THE CAPABILITY APPROACH TO LABOUR LAW AND IMPORTANT LABOUR LAW CONTROVERSIES

# 12

# The Constitution of Capabilities

## The Case of Freedom of Association

*Alan Bogg**

## I. Introduction

The capabilities approach has been prominent as a normative framework for labour law over the last decade. This turn towards capabilities is understandable. It is underpinned by a normative focus on the real opportunities for citizens to achieve flourishing lives: do citizens have the rights, resources, and external supports necessary to empower them to pursue lives that they have reason to value? It has been used in a variety of scholarly and policy contexts: to provide a metric for measuring human development and evaluating policy interventions to alleviate poverty;[1] to sharpen our understanding of human freedom and its relationship with well-being and flourishing; and to provide insights into constitutional design and the content of constitutional rights.

The capabilities approach is strongly aligned with the human rights approach.[2] The capabilities approach can be used to guide deliberations on three basic issues on the implementation of human rights, matters that might otherwise remain unspecified. First, it can help in identifying those rights and determining the reach of duties on governments and private actors to respect and support capabilities. Characteristically, this is done through the legal recognition of 'claim-rights' that are correlative to legal duties, as a basis for supporting human freedoms. Secondly, it can help in determining which political institutions, courts or legislatures, should take the lead in formulating those 'claim-rights'. Thirdly, it can provide guidance on the content and character of legal reasoning when courts are reasoning about the fundamental entitlements of citizens.

* I am extremely grateful to Ruth Dukes, Michael Ford QC, Mark Freedland, Sarah Kanko, and Virginia Mantouvalou for comments on an earlier draft. I am very grateful to Brian Langille for his generous invitation to the capabilities workshop at the University of Toronto, and to the participants at the workshop for critical engagement. I acknowledge my gratitude to the Leverhulme Trust for its generous support of my work.

[1] Sabina Alkire, *Valuing Freedoms: Sen's Capability Approach and Poverty Reduction* (OUP, 2002).
[2] Martha C Nussbaum, 'Capabilities and Human Rights' (1997) 66 *Fordham Law Review* 273.

The Capability Approach to Labour Law. Edited by Brian Langille. Chapter 12 © Alan Bogg 2019.
Published 2019 by Oxford University Press.

In this respect, Martha C Nussbaum has developed a 'capabilities template' for freedom of religion.[3] She suggests that there should be a 'detailed investigation of each concrete area of human capability, as law has specified it through both constitutional text and an ongoing history of judicial interpretation'.[4] In this chapter, I will explore the fundamental right to freedom of association using the capabilities framework. It will draw upon the capabilities approach to provide answers to these three basic issues of implementation.

This exploration will centre upon recent jurisprudence on freedom of association in the Supreme Court of Canada (SCC) and the European Court of Human Rights (ECtHR). Both courts have recognized 'derivative' rights that are constitutionally protected under general 'freedom of association' guarantees.[5] Traditionally, constitutional rights have been protected from vertical encroachment by governments. These courts have gone further in recognizing 'derivative' rights that operate horizontally between private actors. 'Derivative' rights require legislators to impose duties on private actors to respect and protect the rights of other citizens. The centrepiece of these developments has been the recognition of a fundamental *right* to bargain collectively, which the SCC has treated as correlative to a *duty* to bargain.

From a capabilities perspective, the constitutional protection of the right to collective bargaining (and the correlative duty to bargain) seems to epitomize the capabilities approach. Nussbaum's central capabilities of 'affiliation' and 'control over one's material environment' encapsulate the normative salience of collective bargaining.[6] In collective bargaining, workers engage collaboratively and democratically to shape the terms and conditions of their working lives. Where constitutional courts fashion *duties* to bargain collectively, they are empowering workers to exercise important capabilities. What could be problematic about that?

Matters are not so straightforward. There are some important differences between leading proponents of the capabilities approach, especially the work of Amartya Sen and Martha C Nussbaum. There is no single template for freedom of association, because there is no single capabilities approach. These differences are exposed in examining the position of 'derivative' rights, such as the right to collective bargaining and the correlative duty to bargain, under the capabilities approach. The chapter will examine some potential differences between them on the three basic issues of human rights implementation outlined above.

In the first part of the chapter, the potential implications of Sen's work on capabilities will be examined. Sen avoids a prescriptive approach to identifying which capabilities are central. Instead, his account of capabilities emphasizes the intrinsic

---

[3] Martha C Nussbaum, *Liberty of Conscience: In Defense of America's Tradition of Religious Equality* (Basic Books, 2008).

[4] Martha C Nussbaum, *Creating Capabilities: The Human Development Approach* (Harvard University Press, 2011) 167.

[5] This analytical framework of 'derivative' rights is developed in Brian Langille and Benjamin Oliphant, 'The Legal Structure of Freedom of Association' (2014) 40 *Queen's Law Journal* 249. These legal developments are discussed from a socio-legal perspective in Judy Fudge, 'Constitutionalizing Labour Rights in Canada and Europe: Freedom of Association, Collective Bargaining, and Strikes' (2015) 68 *Current Legal Problems* 267.

[6] Nussbaum, *Creating Capabilities* (n 4) 33–4.

value of freedom as a political goal. He has also avoided being prescriptive about matters of constitutional design, and the role of courts in constitutional democracies. This normative abstinence reflects the dominant theoretical concerns of Sen's work. It has often been focused on developing critiques of gross domestic product (GDP) as a measure of human development, and of comparing human development and freedom across different nations in circumstances of moral pluralism.

Sen's work has inspired a democratic and freedom-based critique of an expansive approach to 'derivative' rights, especially the constitutional recognition of a right to collective bargaining. This may be described as 'thin' freedom of association. It is reflected in three fundamental commitments. First, since derivative rights are correlative to duties, and since duties restrict freedoms, such rights should only be recognized exceptionally. Freedom has intrinsic value, and that includes the freedoms of duty-bearers. Accordingly, there is always a normative cost in recognizing derivative rights Secondly, where derivative rights are created, it is better for that to occur democratically through legislation rather than through constitutional litigation. Judges lack the expertise and democratic legitimacy to formulate politically controversial derivative rights such as the right to bargain collectively. Legislators are better-positioned to formulate such rights Thirdly, when courts are reasoning about rights, they should do so by focusing upon formal juridical categories (such as the distinction between 'liberties' and 'claim-rights') and existing legal authorities. They should eschew a broader and more contextual exploration of legal history, moral reasoning, and international law and legal thought.

Sen's work does not lead ineluctably to this 'thin' account. The deeper problem is that Sen's work is too abstract to offer meaningful guidance on constitutional design in specific national contexts. In Robeyns' terms, Sen's theory is 'radically underspecified' as a normative theory.[7] In consequence, the remaining gaps are often filled in by normative commitments that may be left unarticulated by the theorist applying Sen's work.

In the second part of the chapter, I will set out and defend an alternative capabilities template for freedom of association that adopts a more generous approach to the recognition of derivative rights. It will do so using Nussbaum's account of capabilities based upon 'Aristotelian social democracy'. Nussbaum rejects normative abstinence. She has developed an account of the 'central capabilities' which represent areas of human freedom that provide a threshold for a life worthy of human dignity. This provides a strong contrast to thin freedom of association. First, capabilities as fundamental entitlements are correlative to public and private duties. According to Nussbaum, some freedoms are more valuable than others. Drawing upon her work, I argue that where a derivative right is supporting a freedom of great value, and where the correlative duty restricts a freedom of little value, there is a strong normative case for implementing such a derivative right. Secondly, these fundamental entitlements should be protected under constitutional guarantees, and constitutional courts should have a leading role in developing these derivative rights incrementally

---

[7] I Robeyns, 'The Capability Approach in Practice' (2006) 14 *Journal of Political Philosophy* 351, 353.

and expansively. Constitutionalization ensures that the capabilities are secure and resilient, and this contributes to the well-being of citizens. Thirdly, judicial reasoning about capabilities should be rich and contextual, informed by sensitivity to history, ethics, and international law. In this respect, Nussbaum has been highly critical of 'formalistic' legal reasoning which has often been aligned with libertarian and minimalist approaches to the content of constitutional rights.

Whenever labour lawyers use the capabilities approach to examine regulatory problems within national constitutional orders, they would do better to look to Nussbaum's account. By contrast, Sen's work is better suited to the regulatory domain of international labour law and comparative development studies. This indicates a useful methodological division of labour between Sen and Nussbaum when drawing upon their insights in the field of labour law.

In this context, Nussbaum's work provides a strong capabilities justification for the broad recognition of derivative rights. From this perspective, the real problem is not that the courts have gone too far. Quite the contrary, in fact. The courts have not yet gone far enough. In the final section of the chapter, I set out some thoughts on how constitutional courts can realize the constitution of capabilities for the most disadvantaged workers, focusing in particular on the direct promotion of just social and economic outcomes (rather than simply the opportunity to achieve those outcomes). In certain circumstances, constitutional courts should go 'beyond capabilities' as a remedial strategy for supporting capabilities in the longer-term. This requires a greater emphasis on the social democratic rather than the liberal roots of Nussbaum's work on capabilities. I propose some adjustments to Nussbaum's account, to open up space for paternalistic intervention to support the most disadvantaged workers.

## II. The Constitution of Capabilities: The 'Parallel Liberty' Approach

Over the last decade, the scholarship of Brian Langille has had two dominant motifs. The first motif is a defence of 'thin' freedom of association, which begins 'from the premise that the best account of the idea of freedom of association is a very simple one: it is the freedom to do in combination with others what one is free to do alone. Laws that unjustifiably hobble this freedom violate the *Charter*'.[8] As a result, he has been critical of the recent turn in the SCC. Some of this critical work has been undertaken with Benjamin Oliphant, who has also provided his own arguments in favour of 'thin' freedom of association.[9] The second motif is the development of a 'new normativity' for labour law that builds upon Sen's work on capabilities. According to Langille, the virtue of Sen's work is its engagement with our 'true

---

[8] Brian Langille, 'The Freedom of Association Mess: How We Got into It and How We Can Get out of It' (2009) 54 *McGill Law Journal* 177, 183.

[9] Benjamin Oliphant, 'Exiting the Freedom of Association Labyrinth: Resurrecting the Parallel Liberty Standard under 2 (d) & Saving the Freedom to Strike' (2012) 70 *University of Toronto Faculty Law Review* 36.

ends', that 'the point of all our striving is human freedom'.[10] Since the pursuit of real human freedom is 'the intrinsic and ultimate end' of political action,[11] the norms and institutions of labour law should also be configured to promote the capabilities that enable human freedom. These two projects are an integrated package.

Their work emphasizes the pivotal distinction between 'vertical' and 'diagonal' application of constitutional liberties.[12] In 'vertical' situations, the government interferes directly with the citizen's freedom of association. In 'diagonal' cases, by contrast, the court is imposing a constitutional duty on the legislator to introduce legislated duties on (some) private parties to facilitate the exercise of the freedom by (other) private parties. Where these so-called 'derivative rights' are imposed, one person's enhancement of freedom (the right-holder's) is another person's restriction of freedom (the duty-bearer's).

The distinguishing characteristic of 'thin' freedom of association is its circumspection about the constitutional creation of derivative rights. This critique has softened over time. In 'Freedom of Association Mess', for example, Langille describes the constitutionalization of derivative rights as 'crazy': 'look at what the fundamental freedoms include: conscience, thought, expression, and association. It makes no sense to think of freedom of conscience or expression, for example, as a right that I have, corresponding to your duty to think (or not to think) or to say (or not to say) anything. That would be crazy'.[13]

The 'crazy' critique is too categorical. As Webber and others have argued, 'it might be thought that human rights such as the freedom of expression, assembly, and religion are Hohfeldian liberties. The problem with classifying them as such, however, is that their two-term structure does not describe any particular relationship between persons'.[14] Rather, these constitutional formulae are more like directive goals, indicating that a certain kind of activity (i.e. associating) is of such importance that it is something citizens have by right. These 'broad goal-oriented' two-term formulae require further specification and translation into three-term rights through constitutional adjudication and legislative enactment.[15] The implementation of constitutional freedoms such as association or expression requires that 'a series of acts and arrangements—a combination of Hohfeldian relationships—must be selected from

---

[10] Brian Langille, 'Core Labour Rights: The True Story (Reply to Alston)' (2005) 16 *European Journal of International Law* 409, 432.

[11] Brian Langille, 'Labour Law's Theory of Justice' in Guy Davidov and Brian Langille (eds), *The Idea of Labour Law* (OUP, 2011) 104, 114.

[12] Brian Langille, 'Why the Right-Freedom Distinction Matters to Labour Lawyers: And to All Canadians' (2011) 34 *Dalhousie Law Journal* 143.

[13] Langille, 'The Freedom of Association Mess' (n 8) 200.

[14] Gregoire Webber and others, *Legislated Human Rights: Securing Human Rights through Legislation* (CUP, 2018) 127. In other words, 'the two-term structure of rights signifies the importance of the subject matters x (life, liberty, security, privacy, etc) that persons (P) have by right, but does not identify which measures will realise everyone's right by identifying duty-holders and the content of their duties that correlate to the right(s) in question'.'. (21). Langille and Oliphant are astute to recognize this three-term structure of real Hohfeldian rights in Langille and Oliphant, The Legal Structure of Freedom of Association' (n 5) 273–6. However, they do not sufficiently recognize the directive function of two-term rights which have an important role in constitutional texts and constitutional adjudication.

[15] Webber and others, *Legislated Human Rights* (n 14) 21.

among more or less reasonable alternatives and authoritatively established'.[16] The more interesting enquiry is to determine the allocation of law-making responsibility between different constitutional actors.

In later work, they accept that the constitutional creation of 'derivative rights' can be legitimate in certain exceptional situations. They identify *Dunmore* as such an example.[17] In *Dunmore*, agricultural workers were excluded from the general labour relations statute. In the absence of unfair labour practice provisions protecting basic organizational rights, agricultural workers were impeded in their exercise of freedom of association. The SCC directed the legislature to introduce statutory rights that protected agricultural workers from interference, coercion, and discrimination in the exercise of their basic associational freedoms.[18]

Why do they regard *Dunmore* as a legitimate example of derivative rights? There would appear to be three reasons. First, the judicial specification of the 'derivative right' in *Dunmore* was sufficiently complete for it to satisfy the requirement of legality in terms of the right-holder, the duty-bearer, and the relevant acts. The court was able to specify the three-term structure of the relevant derivative right with precision, while allowing the legislator some creative choice in the design of the statutory protections. Secondly, judicial articulation of a narrow core of basic rights did not lead the court into usurping the legislator's role. This limited regulatory task did not engage polycentric issues that would be more amenable to legislative attention.[19] Furthermore, the existence of a legislative template in the general labour relations statute mitigated any deficits in judicial expertise in industrial relations matters. Nor was the subject matter 'political' to the same degree as, say, judicial determination of a 'right to strike'. Thirdly, a high threshold for constitutional intervention ensured that the creation of 'derivative rights' was confined to exceptional cases. The SCC noted that union organization was 'all but impossible' for agricultural workers, in the absence of basic statutory protection for the right to organize.[20]

Where these strict conditions are not satisfied, Langille and Oliphant regard it as constitutionally improper for the courts to create 'derivative rights'.[21] In this respect, they are particularly critical of the Court's creation of a constitutionalized 'right to collective bargaining' (and the correlative 'duty to bargain') in *BC Health Services* which, on their view, fails to meet these conditions.[22] As Langille and Oliphant put it, a low constitutional threshold of 'substantial interference' would mean that 'every individual whose exercise of freedom was rendered unsuccessful by the freedom of third parties could bring a constitutional claim for state action to protect their freedom'.[23]

---

[16] Webber and others, *Legislated Human Rights* (n 14) 42.
[17] *Dunmore v Ontario (Attorney General)* 2001 SCC 94, [2001] 3 SCR 1016.
[18] *Dunmore v Ontario (Attorney General)* (n 17) [67].
[19] On polycentricity and judicial self-restraint in social rights adjudication, see Jeff King, *Judging Social Rights* (CUP, 2012) ch 7.
[20] *Dunmore v Ontario (Attorney General)* (n 17) [48].
[21] Langille and Oliphant, 'The Legal Structure of Freedom of Association' (n 5).
[22] *Health Services and Support: Facilities Subsector Bargaining Association v British Columbia* 2007 SCC 27, [2007] 2 SCR 391.
[23] Langille and Oliphant, 'The Legal Structure of Freedom of Association' (n 5) 291.

From a capabilities perspective, this normative aversion to the constitutional creation of 'derivative rights' seems puzzling. After all, the question of 'derivative rights' only arises in virtue of a concern with the *real opportunities* for citizens to exercise their freedoms in the world. As Langille puts it, 'we create the derivative rights when we know that the freedom would not be worth the paper it's written on without them'.[24] Or again, 'derivative rights' are justified in order 'to protect the substantive or *meaningful* exercise of freedoms'.[25] Yet the capabilities approach is intensely concerned to develop a substantive rather than a formal account of human freedoms. As Sen explains, the capabilities approach is focused 'on the freedom that a person actually has to do this or be that—things he or she may value doing or being'.[26]

There are four main supporting arguments in favour of a limited approach to 'derivative rights', and some of them recur in the work of other labour law scholars who rely on Sen's framework. Let us call them the argument from freedom; the argument from democracy; the argument against contextualism; and the argument from equality.

The first argument is based upon an intrinsic account of freedom's value. Where three-term 'derivative rights' generate correlative duties that are imposed on private parties, 'the individual placed under a constitutional duty to act or not act in a specific way to promote another's freedom would be right to ask: "But what about my freedom?"'.[27] This public ranking of freedoms has been described as a 'condescension on a constitutional scale'.[28] It is incompatible with the idea that freedom is 'an end in itself' or 'intrinsic'.[29] What is needed is *equal* respect for freedoms and their exercise, including the freedom of duty-bearers.[30] There is no doubt that Sen sometimes speaks of 'freedom' as valuable in itself, and he has avoided the specification of central capabilities because of a concern to respect pluralism.[31]

The second argument prioritizes the democratic specification of 'derivative rights'. On this view, it is better to entrust the specification of 'derivative rights' to the democratic process. An extensive role for constitutional courts and strong judicial review would obstruct the scope for elected representatives to design labour codes democratically. Labour codes necessitate controversial *political* judgments, and those judgments should be made *politically* by elected representatives. It is also important that regulatory choices are informed by evidence assembled from a broad range of

---

[24] Langille, 'Why the Right-Freedom Distinction Matters to Labour Lawyers' (n 12) 155 n 32.

[25] Langille and Oliphant, 'The Legal Structure of Freedom of Association' (n 5) 267.

[26] Amartya Sen, *The Idea of Justice* (Harvard University Press, 2011) 231–2.

[27] Langille and Oliphant, 'The Legal Structure of Freedom of Association' (n 5) 291–2.

[28] Brian Langille, 'The Condescending Constitution (or, The Purpose of Freedom of Association is Freedom of Association) (2016) 19 *Canadian Labour and Employment Law Journal* 335, 336.

[29] Langille, 'Labour Law's Theory of Justice' (n 11) 118.

[30] Langille, 'The Condescending Constitution' (n 28) 340.

[31] For critical discussion of Sen's work on this point, see Martha Nussbaum, 'Capabilities as Fundamental Entitlements: Sen and Social Justice' (2003) 9 *Feminist Economics* 33, 43–7. At other times, Sen does speak in terms of ranking freedoms: 'Freedoms can vary in importance . . . For a freedom to count as a part of the evaluative system of human rights, it clearly must be important enough to justify requiring that others should be ready to pay substantial attention to decide what they can reasonable do to advance it'. See Amartya Sen, 'Elements of a Theory of Human Rights' (2004) 32 *Philosophy and Public Affairs* 315, 329).

stakeholders. This is consistent with Sen's aversion to ex ante constraints on the community's identification of valued capabilities through democratic procedures.[32]

This reflects a more general tendency amongst followers of Sen to favour wide democratic space for formulating and implementing social rights. For example, Deakin and Wilkinson observe that the capabilities approach is not even 'prescriptive about the mechanisms that should be employed' to implement social rights.[33] Sen's work is agnostic on constitutional entrenchment in democratic societies.[34] Indeed, Sen countenances that human rights might not be protected through *legal* mechanisms at all, favouring protection through social and political mobilization.[35] This general democratic argument is often supported in labour law by a constellation of more particular concerns about the limited expertise of ordinary courts in the field of collective labour relations, and the 'autonomy' of labour law.[36]

The third argument rejects 'contextual' legal reasoning. In *BC Health Services* the SCC invoked international law and Canadian labour history to justify departing from its earlier position that the right to collective bargaining/duty to bargain was not protected by the Charter. This has attracted vigorous criticism from different quarters. For example, Eric Tucker has criticized the SCC's use of historical sources as selective and instrumental.[37] Tucker demonstrates that prior to the enactment of labour relations statutes there was no *legal* duty to bargain on the employer. The Court regarded this duty as the touchstone of a constitutionalized right to bargain collectively. Yet this right was not a feature of Canada's pre-statutory labour history, hence labour relations history provided weak support for the constitutionalization of a legal duty to bargain. This legal duty was a creature of statute and it was of relatively recent origins.

The Court's use of international law is also castigated as disclosing misunderstandings about the content and institutional mechanics of international labour law.[38] It is alleged that the SCC treats international law as giving rise to binding obligations to constitutionalize a legal duty to bargain. Yet international law does not mandate the constitutionalization of such a legal duty. It would have been better for the court to confine itself to some basic legal distinctions and 'building blocks', and to reason deductively from authoritative legal sources within the national legal system. This envisages a more formalistic account of what counts as legal reasoning, and it has affinities with a concern for the rule of law and the value of legality.

---

[32] Nussbaum, *Creating Capabilities* (n 4) 178–9.
[33] Simon Deakin and Frank Wilkinson, *The Law of the Labour Market* (OUP, 2005) 352.
[34] Nussbaum, *Creating Capabilities* (n 4) 179.        [35] Sen (n 31) 342-345.
[36] Brian Langille and Benjamin Oliphant, 'From Rand to Rothstein: Judges, Fundamental Freedoms, and Labour Law' in Ivo Entchev and Lisa M Kelly (eds), *Judicious Restraint: The Life and Law of Justice Marshall E Rothstein* (LexisNexis, 2016) 251.
[37] Eric M Tucker, 'The Constitutional Right to Bargain Collectively: The Ironies of Labour History in the Supreme Court of Canada' (2008) Comparative Research in Law & Political Economy research Paper No 3/2008.
[38] Brian Langille and Benjamin Oliphant, 'From the Frying Pan into the Fire: Fraser and the Shift from International Law to International "Thought" in Charter Cases' (2011–2012) 16 *Canadian Labour and Employment Law Journal* 181.

Finally, some critics have argued that equality is the correct constitutional response to the marginalization of excluded groups.[39] The problem for agricultural workers in cases like *Dunmore*, for example, is that they have been excluded from the general labour relations regime without appropriate justification. They do not enjoy the equal protection of laws that should apply to them. It would be better to challenge that exclusion directly through a constitutional equality standard. This would give the agricultural workers what is really due to them: the equal protection of the law. It would do so without embroiling courts in the 'political' exercise of designing labour relations statutes.

## III.  The Constitution of Capabilities: Nussbaum and Aristotelian Social Democracy

In contrast to Sen, Nussbaum has developed an account of the 'central capabilities'. These 'central capabilities' identify the basic conditions of human flourishing by setting a minimum threshold for a life that is worthy of human dignity. As fundamental entitlements, the 'central capabilities' provide 'the core of an account of minimal social justice and constitutional law'.[40] Nussbaum has described this project as a form of 'Aristotelian Social Democracy', and this description remains apt. It is reflected in a broad understanding of what counts as 'constitutional'. In particular, the activity of labour is integral to securing the minimal threshold of capabilities for citizens in a well-ordered political community. Whereas for some liberals a labour relations scheme might be left to the legislative stage of implementation, for Aristotelian social democrats 'they are absolutely basic, at least as basic, and perhaps more so, than the scheme of offices and concrete judicial and deliberative institutions'.[41] This would necessitate 'a searching examination of the forms of labor and the relations of production, and for the construction of fully human and sociable forms of labor for all citizens, with an eye to all the forms of human functioning'.[42] 'Aristotelian Social Democracy' emphasizes that the state has a *positive responsibility* to intervene and support the equal freedom of citizens in the economic sphere. It rejects the *laissez-faire* or minimal state as inadequate to the task of supporting human freedom.

Freedom of association provides the constitutional basis for this regulatory task in the domain of work relations. It is underpinned by the capability of 'affiliation', which encompasses 'being able to live with and toward others, to recognize and show concern for other human beings, to engage in various forms of social interaction; to be able to imagine the situation of another. (Protecting this capability means protecting institutions that constitute and nourish such forms of affiliation, and also protecting the freedom of assembly and political speech.)'.[43] It is also underpinned

---

[39]  Langille, 'The Freedom of Association Mess' (n 8) 210–11.
[40]  Nussbaum, *Creating Capabilities* (n 4) 71.
[41]  Martha C Nussbaum, 'Aristotelian Social Democracy' in R Bruce Douglass, Gerald M Mara, and Henry S Richardson (eds), *Liberalism and the Good* (Routledge, 1990) 203, 229.
[42]  Nussbaum, 'Aristotelian Social Democracy' (n 41) 231.
[43]  Nussbaum, *Creating Capabilities* (n 4) 34.

by the capability of 'control over one's political and material environment', specifically 'having the right of political participation, protections of free speech and association' and 'being able to work as a human being, exercising practical reason and entering into meaningful relationships of mutual recognition with other workers'.[44] Nussbaum identifies the principal task of government as securing a threshold of 'combined capabilities' for citizens. This requires attention to the external conditions for the exercise of capabilities, and the different ways in which hostile external environments can impede human flourishing.[45] It follows that 'to secure a right to a citizen ... is to put them in a position of capability to go ahead with choosing that function if they should so desire'.[46]

'Aristotelian Social Democracy' starts from the position that labour relations are a matter of fundamental constitutional concern. It adopts a positive view of judicially created 'derivative rights' and correlative duties as a mechanism for securing the 'combined capabilities' of workers. These derivative rights enable workers to exercise their capabilities where their exercise might otherwise be vulnerable to external constraints in the labour market. In consequence, an Aristotelian social democrat will be much more comfortable with a threshold of 'substantial interference' as a trigger for the creation of derivative rights. By contrast, Langille and Oliphant continue to stress a more stringent 'impossibility' threshold.

We have already encountered the arguments in support of this more limited approach to constitutional derivative rights. To what extent does Aristotelian social democracy undermine those arguments?

## A. The argument from freedom

Why is the Canadian Charter 'condescending' to Canadian citizens? Langille explains that 'the Court seems to have lost the faith it once had in the ability of Canadians to exercise their freedoms as they see fit. It has decided to interpose itself as the gatekeeper to our exercise of our own freedoms'.[47] This is because of the Court's valuation of different freedoms. Some freedoms attract special constitutional protection, in particular 'the right to join with others to meet on more equal terms the power and strength of other groups or entities'.[48] The SCC in *MPAO* also observed that 'the flip side of the purposive approach to freedom of association under s. 2 (d) is that the guarantee will not necessarily protect all associational activity',[49] a proposition that Langille describes as 'alien to and contradictory of the very idea of a freedom. As a result, we really do have a condescending constitution'.[50]

How is this condescending? The description of the court as a 'gatekeeper' to freedom sounds unsettling, for sure. Yet no one is being coerced by the court (or

---

44  Nussbaum, *Creating Capabilities* (n 4).
45  Nussbaum, 'Capabilities and Human Rights' (n 2) 290.
46  Nussbaum, 'Capabilities and Human Rights' (n 2) 293.
47  Langille, 'The Condescending Constitution' (n 28) 336.
48  *Mounted Police Association of Ontario v Canada*, 2015 SCC 1, 1 SCR 3, [66] (*MPAO*).
49  Ibid *MPAO* (n 48) [59].          50  Langille, 'The Condescending Constitution' (n 28) 343.

any other public institution) and subjected to compulsion in their associational choices. Furthermore, though the SCC does indeed state that not all associational activity will be protected, the only example it gives of constitutional exclusion is 'associational activity that constitutes violence'.[51] Nothing in this should surprise us. The legal specification of human rights reflects judgements about the common good and just relations between persons.[52] For example, 'freedom of expression', properly understood, does not encompass the dissemination of child pornography, racist abuse and other forms of hate speech, sexual harassment by managers, and libellous statements. By the same token, we should expect some forms of associational activity, such as violent conspiracies and criminal joint enterprises, to be unprotected by the right to freedom of association.

There may nevertheless be condescension in the *public* ranking of certain forms of association as worthier than others. On Nussbaum's account of capabilities, for example, she observes that 'even a benign religious (or anti-religious) establishment threatens equality by creating an in-group and a variety of out-groups. It says that all citizens do not enter the public square on equal terms'.[53] In elevating groups dedicated to the redressing of social and economic disadvantage, has the SCC effectively created an 'in-group' and thereby prevented citizens from entering the public square on equal terms? This may be the gist of the condescension objection. Ultimately, it fails on the Aristotelian social democratic approach. The SCC's use of 'disadvantage' as a basis for stronger constitutional protection is not analogous to religious establishment. Special support for the disadvantaged is warranted because they are already an 'out-group'. The provision of affirmative support to disadvantaged 'out-groups' is designed to restore substantive equality in the public square, not to undermine it.

From the perspective of Aristotelian social democracy, it is possible for public institutions to value freedoms without this involving any disrespect to citizens. Constitution-building necessitates valuations of freedom. Constitutional rights demarcate specific zones of freedom warranting constitutional protection, such as freedom of religion, freedom of expression, and the right to respect for one's private and family life. Constitutions rarely protect 'liberty' in an undifferentiated way. The value of Nussbaum's account of the 'central capabilities' is in providing a basis for determining which kinds of freedom warrant special protection in a constitutional order. This reflects a basic commitment to 'the idea of the citizen as a free and dignified human being, a maker of choices'.[54] For example, 'practical reason' is a 'central capability' in her list. Indeed, 'practical reason' is characterized by her as an 'architectonic' human functioning because it suffuses all the other capabilities.[55] Practical reason gives *human* shape to the flourishing life. The 'architectonic' positioning of practical reason shows that it is the citizen herself who is responsible for shaping her own life through her own choices. It provides an important check on 'condescension' by public institutions. The Aristotelian social democratic constitution is based

---

[51]  *MPAO* (n 48) [59].      [52]  Webber and others, *Legislated Human Rights* (n 14) 127–8.
[53]  Nussbaum, *Creating Capabilities* (n 4) 90.
[54]  Nussbaum, 'Capabilities and Human Rights' (n 2) 292.
[55]  Nussbaum, 'Aristotelian Social Democracy' (n 41) 226.

upon fundamental respect for the practical reason of citizens. Citizens must *lead* their own lives in accordance with their own determinations of value.

Nussbaum describes her account as based on a 'thick vague' conception of the good. It is thicker than most standard liberal accounts in encompassing the full range of human flourishing. It is vague because the instantiation of these plural and incommensurable forms of human flourishing 'admits ... of many concrete specifications'.[56] This vagueness leaves space for different communities to exercise their practical reason in shaping those more concrete specifications through politics. Nussbaum also endorses a 'political' account of the 'central capabilities'. That is to say, they are offered up for endorsement by citizens who endorse a plurality of different reasonable comprehensive doctrines. Since her 'vague' account of human flourishing is 'articulated in a calculatedly "thin" way ... they can potentially command the approval of a wide range of citizens subscribing to different religious and secular positions'.[57]

Specific capabilities can also be identified as constitutionally important without condescension. For example, freedom of association has particular importance in a constitution shaped by Aristotelian social democracy. This is because 'affiliation', like 'practical reason', is identified by Nussbaum as an architectonic functioning. The architectonic status of affiliation reflects the fact that human plans are relational and associative: 'We do whatever we do as social beings; and the kind of deliberative planning we do for our lives is a planning with and to others'.[58] The making of constitutions is inescapably normative, and it is better to recognize that explicitly, to ensure that the exercise is normative in ways that respect reasonable pluralism.

Aristotelian social democracy also supports the special position of the disadvantaged in the constitution of capabilities, and the political prioritization of strategies to improve the position of the worst off. In their seminal work on disadvantage, Wolff and de-Shalit have drawn attention to 'fertile functionings' and 'corrosive disadvantage'.[59] 'Corrosive disadvantage' describes a situation where certain capability-failures have negative causal impacts on a range of other capabilities so that disadvantages become clustered. 'Fertile functionings' describe certain categories of functioning where targeted support can create a 'virtuous circle' effect in relation to wider functionings. This is valuable in designing effective public policy interventions. The targeted support of functionings that are 'fertile' can have more significant impact in improving the position of the least advantaged. Given the 'architectonic' position of 'affiliation', it is unsurprising that Wolff and de-Shalit identify 'affiliation' as a 'fertile' point of leverage in supporting empowerment and agency, and its absence as a 'corrosive' source of social exclusion and isolation.[60] In our own field, we know that the decline of unionization has been corrosive of capabilities at work. The disintegration of collective regulation has led to the growth in

---

[56] Nussbaum, 'Aristotelian Social Democracy' (n 41) 217.
[57] Nussbaum, *Creating Capabilities* (n 4) 90.
[58] Nussbaum, 'Aristotelian Social Democracy' (n 41) 226–7.
[59] Jonathan Wolff and Avner de-Shalit, *Disadvantage* (OUP, 2007) 120–8.
[60] Wolff and de-Shalit, *Disadvantage* (n 59) 138–42.

precarious and casualized work, and the degradation of decent and secure work. The weakening of workers' political voice has led to further legislative deregulation of labour standards. In turn, the growth of precarity has led to acute challenges for trade unions in organizing precarious workers.[61] This would support the SCC's special focus on the associative rights of disadvantaged groups as a way of breaking into this vicious circle of corrosive capabilities at work.

The enhanced constitutional support for groups focused on redressing disadvantage is not justified by their intrinsic moral goodness. As Nussbaum argues, 'some capabilities ... may justly take priority, and one reason to assign priority would be the fertility of the item in question, or its tendency to remove a corrosive disadvantage'.[62] Wolff and de-Shalit identify 'priority to the worst off' as a political principle upon which 'there is prima facie wide agreement'.[63] This targeting of public support to improve the position of the disadvantaged in cases like *Dunmore* is not condescending. On the contrary, it reflects the special importance of 'affiliation' as a source of 'corrosive disadvantage' and as a 'fertile functioning' leading to empowered agency for marginalized citizens. It is also supported by the political principle that assigns priority to the needs of the most disadvantaged in society in assigning public resources (including legal rights). There is no condescension in that.

Accordingly, we should reject the position in 'thin' freedom of association that restriction of freedoms through the creation of derivative rights always involves a normative cost. Where the freedom restricted by the duty is noxious or inconsequential, for example the freedom of the powerful to oppress the weak, that does not count as a strong reason against creating the derivative right. Admittedly, a constitutional system in which derivative rights are created willy-nilly might lead to an over-juridification that is itself oppressive. It is one thing to create derivative rights to bargain collectively for disadvantaged agricultural workers in order to make their industrial freedom more meaningful. But what about making the street corner preacher's freedom more meaningful by coercing citizens to stop and listen?[64] This requires an answer. Aristotelian social democracy provides one.

Nussbaum argues that 'the very idea of freedom involves the idea of constraint: for person P is not free to action A unless other people are prevented from interfering'.[65] In formal terms, of course, it might be objected that this elides liberties and claim-rights. In response, we might say that where fundamental entitlements are at stake, it is the responsibility of government to secure those entitlements to citizens through the implementation of derivative rights.[66] Once we are in the realm of fundamental entitlements, we move very quickly from 'liberties' to 'rights' and 'duties'. This is because the entitlements correspond to the central capabilities, those conditions that are necessary for people to lead a dignified life. Given their fundamental importance

---

[61] Alan Bogg and Ruth Dukes, 'The Contract of Employment and Collective Labour Law' in Mark Freedland and others (eds), *The Contract of Employment* (OUP, 2016) 96, 122–3.
[62] Nussbaum, *Creating Capabilities* (n 4) 45.     [63] Wolff and de-Shalit (n 59) 155.
[64] Langille and Oliphant. 'The Legal Structure of Freedom of Association' (n 5) 267.
[65] Nussbaum, *Creating Capabilities* (n 4) 71–2.
[66] Nussbaum, *Creating Capabilities* (n 4) 168.

to a dignified life, governments and other actors are subject to duties to respect and protect those fundamental entitlements. In other words, capabilities as fundamental entitlements and derivative rights are highly convergent in the Aristotelian social democratic constitution.

Where we are contemplating the creation of new duties, the public valuation of freedoms is unavoidable. Nussbaum argues that 'no society that pursues equality or even an ample social minimum can avoid curtailing freedom in very many ways, and what it ought to say is: those freedoms are not good, they are not part of a core group of entitlements required by the notion of social justice, and in many ways, indeed, they subvert those core entitlements'.[67] That is why the freedom to sexually harass does not count as a reason against the imposition of a duty not to sexually harass on co-workers.

This also explains why Langille's and Oliphant's street preacher example does not warrant a derivative right, whereas *Dunmore* and *BC Health Services* do. In many derivative rights cases in the labour field, the relevant freedoms of the employer are either inconsequential or noxious: the freedom to refuse to bargain collectively with a representative trade union; the freedom to victimize trade unionists; the freedom to maintain and use blacklists; the freedom to dismiss strikers; the freedom to exploit a precarious workforce. Little of importance is lost where inconsequential or noxious freedoms are restricted through the imposition of duties. Where noxious freedoms are restricted to support valuable freedoms of great significance, such as the freedom from trade union victimization or the opportunity to work in an environment that is free from sexual harassment, the case for creating a new derivative right is very strong.

By contrast, the freedom *not* to listen to a street preacher is a freedom of great importance. It is connected to liberty of conscience and bodily integrity (freedom of movement). It is thus supported by the list of 'central capabilities'. Respect for this freedom should be regarded as a fundamental entitlement. The creation of a derivative right to enforce a 'captive audience' through coercive duties would be a serious injustice. This explains the fundamental difference between the position of the employer in *BC Health Services* and the position of the passers-by in Langille and Oliphant's street preacher example. The employer's freedom not to engage in collective bargaining counts for little in the scheme of Aristotelian social democracy.

From the perspective of capabilities, the SCC's focus on disadvantage as a trigger for intervention is fully justified. It also explains why the creation of a derivative right was justified for the agricultural workers in *Dunmore*. Agricultural work is precarious, subject to poor terms and conditions of employment, and these conditions are exacerbated by unjustified exclusions from standard legislative protections. By contrast, the street preacher has no serious claim for the constitutional creation of derivative rights. She does not experience any form of 'corrosive disadvantage' warranting protective state intervention; and her derivative right would give rise to duties that interfere with the central capabilities of other citizens.

---

[67] Nussbaum, *Creating Capabilities* (n 4) 73.

## B. The argument from democracy

The argument from democracy identifies a leading role for legislatures in the specification of derivative rights, with constitutional courts operating as subsidiary actors. This prioritization of democratic methods in Sen's work, and the capabilities scholarship that it has inspired in labour law, has evident virtues. Democratic specification respects the agency of citizens to determine the meaning of their own freedoms. The specification of derivative rights in the labour field requires complex normative and empirical judgements. The legislative process ensures that a wide range of evidence can be identified and evaluated. By contrast, bipolar litigation is centred on the rights of the parties in dispute and it is not well suited to a wider consideration of policy. Also, the formulation of derivative rights in labour law is intensely political. It is a site where sharp material and evaluative conflicts abound. It is better to entrust those political judgements, and the ongoing adjustment of political conflict, to a democratic process where a plurality of voices can be heard.[68] Finally, the constitutionalization of derivative rights risks the 'ossification' of judicially crafted labour codes.[69] This impedes the scope for legislators to modify the package of derivative rights to keep pace with the rapid changes in the technical and legal organization of work.

There are significant differences between Nussbaum and Sen on constitutional structure. Nussbaum notes that Sen is agnostic on whether fundamental rights should be constitutionally entrenched.[70] There is also a lack of detailed engagement with the basic institutional issues of constitutional design in Sen's work on capabilities. We know that Sen favours democratic methods. But does deliberative democracy depend upon effective constitutional guarantees of political and social rights?[71] If so, how should constitutions underwrite the social conditions of fair democratic deliberation? Might there be some rights with such a well-settled normative core, such as freedom from forced labour, that it would be inappropriate to submit them to a democratic process? These are fundamental questions, and we shouldn't be left guessing.

It might be that constitutional design is something upon which the capabilities approach is silent. It might be possible for theorists to converge on the capabilities approach as the best political account of human flourishing, while holding incompatible views on the constitutional allocation of law-making powers between different political institutions. These constitutional choices are underdetermined

---

[68] For a general analysis of the limitations of the judicial function in labour rights adjudication, see Alan Bogg, 'Common Law and Statute in the Law of Employment' (2016) 69 *Current Legal Problems* 67.

[69] It is worth comparing the US experience. Freedom of association is constitutionally inert, and yet it is one of the most ossified legislative regimes in the world. See Cynthia Estlund, 'The Ossification of American Labor Law' (2002) 102 *Columbia Law Review* 1527. Constitutional litigation could have a disruptive effect which prompts law-making creativity on the part of legislators who might otherwise remain in torpor.

[70] Nussbaum, *Creating Capabilities* (n 4) 179.

[71] J Cohen, 'Procedure and Substance in Deliberative Democracy' in J Bohman and W Rehg (eds), *Deliberative Democracy* (MIT Press 1997) 407.

by the capabilities approach, but reflect other commitments in democratic theory, political science, and constitutional law.

In fact, Nussbaum has been explicit in linking her capabilities approach to constitutional design, and unlike Sen, she favours the entrenchment of fundamental rights. Constitutional entrenchment is justified because the central capabilities are *fundamental* entitlements: 'Support for the specified list of opportunities is not just a kind of handout, or *de haute en bas* charity. It is the right of each and every citizen, and all citizens have equal rights in the specified areas'.[72] The question remains why this should be done through constitutional rights and constitutional courts, rather than through ordinary legislation. We might also wonder whether the capabilities approach has anything to say about that. After all, legislation is not *de haute en bas* charity. It imposes legal duties backed by coercive force.

Nussbaum argues in favour of constitutional entrenchment through the concept of 'capability security'.[73] The constitutional entrenchment of fundamental entitlements, and their removal from the give-and-take of ordinary politics, ensures that rights cannot be 'removed in an hour by an impatient majority'.[74] Wolff and de-Shalit have developed this general idea of security through the concept of 'secure functionings'.[75] According to them, it is a form of disadvantage when achieved functionings are insecure. They give the example of a tenant exposed to the standing risk of eviction. This involuntary exposure to the risk of deprivation is corrosive of wellbeing, even where there is no eviction. It is a form of precariousness that generates fear and anxiety. Exposure to the arbitrary will of the powerful, such as a landlord, is a demeaning relation that violates norms of social equality.[76] We might think of constitutional entrenchment as a security project for capabilities.

Imagine a situation where a neoliberal government repeals its labour relations statutes, leaving freedom of association to basic common law entitlements. Imagine also that there is no constitutional impediment to this legislative act. The very possibility of easy repeal of these protective statutes is itself a form of insecurity. Once the statutes are repealed, this exposes an individual worker to different types of risk corresponding to capability insecurity. Exposure to the common law leaves the specific functioning of affiliation insecure, for the worker can be dismissed at will or lawfully victimized by the employer for trade union membership. Even if our worker is not dismissed, her awareness that she is exposed to this risk is itself a form of disadvantage. Deteriorating terms and conditions expose the worker to diminishing security of employment and income, with knock-on effects on nutrition, social and cultural participation, and housing.[77] Clandestine efforts at unionization might result in dismissal, blacklisting, or even violence and murder in some parts of the world. Blacklisting can destroy the worker's ability to earn a living, feed herself and

---

[72] Martha C Nussbaum, 'Foreword: Constitutions and Capabilities: "Perception" Against Lofty Formalism' (2007) 121 *Harvard Law Review* 4, 13.
[73] Nussbaum, *Creating Capabilities* (n 4) 73.       [74] Nussbaum, *Creating Capabilities* (n 4).
[75] Wolff and de-Shalit (n 59) 3.
[76] This shares much in common with contemporary republican concerns with 'non-domination'. See Philip Pettit, *Republicanism: A Theory of Freedom and Government* (OUP, 2001).
[77] Wolff and de-Shalit (n 59) 70.

her family, participate in social and cultural activities, and enjoy adequate shelter. As these risks propagate across functioning categories, the resulting disadvantages are highly corrosive. This does not answer the question of the substantive scope of constitutional entrenchment. At a minimum, I would suggest that derivative rights protecting organizational activities at work, including the individual right to strike, should be constitutionally entrenched. While constitutional entrenchment of freedom of association is not a failsafe, it provides a brake on deregulatory processes. Without such a constitutional brake, citizens will have insecure functionings.[78] Constitutional equality would be of no assistance here either, because the deregulation of labour standards would be indiscriminate rather than targeted at specific groups of workers.

It is possible to undertake this constitutional entrenchment in a way that is sensitive to the role of legislators, and Nussbaum's approach would support this constitutional complementarity. After all, Nussbaum describes herself as a social *democrat*, and her work is very sensitive to the important role of democracy in specifying the 'thick vague good' in political communities.

In *MPAO*, for example, the SCC deployed general constitutional principles such as 'choice' to conclude that the non-independent staff association imposed on the police violated the constitutional guarantee of freedom of association. The constitutional task of the court was to assess the constitutional compliance of legislation, albeit that 'a variety of labour relations models may provide sufficient employee choice and independence'.[79] This allowed a degree of creative latitude to legislators in the implementation of labour relations regimes that were constitutionally compliant, hence 'the search is not for an "ideal" model of collective bargaining, but rather for a model which provides sufficient employee choice and independence to permit the formulation and pursuit of employee interests in the particular workplace context at issue'.[80] The judicial development of mediate norms such as 'choice' enabled the court to respect democratic legitimacy whilst opening up critical space between abstract constitutional standards and domestic legislation. This emphasis on 'choice' as a general constitutional principle in *MPAO* also fits with the centrality of choice and practical reason in the capabilities approach.[81] It is an exemplar of how constitutional entrenchment can be sensitive to democratic concerns through wise constitutional adjudication.

## C.  The argument against contextualism

The argument against contextualism is critical of the style of judicial reasoning in *BC Health Services*. It will be recalled that the SCC relied upon legal history and

---

[78]  It is important to be realistic about how much of a brake. For a critical discussion of constitutional entrenchment in the era of austerity, see Ioannis Katsaroumpas, 'De-Constitutionalising Collective Labour Rights: The Case of Greece' (2017) 47 *Industrial Law Journal* 465.

[79]  *MPAO* (n 48) [92].        [80]  *MPAO* (n 48) [97].

[81]  'The goal of the CA is capability, because respect for people's power of choice is at the center of the entire approach'. See Nussbaum, 'Foreword: Constitutions and Capabilities' (n 72) 14.

international law to support the proposition that there should be constitutional recognition of a derivative right to collective bargaining. Langille and Oliphant are critical of this because neither legal history nor international law provide deductive support for a legal *duty* to bargain collectively. In historical terms, the legal duty to bargain was a creation of the labour relations statutes; it did not predate these statutory enactments. In international law terms, there is no 'legal duty to bargain' concept that is binding on Canada through its membership and ratification record in the International Labour Organization. Consequently, this appeal to contextualism is illegitimate.

It is possible to read the judgment in a less formalistic way. For example, the court stated that 'the history of collective bargaining in Canada reveals that long before the present statutory labour regimes were put in place, collective bargaining was recognized as a *fundamental aspect* of Canadian society'.[82] Or again, 'This legislation confirmed what the labour movement had been fighting for over centuries and what it had access to in the laissez-faire era through the use of strikes — the right to collective bargaining with employers'.[83] 'Right' is deployed here in a multifaceted way. The right to collective bargaining was a social or moral right long before it was recognized by the Canadian legal system as a legal right. This is compatible with it being described as a 'fundamental aspect' of society—it is a moral rather than a legal claim. It is also possible to read the SCC's use of international law material as supporting the general proposition that collective bargaining is a fundamental aspect of the international law of freedom of association. This is not the same as treating it as binding authority mandating a legal duty to bargain in Canadian constitutional law. The 'right' to collective bargaining in the ILO framework is a two-term goal oriented standard, rather than the three-term Hohfeldian relation between persons. This expresses the special moral value of collective bargaining in the international law on freedom of association, rather than compelling the constitutionalization of a legal duty to bargain in the national system.

This reading of *BC Health Services* is supported by Nussbaum's account of 'contextualism' as a judicial style. 'Contextualism' is a form of reasoning that is a 'realistic, historically and imaginatively informed type of practical reasoning that focuses on the actual abilities of people to choose and act in their concrete social settings'.[84] By contrast, 'lofty formalism' approves of judging legal disputes in 'distanced formal ways', enquiring whether basic freedoms have been respected, using simple rule-based formulae that are abstract and general.[85] Proponents of 'lofty formalism' might argue that it is the best way to ensure consistent judgments and hence respect for the rule of law.[86] As Nussbaum observes, this preference for 'lofty formalism' is usually well-motivated but it is intellectually flawed: 'Throughout the history of human life, people of intelligence and good will have sought such lofty abstractions,

---

[82] *BC Health Services* (n 22) [41].     [83] *BC Health Services* (n 22) [63].
[84] Nussbaum, 'Foreword: Constitutions and Capabilities' (n 72) 8. For a critique of legal reasoning that would be supported by Nussbaum's approach, see Judy Fudge, 'Labour Rights as Human Rights: Turning Slogans into Legal Claims' (2014) 37 *Dalhousie Law Journal* 601, 615.
[85] Nussbaum, 'Foreword: Constitutions and Capabilities' (n 72) 26.
[86] Nussbaum, 'Foreword: Constitutions and Capabilities' (n 72).

perhaps preferring, as Cardozo insightfully sees, a clear, schematic ideal to the sometimes messy and complicated realities of life'.[87]

The 'contextual' approach has important advantages in enabling courts to be imaginatively attuned to the exclusions and obstacles experienced by disadvantaged groups. The flight from historically and contextually situated reasoning favours 'existing power interests: the close scrutiny of history and context is more important for the powerless, who face unequal obstacles to opportunity'.[88] Where legal reasoning is more contextually informed, judges will be more sensitive to the experiences of vulnerable groups of workers. The recent record of the SCC in freedom of association cases supports that view.

To understand the 'contextual' role of legal history and international law in *BC Health Services*, we should recall Nussbaum's account of the 'thick vague' conception of the good:

> The thick vague theory is not, in the sense that worries liberals, a metaphysical theory. That is, it is not a theory that is arrived at in detachment from the actual self-understandings and evaluations of human beings in society; nor is it a theory peculiar to a single metaphysical or religious tradition. Indeed, it is ... both internal to human history and strongly evaluative; and its aim is to be as universal as possible, to set down the basis for our recognitions of members of very different traditions as human across religious and metaphysical gulfs.[89]

This indicates a specific role for historical and international law arguments in judicial reasoning. It is missing the point of those arguments to criticize them against a deductive yardstick, presenting a duty to bargain as a logical necessity derived mechanically from legal premises. The appeal to historical development is better understood as a form of genealogical vindication of values. It is a form of cultural self-interpretation, attentive to the historical contingency of our 'thick' ethical concepts, which would include many of our constitutional concepts.[90] This genealogical approach enables the court to discern the dependence of values on social forms and practices and to trace their historical development. The history of labour struggles, the quest for recognition by organized workers in the face of severe hardship, the portrayal of those struggles in our great art and literature, indicates why *for us* the right to collective bargaining and the right to strike are moral rights of the highest importance. It is particularly appropriate, therefore, that constitutional courts should recognize these as fundamental elements in abstract textual guarantees of freedom of association. The same is also likely to be true of literary and cultural associations, political associations, and so forth.[91] The specification of the 'thick

---

[87] Nussbaum, 'Foreword: Constitutions and Capabilities' (n 72) 28. One wonders whether the simple formula 'the freedom to do collectively that which one is at liberty to do as an individual' is such an example of mechanistic formalism. It seems to stop short of providing helpful guidance in most of the tricky cases that end up in constitutional litigation.

[88] Nussbaum, 'Foreword: Constitutions and Capabilities' (n 72) 30.

[89] Nussbaum, 'Aristotelian Social Democracy' (n 41) 217.

[90] See Bernard Williams, *Ethics and the Limits of Philosophy* (W A Moore (ed), Routledge 2006) 143–5. For further discussion of Williams as a genealogical philosopher, see Colin Koopman, *Genealogy as Critique: Foucault and the Problems of Modernity* (Indiana University Press 2013) 65–73.

[91] Langille is vexed that 'book clubs' are apparently given short shrift by the SCC. It was an unfortunate choice of example by the SCC. The banning of book clubs should frighten all of us. Still, it is

vague' good must always be 'internal to human history', and this supports a genea-logical approach to normative judgements.

Using Nussbaum's framework, the appeal to international law and international thought should be understood as a form of cultural cross-check to ensure that our historically situated practices resonate across different traditions. That is certainly supported by the international law on freedom of association, which identifies col-lective bargaining and strike action as collective activities of great significance. The appeal to international law ensures that the general values underlying constitutional freedoms are, in Nussbaum's terms, 'as universal as possible'. Where local histories and universal values converge, as in *BC Health Services*, the court has likely identi-fied a social practice of great value that warrants strong constitutional protection through derivative rights. This contextualised reasoning is a vital element in consti-tutional adjudication, and a necessary supplement to more conventional modes of legal reasoning characteristic of private law.

'Contextualism' favours the incremental development of legal doctrines, as con-stitutional principles are progressively refined through case law.[92] By contrast, 'lofty formalism' obliterates the human texture from legal reasoning and it is usually aligned with libertarian and minimalist approaches to constitutional rights. From the capabilities perspective, our ideal judge is Justice Sophia. Justice Sophia uses her wise perception to understand the demands of the 'thick vague good', mediated through the constitutional text, always sensitive to the hidden barriers to human freedom. She will also be sensitive to the democratic specification of the 'thick vague' good, understanding that judges do not necessarily enjoy privileged insights into the cultural matrix of social values. The specific content of constitutional freedoms will often be shaped reflexively by the existing legislative framework enacted in order to implement abstract rights such as the right to collective bargaining. This democratic sensitivity has been characteristic of the SCC's interpretive approach to freedom of association. For example, the specific content of Canadian constitutional freedom of association, such as the 'unfair labour practice' provisions in *Dunmore*, has been shaped by the legislated norms specified in labour relations statutes. In the constitu-tion of capabilities, courts and legislatures should work together as complementary institutions in support of human rights and substantive human freedom. The pres-entation of a zero-sum conflict between democracy and constitutional entrench-ment is far too crude to capture this, as the SCC's jurisprudence demonstrates.

## IV. Constitutional Equality and the Capabilities Approach

It has been suggested that much of the constitutional litigation about freedom of association could be addressed in a simple and direct way through constitutional equality. The basic complaint of the agricultural workers in *Dunmore* was their

---

difficult to see how book clubs would need constitutional derivative rights in order to function. Perhaps it is this that marks the difference between labour associations and book clubs.

[92] Nussbaum, *Creating Capabilities* (n 4) 175–6.

unjustified exclusion from the general statutory regime. Constitutional equality responds directly to that complaint, and it does so in a way that avoids the controversies around derivative rights.

From a capabilities perspective, this solution is attractive. For example, Nussbaum has argued that one of the features 'of good judicial interpretation of a constitutional right is its *focus on the rights of minorities to equal treatment*'.[93] In *Wandsworth London Borough Council v Vining and others*, for example, parks constables were excluded from the scope of redundancy consultation provisions under the relevant UK statute.[94] The Court of Appeal held that the right to redundancy consultation was protected under the Article 11 freedom of association provision of the European Convention on Human Rights (ECHR). Where a legislative scheme was in place, any exclusion of particular classes of workers required justification. Since there was no such justification for the exclusions of parks police, the statute was construed to include them within the scope of the right to consultation. *Vining* provides a textbook example of the power and simplicity of an equality-type argument in practice.

There are three general grounds for caution in using equality arguments to improve the position of disadvantaged citizens. The first concerns the role of 'basic equality' arguments in the distribution of legal rights. It is important to recognize the importance of the distinction between what Waldron has described as 'conditional' and 'sortal' statuses.[95] 'Conditional' statuses describe the variety of roles and circumstances that determine our legal rights and duties from time to time: for example, employment, marriage, or alienage. By contrast, 'sortal' status 'categorizes legal subjects on the basis of *the sort of person* they are'.[96] Examples of this would include racial or caste-based distinctions. Now it is certainly true that 'basic equality' would rule out the distribution of fundamental rights like association on the basis of 'sortal' categories. However, 'conditional' categories are central in the allocation of statutory rights. It is not uncommon for statutory freedom of association regimes to draw conditional distinctions based on contract-type (i.e. we confine the statute to 'employees' or 'workers') or occupational distinctions (i.e. special arrangements for civil servants, workers in essential services, police, the army). Conditional statuses are not necessarily incompatible with 'basic equality' in the distribution of fundamental rights through legislation. It is only where the 'conditional status' distinction is unjustified, as in *Vining*, that this gives rise to a legitimate equality objection.

The second concerns the alleged virtue of equality arguments in bracketing controversial policy determinations, so preserving judicial legitimacy. In simple equality cases—*Vining* is such an example—this argument makes sense. It would be crazy for the courts to construct a parallel set of derivative rights where there is a simple equality remedy. Many equality cases are not so simple. For example, imagine a constitutional claim that 'irregular migrants' should be included in general labour

---

[93] Nussbaum, *Creating Capabilities* (n 4) 176.

[94] *Vining v London Borough of Wandsworth* [2017] EWCA Civ 1092.

[95] Jeremy Waldron, *One Another's Equals: The Basis of Human Equality* (Harvard University Press, 2017) 8–9.

[96] Waldron, *One Another's Equals* (n 95) 7.

law protections. This invites a politically controversial exercise. Should it be confined to victims of trafficking? What about situations where there is 'culpability' on the migrant's part in securing employment illegally? Or imagine a constitutional claim that self-employed professionals should be included too. Does this apply to all forms of self-employment including those who wield significant market power? Would this require realignment of the law on anti-competitive practices? In these examples, controversial political and legal judgements are not obviated by an equality approach. Indeed, the equality standard invites them.

Finally, Nussbaum's 'rights of minorities to equal treatment' does not necessarily correspond to formal equality as symmetry. As she reminds us, 'Equality should be understood not in a distanced way, as mere formal symmetry, but in terms of people's actual abilities to do or be'.[97] Where groups experience persistent disadvantage the capabilities approach would advocate affirmative support to those groups. It is well known that 'formal symmetry' can entrench exclusion because general legal norms are not sensitive to the disadvantages experienced by disadvantaged groups. For example, in De Stefano's reflections on the freedom of association of 'non-standard workers', he recommends a suite of substantive reforms designed to ameliorate the specific barriers faced by non-standard workers.[98] It is not sufficient to simply expand the 'personal scope' of existing labour relations statutes so that they apply formally to all workers. For example, he argues for a loosening of restrictions on political and secondary strikes because these rules disproportionately impede the freedom of association of non-standard workers.

It is no surprise that agricultural workers have been at the centre of freedom of association litigation in Canada and the UK. Agricultural workers are sometimes excluded from general labour relations statutes, as in Canada and the US. Often, agricultural work is undertaken by workers under temporary migration programmes, with all the structural vulnerabilities that this entails. Union organization is also impeded because migrant agricultural workers may lack 'English-language skills, and fear of being arbitrarily repatriated or blacklisted from returning to Canada'.[99] The work is hard, dangerous, and conducted under poor working and living conditions.[100] In Wolff and de-Shalit's terminology, these workers experience 'corrosive disadvantage' in the concurrent failure of multiple capabilities: affiliation, control over one's political and material environment, the ability to speak the local language, and bodily health and integrity.

How should a constitutional court respond when presented with a freedom of association claim by agricultural workers? Let us consider two possible responses: (i) the 'equality as symmetry' approach; and (ii) the direct promotion of functionings. I shall argue that only (ii) remedies the 'corrosive disadvantage' experienced by

[97] Nussbaum, 'Foreword: Constitutions and Capabilities' (n 72) 59.
[98] See Valerio De Stefano, "Non-standard Work and Limits on Freedom of Association: A human rights-based approach" (2016) 46 *Industrial Law Journal* 185.
[99] Wayne Hanley, 'The Roots of Organizing Agriculture Workers in Canada' in Fay Faraday, Judy Fudge, and Eric Tucker (eds), *Constitutional Labour Rights in Canada: Farm Workers and the Fraser Case* (Irwin, 2012) 57, 59.
[100] Hanley, 'The Roots of Organizing Agriculture Workers in Canada' (n 99).

agricultural workers. Although it appears to be ruled out on Nussbaum's account of capabilities, I will propose a modification of Nussbaum's account that would allow for direct promotion of functionings in appropriate cases.

## A.  The 'equality as symmetry' approach

The problem with constitutional equality arguments is demonstrated by the recent decision in *Unite v United Kingdom*.[101] In 2013, the UK government abolished the Agricultural Wages Board of England and Wales (AWB). The AWB was composed of employer and worker representatives and independent members, and it set minimum wages and conditions of employment in the agricultural sector. On Langille's account of constitutional equality, the abolition of the AWB would appear to be a desirable restoration of symmetry in the legal system. The agricultural workers enjoy access to the general legislative machinery for collective bargaining certification. By removing special legal arrangements for agricultural workers, constitutional equality is secured.

In *Unite*, however, the trade union was challenging the abolition of the AWB as a violation of Article 11 and the right to collective bargaining. The basis of its challenge was that the general labour laws were practically unavailable to agricultural workers. The certification procedure in the U.K. is confined to employers employing at least 21 workers. Given the structure of employment in the agricultural sector, the vast majority of employers failed to meet this threshold; hence the statute was practically unavailable to most agricultural workers. While it was theoretically possible for agricultural workers to strike for union recognition, the highly dispersed and precarious nature of employment meant that this means of securing collective bargaining was likely to be ineffective. The equal protection of the general collective bargaining and strike laws had the practical effect of extinguishing the collective bargaining rights of agricultural workers.

In a controversial judgment, the ECtHR rejected the union's claim as inadmissible. The formal access for agricultural workers to the general statutory framework was sufficient for Article 11. In its embrace of formal equality, *Unite* is a *tour de force* of 'lofty formalism'. This is reflected in three features of its reasoning. First, the ECtHR is obtusely inattentive to the practical disadvantages experienced by agricultural workers in the real world of work. In this respect, it is the antithesis of the imaginative 'contextualism' defended by Nussbaum that is necessary for judges to appreciate the hidden exclusionary barriers faced by disadvantaged groups. While transnational courts face genuine obstacles in this regard, given their distance from the local context, the substantial evidence provided by the trade union appeared to fall on deaf judicial ears. For example, given the dominance of small employers in the UK agricultural sector, and the 21-worker threshold in the statute, it did not require too much imagination to grasp the specific barrier faced by these workers. The

---

[101]  *Unite the Union v United Kingdom*, App No 65397/13 (3 May 2016). For an excellent analysis, see Kalina Arabadijeva, 'Another Disappointment in Strasbourg' (2017) 46 *Industrial Law Journal* 289.

blithe assumption that workers can strike for recognition displays a basic failure to understand what was being asked of workers who can sometimes barely afford to eat and keep a roof over their heads.

Secondly, the judgment is focused narrowly on the paper rights of agricultural workers, rather than whether those rights are 'practical and effective'.[102] The capabilities approach is concerned with what citizens are *really* able to do and be, not what they can do on paper. Finally, the ECtHR used its 'margin of appreciation' doctrine to adopt a highly deferential stance to the national government's decision-making in abolishing the AWB. The Court attached particular weight to the implementation of a consultation process by the Government prior to abolition. The democratic quality of the consultation process was not subjected to robust interrogation, nor was there an acknowledgment of the obvious threat posed by democratic processes to disadvantaged groups who lack political clout. Certainly, there was little engagement with the idea that capabilities need to be secured through some form of constitutional entrenchment.

## B. The direct promotion of functionings

Why was the restoration of the AWB so important to the agricultural workers in *Unite*? The AWB provided a legal mechanism that guaranteed social and economic outcomes for workers who were practically unable to organize and seek their own improved terms and conditions through collective action. Historically, Wages Councils in the UK operated on similar principles. It provided a mechanism for catalysing collective bargaining, so that the principal objective of a Wages Council was to render itself redundant because autonomous union organization had taken root.[103] In the North American context, proposals for 'first contract arbitration' or arbitration as a remedy for unfair labour practices provide another example where the state underwrites substantive outcomes to support enduring collective bargaining procedures.

Where does the capabilities approach stand on these more radical strategies? The capabilities approach draws a crucial distinction between capabilities and functionings. Functionings describe those valuable beings and doings that are the 'outgrowths or realizations of capabilities'.[104] Functioning describes the flourishing itself—being well nourished, enjoying health, exercising control over one's material environment—rather than the effective opportunity of achieving it. For Nussbaum, it is illegitimate for the state to promote functionings directly because this involves a failure to respect the self-directed agency of persons. The political focus on capabilities ensures that the state is respectful of reasonable pluralism amongst its citizens.

To use Langille's terminology, the direct promotion of functionings is a form of condescension, whereas the promotion of the capabilities respects the agency of

---

[102] *Artico v Italy* (1981) 3 EHRR 1 [33].
[103] See Alan Bogg, 'Subsidiarity or Freedom of Association? A Perspective from Labor Law' (2016) 61 *The American Journal of Jurisprudence* 143, 156–7.
[104] Nussbaum, *Creating Capabilities* (n 4) 25.

citizens to decide for themselves. This would seem to provide a strong argument against 'substantive' constitutional remedies for disadvantaged workers, for these appear to promote the functioning directly. This anti-paternalist approach also supports the emphasis on 'choice' as a constitutional principle in *M.P.A.O*, and the strict insistence in *BC Health Services* that the right to collective bargaining 'does not guarantee the particular objectives sought through this associational activity. However, it guarantees the process through which those goals are pursued'.[105]

*Pace* Nussbaum, it is not disrespectful to support the direct promotion of functioning in certain circumstances, subject to the following conditions. First, where there are 'adaptive preference' effects in play, so that citizens' preferences have adjusted to past deprivations and the unavailability of options, the provision of the relevant capability may not be sufficient to ensure that freedom of choice is genuinely facilitated. As Sunstein has pointed out, workers may not value the option of industrial self-rule if they have been inured to domination and subordination.[106] It may be necessary to expose them to the functioning so that they have an opportunity to assess its value in their lives. That would be the only way to ensure an effective opportunity to exercise the capability.

Secondly, there is an important normative difference between voluntary and non-voluntary contexts of direct state provision of functionings. In voluntary contexts, *the disadvantaged workers themselves* are seeking a substantive constitutional remedy, for example through constitutional litigation. This is significantly different to an overweening state foisting the functioning onto unwilling citizens. There is no disrespect where help in the form of direct provision is being actively sought and welcomed by disadvantaged groups. Indeed, it would seem not a little callous to disregard the request for help in achieving the functioning where that denial is justified in terms of the 'best interests' of the disadvantaged.

Thirdly, the direct provision of the functioning should always be conceived as a short-term remedial intervention whose aim is to catalyse the relevant capability. This could be achieved through imposing temporal limits on such remedies (for example, targeting arbitration at 'first contract' negotiations but not subsequent bargaining rounds). The aim must always be to achieve empowered agency for the beneficiaries of direct state support of functionings, and to avoid situations where disadvantaged groups become dependent on state help.

Fourthly, the direct promotion of the functioning should not interfere with the valuable freedoms of other citizens who are affected by the intervention. For example, imposing compulsory arbitration on employers interferes with their freedom to impose poor terms and conditions on disadvantaged workers. This freedom should not count for very much in assessing the legitimacy of the intervention. Matters might be different where the substantive remedy interferes with a central capability.

---

[105] *BC Health Services* (n 22) [89].
[106] Cass Sunstein, 'Legal Interference with Private Preferences' (1986) 53 *University of Chicago Law Review* 1129, 1148. Both Nussbaum and Sen have rejected utilitarian theories on the basis of adaptive preference effects: for discussion; see Nussbaum, *Creating Capabilities* (n 4) 54–5.

Finally, it is important to ensure that, in Wolff and de-Shalit's terms, disadvantage is addressed while respecting people. Some forms of targeted support for disadvantaged groups can be experienced as demeaning and humiliating. For example, where there are free school meals for poor children and the children are required to line up in a separate 'free school dinner' queue, that arrangement will be experienced as humiliating by the beneficiaries of public support.[107] Wolff and De-Shalit argue that 'the types of policies which seem most likely to undercut affiliation are those which divide society into two groups by identifying, and thereby stigmatizing, those who need help'.[108] This is undoubtedly very important. Political strategies should focus on a universal floor of fundamental social rights to eradicate precarious work in the labour market for everyone. The crafting of targeted constitutional remedies for disadvantaged groups is a sign of political failure, not success. In a just society, there would not be groups that suffer from corrosive disadvantage. However, provided that the four preceding conditions are satisfied, the direct promotion of functionings should operate as a remedial backstop in the constitution of capabilities.

## V.  Conclusion

This chapter has proposed a 'capabilities template' for freedom of association inspired by Nussbaum's Aristotelian social democracy. In so doing, it has rejected an alternative 'capabilities template' developed by Langille and Oliphant. The thinness of their account of freedom of association reflects the normative abstinence of Sen's account. Sen's work is ill-suited to providing meaningful guidance on constitutional design in specific national contexts. In Robeyns' terms, Sen's theory is 'radically underspecified' as a normative theory.[109] This abstraction is a virtue where the theoretical concern is to measure comparative human development within and across countries in circumstances of cultural pluralism. Sen's theoretical work is also well-suited to the sphere of international labour law and development. However, it is too abstract to guide deliberation about fundamental rights within national constitutional orders. There are too many basic constitutional points that are left unresolved. Nussbaum's richer account of capabilities provides a much better framework for guiding our reflections on constitutional rights.

We might do better, however, to avoid thinking in terms of 'templates' for fundamental rights. Constitutions should not be in the business of ossifying political ideologies. Their function is to provide an 'overlapping consensus', to provide public structures within which citizens with a plurality of comprehensive worldviews can disagree in conditions of mutual respect.[110] In this way, the constitution of capabilities should provide discursive space for political deliberation between free and equal

---

[107] I draw that example from my own childhood. Fortunately, I can now afford an expensive psychoanalyst. Not everyone is so lucky.

[108] Wolff and de-Shalit (n 59) 172.

[109] I Robeyns, 'The Capability Approach in Practice' (2006) 14 *Journal of Political Philosophy* 351, 353.

[110] Nussbaum, *Creating Capabilities* (n 4) 89–93.

persons in circumstances of reasonable pluralism. There is no single authoritative account of the capabilities approach, and we should expect contesting visions of fundamental rights to flow from this pluralistic intellectual tradition.

Nussbaum has emphasized that one of the crucial enquiries for the capabilities approach in the next phase of its development is to bring more precision to its constitutional and institutional commitments. It would be a mistake to regard these enquiries as external to the capabilities approach. The constitution of capabilities is not silent on issues of constitutional design and the content of fundamental rights. In the hands of Nussbaum, the idea of capabilities provides determinate guidance in addressing some fundamental constitutional matters. The notion of 'capability security' would support some form of constitutional entrenchment of fundamental entitlements such as freedom of association. It is strongly aligned with the constitutional creation of derivative rights, given the close connection between fundamental entitlements, and duties to respect and to protect those entitlements. It supports judicial reasoning that is 'contextual' rather than 'formalistic'. It also favours deliberative modes of democratic engagement, and it envisages a complementary relation between legal and political institutions in supporting the realization of the central capabilities. Finally, and most controversially, the basic duty to support the most disadvantaged will sometimes require the direct promotion of functionings, as a strategy for supporting their capabilities in the longer-term.

The SCC has gone some way towards the constitution of capabilities, while the ECtHR has been in retreat. Neither constitutional court has gone far enough. The constitution of capabilities is a work in progress. The political and economic forces arrayed against human freedom have never been stronger, the intellectual and practical tasks for the constitution of capabilities never so urgent.

# 13

# Capabilities and Age Discrimination

*Pnina Alon-Shenker* *

## I. Introduction

In *Aging Thoughtfully*, Martha C. Nussbaum argues that current U.S. policies fail to meet an acceptable level of capabilities for its ageing citizens.[1] Employing her well-known list of ten central capabilities,[2] Nussbaum identifies deficiencies related to issues such as physician-assisted suicide, access to healthcare, retirement communities, and elder abuse.[3] Specifically regarding the seventh central capability—affiliation—Nussbaum notes that the "capabilities list speaks of nondiscrimination, but (formulated a long time ago) it did not mention age discrimination, a great evil ... Here the CA was short-sighted, and ought to be changed!"[4]

The purpose of this chapter is to explore the particular relevance and usefulness of the capabilities approach (CA) to age discrimination in the workplace. Indeed, ageism has become one of the most tolerated forms of social prejudice of our times.[5] Yet workplace discrimination laws and policies often fail to respond effectively to its increasingly subtle, unconscious, and structural forms.[6] This chapter argues that the CA provides a fresh theoretical framework for addressing significant barriers experienced by older workers in the labour market.[7]

This chapter is organized as follows. Section II highlights the appeal of the CA to workplace discrimination law and illustrates the close relation between the two. Section III critically assesses some contemporary challenges faced by older workers

* Associate Professor, Department of Law & Business, Ted Rogers School of Management, Ryerson University, Canada. I am grateful to Brian Langille, Guy Davidov, Therese MacDermott, Virginia Mantouvalou, and Supriya Routh for comments on an earlier draft of this chapter.

[1] Martha C. Nussbaum and Saul Levmore, *Aging Thoughtfully: Conversations about Retirement, Romance, Wrinkles, and Regret* (Oxford University Press, 2017) 195 ff.
[2] Martha C. Nussbaum, *Frontiers of Justice: Disability, Nationality, Species Membership* (Harvard University Press, 2006) 76–8.
[3] Nussbaum and Levmore, *Aging Thoughtfully* (n. 1) 197–207.
[4] Nussbaum and Levmore, *Aging Thoughtfully* (n. 1) 205.
[5] See *Revera Report on Ageism: Independence and Choice as We Age* (Sheridan Centre for Elder Research & Revera, 2016).
[6] See discussion in section III.
[7] While there are various versions of the CA, this chapter primarily adopts Nussbaum's CA and builds specifically on her work in *Frontiers of Justice*. See Nussbaum, *Frontiers of Justice* (n. 2).

in the labour market, which discrimination laws and policies often fail to address effectively. Finally, section IV demonstrates how some unique features of the CA are significant and useful in tackling some of these difficulties. First, the compelling evidence that ageism poses major obstacles to attaining and maintaining decent work is examined against Sen's idea of "the 'capabilities' of persons to lead the kind of lives they value—and have reason to value,"[8] and Nussbaum's idea of core entitlements "implicit in the very notions of human dignity and a life that is worthy of human dignity."[9] Second, the CA provides a strong critique of the popular view that age discrimination is a justifiable and reasonable way of ordering our society by distributing benefits and burdens over a lifespan. Third, the CA's sensitivity to variations in need highlights heterogeneity within the group of older workers and advances the consideration of intersectionality issues. Finally, the CA is useful in justifying regulatory reforms and policies that foster positive action and shift responsibility back to governments.

## II. The CA and Workplace Discrimination Law

The notion of capabilities was invoked by Amartya Sen in development economics theory, as an alternative measurement of the quality of life to the commonly applied welfare metrics, such as gross domestic product (GDP). Capabilities, according to Sen, are the substantive freedom to achieve what people value doing or being ("functionings")—from being well nourished and healthy, to being able to participate socially in the community.[10] Central to Sen's work is the idea that people are different in their ability to convert resources, such as wealth and income, into desired functionings.[11] That is, difference in conversion factors (which may be caused by personal characteristics but also often by external conditions) determines people's sets of capabilities, their "substantive freedom to achieve alternate functioning combinations."[12] Therefore, society's goal should be to enhance people's capabilities, their substantive freedom, "to lead the lives they have reason to value and to enhance the real choices they have."[13]

Premised on a similar idea of capabilities,[14] Nussbaum developed a philosophical account of minimum core human entitlements, which are necessary for realizing a "life that is worthy of the dignity of the human being," and as such, ought to be respected and pursued for each and every person by governments across the world.[15] The core human entitlements are articulated in a list of ten central capabilities, which "provides the underpinnings of basic political principles that can be embodied in constitutional guarantees."[16] Nussbaum distinguishes between basic

---

[8] Amartya Sen, *Development as Freedom* (Oxford University Press, 1999) 18.
[9] Nussbaum, *Frontiers of Justice* (n. 2) 155.    [10] Sen, *Development as Freedom* (n. 8) 75.
[11] Sen, *Development as Freedom* (n. 8) 70–1.    [12] Sen, *Development as Freedom* (n. 8) 75.
[13] Sen, *Development as Freedom* (n. 8) 293.
[14] Nussbaum, *Frontiers of Justice* (n. 2) 164.
[15] Nussbaum, *Frontiers of Justice* (n. 2) 70.
[16] Martha C. Nussbaum, *Women and Human Development: The Capabilities Approach* (Cambridge University Press, 2000) 74.

capabilities (which one is born with, such as seeing or hearing), internal capabilities (which one develops throughout his or her life, such as ability to play, love, or exercise political choice), and combined capabilities (which are "internal capabilities *combined with* suitable external conditions for the exercise of the function," such as the capability to exercise religious freedom or freedom of speech in various political regimes).[17] As one's capabilities depend not only on their personal internal characteristics but also on external economic, social, political, and legal circumstances, the list of ten core entitlements comprises combined capabilities.[18] Each capability has to be guaranteed to all citizens at some appropriate threshold level.[19] A failure to meet this threshold is considered "a particularly grave violation of basic justice" because these entitlements are "held to be implicit in the very notions of human dignity and a life that is worthy of human dignity."[20]

There seems to be a wide consensus that the CA is relevant to and compatible with workplace discrimination laws.[21] One can identify four main aspects of the CA that are of specific appeal and interest to discrimination law. First is the notion of capabilities as substantive freedom and the idea of conversion factors. Second is the CA's reliance on an Aristotelian notion of dignity and its insistence that core human entitlements are correlative with duties of governments and others. Third is its critique of Rawls's theory of justice. Fourth is Nussbaum's list of ten central capabilities, which include several references to discrimination issues. Each is discussed below.

## A. Capabilities as substantive freedom and the idea of conversion factors

The idea of enhancing people's substantive freedom to achieve what they have reason to value is closely connected to workplace discrimination laws. Indeed, Nussbaum's work on women and people with disabilities touches upon work-related issues, including workplace discrimination.[22] Work is considered a desired functioning.[23] Furthermore, good and decent work is viewed as a fertile functioning because it is both intrinsically valuable and instrumental to the securing of other capabilities and functionings.[24] Clearly, having the same level of

---

[17] Nussbaum, *Women and Human Development* (n. 16) 84–5.
[18] Nussbaum, *Women and Human Development* (n. 16) 85.
[19] Nussbaum, *Frontiers of Justice* (n. 2) 75.
[20] Nussbaum, *Frontiers of Justice* (n. 2) 155.
[21] See Hugh Collins, "What Can Sen's Capability Approach Offer to Labour Law?"; Riccardo Del Punta, "Is the Capability Theory an Adequate Normative Theory for Labour Law?"; Alan Bogg, "The Constitution of Capabilities: The Case of Freedom of Association"; Guy Davidov, "The Capability Approach and Labour Law: Identifying the Areas of Fit"; Virginia Mantouvalou, "Work, Human Rights, and Human Capabilities"; and Brian Langille, "What is Labour Law? Implications of the Capability Approach," all chapters in this volume.
[22] Nussbaum, *Frontiers of Justice* (n. 2); Nussbaum, *Women and Human Development* (n. 16); Martha C. Nussbaum, "Women and Equality: The Capabilities Approach" (1999) 138(3) *International Labour Review* 227.
[23] See e.g. Virginia Mantouvalou, "Work, Human Rights, and Human Capabilities," Chapter 10 in this volume.
[24] See Brian Langille, "What is Labour Law? Implications of the Capability Approach" and Virginia Mantouvalou, "Work, Human Rights, and Human Capabilities," Chapters 6 and 10, respectively, in this volume.

resources (including skills and expertise) does not always yield the same level of capabilities to convert resources into meaningful access and substantive participation in the labour market. Discrimination may often affect people's capability to achieve this desired and fertile functioning. On the CA, the purpose of workplace discrimination laws is to remove discriminatory barriers and to enhance the real choice and substantive freedom of workers to be able to achieve good and decent work.[25]

Simon Deakin finds the CA particularly useful in justifying discrimination laws by illuminating their market-constituting role. Employing Sen's idea of conversion factors, Deakin explains how discrimination laws create circumstances and institutions that act as conversion factors. Alongside personal conversion factors (internal characteristics) and environmental conversion factors (the characteristics of the environment in which people live), social conversion factors (such as social norms, practices, and institutions created by the presence or absence of legal rules, and public policies) determine how people vary in their capabilities to transform resources into functionings. For example, social norms and structural barriers, such as stereotypes and unconscious bias, can diminish some people's set of capabilities to meaningfully participate in the labour market. Discrimination laws are therefore justified as creating circumstances and institutions, which act as a conversion factor, because they can alter such norms and barriers to provide individuals with substantive and effective access to various processes, such as socialization, education, and training, thereby opening up the labour market to disadvantaged groups and extending its scope to benefit all market participants.[26] Discrimination laws prevent forms of inequality and social exclusion, which might also diminish the scope of the market and threaten its existence.[27] To demonstrate the market-constituting role of discrimination laws, Deakin provides the example of legal protection against dismissal of pregnant women.[28] This legal protection can be seen as "a form of institutionalised capability" because it provides "the conditions under which, for women workers, the freedom to enter the labour market becomes more than merely formal; it becomes a substantive freedom."[29] In the absence of legal protection, women will be expected to exit the market upon marriage or pregnancy and investment in skills and training will be lost, making society worse

---

[25] See Brian Langille, "What is Labour Law? Implications of the Capability Approach," Chapter 6 in this volume (who makes this argument more broadly as to the overarching purpose of labour law); Riccardo Del Punta, "Labour Law and the Capability Approach" (2016) 32 *International Journal of Comparative Labour Law and Industrial Relations* 383.

[26] Simon Deakin, "The 'Capability' Concept and the Evolution of European Social Policy," ESRC Centre for Business Research, University of Cambridge Working Paper No. 303 (2005).

[27] Simon Deakin, "Equality, Non-discrimination and the Labour Market," in Richard A. Epstein, *Equal Opportunity or More Opportunity? The Good Thing about Discrimination* (Institute for the Study of Civil Society, 2002), 41 41–2, 47.

[28] Deakin, "Equality, Non-discrimination and the Labour Market" (n. 27) 47–8.

[29] Deakin, "Equality, Non-discrimination and the Labour Market" (n. 27) 48. See also Simon Deakin and Frank Wilkinson, *The Law of the Labour Market: Industrialization, Employment and Legal Evolution* (Oxford University Press, 2005) 290–2.

off. Discrimination laws may not only remedy the injustice caused to dismissed pregnant workers, but also alter market incentive structures to encourage women to seek out and employers to provide training for skill-specific jobs.[30] Deakin, together with Wilkinson, then develops this idea to justify social rights more broadly as having a market-constituting function because they work as "institutionalized forms of capabilities which provide individuals with the means to realize the potential of their resource endowments and thereby achieve a higher level of economic function."[31]

## B. Aristotelian notion of dignity and human entitlements as correlative with duties

Responding to critique,[32] Deakin clarifies that labour laws should not be seen in exclusively economic terms and that they do aim to achieve other goals like economic security, human dignity, freedom of collective action, and democratic participation.[33] This is an important clarification as Nussbaum's CA is premised on an Aristotelian notion of dignity, which acknowledges that not every person can be productive in economic terms, but is still worthy of dignity because "[s]ociety is held together by a wide range of attachments and concerns, only some of which concern productivity."[34] That is, the CA significantly contributes to the long standing debate between human rights and economic approaches to discrimination laws.[35] While productivity is important, "it is not the main end of social life."[36] The main end is the realization of people's capabilities, which are core human entitlements. These core human entitlements are necessary for the realization of life worthy of human dignity, and are therefore correlative with duties: "if people have entitlements, then there is a duty to secure them."[37] This duty belongs to the government "as well, to non-governmental organizations, to corporations, to international organizations, and to individuals."[38] While other liberal theories recognize linkages between equality and dignity, the CA more clearly spells out the duties and, specifically, the affirmative task of securing basic entitlements to all.[39] This strong commitment to proactive measures can be demonstrated in the CA's critique of John Rawls's theory of justice discussed below.

---

[30] Deakin, "Equality, Non-discrimination and the Labour Market" (n. 27) 48.
[31] Deakin and Wilkinson, *The Law of the Labour Market* (n. 29) 347–8.
[32] See Supriya Routh, "The Need to Become Fashionable," Chapter 5 in this volume.
[33] See Simon Deakin, "The Capability Approach and the Economics of Labour Law," Chapter 7 in this volume.
[34] Nussbaum, *Frontiers of Justice* (n. 2) 160.
[35] See e.g. Richard A. Posner, "The Efficiency and the Efficacy of Title VII" (1987) 136 *University of Pennsylvania Law Review* 513; Richard A. Epstein, *Forbidden Grounds: The Case Against Employment Discrimination Laws* (Harvard University Press, 1992).
[36] Nussbaum, *Frontiers of Justice* (n. 2) 160.
[37] Martha C. Nussbaum, "Capabilities, Entitlements, Rights: Supplementation and Critique" (2011) 12(1) *Journal of Human Development and Capabilities* 23, 26.
[38] Nussbaum, "Capabilities, Entitlements, Rights: Supplementation and Critique" (n. 37).
[39] Nussbaum, "Capabilities, Entitlements, Rights: Supplementation and Critique" (n. 37) 32.

## C. Considering differences behind the veil of ignorance

Both Sen's and Nussbaum's accounts entail an important critique of social contract theories and especially Rawls's theory of justice. In short, Rawls's theory is based on the idea that the principles of justice are those that free and rational people, who get together for their mutual benefit, would accept in the original position of fair and equal bargaining.[40] Namely, they would agree that all citizens should be entitled to a certain set of primary goods if they were placed behind a veil of ignorance as to what they would be and how well they would do in their lives.[41] Sen's and Nussbaum's critique is twofold. First, Sen argues that Rawls's list of primary goods, which predominantly uses resources (income and wealth) as proxies for well-being, is wrong and should be replaced with capabilities.[42] Even if two individuals have an equal set of resources, they would not be equal because of their varying abilities to convert resources into functionings and satisfy their preferences and desires. For example, "a person in a wheelchair may have the same income and wealth as a person of 'normal' mobility and still be unequal in capacity to move from place to place."[43] In response, Rawls argued, "the idea of primary goods is closely connected with the conception of citizens as having certain basic capabilities."[44] While Nussbaum accepts that,[45] she insists that income and wealth considerations do not address variations in need when measuring well-being and are not good proxies for important social goods like mobility and social inclusion.[46]

Second, people behind the veil of ignorance are asked to imagine themselves as "normal and fully cooperating members of society over a complete life,"[47] and therefore as citizens with no need for care. But as Nussbaum explains, for many people, health care and other forms of care (for children, elderly people, and people with mental and physical impairments) are important goods that make well-being possible.[48] In response, Rawls argues that when some citizens fall for a time below the minimum essentials due to illness or accident, the index of primary goods can be specified later, at the legislative stage, and over the normal course of a complete life.[49] But the issue of timing is significant. The omission of various forms of need and dependency that human beings may experience in the initial choice of basic political principles has significant impact on their equal citizenship.[50] As Nussbaum maintains, "any theory of justice needs to think about the problem from the beginning, in the design of the basic institutional structure, and particularly in its theory of the primary goods."[51] Furthermore, Rawls's focus on the temporary health needs of "normal" citizens and balancing them through various life phases suggests that the goal is mutual advantage in economic terms. It gives priority "to those who have the

---

[40] John Rawls, *A Theory of Justice* (Harvard University Press, 2005) 11.
[41] John Rawls, *Justice as Fairness: A Restatement* (edited by Erin Kelly, Harvard Press, 2003) 15–16.
[42] Amartya Sen, *Inequality Reexamined* (Harvard University Press, 1992) ch. 5.
[43] Nussbaum, *Frontiers of Justice* (n. 2) 74.    [44] Rawls, *Justice as Fairness* (n. 41) 175.
[45] Nussbaum, *Women and Human Development* (n. 16) 88.
[46] Nussbaum, *Frontiers of Justice* (n. 2) 116, 125.    [47] Rawls, *Justice as Fairness* (n. 41) 8.
[48] Nussbaum, *Frontiers of Justice* (n. 2) 127.    [49] Rawls, *Justice as Fairness* (n. 41) 175.
[50] Nussbaum, *Frontiers of Justice* (n. 2) 109.
[51] Nussbaum, *Frontiers of Justice* (n. 2) 127.

capacity to return to the workforce and resume their productivity" and has significant implications for "those who fall beneath the 'line' of normalcy."[52]

The CA's insistence on considering various forms of need and dependency from the outset is particularly useful in justifying discrimination laws and policies that promote proactive measures such as reasonable adjustments and affirmative action.[53] Here, the CA provides an important alternative to other classical liberal theories of equality in justifying workplace discrimination laws and policies that take both negative and positive steps to ensure these forms of need and dependency are actually addressed.[54] Otherwise, workplace equality and access to the labour market would be merely formal, not substantive. The purpose of discrimination laws is not simply to prohibit unequal treatment, but also to enhance real choice and meaningful access to work through the promotion of various education and training opportunities, accommodation, and special treatment programs. As Nussbaum stresses, "securing core human capabilities clearly involves affirmative material and institutional support, not simply a failure to impede."[55] This means that the government is directed "to think from the start about what obstacles there are to full and effective empowerment for all citizens, and to devise measures that address these obstacles."[56] The government has a positive duty to protect and secure an acceptable threshold level of capabilities for all its citizens using law and public policy.[57] While Nussbaum focuses on constitutional entitlements, "capabilities need not always be secured by legislation"; all three branches are relevant (the executive, the judiciary, and the legislature).[58] Furthermore, the CA may also justify the enforcement of positive duties upon employers to accommodate workers or adjust workplace practices to enable workers with special needs to enjoy meaningful access and participation.[59]

## D. The ten central capabilities

Finally, Nussbaum's list of ten central capabilities includes several explicit and implicit references to workplace discrimination issues.[60] Not being discriminated against is an important functioning. Certainly, the CA does not suggest that we focus only on capabilities. When the goal is self-respect and dignity, "actual functioning

[52] Nussbaum, *Frontiers of Justice* (n. 2) 145.
[53] Hugh Collins, "What Can Sen's Capability Approach Offer to Labour Law?" Chapter 1 in this volume; Nussbaum, "Capabilities, Entitlements, Rights" (n. 37) 31.
[54] For alternative justifications for discrimination laws which move beyond the traditional conceptions of equality see e.g. Hugh Collins, "Discrimination, Equality and Social Inclusion" (2003) 66(1) *Modern Law Review* 16; Cynthia Estlund, *Working Together: How Workplace Bonds Strengthen a Diverse Democracy* (Oxford University Press, 2003).
[55] Nussbaum, "Capabilities, Entitlements, Rights" (n. 37) 31.
[56] Nussbaum, "Capabilities, Entitlements, Rights" (n. 37) 32.
[57] Nussbaum, "Capabilities, Entitlements, Rights" (n. 37) 26.
[58] Nussbaum, "Capabilities, Entitlements, Rights" (n. 37) 28.
[59] Hugh Collins, "What Can Sen's Capability Approach Offer to Labour Law?" Chapter 1 in this volume.
[60] See Del Punta, "Labour Law and the Capability Approach" (n. 25); Kevin Kolben, "Labour Regulation, Capabilities, and Democracy" in Colin Fenwick and Shelley Marshall (eds.), *Labour Law and Development* (Edward Elgar Publishing, 2016) 60.

is the appropriate aim of public policy," as it would be incompatible with basic justice to provide choice on these matters.[61] Accordingly, the seventh capability—affiliation—is not about providing people with the choice of whether to be treated with dignity or not. Rather, it is about:

Having the social bases of self-respect and non-humiliation; being able to be treated as a dignified being whose worth is equal to that of others. This entails, at minimum, protections against discrimination on the basis of race, sex, sexual orientation, religion, caste, ethnicity, or national origin. In work, being able to work as a human being, exercising practical reason and entering into meaningful relationship of mutual recognition with other workers.[62]

This means that the capability to work in an environment that is free of various forms of discrimination is a central capability. This basic entitlement can only be secured by a correlative duty. Again, this is not limited to a duty to refrain from discrimination. Securing a real capability to exercise practical reason and enter into meaningful relationships at work also requires positive action by governments and the enforcement of positive duties upon employers to ensure meaningful inclusion and participation in the workplace.

Discrimination laws and policies that entail positive action are also vital in securing other capabilities. The tenth capability—control over one's environment—is about "having the right to seek employment on an equal basis with others" and "being able to work as human, exercising practical reason and entering into meaningful relationships of mutual recognition with other workers."[63] Furthermore, Nussbaum explains that the ninth capability—play—means among other things, "not being stuck with the 'double day' of a demanding job plus full responsibility for domestic labor and child and elder care."[64] Here, the central capabilities require us to take into consideration the current distribution of rights and entitlements, which may lead to exploitation and abuse of power in unequal bargaining situations. The goal is not merely to eliminate barriers to participation in the labour market but also to promote substantive rights to ensure effective participation. For example, the right to be free from gender discrimination has to be supplemented by maternity leave, pay equity, and a positive duty to accommodate domestic care responsibilities, which often fall on women.[65]

One might argue that the central capabilities are simply a descriptive account of human rights.[66] Indeed, the idea of central capabilities is closely related to human rights.[67] But the language of capabilities has an important added value. First, the CA makes it clear that it is not enough to have "rights on paper." Governments

[61] Nussbaum, *Frontiers of Justice* (n. 2) 172.
[62] Nussbaum, *Women and Human Development* (n. 16) 79–80.
[63] Nussbaum, *Frontiers of Justice* (n. 2) 77–8.
[64] Martha C. Nussbaum, *Creating Capabilities: The Human Development Approach* (Harvard University Press, 2011) 10–11.
[65] See Judy Fudge, "The New Discourse of Labor Rights: From Social to Fundamental Rights?" (2007) 29 *Comparative Labor Law and Policy Journal* 29, 61.
[66] See e.g. Guy Davidov, "The Capability Approach and Labour Law: Identifying the Areas of Fit," Chapter 2 in this volume.
[67] Nussbaum, *Women and Human Development* (n. 16) 97.

have to take effective measures to ensure people are actually capable of exercising these rights.[68] Second, the CA does not view economic and material human rights (such as the right to shelter) as resources because providing the same of level of resources cannot guarantee that all people meet an appropriate level of capabilities or functionings. Rather, it views rights as capabilities that may justify distributing more resources to and promoting special programs for the disadvantaged to bring them to an acceptable level of capabilities.[69]

## III. Age Discrimination in the Workplace

Older workers face a myriad of barriers in the labour market to which contemporary discrimination laws and policies in most Western societies only provide a limited response. Before examining how the CA can be helpful in this context, this section provides a brief assessment of the current challenges in this field.

Research shows that older workers often perceive age discrimination as a major obstacle to obtaining and retaining jobs.[70] Some employers hold ageist stereotypes about older workers, especially regarding their declining productivity or performance and their retirement desires.[71] Numerous experimental studies examining the reception of identical fictitious résumés (except for age) provide compelling evidence of age discrimination in hiring.[72] While the experience and expertise of older workers are often acknowledged, assumptions are made regarding their higher labour costs, health and disability issues, and technological adeptness.[73] Certainly, older workers may experience age-related losses or declines, yet many are more active and productive than they have been stereotypically portrayed.[74] Although the ageing process is highly individualized and age has been proven to be a poor proxy for job performance,[75] stereotyping and unconscious biases continue to have

---

[68] Nussbaum, *Women and Human Development* (n. 16) 98.

[69] Nussbaum, *Women and Human Development* (n. 16) 99.

[70] See e.g. Ellie D. Berger, "'Aging' Identities: Degradation and Negotiation in the Search for Employment" (2006) 20(4) *Journal of Aging Studies* 303; Richard L. Weiner and Steven L. Willborn (eds.), *Disability and Aging Discrimination: Perspectives in Law and Psychology* (Springer, 2011).

[71] See e.g. Kène Henkens, "Stereotyping Older Workers and Retirement: The Managers' Point of View" (2005) 24(4) *Canadian Journal on Aging* 353; Michèle Céline Kaufmann, Franciska Krings, and Sabine Sczensny, "Looking Too Old? How an Older Age Appearance Reduces Chances of Being Hired" (2016) 27(4) *British Journal of Management* 727.

[72] See e.g. Ben Richardson et al., "Age Discrimination in the Evaluation of Job Applicants" (2013) 43(1) *Journal of Applied Social Psychology* 35; David Neumark, Ian Burn, and Patrick Button, "Experimental Age Discrimination Evidence and the Heckman Critique" (2016) 106(5) *American Economic Review* 303.

[73] See e.g. *A Little Bit Older, A Little Bit Wiser* (Investors Group, 2012) www.investorsgroup.com>.

[74] See e.g. Eddy S.W. Ng and Alan Law, "Keeping Up! Older Workers' Adaptation in the Workplace after Age 55" (2014) 33(1) *Canadian Journal of Aging* 1, 10–11.

[75] See e.g. Geoffrey Wood, Adrian Wilkinson, and Mark Harcourt, "Age Discrimination and Working Life: Perspectives and Contestations—A Review of the Contemporary Literature" (2008) 10(4) *International Journal of Management Reviews* 425; Thomas W.H. Ng and Daniel C. Feldman, "The Relationship of Age to Ten Dimensions of Job Performance" (2008) 93 *Journal of Applied Psychology* 392.

a potent impact on workplace decision-making.[76] Studies show that older workers are often deprived of proper training and accommodation, which negatively affects their job retention and reemployment prospects.[77] Furthermore, older workers generally spend longer periods in unemployment than younger workers, and are often faced with two bad options: either settle for non-standard, lower-wage jobs, or exit the labour market.[78]

There is also overwhelming evidence that contemporary age discrimination laws and policies fail to respond to these current challenges. A systematic literature review of studies published during 2006–2015 found that "although governments in many nations have enacted anti age discrimination policies and are promoting extended work lives, ageism presents a barrier to attaining and maintaining satisfactory work."[79] In the U.S., the law has been criticized for imposing significant burden on plaintiffs and making it easier for employers to justify discrimination.[80] In the U.K., a comprehensive study found that age discrimination laws fail to address the challenges faced by older workers and neglect to achieve attitudinal change, as employers often adopt a compliance-based approach to the law and rarely take proactive measures to support older workers.[81] Similar critiques were made in the EU,[82] Australia,[83] and Canada.[84] Against this background, four main difficulties can be identified. First, compared to other forms of prejudice, the wrongness of age discrimination seems uncertain. Second, age discrimination laws and policies reflect

---

[76] Ageist stereotypes can be explicit but are often implicit and may involve aversive reactions to ageing bodies. See Nussbaum and Levmore, *Aging Thoughtfully* (n. 1) 108 ff; Martha C. Nussbaum, "Ageing, Stigma, and Disgust," in Zoya Hasan, Aziz Z. Huq, Martha C. Nussbaum, and Vidhu Verma (eds.), *The Empire of Disgust: Prejudice, Discrimination, and Policy in India and the U.S.* (Oxford University Press, 2018).

[77] See e.g. Jungwee Park, "Job-Related Training of Older Workers" (2012) 24 *Perspective on Labour and Income* 4; Kevin Banks, Richard P. Chaykowski, and George A. Slotsve, "Disability Accommodation Gap in Canadian Workplaces: What Does It Mean for Law, Policy, and an Aging Population?" (2013) 17(2) *Canadian Labour and Employment Law Journal* 295.

[78] See e.g. Susan Bisom-Rapp, Andrew D. Frazer, and Malcolm Sargeant, "Decent Work, Older Workers, and Vulnerability in the Economic Recession: A Comparative Study of Australia, the United Kingdom, and the United States" (2011) 15 *Employee Rights and Employment Policy Journal* 43; Tammy Schirle, "Wage Losses of Displaced Older Men: Does Selective Retirement Bias Results?" (2012) 38(1) *Canadian Public Policy* 1; Matthew S. Rutledge, Natalia Orlova, and Anthony Webb, "How Will Older Workers Who Lose Their Jobs During the Great Recession Fare in the Long-Run?" Centre for Retirement Research at Boston College (2013) www.crr.bc.edu.

[79] Kelly Harris et al., "Ageism and the Older Worker: A Scoping Review" (2018) 58(2) *The Gerontologist* 1.

[80] See Susan Bisom-Rapp and Malcolm Sargent, "Diverging Doctrine, Converging Outcomes: Evaluating the Age Discrimination Law in the United Kingdom and the United States" (2013) 44 *Loyola University Chicago International Law Review* 717.

[81] See Alysia Blackham, *Extending Working Life for Older Workers: Age Discrimination Law, Policy and Practice* (Hart Publishing, 2016).

[82] See Ann Numhauser-Henning, "The EU Ban on Age-Discrimination and Older Workers: Potentials and Pitfalls" (2013) 29(4) *International Journal of Comparative Labour Law and Industrial Relations* 391.

[83] See Therese MacDermott, "Affirming Age: Making Federal Anti- Discrimination Regulation Work for Older Australians" (2013) 26 *Australian Journal of Labour Law* 141.

[84] See Pnina Alon-Shenker, "Legal Barriers to Age Discrimination in Hiring Complaints" (2016) 39(1) *Dalhousie Law Journal* 289.

an unsolved tension between a human rights approach and an economic approach. Third, it is hard to define the group that age discrimination laws and policies aim to protect. Finally, while older workers are increasingly pressured to prolong their working lives, they are not provided with adequate support and protection as most age discrimination laws and policies build mainly on compliance-based action and lack proactive measures. Each difficulty is discussed below.

## A. Is age discrimination wrong?

It seems that ageism is more difficult to eradicate because it is perceived as less harmful and not as morally wrong as other forms of prejudice such as sexism and racism. The literature seems obsessed with whether or not age discrimination law is efficient,[85] often finding that it is not,[86] rather than viewing age discrimination as a human rights issue.[87] Indeed, there is great uncertainty about whether and when differential treatment on the basis of age is considered wrongful. As O'Cinneide explains, while "age discrimination can be viewed as a form of crude and irrational stereotyping," which is an affront to human dignity "because it denies individuals the opportunity to be judged according to their specific attributes, needs and qualities ... the use of age-based distinctions is not linked to deeply embedded historical patterns of group subordination, and does not in general give rise to the sense of moral opprobrium that other forms of illegitimate discrimination attract."[88]

Indeed, ageism can be motivated by different feelings than those behind sexism and racism, namely disgust (which includes self-disgust and may lead to avoidance), and fear of the inevitability of becoming "like them" (i.e., death and ageing anxiety).[89] These feelings are often ambivalent and complex, operating on both conscious and unconscious levels.[90] They often couched in the language of cost and other rational business needs that do not fit well within a narrow stereotyping/prejudice definition, and are easily overlooked for lack of "smoking gun" evidence.[91] Furthermore, unlike other personal characteristics, such as gender and race, age is

---

[85]  Lawrence M. Friedman, "Age Discrimination Law: Some Remarks on the American Experience," in Sandra Fredman and Sarah Spencer (eds.), *Age as an Equality Issue* (Hart Publishing, 2003) 175, 186–7.

[86]  See e.g. Richard A. Posner, *Aging and Old Age* (University of Chicago Press, 1995) ch. 13; Samuel Issacharoff and Erica Worth Harris, "Is Age Discrimination Really Age Discrimination?: The ADEA's Unnatural Solution" (1997) 72 *New York University Law Review* 780. But see Christine Jolls, "Hands-Tying and the Age Discrimination in Employment Act" (1996) 74 *Texas Law Review* 1813.

[87]  With some exceptions, e.g. Fredman and Spencer, *Age as an Equality Issue* (n. 85); Bisom-Rapp and Sargent, "Diverging Doctrine, Converging Outcomes" (n. 80).

[88]  Colm O'Cinneide, "Constitutional and Fundamental Rights Aspects of Age Discrimination," in Ann Numhauser-Henning and Mia Rönnmar (eds.), *Age Discrimination and Labour Law: Comparative and Conceptual Perspectives in the EU and Beyond* (Kluwer, 2015) 51, 54.

[89]  Nussbaum and Levmore (n. 1) 112. See also Jeff Greenberg, Jeff Schimel, and Andy Martens, "Ageism: Denying the Face of the Future," in Todd D. Nelson (ed.), *Ageism: Stereotyping and Prejudice against Older Persons* (MIT Press, 2002) 27.

[90]  See e.g. Becca R. Levy, "Unconscious Ageism," in Erdman B. Palmore, Laurence Branch, and Diana K. Harris (eds.), *Encyclopedia of Ageism* (Haworth Pastoral Press, 2005) 335–9; Becca R. Levy and Mahzarin R. Banaji, "Implicit Ageism," in Todd D. Nelson (ed.), *Ageism: Stereotyping and Prejudice against Older Persons* (MIT Press, 2002) 49.

[91]  See e.g. Alon-Shenker, "Legal Barriers to Age Discrimination in Hiring Complaints" (n. 84).

temporal and mutable. We were all young once, and we all expect to grow older. Since ageing is a natural process that affects us all (though at different times and varying degrees), "[t]he feeling that discrimination against older workers is just 'natural' and is not discrimination at all is extremely widespread."[92] The result is that age discrimination law is often treated as "a sui generis area of discrimination law" subject to different rules and broader exceptions and provides weaker protection.[93] In the U.S., for example, unlike Title VII of the federal Civil Rights Act, which allows for a mixed motive analysis, the Age Discrimination in Employment Act has been interpreted as requiring the plaintiff to prove that age was the determinative factor (the "but-for" cause) of the adverse employment action.[94] Furthermore, indirect age discrimination can be justified if it was based on a "reasonable factor other than age," which is broader than the "business necessity" exception under Title VII.[95] And although mandatory retirement was strictly outlawed many years ago, many employees are forced to retire against their will because the law fails to protect them from employer practices that are indirectly discriminatory.[96]

## B. Tension between different rationales

Discrimination laws often reflect a tension between a human rights approach, protecting from differential treatment that undermines the dignity of individual workers, and a collective approach, promoting broader distributional and societal purposes. This tension, referred to as the "double bind," is specifically evident in the context of age discrimination.[97] Age has been widely used as a social stratifier in the labour market and beyond.[98] It has been considered an efficient and "neutral" tool to distribute employment opportunities and various forms of social protection among different age groups.[99] For example, while

[92] Nussbaum and Levmore, *Aging Thoughtfully* (n. 1) 116.
[93] See O'Cinneide, "Constitutional and Fundamental Rights Aspects of Age Discrimination" (n. 88) 64.
[94] See *Gross v. FBL Financial Services Inc.*, 557 U.S. 167 (2009); Gillian Lester, "Age Discrimination and Labor Law in the United States," in Ann Numhauser-Henning and Mia Rönnmar, *Age Discrimination and Labour Law* (Kluwer, 2015) 397, 405.
[95] See *Smith v. City of Jackson*, 544 U.S. 228 (2005); Lester, "Age Discrimination and Labor Law in the United States" (n. 94) 405.
[96] See Anja Wiesbrock, "Mandatory Retirement in the EU and the US: The Scope of Protection Against Age Discrimination in Employment" (2013) 29(3) *International Journal of Comparative Labour Law and Industrial Relations* 305.
[97] See Frank Hendrickx, "Age and European Employment Discrimination Law," in Frank Hendrickx (ed.), *Active Ageing and Labour Law: Contributions in Honour of Professor Roger Blanpain* (Intersentia, 2012) 3; Ann Numhauser-Henning, "The Elder Law Individual versus Societal Dichotomy: A European Perspective," in Ann Numhauser-Henning (ed.), *Elder Law: Evolving European Perspectives* (Edward Elgar Publishing, 2017) 86.
[98] See Ann Numhauser-Henning, "Labour Law, Pension Norms and the EU Ban on Age Discrimination: Towards Ultimate Flexibilization?," in Ann Numhauser-Henning and Mia Rönnmar, *Age Discrimination and Labour Law* (Kluwer, 2015) 115, 118. See also Dagmar Schiek, "Age Discrimination before the ECJ: Conceptual and Theoretical Issues" (2011) 48 *Common Market Law Review* 777.
[99] O'Cinneide, "Constitutional and Fundamental Rights Aspects of Age Discrimination" (n. 88) 54–5.

discriminatory on its face, mandatory retirement, coupled with a pension plan, has been justified as promoting the redistribution of job opportunities from older to younger workers, and hence as economically and socially beneficial to society as a whole.[100] Furthermore, age-based distinctions, which apply to all people as they move through various life stages, have enjoyed a veneer of legitimacy because the view is that the same burdens imposed on older people will be borne by younger people as they, too, grow old.[101] According to this popular view, referred to as "Complete Lives Egalitarianism," given that resources are scarce, whether any two people are treated equally should be assessed on the basis of their lifetime experience.[102]

The result is often a weaker ban on age discrimination. For example, the 2000/78/EC Directive, which introduced the ban on age discrimination in the EU,[103] allows age discrimination under various defenses and justifications more than any other ground of discrimination. Most notably, direct differential treatment on the basis of age can be justified if it is for a "legitimate employment policy, labour market and vocational training objectives" and the measure at issue was appropriate and necessary.[104] In Canada, even though mandatory retirement has been generally outlawed, it is still allowed through broad statutory exemptions.[105] Furthermore, age-based distinctions in the provision of pension and benefits plans to workers over the age of 65 are widely allowed as a reasonable compromise between the right of older workers, as individuals, to continue working past 65 and the collective interest in maintaining the viability of employment pension and benefits plans.[106]

Courts, influenced by this "double bind," tend to apply variable levels of scrutiny, under which the deleterious impact on the dignity of individuals is often outweighed by broader social and economic considerations.[107] For example, against the background of increasing rates of youth unemployment, the Court of Justice of the European Union under Article 6 has readily upheld mandatory retirement

---

[100] See Edward P. Lazear, "Why is There Mandatory Retirement?" (1979) 87(6) *Journal of Political Economy* 1261; Stewart J. Schwab, "Life-Cycle Justice: Accommodating Just Cause and Employment at Will" (1993) 92(1) *Michigan Law Review* 8.

[101] See e.g. John Chandler, "Mandatory Retirement and Justice" (1996) 22(1) *Social Theory and Practice* 35.

[102] See Dennis McKerlie, "Equality between Age-Groups" (1992) 21(3) *Philosophy & Public Affairs* 275; Pnina Alon-Shenker, "The Unequal Right to Age Equality: Towards a Dignified Lives Approach to Age Discrimination" (2012) 25(2) *Canadian Journal of Law and Jurisprudence* 243, 247–8.

[103] Council Directive, 2000/78/EC, 2000 O.J. (L 303/16) 16–22 (EC).

[104] Article 6.

[105] See e.g. Human Rights Act, RSNB 2011, c. 171, ss. 4(1), 4(5)–(6) and *New Brunswick (Human Rights Commission) v Potash Corporation of Saskatchewan*, 2008 SCC 45, 2 SCR 604. See also Pnina Alon-Shenker, "Ending Mandatory Retirement: Reassessment" (2014) 35 *Windsor Review of Legal and Social Issues* 22; Kenneth Wm Thornicroft, "The Uncertain State of Mandatory Retirement in Canada" 67(2) (2016) *Labor Law Journal* 397.

[106] See Robert E. Charney and Matthew Horner, "Employee Benefits after the Elimination of Mandatory Retirement" (2013) 17 *Canadian Labour and Employment Law Journal* 255; *Ontario Nurses' Association v Chatham-Kent (Municipality of)* (2010), 88 CCPB 95, 202 LAC (4th) 1. But more recently see *Talos v Grand Erie District School Board*, 2018 HRTO 680.

[107] O'Cinneide, "Constitutional and Fundamental Rights Aspects of Age Discrimination" (n. 88) 69.

policies.[108] However, these decisions often do not establish clear evidence of societal benefits,[109] and assume the existence of long-term employment arrangements and adequate pension plans, assumptions that no longer reflect the reality of many workers and were never relevant to many disadvantaged workers (such as older female or racialized workers).[110]

## C. Are all older workers at a disadvantage?

It is not clear how to define the group that age discrimination laws and policies aim to protect. All of us may potentially belong to the group "older workers" one day. Furthermore, since older people are not a typical "minority group" and are often considered privileged, it has been argued that they do not warrant special protection.[111] While some older workers are doing fairly well in the labour market and beyond, others experience difficulties and challenges with ageism, financial insecurity, and work displacement.[112] Yet, age discrimination laws and policies often treat older workers as a homogeneous group and take "one size fits all" measures to protect them, which are weak and ineffective. Vulnerability among older workers is often linked to intersectionality.[113] Most notably, older female workers, racialized workers, and those with disabilities experience more difficulties than white, male, and able-bodied older workers do.[114] Other groups of people who might be at greater risk are displaced older workers, low-skilled, and low-literacy older workers, older indigenous workers, recent immigrant older workers, and older workers with significant unpaid caregiving responsibilities.[115] However, intersectionality is still not

---

[108] See Judy Fudge and Ania Zbyszewska, "An Intersectional Approach to Age Discrimination in the European Union: Bridging Dignity and Distribution?," in Ann Numhauser-Henning and Mia Rönnmar, *Age Discrimination and Labour Law* (Kluwer, 2015) 141, 144.

[109] For example, research suggests that the continued employment of older workers does not reduce job opportunities for younger workers. To the contrary. See e.g. Alicia H. Munnell and April Yanyuan Wu, "Will Delayed Retirement by the Baby Boomers Lead to Higher Unemployment among Younger Workers?" Center for Retirement Research at Boston College (October 2012); Werner Eichhorst et al., "How to Combine the Entry of Young People in the Labour Market with the Retention of Older Workers?" IZA DP No. 7829 (December 2013) http://ftp.iza.org/dp7829.pdf.

[110] Fudge and Zbyszewska, "An Intersectional Approach to Age Discrimination in the European Union" (n. 108) 141–2.

[111] See e.g. Peter H. Schuck, "Age Discrimination Revisited" (1981) 57 *Chicago Kent Law Review* 1029.

[112] See Rebecca Casey and Ellie Berger, "Encouraging or Discouraging? Competing Pictures of Aging and Paid Work in Later Life" (2015) 3(3) Population Change and Lifecourse Strategic Knowledge Cluster Discussion Paper Series 13 http://ir.lib.uwo.ca/pclc/vol3/iss3/3.

[113] See e.g. Kimberlé Crenshaw, "Mapping the Margins: Intersectionality, Identity Politics, and Violence Against Women of Color" (1990–1991) 43 *Stanford Law Review* 1241; Dianne Pothier, "Connecting Grounds of Discrimination to Real People's Real Experiences" (2001) 13 *Canadian Journal of Women & Law* 37.

[114] See e.g. Malcolm Sargeant (ed.), *Age Discrimination and Diversity: Multiple Discrimination from an Age Perspective* (Cambridge University Press, 2011); Susan Bison-Rapp and Malcolm Sargeant, *Lifetime Disadvantage, Discrimination and the Gendered Workforce* (Cambridge University Press, 2016).

[115] See National Seniors Council, *Older Workers at Risk of Withdrawing from the Labour Force or Becoming Unemployed: Employers' Views on How to Retain and Attract Older Workers* (2013).

fully acknowledged or developed in the case law.[116] Furthermore, policies are not tailored to tackle the challenges of those affected by intersectionality. They are often designed for the "mainstream" older workers—white-collar educated male workers, who are able and wish to prolong their participation in the labour market.[117] Policies fail to account for gender, marital status, disability, work environment, and other factors that may affect one's capability or desire to work longer.[118]

## D. Pressured to work longer without adequate support

While older workers are increasingly pressured to prolong their working lives, they are not provided with adequate support and protection since most age discrimination laws and policies build mainly on compliance-based action and lack proactive measures and strong enforcement mechanisms. Active ageing policies aim to address the concern that increased life expectancy, combined with lower fertility rate and the mass retirement of baby boomers, will negatively affect the economy and labour force growth, as well as pension and healthcare systems. But often these policies promote only one "good choice," which is to extend working lives, and put pressure on older workers to make that choice. Focusing on pension age increases, privatization of pensions, and penalties on early exits, these policies heavily rely on individual, rather than government, responsibility for active ageing and improved employability. As older workers are pressured to take prime responsibility for managing the development and upgrading of their skills, they often bear the full risk of inadequate retirement savings and increased vulnerability in the workplace.[119] While some workers wish to work longer, others are unable to do so for a variety of reasons including disabilities, health concerns, and elder care responsibilities. And those who wish to work longer are not provided with effective government protection and support to ensure meaningful access to decent work, such as training, accommodation, flexible work arrangements, and re-employment opportunities.[120] Furthermore, employers rarely take proactive measures to support older workers by

---

[116] See Ben Smith, "Intersectional Discrimination and Substantive Equality: A Comparative and Theoretical Perspective" (2016) 16 *The Equal Rights Review* 73; Fudge and Zbyszewska, "An Intersectional Approach to Age Discrimination in the European Union" (n. 108) 162.

[117] For example, increasing the age of eligibility for Social Security benefits in the U.S. harms women as it fails to take their unique circumstances (e.g. long career breaks due to caregiving duties) into account. See Bison-Rapp and Sargeant, *Lifetime Disadvantage, Discrimination and the Gendered Workforce* (n. 114) 188.

[118] In the U.K., for example, the state pension age will increase for both women and men to 67 by 2028 and various active ageing policies assume that all workers are able and willing to extend their working lives. See Alysia Blackham et al., "The Rationale of Government Action on Ageing and the Extension of Working Lives," in Ann Numhauser-Henning (ed.), *Elder Law: Evolving European Perspectives* (Edward Elgar Publishing, 2017) 179, 202–203.

[119] Blackham et al., "The Rationale of Government Action on Ageing and the Extension of Working Lives" (n. 118). See also Mia Rönnmar et al., "Employment Protection and Older Workers," in Ann Numhauser-Henning (ed.), *Elder Law: Evolving European Perspectives* (Edward Elgar Publishing, 2017) 204.

[120] See e.g. Pnina Alon-Shenker, "The Duty to Accommodate Senior Workers: Its Nature, Scope and Limitations" (2012) 38(1) *Queen's Law Journal* 165.

adapting practices and policies to their needs.[121] The result is that many workers have to exit the labour market without adequate pension or retirement savings.[122]

## IV. Applying the CA to Age Discrimination in the Workplace

As we have seen, the CA has a special appeal to workplace discrimination laws. Given the difficulties associated with contemporary age discrimination laws and policies, this section identifies a few ways in which the CA can be insightful in addressing them.

### A. The wrongness of age discrimination in employment

Supplemented by other theories such as critical gerontology, the CA can be helpful in underlining the wrongness of age discrimination in employment. It stresses that while some internal capabilities may decline due to the process of ageing, it is the combined capabilities that are mostly constrained for older workers.[123] True, declining physical and mental abilities can negatively affect older workers' sets of capabilities. However, like in the case of people with disabilities, this is exactly where the CA becomes valuable and distinct from other theories of just distribution. Premised on the idea that each person differs in their conversion factors, and therefore in their need for resources and their ability to convert them into functionings, the CA urges us to provide more attention to older people so that they reach an acceptable adequate level of capabilities regardless of their current economic productivity.

Furthermore, the effects of ageing vary significantly amongst individuals. Often, it is the perceived (rather than actual) declining abilities that diminish older workers' substantive freedom. That is, ageist stereotypes and age-based assumptions held by governments, policy-makers, and employers weaken the combined capabilities of older workers. Society has expectations about proper behavior at different ages ("age norms"), which are expressed in familiar phrases like "act your age" or "shouldn't you be retired by now?" Age norms and expectations are enforced through various mechanisms of social control.[124] For example, while society worships youth, older workers are portrayed as a burden on society and are expected to retire and "make room" for younger workers, or to continue working to ensure the stability of pension plans. On the CA, age norms and expectations negatively affect older workers' conversion factors and therefore their capability to lead the life they have reason to value. They often work as self-fulfilling prophecies and are internalized by older workers, who adjust their real aspirations and act as they are expected to.[125] Furthermore, ageism

---

[121] See e.g. Blackham, *Extending Working Life for Older Workers* (n. 81); National Seniors Council, *Older Workers at Risk of Withdrawing from the Labour Force or Becoming Unemployed* (n. 115).

[122] See e.g. Richard Shillington, *An Analysis of the Economic Circumstances of Canadian Seniors* (Broadbent Institute, 2016).

[123] See Peter Lloyd-Sherlock, "Nussbaum, Capabilities and Older People" (2002) 14 *Journal of International Development* 1163.

[124] See Diana K. Harris, "Age Norms" in Palmore et al., *Encyclopedia of Ageism* (n. 90) 14.

[125] Nussbaum and Levmore, *Aging Thoughtfully* (n. 1) 58–9.

and age-based assumptions weaken the real substantive freedom of older workers to choose how, where, and when to work and retire. Placing choice and agency at the center, the CA recognizes that the choices and preferences of older workers may vary. Some want to work longer, some want to retire, while others prefer a variety of hybrid solutions. Yet, often they are not capable of doing and being what they want. There is compelling evidence that ageism poses major obstacles in attaining and maintaining decent work. Older workers are often denied meaningful access to various processes, such as education and training, and consequently to substantive participation in the labour market. While some are forced to exit the labour market due to mandatory retirement policies or lack of sustainable working conditions, others are forced to extend their working lives due to lack of adequate pension and retirement savings.

On the CA, age-based distinctions are not merely wrong when they are based on stereotypes and prejudice; they are primarily wrong because they fail to treat older workers as real agents who are capable of making their own choices, and because they undermine their sets of capabilities. The CA's focus on capabilities, rather than on goods or resources, helps substantiate the argument that even if some older workers are privileged and have sufficient income or wealth, experience, and skills, they may still not be capable of using these goods to live a life worthy of the dignity of a human being. Age discrimination laws and policies are therefore necessary in creating conversion factors, in altering social norms, removing barriers, and providing the conditions under which older workers enjoy the substantive freedom to achieve various desired functionings. They should "*support and protect agency*, seeing aging people as choosers and makers of their lives ... not as passive recipients of benefits."[126]

## B. Critique of complete lives egalitarianism

The CA provides a strong critique of the popular view that age is a justifiable and reasonable way of ordering our society by distributing benefits and burdens over a lifespan and promoting broad social and economic goals. The CA "starts from the basic idea that policies about core entitlements must respect the equal human dignity of all citizens, regardless of their current economic productivity."[127] That is, the CA looks beyond economic considerations to the well-being of all citizens including older workers. As Nussbaum explains, "[w]e do not have to win the respect of others by being productive. We have a claim to support in the dignity of our human need itself ... Productivity is necessary, and even good; but it is not the main end of social life."[128] Even if older workers are (or are perceived as) less productive than others, their equal human dignity should be respected at any given time, and not only considered simply in terms of their experience over a lifetime.

Furthermore, the CA stresses the importance of treating *each person* as an end, and not merely a means to the ends of others. It opposes "the pursuit of a glorious

---

[126] Nussbaum and Levmore, *Aging Thoughtfully* (n. 1) 197.
[127] Nussbaum and Levmore, *Aging Thoughtfully* (n. 1) 196.
[128] Nussbaum, *Frontiers of Justice* (n. 2) 160.

total or average in ways that subordinate certain groups or individuals" because "one person's exceeding well-being is not permitted to compensate for another person's misery."[129] For example, a mandatory retirement policy, justified as providing employment opportunities for younger workers, treats older workers as the supporters of the ends of others rather than as ends in their own rights.[130] On the CA, "the capabilities sought are for each and every person"; while groups are important, "the ultimate political goal is always the promotion of the capabilities of *each person*."[131] This means that various age-based distinctions, which promote important social and economic goals, cannot be justified if they diminish the central capabilities of older workers.

While equality is not the goal with regard to all the central capabilities,[132] securing an adequate threshold of each core capability for each person is crucial and "the relevant goods must be available at a sufficiently high level."[133] Equality with respect to the central capability to work in an environment free from age discrimination is an essential goal because "its absence would be connected with a deficit in dignity and self-respect."[134] But for other capabilities related to property and instrumental goods, like pensions, adequacy should be the goal, though this goal is often unmet.[135] Regardless of whether the goal is equality or a threshold of adequacy, each capability is important and cannot compensate for the absence of another capability. That is, the list is a list of separate components: "We cannot satisfy the need for one of them by giving a larger amount of another one."[136] This means that age-based distinctions cannot be justified even if they enhance some capabilities of older workers if they also diminish their other capabilities below an acceptable adequate threshold, and even if younger workers will be treated similarly in the future. This would be considered "a failure of basic justice, no matter how high up they are on all the others."[137]

But age-based distinctions may still be allowed. The CA's principle of adequacy may actually help reconcile the difficulty associated with the "double bind" of balancing between the concern for the individual worker's dignity and broader societal goals. For example, the CA may allow mandatory retirement policies when these are supported by evidence of declining abilities (e.g., in physically demanding jobs), aimed to promote legitimate goals on the basis of compelling evidence, and are supported by an adequate pension scheme. They also must include alternative ways to pursue desired functionings, including real access to, and meaningful participation in, various social spheres (e.g., creating opportunities for post-retirement part-time or voluntary work, consultancy and mentorship, and promoting continuing education and gradual and flexible approaches to retirement).

[129] Nussbaum, *Frontiers of Justice* (n. 2) 80.
[130] Nussbaum, *Frontiers of Justice* (n. 2) 70–1.
[131] Nussbaum, *Women and Human Development* (n. 16) 74.
[132] Nussbaum, *Frontiers of Justice* (n. 2) 295.
[133] Nussbaum, *Frontiers of Justice* (n. 2) 292.
[134] Nussbaum, *Frontiers of Justice* (n. 2).
[135] Nussbaum, *Frontiers of Justice* (n. 2) 293.
[136] Nussbaum, *Women and Human Development* (n. 16) 81.
[137] Nussbaum, *Frontiers of Justice* (n. 2) 167.

## C. Variations in need, heterogeneity, and intersectionality

The CA's sensitivity to variations in need, "which are pervasive features of human life,"[138] highlights heterogeneity within the group of older workers and advances the consideration of intersectionality issues. First and foremost, the CA recognizes "the *variety and non-homogeneity* of lives that aging people lead."[139] Older workers may have different preferences when it comes to work and retirement, and their capabilities to achieve alternate functioning combinations should be secured. Second, while other theories of equality and distributive justice promote entitlements that are "basic all-purpose resources, such as income and wealth," the goal of the CA is to secure each person's capabilities to an acceptable adequate level. This is because each person differs in their personal and social conversion factors and therefore differs in their need for resources and their ability to convert them into functionings.[140] Recognizing that personal and social conversion factors may vary among people, the CA is sensitive to the numerous forms that disadvantage might take as an individual's age advances and to the great variety of experiences and needs within the group of older workers. It suggests that age may intersect with other characteristics (such as sex or race), but also with a variety of experiences and backgrounds that increases disadvantage and vulnerability by directly affecting people's sets of capabilities. Consideration of intersectionality issues is required when drafting laws and policies to ensure that such disadvantaged groups are not invisible and marginalized because assumptions were made on the basis of an "average image" of an older worker. Indeed, consideration of intersectionality has the potential to reconcile the tension between dignity and distributional concerns.[141] For example, age-based distinctions, which allow for the provision of fewer or no benefits to workers above the age of 65, assume they have accrued sufficient pension and are close to retirement. This assumption may not reflect the reality of those who spent long spans of time unemployed or caring for others (e.g., immigrants or women). Another example is a penalty for early exit, which assumes that workers who exit early made a "poor choice" of not staying active and that they should be encouraged to work longer or else their vulnerability will increase. Yet, most often, increased vulnerability is not the result of a "poor choice" but, rather, is embedded in the systemic effects of mainstream policies that ignore the unique circumstances of some older workers.[142] Finally, sensitivity to variations in need also requires attention to the actual source of need, rather than an assumption that it is disability-related. Policies and workplace adjustments should take into account a variety of age-related needs that older workers may have. This may include, for example, physical and mental declines that are linked to the ageing process but do not amount to disability, as well as other

---

[138] Nussbaum, *Frontiers of Justice* (n. 2) 165.
[139] Nussbaum and Levmore, *Aging Thoughtfully* (n. 1) 197.
[140] Nussbaum and Levmore, *Aging Thoughtfully* (n. 1) 196.
[141] See Fudge and Zbyszewska, "An Intersectional Approach to Age Discrimination in the European Union" (n. 108).
[142] See Titti Mattsson and Mirjam Katzin, "Vulnerability and Ageing," in Ann Numhauser-Henning (ed.), *Elder Law: Evolving European Perspectives* (Edward Elgar Publishing, 2017) 113.

needs arising from factors more common among older workers, such as job burnout and fatigue, outdated skills, fears of sharp transition to retirement, the burden of taking care of elderly family members, or the need to work longer due to inadequate retirement savings.[143]

## D. Effective protection and support require proactive measures

The CA is useful in justifying regulatory reforms and policies that foster positive action and shift responsibility back to governments. The CA urges us to think about various forms of need and dependency—physical and mental, permanent and temporary—that older people may experience. Such consideration is done from the outset, when designing the basic institutional structure of a society, and even in the absence of mutual gains—that is, even if some old people are unable to return to the workplace and resume their productivity.[144] While the right of older workers to equality is legally protected, the CA goes deeper and asks whether and to what extent older workers are actually able to enjoy this right.[145] Exposing the various blatant and subtle barriers that affect the capabilities of older workers, the CA puts greater emphasis on proactive and preventive measures than those advanced by contemporary age discrimination laws and policies. It directs us not only to remove structural barriers to meaningful choice, such as ageism, but also proactively to promote substantive rights to ensure the effective freedom of older workers to do what they have reason to value, including to work, to study, and to retire, if and however they choose to do so. While private actors may share responsibilities, the CA holds that it is the responsibility of the government "to promote a set of core necessary conditions for reasonably flourishing lives, lives worthy of human dignity" because "[s]upport for citizens' capabilities is not mere charity, it is their right — what they are entitled to expect from the nation in which they live, as a matter of basic justice, and out of respect for their equal worth."[146] As Nussbaum explains, "[t]o realize one of the items on the list [of central capabilities] for citizens of a nation entails not only promoting appropriate development of their internal powers, but also preparing the environment so that it is favorable for the exercise of practical reason and the other major functions."[147]

Such responsibility requires a commitment to the development of systems and environments that will allow older workers to make meaningful choices about work, education, and retirement. This entails stronger protection under age discrimination laws and the abolishment of mandatory retirement in most circumstances.[148] It also

---

[143] See Alon-Shenker, "The Duty to Accommodate Senior Workers" (n. 120).

[144] See discussion in section II.C.

[145] Martha C. Nussbaum, "Foreword: Constitutions and Capabilities: 'Perception' against Lofty Formalism" (2007) 121 *Harvard Law Review* 4, 25.

[146] Nussbaum, "Foreword" (n. 145) 24.

[147] Nussbaum, *Women and Human Development* (n. 16) 85.

[148] While some studies suggest that stronger discrimination laws deter the hiring of older workers, others show that stronger discrimination laws are associated with increased employment and employment prospects of older workers. See e.g. Joanna Lahey, "State Age Protection Laws and the Age Discrimination in Employment Act" (2008) 51 *Journal of Law and Economics* 433; David Neumark

extends adjustments to the onus of proof and statutory exemptions, more effective enforcement mechanisms, and greater variety of remedies. But effective protection and support also require more proactive measures, such as policies aimed to promote accommodation and adjustments with respect to time, layout, and work organization. These include flexible work arrangements, part time opportunities, bridge positions, phased retirement, and training and retraining opportunities. These also entail affirmative action strategies, including reporting duties on age compositions, selection practices, and structural barriers. It also requires government grants, incentives, or subsidies for the recruitment of older workers and for ergonomic improvements and business expansions that would lead to their recruitment. Policies that encourage collective action through unions, class actions, and public interest complaints also enhance the capabilities and effective choice of older workers. Together these changes will alter social norms and advance proactive self-regulatory measures such as the implementation of standardized and objective criteria for hiring and other workplace practices, and the development of age-conscious hiring and other workplace policies.

More importantly, promoting the substantive freedom of older workers requires that the responsibility for adequate retirement income should be reassumed by governments, directly through social security benefits and public pension funds, and indirectly through closer and improved supervision of registered pension funds. Similarly, a conceptual shift from a neo-liberal use of the idea of employability to workability is warranted. While employability emphasizes the individual's responsibility to enhance and upgrade his or her skills and qualifications, workability takes a proactive and holistic approach to people's working lives.[149] This requires the development of institutions and infrastructure that are meaningful to the enhancement of workplace health and safety, quality jobs, and sustainable working conditions through various labour market systems starting from early in the working life cycle. This also entails policies aimed to advance real and substantive access to lifelong learning, training, and competence development through, for example, subsidies for specific training at the organizational level and the establishment of effective government centers and programs for retraining and job placements. This also includes the provision of financial and educational assistance for older workers who, failing to find a job, often choose to become self-employed. Financial assistance should also be provided to unemployed older workers as a bridge between involuntary exit (e.g., due to dismissal or health issues) and pensionable age, especially for those who worked in physically demanding, low-skilled jobs. Finally, this requires the promotion of public elderly care to allow older (especially female) workers to participate more meaningfully in the labour market.

---

and Patrick Button, "Did Age Discrimination Protections Help Older Workers Weather the Great Recession?" (2014) 33(4) *Journal of Policy Analysis and Management* 566; David Neumark, Joanne Song, and Patrick Button, "Does Protecting Older Workers from Discrimination Make it Harder to Get Hired? Evidence from Disability Discrimination Laws" (2017) 39(1) *Research on Aging* 29.

[149] Tony Maltby, "Extending Working Lives? Employability, Work Ability and Better Quality Working Lives" (2011) 10(3) *Social Policy & Society* 299, 301–2.

# V. Conclusion

Nussbaum's CA is premised on the idea of social cooperation between human beings from the very start, which among other reasons, is motivated by their moral compassion for those who have less than they need to lead a life worthy of human dignity.[150] Inclusiveness is an intrinsically valuable end under the CA because each person views the good of others as an essential part of his or her own good and "cannot imagine living well without shared ends and a shared life."[151] The CA is therefore distinct from other theories of just distribution, including Rawls's theory of justice, because instead of being a matter left to individual conceptions of the good, the CA advances a strong commitment to the good of others, which is "a part of the shared *public* conception of the person from the start."[152]

This central idea of social cooperation, which is not based on mutual advantage and emphasizes the importance of care as a social primary good, is of paramount relevance to workplace discrimination laws and policies. Specifically, the CA offers a fresh perspective for contemporary age discrimination laws and policies that often fail to effectively respond to the challenges faced by older workers in the labour market. First, it helps underline the wrongness associated with age discrimination by demonstrating how the combined capabilities and substantive freedom of older workers are diminished by various overt and subtle impediments. Second, it emphasizes the importance of *each* person's capabilities and of securing an adequate level of *each* capability, which provides guidance for reconciling tensions between dignity and distributional concerns. Third, its sensitivity to variations in need highlights heterogeneity within the group of older workers and advances the consideration of intersectionality issues. Finally, the CA helps justify regulatory reforms and policies that foster positive action to ensure older workers are able effectively to exercise real choice and substantive freedom.

---

[150] Nussbaum, *Frontiers of Justice* (n. 2) 156–7.
[151] Nussbaum, *Frontiers of Justice* (n. 2) 158.
[152] Nussbaum, *Frontiers of Justice* (n. 2).

# 14

# (Re)Imagining the Trade–Labour Linkage

## The Capabilities Approach

*Clair Gammage*

> *We must work together to ensure the equitable distribution of wealth, opportunity, and power in our society*
>
> Nelson Mandela, 1996

## I. Introduction

The purpose of this chapter is to revisit the debate that dominated trade talks in the early days of the World Trade Organization (WTO): *should* WTO rules protect and promote workers' rights? As one of the key factors of production, labour is a key determinant in defining fair conditions of trade. Exploring the close and evolving relationship between trade and labour, this chapter uses Sen's concept of human freedom[1] to invert the dominant rationalist economic analyses of trade which conceive of the 'ends' of trade as development defined by economic growth. Refocusing the debate around the concept of freedoms allows for a (re)conceptualization of the normative foundation of the international trading system where the expansion of 'human freedom' is seen as the 'ends' of trade.

This chapter begins by mapping the origins of the trade–labour linkage and identifies key conceptual shifts in the global economy that have shaped the relationship between these two distinct but interrelated disciplines. The chapter continues by (re) imagining the concept of sustainability through the lens of capabilities to evaluate the significance of this normative framework for the promotion and protection of labour standards in the context of trade. In 2015, the enunciation of the 2030 Agenda for Sustainable Development, with its seventeen Sustainable Development Goals (SDGs) and 169 targets, reinvigorated the debate on how the international community can work together to create more inclusive, just, and sustainable societies. Trade liberalization plays a central role in sustainability and the SDGs call for a 'universal,

---

[1] Amartya Sen, *Development as Freedom* (OUP, 1999); Amartya Sen, *The Idea of Justice* (Penguin, 2009).

The Capability Approach to Labour Law. Edited by Brian Langille. Chapter 14 © Clair Gammage 2019. Published 2019 by Oxford University Press.

rules-based, open, non-discriminatory and equitable' multi-lateral trading system.[2] While the 2030 Agenda does not provide an exhaustive list of the characteristics constituting an *equitable* trading system, the promotion and protection of labour standards is one such feature (Goal 8).[3]

It is suggested that the point of intersection between sustainable development, labour law, and international trade is 'removing obstacles to human freedom'[4] and the purpose of redistribution through the international trading system is to promote and enhance freedoms. Freedom, in the context of this analysis, should be properly understood as advancing the notion of capabilities as 'real opportunities' that are both formally and legally available as well as being effectively available in practice to the individual.[5] Situating capabilities and freedoms in the context of sustainability, with its emphasis on the three dimensions of development (environmental, human, and economic), this chapter argues that the international trade regime can play a significant role in enhancing freedoms that will enable individuals to live a life they value.

With this in mind, the remaining parts of the chapter consider the significance of free trade agreements (FTAs) for the realization of labour standards. Analysing the US-Guatemala labour dispute—the first and only labour dispute to be brought in the context of a trade agreement—through the lens of capabilities illustrates the way in which trade-oriented legal reasoning can perpetuate *un*freedoms and limit agency. This chapter concludes by arguing that while Sen's capability approach (CA) offers an alternative vision for development, the transformative potential for a just and equitable trade regime can only be realized if there is a meaningful commitment to agency and participation.

## II.  Trade and Labour

Founded on a normative conception of social justice, the International Labour Organization (ILO) was created in 1919 with the purpose of promoting and protecting workers' rights.[6] It was not until the end of the Second World War that states sought to create an institution to regulate international trade. The International Trade Organization (ITO), which was supposed to support the restructuring of markets, ultimately failed and instead, the General Agreement on Tariffs and Trade (GATT) entered into force in 1948. As both a body of rules and a loose organization of states, the purpose of the GATT was (and still is) the liberalization of trade among

---

[2] Goal 17.10, United Nations, 'Transforming our World: The 2030 Agenda for Sustainable Development' (UN Publishing, 2015).

[3] Goal 8, entitled 'Decent Work and Economic Growth' calls for the promotion of 'sustained, inclusive, and sustainable economic growth, full and productive employment and decent work for all'.

[4] Brian Langille, 'Labour Law's Theory of Justice' in Guy Davidov and Brian Langille (eds), *The Idea of Labour Law* (OUP, 2011) 113.

[5] Amartya Sen, *The Idea of Justice* (Penguin, 2009) 231.

[6] Preamble, Part XIII Treaty of Peace of Versailles establishing the International Labour Organization (1919).

countries by eliminating trade barriers. From a liberal perspective, economic inter-dependence has been shown to decrease the likelihood of war as states would 'rather trade than invade'[7] and, in this regard, the GATT can be seen as serving a social pur-pose. However, unlike the ILO which is founded on a conception of social justice, the international trading system favours a concept of justice that is concerned with economic efficiency and utility maximization.

Early expressions of the relationship between trade and labour can be found in international legal instruments.[8] The Havana Charter of 1948, the legal basis for the ITO, dedicated an entire chapter to the governance of 'employment and economic activity' and recognized the importance of 'fair labour standards' as a condition for the liberalization of international trade:

> The Members recognize that measures relating to employment must take fully into account the rights of workers under inter-governmental declarations, conventions and agreements. They recognize that all countries have a common interest in the achievement and mainten-ance of fair labour standards related to productivity, and thus in the improvement of wages and working conditions as productivity may permit. The Members recognize that unfair labour conditions, particularly in production for export, create difficulties in international trade, and, accordingly, each Member shall take whatever action may be appropriate and feasible to eliminate such conditions within its territory.[9]

However, the first significant attempt to protect and promote workers' rights in the context of international trade subsequently occurred in negotiations towards the creation of the World Trade Organization (WTO). For some time, the EU and USA had been advocating for the inclusion of a 'social clause' into the WTO agree-ments which would explicitly link trade and labour concerns. At the 1996 Singapore Ministerial Conference, the WTO Members remained divided on the question of whether the international trade regime was the appropriate mechanism for the gov-ernance of labour standards.[10] From an economic perspective, the purpose of labour standards is twofold. First, labour standards can correct market failures, for labour markets left unsupervised 'will not achieve an optimal level of workplace safety, em-ployment, security and skills training'.[11] Secondly, promoting and protecting high

---

[7] Dale Copeland, 'Economic Interdependence and War: A Theory of Trade Expectations' (1996) 20(4) *International Security* 5, 5–41.

[8] The first multi-lateral labour treaty to incorporate a trade dimension was the Convention re-specting the Prohibition of the Use of White (Yellow) Phosphorus in the Manufacture of Matches of 26 September 1901, while the first multi-lateral trade treaty to address labour standards was the International Convention for the Abolition of Import and Export Prohibitions and Restrictions of 8 November 1927, LNTS Vol 96, No 2238, Protocol Section IV. Although the latter legal instrument did not come into force, both multi-lateral treaties demonstrate the willingness of states to acknowledge the connection between trade and labour. See Steve Charnovitz, 'The International Labour Organisation in its 2nd Century' in Jochen A Frowein and Rüdiger Wolfrum (eds), *Max Planck Yearbook of United Nations Law* (2000) 147–84.

[9] Havana Charter for an International Trade Organization 1948, UN Doc E/CONF.2/78.

[10] Steve Charnovitz, 'Trade, Employment and Labour Standards: The OECD Study and Recent Developments in The Trade and Labour Standards Debate' (1997) *Temple International and Comparative Law Journal* 131, 154–8.

[11] Steve Charnovitz, 'The International Labour Organisation in its 2nd Century' in Jochen A Frowein and Rüdiger Wolfrum(eds), *Max Planck Yearbook of United Nations Law* (2000) 165.

labour standards prevents circumvention of the non-discrimination principle—a fundamental rule of WTO law. Low labour standards mean that labour is cheaper, which can confer a comparative advantage in the production of goods. Developing countries were concerned at the rationale behind the social clause, which they perceived to be a mechanism for developed economies to protect their markets from the threat posed by developing countries where labour standards are typically lower and the costs of production cheaper. From this perspective, requiring higher labour standards in the context of international trade was protectionism 'masking behind a moral face'.[12] The proposal to include a social clause at the WTO was eventually abandoned.[13]

As efforts to embed a social dimension in international trade rules at the multilateral level through the negotiation rounds faltered, some states found other avenues through which the trade–labour linkage could be promoted. Labour conditionality has been a requirement of unilateral preference schemes for decades, with the both the US and the EU offering preferential terms of trade to developing countries that agree to sign up to ILO Conventions and respect labour standards.[14] Free trade agreements (FTAs) have also become an increasingly important market-oriented tool to further social norms, including labour standards. The first FTA to include labour standards was the North American Free Trade Agreement (NAFTA), which proclaimed a commitment to 'protect, enhance and enforce basic worker's rights'.[15] With NAFTA now under review, labour standards have once again become a site of contestation among the three trading partners.[16]

Important conceptual shifts were also taking place at the ILO at this time, and in 1998 a soft law instrument, the Declaration on Fundamental Principles and Rights at Work (the Declaration) was adopted. Promoting the universalization of labour standards, the Declaration was celebrated by many scholars as a significant constitutional moment in labour law.[17] The Declaration set out four 'core labour standards' in the eight legally binding Conventions of the ILO and recognized as fundamental

---

[12]  Jagdish Bhagwati, 'Trade Liberalisation and 'Fair Trade' Demands: Addressing the Environmental and Labour Standards Issues' (1995) 18(6) *The World Economy* 756.

[13]  See Economic and Social Committee of the EU, 'Opinion on the Effects of the Uruguay Round Agreements' 94/C 393/31 of 26 February 1994. In particular, paragraph 12.2 identified those labour standards considered to be fundamental to the creation of the social clause: the abolition of forced labour, the right to organize and collective bargaining, minimum age for work and abolition of child labour, and a ban on discrimination in the workplace and equal pay for equal work.

[14]  Steve Charnovitz, 'The Influence of International Labour Standards on the World Trade Regime: A Historical Overview' (1987) 126(5) *International Labour Review* 565, 565–84.

[15]  'North American Agreement on Labour Cooperation' Between the Government of the United States of America, the Government of Canada and the Government of the United Mexican States of 13 September 1993.

[16]  Dave Graham and Sharay Angulo, 'Sharp Differences over Labour Surface at NAFTA Talks in Mexico' *Reuters Business News* (4 September 2017) https://www.reuters.com/article/us-trade-nafta-labor/sharp-differences-over-labor-surface-at-nafta-talks-in-mexico-idUSKCN1BF00H.

[17]  For a comprehensive debate on the constitutional significance of the Declaration, see Philip Alston, 'Core Labour Standards and the Transformation of the International Labour Rights Regime' (2004) 15(3) *European Journal of International Law* 457, 457–521 and Brian Langille, 'Core Labour Rights: The True Story (A Reply to Alston)' (2005) 16(3) *European Journal of International Law* 409, 409–437.

principles and rights at work: freedom of association and collective bargaining;[18] the elimination of forced labour;[19] the abolition of child labour;[20] and the elimination of discrimination and equal pay for equal work in the workplace.[21] Identifying four standards that were 'core' to the ILO's focus on social justice appeared to create a new 'normative hierarchy' of labour standards,[22] with many questioning whether labour standards are properly conceived as labour *rights* and, if so, are labour rights, then, human rights?

The labour rights as human rights debate has been heavily scrutinized and it is not the purpose of this chapter to restate at length the arguments set out by supporters and detractors.[23] However, this chapter draws insights from the debate to assess whether the language of labour rights as human rights carries normative weight in the context of the multi-lateral trading system. Labour rights have been defined as 'entitlements that relate specifically to the role of being a worker',[24] and while they may refer to individual and collective entitlements, such rights can only apply to those in paid employment or 'employment-like relationships'.[25] Articulating labour rights as human rights can be defended on the grounds of the Dworkinian metaphor that rights are 'trumps' which confer certain fundamental entitlements on workers in the context of their employment relationship.[26] Three approaches to the debate have been identified in the scholarship that examines labour rights as human rights, although these are not always clearly distinguished from one another.[27] The first approach is positivistic in nature and identifies labour standards as human rights where they have been laid down by legally binding instruments. At the international level, the earliest expression of labour rights is found in the United Nations Declaration of Human Rights (UNHDR). Core labour standards/rights find their expression in international human rights instruments including the International Covenant for Civil and Political Rights (ICCPR) and the International Covenant for Economic,

---

[18] ILO, Freedom of Association and Protection of the Right to Organise Convention CO87 (No 87) of 1948 (entered into force on 4 July 1950) and ILO, Right to Organise and Collective Bargaining Convention CO98 (No 98) of 1949 (entered into force on 18 July 1951).

[19] ILO, Forced Labour Convention CO29 (No 29) of 1930 (entered into force on 1 May 1932) and ILO, Abolition of Forced Labour Convention C105 (No 105) of 1957 (entered into force on 17 January 1959).

[20] ILO, Minimum Age Convention C138 of 1973 (entered into force on 19 June 1976) and ILO, Worst Forms of Child Labour Convention C182 of 1999 (entered into force on 19 November 2000).

[21] ILO, Equal Remuneration Convention (C100) of 1951 (entered into force on 23 May 1953) and ILO, Discrimination (Employment and Occupation) Convention (C111) of 1958 (entered into force on 15 June 1960).

[22] Philip Alston, 'Core Labour Standards and the Transformation of the International Labour Rights Regime' (n 17) 457–521.

[23] Jay Youngdahl and Lance A Compa, 'Should Labor Defend Worker Rights as Human Rights? A Debate' (2009) 18(1) *New Labour Forum* 31, 31–7; Hugh Collins, 'Theories of Rights as Justifications for Labour Law' in Guy Davidov and Brian Langille, *The Idea of Labour Law* (OUP, 2011).

[24] Virginia Mantouvalou, 'Are Labour Rights Human Rights?' (2012) 3(2) *European Law Journal* 152.

[25] Collins, 'Theories of Rights as Justifications for Labour Law' (n 23) 142.

[26] Ronald Dworkin, 'Rights as Trumps' in Jeremy Waldron (ed), *Theories of Rights* (OUP, 1984).

[27] Mantouvalou, 'Are Labour Rights Human Rights?' (n 24).

Social, and Cultural Rights (ICESCR).[28] When codified into legally binding in-struments, the status of labour rights as human rights is unquestionable. The second approach is instrumental and is concerned with 'the consequences of using strat-egies, such as litigation or civil society action, which promote labour rights as human rights'.[29] Classifying labour rights as human rights under the instrumental approach hinges on the success of the strategy employed. Finally, the question of whether la-bour rights are properly conceptualized as human rights can be approached from a normative perspective.

It is the latter approach that bears significance for the trade–labour linkage in the context of FTAs since recasting labour standards as international human rights can serve to not only 'elevate their moral appeal'[30] but also to impose legally binding commitments on trade partners in the context of FTAs. For example, in EU FTAs the respect for human rights constitutes an 'essential element' of the agreement. If a party to the FTA violates human rights then 'appropriate measures' may be taken in the form of trade concessions.[31] Human rights clauses are considered to be 'sufficiently robust and flexible' to enable a party to withdraw from the FTA if a violation of human rights occurs.[32] Rights-talk can, therefore, be a powerful tool for harnessing capabilities and promoting human freedom. However, labour stand-ards are now increasingly being reframed in the context of sustainability and *not* as human rights.

## III.  Trade, Labour, and Sustainability: Towards Freedom?

Labour standards fall within the social and economic dimension of sustainability development and they are increasingly articulated in the context of sustainability.[33] First articulated in the 1987 Brundtland Report as 'development that meets the needs of the present without compromising the ability of future generations to meet their own needs', sustainability was recognized to encompass social, economic, and political dimensions of justice. The vagueness of the Brundtland conception of sus-tainability, with its failure to define 'development', has led many over the years to

---

[28]  There is a normative distinction between the rights set out in these two international legal instru-ments. Rights expressed in the ICCPR are justiciable while rights laid down in the ICESCR are believed to be progressive.

[29]  Mantouvalou, 'Are Labour Rights Human Rights?' (n 24) 151.

[30]  Judy Fudge, 'Labour Rights and Human Rights: Turning Slogans into Legal Claims' (2014) 37(2) *The Dalhousie Law Journal* 609.

[31]  For examples of non-execution clauses see Article 455 of the EU–Moldova Association Agreement; Article 422 EU–Moldova Association Agreement; and Article 96 Cotonou Partnership Agreement (CPA) between the EU and African, Caribbean and Pacific States. Overall, the EU has invoked non-execution clauses in 24 cases. The EU has taken 'appropriate measures' most recently in the context of Article 96 of the CPA, in response to the human rights crisis in Burundi.

[32]  Lorand Bartels, 'The EU's Human Rights Obligations in Relation to Policies with Extraterritorial Effects' (2014) 25(4) *European Journal of International Law* 1074.

[33]  Tonia Novitz, 'Labour Standards and Trade: Need We Choose Between 'Human Rights' and 'Sustainable Development'?' in Henner Gött, *Labour Standards in International Economic Law* (Springer, 2018) 113–34.

question the utility of this concept. Proponents of welfare economics and sustainable economic development understand sustainability in terms of utility and the maximization of aggregate utility.[34] From this perspective, sustainability is achieved if there is an overall increase in a particular measure, for example, income or happiness. Early and influential accounts from sustainable economic development theorists explain the Brundtland concept of sustainability in exhaustible-resource economies through the 'savings-investment' rule, also known as the 'Hartwick rule', which identifies the amount of investment needed in capital stock to replenish the declining stock of exhaustible resources.[35] In effect, the rule evaluates the amount of investment needed to ensure that the standard of living is maintained for future generations as exhaustible resources diminish. Sustainability, according to economist Robert Solow, 'is an injunction not to satisfy ourselves by impoverishing our successors'.[36]

While these earlier accounts offer insight into the many ways in which the concept of sustainability might be analysed and measured, it would be a 'terribly hollow ring' if the focus were only on maintaining the stock of capital for future generations without enhancing the well-being of present generations.[37] Furthermore, they tell us little about what values are constitutive of development. Over the past ten years, a new and powerful conceptual framework for sustainability which articulates a more robust account of the three dimensions of sustainability has emerged, known as the 'planetary boundaries' model of sustainability. Originating in the discipline of natural sciences, this model seeks to identify the 'safe operating space for humanity' through the measurement of nine environmental factors.[38] Transgressing one or more of the planetary boundaries could have catastrophic effects for humanity, and for this reason the approach endorses a strong reading of the precautionary principle by 'setting the discrete boundary value at the lower and more conservative bound of the uncertainty range'.[39] Shifting the focus onto the environmental limits of our planet defines the 'planetary playing field' for humanity and for sustainability.

However, prioritizing the environmental dimension of sustainability over the social and economic dimensions is problematic for it obscures the relationship between

---

[34] The liberal writings of John Rawls and Ronald Dworkin have been particularly persuasive from a political philosophy perspective. See John Rawls, *A Theory of Justice* (Harvard University Press, 1971) and for a commentary on Dworkin's contribution, see Alexander Brown, *Ronald Dworkin's Theory of Equality: Domestic and Global Perspectives* (Palgrave Macmillan, 2009).

[35] See Robert M Solow, 'Intergenerational Equity and Exhaustible Resources' (1974) *Review of Economic Studies* Symposium and John M Hartwick, 'Substitution Among Exhaustible Resources and Intergenerational Equity' (1978) 45(2) *Review of Economic Studies* 347, 347–54.

[36] Robert M Solow, 'Sustainability: An economist's perspective' (1991) The Eighteenth J Seward Johnson Lecture. Woods Hole (Woods Hole Oceanographic Institution), cited in Sudhir Anand and Amartya Sen, 'Human Development and Economic Sustainability' (2000) 28(12) *World Development* 2031.

[37] Anand and Sen, 'Human Development and Economic Sustainability' (n 36) 2038.

[38] The nine planetary boundaries are identified as: stratospheric ozone depletion; loss of biosphere integrity; chemical pollution; climate change; ocean acidification; freshwater consumption and the global hydrological cycle; land system changes; nitrogen and phosphorous flows to the biosphere and oceans; and atmospheric aerosol loading.

[39] Johan Rockström and others, 'Planetary Boundaries: Exploring the Safe Operating Space for Humanity' (2009) 14(2) *Ecology and Society* 32.

individuals and the nine planetary boundaries. Recognizing the limitations with the dominant 'rational economic man' model of economics which correlates economic growth with wellbeing, Kate Raworth offers an alternative socially informed conception of the planetary boundaries framework. She proposes that the aim, or 'ends', of economic activity should be 'meeting the needs of all within the means of the planet' so that each individual can live in the 'ecologically safe and just social space' (as Raworth describes it, getting 'into the doughnut').[40] Our focus, Raworth argues, should be on 'what enables human beings to thrive'.[41] Building on the respective works of Johan Rockström and Kate Raworth, recent research has sought to 'close the loop'[42] between the economic, environmental, and social dimensions of the planetary boundary conception of sustainability. By situating the 'social' in the planetary boundaries model, the important but complex role of human agency and social networks for ensuring that humanity remains within a safe operating space is made more explicit. Human agency is 'more multi-dimensional than single purpose organisation'.[43] It is the inherent complexity and unpredictability of the social dimension that makes for an uncomfortable bedfellow to the inherently rational approaches of economics and natural sciences. However, bridging the gap, or 'closing the loop', between these dimensions is necessary if humanity is to strive to live in the ecologically safe and socially just operating space.

The socially sensitive account of environmental sustainability presented by Raworth is complementary to the human development approach advanced by capability theorists. Bridging the schools of ethics and economics, Amartya Sen proposes a theory of development where freedom is both the principal means and the principal end of development.[44] Amartya Sen argues that the focus of development should be on human capabilities to achieve a life that each individual values and, in order to do so, the means to realizing substantive freedom must be established.[45] Freedoms can be either constitutive or instrumental, or both.[46] Constitutive freedoms are those freedoms that we intrinsically value, like the ability to be nourished, the ability to live a peaceful life, the ability to access education so that we can learn to read and write, the ability to participate in political processes, and so on. Instrumental freedoms are those freedoms which contribute to, or expand, the realization of constitutive freedoms. For example, the ability to participate in the market and sell one's labour (an *instrumental* freedom) will generate income with which one can buy food and access nourishment (a *constitutive* freedom). Constitutive freedoms may also be instrumental insofar as they contribute to the realization of other

---

[40]  Kate Raworth, *Doughnut Economics: Seven Ways to Think Like a 21st Century Economist* (Chelsea Green Publishing, 2017).

[41]  Raworth, *Doughnut Economics* (n 40) 43.

[42]  Jonathan F. Donges and others, 'Closing the Loop: Reconnecting Human Dynamics to Earth System Science' (2017) 4(2) *The Anthropocene Review* 151, 151–7.

[43]  Donges and others, 'Closing the Loop' (n 42) 154.

[44]  Amartya Sen, *Development as Freedom* (OUP, 2001).

[45]  Martha C Nussbaum, 'Capabilities as Fundamental Entitlements: Sen and Social Justice' (2003) 9(2–3) *Feminist Economics* 33.

[46]  Sen, *Development as Freedom* (n 44) 36–41.

constitutive freedoms. While the concept of sustainability is 'malleable'[47] the focus for development as a *process* has been to alleviate poverty. Sen conceives of poverty as 'capability deprivation' and the process of development is, therefore, one that achieves freedom from the deprivation of capabilities.[48]

Sen identifies five types of distinct, but interrelated, freedoms that advance the capabilities of a person: political freedom, economic facilities, social opportunities, transparency guarantees, and protective security.[49] Development as a process should, therefore, play an instrumental role in promoting these freedoms so that people can have lives that they value:

> Expanding the freedoms that we have reason to value not only makes our lives richer and more unfettered, but also allows us to be fuller social persons, exercising our own volitions and interacting with—and influencing—the world in which we live.[50]

Moving against the instrumentalist assumption that economic growth presupposes other substantive freedoms, Sen argues that these values should be seem as primary goals which will in turn stimulate economic growth. Development is, therefore, conceptualized as 'a process of expanding the real freedoms that people enjoy'[51] with economic growth perceived as a 'means' towards the realization of those substantive freedoms. Sen offers an alternative vision of justice through which human agency plays a central role. Sen's CA is 'people-centred'; it places individuals at the centre of its discourse as opposed to institutions, governments, and markets. Wellbeing and agency are central, albeit distinguishable, concepts.[52] From this perspective, social opportunities serve to 'expand the realm of human agency and freedom, both as an end in itself and as a means of further expansion of freedom'.[53] Sen defines 'agency' as 'what a person is free to do and achieve in pursuit of whatever goals or values he or she regards as important'.[54] An agent is 'someone who acts and brings about change, and whose achievements can be judged in terms of her own values and objectives, whether or not we assess them in terms of some external criteria as well'.[55] However, it is important not to view the individual in isolation from others or from social opportunities. Sen's CA is inherently *relational*: the capabilities of an individual can only be properly understood in light of their relationships with social opportunities and with others.

Economic arrangements, including that of market mechanisms, and political participation play a central role in shaping our social opportunities and there is a 'deep-seated complementarity' between the social, political, and economic arrangements

[47] Virginie Barral, 'Sustainable Development in International Law: Nature and Operation of an Evolutive Legal Norm' (2012) 23(2) *European Journal of International Law* 377, 377–400.
[48] Sen, *Development as Freedom* (n 44) 87.    [49] Sen, *Development as Freedom* (n 44) 10.
[50] Sen, *Development as Freedom* (n 44) 16–17.
[51] Sen, *Development as Freedom* (n 44) 3.
[52] David A Crocker and Ingrid Robeyns, 'Capability and Agency' in Christopher W Morris (ed), *Amartya Sen: Contemporary Philosophy in Focus* (CUP, 2010) 62.
[53] Jean Drèze and Amartya Sen, *India: Development and Participation* (2nd edn, OUP, 2002) 6.
[54] Amartya Sen, 'Well-being, Agency and Freedom: The Dewey Lectures 1984' (1985) 82(4) *Journal of Philosophy* 203.
[55] Sen, *Development as Freedom* (n 44) 19.

of society.[56] As such, Sen's CA offers a perspective of distribution that is broader than, but not inconsistent with, mainstream economic theories of development underpinning the rationale of the multi-lateral trading system. Sen's CA appeals to the view that egalitarian theories should look beyond distribution based on welfare and resources.[57] The real problem of the wealth maximization and economic efficiency approaches is the failure to consider the *real* opportunities that individuals have in any particular society:

The exclusive concentration only on incomes at the aggregative or individual levels ignores the plurality of influences that differentiate the real opportunities of people, and implicitly assumes away the variations—related to personal characteristics as well as the social and physical environment—in the possibility of converting the means of income into the ends of good and liveable lives which people have reason to value.[58]

However, critics have argued that Sen's theory is incomplete.[59] Martha C Nussbaum, a leading proponent of the CA and feminist philosopher, has criticized Sen's theory for failing to articulate a central or core set of inviolable freedoms.[60] She offers ten central capabilities[61] of which two—affiliation and practical reason—play an 'architectonic role' in pervading and organizing the other central capabilities.[62] Nussbaum's work has significant implications for policy as it identifies 'each individual as an end' and provides that no individual should be used a means to the capabilities of others. There are nonetheless similarities in their normative frameworks, for the accounts of freedom in Sen and Nussbaum's accounts of the CA both rest on the anti-paternalistic conception that we should not advance a particular conception of what constitutes the 'good life'; rather, in focusing on capabilities (and not functionings), each agent can pursue a life that they value.

The market does not stand outside the realm of moral justification and 'we need a theory which explains why market activity and economic growth are desirable in the first place'.[63] Setting rules to liberalize trade in favour of human development remains the challenge for the WTO. Abandoning the social clause at the WTO required the (re)imagination of how the language of capabilities and freedom could be framed in the context of trade. Increasingly, states have sought to embed a social dimension to FTAs, many of which now cover a wide range of economic, social, and environmental issues. The remaining parts of this chapter will consider the

---

[56] Drèze and Sen, *India* (n 53) 7.
[57] For a comprehensive account of the distinctions between the works of Ronald Dworkin and Amartya Sen, see Andrew Williams, 'Dworkin on Capability' (2002) 113(1) *Ethics* 23, 23–9.
[58] Anand and Sen, 'Human Development and Economic Sustainability' (n 36) 2031.
[59] Robert Sugden, 'Welfare, Resources, and Capabilities: A Review of Inequality Reexamined by Amartya Sen' (1993) 31 *Journal of Economic Literature* 1947, 1947–62.
[60] Martha C Nussbaum, *Creating Capabilities: The Human Development Approach* (Harvard University Press, 2011).
[61] The ten central capabilities are: life; bodily health; bodily integrity; senses, imagination, and thought; emotions; practical reason; affiliation; other species; play; and, control over one's environment.
[62] See Nussbaum, *Creating Capabilities* (n 60) 33–40.
[63] Langille, 'Labour Law's Theory of Justice' (n 4) 119.

significance of this ideological shift for expanding capabilities through trade liberalization, with a focus on workers' rights and labour standards.

## IV.  Labour Standards in FTAs: A Normative Shift

In the absence of a multi-lateral social clause, labour standards have provided a social foundation to FTAs since the early 1990s. The North American Agreement on Labour and Cooperation (NAALC), a side agreement to NAFTA, was the first US FTA to include labour standards and the US, Canada, and the EU have been the most active proponents of labour clauses in FTAs. Early iterations of labour standards in EU trade agreements, like the Trade and Development Cooperation Agreement between the EU and South Africa (1999) and the EU–Chile FTA (2003), included labour standards, but these were expressed as non-binding commitments and the agreements did not include a mechanism for their enforcement.[64] However, labour standards are increasingly being reframed in the context of sustainability. Contemporary EU FTAs, such as the EU–Korea FTA, favour a more expansive approach to labour standards and call for the parties to adopt 'high levels' of protection 'consistent with internationally recognised standards'.[65] Respect for core labour standards as 'fundamental' entitlements is now commonplace[66] and explicit reference is made to the ILO's Decent Work Agenda in recent EU-FTAs, including the 'deep and comprehensive' FTAs with Moldova, Georgia, and the Ukraine. [67] Tonia Novitz argues that conceiving of labour standards in the context of sustainability may enable the broader objectives of the Decent Work Agenda (2008) to be pursued and therefore 'add new labour standards as worthy of protection and to seek durability of a fairer economic settlement for workers'.[68] However, and as noted by Novitz, the success of this approach hinges on the extent to which agency and participation can be facilitated through the FTA.

Over time, an increasing judicialization of labour provisions has been observed, with FTAs including different and more effective means for enforcing labour standards in the context of trade. In EU FTAs the 'soft incentives-based' approach to enforcement of labour standards is promoted. Labour standards are typically found in the trade and sustainable development (TSD) chapters of EU FTAs, under which consultative mechanisms encourage 'dialogue and cooperation between the parties, transparency in introducing new labour standards measures, monitoring and review of the sustainability impacts of the agreement, and a commitment to upholding

---

[64] Article 44(1) EU–Chile FTA of 2003.          [65] Article 13.3 EU–Korea FTA of 2011.

[66] Article 13.4.3 recognizes the following rights as fundamental: (a) freedom of association and the effective recognition of the right to collective bargaining; (b) the elimination of all forms of forced or compulsory labour; (c) the effective abolition of child labour; and (d) the elimination of discrimination in respect of employment and occupation.

[67] See Articles 364–5 EU–Moldova DCFTA, Articles 228–9 EU–Georgia DCFTA, and Articles 290–1 EU–Ukraine DCFTA.

[68] Novitz (n 33) 124.

levels of domestic labour protection'.[69] Implementation and monitoring of the TSD falls to a civil society mechanism, such as a domestic advisory group (DAG), and a panel of experts that can examine any complaint and make recommendations to the parties.[70] In relation to labour standards in FTAs, the ILO offers technical assistance and expertise to ensure that contradictions in the application of national labour standards, labour provisions in FTAs, and multi-lateral obligations are avoided.[71]

The legal consequences of this normative shift render the context of labour standards 'blurred' and it is not entirely clear how violations of labour standards are to be addressed.[72] Many countries ratify the ILO Conventions but do not comply with labour standards in practice.[73] There is evidence to suggest that the institutional frameworks to promote dialogue and cooperation in EU-FTAs are not as effective as they could be.[74] For example, in the context of the CARIFORUM-Economic Partnership Agreement the creation of the DAG was delayed while other FTAs, like EU–Korea and EU–Colombia-Peru, have failed to engage constructively with the recommendations of the civil society mechanisms. In the context of the EU-Colombia-Peru FTA[75] and the EU–Vietnam FTA[76] labour standards in the third country were *lowered* on the implementation of some bilateral agreements. To what extent the EU might be accountable for contributing to the lowering of labour standards very much hinges on the effectiveness of the civil society mechanism and the DAG.

While the depth and breadth of labour provisions in EU-FTAs stands in stark contrast to their weak enforcement mechanisms, the soft incentive-based approach of the EU 'should not be dismissed as cheap rhetorical commitment'[77] since certain labour standards, especially core labour standards, could be protected under the essential elements clause. Arguably, it is the lack of a formal complaint framework through which the State must react to the issues raised by the civil society mechanism that 'allows the parties to these agreements to remain inactive, even when confronted with allegations of severe labour standards violations'.[78] It seems that

---

[69] James Harrison and others, 'Governing Labour Standards through Free Trade Agreements: Limits of the European Union's Trade and Sustainable Development Chapters' (2018) *Journal of Common Market Studies* doi: 10.1111/jcms.12715.

[70] An exception to this type of arrangement is the EU–CARIFORUM EPA, for which the implementation of the entire agreement is overseen by the civil society mechanism.

[71] International Labour Organization, 'Labour-Related Provisions in Trade Agreements: Recent Trends and Relevance to the ILO' (29 September 2016) GB.328/POL/3.

[72] Lore van den Putte and Jan Orbie, 'EU Bilateral Trade Agreements and the Surprising Rise of Labour Provisions' (2015) 31(3) *The International Journal of Comparative Labour Law and Industrial Relations* 281.

[73] Emilie Hafner-Burton, *Making Human Rights a Reality* (Princeton University Press, 2013).

[74] Franz Ebert, 'Labour Provisions in EU Trade Agreements: What Potential for Channelling Labour Standards-Related Capacity Building?' (2016) 155(3) *International Labour Review* 407, 407–33.

[75] Axel Marx and others, 'The Protection of Labour Rights in Trade Agreements: the Case of the EU-Colombia Agreement' (2016) 50(4) *Journal of World Trade* 587, 587–610.

[76] Daniella Sicurelli, 'The EU as a Promoter of Human Rights in Bilateral Trade Agreements' (2015) 11(2) *Journal of Contemporary European Research* 230, 230–45.

[77] van den Putte and Orbie, 'EU Bilateral Trade Agreements and the Surprising Rise of Labour Provisions' (n 72) 269.

[78] Ebert, 'Labour Provisions in EU Trade Agreements' (n 74) 413.

the enforcement mechanism under the essential elements clause is more robust than the 'soft incentive-based' approach for resolving labour standard disputes and the even weaker protection afforded to the objective of sustainable development under the TSD Chapter.

Unlike the EU, the US has not sought to frame labour standards in the context of sustainability. Instead, the US has included labour chapters that set out labour standards as justiciable and subject to the dispute settlement mechanism of the FTA.[79] As noted earlier in this chapter, classifying labour standards as human rights has normative import for dispute settlement under FTAs. The violation of labour standards could result in trade concessions or a financial penalty. In 2017, the first labour dispute under a FTA was brought to arbitration.[80] In this case, the US complained that Guatemala had failed to comply with its obligations under the labour chapter of the CAFTA-DR FTA in relation to respecting and promoting the right of association, the right to organize and bargain collectively, and ensure acceptable conditions of work. When the CAFTA-DR FTA was implemented in Guatemala in 2006, it was expected that labour rights protection would be strengthened. However, Guatemala continues to be ranked by the International Trade Union Confederation (ITUC) as one of the worst countries for workers for its poor record of labour rights protection:

> The pervasive climate of repression, physical violence and intimidation was compounded by the government's failure to provide timely and adequate protection to trade unionists who received death threats and to pursue the many historic cases of murders of trade unionists.[81]

Since 2004, records show that eighty-seven workers have been assassinated for participating in trade union activities[82] and the failure to enforce and uphold labour standards has even led to the opening of a Commission of Inquiry at the ILO for a review of Guatemala's non-observance of the right to freedom of association and the right to organize.[83] Gender, ethnicity, and socio-economic class play a significant role for realizing capabilities in Guatemala and studies show that women and indigenous individuals are likely to have a lower level of educational attainment and earn lower wages.[84] Although non-indigenous men and women have similar educational

[79] The approach of the US has been evolutive since the NAALC and there have been a number of important progressive shifts in the framing of labour standards in FTAs. For an excellent comparative account, see J Vogt, 'The Evolution of Labour Rights and Trade: A Transatlantic Comparison and Lessons for the Transatlantic Trade and Investment Partnership' (2015) 18 *Journal of International Economic Law* 827, 827–60.

[80] It should be noted that the US has investigated alleged violations of labour standards in four separate cases under the DR-CAFTA with respect to Colombia, Dominican Republic, Guatemala, and Peru. For full documentation relating to the investigations, see Bureau of International Labor Affairs, 'Submissions under the Labor Provisions of Free Trade Agreements' (undated) https://www.dol.gov/agencies/ilab/our-work/trade/fta-submissions.

[81] ITUC, 'Global Rights Index: The World's Worst Countries for Workers' (2018) 24.

[82] ITUC, 'Global Rights Index' (n 81).

[83] See ILO, 'Decision on the complaint concerning non-observance by Guatemala on the Freedom of Association and Protection of the Right to Organise Convention, 1948 (No 87) made by delegates to the 101st Session (2012) of the International Labour Conference under Article 26 of the ILO Constitution: Information on Progress Achieved' (9 June 2018).

[84] Carla Canelas and Rachel M. Gisselquist, 'Human Capital, Labour Market Outcomes, and Horizontal Inequality in Guatemala' (2017) UNU-WIDER Working Paper 2017/91.

attainment levels, men typically earn on average twice that of women.[85] In 2018, the UN Human Rights Committee documented its concerns about the lack of social and labour protection in the maquila industry (export processing zones) and agriculture and services sectors, the effects of which are more acutely felt by women and indigenous persons.[86] Although the government of Guatemala drafted a Roadmap for the Prevention and Elimination of the Worst Forms of Child Labour, children continue to work and to perform dangerous tasks in the agriculture industry.[87]

The analysis that explores the recent arbitral decision in the Guatemala case and draws insights from Sen's CA to argue that the formalization of legal reasoning adopted by the panel, with its focus on economic efficiency and trade, has contributed to the perpetuation of *un*freedoms for workers in Guatemala. In doing so, this marks a regressive step in the evolution of the labour–trade linkage.

## V. Contesting Labour Standards in the Context of Trade: A Test Case

The Guatemala case was a protracted dispute, lasting almost ten years, and was initially brought by the American Federation of Labour and Congress of Industrial Organizations (AFL-CIO) in conjunction with six Guatemalan trade unions in 2008. A public submission setting out their complaint against Guatemala in relation to five case studies was submitted to the US Department of Labour's Office of Trade and Labour Affairs (OTLA) and it was asserted that Guatemala had failed to effectively enforce its labour laws in accordance with its legal commitments under the CAFTA-DR FTA.[88] Furthermore, the submission pointed to instances of violence against trade unionists in Guatemala resulting in a climate where the rights of trade unionists were undermined and weakened. OLTA began a review process of the alleged labour violations, which lasted six months. On completion of the review, OLTA published its report which identified 'serious problems' in relation to the enforcement of court orders and notable failings on the part of the Guatemalan Ministry of Labour to enforce its labour laws effectively.[89]

On 30 July 2010, the US requested consultations with the government of Guatemala to discuss matters arising in relation to Chapter 16 ('Labour') of the CAFTA-DR. In the original letter requesting the panel to be convened, the US

---

[85] UNDP, 'Human Development for Everyone: Briefing Note for Countries on the 2016 Human Development Report: Guatemala' *UNDP Briefing Note* (2016).

[86] UN Human Rights Committee, 'Concluding Observations on the Fourth Periodic Report of Guatemala' (7 May 2018) CCPR/C/GTM/CO/4.

[87] United States Department of Labour, '2016 Findings on the Worst Forms of Child Labour: Guatemala' *Bureau of International Labour Affairs Report* (2016) https://www.dol.gov/agencies/ilab/resources/reports/child-labor/guatemala.

[88] For a comprehensive account of the dispute see, International Labour Rights Forum, 'Wrong Turn for Workers' Rights: The U.S.–Guatemala CAFTA Labour Arbitration Ruling—and What to Do About It' (March 2018) https://laborrights.org/publications/wrong-turn-workers%E2%80%99-rights-us-guatemala-cafta-labor-arbitration-ruling-%E2%80%93-and-what-do.

[89] Public Report of Review of Office of Trade and Labor Affairs U.S. Submission 2008-01, Guatemala (16 January 2009).

complained that Guatemala had acted in violation of Article 16.2.1(a) of the
CAFTA-DR and identified three 'significant failures' by Guatemala to effectively
enforce its labour laws in relation to a number of different companies, predominantly operating in the agricultural sector: a failure by the Ministry of Labour to
investigate alleged labour law violations; a failure by the Ministry of Labour to take
enforcement action after identifying violations of its labour law; and a failure by
the domestic courts to enforce Guatemala's Labour Court orders in cases involving
violations of labour laws.[90] In 2011, the US requested that an arbitral panel be convened, and on 30 November 2012 the panel was constituted. At the heart of the
dispute was the legal interpretation of Article 16.2.1(a) of the CAFTA-DR, which
states:

A Party shall not fail to effectively enforce its labour laws, through a sustained or recurring
course of action or inaction, in a manner affecting trade between the Parties, after the date of
entry into force of this Agreement.

Three elements of Article 16.2.1(a) were identified by the panel, who noted that
the failure of a Party 'to effectively enforce its labour laws' must occur: (i) 'through a
sustained or recurring course of action or inaction;' (ii) 'in a manner affecting trade
between the Parties'; and (iii) after the FTA has entered into force.[91] Central to the
dispute was the question of how these three elements of Article 16.2.1(a) relate to
one another. Concluding that these three elements are 'cumulative', the panel established a high threshold for establishing a breach under Article 16.2.1(a). In this
dispute, it became clear from the evidence submitted that there were numerous and
cumulative failings on the part of the Guatemalan government to effectively enforce
its labour laws. This was not disputed by the panel. However, the question before the
panel was whether Guatemala was in breach of Article 16.2.1(a) if only one failure to
effectively enforce its labour laws in a manner affecting trade had occurred. Defining
the scope and meaning of Article 16.2.1(a), the panel found:

a failure to effectively enforce a Party's labour law through a sustained or recurring course of
action or inaction is 'in a manner affecting trade between the Parties' if it confers some competitive advantage on an employer or employers engaged in trade between the Parties . . .[92]

In determining the requirement for a competitive advantage to be conferred in the
context of trade between the members of CAFTA-DR, the panel established a three-
tier test.[93] First, it must be shown that that there is a competitive relationship between the enterprise in question and other enterprises in CAFTA-DR. Secondly,
the effects of the state's failure to properly enforce its labour laws must be identified.
It is important to note that the 'effects' to which the panel refer are framed in *economic* terms and relate to the effects of non-enforcement of labour law in Guatemala
for the competitive relationship between companies operating in CAFTA-DR. The

[90]  The original letter is reproduced in the arbitral report at para 73.
[91]  Final Report of the Panel, *Guatemala: Issues Relating to the Obligations Under Article 16.2.1(a) of
the CAFTA-DR* (14 June 2017).
[92]  Final Report of the Panel, *Guatemala* (n 91) para 191.
[93]  Final Report of the Panel, *Guatemala* (n 91) para 196.

panel did not interpret this part of the three-tier test to require an analysis of the *social* effects of non-enforcement or to consider how workers' rights were violated in the context of the FTA. Finally, it must be established that the effects are 'sufficient to confer some competitive advantage' on the enterprise in question.

On the application of this test to the facts of the dispute, the panel found that 'when Guatemala's law enforcement failures are looked at collectively, they show (on an *arguendo* basis) a sustained or recurring course of action or inaction, but not conduct in a manner affecting trade'.[94] In the one case that the panel did find a failure to have taken place in a manner affecting trade, it was not deemed to be a 'sustained or recurring course of action or inaction'.[95] While the US was found to have successfully proven that, at eight worksites and with respect to seventy-four workers, the Guatemalan Ministry of Labour had failed to effectively enforce its labour laws by failing to secure compliance with court orders, this action was *not* found to be in a manner affecting trade.[96] Remarkably, even in the face of evidence that indicated widespread and systematic violations of labour rights, the panel did not find a violation of Article 16.2.1(a). As there is no appeal mechanism under the CAFTA-DR, the findings of the panel are final and cannot be challenged.

In light of Guatemala's historic record of labour rights violations, the findings of the panel were a surprise to many. However, the trade-oriented approach of legal reasoning in the dispute should not be surprising given that two of the three panellists reviewing this dispute are experts in international trade law[97] while only one has extensive expertise in labour law.[98] In its submission, Guatemala urged the panel to draw insights from WTO law perhaps in an attempt to construct this dispute primarily as a trade matter, rather than a labour rights matter. Accordingly, the Parties relied on the recommendations of the WTO Appellate Body and Panels to the extent that these 'shed light on the interpretation of the CAFTA-DR'.[99] Further, although the panel noted that the AB and Panel recommendations were not 'clarifying provisions of the CAFTA-DR' these recommendations were taken into account 'where appropriate'.[100] In constructing their argument, the panel drew little insight from ILO references.

The trade-oriented reasoning of the panel has far-reaching implications, both substantively and procedurally, for the enforcement of labour standards in the context of FTAs. Constructed much like a trade dispute, a substantial amount of the arbitral report is dedicated to establishing whether the requisite burden of evidential proof has been satisfied.[101] The authenticity of the evidence was called into question

---

[94] Final Report of the Panel, *Guatemala* (n 91) para 505.

[95] Final Report of the Panel, *Guatemala* (n 91).

[96] Final Report of the Panel, *Guatemala* (n 91) para 201.

[97] Professor Ricardo Ramírez Hernández has served as a member of the WTO Appellate Body (2009–2017) and Mr Theodore R Posner is a partner at global law firm Weil, Gotshal & Manges LLP and a celebrated expert in international trade law and arbitration.

[98] Professor Kevin Banks, who served as Chair of the arbitral panel in this dispute, is an academic at Queen's University, Toronto.

[99] Final Report of the Panel, *Guatemala* (n 91 ) para 69.

[100] Final Report of the Panel, *Guatemala* (n 91).

[101] In accordance with Article 65 of the DR-CAFTA FTA, the burden of proof is on the complainant.

in respect of the evidence submitted by workers. In one instance, the panel noted that the statements of individuals alleging non-compliance with labour standards are 'almost verbatim' which 'raises important questions about how they were prepared and therefore whether they are reliable'. The panel continues:

One can reasonably infer from their similarities that the statements are not entirely the product of spontaneous declarations by the witnesses. *But because we do not know how the statements were created, we do not know the precise explanation for the common text.*[102]

A central tenet of the CA is to conceive of individuals as more than a 'means' to economic growth. Instead, economic freedom was privileged over other freedoms throughout the panel's reasoning. Various reports from international institutions, including the ILO, were submitted in support of the US claim that Guatemala had engaged in a prolonged course of *inaction* and, while the panel did not contest the findings set out in those reports, they were found to offer an account of the situation in Guatemala more generally. Effectively disregarding the reports, the panel limited their analysis to the subject-matter of the dispute as set out in the claims by the US in this dispute.[103] That the panel can disregard the evidence of workers, without offering those workers the opportunity to clarify their submissions, reveals a democratic deficit in the FTA dispute settlement mechanism and undermines the close relationship between trade and labour. It should be recalled that human agency plays a central role in Sen's theory of capabilities and justice, and the participatory aspect of the FTA dispute settlement mechanism was significantly weakened by the lack of meaningful engagement with different stakeholders. As a consequence, the voices of marginalized workers were silenced and their lived experiences disregarded, which undermines their potential to achieve lives that they value.

Extraordinarily, the purpose of the Article 16.2.1.(a) was *not* found to be protecting and promoting labour rights in the context of the FTA as the literal reading of the provision might suggest. Rather, the panel determined that the 'ends' of Chapter 16 are 'centered around ensuring fair conditions of competition within CAFTA-DR trade'.[104] Reframing labour rights in the language of 'fair conditions of competition' can be defended on the basis that the principle of non-discrimination in trade must be upheld. Guatemala's lower level of labour standards could serve as a competitive advantage and distort competition among the CAFTA-DR group. While concerns of social dumping are real,[105] the language used in the panel's report has the effect of shifting the focus away from social concerns (labour standards) towards economic goals (fair conditions of competition). However, to assert that a labour violation can take place in a manner that does *not* affect trade is nonsensical. Non-enforcement and violations of labour standards will always affect trade. Nevertheless, in prioritizing the trade qualifier of Article 16.2.1(a), the panel reinforced the notion that

[102] Final Report of the Panel, *Guatemala* (n 91) para 561 (emphasis added).
[103] Final Report of the Panel, *Guatemala* (n 91) para 514.
[104] Final Report of the Panel, *Guatemala* (n 91) para 506.
[105] For an account of the relationship between trade, labour standards, and social dumping, see Magdalena Bernaciak, 'Social Dumping: Political Catchphrase or Threat to Labour Standards' (2012) ETUI Working Paper 2012.06.

trade and labour standards can be separated. The trade-oriented approach of the panel was considered to be a 'fundamental flaw' of the proceedings since this matter 'was treated primarily as a trade dispute and handled like a WTO case. Trade considerations, not workers' rights, drove the dynamic of the Panel's deliberations and analysis'.[106] Engaging in the formalization of law, the panel has adopted a narrow economic interpretation of the matter, which is entirely detached from the social reality of workers in Guatemala. A consequence of formalization is to further perpetuate capability deprivations for workers across the maquila, agricultural, and services industries, and deepen pre-existing socio-economic inequalities. Failing to uphold the fundamental labour entitlements of workers in the Guatemalan context undermines the normative basis of sustainable development. The dispute illustrates the dangers of a trade-oriented analysis for labour standards and, while this is the first dispute of its kind, it raises important concerns about the normative status of labour standards in the context of trade. More specifically, it also draws into question the strength of labour provisions under FTAs with US representatives calling for the removal of the requirement that labour violations occur 'in a manner affecting trade' in future FTAs.[107]

## VI.  Concluding Thoughts: Challenges and Opportunities

Moving forward, this chapter concludes by offering some thoughts about how the international trade system can harness the discourse of capabilities to reimagine its purpose as a system to promote and enhance many freedoms, and not just economic freedom. To (re)imagine the transformative potential of an *equitable* multi-lateral trading system is to envisage a framework through which fairer conditions of work can be realized. In doing so, it should be recalled that 'law and laws do not exist as ends in themselves but for the welfare of society'.[108]

The first proposition relates to reframing existing multi-lateral rules in a manner that reflects the capabilities conception of development. While the multi-lateral trade agreements do not explicitly provide for the protection and promotion of labour standards, the General Exceptions of the GATT and General Agreement on Trade in Services (GATS) offer the potential for a rights-sensitive interpretation of WTO rules. Already, the Appellate Body of the WTO's Dispute Settlement Body has considered the relationship between trade, the environment, and sustainable development in a number of high-profile disputes relating to Article XX of the GATT.[109] Of interest to the trade–linkage debate is the extent to which the public

---

[106] International Labour Rights Forum, 'Wrong Turn for Workers' Rights' (n 88) 6.
[107] Bloomberg Law, 'US Labor Dispute Failure Prompts Calls for NAFTA Changes' *International Trade Daily Bulletin No 125* of 30 June 2017.
[108] Langille, 'Core Labour Rights' (n 17) 417.
[109] For an example of notable disputes, see *United States-Import Prohibitions of Certain Shrimp and Shrimp Products* Report of the Appellate Body WT/DS58/AB/R (12 October 1998); *United States: Standards for Reformulated and Conventional Gasoline* Report of the Appellate Body WT/DS2/AB/R (29 January 1996); *United States – Measures Concerning the Importation, Marketing and Sale of Tuna and Tuna Products* Report of the Appellate Body WT/DS381/AB/R (16 May 2012); *European*

morals exception under the GATT and GATS might create policy space for WTO Members to implement trade-restrictive measures in the name of protecting and promoting labour standards. From a capabilities perspective, the public morality exception raises two important normative questions: (i) does the public morals exception enable human freedom to be the 'ends' of a trade measure? And (ii) is the WTO the appropriate international arbitration setting to determine whether the interests and rights of other trading nations can be circumscribed on the grounds of public morality?

To date, the public morals exception under the GATT has been considered in only a handful of disputes.[110] Thomas Cottier cautiously advances the argument that the reasoning of the Appellate Body in relation to the public morals exception could provide space to establish closer connections between trade and labour standards.[111] Public morals are understood by the Appellate Body to mean 'standards of right and wrong conduct maintained by or on behalf of a community or nation',[112] although the content of these standards 'may vary in time and space, depending on a range of factors, including prevailing social, cultural, ethical, and religious values'.[113] Analysing the interpretive reasoning of the Appellate Body in the *EC–Seals* dispute, Cottier proposes that, in theory at least, trade measures can be justified on moral grounds including, for example, imposing an import ban on products originating from factories known to use child labour. This suggestion appeals to the capabilities perspective as it places human freedom as a means and end of the trade measure. However, the trade-oriented interpretive approach of the arbitral panel in the Guatemala dispute does not offer much hope for such an expansive reading of the public morals exception if such a case were to be brought before the DSB.

The second proposal for strengthening the trade–labour linkage is to make better use of existing mechanisms. As noted earlier in this chapter, the trade–labour linkage is more advanced in the case of FTAs where labour standards are increasingly framed in the context of sustainability. The infrastructure to promote agency and participation within these agreements already exists in the form of civil society mechanisms and DAGs. However, engaging non-state actors at the multi-lateral level has been a slow process.[114] Article V.2 of the Marrakech Agreement provides the legal basis for

---

*Communities—Measures Prohibiting the Importation and Marketing of Seal Products* Report of the Appellate Body WT/DS401/AB/R (22 May 2014).

[110] *United States—Measures Affecting the Cross-Border Supply of Gambling and Betting Services* Report of the Appellate Body DS/285/AB/R (7 April 2005); *China—Measures Affecting Trading Rights and Distribution Services for Certain Publications and Audiovisual Entertainment Products* Report of the Appellate Body WT/DS363/AB/R (21 December 2009); and *European Communities—Measures Prohibiting the Importation and Marketing of Seal Products* Report of the Appellate Body WT/DS401/AB/R (22 May 2014).

[111] Thomas Cottier, 'The Implications of *EC–Seal Products* for the Protection of Core Labour Standards in WTO Law' in Henner Gött (ed), *Labour Standards in International Economic Law* (Springer, 2018) 69–92.

[112] *United States—Measures Affecting the Cross-Border Supply of Gambling and Betting Services* Panel Report WT/DS285/R (10 November 2004) para 6.465.

[113] *United States—Measures Affecting the Cross-Border Supply of Gambling and Betting Services* (n 112) para 6.461.

[114] The Appellate Body has welcomed amicus curiae briefs in relation to the public interest clauses but there are considerable constraints on non-government actors.

'effective cooperation' between the WTO and other non-government organizations 'concerned with matters related to those of the WTO'.[115] Cooperation with NGOs is seen as a way to increase the transparency of the WTO although civil society is not directly involved in the work of the WTO or its meetings.[116] In the Guatemala dispute, amicus curiae briefs were submitted from a number of non-governmental organizations, which demonstrates a progressive step forward in recognizing the importance of agency, dialogue, and participation. Even though the legal effects of other social norms like sustainable development expressed in FTAs may lack definitional clarity, these clauses are 'not simply a matter of discretionary foreign policy'.[117] While the limitations of the civil society mechanisms and DAGs have been acknowledged, this chapter does not propose that labour provisions in FTAs should be abandoned. Rather, further research should be carried out into the potential for the alternative functions of labour provisions, such as national capacity-building and the strengthening of dialogue mechanisms to promote compliance.[118]

The third proposal for enhancing freedoms relates to the gendered dimension of trade and labour. Martha C Nussbaum's work has been extremely influential in highlighting the intersectionality between capabilities, trade, labour, and gender. For decades, women have been found to provide a disproportionate share of unpaid work, and in the early-mid 1990s, processes of economic globalization were expected to restructure the means of production in a way that resulted in the *feminization* of the labour market.[119] An increase in the number of women in the formal workplace should result in economic growth and expand their capabilities.[120] However, women have not enjoyed the expected benefits of economic restructuring. Women are less likely to work in formal employment, bear a disproportionate responsibility to do unpaid work, and are less likely to be represented in unions.[121] The feminization of labour did not yield the expected benefits for women globally and, instead, we have witnessed the feminization of poverty. But low income is not the sole factor for poverty, defined by Sen as 'capability deprivation'. Recognizing the multi-faceted nature of poverty and identifying the intersections of capability deprivations is key

---

[115] Marrakech Agreement Establishing the World Trade Organization, 15 April 1994, 1867 UNTS 154, 33 ILM 1144 (1994).

[116] Article V.2 Marrakech Agreement was clarified in the mandate (WT/L/162): 'Guidelines for Arrangements on Relations with Non-Governmental Organisations' WTO Decision Adopted by the General Council on 18 July 1996.

[117] Lorand Bartels, 'Human Rights and Sustainable Development Obligations in EU Free Trade Agreements' (2012) *University of Cambridge Legal Studies Research Paper Series* No 24/2012, 17.

[118] For an excellent account of alternative functions of labour provisions, see Ebert, 'Labour Provisions in EU Trade Agreements' (n 74) 407–33.

[119] Judy Fudge defined the feminization of labour as a 'twofold process' consisting of 'the dramatic increase in both the labour market participation of women and in forms of work which are traditionally associated with women'. See Judy Fudge, 'Reconceiving Employment Standards Legislation: Labour Law's Little Sister and the Feminization of Labour' (1991) 7 *Journal of Law and Social Policy* 73, 73–89.

[120] Stephan Klasen and Francesca Lamanna, 'The Impact of Gender Inequality in Education and Employment on Economic Growth: New Evidence For a Panel of Countries' (2009) 15(3) *Feminist Economics* 91, 91–132.

[121] UN Women, 'Facts and Figures: Economic Empowerment' (July 2017) http://www.unwomen.org/en/what-we-do/economic-empowerment/facts-and-figures#notes.

to understanding the challenges facing women and other vulnerable groups in the modern workforce.[122] More generally, the precariousness of work for both men and women—in part, a consequence of the 'gig' economy[123] and the casualization of labour—coupled with rising inequality has undermined social cohesion through the creation of 'fissures and tensions in the social fabric'.[124] At the 2017 Buenos Aires Ministerial Conference, the WTO launched the first Joint Declaration on Trade and Women's Economic Empowerment which sets out modest objectives to improve women's participation in the economy. However, it is suggested that more detailed empirical work is needed to identify the barriers that limit women's participation in the economy so as to evaluate the ways in which the economic empowerment can enhance other capabilities.

The final thought relates to the SDGs and proposes that greater clarification is needed in order to promote labour standards as part of an 'equitable' and fair multi-lateral trading system. Labour and trade, and their interrelationship, are a central feature of sustainability. However, while there is high-level policy support for the SDGs, the goals are framed in ambiguous and vague language providing little substantive detail as to how sustainability can be achieved. The 2030 Agenda is further weakened by the failure to articulate a hierarchy of the SDGs and I argue that the goals should be organized around SDG 17, which sets out targets for inter-institutional cooperation for the achievement of sustainable development. More specifically, SDG17.14 identifies the systemic issue of 'ensuring policy coherence for sustainable development'. However, there is no further elaboration on what 'policy coherence for sustainable development' (PCSD) means in the context of the SDGs nor is there any finite means for measuring and monitoring the implementation of this target. In failing to clarify the meaning of PCSD there is a danger that 'it is dropped altogether, and referred to only as a vague commitment in the preamble to the SDGs'.[125] In spite of its conceptual vagaries, the 2030 Agenda has cemented the trade–labour linkage in the framework of sustainability and this conceptual frame is worthy of deeper exploration.

---

[122] Sakiko Fukuda-Parr, 'What does Feminization of Poverty Mean? It Isn't Just Lack of Income' (1999) 5(2) *Feminist Economics* 99, 99–103.

[123] For an overview of the implications of the gig economy on labour law governance see Valerio de Stefano, 'The Rise of the "Just-in-Time" Workforce: On-Demand Work, Crowdwork, and Labour Protection in the "Gig-Economy"' (2016) 37 *Comparative Labor Law Journal & Policy Journal* 471, 471–504.

[124] Fudge, 'Labour Rights and Human Rights' (n 30) 608.

[125] OECD, 'Policy Coherence for Development in the SDG Framework: Shaping Targets and Monitoring Progress' (2015) http://www.oecd.org/development/pcd/Note%20on%20Shaping%20Targets.pdf.

# 15

# Freedom in Work and the Capability Approach

## Towards a Politics of Freedoms for Labour?

*Robert Salais*

Let us transport ourselves to a world where labour as a social practice has been re-configured along the lines of a capability approach. In other words, a world in which labour has been transformed by implementing a politics of freedoms in line with the one suggested by Amartya Sen in his works, in particular in the opening sentence of *Development as Freedom*:[1] 'Development should be grasped as a process of expanding the real freedoms enjoyed by individuals'. Freedoms become the ultimate ends of development and, in the same process, the primary means to achieve those ends. What does it mean with regard to labour? Amartya Sen, except for some occasional insights, has not tried to answer to that 'Herculean' question. One can easily understand why. It is nevertheless vital to grasp the implication of such a politics of freedoms for the transformation of labour, or at least to begin to debate on possible lines of reflection. For how can economic development centred on the progress of real freedoms be implemented without including labour? It cannot be implemented without having, as its core concern, capabilities for work, and more widely for labour, its responsibilities in economy, society, and politics, individual and collective, because all these features condition any possible development.

Far from being remote in an idealized world, some empirical trends born (or the awareness of which has grown) during these last years of global crisis illustrate the relevance of this issue of a politics of freedoms for labour. I will limit myself to focusing on two trends of the workplace. First, on sexual and, more broadly, moral harassment, which points to the need to be truly freed *from* such attacks against the freedom and dignity of the person.[2] Secondly, on the rising contradiction between asking workers to engage their capabilities as persons in the firm while treating them as pure factors of production, reduced to numbers and to quantitative performance indicators. This trend points to the freedom *to* engage one's being and humanity in work. These freedoms in work *from* and *to*, in my view, belong to a research agenda

---

[1] Amartya Sen, *Development as Freedom* (Oxford University Press, 1999).
[2] The importance of which has been underlined by Martha C Nussbaum during the presentation of my contribution in the workshop at the origin of this book.

The Capability Approach to Labour Law. Edited by Brian Langille. Chapter 15 © Robert Salais 2019. Published 2019 by Oxford University Press.

built along the lines of a capability approach. They also belong to a political agenda, intuited by the UN Universal Declaration of Human Rights since 1948, which should be actualized.[3]

Section I explores what 'capability' means in comparison to the misunderstanding of European authorities. Section II analyses moral harassment and new forms of work organizations as illustration of freedom in work. Section III addresses the issue of institutionalizing freedom in work. The conclusion emphasizes the political relevance of such institution.

The material on which I rely for this chapter is from the results of a series of research programmes funded by the European Commission from 2003 to 2010,[4] centred on the capability approach (CA),[5] which I coordinated as head of the IHDES[6] French Research Centre. Our methodology in these programmes was not, strictly speaking, applying a theory about capability. This aim would have been nonsense and has never been the purpose of Amartya Sen (who leaves explicitly open his theoretical frame). We carefully and collectively read a series of research papers and books written by Amartya Sen, Martha C Nussbaum, and others. Our perspective was to look for promising assumptions or theoretical developments in works related to capability that could offer lines of research for problems we encounter in European policies and institutions. The end goal of this approach was to transform these problems into theoretical issues and, ultimately, to make propositions to operationalize the capability approach in Europe. In brief, we did not start from academic debates to clear points that will never be totally clarified, but from practical issues that could lead to possible theoretical innovations in the line of Amartya Sen's thought.

## I. Preliminaries: What Is and What Is Not Capability?

In a paper on 'Providing security in a flexible economy' I presented in 1997 at Mondorf-les-Bains, Luxemburg,[7] promoting 'capability' would have meant

---

[3] Rightly underlined by Martha C Nussbaum, 'Political Liberalism and Respect: A Response to Linda Barclay' (2003) 4(2) *Sats-Nordic Journal of Philosophy* 25, 25–44.

[4] Mainly EUROCAP and CAPRIGHT programmes.

[5] The terrain, empirical and political, was European social and employment policies. See, for the capability approach applied to employment and social domains: Robert Salais, 'The Contours of a Pragmatic Theory of "Situated" Institutions and Its Economic Relevance' (English revised version of Robert Salais, 1998) https://hal.archives-ouvertes.fr/halshs-00430543); Robert Salais and Robert Villeneuve (eds), *Europe and the Politics of Capabilities* (Cambridge University Press, 2004); Jean De Munck, and Bénédicte Zimmermann (eds), *La liberté au prisme des capacités. Amartya Sen au-delà du libéralisme* (Editions de l'EHESS, Raisons pratiques 18, 2008); Jean-Michel Bonvin, and Nicolas Farvaque, *Amartya Sen, Une politique de la liberté* (Michallon, 2008); Ralf Rogowski, , Robert Salais, and Noel Whiteside (eds), *Transforming European Employment Policy: Labour Market Transitions and the Promotion of Capability* (Edward Elgar Publishing, 2011); Bénédicte Zimmermann, *Ce que travailler veut dire. Une sociologie des capacités et des parcours professionnels* (Economica, 2011).

[6] 'Institutions and Historical Dynamics of the Economy and the Society'.

[7] The European Employment Strategy was officially launched in November 1997 at Mondorf-les-Bains (Luxemburg) at an event, involving both policy-makers and researchers, under the Presidency of Jean-Claude Juncker, the Prime Minister of Luxemburg at the time. My paper, I guess, was the first one sketching to Eurocrats what could be a capability approach for a European Employment Strategy. See, for a slightly different version Robert Salais, , 2002, 'Security in a flexible economy. Towards a third age

employment policies and management devoted to enlarging the capabilities of workers to find good jobs. The idea, then, was that public employment policies could make progress in that direction by improving qualifications, developing real and serious manpower reconversion plans, long term training, and so on. Firms' management should pay attention to defining jobs as capacitating their employees—that is, offering more autonomy, better training, enlarged job experiences, promotion plans, and so on. Flexibility should be in priority internal to the firm; when external, workers arriving on the labour market could find a wider and better set of job offers. All in all, I tried to demonstrate that more security (which we later label as 'active security') could favour flexibility, not the reverse. It would have been a mix of freedom of choice, collective negotiation, and European legislation.[8]

However, it was not the line taken by the European Commission since then.

## A. What capability is not: The European misunderstanding

In the CA research field, a current mistake being made is in identifying capability with productivity. The more you are capable, the more you will be productive and employable on the labour market. After years of not being interested in the capability approach and of refusing to mention the word, the only use of the theory that the European Commission is making is to connect capability and productivity. Despite several programmes, books, special issues of international review, individual papers, seminars, and presentations, understanding of the CA has not permeated the invisible walls surrounding European authorities. Unfortunately, as I demonstrated in my book on the history of Europe,[9] this lack of uptake is becoming the normal state of Europe today. Its authorities adapt duly established concepts as a pretence for the political ideas they want to publicize. They develop a mostly neoliberal conception of work and of the labour market. This conception is very simple and can be summed up by the value it gives to the individual as either a 'one' or a 'zero'. If you have a job, whatever it is (regardless of quality or legal and social protection), you count as a 'one'. If you have no job at all, you are a 'zero'. In terms of politics, the only political purpose—by any possible means including systems of penalties and incentives, deregulating the labour market, reforming law, and social protection—is to push you to some job, whatever it is and as fast as possible, to change you from a 'zero' to a 'one'. It is called the politics of employability, around which law and social reforms are thought to be reformed. Even the word of politics is mistaken. It is not

in relations between work and social protection' in Hedva Sarfati and Giuliano Bonoli (eds), *Labour Markets and Social Protection Reforms in International Perspective: Parallel or Converging Tracks* (Ashgate, 2002) 437–50.

[8] I much later discovered that the core lines of this strategy had already been debated and confirmed within a US–EU Working Group and a Symposium held in Washington DC in May 1997, 'Employment Policy and the Promotion of Employability'. Promoting employability meant for the Commission that economic hazards should be entirely supported by employed workers who have to adjust their employment demand and to be perfectly mobile on the labour market.

[9] Robert Salais, *Le viol d'Europe. Enquête sur la disparition d'une idée* (Presses Universitaires de France, 2013).

politics, but about management of the social dimension. There is no place for the concepts (and for the underlying realities) of capability, labour, and politics. The only thing they keep is the valuation of people, from which one can deduce how to manage them at the different levels and spheres. And this valuation is reduced to the simplest one.

However, the issue of how to value people is a fundamental one. We will start by addressing this issue. Then we will discuss the CA principle of justice and what one can call the 'elementary matrix of the capability approach'.

## B. What is capability? The valuation issue

The valuation problem of people is at the core of the capability approach. It is one of the richest conceptions one can find in the literature. From it, one can make explicit what concepts and practices of labour and of politics with regard to labour are at work, sometimes implicitly, in the CA.

The valuation problem is addressed by Amartya Sen in his concept of 'Informational Basis of Judgment in Justice' (IBJJ). I quote:

The informational basis of judgment in justice identifies the information on which the judgment is directly dependent – and no less important – asserts that the truth or falsehood of any other type of information cannot *directly* influence the correctness of the judgment. The informational basis of judgment in justice thus determines the factual territory over which considerations of justice would *directly* apply.[10]

Establishing an informational basis is to find the correct and fair value one should attribute to a person in relation to considerations of justice when considering her situation with regard to the collective issue to solve. Such a basis serves both to form and to implement any collective decision that has an impact on the life and work of that person. Such decision should, as far as possible, respects a principle of justice. I have no place here to enter the huge literature about social justice. But Amartya Sen has an original position in the literature that necessitates some comments.

## C. The CA conception of justice

The CA principle of justice taken as reference for judgment is to provide people, as they are and where they are, *with real freedoms to lead the life (and work, as we have added with our research) that they value.* Each word here deserves comments.

First, the judgment should be *substantial*, not just relative through the ranking of people. The standard literature is mostly concerned with ranking people along a given scale. For Sen, the right question is a dynamic, procedural one, in which the ethical issue is how to allow people, each individually, to accomplish the basic objectives he/she assigns to her life (and work) and, more precisely, to make progress

---

[10] Amartya Sen, 'Justice: Means versus Freedom' (1990) 19(2) *Philosophy and Public Affairs* 111, 111–21, 111 (emphasis by Sen).

towards such accomplishment.[11] So the judgment of justice should result in quantitative and qualitative data on each person. It should measure her situation, from where she starts, and whether she makes progress or not over time.

Secondly, and no less important, freedom is at the core of the CA. 'Allowing' does not at all mean 'providing' as in the classical welfare State model, which only considers negative freedoms (for instance, freedom from want as for Beveridge or Roosevelt). In the CA, people are considered to need the freedom of choose or not to choose. They take or not what is available in resources or procedures offered by political or organizational schemes. However, for Amartya Sen and even more for Martha C Nussbaum, some capabilities must be ensured by the State (those said to be intrinsic by Sen, or those included in a list of basic capabilities by Nussbaum). These intrinsic or basic capabilities lead to a gradation of personal responsibility that depends on the level and type of capabilities to which each person has access. In contrast, for the standard liberals, people are considered as to be free a priori; it is up to them to take or not. They are totally responsible for their own choices.

Thirdly, for Sen, freedom is not an *a priori* axiom. It is an objective to be aimed at by all collective decisions that influence the lives and work of people. Freedoms should be *effective* freedoms, not only formal. Such objective cannot be achieved, of course, but should always be present at the horizon of collective decisions. Effective freedom means that, when undertaking an action, a functioning, or struggling for a general cause (belonging to her agency), a person should ideally have the capability to do so. Capability, here (see part II), also means having the power to achieve what we undertake, if we freely engage in such objectives. Again, it is a horizon, a moving target, a potentiality that motivates the person more than reality. Public policies, in particular, should have as one of their objectives to extend the level of capability and the extent of effective freedom for each person in order to reduce inequalities of capabilities. This leads to the fourth point.

Fourthly, one of the most beautiful concepts I have ever come across is the one of 'factual territory' that one finds in the definition of the informational basis of judgment of justice. Factual territory delineates the set of information (qualitative and quantitative) required to make a correct and fair evaluation of the capabilities of a person (their degree and nature). This set of information has to be collected or, if not yet existing, produced by the creation of statistics and inquiries. In the views elaborated in the research leading up to this book, there was a sense that Sen has not truly grasped in his works the extreme—empirical and ethical—ambition of the concept of factual territory. Being fair requires that the data used should be produced through a grid that operationalizes the corresponding principle of justice, that is, to build questions able to elicit the capabilities of those being inquired. Being correct requires that the data produced truly tells us what we intend to measure, which means that, in the case of inquiry, persons understand what is at stake and can correctly answer, or, in case of pre-existing administrative data, that data were built

---

[11] And then, how to allow for the readjustment, revisions, developing of more ambitious expectations, and so on.

along categories close to the capability approach. Both requirements, especially the second one, are demanding as well as motivating. See Table 1 for what one can call the 'elementary capability matrix', sketching the information that any IBJJ should include if it claims to correct and fair.[12]

Table 1  The Elementary Capability Matrix

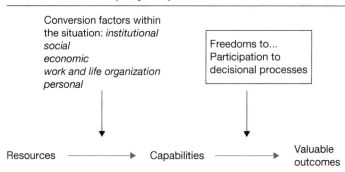

No person can be considered as responsible of his/her future without effective freedome of choice and without being put in a position to achieve a valuable outcome

The more capabilities a person has, the more responsible can she be considered; idem, the less....., the less

## II.  The CA, Freedom in Work, Moral Harassment, and New Forms of Work Organization in Firms

To trace the track that leads to capabilities as applied to work, it is worth starting from the 1948 UN Universal Declaration of Human Rights.

In Article 23.1, the 1948 UN Declaration states that 'everyone has the right to work, to free choice of employment, to just and favourable conditions of work and to protection against unemployment'.[13] And in Article 1, it claims that 'all human beings are born free and equal in terms of dignity and rights'. In so doing,

---

[12]  Borrowed from Jean-Michel Bonvin and Nicolas Farvaque *Amartya Sen, Une politique de la liberté* (Michallon, 2008).

[13]  It is cruel to compare this 1948 UN article with the similar one of the 2001 Charter of Fundamental Rights of the European Union (Official Journal of the European Union, 26 October 2012 (2012/C 326/ 02)). The 'right to work' is replaced by the 'right to engage in work'. Article II.15 of the Charter states:

1. Everyone has the right to engage in work and to pursue a freely chosen or accepted occupation.
2. Every citizen of the Union has the freedom to seek employment, to work, to exercise the right of establishment and to provide services in any Member State.

it paraphrases the famous Article 1 of the 1789 French Declaration of Human and Civic Rights, although with some signifying modifications, as we will see below.

Often, one hears talk of the post-Second World War social reforms as the recognition of the concept of 'freedom from', or negative freedom, that introduces a logic of protection against poverty and insecurity of life, or against work uncertainties like unemployment, professional maladies, or accidents. In other terms, following Jean De Munck,[14] a 'resources' approach that is intended to compensate for these hazards by social provision (through monetary allocations and social services, in whatever diverse form they exist in different countries). One considers the right to work mostly in relation with full employment as the core objective of macroeconomic policies and with the creation of efficient labour markets. I would not deny these key points.

But there are, in Article 23.1, two meaningful words, namely 'free' and 'just'. Allusion is made, too, to the concrete situation where work is delivered, that is, 'the conditions of work'. They all sound like prescience of the capability approach, and in particular of its claim for a just and effective access to 'freedoms to'. The CA closely links freedom and justice; such linkage should be verified in the situations of life and work ('the conditions of work'). If not, remedies should be sought for by acting, in some way or another, on the 'focal features' of the situations under review—the features that precisely have an impact, positive or negative, on the capabilities of the person.

The UN Declaration of Rights suggests us to be circumspect with regard to strict opposition between political liberalism and comprehensive liberalism.[15] The former supposedly leaves choice to people while the latter is inclined to favour obligatory measures coming from the state. The UN Declaration takes a pragmatic position; it depends of the issue. One cannot imagine law or social protection as voluntary choices, at least for the most basic issues like unemployment. 'Free choice of employment' is, on its own, evident. The phrase 'just and favourable conditions of work' appears susceptible to a variety of treatments, from free bargaining at several levels, individual or collective, to legal treatments, with possible mixed or multi-level arrangements.[16] Harassment, whatever its forms, requires legal obligation.

While (or because) the capability approach has a universal dimension, its concretization in social reality, policies, and law should be sought at the politically levels that the community at stake recognizes as relevant and as its own. In what follows, I have taken a mostly French perspective.

---

[14] Jean De Munck, 'Qu'est-ce qu'une capacité?' in Jean De Munck and Bénédicte Zimmermann (eds), *La liberté au prisme des capacités. Amartya Sen au-delà du libéralisme* (Editions de l'EHESS, Raisons pratiques 18, 2008) 21–49.

[15] See the answer of Martha C Nussbaum to Linda Barclay in Nussbaum, 'Political Liberalism and Respect' (n 3) 25.

[16] For instance, though criticizing the priority given to functioning at the expense of capability, Rutger Claassen considers that entitlements for citizens 'are not only created by political authorities, by citizens themselves in the *exercise* of their autonomy ... depending for instance "on the spontaneous processes of economic life"'. See Rutger Claassen, 'The Place of Autonomy in a Capability Theory of Justice' https://soc.kuleuven.be/web/files/11/72/W11-177.pdf.

## A. Work and moral harassment

From 2008 to 2010, a series of suicides among the France Telecom (FT) personnel happened that alarmed the public and the trade unions.[17] These suicides happened during the process of privatization of this state monopoly that led to the multi-national corporation, 'Orange'. In 2016, following a union's complaint against Orange for moral harassment, the prosecutor[18] decided to sue in justice, not only the director and his team of the ex-France Telecom, but also the firm, Orange, as a legal moral personality. The trial process was scheduled for the end of 2018. It will be the first important trial following the passing of a French law on moral harassment, and will be the first test of this law.[19]

The new FT director, chosen by the state, was eager to reduce the number of employees under public statute (civil servants). Its target was get rid of 22,000 people in three years (20% of the staff). It is impossible to fire public employees; the only way for the director to reduce the numbers of workers was to obtain voluntary departures. As the Head Director Didier Lombard elegantly said in an FT executives' meeting in 2006: 'That will be a little bit more dirigist than in the past … I will obtain [these departures] whatever the method, through the window or through the door'. For the prosecutor, at France Telecom in these years, harassment had become a management method. Executives[20] were trained to discourage their staff; their bonuses depended on their performance in this matter. Each new departure was a promise for an extra bonus at the end of the year. A management school, specially created in 2005 for that purpose, trained them 'to make people move' by 'putting on them any conceivable pressure'. More than 4000 executives were following the curriculum each year. Any tactic was available for their use. To assign mothers to work-posts two hours away from their home; to offer executives responsibilities neatly inferior to their preceding ones; to 'forget' employees during a relocation of their service; to leave them during weeks on a platform with neither table nor chair, far removed from their colleagues; to send, every Friday evening, an e-mail praising the merits of a post in some local administration or the possibility of obtaining subsidies to become a beekeeper,[21] and so on.

The interesting thing here is that French law had already ruled on the case of moral harassment on 12 January 2002 (Art. L 1152-1 of the Labour Code), before the case of sexual harassment (6 August 2012, Art. 222-33 of the Penal Code).[22] Moral harassment has been defined by the 2002 Law with regard to salaried workers as 'repeated actions having as object or effect a degradation of her work conditions susceptible to violate her rights and her dignity, to alter her physical or mental health or to compromise her professional future'.[23] As a consequence,

---

[17] There were dozens of suicides—at least 60 (the precise number being difficult to establish).
[18] 'Procureur' in French.       [19] Information from *Le Monde* (7 July 2016).
[20] 'Cadres' in French.       [21] All these examples are authentic. See *Le Monde* (7 July 2016).
[22] In the 2012 law, sexual harassment is defined as 'to repeatedly impose on a person remarks or behaviors with sexual connotation that either harm her dignity by their degrading or humiliating characteristics, or create against her an intimidating, hostile or abusing situation'.
[23] Article 1152-1 of the Labour Code.

'any rupture of the labor contract intervening in disregard of the dispositions of Articles L. 1152 1 and L. 1152 2 [of Labour Code], any opposite disposition or act is considered as null', (Art. L. 1152 3). Later, a National Collective Agreement (26 March 2010) between employers and unions defines moral harassment as existing 'when one or several salaried workers are the object of abuses, repeated and deliberate threats and/or humiliations in circumstances linked to work, either in workplaces or in situations linked to work'. It focused less on effects than on actions aiming at demoralizing workers up to the point to provoke depression, incapacity to work, and, possibly, suicide.

It is likely that the FT directors knew the 2002 Law on moral harassment forbade any rupture of contract based on moral harassment, but decided to play the scenario of pushing workers to quit the firm by themselves. The Orange strategy of defence will likely be to plead that France Telecom had solid reasons for managing its personnel as it did: competition, problems of efficiency, and the need for restructuring a decrepit public administration. One of the judicial difficulties will be to materially prove the link between these 'supposed' moral harassments and suicides.

It is also worth noting that the main argument of the French laws is about dignity of the person, and not about her freedom, and conforms to the UN 1948 Declaration that puts the main emphasis on dignity. However, the UN 1948 Declaration makes a subtle variation of the Article 1 of the 1789 French Declaration of Human and Civic Rights: 'Men are born and *remain* free and equal in rights'. Notwithstanding the replacement of 'men' by 'human beings', in order not to forget women, the UN Declaration forgets the key precision that not only are human beings born free and equal in rights, but should also *remain* in those same conditions through life and history. I am tempted to say that in 'remain' one finds an anticipation of the problem of how to ensure, materially and institutionally, the effectiveness of equal access to rights, which is not foreign to the CA programme. So the open question, some answer to which could come during the FT trial, is the following one: is relying upon dignity as a basic value, instead of freedom, a failure of the French law on harassment, fundamentally and operationally? This question is legitimate. For, in practice all witnesses are examples of losses of freedom in work and one is not facing relations between individuals, but a management based on 'active' and rational denial of such freedom.

## B. Introducing freedom in work into new forms of work organization

Contemporary capitalism, at least in developed countries, has dramatically transformed the standard organization of work. Inadvertently, it has put on the public scene the concept of 'freedom in work'.

In brief, contemporary capitalism tries to mobilize, in favour of its interests and by its own way, the aspirations of workers to freedom, autonomy, and initiative. We are no longer in the realm of pure prescription by hierarchical vertical lines of the elementary tasks to be executed at each work-post. Under dire control, of course, the responsibility of determining what to do has been largely transferred to the levels of the individual. Operators, technicians, engineers, and executives are now, in large firms, submitted to such shifting.

There is no benevolence here, only necessity. In an economic universe of uncertainties, of reactivity, of technical complexities of products and services, and of long worldwide chains of value, it has become inefficient to detail and prescribe in advance and from the top what tasks to do, in what order, and by whom. For instance, organizations that must adjust their products to the desires of their clients, relative to quantity and quality, require labour flexibility that relies upon the capacity of the collective to adapt itself in time. Clients, even markets themselves, penetrate into the enterprise. So the organization must leave to the worker and his collective a space of freedom to decide and to act by himself as the only way to find, among the surrounding uncertainties, the right solution. Workers must have the capability to do so (competencies plus right exercise of their freedom) or, at least, are supposed to have it. The control of the use of this freedom to act is made by an ex post monitoring through indicators of performance. And the performance level to be achieved is already decided with neither the workers' nor trade unions' participation. In practice, such monitoring leads to the denial by the firm of the capability mobilized by the worker. Freedom and capability to act are trapped into a severe contradiction, being at the same time required, mobilized, and denied.

Such combination, to be clarified and understood by social actors, requires the intervention of the capability approach. There are many obstacles to overcome for the awareness of this issue (section 1, below). To introduce work in a CA approach, one must remember some of the CA's technicalities (section 2). And one must ask if work is an object of value or an instrument only for people (section 3).

## 1. Some obstacles for awareness of freedom in work

It is controversial, first. It smells of the neoliberal to many left-wing people, social organizations, and trade unions who identify freedom with employers' power and refined exploitation. When considering the new forms of organization we mentioned before, they only see the negative, black side of 'freedom'. Not the least, I would say again, because the way it is implanted is the monitoring of work by performance indicators. It pushes work intensity and its consequences in terms of physical and mental health always further. But there is also a potentially positive—although hidden—side, to be pushed in full light: the exercise by workers of their freedoms and of denied capabilities. But behind the façade of objective evaluation by performance indicators, freedoms to act, to choose, and other ones are manipulated. Workers are *obliged to mobilize their freedoms* (a dire contradiction in the course of work, which is at the root of new professional diseases, even suicides), the most often with no, or perverse, rewards.

Secondly, such denial of freedom in work is too often considered as a minor point within an ocean of capitalist turpitudes. This downplaying is not the case. Work is a human activity at the basis of personal accomplishment and of the utopia of collective emancipation. The new methods of management create an aggregation of quantitative performances measures that, in the same process, goes up and down between the bottom (the work done by individual workers) and the top (financial return). In this process, work as activity disappears from the view, plays no 'official' role in the functioning of the firm, and is replaced by pure numbers.

Thirdly, the individual versus collective problem is a standard critique made against Sen's CA; the approach would be individualistic. One can answer that: 1. Sen does not consider the neoclassical opportunistic individual, but the person embedded into a situation, socially, and historically built; 2. As Jean De Munck suggests,[24] capabilities, as they are related to the focal features of social situations, institutional arrangements included, have a collective, even multi-levelled (from the family, the territory, the enterprise, the branch, the national, and the global) dimension. Much depends on these multi-level features as to whether they are favourable or hostile to the deployment of capabilities.

Fourthly, last but not least, the individual versus collective issue points to the conceptions of labour law at national and international levels (especially the European one).[25] The French architecture of labour law, for instance, articulates the individual work contract and collective conventions at the level of the branch or at national level.[26] At its basis is the recognition by law of the principle of subordination as the foundation of a work relationship. Employees and Representatives accept the legitimacy of the power of the employer, and draw collective rights by the fact of their acceptance of subordination on wage and on some work conditions negotiation with regard to strikes, hours worked by week or year, and so on. These regulations apply to work contracts; the negotiators are mostly trade unions, or they are decided at the State level. Such architecture remains asymmetric as it is formulated in terms of inequality of power and its acceptance, which in my view weakens the strength of the collective (and the individual) rights.

## 2. Remembering some technicalities of the capability approach[27]

One starts from the two main critiques Sen has addressed to Rawls. Inequalities to be corrected are, for Rawls, inequalities with regard to the means constituted by the initial endowments in primary goods. What remains—the realization of individuals' life projects—are only the responsibility of the individuals and of their use of rationality. To this point, Sen answers that: 1. Persons having at their disposal equal means

---

[24] De Munck, 'Qu'est-ce qu'une capacité?' (n 14) 30.

[25] See, for a comparison between France, Germany, and Great Britain during the interwar period, Robert Salais, , 2011, 'Labour-Related Conventions and Configurations of Meaning: France, Germany and Great-Britain prior to the Second World War' in Rainer Diaz-Bone and Robert Salais (eds), 'Conventions and Institutions from a Historical Perspective' (2011) 36(4) *Historical Social Research* 218, 218–47.

[26] See Claude Didry, *Naissance de la convention collective. Débats juridiques et luttes sociales en France au début du XX e siècle* (Éditions de l'EHESS, 2002).

[27] For an extensive presentation of this issue, see Sabina Alkire, 'The Capability Approach as Development Paradigm?' Material for the training session preceding the 3rd international conference on the capability approach (Pavia, 7 September 2003) https://www.researchgate.net/publication/228832403_The_Capability_Approach.

can remain unequal with regard to their possibilities to convert means into valuable outcomes for them, owing to the very diverse life (and work) conditions they face; and 2. Some goods have an intrinsic value in themselves, independent from individual preferences and evaluations. These preferences can be biased by the impact of their life conditions, current and past—in particular what Sen calls 'entrenched deprivation' for the poor. So whatever their preferences, equal access, for all people, should be ensured to these intrinsic goods. The list of intrinsic goods is a priori incomplete and open; it depends of the community and its values, and has historical and social dimensions. These goods do not fall within a particular doctrine. They can be utilitarian (being happy), liberal (acting freely), Rawlsian (having self-respect), or from the order of necessities (Adam Smith). With regard to our concern, Sen never mentions work as an intrinsic good. However, nothing in his formalization impedes work from being considered by part of the people at least as an 'object-of-value' for them, which means that when evaluating their situation with regard to their capabilities, the value they accord to work has to be taken into account.

The CA approach has basically a pragmatic component (in the sense of the pragmatists like Pierce, Dewey, and others) that should not be forgotten. The CA axiomatically defines the life course of a person (her *living*) as a set of elementary *functionings*, themselves composed of *doings* and *beings*. Such functionings are multiple; they are relative to access, not only to intrinsic goods, but also to goods freely chosen by the person. Terms ending with 'ing' indicate that Sen has in view, not only the *state* of the person, but also the *process of action and* even *of realization* in which she is engaged at a moment and a given situation. People select the functionings composing the life they value and want to accomplish.

The last complexity, as observed by Nicolas Farvaque[28] is with regard to the fact that the consideration of capabilities of the person has to be made at two levels: what chosen functionings can be considered *of objects of value?* And what is the *weight* attributed to each by the person?

### 3. *Work activity: object of value or instrument?*

Most of the literature on work treats work activity as a disutility (neoclassical economics) or, which is more or less the same, as purely instrumental (Jürgen Habermas, for instance, see the critics of Axel Honneth).[29] Work is a means to gaining something else (wage especially); it does not have its own value for the person. Such a position is not tenable in a capability approach. Claiming effective freedom in work—which would have, as a consequence, to search for new conceptions of work organization—implies that work is an object of value for people. The weighing of

---

[28] Nicolas Farvaque, 'Faire surgir des faits utilisables' in Jean De Munck and Bénédicte Zimmermann (eds), *La liberté au prisme des capacités. Amartya Sen au-delà du libéralisme* (Editions de l'EHESS, Raisons pratiques 18, 2008) 51–80.

[29] Axel Honneth, 'Travail et agir instrumental. A propos des problèmes catégoriels d'une théorie critique de la société' (French translation 2007) in (1980) 2(18) *Travailler* 17, 17–58), published originally in German in Axel Honneth and Urs Jaeggi (eds), *Arbeit, Handlung, Normativität, Theorien des Historischen Materialismus* (Suhrkamp, 1980) 285–333.

work activity among the objects to which people accord value may vary as far as it is linked to individual characteristics. It is possible that some people attribute a zero weight to work activity.

Converting human rights into real and valuable outcomes for people has opened a wide discussion in the field on the concept 'reason to value'.[30] These are not any whim or desire of the person, but those that the community to which the person belongs considers of value, by mutual agreement or convention. Amartya Sen quotes, for instance, self-esteem, participating in the community, being fairly treated, having good housing, and so on. Our position is to add work activity to the list. As Hannah Arendt concludes in another domain (but the quotation can be transposed to freedom in work) one can consider it as the 'power that men have to begin something new starting from their own resources, something that cannot be explained in terms of reactions to the environment and events'.[31]

There remains a hard question: how to subsume the dire contradiction we spoke of before between freedom and the constraint to use it towards objectives prefixed by top management? And, not the least in French case, the contradiction between freedom in work and the principle of subordination?

At this step of our reasoning, freedom in work when deployed should reveal several facets: at least mutual respect[32] in case of disagreement, autonomy, initiative, engagement, responsibility, and aptitude to coordinate with others. In a CA approach, there are more or less explicit quasi-Aristotelian principles guiding the search for a good life. A person is motivated by her awareness to make progress towards self-accomplishment (principle of perfection); and such progress is the outcome of a learning process that could have individual and collective dimensions (principle of learning). Both imply reflexivity and some capacity for it. Many authors have questioned this dimension of the CA. Martha C Nussbaum, herself, in her early works had explored it.[33] Even Amartya Sen was attracted by this Aristotelian aspect:

Though at the time of proposing the approach, I did not manage to seize its Aristotelian connections, it is interesting to note that the Greek word *dunamin* used by Aristotle to discuss an aspect of the human good, which is sometimes translated as 'potentiality', can be translated also as 'capability of existing or acting'. The Aristotelian perspective and its connections with the recent attempts at constructing a capability-focused approach have been illuminatingly discussed by Martha Nussbaum (1988).[34]

---

[30] Sen, *Development as Freedom* (n 1). Also see section III of this chapter.

[31] Quotation from Hannah Arendt, *Les origines du totalitarisme* (Seuil, 1972) [First publication, 1951, *The origins of totalitarianism*, Harcourt Bruce and Co] 271: 'Détruire l'individualité, c'est détruire la spontanéité, le pouvoir qu'a l'homme de commencer quelque chose de neuf à partir de ses propres ressources, quelque chose qui ne peut s'expliquer à partir de réactions à l'environnement et aux évènements' (my own translation).

[32] All the more necessary than 'reasonable persons cannot be expected to converge' in case of 'incompatible comprehensive views of human life and its goals' (from Nussbaum, 'Political Liberalism and Respect' (n 3) 26). Such statement can be extended to work milieu, especially but not only between employers and workers.

[33] Martha C Nussbaum, , 1993, 'Non Relative Virtues: An Aristotelian Approach' in Martha C Nussbaum, and Amartya Sen (eds), *The Quality of Life* (Clarendon Press, 1993) 242–69.

[34] Amartya Sen, 'Capability and Well-Being' in Martha Nussbaum and Amartya Sen (eds), *The Quality of Life* (Clarendon Press, 1993) 30.

Such principles help us imagine the plausibility of a virtuous circle between work practice and expectation of a good life to be developed, and to subsume the contradiction we spoke of earlier between freedom in work and authoritarian management of firms. But they say nothing about the ways to generate such a circle. In other terms, is the capability approach self-sufficient to adequately pose the issue of freedom in work? Or should it be supplemented by other institutional approaches? One needs to address the question of institutionalizing freedom in work.

## III.  Institutionalizing Freedom in Work

In Sen's work, there are three canonical meanings of capability that are deployed in various combinations, depending on what is at stake (to choose, to accomplish her life, to do, or realize). A fourth one has been added by James Bohman: the capability to deliberate (with a variant introduced by Jean-Michel Bonvin as the capability for voice). (A) To what rights and resources each meaning calls for workers to have access? (B) How to institutionalize and implement freedom in work into firms?

## A.  Work and the four interconnected meanings of capability

### 1.  *The capability to choose*

The capability to choose is at the core of Sen's reflections. He defines it as the freedom that people 'have to effectively choose among several livings for which they have reasons to value'.[35] This conception of capability takes seriously into account the ontological importance for people of their 'reasons to value'. Choice supposes an autonomous evaluation leading to an act in order to live the chosen living; to be possible such a choice implies to be guiding by a reason to value. Choice focuses on the two sides of freedom: an opportunities aspect and a process aspect. First, to have a real freedom to choose, the person should have a true array of options (leading to a plurality of possible worlds) among which she can choose autonomously and detached from any interference. Secondly, she should participate in the process defining these options and their contours, either individually or through her representatives. This draws attention to freedom of deliberation (see below point 4) and to situations of life and work whose focal features provide the capability to choose.

What might this imply for having a true freedom in work? My conjectures are that: 1. Each worker, even within a given work-post, should have access to a set of opportunities (or to be put in a work situation that enables her to find possibilities she can explore[36] and among which she can choose, either today or in the future of her career); 2. These opportunities should have to develop (or at least maintain) the

---

[35] Among others, Sen, *Development as Freedom* (n 1) 291.
[36] Or discover, even generate and realize the 'potentialities' in which he could invest towards his personal development.

worker's capabilities, not only to choose, but to all of the others capabilities (personal accomplishment, realization and deliberation); 3. One cannot separate work and life. Freedom of choice includes, in my view, the freedom to choose how to organize and connect private life and work time, in quantity and quality.

## 2. The capability in personal accomplishment perspective

The concept of capability does not value freedom in itself as in classical liberalism. Freedom has among its finalities the substantial accomplishment of people—not anyone, but the ones in line with the set of livings they have the possibility to choose. These accomplishments are diverse, depending on the chosen objects-of-value and the values attributed to them, and also on people's agencies (those are the collective causes—social, humanitarian, political, common goods—the participation in which they accord a personal accomplishment value).

For this second dimension of capability, to enjoy freedom in work requires: 1. That work activity is, by itself and its process of effectuation, a potential source of accomplishment for people; 2. In consequence that the definition of jobs, the chains of collective work that connect people, training and more generally formation, have to be designed in order to make such accomplishment possible (to offer a true choice, whatever people will do); 3. That the 'out' (private life in its widest sense) cannot be separated from the 'in' (work activity). For instance the content of the formations offered by the firm should take in consideration both sides.

## 3. The capability to do (to realize)

The third dimension of capability is the capability to realize. As such, capability is also the power to do what we have decided to do. As we have seen above (Table 1), the conversion factors at work in people's situations play a core role in the scope of the capabilities they have, especially in this power to do what they undertake and its development or regression. Discovering the relevant conversion factors on which to act or develop relevant policies or work organizations must be done in relation to the capability to deliberate.

The link between freedom in work and power to do appears evident, all the more as one remembers the organizational shift of contemporaneous capitalism towards the creation of local spaces of freedom aiming at putting individual freedom and capability at the service of prefixed quantitative objectives. To enjoy a power to do implies that: 1. At the minimum, workers have the competencies (in its narrow definition) to be able what is asked for; and 2. In practice, that freedom instrumentalization should be converted into free deployment by people. At the core of such requirement is the right valuation of work effectuated and of its resulting realization. It is a question for work not to be attributed a quantity (in forms of numbers) only, but to recover its *true value* in the global meaning of value, ethical, moral, and participation in some common good. It includes wage classification or standard trade-unions claims, but goes beyond. Not only should workers and their representatives intervene in the definition of evaluation criteria, but they should build up their own methodologies that could oppose the capitalist measurement methodologies, which implies inquiries, participation of the workers and their representatives, and so on.

Such issues are, at their basis, democratic issues. They lead to the fourth dimension of capability (to deliberate and for voice) and to the type of right to be implemented and of the state able to do the job.

## 4. *The capability to deliberate, the capability for voice*

The capability to deliberate does not come from Amartya Sen, but from James Bohman in his critical works on deliberative democracy. [37] I will enter in some detail here.[38] Standard research on deliberative democracy (from Jürgen Habermas and John Rawls to Joshua Cohen) argues that one can find optimal rules of procedures that, when respected by all the deliberants, allow the achieving of a political consensus. Such research is, above all, normative, and does not care about the many inequalities between the deliberants.[39] Critical research focuses on observing real situations and reincorporating the virtues of disagreement.[40] James Bohman emphasizes that, for free and equal exchange of arguments (reasons) to take place, a deliberative procedure must satisfy the requirement of equal capabilities to deliberate, or, what he called an 'equal capability for public functioning'. To be efficiently heard and to influence collective decisions in a given area, social criticism must build a 'new understanding' of the economic and social phenomena that develop within this area. In Bohman's view, this new understanding entails building new collective causes, endowing them with legitimacy and mobilizing communities of influence within civil society able to share that cause and to commit to it. Samantha Besson and Chantal Mouffe[41] encourage us to abandon the dream of rational consensus because it is unattainable—and we would add—too easily manipulated. Trying to achieve consensus by avoiding the substantial issues or through negotiated accommodation may, in fact, overpower the need to bring the reasons (or the scope of what can be considered reasonable) to the attention of the public. By clarifying the basis of disagreement for the participants, deliberation can, on the contrary, have the beneficial effect of enriching their conceptions and making the process more informative,

[37] James Bohman, 'Deliberative Democracy and Effective Social Freedom: Capabilities, Resources, and Opportunities' in James Bohman and William Rehg (eds), *Deliberative Democracy* (The MIT Press, 1999) 321–34.

[38] See also Ota De Leonardis, , Serafino Negrelli, and Robert Salais (eds), *Democracy and Capabilities for Voice* (Peter Lang, 2012).

[39] The work of Joshua Cohen, which is remarkable in other respects, is a good example of this. See his contribution in James Bohman, and William Rehg (eds), *Deliberative Democracy* (The MIT Press, 1999).

[40] To achieve 'reasonable disagreement', to quote the words of Martha C Nussbaum, 'Political Liberalism and Respect' (n 3).

[41] Samantha Besson, 'Disagreement and Democracy: From Vote to Deliberation and Back Again?' in Jordi Ferrer and Marissa Iglesias (eds), *Law, Politics and Morality: European Perspectives, vol* I (Duncker & Humblot, 2003) 101–35. Chantal Mouffe, 'Deliberative Democracy and Agonistic Pluralism', *Working paper*, Institute for Advanced Studies (IHS), Vienne, December 2000.

consistent, and thoughtful. For Samantha Besson, disagreement must be seen as a creative resource for deliberation. Disagreement does not rule out the possibility of partial agreements, for example, on which variables are relevant to the problem or how some of their aspects should be dealt with; the possibility of partial agreements will become even more visible.

At this point, one is not so far from the capability for voice (as introduced by Jean-Michel Bonvin[42]). Even if not, to my knowledge, this idea is precisely Bonvin's argument, from the quoted works emerges the idea that to efficiently voice their claim, deliberants should build, not only denunciations as usual, not only counterarguments, but also a 'new understanding' of the economic, social, and political situation. To be built, this new understanding, first, should discover its own internal coherence and search for its adequacy to the reality of the situation; secondly, should be understood by the other deliberants; and, thirdly, be tightly connected to the problem at stake in the deliberation. We have there the different dimensions of the political construction of what is necessary for a capability to deliberate.

## 5. Collective negotiation and deliberation

It follows that, to be implemented or to claim for, effective freedom in work requires the mobilization and, even more, the elaboration of a new culture for collective negotiation by the workers and their representatives. Negotiation should be equipped with and backed by the building of new understandings, a building that cannot be undertaken without the main interested people, the workers. Other deliberants, especially employers, might do all that is possible to deny the validity of such understandings. Equal capability for public functioning is not only a question of rhetoric or of the use of the right language, concepts, words, expressions. Proof of the adequacy of understandings of the reality at stake should be publicly provided and debated, in qualitative and quantitative forms. And the solidity and legitimacy of such proof will be increased by the participation of workers and the taking into account of their knowledge and experience of work. It means that unions and representatives must be aware that negotiation is not reducible to pure strategic bargaining between interests, but should incorporate more and more elements of deliberation aiming at achieving (at least) partial agreements and well-funded disagreements about what is the reality at stake.

## B. Institutionalizing and implementing freedom in work

Implementing freedom in work requires the development of all the dimensions of capability: choice, personal accomplishment, realization, and deliberation. If work organization was reframed as some combination of the four capability dimensions, workers could expect their employment to lead them to enjoy true freedom of

---

[42] Jean-Michel Bonvin, 'Capacités et démocratie' in Jean DeMunck and Bénédicte Zimmermann (eds), *La liberté au prisme des capacités. Amartya Sen au-delà du libéralisme*, (Editions de l'EHESS, Raisons pratiques 18, 2008) 237–62.

choice, of accomplishment, and of realization. They can verify whether the corresponding commitments have been taken in due account, at the different levels: firms, branches, public policies, and law. By repetitive and dynamic feedback, the convergence of mutual expectations between social organization (especially the firm) and workers can lead the latter to include reciprocity and good work (in other terms mobilizing the capability to realize) as guidelines for their work. Room will be opened for the rise of mutual expectations, or, in other words, the birth and development of *conventions* between workers and between workers and their employer. I cannot truly develop here what the economics of convention[43] means by 'convention'. Let me say that, as any process of coordination between people or actors is uncertain— in that when you act you face so many a priori unpredictable contingencies—so the only way to proceed is to refer to some convention we believe shared by the other and to use it a reference (a guide) to nevertheless act. When entered in the coordination, it also will help people appreciate, in the process, whether the others are following the same convention or not, to agree or disagree.

Most of research in the capability field focuses on moral and ethical behaviour of individuals, which leads to some feeling of helplessness.[44] This focus does not suffice for freedom in work. In the case of French labour law for instance,[45] implementing freedom in work is in frontal opposition to the principle of subordination. So it puts in question not only the legal foundation of the labour contract, but also the legal statute of firms and the respective roles recognized by the main stakeholders (shareholders, workers, representatives of civil society, local communities, not to speak of the state). It also contradicts the main trends of work organization theories.

Nevertheless, the capability approach puts at its core the valuation of work activities. It is precisely to what Amartya Sen points with his notion of informational basis of judgment in justice (IBJJ). Valuation has a double perspective: firstly, as the recognition of the worth attached by people to work as freedom of choice and of personal accomplishment (work as object of value);[46] secondly, as a just and fair evaluation of their work (criteria and measures) as done by the new organizations of work. Here resides the basic contradiction between workers and the firm. When informed by the capability approach, workers and their representatives would demand that a just and fair evaluation of their capabilities is realized. The perspective of the firm, instead, is to build a quantitative evaluation in terms of minimizing costs and maximizing profitability.

---

[43] The seminar work is the special issue of the *Revue économique*, March 1989. In English, see Michael Storper and Robert Salais, *Worlds of Production? The Action Frameworks of the Economy* (Harvard University Press, 1997). A wonderful quasi-exhaustive review in German can be found in Rainer Diaz-Bone, *Die 'Economie des conventions'. Grundlagen und Entwicklungen der neuen französischen Wirtschaftssoziologie* (Springer, 2018, 1st edn, 2015).

[44] For instance in Ingrid Robeyns, 'Freedom and Responsibility: Sustainable Prosperity through a Capabilities Lens' *Working Paper*, Centre of the Understanding of Sustainable Prosperity, 2017 https://www.cusp.ac.uk/themes/m/m1-4/.

[45] Remember that in a process of institutionalizing, one cannot abstract oneself from the specific social-historical characteristics of law and public policies.

[46] For instance, in the case of moral (or sexual) harassment.

But here enters on the scene the capability to deliberate (and for voice), which can help establish a balance between these claims and leave real room for workers' claims. Establishing such a balance by deliberation requires a process of institutionalizing freedom in work, allowing democracy to enter the sphere of work.

Amartya Sen has proposed a conception of rights as goals to be implemented by law and policies.[47] As Jean De Munck[48] suggests, law starts from the foundational assumption that rights are intrinsic orientations for people and actors. Could rights as goals be read as favouring the emergence of conventions that balance the taking of responsibility and commitment with an expectation of reciprocity from the other side (especially the employers and the state)? Could we, at the same time, reciprocally back the effectiveness of rights on the emergence of conventions?

What type of state would be able to implement such conception of rights as goals? With Michael Storper, we have distinguished different types of state depending on the extent to which, as a convention, citizens and/or intermediaries bodies (professions, regions, territories, and other levels of the society) share with the state such defining and implementing common goods. Briefly said,[49] we conceive of different types of states (or conventions of the state); for instance, the external state that takes charge in all the tasks through aggregation and top-down policies founded on general and abstract categories (the French state, typically); or the absent state that denies the existence of common goods, leaving people at their risk to look for their private goods only (corresponding to the free perfect market).

The situated state is the most relevant for our purpose. It roughly corresponds to the principle of subsidiarity as elaborated in social philosophy.[50] In our definition, a situated state considers that it is impossible to a priori describe the common good, beyond formulating a fundamental objective such as, in our case, implementing effective freedom in work. Only when referring to specific situations of work (for instance in firms or branches or territories), freedom in work as fundamental objective becomes collectively definable and knowable, even in the course of collective action through disagreements and partial compromises. A situated state aims at promoting processes of collective knowledge (with intermediate levels that vary in their results and can be dynamically revised). It therefore orients its action not to achieve political consensus on procedures, but towards seeking adjustable compromises at the relevant levels. For such tasks, it provides free spaces and adequate resources within and with which relevant actors deliberate to find the relevant implementation; hence the importance of capabilities to deliberate or to voice. Coming back to rights as goals, such a situated state will define them at the general level as guidelines for the relevant lower levels. It would leave these levels to try to define, specify, and implement rights along the built IBJJ, while following the process. If it appears

[47] Amartya Sen, 'Elements of a Theory of Human Rights' (2004) 32(4) *Philosophy and Public Affairs* 315, 315–56.
[48] De Munck, 'Qu'est-ce qu'une capacité?' (n 14) 46.
[49] See Storper, and Salais, *Worlds of Production?* (n 42), 328–48.
[50] Chantal Millon-Delson, *L'Etat subsidiaire* (Presses Universitaires de France, 1992).

necessary, it would offer ex post incentives (or making it compulsory) to revise the outcomes and continue the process.

## IV. Conclusion: Towards a Politics of Freedoms for Labour?

I hope that in this contribution I have succeeded in persuading labour lawyers and others that, as it can be formalized by a capability approach, freedom in work is an important freedom for labour—maybe the most important one of a politics of freedoms for labour.[51] There are two reasons for this hope. Firstly, a key issue is for work to have its true value recognized in its several dimensions, not only in economic terms of quality and performance, but also in moral, ethical, political, legal and social dimensions. Secondly, if one follows our analysis, the capability approach puts at its core the right and fair valuation of work activities. It is precisely to what Amartya Sen points with his notion of informational basis of judgment in justice (IBJJ). To be persuaded, it is enough to consider the wide array of connections one finds in the contribution between freedom in work and issues treated in labour law and elsewhere (other branches of law, political philosophy, economics *à la* Sen, and so on). To make progress towards the elaboration of a politics of freedom, labour law should penetrate these other territories.

This is far from uncommon when one returns, even schematically, to history or literature. I will just pick one significant example. The European Commission in the 1970s proposed a Directive on the European Company Statute that, in retrospect, tried to take on board, at least partially, such objectives. At the end of process in 1975, the most advanced propositions were:

1. That workers should be represented in the Supervisory Board at equality: one third for workers' representatives, one third for shareholders and one third for representatives of the 'general interest' chosen by common agreement by the two others thirds. The idea was 'to enable [workers] to express their point of view when important economic decisions are made upon matters of company management and on the appointment of members of the Board of Management'.

2. That 'decisions concerning the following matters may be made by the Board of Management *only with the agreement of the European Works Council' (article 123).*[52]

These matters were (and I quote):

a) Rules relating to recruitment, promotion, and dismissal of employees;
b) Implementation of vocational training;
c) Fixing of terms of remuneration and introduction of new methods of computing remuneration;

---

[51] For an essay to conceptualize a politics of freedom for labour, Robert Salais, 'Labour and the Politics of Freedom' in Ota De Leonardis, Serafino Negrelli, and Robert Salais (eds), *Democracy and Capabilities for Voice* (Peter Lang, 2012) 227–44.
[52] European Commission COM(75) 150 final (my emphasis).

d) Measures relating to industrial safety, health and hygiene;
e) Introduction and management of social facilities;
f) Daily time. of commencement and termination of work;
g) Preparation of the holiday schedule.

All of these matters could be addressed through a capability approach. Freedom in work and workers evaluation, in particular, could be treated by relying on items a, b, c, and d. It is not difficult to imagine worker representatives on the Supervisory Board involved in a strategy of alliances with at least part of the representatives of the general interest and, we never know, with one or two shareholder representatives, alliances that favour something like a politics of freedom for workers. Not easy of course, but ...

These projects of the European Commission were not accepted and later disappeared from the European social agenda owing to the process of financial liberalization. But they remain present as references and resources in the still-brief history of the construction of Europe. Furthermore, research continues to explore the field, like those about the firm as political entity (see the works of Jean-Philippe Robé and Isabelle Ferreras, in particular).[53] There is no reason to despair, even today. Good luck, lawyers!

---

[53] Jean-Philippe Robé, 'L'entreprise oubliée par le droit' *Séminaire Vie des Affaires*, Les Amis de l'Ecole de Paris (1 June 2001) https://www.ecole.org/fr/398/VA010601.pdf; Isabelle Ferreras, *Firms as Political Entities: Saving Democracy through Economic Bicameralism* (Cambridge University Press, 2017).

# 16

# Capabilities, Contract, and Causality

## The Case of Sweatshop Goods

*Lyn K.L. Tjon Soei Len\**

## I.  Introduction

Deplorable working conditions (e.g., sweatshops) in global supply chains represent a serious justice concern for globalization and for those who advocate for international labor rights. Legal regimes on national, transnational, and international levels struggle to address deplorable labor conditions that occur in global supply chains in an effective manner.[1] Common approaches pursued by international labor rights advocates include the pursuit of minimum labor standards, as well as the articulation of corporate social responsibility standards.[2] Attempts to restrict corporate conduct on the basis of voluntary commitments (e.g., codes of conduct) are informed by the idea that deplorable labor conditions are, first and foremost, a matter of irresponsible (cross-border) corporate conduct for which we need to develop effective forms of (transnational) regulation. In line with this perspective, contractual approaches offer a range of complementary strategies to address deplorable working conditions. For instance, some scholars have argued that supply chain contracts provide an opportunity to transform soft corporate social responsibility commitments into legally binding obligations.[3] This argument is in line with the

---

* Visiting Assistant Professor, The Ohio State University, tjonsoeilen.1@osu.edu.

[1] See Dagan and Dorfman, "Interpersonal Human Rights and Transnational Private Law" (Sept. 17, 2017) https://ssrn.com/abstract=3038380.

[2] See Ruggie, "Guiding Principles on Business and Human Rights: Implementing the United Nations 'Protect, Respect and Remedy' Framework," *United Nations Report HR/PUB/11/04*, 2011 or the OECD Guidelines for Multinational Enterprises (OECD Publishing, 2011).

[3] See Beckers, *Enforcing Corporate Social Responsibility Codes. On Global Self-Regulation and National Private Law* (Hart Publishing, 2015), who argues that CSR codes should be legally enforced as private legal obligations. See also McBarnet, "Corporate Social Responsibility Beyond Law, Through Law, for Law: The New Corporate Accountability," in McBarnet, Voiculescu, and Campbell (eds.), *The New Corporate Accountability: Corporate Social Responsibility and the Law* (Cambridge University Press, 2007); and Vytopil, *Contractual Control in the Supply Chain* (Boom Juridische Uitgevers, 2015); and Cafaggi, "The Regulatory Functions of Transnational Commercial Contracts: New Architectures," 36 *Fordham International Law Journal* (2013): 1557–618.

broader idea that labor rights—as human rights—need to be given direct effect in contractual, horizontal relationships in order to advance justice.[4]

A capabilities perspective to minimum contract justice, however, invites a broader set of questions that directs our attention not only to corporate responsibility, but to the wider issue of the legal permissibility of market exchanges, and their terms, for goods produced under deplorable production conditions.[5] How should societies treat, for instance, consumer contracts for sweatshop produced goods? What are the minimum standards for contractual behavior applicable to private actors, whether they are corporate or consumer actors? What does minimum justice require of contract law?[6] A capabilities perspective to minimum contract justice suggests that societies ought to refuse facilitating and enforcing market exchanges *as contracts* if they have impairing implications for the central capabilities of others.[7] If sweatshops reflect working conditions that are incompatible with human dignity expressed through a minimum threshold of central capabilities, then contract law ought to refuse to make state power available for the enforcement of contracts the performance of which relies on sweatshop conditions.[8] A capabilities perspective offers a compelling interpretation of the demands that minimum justice requires of the institution of contract. Moreover, it offers a normative argument that could encourage a complementary legal strategy for those who battle labor rights violations by addressing irresponsible private market conduct.

However, the idea that states would refuse to provide their support to market exchanges for goods made in sweatshops, in particular consumer sales, encounters a common objection. Critics deem it inappropriate to include potential supply chain labor rights violations in the normative evaluation of consumer contracts. In most instances, the objection is expressed through the idea of a missing causal link between consumer conduct and sweatshop conditions. In other instances, the objection is expressed as, or combined with, a positive legal claim about the correct interpretation of legal doctrine, including the notion of contractual privity.

This chapter aims to do two things in response to this common criticism of a capabilities-based notion of minimum contract justice. First, the chapter addresses

---

[4] See Beckers, *Enforcing Corporate Social Responsibility Codes* (n. 3). Also, Trakman, "Public Responsibilities beyond Consent: Rethinking Contract Theory," (45) 2016 *Hofstra Law Review* 217–62, who argues for an account of contract in which public values and responsibilities are central.

[5] See Tjon Soei Len, *Minimum Contract Justice: A Capabilities Perspective on Sweatshops and Consumer Contracts* (Hart Publishing, 2017).

[6] For an elaborate discussion of this set of questions, see (n. 5) 42–57.

[7] Doctrinal analysis across several European legal systems shows that the idea that the state should refuse to support such market activities is not quixotic but can be realized through legal doctrines of contractual immorality and invalidity. Under such rules, states are to refuse support to private market exchanges that are contrary to society's fundamental values. See Tjon Soei Len, *Minimum Contract Justice* (n. 5) ch. 5; and Kötz, *Illegality of Contracts in The Max Planck Encyclopedia of European Private Law Vol I* (Oxford University Press, 2012), 847.

[8] See Bang, "Unmasking the Charade of the Global Supply Contract: A Novel Theory of Corporate Liability in Human Trafficking and Forced Labor Cases," 35 *Houston Journal of International Law* (2013): 257: "Although the global economy has enabled average people access to a diverse and ready supply of inexpensive clothing and electronics, the dark reality is that this access comes at great human expense. The by-products of these cheap products are human trafficking and forced labor."

the causality objection on its own terms. Second, it articulates a revised version of the criticism leveled against the project. The chapter aims to show how both renditions fall short of undermining the core argument of minimum contract justice from a capabilities perspective.

After briefly outlining the capabilities-based argument from minimum contract justice as it applies to consumer contracts for sweatshop goods, I aim to address the causality objection on its own terms and show why it does not speak to the core argument of minimum contract justice. This part of the chapter offers two distinct articulations of the causality objection: 1) an individual (consumer) contract does not impact working conditions and therefore is not their cause; and 2) goods that are made in sweatshops have already been produced when consumers buy them, and therefore contracts for their sale cannot be their cause. This chapter offers a discussion of the underlying notion and purpose of causality and hypothesizes two implicit motivating factors for the causality objection in the case of consumer contracts that we ought to reject: 1) intuitions about blame and culpability that are in principle immaterial for questions of contractual recognition; and 2) a bias in favor of consumers that we should abandon. The chapter will also articulate a revised version of the causality objection in a way that addresses the project and will show why even this elevated version of the objection fails to undermine the core argument of minimum contract justice that consumer contracts for sweatshop goods should be deemed invalid.

## II. Minimum Contract Justice and Consumer Contracts for Sweatshop Goods

Contract law is the legal institution that underwrites a just market order; it reflects a society's fundamental values and contemporary vision of a way of life through minimum standards for contractual behavior.[9] Contract law contains normative standards that reveal how transacting parties should behave toward each other, others, and society as a whole when engaging in market activities if they wish to invoke public support for the realization of their private pursuits (i.e. state power for the enforcement of their transactions). Of special significance are contract law rules that portray the *defining structure of contract* and articulate the minimum standards for transactions that society recognizes *as contracts*—those contracts that are compatible with the public values that are ensconced in society's basic institutions. A capabilities approach to minimum justice offers a partial articulation of what justice requires of a society's basic institutions.[10] As part of this basic structure, contract law is subject to minimum requirements of justice. A capabilities perspective on minimum contract

---

[9] See Singer, "Things that We Would Like to Take for Granted: Minimum Standards for the Legal Framework of a Free and Democratic Society," 2 *Harvard Law & Policy Review* (2008): 139–59.
[10] As such, the capabilities approach informs how we ought to understand the role of contract law in a liberal society, that is, an understanding of what contract law is for. Compare in this volume Langille, "What is Labour Law For? Implications of the Capability Approach".

justice informs—as a matter of what justice more generally requires of us—when a society ought to withhold public recognition of private transactions *as contracts*.

For the specific case of market transactions for goods produced under deplorable production conditions we may ask: how, from a capabilities perspective of minimum contract justice, ought a decently just society deal with exchanges for goods that are made under deplorable production conditions? Specifically, how ought a society that strives toward minimum justice treat consumer contracts for sweatshop goods? A capabilities-based response starts with the idea that there is a set of central capabilities that reflects individuals' fundamental entitlements based in justice. While the threshold levels for each of the central capabilities is to be determined within a society and can thus diverge on a global level, the set of central capabilities is fully universal.[11] The central capabilities are imperative for human beings wherever they may be situated and for human dignity regardless of a person's membership in a particular society.

The case of consumer contracts for sweatshop goods then raises the following set of questions. First, are sweatshop conditions compatible with (a threshold level of) central capabilities? Second, ought contract law enforce contracts for sweatshop goods? And third, ought contract law distinguish between goods produced in sweatshops by human beings within and beyond the borders of its jurisdiction? Minimum contract justice argues that the answer to all three questions is negative; mutually beneficial transactions for sweatshop goods should not be recognized *as contracts* (i.e. enforceable by means of the power of the state), because they have implications for others that are incompatible with society's commitments to minimum justice. Sweatshops entail infringements of labor rights and human rights that, from a capabilities perspective, represent universal fundamental entitlements based in justice.[12] Sweatshop conditions preclude workers' abilities—predominantly women—"to work as human beings." They lack adequate control over the content and conditions of their work, and valuable exit options from and alternatives to exploitative work.[13] Sweatshop conditions are thus incompatible with the universal core and set of central capabilities that reflects human dignity. Market activities that advance and rely on the exploitation of others, regardless of their national membership, should not be considered as part of "normal" market functioning that a society, which strives toward minimum justice, should wish to facilitate, assist, and endorse. In light of its commitment to minimum justice, the state may have what Shiffrin refers to as a legitimate "self-regarding concern"[14] not to make its support available for the realization of private pursuits that are incompatible with the public values

---

[11]  See Nussbaum, *Frontiers of Justice* (Harvard University Press, 2006), ch. 5.

[12]  See related, Chapter 10 in this volume, Mantouvalou, "Work, Human Rights, and Human Capabilities," who argues that from a capabilities perspective the right to work should be interpreted to include the option to work under conditions that respect human rights and that working conditions that undermine people's capabilities are incompatible with the right to work.

[13]  See for the capability to exercise control over one's environment, the list of central human capabilities under 10B, Nussbaum, *Frontiers of Justice* (n. 11) ch. 1 at 77.

[14]  Shiffrin, "Paternalism, Unconscionability, and Accommodation," 29 *Philosophy and Public Affairs* (2009): 205–50, 224.

ensconced in society's basic institutions, e.g. market exchanges that are incompatible with a commitment to central capabilities as fundamental entitlements.

This interpretation of minimum contract justice encounters a common objection expressed as an issue of causality: if a consumer sale does not *cause* the sweatshop conditions under which a good is produced, why ought private parties—e.g., consumers and retailers—not be able to rely on state support for their private pursuits? The objection reflects the idea that in the absence of a causal link there is no justification for disapproval and consequent exclusion from contractual recognition by the state. In particular, such disapproval seems out of place where it affects ordinary consumer transactions. However, the minimum contract justice argument means to affect transactions that occur on a regular basis on the market but aims to challenge the presumption of their normality—that is, their acceptability. First, the content of the exchange resembles an everyday sales contract where the consumer obtains a right to delivery of goods (e.g., clothes), and the seller to the agreed-upon price. For the sake of the argument, there is no need to distinguish between the order of the performances, that is, whether the consumer pays first, the seller delivers the goods first, or whether they occur simultaneously (e.g., buying clothes in a physical store vs. ordering them online). Second, the parties generally have ordinary reasons and motivations to engage in exchange—the consumer wants to buy clothes while the seller wants to receive money. They are usually indifferent to their production conditions, such that production conditions do not form a motivating reason for either party to enter into, or refrain from, exchange. Third, in relevant cases parties are aware, or at least should be aware, that the goods are produced under sweatshop conditions. Knowledge arises from awareness of general facts about the world; the agreed upon price; available brand information; supply chain knowledge; media attention; etc. Awareness does not dissuade parties from engaging in exchange, nor does it deter them from seeking state supports, that is, pursuing enforcement in the event of a dispute. With this case illustration in mind, the following section addresses the causality objection.[15] Before doing so, it is helpful to note that the question of whether the state should withhold recognition from an exchange on the basis of its incompatibility with a society's fundamental values is always pertinent in the event of a dispute, regardless of the issues that the parties may raise. First, the state's moral objections to contractual recognition and enforcement often have to be raised *ex officio* by courts.[16] Second, how a society responds to exploitative market

---

[15] The argument is also applicable to other exchanges in supply chains. One may, for instance, consider contracts between retailers, distributors, brands, and suppliers. The issue becomes pertinent for courts to consider in any dispute, as their outcomes rely on the enforceability of contractual rights and obligations. Thus, one may think of any dispute that results from defaults on, e.g., payments or deliveries.

[16] See Tjon Soei Len, *Minimum Contract Justice* (n. 5) ch. 5. In relation to Dutch, German, and French law: Asser, Hartkamp, and Sieburgh (eds.), *Mr. Asser's Handleiding tot beoefening van het Nederlandse recht. 6. Algemeen overeenkomstenrecht* (Kluwer, 2010), 312; Loth, MA, *Dwingend en aanvullend recht* (Monografieën Nieuw BW A-19, Kluwer, 2009), 19; Ellenberger, *Palandt Bürgerliches Gesetzbuch* (69 Auflage edn, Verlag CH Beck, 2010), 21; Fabre-Magnan, *Droit de Obligations. 1-Contrat et engagement unilatéral* (Presses Universitaires de France, 2012), 465–6.

activities through contract says something about the acceptability of such conduct in the market, and in society at large.

## III.  Contractual Invalidity and Causality

In this section, I will argue that the causality objection to considerations of minimum contract justice regarding contractual invalidity for immorality is a mistake. First, I identify the causality objection that minimum contract justice encounters and articulates it in two common renditions. Then, I will discuss the notion of causality in its most dominant usage in legal contexts: as a central criterion for questions of liability. I will suggest that the causality objection is motivated by the specific function that causality serves in that context and I will highlight that this notion is erroneously transposed into the context of contractual immorality; for questions of contractual immorality and invalidity, this notion of causality is mistakenly put forward as a necessary requirement. The causality objection confuses what is pivotal for questions of liability with the potential concerns of foreseeability that play a role in the context of contractual validity. Moreover, I will hypothesize that a normative bias in favor of consumers propels the causality objection further.

### A.  The causality objection

Many opponents of sweatshops share the idea that their occurrence and continued existence is causally linked to private actors' market conduct in the supply chain and the structural features of specific markets where sweatshop conditions are endemic. In this context, corporate actors in the supply chain, notably retailers and brands, are under severe scrutiny for their role in creating and maintaining a systemic demand for sweatshop produced goods.[17] Alongside this focus on corporate actors, others express ideas about how the ways in which consumers are capable of affecting social change through their contracting behavior (e.g., by not contracting with certain brands, or by choosing alternative goods) and offer critical analyses.[18] Yet, the idea that there is a salient link between consumer sales and sweatshop working conditions so as to render *consumer contracts* invalid is controversial. Specifically, the idea that consumer contracts lack a *causal* link to sweatshop conditions leads opponents to reject, or at least be skeptical of, the argument that such contracts should be

---

[17]  See, for instance, in response to the collapse of the Rana Plaza: Bader, "The Bangladesh Factory Collapse: Why CSR Is More Important Than Ever" (May 7, 2013) https://www.theguardian.com/sustainable-business/blog/bangladesh-factory-collapse-csr-important; or Abrams, "Retailers Like H&M and Walmart Fall Short of Pledges to Overseas Workers" (May 31, 2016) https://www.nytimes.com/2016/05/31/business/international/top-retailers-fall-short-of-commitments-to-overseas-workers.html.

[18]  See Kysar, "Preferences for Processes: the Process/Product Distinction and the Regulation of Consumer Choice," 118 *Harvard Law Review* (2004): 525–642. For a critical analysis of social change ethical consumerism, see Hussain, "Is Ethical Consumerism an Impermissible Form of Vigilantism?" 40 *Philosophy & Public Affairs* 2(012): 111–42.

regarded as invalid for immorality. Those who convey this point of view often argue that consumers should not be held responsible for sweatshop conditions, as the consumer conduct cannot be considered the latter's cause.

There is something quite appealing about the rejection of the idea that there is a causal link between consumer contracts and sweatshop conditions, especially if the purpose of causality is to identify responsible agents for sweatshop conditions. Within the legal context, responsibility is closely linked to ideas about legal liability. The notion of causality serves the role of establishing attribution; if a consumer's action of buying a good causes its deplorable production conditions, then the consumer is responsible and should potentially be liable for remedying any resulting harm. Moreover, causality concepts in law that serve to answer liability questions often resemble everyday intuitions about blame and culpability. And our intuitions about who is to blame for sweatshop conditions generally do not lead us to focus on consumers, as there are other, more proximate, actors in the supply chains of sweatshop goods. Why then should we blame and hold consumers responsible for deplorable production conditions? When the argument regarding consumer contracts' invalidity for immorality encounters the causality objection, it is often this set of questions that forms the background for two claims: first, that there should be a causal link between consumer contracts and sweatshop conditions; and second, that there is a failure to establish such a causal link. There are two specific renditions in which the causality objection is most often expressed.

## 1. Single contracts vs. contractual chains and aggregate consumption

The first rendition of the causal criticism goes as follows: sweatshops occur within a complex context of interconnected and interdependent contractual chains and no single consumer contract *causes* sweatshop conditions to occur. More specifically, there is no consumer contract that can be said to impact meaningfully the working conditions under which consumer goods are made, nor to sustain the continued existence of such networks or the place of sweatshop within them. In other words, whether or not I buy a sweatshop produced good has no impact on its production or production conditions. This link is important because, doctrinally, the issue of contractual invalidity for immorality is dependent on the individual circumstances of a case, and courts evaluate contracts on a case-by-case basis. Therefore, even if the aggregate activity of consuming sweatshop goods could be a causal factor in generating and sustaining sweatshops, there is no single consumer contract that would be identifiable as *causing* sweatshop conditions such that a court could deem it invalid for contractual immorality.

## 2. The direction of causation

The second rendition of the objection addresses the issue of the direction of causation: consumers generally buy goods that have already been produced (e.g., in physical stores) and the deplorable production conditions have thus already materialized prior to the contract under scrutiny. In other words, any potential harm that is entailed in sweatshop production has already occurred before the consumer engages in a sales contract. Therefore, a consumer contract for sweatshop good cannot be said to have *caused* its production conditions; the occurrence of sweatshops and consumer contracts do not align with the required temporal direction of relationships of cause and effect.

## B.  Causality in context: examined

To determine whether the causality objection—in either rendition—is successful, we must gain some further insight into the notion of causality and its usage in private legal contexts. Since causality is notoriously subject to disagreement among legal scholars, I will begin by discussing the private legal contexts in which questions of causality are most common. This helps us understand the motivation behind the causality objection and assists in identifying why and when causality matters.

The primary purpose of the notion of causality in law is to justify responsibility for harm. Whether in the context of criminal law or the private legal context of tort or contract, causality functions as the basis for attribution of liability. In the private legal context of tort, causality is intimately tied to questions of civil liability for private wrongs outside of contract.[19] In this context, causality helps to determine whether private party, A, should be held liable for the occurrence of a harmful outcome for another private party, B. There are various ways to establish a causal link between A's action and a harm incurred by B. In particular, causality may involve two distinct legal inquiries, the first relating to "cause-in-fact" and the second relating to "proximate cause." Cause-in-fact determines whether A's conduct is a factor that factually lead to the harmful outcome for B. Proximate cause determines whether the law attributes the harmful outcome to A's conduct. While some actions may be part of the factual causal chain, the law may determine one's conduct to be too remote from the harm to justify legal liability. The most common causality test that establishes cause-in-fact is the "but for" or *conditio sine qua non* test. Simply stated, this test asks whether a harm would have occurred in the absence of the (suspect-causal) action; but for A's action, B's harm would not have occurred. If, in fact, but for A's action, B's harm would not have occurred, the question remains whether the cause-in-fact is significant enough (i.e. proximate enough to the harmful outcome) to justify legal liability. Proximate cause—that is, the question of remoteness—is often established through the standard of reasonable foreseeability. If A could not have reasonably foreseen the harmful outcome, then liability is not justified.

---

[19]  See Hart and Honoré, *Causation in the Law* (OUP, 1985); Stapleton, "Unpacking Causation," in Cane and Gardner (eds.), *Relating to Responsibility: Essays in Honour of Tony Honoré on his 80th Birthday* (Hart Publishing, 2001), 145–85; Moore, *Causation and Responsibility. An Essay in Law, Morals, and Metaphysics* (OUP, 2009); Kahmen and Stepanians, *Critical Essays on Causation and Responsibility* (de Gruyter, 2013); Ben-Shahar, "Causation and Foreseeability," in Faure (ed.), *Tort Law and Economics* (Edward Elgar Publishing, 2009); Golberg, *Perspectives on Causation* (Hart Publishing, 2011).

While the *conditio sine qua non* test presents itself as an inquiry in fact, it provides a normative basis for qualifying certain acts and factors as *causal* rather than others. Alternative tests identify different sets of factual causes. For instance, the "NESS" test—asking whether A's conduct is a necessary element of a set of conditions that is sufficient for B's harm to occur—leads to a different selection and identification of causal facts.[20] I reference this rival notion of causality not to adjudicate between them, but to illustrate that the selection of a cause-in-fact test already imports, at least implicitly, ideas about what acts or factors *ought* to qualify as being historically engaged in bringing about the harmful outcome. It can thus be informative to examine what the driving forces behind the causality objection to the invalidity of consumer contracts for sweatshop goods are.

This description of the notion of causality in law provides an important insight for our understanding of the causal objection. Namely, the primary function of causality is to determine whether a harm should be ascribed to the action undertaken by a private actor such that they should be held legally liable. Causality fulfills not only the function of identifying a factual set of circumstances involved in bringing about an outcome, but also a normative or attributive function that legally demarcates where the limits of liability ought to be drawn. Relatedly, the purported objectivity of causality may obscure implicit yet motivating normative commitments that are imported into the causal objection. Causality may incorporate normative ideas about: 1) the conduct that we ought to regard as bringing about sweatshop conditions; and 2) what sort of conduct justifies attribution of legal responsibility for sweatshop conditions. It can be insightful to examine the normative framework that informs our view of consumers in the private legal context. From the private legal viewpoint, consumers are generally regarded as weaker parties deserving of legal protection from the state. If our ideas about consumers inform the objection against contractual immorality in the case of consumer contracts for sweatshop goods, then it may impede our ability to appropriately recognize and respond to consumer conduct that is incompatible with our broader commitments to justice. In particular, it may impede our ability to recognize consumers as actors capable of making consumption choices for which a society may, with legitimate and compelling reasons, not want to offer public support. The following section will explore an image of the consumer as a weaker and potentially ethical agent on the market, which may inform why the causality objection mistakenly transposes the normative function of causality from questions of liability into the question of contractual recognition.[21]

---

[20] E.g., unlike the *conditio sine qua non*-test, the NESS-test allows for the possibility that there is more than one unique set of conditions that is sufficient for the harm to occur. Comparatively, under Dutch law, liability depends on what can reasonably be attributed to a party. Whether attribution is "reasonable" depends on the type of liability and type of harm involved. An important criterium is foreseeability assessed on the basis of proximity and likelihood of the harm.

[21] See Leczykiewicz and Weatherill (eds.), *The Images of the Consumer in EU Law* (Hart Publishing, 2016). In particular, ch. 12: Miller, "Ethical Consumption and the Internal Market" and ch.13 Collins, "Conformity of Goods, the Network Society, and the Ethical Consumer."

## *1. The image of the consumer: an implicit bias?*

Deplorable production conditions, and sweatshops in particular, are subject to critical scrutiny, and even moral outrage in the event of disaster.[22] At the core of common responses, in the areas of corporate responsibility initiatives and of international labor rights, is the idea that corporations are irresponsible and should be held accountable.[23] Similarly, this perspective dominates private legal inquiries, which focus on questions of how legal claims for damages can be effectively made in relation to corporate actors.[24] There is a vast literature relating to corporate liability for infringements of fundamental rights in supply chains.[25] Even in the context of contract law, certain questions reveal a similar focus on corporate transgressions: what is the legal significance of publicly expressed corporate commitments to non-binding frameworks for corporate responsible conduct?[26] Do consumers have the right to rescind a sales contract if a sweatshop-produced good does not meet her reasonable expectations regarding decent production conditions?[27]

These inquiries do not only reveal an image of the corporation as a transgressor of norms, but also an image of the consumer as a (potential) victim of corporate transgressions. Within private legal literature, this image dovetails with the dominant narrative in contract and consumer law, where the consumer is depicted as a weaker, vulnerable party in need of legal protection against corporate advantage-taking. When it comes to the image of the consumer, the unequal power balance in business-to-consumer relations permeates the entire private legal sphere. Early on, the "consumer" was created in the realm of private law precisely because of a motivation to offer legal protection.[28] Within private legal frameworks, the consumer is thus, by definition, viewed through a lens and presumption of weakness. The predominant protective response to consumer weakness is through legally mandated disclosures,[29] informed by the idea that more information will lead to adequate decision making and consumer choices that meet the appropriate minimum standards of personal autonomy. This dominant response suggests that adequate information remedies faulty consumer decisions, but it neglects the idea that consumers can be capable private parties who, with full information of the relevant facts, can choose

---

[22] See Bader, "The Bangladesh Factory Collapse" (n. 17) and Abrams, "Retailers Like H&M and Walmart Fall Short of Pledges to Overseas Workers" (n. 17).
[23] See Bang, "Unmasking the Charade of the Global Supply Contract" (n. 8) and Dagan and Dorfman, "Interpersonal Human Rights and Transnational Private Law" (n. 1).
[24] See literature in (n. 3).
[25] See also Gatto, *Multinational Enterprises and Human Rights* (Edward Elgar Publishing, 2011).
[26] See for instance, Beckers, *Enforcing Corporate Social Responsibility Codes* (n. 3) and Vytopil, *Contractual Control in the Supply Chain* (n. 3).
[27] See Wilhelmsson, "Varieties of Welfarism in European Contract Law," 10 *European Law Journal* (2004): 712–33; Collins, "Conformity of Goods, the Network Society, and the Ethical Consumer," 22 *European Review of Private Law* (2014): 619–40.
[28] Micklitz, "Do Consumers and Businesses Need a New Architecture of Consumer Law? A Thought Provoking Impulse," 32 *Yearbook of European Law* (2013): 266–367 and Leczykiewicz and Weatherill (eds.), *The Images of the Consumer in EU Law* (n. 21).
[29] See for a critical view Ben-Shahar and Schneider, *More Than You Wanted to Know: The Failure of Mandated Disclosure* (Princeton University Press, 2014).

to engage in exchanges that are, or ought to be, legally impermissible. In the case of consumer contracts for sweatshop-produced goods, full information of the relevant facts is unlikely to move consumers to avoid such transactions.[30] Without having to accept a more general anti-consumption position, it is reasonable to consider the possibility that consumers need not have been deceived, misinformed, or otherwise taken advantage of when engaging in transactions for sweatshop goods. In fact, research shows that it is entirely plausible that consumers are, by and large, indifferent to production conditions as far as their purchasing decisions goes, or at least that they prioritize other considerations (e.g., low price, trend, rapid product availability).[31] Viewing consumers almost exclusively as vulnerable private actors can limit our ability to recognize them as private actors who engage in objectionable market conduct. The causality objection may import this view, resulting in an implicit bias of protection that favors consumers over corporate actors. However, while attempting to pin responsibility for deplorable production conditions on corporations is politically attractive, and sometimes legally expedient, it should not exhaust the spectrum of legally relevant questions that arise from sweatshop-produced goods.

## 2. *Contractual immorality and foreseeability*

Why should the notion of causality play the same role in questions of contractual validity as it does in questions of liability? The normative function of causality in questions of liability is often interpreted as an attribution of blame or responsibility, but these normative functions have no (necessary) role to play in determining contractual invalidity for immorality in the case of sales of sweatshop goods. The question of whether the state ought to support or refuse to support a private endeavor through the institution of contract does not rely on the existence of a causal relationship of the sort that private wrongs may demand. While contractual invalidity may serve a variety of purposes, an important function is the state's self-regarding concern for protecting society, and its fundamental values as a whole, against the (market) activities that private parties may undertake, and for which they seek state support in the form of recognition and enforcement.[32]

In this context, it is a mistake to import the notion of causality from liability to contractual recognition. It is inappropriate, and at least unnecessary, to require causality in the same way for contractual invalidity based on immorality as we do for assigning responsibility for harm. The question of which contractual terms are

---

[30] Consumers may also avoid "inconvenient" facts as a form of willful ignorance: see Ehrich and Irwin, "Willful Ignorance in the Request for Product Attribute Information," 42 *Journal of Marketing Research* (2005): 266–77 and Van der Weele, "When Ignorance Is Innocence: On Information Avoidance in Moral Dilemmas" (Aug. 20, 2012) https:// papers.ssrn.com/sol3/papers.cfm?abstract_id=1844702.

[31] There is little evidence that consumers who have preferences for ethically produced goods actually seek out to purchase those goods over others. See Hiscox, Broukhim, and Litwin, "Consumer Demand for Fair Trade: New Evidence from a Field Experiment Using eBay Auctions of Fresh Roasted Coffee" (Mar. 16, 2011) https://papers.ssrn.com/sol3/papers.cfm?abstract_id=1811783.

[32] See for a compelling account of self-regarding refusal Shiffrin, "Paternalism, Unconscionability, and Accommodation" (n. 14).

permissible in a society is not exhaustively answered by adequately demarcating and identifying those terms that ought to be regarded as the cause-in-fact and proximate cause of a harm. If it were, the doctrine of contractual immorality would be severely limited to only those contracts whose performance involves private wrongs. Such a reading would be unnecessarily restrictive and normatively unattractive, while at the same time inconsistent with the established and more compelling role that contractual immorality plays in most legal systems.

Doctrinal analysis shows that contractual immorality is often used to block from public support both arrangements that are objectionable in content (i.e. contractual obligations and their performance that would constitute immoral acts), as well as those that have objectionable, necessary implications.[33] The latter category includes a range of relevant features that are subject to assessment under contractual immorality doctrines, including an agreement's foreseeable consequences. In the context of questions of liability, reasonable foreseeability performs in contract a similar task to that of causality in tort. To recall, causality in tort forms the basis for demarcating the scope of liability for wrongdoing. In turn, reasonable foreseeability is often used to determine the limits of contractual liability for harm caused by breach.[34] If a harm from a breach was foreseeable to the breaching party, then they are liable for damages. Thus, similar to its parallel context in tort, foreseeability of the harm from a contractual breach is about attribution of responsibility and blame.

However, in the context of contractual immorality there is an alternative, and more compelling, interpretation available regarding the function of foreseeability. The foreseeability standard manifests itself in the form of a requirement of the parties' knowledge regarding the agreement's immoral implications.[35] In this context, foreseeability appears to function as a way to balance the interests of private parties with those of others, or of society at large. These knowledge requirements diverge significantly between legal systems. While some legal systems require that both parties should have foreseen the immoral implications of their exchange, others require knowledge of only one of the parties for contractual invalidity.[36] The standards of foreseeability are normative and need not entail actual, factual knowing of the parties. They provide an objective standard that parties should have been aware of the agreement's implications—that is, what should parties have expected.

The question, here, is: did the parties have reason to believe that the good was made under sweatshop conditions? One may interpret this question as addressing the idea of blameworthiness, and hence consider it a prerequisite for the justification of the refusal of contractual recognition. But this interpretation seems to insufficiently distinguish between two separate categories of immoral contracts: on the one hand, contracts deemed immoral based on aspects relating to the contracting parties (e.g., their motives and intentions), and on the other hand, contracts

---

[33] See doctrinal analysis in Tjon Soei Len, *Minimum Contract Justice* (n. 5) ch. 5.
[34] See Posner, *Contract Law and Theory* (Wolters Kluwer, 2016), 195–6.
[35] See doctrinal analysis in Tjon Soei Len, *Minimum Contract Justice* (n. 5) ch. 5.
[36] Tjon Soei Len, *Minimum Contract Justice* (n. 5) ch. 5.

immoral due to their implications for others or for society at large. For the latter category, rather than interpreting knowledge in light of the parties' responsibility, a more compelling interpretation of what is at stake is the balance of interests between the contracting parties (e.g., legal certainty) and, on the other side, others or society at large. If society's self-regarding concerns for justice are in play, attributive causality (i.e. causality as liability) misfires in two distinct ways. First, it fails to adequately capture the interests of private parties in contractual enforcement. Party interests are better expressed by ideas of legal certainty, their reliance or expectation regarding the actual realization of their transaction, or in the availability of contractual remedies. Second, and more fundamentally, causality misfires because it fails to recognize that in the relevant category of immoral contracts—those deemed invalid because of self-regarding or other reasons—the private interests of contracting parties ought to be subordinate to the interest of others and society at large.[37] In this context of contractual immorality, the notion of causality as attribution is out of place because its purpose is not to allocate responsibility to remedy a specific instance of harm, but to support a just market order where market activities that have exploitative implications are not endorsed. In the relevant categories of contractual immorality, the state is performing its task of protecting the fundamental values of society, and its minimum standard of justice as ensconced in the public institutions.

This interpretation gains support from the fact that proposals for instruments of transnational contract law have gone one step further in suggesting that party knowledge ought be entirely irrelevant when it comes to questions of contractual immorality; what matters is a society's interests in establishing the minimum standards of a just market order.[38] This latter position resonates with criticism voiced against the requirement of parties' knowledge in national legal systems; requiring that parties know of the immoral implications of their transaction undermines the protection of others and society at large in favor of private interests.[39] Furthermore, other aspects of the assessment of contractual immorality support this view. In particular, contractual immorality is not a default rule, only relevant unless parties agreed otherwise, but a mandatory one that comes into play regardless of, and superseding to, what parties may agree among themselves. What is more, the court's public task of self-regarding protection is performed *ex officio*: regardless of whether parties raise the issue themselves, courts must raise it on their own motion.

---

[37] A difficult dilemma arises when the recognition of a contract *and* the claim of its invalidity are both informed by justice commitments. I don't believe that the sweatshop case represents such a hard case (See below). See related Dagan and Dorfman, "Interpersonal Human Rights and Transnational Private Law" (n. 1); Tjon Soei Len, "Equal respect, capabilities and the moral limits of market exchange: denigration in the EU internal market," 8 *Transnational Legal Theory* (2017): 103–18.

[38] See for instance earlier attempts to harmonize European contract laws: The Study Group on a European Civil Code and Research Group on EC Private Law (ed.), *Draft Common Frame of Reference* (Sellier, 2009).

[39] See Ghestin, *Cause de l'engagement et validité du contrat* (Librarie Générale de Droit et de Jurisprudence, 2006).

## IV. The Causality Objection Revised: A Capabilities Objection?

So far, I have discussed why the causality objection, understood as a claim about a factual causal chain and as a tool for normative attribution, does not speak to the core of the argument from minimum contract justice. In this section, I attempt to articulate a revised version of the causality objection leveled against the project. This revised objection addresses the argument's normative framework: a capabilities-based perspective on minimum contract justice. The basic outline for this revision is as follows: the normative basis of the causality objection specifies which elements (e.g., whose conduct, whose interests) we should count as salient for—and also which should be excluded from—our evaluation of contractual immorality. This normative basis presupposes an account of contract law and relies on the criteria that are congruent with that account of contract (i.e. its purpose and function). The causality objection holds that in the assessment of the validity of consumer transactions (and presumably other market transactions), the interests of others located elsewhere should be excluded. As such, it resonates with accounts of contract that view the consideration of third party interests, generally, as an inappropriate burden on freedom of contract and the bilateral nature of contractual relationships. Notably, such accounts generally exclude distributive concerns from questions of contract justice. However, such accounts are incompatible with the capabilities-based perspective on contract law that is at the heart of the argument of minimum contract justice. We ought to articulate, then, a revised version of the causality objection leveled against the capabilities-based interpretation of contract justice.

### A. A capabilities-based approach to minimum contract justice

Dominant contract law theories generally focus on the internal, bilateral relationship between the contracting parties. These theories often understand the principle of freedom of contract to shield private parties from the burden entailed in having to assess if, and how, their contracts affect others and society at large (i.e. parties should be free to decide whether or not to contract, with whom, and on what terms).[40] As Aditi Bagchi observes, in present-day contract theory, "bilateralism threatens to crowd out the interests and concerns of third parties, denying them any role in determining the rights and duties that two people hold against each other."[41] Within dominant accounts of contract law, contractual immorality is considered to be in tension with freedom of contract that resembles Keren's description of the neoliberal account in which:

[c]ontracts are seen as the shrine of the market and as crucial to its proper functioning. Accordingly, and almost without exception, contracts should be enforced in order to facilitate

---

[40]  See Weinrib, *The Idea of Private Law* (Harvard University Press, 1995) and Weinrib, *Corrective Justice* (Oxford University Press, 2012); Ripstein, "Private Order and Public Justice: Kant and Rawls," 92 *Virginia Law Review* (2006): 1391–438. See for an economic explanation: Posner, *Contract Law and Theory* (Wolters Kluwer, 2016), 27–8: *"Contract law itself presumes that contracts do not produce negative externalities, or, if they do, that they will be governed by other laws. . . . the common law of contract evolved to address the problems of contracting parties."*
[41]  See Bagchi, "Other People's Contracts," 32 *Yale Journal on Regulation* (2015): 223.

the market's work. At the same time, the state is supposedly removed from the market, and consequently its role vis-à-vis the market is by and large limited to enforcement of contracts via its courts. Courts are thus very limited: any decision to invalidate a contract produced by the market is perceived as an extreme measure that jeopardizes the sacred freedom of contract and amounts to unwanted intervention by the state.[42]

In other words, dominant contract law theories provide accounts of *contract justice* that are (largely) independent of a contract's implications on others, and explain and justify why contract law is, and ought to be, disinclined to take the interests of others into account. While such contract accounts may have explanatory power for some key features of contract law, they tend to overlook the ways in which other established rules of contract law seek to advance social justice,[43] and they ways in which contractual immorality, in particular, functions as a tool for the purpose of safeguarding fundamental rights.[44]

However, from a capabilities-based perspective, the relation between contract law and market exchange is informed by the notion of *substantive* freedom. Contractual immorality serves our substantive freedom of contract, that is, "the substantive freedom to realize, through participation in the market, a range of desired end-states and activities."[45] In light of society's overall commitments to minimum justice, a particular set of substantive freedoms—the central capabilities as fundamental entitlements—qualifies the support that society ought to provide to the exercise of freedom in the market order. Contractual relationships function as mechanisms for activities that move individual life projects forward, but not all projects are equally worthy of support by the state.[46] While market exchanges may form important means through which to pursue valuable ends, they can also undermine the central capabilities, both of contracting parties and of others. In such cases, refusal of contractual recognition can serve to enhance, rather than interfere with, individual substantive freedom.[47] In this case, refusal is not an interference with individual freedoms, but constitutive of contractual freedom in a just market order. The state's self-regarding action is not just an attempt to avoid complicity with objectionable market activities but, instead, a reflection of its pursuit of minimum justice. While capabilities-based requirements of minimum justice may offer limited guidance to

---

[42] See Keren, "In the Land of Choice. Privatized Reality and Contractual Vulnerability," in Fineman, Andersson, and Mattsson (eds.), *Privatization, Vulnerability, and Social Responsibility. A Comparative Perspective.* (Routledge, 2017), 69–70.

[43] See Kronman, "Contract Law and Distributive Justice," 89 *Yale Law Journal* (1980): 472–511; Study Group on Social Justice in European Private Law, "Social Justice in European Contract Law: A Manifesto," 10 *European Law Journal* (2004): 653–74; Hesselink, *CFR & Social Justice* (Sellier European Law Publishers, 2008); Bagchi, "Distributive Justice and Contract," in Klass, Letsas, and Saprai (eds.), *Philosophical Foundations of Contract Law* (OUP, 2014).

[44] See Micklitz (ed.), *Constitutionalization of European Private Law* (OUP, 2014); Brüggemeier, Colombi Ciacchi, and Comandé (eds.), *Fundamental Rights and Private Law in the European Union* (CUP, 2010).

[45] See Deakin, "'Capacitas': Contract Law and the Institutional Preconditions of a Market Economy," 2 *European Review of Private Law* (2006): 317–41.

[46] See for a related argument: Dagan, "The Utopian Promise of Private Law," 66 University of Toronto Law Journal (2016): 392–417.

[47] See Deakin, "Capacitas" (n. 45).

evaluate individual contracts or contract terms, there are structural implications for (1) how we understand contract law, and (2) state's construction of the defining structure of contract.

## 1. Capabilities and contract law

Contract law is the law that governs economic transactions and represents the primary legal institution upon which markets are built. It defines the minimum standards for market transactions and terms of transactions that are legal permissibility in a market order. Contract law sets the standards for our access to the legal institution of contract and determines the advantages and disadvantages that come with contractual recognition. In order to understand contract law's role in human lives, we need to say something about the role that market transactions play in people's real abilities to pursue their own life plans, whatever those may be.

Contract law has an important role for people's capabilities. In modern societies, market participation is crucial to individual well-being, as market exchange is the primary mechanism through which individuals fulfill their basic needs. Our abilities to obtain housing, credit, employment, food, electricity, and education is by and large mediated through exchange relationships and depend, in part, on the legal institution of contract law. Market relationships are crucial for our ability to exercise control over our material environment. The latter does not only entail the ability to hold property and have property rights, but also the freedom to exercise those rights. The ability to hold property and property rights seems devoid of real significance for our abilities to shape our own lives if it does not include the possibility of exchange. In other words, our effective exercise of property rights necessarily includes some ability to engage in exchange.[48]

Market transactions are thus pivotal for areas of human life that are central to evaluations of justice. Contract law shapes the market order and functions as a determining factor for the extent to which the state allows market transactions as sources, or as facilitating factors of severe deprivations in human lives and potential infringements of fundamental entitlements.[49] While the extent to which individuals are exposed to markets may be governed by other laws, contract law sets minimum standards for market conduct and articulates the state's response to potential market exploitation. Contract law rules determine to what extent, if at all, capability deprivations are salient for the availability of public enforcement mechanisms in private exchanges. As an institution that is pertinent to individual capabilities, contract law must be considered part of the responsibility-bearing structure of a society that strives for minimum justice.

---

[48] On the ability to hold property and property rights, see the list of central human capabilities under 10B: Nussbaum, *Frontiers of Justice* (n. 11) 77. Also, see for the importance of the ability to exchange, Satz, *Why Some Things Should Not Be For Sale: The Moral Limits of Markets* (OUP, 2010), 26–27.

[49] See Keren, "In the Land of Choice (n. 42) 60–84.

## 2. The defining structure of contract

An important function of the institution of contract is to specify the conditions under which economic transactions become *contracts*, that is, transactions that are legally permissible and enforceable. People can, in principle, engage in exchange and agree to whatever conditions and terms they see fit. However, what the legally recognized set of rights and obligations between transacting parties will be and, ultimately, whether or not state power will be available for legal enforcement, does not fall within the sphere of authority of private parties. In short, contract law determines which transactions the state would be willing to enforce and how. Contract law is the institution that transforms a limited and favored set of transactions between individuals into *contracts*, that is, those that meet the minimum substantive standards that a society sets for market conduct. Contract law's conditions are selective and set a minimum standard of legal permissibility that determines the availability of public support for private endeavors. The conditions exclude from the contractual recognition a range of transactions that private actors may wish to pursue, but for which they cannot invoke the support of society at large.

Rules on contractual immorality are part of the broader set of contract law rules that serve this function. The broader set of rules lays out the requirements of contractual validity. This set includes rules that pertain to the qualities of the contracting parties (e.g., age as a proxy for legal capacity); the circumstances surrounding the formation of parties' consent and intention (e.g., defects of consent); and the substantive standards of morality with which agreements, if they are to be recognized as *contracts*, must comply.[50] Contractual immorality offers a legal basis on which courts can refuse the availability of state power for the realization of private pursuits deemed contrary to fundamental values of society.[51] The rules of contract law that provide the standards of contractual validity reveal the contours of the *defining structure of contract* and, as such, provide the minimum normative standards that reveal how private actors ought to behave toward each other, toward others, and toward society as a whole if they wish to receive the advantages that come with contract law's recognition. In other words, contract law does not just facilitate or simply assist the activity of exchange but defines the structure of contractual relations that is compatible with the public values that are ensconced in society's basic institutions. It sets out the basic or defining structure of contractual relations—agreements that are legally binding between private parties and for which the power of the state can be invoked for their enforcement. While minimum justice leaves open whether individuals choose to function in valuable areas encompassed by central capabilities, it does not leave it to the authority of private parties—that is, the market—what spaces of substantive freedom are available and to whom. Again, it is not to the authority of private actors to determine the legal standards of permissible contracts and contract terms.

---

[50] Under substantive standards I mean to include those legal doctrines that refer to good morals, illegality, transactions incompatible with public order or public policy, and unconscionable contracts.
[51] See for instance, art 3:40 of the Dutch Civil Code and art 138 of the German Civil Code.

Contrary to a neoliberal understanding of contractual immorality, a capabilities perspective shows that these substantive standards do not impose constraints on existing contractual relations as though they were phenomena of nature, but constructs and defines what contractual relations are from the start. There is no (natural) relationship between individuals into which the state intervenes by means of contract law. Out of many, the law identifies the ones that will be recognized *as contract*.

Given the importance of market exchange for human lives, the state must perform this task, through contract law, in a way that is compatible with the requirements of minimum justice. Notably, it must assess when market activities impose barriers to people's abilities to engage in valuable functioning within the spheres of central capabilities such that these barriers ought to inform the demarcation of freedom of contract.

## B. The causality objection as capabilities objection

We can now modify the causality objection to contractual invalidity of consumer contracts for sweatshop goods into a capabilities objection. As a capabilities objection, excluding such exchanges from contractual recognition and enforcement would impose a constraint too grave for freedom of contract, that is, consumers should have the ability to contract for goods without the burden of having to consider its production conditions. If contract law would take into account what capabilities-implications our market exchanges have, not only for our transactional parties, but for others elsewhere, then the burdens on our freedom to engage in market activities in pursuit of our own conceptions of the good is too severe. So understood, the capabilities objection is forceful and addresses the core of minimum contract justice, capturing the spirit of a capabilities-based project. The primary concern is to enable individuals to choose and expand their valuable options for choice. If the capabilities-based argument would amount to a restriction of individuals' abilities to engage in valuable activities then it may fail on its own terms. In short, the capabilities objection holds that closing contracting options that are deemed incompatible with the central capabilities of others elsewhere would be too restrictive of contracting parties' capabilities (i.e. the abilities to engage in market exchange without severe burdens to consider the interests of others) and would therefore be self-defeating.[52]

Moreover, in the case of a conflict between individual competing central capabilities, a state may have good reasons to prioritize the central capabilities of its own citizens. While the central capabilities are of universal normative importance, the capabilities deemed central to human life and the relevant threshold levels ought to be determined in each society.[53] Provided that the argument regarding contractual invalidity of consumer contracts features the instance of cross border sweatshops, a

---

[52] See Nussbaum, *Frontiers of Justice* (n. 11) 309.
[53] Nussbaum, *Frontiers of Justice* (n. 11) 78–9.

court (as representative of the state) may not only be severely restrained in making the required assessment, but may also lack the legitimate authority to do so.

A response to this revised objection may take the following form. It is important to acknowledge the possibility of difficult cases that entail a conflict between competing capabilities claims. For instance, the specific construction of contracting options as open or closed might have diverging impacts on various spaces of substantive freedom, and on the capabilities of various individuals. How we address such issues is important, and minimum contract justice does not address or resolve this predicament. However, we should be cautious in characterizing the case of consumer contracts for sweatshop goods as a difficult case of this sort. If we take, as an archetypal example, a consumer sale for clothes produced by brands that engage in "fast fashion" strategies, we have compelling reasons to doubt that such a conflict is at stake. Fast fashion strategies are pursued by a portion of the garment industry that seeks to meet consumer demand for items that meet the latest fashion trends at exceptionally low prices. These brands produce many collections throughout the year; replenish clothing items routinely; closely follow highly unpredictable trends and trendsetters; and design and produce clothes with extremely short lead-times. These features of fast fashion allow consumers to replenish their wardrobe on a regular basis as fashion trends shift.

These features also are distinct for a clothing market dynamic in which sweatshops are endemic. Fast fashion requires corporations to be flexible in their ability to fulfill orders that meet volatile and unpredictable demand. Retailers that meet consumer demands for fast fashion pursue flexible and inexpensive means of production. Consumer demand for inexpensive and trendy products that are immediately available as trends appear requires—and is dependent on—supply factors that enable production and that make products available on the market. In particular, the low prices paid for products that follow the latest fashion trends require inexpensive production conditions with short lead times. These market dynamics sustain the systemic occurrence of sweatshops in a portion of the garment industry.[54] The transaction terms that accompany sales of fast fashion products (e.g., immediate availability and low prices) cannot be realized without sweatshops. The availability of such contracting options and the price as a central contract term are two important factors that link consumer contracts to sweatshop conditions. The example of demand for fast fashion goods illustrates how consumer contracts can advance and sustain, in a foreseeable manner, sweatshop exploitation. The revised objection raises the question whether we ought to recognize the abilities of consumers to buy such goods as pivotal from a viewpoint of central capabilities and whether it represents a fundamental entitlement that conflicts with the fundamental entitlements of others to work in conditions reflective of human dignity. It seems to me that this case is not a difficult case that involves the consideration of competing central capabilities. The point is not to deny that such difficult cases are possible, but rather to illustrate

---

[54] See Ross, *Slaves to Fashion* (University of Michigan Press, 2004); Rosen, *Making Sweatshops: The Globalization of the U.S. Apparel Industry* (University of California Press, 2002); Klein, *No Logo* (Macmillan, 2003).

that there is a sphere and practice of contract where the argument from minimum contract justice applies.

Additionally, much will depend on empirical data. For instance, if closing contracting options through contractual immorality of consumer contracts will lead to fewer valuable options for women working in sweatshops, this is a serious concern that ought to inform our course of action. While courts have legitimate authority to determine the legal permissibility of contracts over which they govern, the real consequences for the lives that others are able to live should not remain invisible. Instead of transforming the assessment of minimum contract justice, such facts illustrate that the responsibility for minimum justice is shared by a wide range of institutions, and it certainly cannot be pursued and achieved through contract law alone.

## V. Conclusion

While sweatshop production is widely criticized, consumer contracts for sweatshop produced goods are rarely scrutinized for their legal permissibility. Consumer sales contracts are considered too remote to be regarded as suspect or worthy of legally relevant moral disapproval. An important reason for this point of view is the idea that consumer contracts lack a causal link to sweatshops and, therefore, consumers should bear no blame or responsibility for deplorable production conditions under which their goods are produced. As suggested in this chapter, this idea is based on a mistaken transposition of the notion of causation from the context of liability to the context of contractual recognition. Whether the state ought to refuse recognition of consumer contracts ought not be based on the question of whether consumers should bear responsibility or blame for sweatshops, but rather on the question of whether the state's support for such exchanges is compatible with its broader commitments to minimum justice. A capabilities perspective on minimum contract justice produces a legal strategy that could be complementary pathway for those who battle labor rights violations.

# Index

affiliation 69n19, 205, 221–22, 225–26
  age discrimination 268, 274–75
  architectonic status 252–53
  demeaning and humiliating, support as 266
  freedom of association 242, 249–50, 252–53, 256–57
  justifications for labour law 56
  restorative justice 225–26, 229–30
  robot-like jobs 214–15
  work-life balance 233–34
affirmative/positive action
  age discrimination 15–16, 268, 273–74, 275, 287–88
  development of capabilities 96
  equality 251
  gender 96
  quality of life 66–67
  theory of justice 8–9, 22, 38–39, 40–41
  unions 173
Agarwal, Bina 80–81
age discrimination 54–55, 268–89
  affirmative action 15–16, 268, 273–74, 275, 287–88
  application of CA 283–88
  combined capabilities 269–70, 283–84
  complete lives egalitarianism 284–85
  conversion factors 15–16, 269, 270–72, 283–84, 286–87
  critical gerontology 283
  effective protection and support, proactive measures for 287–88
  equality 15–16, 272, 285, 287
  EU law 280–81
  gender 79, 281–82
  heterogeneity 268, 286–87, 289
  human dignity 15–16, 268, 269–70, 272, 274–75, 280–81, 284–87
  human rights 275–76, 277–80
  indirect age discrimination 278–79
  intersectionality 15–16, 268, 281–82, 286–87
  motivations 278–79
  pensions 280, 282–84, 285
  perceived deficits in older workers 15–16, 276–77, 283–84
  proactive measures 277–78, 282–83, 287–88
  regulatory reform 268, 287, 289
  retirement
    mandatory 54–55, 280, 283–84, 285, 287–88
    savings 282–84, 286–87, 288
  stereotypes and prejudice 268, 271–72, 276–79, 283–84
  substantive freedom 269, 270–72, 283–84

  pressure to work longer without adequate support 277–78, 282–83
  tension between different rationales 279–81
  theory of justice 270, 272–74, 289
  variations in need 286–87
  well-being 273–74
  wrong, whether age discrimination is 15–16, 278–79, 283–84
agency 5–6, 16–17
  development of capabilities 95
  free trade agreements (FTAs) 308–9
  heterogeneous workers 118
  restorative justice 222–23
  trade and labour standards 16, 291
agricultural workers
  collective bargaining 15, 253, 263–64
  constitutional equality 260–61
  derivative rights 246, 253, 260–61
  exclusion from labour law 15, 249, 253, 260–61, 262
  functionings 264
  Guatemala's failure to enforce labour standards in CAFTA-DR FTA 302–4, 306–7
  labour law, suitability for 200
  migrant workers 262
  precarious, work as 254
Alston, Philip 186
alternative concepts 13, 181, 187–91
  freedom of association 243–44, 266–67
  template 243–44, 266–67
altruism 13, 181, 184, 197–98, 200
Amazon warehouse, working conditions in 14, 202, 212–13
  exploitation 204–5
  human rights 217
  labour standards 202, 204–5, 217
  mental health and physical health 216–17
American Civil Liberties Union (ACLU) 159–60, 168–69, 172, 175
American Federation of Labor (AFL) 163–65, 166
Anderson, Elizabeth 44, 56–57, 110, 118
animals 62–65, 69n19, 205, 221–22
approach, CA as an 10–11
  fit between current labour laws and CA 45–46, 49, 54–55, 59–61
  potential role of CA in labour law 103–21
arbitration 14, 218–19, 227–29, 303–7
Arendt, Hannah 88, 323
Aristotle 15, 72, 92, 185, 243–44, 249–60, 270, 272, 323
Arrow-Debreu general equilibrium model 181–82
Arrow, Kenneth 198
Arthurs, Harry 25–26